29.95

Law, Pol

and the J

in Canad

SECOND EDI

D0110699

Law, Politics and the Judicial Process in Canada

SECOND EDITION

Edited by F.L. Morton

University of Calgary Press

© 1992 F.L. Morton

University of Calgary Press
2500 University Dr. N.W.
Calgary, Alberta, Canada T2N 1N4

Canadian Cataloguing in Publication Data
    Main entry under title:
    Law, politics and the judicial process
        in Canada

        Includes bibliographical references and index.
        ISBN 0-919813-83-6

        1. Courts — Canada.   2. Judicial process — Canada.
    3. Political questions and judicial power — Canada.
    I. Morton, F. L. (Frederick Lee), 1949–
    KE8200.Z85L39 1992   347.71'012   C92-091322-9

Printed and bound in Canada by John Deyell Company Limited

 This book is printed on acid-free paper.

Table of Contents

---

* Reprinted elsewhere in the book.

Preface

I completed the first edition of this book in May, 1984, the month that the Supreme Court issued its first Charter of Rights decision. In the preface to that first edition, I speculated that the adoption of the Charter was going to "force the Canadian judiciary into a much more explicit political function than it had previously exercised." This was indeed speculation. No one knew at the time what the Charter would hold. The impact—if any—of the Charter was clearly going to be a function of judicial interpretation and choice. If past Canadian practice was any guide, and given provincial opposition, especially Quebec's, to the Charter, there was good reason to suspect no more than modest deviation from the *status quo ante*.

Today, ten years down the road into "Charterland," Canadians live in a different legal and political world. There have been more than six thousand reported Charter decisions, almost two hundred by the Supreme Court of Canada. While the Supreme Court's Charter decisions are the most visible and often dramatic indicators of the impact of the Charter, they represent only the tip of the iceberg of Charter-induced activities. The Charter has acted as a catalyst for changes throughout the legal and political systems: the docket and decision-making procedures of the Supreme Court, law schools, legal scholarship, interest group activity, and government expenditures. These changes are recounted in the revised introductions to each chapter, and many of the thirty new readings. While the merits of these changes have become a topic of growing debate, the change itself is not. In a recently published comparative study of judicial activism, Canada was ranked second only to the United States.[1] England, the model followed by Canadian jurists until recently, was ranked ninth out of the ten democracies in the study. Had the same survey been done twenty years ago, when the Canadian Court was still "the quiet court in the unquiet country," Canada would have quietly taken its place next to the mother country. No longer! Indeed, a strong case can now be made that the Supreme Court of Canada is actually more activist than the contemporary (as opposed to the historical) American Supreme Court. The heydays of American judicial activism are fast receding under the impact of the judicial appointments of the conservative Reagan administration. And unlike its American counterpart, the Canadian Court remains an active player in the law and politics of federalism.

In the preface to the first edition, I also hazarded the observation that the study of the judicial process in Canada had been relatively neglected

---

[1] Kenneth Holland, *Judicial Activism in Comparative Perspective* (London: Macmillan, 1991).

because it was "too political for law professors but too legal for political scientists." There is hardly any danger of this today. The Charter has dissolved any bright-line distinction between law and politics. Much of the best political analysis of the Charter has come from the law schools, while Canadian political scientists have rediscovered constitutional law and the courts. Leading examples of both are included among the new readings selected for this edition.

I am indebted to many people who assisted in the production of this edition of the book. I would like to thank all the contributing authors, without whom there would be no book. I also acknowledge the helpful suggestions of the many teachers and students who used the first edition. Their suggestions for improvements, additions and deletions have been welcomed. (Keep them coming for the third edition!) Lou Pedder, the administrative secretary for the Research Unit for Socio-Legal Studies, assisted in the preparation of the manuscript in more ways than I can count. Finally, I want to thank the staff at the University of Calgary Press, especially Sharon Boyle, my very patient editor, and Eileen Eckert, who has done such a splendid job on page layout and format. Any shortcomings in this second edition, I cheerfully blame on the twelve fifteen-year-old boys on the baseball team which I manage, who despite posting a respectable 13–6 season record, have driven me to distraction for the past two months!

This book has been published with the help of a grant from the Alberta Foundation for the Arts.

1

The Rule of Law in the Canadian Constitution

On December 4, 1946, Frank Roncarelli was informed by the Quebec Liquor Commission that the liquor license for his Montreal restaurant had been revoked "forever." Mr. Roncarelli had not violated any Liquor Commission guidelines, nor had he been charged with or convicted of any criminal wrongdoing. The license was revoked because, as Mr. Roncarelli and indeed everyone else knew, Maurice Duplessis, the Premier of Quebec, wanted to punish him for his membership in and financial support of the Jehovah's Witnesses. The Jehovah's Witnesses are an evangelizing, fundamentalist protestant sect, who had outraged Duplessis and the French Catholic majority in Quebec through their outspoken criticisms of the Catholic Church and its priests. The Duplessis government had begun a campaign of legal harassment against the Witnesses, by arresting them for distributing their printed materials without a license. Roncarelli frustrated this plan by regularly providing bail money for his arrested fellow-believers, who would then return to the streets. Roncarelli thus became a special target of the harassment policies of the Quebec government.

After a thirteen-year legal battle, the Supreme Court of Canada finally ruled that the government of Quebec's treatment of Roncarelli had been arbitrary and illegal. Moreover, Duplessis could not hide behind the civil immunity normally enjoyed by state administrators under Quebec law. By grossly abusing his administrative discretion, Duplessis was deemed to have acted outside the law and was thus subject to being sued by Roncarelli for damages.[1] (See Reading 1.1) A majority of the Court held that in Canada there is a general right not to be punished by the arbitrary exercise of government power. A government, federal or provincial, can only move against an individual in accordance with known rules, and the Duplessis government had failed to meet this standard. In so ruling, the Supreme Court re-asserted one of the fundamental principles of the "unwritten constitution" of Canada — "the rule of law."

---

[1] For an excellent account of both the Roncarelli Case and the larger conflict between the Jehovah's Witnesses and the Quebec government, see William Kaplan, *State and Salvation: The Jehovah's Witnesses and Their Fight for Civil Rights* (Toronto, ON: University of Toronto Press, 1989).

The Roncarelli case was just the most recent chapter in a living tradition that can be traced back through the nineteenth-century writings of A.V.C. Dicey (Reading 1 .4); the American Declaration of Independence of 1776 (See Reading 1.3); the political theory of the seventeenth-century philosopher John Locke (See Reading 1.2); and back to the fields of Runnymede in June of 1215, when the English nobles forced King John to sign Magna Carta and to agree to rule *per legem terrae* — according to the laws of the land.[2]

Magna Carta marked the beginning of the "rule of law" tradition. The "Glorious Revolution of 1688" deposed the Stuart kings and established the supremacy of Parliament over the Crown. This landmark event initiated the practice of government that we now take for granted (too much so!) — representative government, or government by consent of the governed. The second reading is from the writings of John Locke, often referred to as the "theorist of the Glorious Revolution." Locke's *Second Treatise on Government*, first published in 1690, has been the most influential defence and advocacy of "government by consent," or liberal democracy, ever written. In it, we find not only a defence of "government by consent of the governed," but also a restatement of the principle of *per legem terrae*. Locke explicitly declares that even the new sovereign, the legislature, must rule "by declared and received laws . . . interpreted by known authorized judges."

A careful reading of the passage from Locke reveals that in addition to these procedural restrictions, he imposes a second major restriction on the legislative, or "law-making," power of the state — "the law of Nature." This substantive restriction means that not only must laws be duly enacted and fairly administered, but also that the laws themselves must not violate the "natural rights" of individuals that exist by the "law of Nature." This law of nature is understood to transcend human society and to exist independently of the positive law of any given state.

This double limitation on just government was given its most striking and memorable articulation in the American Declaration of Independence of 1776, written primarily by Thomas Jefferson. (See Reading 1.3) The Americans justified their revolution, and subsequently founded their new republic, on the two fundamental principles of Locke's political theory: that "all men are by Nature equal," and that they possess "certain inalienable (i.e., natural) rights." There is a critical tension between these two

---

[2] The full text of s. 39 of Magna Carta reads as follows: "No freeman shall be taken or (and) imprisoned or disseised or outlawed or exiled or in any way destroyed, nor will we go upon him nor send upon him, except by the lawful judgement of his peers or (and) by the law of the land." This 700 year-old rule is the direct ancestor of the 1982 Charter of Rights and Freedoms, whose preamble declares: "Whereas Canada is founded upon principles that recognize the supremacy of God and the rule of law." Section 7 of the Charter essentially restates the modern formulation of *per legem terrae*, that no person can be deprived of his life, liberty, or security of the person. except according to the due process of law. Sections 8 through 15 then elaborate specific aspects of due process.

fundamental concepts of equality and liberty. The principle of natural equality essentially means that no person (or group of persons) is so inherently superior as to rule others without their consent. This banishes the traditional claims of priests, kings, and nobles to rule on the basis of their alleged natural superiority, and replaces it with government by consent of the governed. In practice, this has meant some form of "majority rule" democracy. The principle of natural rights means that a just government cannot violate these rights, since the very purpose of government is to secure such rights. The tension arises from the fact that "majority rule" does not always produce laws that respect the rights of individuals or groups who are not part of the majority.

This tension is more of a theoretical problem than a practical one. Most of the time the combined practice of "government by consent" and "the rule of law" is a strong guarantee that the twin requirements of equality and liberty will both be met. It is unlikely that a governing majority will ever (knowingly) consent to policies that are destructive of their rights. The "rule of law" provides additional safeguards by detering rulers from pursuing ends and using means that "they would not like to have known by the people, and own not willingly."[3] But what happens when the majority consents to laws that are destructive of the natural rights of a minority? What happens when government by the "consent of the governed" no longer "secures these rights"? Neither Locke nor Jefferson answered this question. The practical problem of reconciling "majority rule" with "minority rights" was left to the founders of new liberal democracies such as the United States and Canada.

There have been two principal approaches to giving institutional expression to the principles of equality and liberty in modern liberal democracies: the British parliamentary or Westminster model, and the American "separation of powers" model. Because of two major differences in the Parliamentary and American systems, the courts in each system have very different functions and characteristics. The American model is ultimately based on and organized by a single basic document — a written constitution. This single document sets down in writing "the rules governing the composition, powers and methods of operation of the main institutions of government, and the general principles applicable to their relations to the citizens."[4] By contrast, the Westminster model is based on an "unwritten constitution" — a combination of historically important statutes, the common law, and numerous unwritten conventions and usages. The second difference is that the "written constitution" of the Americans includes an enumeration of the fundamental rights and

---

[3] See Locke, *The Second Treatise*, Ch. 1. Reading 1.2.

[4] Sir Ivor Jennings, *The Law and the Constitution*. 5th ed. (London: University of London Press, 1959), p. 33.

liberties of the individual against government, known collectively as the Bill of Rights. While individuals enjoy basically the same rights and freedoms under the British parliamentary model of democracy, they are not "spelled out" in any single, basic document of government, i.e., they are not "constitutionally entrenched."

The result of these two differences is that under the American model of democracy, the courts, and especially the Supreme Court, play a more explicit and influential political role. Ever since the 1803 case of *Marbury v. Madison,* American courts have assumed the function of interpreting and enforcing "constitutional law" just as they do all other law. This "judicial review" of legislative and executive actions is intended to ensure that they conform to the procedures and limitations laid down in the Constitution. If they do not conform, the court declares them to be "unconstitutional," invalid and therefore without legal effect.

It is easy to see how, in theory at least, combining the American practice of judicial review with an entrenched Bill of Rights resolves the tension between liberty and equality, majority rule and minority rights. If the majority enacts a law that infringes a person's constitutional right, the individual can go to court and ask the judges to strike down the law as unconstitutional. This approach to protecting civil liberties was particularly effective in promoting racial justice in American society during the 1950s and 1960s. While the more "democratic" (majoritarian) institutions of government refused to take action, the American Supreme Court used the Bill of Rights guarantee of "equal protection of the laws" to strike down the legal barriers of racial discrimination in American society. However, as the American Supreme Court expanded its "judicial activism" into more and more areas of public policy and local government, serious questions began to arise about the "undemocratic" character of its use of judicial review. In protecting the "individual rights" side of the liberal equation, the Court was perceived as neglecting and even violating the equality requirement of government by consent of the governed.[5]

The British model of parliamentary supremacy combined with "the rule of law" tradition avoids this problem. There are no written constitutional prohibitions for the British courts to enforce against Parliament, and the courts do not interpret or enforce constitutional conventions, the "unwritten constitution."[6] The critics of parliamentary democracy, however, contend that it is prone to the opposite problem — that there is no adequate mechanism to protect individuals or minorities from democratic majorities that violate their rights. While this may be true in theory, in

---

[5] This problem is the subject of Chapter 13.

[6] The Canadian Supreme Court's decision in the 1981 *Constitutional Amendment Reference* was contrary to this generally accepted practice and is probably best understood as an exception to an otherwise still valid rule.

practice it has not proven to be a serious problem in either Great Britain or Canada. While Canada's civil liberties record is far from perfect,[7] it remains much better than the vast majority of modern nation states.

The key to the practical success of the British parliamentary system is conveyed in the reading from Dicey on "the rule of law," and especially his quotation from Tocqueville. (See Reading 1.4) Comparing the governments of England and Switzerland, Tocqueville observed that, "In England there seems to be more liberty in the customs than in the laws of the people," while the opposite holds for Switzerland. For both Tocqueville and Dicey, the British condition is far preferable. For in the long run, the customs, habits, beliefs — the moral quality public opinion — of a society is a more dependable guarantee of just laws than the "paper barriers" of constitutional "guarantees." Put very simply, a written constitution cannot "guarantee" that the laws of a democratic society will be any more just or fair than the people who make up that society.

The government of Canada was basically modeled after the British parliamentary system. The one important exception is the federal form of the union of the Canadian provinces, and the defining of the forms and limits of this union in a single, written document — the British North America Act, 1867, now known as the Constitution Act, 1867. This aspect of Canadian government is especially important for the courts, because it has thrust upon them the function of judicial review, or "umpire" of the federal system.[8] Federalism aside, both levels of government in Canada were formed after the Westminster model, which meant parliamentary supremacy within their respective spheres of jurisdiction.

Accordingly, Canada has, until very recently, followed the British approach to the protection of civil liberty — parliamentary supremacy combined with "the rule of law," and a healthy self-confidence in the basic sense of fairness and toleration for diversity in the Canadian people. Inevitably, the proximity of the United States has prompted constant comparisons. One of the most eloquent and forceful defences of the Anglo-Canadian approach to protecting civil liberties was given by the dean of Canadian political science, R. MacGregor Dawson. In discussing the various components of Canada's unwritten constitution, Dawson argued:

> The mere fact that a constitutional doctrine is not explicitly enunciated and formally committed to writing may affect the external appearance but not disturb the genuineness or force of that doctrine. Thus the broad tolerance which will permit differences of opinion and will disapprove of punitive or repressive measures against the dissenters is of as great constitutional significance and may conceivably under some circumstances afford

---

[7] See Thomas Berger, *Fragile Freedoms: Human Rights and Dissent in Canada* (Vancouver, BC: Clarke, Irwin and Co., 1981).

[8] This is the subject of Chapter 10.

an even more assured protection than an explicit guarantee of freedom of speech, written into a constitution, yet with no solid conviction behind it.[9]

The force of Dawson's argument notwithstanding, Canadian political leaders have been increasingly attracted to the American approach to protecting civil liberties. In 1960 the Diefenbaker government enacted the Canadian Bill of Rights. It took the form of a statute, not a constitutional amendment, and applied only to the federal government and not to the provinces.[10] Partly because of dissatisfaction with this document and partly in response to political developments within Canada during the 1970s, the Trudeau government undertook a major program of constitutional reform in 1980. Prime Minister Trudeau's constitutional agenda included "patriating" the B.N.A. Act, an amending formula, and a new Charter of Rights that applied to both levels of Canadian government. After a year and a half of political maneuvering, confrontation, and finally compromise, modified versions of all three objectives were achieved.

The adoption of a constitutionally entrenched Charter of Rights (reproduced in the Appendix) fundamentally altered the Canadian system of government by placing explicit limitations on the law-making power of both levels of government. Parliament was no longer supreme; the Constitution was. Or almost. The Charter was not adopted in its original "pure" form. Attachment to the tradition of Parliamentary supremacy, combined with provincial suspicion and opposition, were too strong, and forced an important compromise. Added in the eleventh hour of constitutional negotiations between the federal government and the provinces, section 33 of the Charter allows both levels of government to ignore certain Charter provisions if they deem it necessary. Parliamentary supremacy was thus preserved, albeit in a qualified form.

As a result, Canada finds itself today almost equidistant between the British and American models of liberal democracy, with their differing approaches to civil liberties. As a result, the debate over which form of liberal democracy is best designed to protect the liberties of its citizens remains very much alive. The truth of this debate lies somewhere between the two contending positions, for as Dawson pointed out: "Written law and the conventions will normally complement one another and each becomes necessary to the proper functioning of the other."[11]

While this debate is ongoing, there is one undisputed fact about the effect of enumerating individual rights in a written constitution: it thrusts the courts, and the judges who constitute them, into a much more explicit

---

[9]   R. MacGregor Dawson, *The Government of Canada*. 4th ed. (Toronto, ON: University of Toronto Press, 1963), p. 70.

[10]   This is discussed in greater detail in Chapter 11.

[11]   Dawson, p. 71.

and influential political role. This is the subject of the next chapter, while the details and consequences of this new role for Canadian judges and courts are elaborated in the remainder of the book.

1.1

RONCARELLI v. DUPLESSIS
Supreme Court of Canada (1959)

The judgment of Rand and Judson JJ. was delivered by

RAND J.: The material facts from which my conclusion is drawn are these. The appellant was the proprietor of a restaurant in a busy section of Montreal which in 1946 through its transmission to him from his father had been continuously licensed for the sale of liquor for approximately 34 years; he is of good education and repute and the restaurant was of a superior class. On December 4 of that year, while his application for annual renewal was before the Liquor Commission, the existing license was cancelled and his application for renewal rejected, to which was added a declaration by the respondent that no future license would ever issue to him. These primary facts took place in the following circumstances.

For some years the appellant had been an adherent of a rather militant Christian religious sect known as the Witnesses of Jehovah. Their ideology condemns the established church institutions and stresses the absolute and exclusive personal relation of the individual to the Deity without human intermediation or intervention.

The first impact of their proselytizing zeal upon the Roman Catholic church and community in Quebec, as might be expected, produced a violent reaction. Meetings were forcibly broken up, property damaged, individuals ordered out of communities, in one case out of the province, and generally, within the cities and towns, bitter controversy aroused. The work of the Witnesses was carried on both by word of mouth and by the distribution of printed matter, the latter including two periodicals known as "The Watch Tower" and "Awake," sold at a small price.

In 1945 the provincial authorities began to take steps to bring an end to what was considered insulting and offensive to the religious beliefs and feelings of the Roman Catholic population. Large scale arrests were made of young men and women, by whom the publications mentioned were being held out for sale, under local by-laws requiring a licence for peddling any kind of wares. Altogether almost one thousand of such charges were laid. The penalty involved in Montreal, where most of the arrests took place, was a fine of $40, and as the Witnesses disputed liability, bail was in all cases resorted to.

The appellant, being a person of some means, was accepted by the Recorder's Court as bail without question, and up to November 12, 1946, he had gone security in about 380 cases, some of the accused being involved in repeated offenses. Up to this time there had been no suggestion of impropriety; the security of the appellant was taken as so satisfactory that at times, to avoid delay when he was absent from the city, recognizances were signed by him in blank and kept ready for completion by the Court officials. The reason for the accumulation of charges was the doubt that they could be sustained in law. Apparently the legal officers of Montreal, acting in concert with those of the Province, had come to an agreement with the attorney for the Witnesses to have a test case proceeded with. Pending that, however, there was no stoppage of the sale of the tracts and this became the annoying circumstance that produced the volume of proceedings.

On or about November 12 it was decided to require bail in cash for Witnesses so arrested and the sum set ranged from $100 to $300. No such bail was furnished by the appellant; his connection with giving security ended with this change of practice; and in the result, all of the charges in relation to which he had become surety were dismissed.

At no time did he take any part in the distribution of the tracts: he was an adherent of the group but nothing more. It was shown that he had leased to another member premises in Sherbrooke which were used as a hall for carrying on religious meetings: but it is unnecessary to do more than mention that fact to reject it as having no bearing on the issues raised. Beyond the giving of bail and being an adherent, the appellant is free from any relation that could be tortured into a badge of character pertinent to his fitness or unfitness to hold a liquor licence.

The mounting resistance that stopped the surety bail sought other means of crushing the propagandist invasion and among the circumstances looked into was the situation of the appellant. Admittedly an adherent, he was enabling these protagonists to be at large to carry on their campaign of publishing what they believed to be the Christian truth as revealed by the Bible; he was also the holder of a liquor licence, a "privilege" granted by the Province, the profits from which, as it was seen by the authorities, he was using to promote the disturbance of settled beliefs and arouse community disaffection generally. Following discussions between the then Mr. Archambault, as the personality of the Liquor Commission, and the chief prosecuting officer in Montreal, the former, on or about November 21, telephoned to the respondent, advised him of those facts, and queried what should be done. Mr. Duplessis answered that the matter was serious and that the identity of the person furnishing bail and the liquor licensee should be put beyond doubt. A few days later, that identity being established through a private investigator, Mr. Archambault again communicated with the respondent and, as a result of what passed between them, the licence, as of December 4, 1946, was revoked.

In the meantime, about November 25, 1946, a blasting answer had come from the Witnesses. In an issue of one of the periodicals, under the heading "Quebec's Burning Hate," was a searing denunciation of what was alleged to be the savage persecution of Christian believers. Immediately instructions were sent out from the department of the Attorney-General ordering the confiscation of the issue and proceedings were taken against one Boucher charging him with publication of a seditious libel.

It is then wholly as a private citizen, an adherent of a religious group, holding a liquor licence and furnishing bail to arrested persons for no other purpose than to enable them to be released from detention pending the determination of the charges against them, and with no other relevant considerations to be taken into account, that he is involved in the issues of this controversy.

The complementary state of things is equally free from doubt. From the evidence of Mr. Duplessis and Mr. Archambault alone, it appears that the action taken by the latter as the general manager and sole member of the Commission was dictated by Mr. Duplessis as Attorney-General and Prime Minister of the province; that that step was taken as a means of bringing to a halt the activities of the Witnesses, to punish the appellant for the part he had played not only by revoking the existing licence but in declaring him barred from one "forever," and to warn others that they similarly would be stripped of provincial "privileges" if they persisted in any activity directly or indirectly related to the Witnesses and to the objectionable campaign. The respondent felt that action to be his duty, something which his conscience demanded of him; and as representing the provincial government his decision became automatically that of Mr. Archambault and the Commission....

... In these circumstances, when the *de facto* power of the Executive over its appointees at will to such a statutory public function is exercised deliberately and intentionally to destroy the vital business interests of a citizen, is there legal redress by him against the person so acting? This calls for an examination of the statutory provisions governing the issue, renewal and revocation of liquor licences and the scope of authority entrusted by law to the Attorney-General and the government in relation to the administration of the Act....

... The provisions of the statute, which may be supplemented by detailed regulations, furnish a code for the complete administration of the sale and distribution of alcoholic liquors directed by the commission as a public service, for all legitimate purposes of the populace. It recognizes the association of wines and liquors as embellishments of food and its ritual and as an interest of the public. As put in *Macbeth*, the "sauce to meat is ceremony," and so we have restaurants, cafes, hotels and other places of serving food, specifically provided for in that association.

At the same time the issue of permits has a complementary interest in those so catering to the public. The continuance of the permit over the years, as in this case, not only recognizes its virtual necessity to a superior class restaurant but also its identification with the business carried on. The provisions for assignment of the permit are to this most pertinent and they were exemplified in the continuity of the business here. As its exercise continues, the economic life of the holder becomes progressively more deeply implicated with the privilege while at the same time his vocation becomes correspondingly dependent on it.

The field of licensed occupations and businesses of this nature is steadily becoming of greater concern to citizens generally. It is a matter of vital importance that a public administration that can refuse to allow a person to enter or continue a calling which, in the absence of regulation, would be free and legitimate, should be conducted with complete impartiality and integrity; and that the grounds for refusing or cancelling a permit should unquestionably be such and such only as are incompatible with the purposes envisaged by the statute: the duty of a Commission is to serve those purposes and those only. A decision to deny or cancel such a privilege lies within the "discretion" of the Commission; but that means that decision is to be based upon a weighing of considerations pertinent to the object of the administration.

In public regulation of this sort there is no such thing as absolute and untrammelled "discretion," that is, that action can taken on any ground or for any reason that can be suggested to the mind of the administrator; no legislative Act can, without express language, be taken to contemplate an unlimited arbitrary power exercisable for any purpose, however capricious or irrelevant, regardless of the nature or purpose of the statute. Fraud and corruption in the Commission may not be mentioned in such statutes but they are always implied as exceptions. "Discretion" necessarily implies good faith in discharging public duty; there is always a perspective within which a statute is intended to operate; and any clear departure from its line or objects is just as objectionable as fraud or corruption. Could an applicant be refused a permit because he had been born in another province, or because of the colour of his hair? The ordinary language of the legislature cannot be so distorted.

To deny or revoke a permit because a citizen exercises an unchallengeable right totally irrelevant to the sale of liquor in a restaurant is equally beyond the scope of the discretion conferred. There was here not only revocation of the existing permit but a declaration of a future, definitive disqualification of the appellant to obtain one: it was to be "forever." This purports to divest his citizenship status of its incident of membership in the class of those of the public to whom such a privilege could be extended. Under the statutory language here, that is not competent to the Commission and *a fortiori* to the government or the respondent: *McGillivray v. Kimber*. There is here an administrative tribunal which, in certain respects, is to act in a judicial manner; and even on the view of the dissenting justices in *McGillivray*, there is liability: what could be more malicious than to punish this licensee for having done what he had an absolute right to do in a matter utterly irrelevant to the Liquor Act? Malice in the proper sense is simply acting for a reason and purpose knowingly foreign to the administration, to which was added here the element of intentional punishment by what was virtually vocation outlawry.

It may be difficult if not impossible in cases generally to demonstrate a breach of this public duty in the illegal purpose served; there may be no means, even if proceedings against the Commission were permitted by the Attorney-General, as here they were refused, of compelling the Commission to justify a refusal or revocation or to give reasons for its action; on these questions I make no observation; but in the case before us that difficulty is not present: the reasons are openly avowed.

The act of the respondent through the instrumentality of the Commission brought about a breach of an implied public statutory duty toward the appellant; it was a gross abuse of legal power expressly intended to punish him for an act wholly irrelevant to the statute, a punishment which inflicted on him, as it was intended to do, the destruction of his economic life as a restaurant keeper within the province. Whatever may be the immunity of the Commission or its member from an action for damages, there is none in the respondent. He was under no duty in relation to the appellant and his act was an intrusion upon the functions of a statutory body. The injury done by him was a fault engaging liability within the principles of the underlying public law of Quebec: *Mostyn v. Fabrigas*, and under art. 1053 of the Civil Code. That, in the presence of expanding administrative regulation of economic activities, such a step and its consequences are to be suffered by the victim without recourse or remedy, that an administration according to law is to be superseded by action dictated by and according to the arbitrary likes, dislikes and irrelevant purposes of public officers acting beyond their duty, would signal the beginning of disintegration of the rule of law as a fundamental postulate of our constitutional structure. An administration of licences on the highest level of fair and impartial treatment to all may be forced to follow the practice of "first come, first served," which makes the strictest observance of equal responsibility to all of even greater importance; at this stage of developing government it would be a danger of high consequence to tolerate such a departure from good faith in executing the legislative purpose. It should be added, however, that that principle is not, by this language, intended to be extended to ordinary governmental employment: with that we are not here concerned.

It was urged by Mr. Beaulieu that the respondent, as the incumbent of an office of state, so long as he was proceeding in "good faith," was free to act in a matter of this kind virtually as he pleased. The office of Attorney-General traditionally and by statute carries duties that relate to advising the Executive, including here, administrative bodies, enforcing the public law and directing the administration of justice. In any decision of the statutory body in this case, he had no part to play beyond giving advice on legal questions arising. In that role his action should have been limited to advice on the validity of a revocation for such a reason or purpose and what that advice should have been does not seem to me to admit of any doubt. To pass from this limited scope of action to that of bringing about a step by the Commission beyond the bounds prescribed by the legislature for its exclusive action converted what was done into his personal act.

"Good faith" in this context, applicable both to the respondent and the general manager, means carrying out the statute according to its intent and for its purpose; it means good faith in acting with a rational appreciation of that intent and purpose and not with an improper intent and for an alien purpose; it does not mean for the purposes of punishing a person for exercising an unchallengeable right; it does not mean arbitrarily and illegally attempting to divest a citizen of an incident of his civil status. . . .

1.2

OF THE EXTENT OF THE LEGISLATIVE POWER
John Locke, *The Second Treatise* (1690)

The great end of Mens entring into Society, being the enjoyment of their Properties in Peace and Safety, and the great instrument and means of that being the Laws establish'd in that Society; the first and fundamental positive Law of all Commonwealths, is the establishing of the Legislative Power; as the first and fundamental natural Law, which is to govern even the Legislative itself, is the preservation of the Society, and (as far as will consist with the publik good) of every person in it. This Legislative is not only the supream power of the Commonwealth, but sacred and unalterable in the hands where the Community have once placed it; . . .

. . . Though the Legislative, whether placed in one or more, whether it be always in being, or only by intervals, tho' it be the Supream Power in every Common-wealth; yet,

First, It is not, nor can possibly be absolutely Arbitrary over the Lives and Fortunes of the People. For it being but the joynt power of every

Cambridge and New York: Cambridge University Press, 1960, from pages 401–409. Edited by Peter Laslett. Reprinted with permission.

Member of the Society given up to that Person, or Assembly, which is Legislator, it can be no more than those persons had in a State of Nature before they enter'd into Society, and gave up to the Community. . . . Their Power in the utmost Bounds of it, is limited to the publik good of the Society. It is a Power, that hath no other end but preservation, and therefore can never have a right to destroy, enslave, or designedly to impoverish the Subjects. The Obligations of the Law of Nature, cease not in Society but only in many Cases are drawn closer, and have by Humane Laws known Penalties annexed to them, to inforce their observation. Thus the Law of Nature stands as an Eternal Rule to all Men, Legislators as well as others. . . .

. . . Secondly, The Legislative, or Supream Authority, cannot assume to its self a power to Rule by extemporary Arbitrary Decrees, but is bound to dispense Justice, and decide the Rights of the Subject by promulgated standing Laws, and known Authoris'd Judges. For the Law of Nature being unwritten, and so no where to be found but in the minds of Men, they who through Passion or Interest shall mis-cite, or misapply it, cannot so easily be convinced of their mistake where there is no establish'd Judge: And so it serves not, as it ought, to determine the Rights, and fence the Properties of those that live under it, especially where every one is Judge, Interpreter, and Executioner of it too, and that in his own Case: And he that has right on his side, having ordinarily but his own single strength, hath not force enough to defend himself from Injuries, or to punish Delinquents. To avoid these Inconveniencies which disorder Mens Properties in the state of Nature, Men unite into Societies, that they may have the united strength of the whole Society to secure and defend their Properties, and may have standing Rules to bound it, by which every one may know what is his. To this end it is that Men give up all their Natural Power to the Society which they enter into, and the Community put the Legislative Power into such hands as they think fit, with this trust, that they shall be govern'd by declared Laws, or else their Peace, Quiet, and Property will still be at the same uncertainty, as it was in the state of Nature.

Absolute Arbitrary Power, or Governing without settled standing Laws, can neither of them consist with the ends of Society and Government, which Men would not quit the freedom of the state of Nature for, and tie themselves up under, were it not to preserve their Lives, Liberties and Fortunes; and by stated Rules of Right and Property to secure their Peace and Quiet. . . . And therefore whatever Form the Common-wealth is under, the Ruling Power ought to govern by declared and received Laws, and not by extemporary Dictates and undetermined Resolutions. For then Mankind will be in a far worse condition, than in the State of Nature, if they shall have armed one or a few Men with the joynt power of a Multitude, to force them to obey at pleasure the exorbitant and unlimited Decrees of their sudden thoughts, or unrestrain'd, and till that moment unknown Wills without having any measures set down which may guide and justifie their actions. For all the power the Government has, being only for the good of the Society, as it ought not to be *Arbitrary* and at Pleasure, so it ought to be exercised by *established and promulgated Laws*: that both the People may know their Duty, and be safe and secure within the limits of the Law, and the Rulers too kept within their due bounds, and not to be tempted, by the Power they have in their hands, to imploy it to such purposes, and by such measures, as they would not have known, and own not willingly.

... Thirdly, The Supream Power cannot take from any Man any part of his Property without his own consent. . . .

... Fourthly, The Legislative cannot transfer the Power of Making Laws to any other hands. For it being but a delegated Power from the People, they, who have it, cannot pass it over to others. The People alone can appoint the Form of the Commonwealth, which is by Constituting the Legislative, and appointing in whose hands that shall be.

... These are the Bounds which the trust that is put in them by the Society, and the Law of God and Nature, have set to the Legislative Power of every Commonwealth, in all Forms of Government.

First, They are to govern, by promulgated establish'd Laws, not to be varied in particular Cases, but to have one Rule for Rich and Poor, for the Favourite at Court, and the Country Man at Plough.

Secondly, These Laws also ought to be designed for no other end ultimately but the good of the People.

Thirdly, they must not raise Taxes on the Property of the People, without the Consent of the People, given by themselves, or their Deputies. And this properly concerns only such Governments where the Legislative is always in being, or at least where the People have not reserv'd any part of the Legislative to Deputies, to be from time to time chosen by themselves.

Fourthly, The Legislative neither must nor can transfer the Power of making Laws to any Body else, or place it anywhere but where the People have.

1.3

THE DECLARATION OF INDEPENDENCE
Thomas Jefferson (1776)

When in the course of human events, it becomes necessary for one people to dissolve the political bands which have connected them with another, and to assume among the Powers of the earth, the separate and equal station to which the Laws of Nature and of Nature's God entitle them, a decent respect to the opinions of mankind requires that they should declare the causes which impell them to the separation.

We hold these truths to be self-evident, that all men are created equal, that they are endowed by their Creator with certain unalienable Rights, that among these are Life, Liberty and the pursuit of Happiness. That to secure these rights, Governments are instituted among Men, deriving their just powers from the consent of the governed, that whenever any Form of Government becomes destructive of these ends, it is the Right of the People to alter or to abolish it, and to institute new Government, laying its foundation on such principles and organizing its powers in such form, as to them shall seem most likely to effect their Safety and Happiness. Prudence, indeed, will dictate that Governments long established should not be changed for light and transient causes; and accordingly all experience hath shown, that mankind are more disposed to suffer, while evils are sufferable, than to right themselves by abolishing the forms to which they are accustomed. But when a long train of abuses and usurpations, pursuing invariably the same Object evinces a design to reduce them under absolute Despotism, it is their right, it is their duty, to throw off such Government, and to provide new Guards for their future security. . . .

1.4

THE RULE OF LAW
A.V. Dicey, *The Law of the Constitution*, 7th ed. (1885)

Two features have at all times since the Norman Conquest characterised the political institutions of England.

The first of these features is the omnipotence or undisputed supremacy throughout the whole country of the central government. This authority of the state or the nation was during the earlier periods of our history represented by the power of the Crown. The King was the source of law and the maintainer of order. The maxim of the Courts, *tout fuit in luy et vient de lui al commencement*, was originally the expression of an actual and undoubted fact. This royal supremacy has now passed into that sovereignty of Parliament. . . .

London: MacMillan, 1908, from pages 179–201. Reprinted with permission.

The second of these features, which is closely connected with the first, is the rule or supremacy of law. This peculiarity of our polity is well expressed in the old saw of the Courts, "*La ley est le plus haute inheritance, que le roy ad; car par la ley il meme et toutes ses sujets sont rules, et si la ley ne fuit, nul roi, et nul inheritance sera.*"

This supremacy of the law, or the security given under the English constitution to the rights of individuals looked at from various points of view, forms the subject of this part of this treatise.

Foreign observers of English manners, such for example as Voltaire, De Lolme, Tocqueville, or Gneist, have been far more struck than have Englishmen themselves with the fact that England is a country governed, as is scarcely any other part of Europe, under the rule of law; and admiration or astonishment at the legality of English habits and feeling is nowhere better expressed than in a curious passage from Tocqueville's writings, which compares the Switzerland and the England of 1836 in respect of the spirit which pervades their laws and manners.

"I am not about," he writes, "to compare Switzerland with the United States, but with Great Britain. When you examine the two countries, or even if you only pass through them, you perceive, in my judgment, the most astonishing differences between them. Take it all in all, England seems to be much more republican than the Helvetic Republic. The principal differences are found in the institutions of the two countries, and especially in their customs(*moeurs*)." . . .

The Swiss do not show the love of justice which is such a strong characteristic of the English. Their Courts have no place in the political arrangements of the country, and exert no influence on public opinion. The love of justice, the peaceful and legal introduction of the judge into the domain of politics, are perhaps the most standing characteristics of a free people.

Finally, and this really embraces all the rest, the Swiss do not show at bottom that respect for justice, that love of law, that dislike of using force, without which no free nation can exist, which strikes strangers so forcibly in England. I sum up these impressions in a few words. Whoever travels in the United States is involuntarily and instinctively so impressed with the fact that the spirit of liberty and the taste for it have pervaded all the habits of the American people, that he cannot conceive of them under any but a Republican government. In the same way it is impossible to think of the English as living under any but a free government. But if violence were to destroy the Republican institutions in most of the Swiss Cantons, it would be by no means certain that after rather a short state of transition the people would not grow accustomed to the loss of liberty. In the United States and in England there seems to be more liberty in the customs than in the laws of the people. In Switzerland there seems to be more liberty in the laws than in the customs of the country.

Tocqueville's language has a twofold bearing on our present topic. His words point in the clearest manner to the rule, predominance, or supremacy of law as the distinguishing characteristic of English institutions. They further direct attention to the extreme vagueness of a trait of national character which is as noticeable as it is hard to portray. Tocqueville, we see, is clearly perplexed how to define a feature of English manners of which he at once recognises the existence; he mingles or confuses together the habit of self-government, the love of order, the respect for justice and a legal turn of mind. All these sentiments are intimately allied, but they cannot without confusion be identified with each other. If, however, a critic as acute as Tocqueville found a difficulty in describing one of the most marked peculiarities of English life, we may safely conclude that we ourselves, whenever we talk of Englishmen as loving the government of law, or of the supremacy of law as being a characteristic of the English constitution, are using words which, though they possess a real signifi- cance, are nevertheless to most persons who employ them full of vagueness and ambiguity. If therefore we are ever to appreciate the full import of the idea denoted by the term "rule, supremacy, or predominance of law," we must first determine precisely what we mean by such expressions when we apply them to the British constitution.

When we say that the supremacy or the rule of law is a characteristic of the English constitution, we generally include under one expression at least three distinct though kindred conceptions. . . .

. . . It means, in the first place, the absolute supremacy or predominance of regular law as opposed to the influence of arbitrary power, and ex- cludes the existence of arbitrariness, of prerogative, or even of wide discretionary authority on the part of the government. Englishmen are ruled by the law, and by the law alone; a man may with us be punished for a breach of law, but he can be punished for nothing else.

It means, again, equality before the law, or the equal subjection of all classes to the ordinary law of the land administered by the ordinary Law Courts; the "rule of law" in this sense excludes the idea of any exemption of officials or others from the duty of obedience to the law which governs other citizens or from the jurisdiction of the ordinary tribunals; there can be with us nothing really corresponding to the"administrative law" (*droit administratif*) or the "administrative tribunals" (*tribunaux administratifs*) of France. The notion which lies at the bottom of the "administrative law" known to foreign countries is, that affairs or disputes in which the govern- ment or its servants are concerned are beyond the sphere of the civil Courts and must be dealt with by special and more or less official bodies. This idea is utterly unknown to the law of England, and indeed is fundamen- tally inconsistent with our traditions and customs.

The "rule of law," lastly, may be used as a formula for expressing the fact that with us the law of the constitution, the rules which in foreign countries naturally form part of a constitutional code, are not the source but the consequence of the rights of individuals, as defined and enforced by the Courts; that, in short, the principles of private law have with us been by the action of the Courts and Parliament so extended as to determine the position of the Crown and of its servants; thus the constitution is the result of the ordinary law of the land.

General propositions, however, as to the nature of the rule of law carry us but a very little way. If we want to understand what that principle in all its different aspects and developments really means, we must try to trace its influence throughout some of the main provisions of the constitution. The best mode of doing this is to examine with care the manner in which the law of England deals with the following topics, namely, the right to personal freedom; the right to freedom of discussion; the right of public meeting; the use of martial law; the rights and duties of the army; the collection and expenditure of the public revenue; and the responsibility of Ministers. The true nature further of the rule of law as it exists in England will be illustrated by contrast with the idea of *droit administratif*, or administrative law, which prevails in many continental countries. These topics will each be treated of in their due order. The object, however, of this treatise, as the reader should remember, is not to provide minute and full information, e.g., as to the *Habeas Corpus* Acts, or other enactments protecting the liberty of the subject; but simply to show that these leading heads of constitutional law, which have been enumerated, these "articles," so to speak of the constitution, are both governed by, and afford illustrations of, the supremacy throughout English institutions of the law of the land. If at some future day the law of the constitution should be codified, each of the topics I have mentioned would be dealt with by the sections of the code.

1.5

THE INDEPENDENCE OF THE JUDICIARY
W.R. Lederman

This excerpt is reprinted as Reading 5.1.

1.6

KEY TERMS

Concepts

"the rule of law"
per legem terrae
natural right theory of government
"All men are by nature equal"
natural law
positive law
"written constitution"
"limited government"
judicial review
"unwritten constitution"
Parliamentary or Westminster form of democracy
"Separation of powers" or American form of democracy
judicial independence

Institutions, Events and Documents

Magna Carta (1215)
Habeas Corpus Act (1679)
"Glorious Revolution of 1688"
John Locke, *Second Treatise on Government* (1690)
Declaration of Independence (1776)
Constitution of the United States of America (1788)
U.S. Bill of Rights (1790)
Constitution Act, 1867 (British North American Act, 1867)
A.V.C. Dicey, *The Law of the Constitution* (1885)
Roncarelli v. Duplessis (1959)
Canadian Bill of Rights (1960)
Canadian Charter of Rights and Freedoms (1982)

2
Political Jurisprudence

This chapter addresses a deceptively simple set of questions. What do judges do? Do they just interpret and apply the law? Or, in the process of interpreting and applying the law, do the judges also "make law"? If the answer to this second question is yes, then how do courts differ from legislatures? Ultimately these questions take on a normative character: Should judges restrict themselves to declaring what the law is, as determined by statute and precedent? Or, if a judge finds the relevant statutes and precedents inadequate or even "wrong," is the judge free to "make new law"?

These are old and much debated questions, and they have been given very different answers by scholars and judges. There is some truth in each of these conflicting answers, because the character of the judicial process varies from nation to nation, and even within a single nation. What is true of trial courts is not applicable to appeal courts, and what is true for torts and contracts does not apply to constitutional law. Different judges on the same court may conduct themselves according to different judicial philosophies.

Canadian legal and political thought has traditionally held that judges do not, and should not, "make law" in any significant sense. "The law" has been portrayed as something that already exists "out there," and the role of the judge is merely to "find" it and declare its meaning to the interested parties. This view of judicial decision-making is known as the "declaratory model," and is closely associated with the British common law tradition, from which it evolved. In both Britain and Canada, this view of the judges as exercising "neither force nor will, but only judgment," has been reinforced by the practice of parliamentary supremacy and the theory of legal positivism.

The parliamentary model of government stresses that only the representative legislature can "make law," because only the elected legislators have the consent of the people to govern. This understanding of just laws comes directly from the equality-consent dimension of liberal political theory, as articulated by John Locke in the preceding chapter. According to its logic, it would be unjust and unjustifiable for judges to "make law," since judges are neither representative of nor responsible to the citizenry. This precise and limiting understanding of the judicial function has been reinforced by the theory of legal positivism. Legal positivism defines law as "the command of the sovereign," in this case, the Queen in Parliament. This definition stresses the form and function of the law, not its content. The notion of judicial law-making is logically incompatible with this view.

It is important to remember that the "declaratory model" of judging is drawn from British experience. This explains both its original dominance of Canadian jurisprudence, and also its more recent decline. As we saw in Chapter One, Canada differs from Great Britain by being a federal not a unitary state, and by having the boundaries of federalism defined in a "written constitution"—the Constitution Act, 1867.[1] Because of this difference, Canadian courts and judges have had to fulfill an important function unknown in British legal experience — judicial review. Since its creation in 1875, the Supreme Court of Canada has acted as the "neutral umpire" of the federal division of powers between Ottawa and the provinces.

A constitutional law of federalism is political in a way other kinds of law are not. It defines and therefore limits the law-making powers of rival levels of government. Questions of constitutional law often arise in the context of heated political struggles between Ottawa and one or more provinces. Political passions run high, and all of Canada awaits the Court's decision with interest. Major government policy often hangs in the balance. In such circumstances, it becomes difficult to believe that judges are not aware of the policy consequences of their "legal" decisions and that these decisions are not influenced by the anticipation of their consequences. Indeed, in 1985, the former Chief Justice of the Supreme Court of Canada, Brian Dickson, cautioned his fellow judges against adopting a "mechanical legalism," advising them instead to "be aware of the underlying principles and practical consequences of questions before [them], paying close attention to the policy aspects of each issue."[2] Under these circumstances, final appeal courts inevitably come to be regarded as hybrid institutions, part-judicial, part-political.

In view of this dimension of Canadian law, it is not surprising that Canadian jurists began to be attracted by the "legal realism" theory of judging that had developed in the United States in the early decades of this century. The Americans had lived with the practice of judicial review since 1803. Moreover, the American Supreme Court exercised judicial review not just over the boundaries of federalism, but also enforced the more absolute limitations of the Bill of Rights. By the end of the nineteenth century, the U.S. Supreme Court had come to play an influential role in the major political issues of the day. The traditional "declaratory model" of judging, inherited with the common law from Great Britain, seemed to

---

[1] Originally known and still commonly referred to as the British North America Act.

[2] "Dickson discourages mechanical legalism," *Globe and Mail*, Oct. 5, 1985, p. A4. This message seems somewhat inconsistent with Dickson's opinion in the 1976 case of *Harrison v. Carswell* (See Reading 2.3), and suggests that Dickson may have changed his mind.

provide a less and less satisfactory explanation of what American courts and judges were actually doing in the area of constitutional law. A new generation of American jurists began to rethink and reformulate the relationship between judges and law. Through the writings of men like Oliver Wendell Holmes, Benjamin Cardozo, and Roscoe Pound, the "legal realism" theory of judging was developed.

The legal realists stressed the creative and personal connection between judges and law. Holmes declared that the law is "the prophecies of what the courts will do in fact, and nothing more pretentious."[3] Pound and Cardozo extended Holmes's critique by elaborating the subjective, personal dimension of judging. The key to this analysis was the "unfinished" quality of law, and the resulting discretion and freedom of the judge to give the law its practical meaning when applied to a novel set of circumstances. The inescapably personal dimension of judging is explored in former Justice Bertha Wilson's discussion of the question, "Will Women Judges Make a Difference?" (See Reading 2.2) Justice Wilson's acceptance of the argument that the gender of a judge may influence his or her decisions reveals the extent to which legal realism has triumphed. However, acceptance of the legal realist view still leaves open the question whether this is desirable or should be encouraged, especially in appeal court judges and especially in the area of constitutional law. The first generation of legal realists were almost all supporters of judicial self-restraint and deference to legislative judgments, while today many of their followers support a more activist exercise of judicial review.

The preceding example of Justice Wilson notwithstanding, Canadian jurists were initially unreceptive to the theory of judicial realism which they considered an American idiosyncrasy. Predictably, it was the constitutional law decisions of Canada's first final court of appeal — the Judicial Committee of the Privy Council (JCPC) — that provoked the first appearance of judicial realism in Canadian legal and political thought. Beginning in the 1890s, the JCPC made a series of important constitutional decisions that progressively narrowed the scope of the legislative powers of the federal government. This trend reached a climax in the mid-thirties, when the Privy Council struck down a number of federal "New Deal" programs designed to cope with the economic and social devastation of the Great Depression. This provoked an angry reaction among some Canadian leaders, culminating in the *O'Connor Report* (1939) to the Senate, which advocated the abolition of appeals to the JCPC. The *O'Connor Report* argued that questions of Canadian constitutional law could be better answered by Canadian judges, judges with first-hand familiarity with the political and economic realities of Canadian life. Implicit in this argument was a tacit acceptance of the legal realist view that the personal background and political formation of a judge is an important factor in his

---

3 *Harvard Law Review*, 10 (1897), p. 39.

legal decision-making. Because the goal of this movement was to make the Supreme Court the final court of appeal "of and for Canadians," it came to be known as "judicial nationalism."[4]

In 1949, appeals to the JCPC were abolished, and the Supreme Court of Canada became the final and exclusive court of appeal for Canada. But this has not stopped the debate over the nature of the judicial process in Canada. The adoption in 1960 of the Bill of Rights stimulated new debate on this old issue. The broadly worded prohibitions of the Bill of Rights — such as freedom of religion and equality before the law — seemed to invite and even require judicial choice and creativity in giving them practical application. By and large the Canadian judiciary declined this invitation. Stressing the statutory (as opposed to constitutional) character of the 1960 Bill of Rights, and the absence of any explicit qualification of the tradition of parliamentary supremacy, the Supreme Court gave a limited and traditional interpretation to the Bill's major provisions. Partly in response to the courts' cautious use of the Bill of Rights, it was superceded in 1982 by the Charter of Rights and Freedoms. A constitutionally entrenched document that applies to both levels of government, the Charter raises the issue of proper judicial decision-making in an even more pointed and pressing manner.

The competing views of proper judicial conduct are the subject of Paul Weiler's 1967 article, "Two Models of Judicial Decision-Making." (See Reading 2.1) One—the "adjudication of disputes" model—stresses the traditional understanding of the judicial function, and the institutional characteristics that distinguish the judicial process from the legislative process. Weiler's second model, the "policy-making" model, asserts that there is no essential difference between judges and legislators, that "they make policy, or legislate, through essentially the same mode of reasoning."

Weiler's two models are not coterminous with the declaratory and judicial realist theories of judging. While most informed observers now reject the declaratory model of judging, acceptance of judical realism does not require acceptance of Weiler's "policy-making" model. While conceding that the personal characteristics of judges do influence their legal choices, many Canadian commentators continue to stress the "interstitial" character of judicial law-making. They argue that while some judicial law-making may be an inevitable by-product of judicial interpretation, it is and should remain secondary to the main function of adjudication of disputes. While this prescription for minimizing the law-making potential of judges may seem to rob the courts of influence, Peter Russell argues that it may do more to preserve judicial authority. Russell notes that the *O'Connor Report* and the increased acknowledgement of judical power in Canadian legal

---

[4] See Peter H. Russell, "Judicial Power in Canada's Political Culture," in *Courts and Trials: A Multidisciplinary Approach*, ed. M .L. Friedland. (Toronto, ON: University of Toronto Press, 1975), p. 75. This article was reprinted in the first edition of this book.

culture resulted in a loss of authority for the Supreme Court in Quebec. "Just as nationalist Canadian jurists denounced the British judges for their insensitive interpretation of the Canadian constitution, nationalist lawyers in Quebec resumed their protest against the Supreme Court of Canada's insensitive interpretation of Quebec's Civil Code."[5] Russell's thesis that "less may be more" is especially relevant to judicial decision-making under the 1982 Charter of Rights. While the Charter clearly expands the potential for judicial law-making, the section 33 legislative override explicitly arms governments with a power to fight back against perceived abuses of judicial review. Is it by accident that Quebec has had more statutes declared invalid under the Charter than any other province and has also been the province to make the most use of the section 33 override?[6]

Weiler's model provides a conceptual framework through which we can better understand the differences between Canadian, British, and American judicial process, and better evaluate recommendations that Canadian judges adopt a greater "policy-making" role. The "two models" analysis also demonstrates that different institutional consequences follow from the two different conceptions of judging. Traditional Canadian practices regarding judicial recruitment, judicial independence, jurisdiction, access to the courts, judicial fact-finding, and modes of legal argument — were all premised on the understanding that judges do not, and should not, "make law." As Canadian judges have moved away from the "adjudication of disputes" approach and toward a greater "policy-making" role, especially since the 1982 adoption of the Charter, the continued adequacy of traditional institutional practices has been challenged. Weiler's elaborations of the different institutional consequences of the two models are not included in this chapter, but are discussed in the introductions to the subsequent chapters. We can thus use Weiler's analytical framework to understand the traditional aspects of the judicial process and to evaluate the changes that have occurred in recent decades.

The last two readings demonstrate the contemporary character of the debate over the proper role of the judiciary in Canadian law and politics. In the 1976 case of *Harrison v. Carswell*, we find a sharp disagreement over proper judicial role between the then Chief Justice of Canada, the late Bora Laskin, and his successor as Chief Justice, Brian Dickson. (See Reading 2.3) The principal difference between Dickson's majority opinion and Laskin's dissent is not about the law but about the limits of the Supreme Court's responsibility. Both agree that there is a serious legal problem raised by the *Harrison* case. Laskin argues that the Supreme Court should solve it, while Dickson maintains that law reform is the business of the legislatures, not the courts.

---

[5] Russell, p. 75.

[6] See Readings 11.5 and 13.4.

Michael Mandel's analysis of the Supreme Court's decision in the 1981 *Patriation Reference* provides strong evidence to support the judicial realist school. (See Reading 2.4) The Supreme Court's decision in the *Patriation Reference* was arguably the most important it has ever made. It broke the political deadlock between the Federal government and eight of the ten provinces and led to the adoption of the Constitution Act, 1982, of which the Charter of Rights was an integral part. At stake was whether Prime Minister Trudeau's plan to "patriate" the constitution unilaterally—that is, add an amending formula and the Charter to the Constitution without first obtaining the consent of all the provinces—was constitutionally permissible. While it was generally agreed that constitutional convention required the unanimous consent of the provinces for a formal amendment of this magnitude, it was also agreed that constitutional conventions were political matters and could not be recognized or enforced in courts of law. The federal lawyers argued that unilateral amendment was both constitutional (i.e., there was no convention of unanimity) and "legal" (i.e., even if there was, it could not be enforced by the courts). The opposing provinces argued that Trudeau's unilateralism was both unconstitutional and illegal (i.e., that it violated the convention and that the convention could be enforced by the courts). In the end, a sharply divided Supreme Court split the difference and ruled that the federal government's plan was "unconstitutional but legal."

Mandel shows that the division of the judges closely followed their political and regional affiliations. The three judges from Quebec all agreed that unilateralism was unconstitutional. The two judges who said that Trudeau's plan was both unconstitutional and illegal were Tory appointees from provinces that opposed the Liberal plan (Alberta and Nova Scotia). The three judges who took the other extreme—that unilateralism was both legal and constitutional—were all Trudeau appointees, two from Ontario, a province that supported the Trudeau initiative. Of the seven-judge coalition that held unilateralism was legal, six were Trudeau appointees. "If we were paying attention," writes Mandel, this "gave us a good idea of what Canada could expect with the Charter."

2.1

TWO MODELS OF JUDICIAL DECISION-MAKING
Paul Weiler

I. Introduction

The philosophy of the judicial process will soon be of great practical significance for the Canadian legal scene. The traditional, inarticulate, legal positivism of Canadian lawyers and judges is rapidly becoming outmoded by recent developments. First, the determination of our new Prime Minister [Ed. note: In 1968, Pierre Trudeau had just been elected P.M.] to achieve an entrenched Bill of Rights will, of necessity, confer on the courts the power and the duty to make fundamental value judgments which cannot flow mechanically and impersonally from the language of the document. Second, the British House of Lords has decided to change its long-standing rule that its earlier precedents could not be overruled. Presumably, and hopefully, the Canadian Supreme Court will continue to imitate slavishly its English counterpart by following this decision. Third, Canadian scholarship about the Supreme Court has begun to utilize some of the advanced techniques of the behavioural sciences in order to study judicial decision-making. Two related developments should follow. Our judges will grow increasingly conscious of the freedom and the responsibility they have to develop and alter the law. Both academics and the public will become aware of the fact of judicial power and then go on to question its legitimacy.

It is only too true that we will be decades behind the same course of developments in our neighbour to the south. There is a favourable cast to this situation. We have available to us a significant body of American experience, and of jurisprudential reflection concerning it, which we can use in intelligently understanding and evaluating the process of change that the Canadian judicial process is likely to undergo. Moreover we can choose between at least two, substantially different conceptions of judicial decision-making which have been elaborated in some detail in American legal thinking. One theory characterizes the judicial function as, essentially, the "adjudication of disputes" within the legal system. The other holds that at least some courts are primarily engaged in "policy-making," in a manner largely indistinguishable from the other political agencies in our society. It is my intention to draw together, in a systematic way, these two very sophisticated theories, to show the conclusions which flow from the insights that lie at the root of each "model," and to indicate the impor-

Canadian Bar Review 46 (1968), from pages 406–471. Reprinted with permission.

tant problems which, as yet, detract from the adequacy of each. In doing so, I shall also record the significance of many apparently unrelated phenomena within the Canadian judicial system.

What theoretical significance do I attach to the use of these models? Sociological theory tells us that the position of judge in any society carries with it a set of shared expectations about the type of conduct that is appropriate to that position. These expectations have reference not only to the proper *physical* behaviour of one who occupies that position but also to the mode of reasoning to be used in making his judicial decisions. There are several possible decision-making roles that can be proposed by society for its judges, each having different supporting reasons for their acceptance. Two of these roles are the subject of this article, "adjudicator" and "policy-maker." Both embody fundamental value choices for the society which, presumably, are made after some consideration of these competing justifications. Once the choice is made, the expectations that are connected with this one role must be shared by at least a substantial majority of the participants within the system in order that it have some institutional stability. Finally, the institutional position of the judge is reciprocally connected with society's wishes about how they should behave in their decision-making capacity. It is this connexion between the role we give to our judges and the design of the structure within which they operate that the two models are intended to display.

Hence, the function of each model is to trace the institutional implications of each of these fundamental value judgments about the appropriate mission of the judge. One model is based on the value judgment that judges should make policy choices as a political actor; the other assumes it is desirable that judges confine their activity to the settlement of private disputes. As we shall see, there are real differences in the social arrangements which are most compatible with these two distinctive judgments about the appropriate judicial role. We should be able to verify the existence of these proposed differences in actual practice, or in recommendations about changes in the existing system. Moreover, not only do these theoretical models serve as a framework for explanations of how judges do behave, they also assist our appraisal of how judges ought to behave.

Finally, the use of these two schematic representations of the judicial process should serve to illuminate a significant moral problem that has surfaced recently in American legal discussion of the role of the judiciary. Once an institution has gained inertial force and power as a result of shared expectations about how it is and ought to operate, it is then available as an instrument for serving social purposes that are not compatible with the original model. Is it legitimate for those who believe in a alternative model of judicial behaviour to make covert use of the existing organization? To what extent will such "parasitic" utilization of one version of the judicial process induce actual changes in the existing system which make it more compatible with the form that naturally flows from a new conception of appropriate judicial decision-making? To these, and other problems, this article is addressed in a preliminary way.

II. The Adjudication of Disputes Model

The two models whose traits I am going to describe both agree in rejecting the viability and the desirability of the traditional Anglo-Canadian model of judicial decision-making. The latter suggests that a judge decides his cases by the somewhat mechanical application of legal rules which he finds *established* in the legal system. They are, in this sense, *binding* on him completely apart from his own judgment as to their fitness. This theory has a historical, if not a logical, relationship with the dictates of an Austinian, positivist conception of law and a rigid notion of the division of powers. The "adjudication of disputes" model shares, to some extent, the assumption that judges have a distinctive and limited function. However, it emphatically denies the conclusion that it is *possible* for a judge to be purely passive, and *desirable* that he makes decisions without a necessary exercise of his judgment about what the law ought to be.

As was stated earlier the purpose of the model is to show the necessary inter-relationship between the function which judicial decision-making is primarily intended to perform, the institutional characteristics which are implied by such a function, and the qualities in judicial decision-making which flow naturally from this institutional background. In short, the job we give judges to perform determines the design of the judicial process; the nature of the structure influences the manner in which judges carry out their tasks; the form of judicial action limits the issues judges may appropriately resolve. Hence the adjudication model rejects the tacit assumption, often made, of "institutional fungibility." The latter holds that the same substantive policies can and should be achieved in the same undifferentiated way, whatever be the organizational form in which various actors are allowed to strive for these ends. To the contrary, the specific institutional form of adjudication, by comparision with that of legislation, for instance, limits both the goals for which judges should strive and the means they should use for achieving these goals.

To summarize the model very briefly, it conceives of the judge as the adjudicator of specific, concrete disputes, who disposes of the problems within the latter by elaborating and applying a legal regime to facts, which he finds on the basis of evidence and argument presented to him in an adversary process. The body of rules and principles which are to govern the private conduct of the participants in the legal order are largely settled by forces outside adjudication, although the judge does play a collaborative role in articulating and elaborating these principles. However, the primary focus of adjudication is the settlement of disputes arising out of private line of conduct, by evaluating such conduct in the light of established rules and principles. As we shall see, the whole institutional structure of adjudication — its incidence, access to it, the mode of participation in it, the bases for decision, and the nature of the relief available in it — are all defined by and flow naturally from this function. The key elements within the adjudicative model are (1) settlement of disputes, (2) the adversary process and (3) an established system of standards which are utilized in the process to dispose of the disputes.

Settlement of Concrete Disputes

The first characteristic of "adjudication" is that it has the function of settling disputes (between private individuals or groups, or the government and the individual). These disputes are not future-oriented debates over general policy questions, although, as we shall see, the latter can enter into the final resolution of the problem. Rather, the disputes which are necessary to set the process of adjudication in motion involve "controversies" arising out of a particular line of conduct which causes a collision of specific interests. There is no *logical* or *factual* necessity about this proposition. There can be exceptions and the question of defining the limits of the adjudicative function can be difficult and debatable in the marginal areas. . . .

. . . To summarize, a court should confine itself to settling concrete, private disputes between individuals who apply to the adjudicator for the resolution of their problem.

An Adversary Process

An adversary process is one which satisfies, more or less, this factual description: as a prelude to the dispute being solved, the interested parties have the opportunity of adducing evidence (or proof) and making arguments to a disinterested and impartial arbiter who decides the case on the basis of this evidence and these arguments. This is by contrast with the public processes of decision by "legitimated power" and "mediation-agreement," where the guaranteed private modes of participation are voting and negotiation respectively. Adjudication is distinctive because it guarantees to each of the parties who are affected the right to prepare for themselves the representations on the basis of which their dispute is to be resolved.

The Need for Standards

. . . Why does the institution of adjudication require the existence of standards for decision? Of what type are these standards and what does it mean to say that they "exist"? Taking these questions in reverse order, in order that standards "exist," there must be a shared consensus between the adjudicator and the parties about what the standards are which the former is going to apply. Secondly, the parties must reasonably have expected, at the time they acted, that these standards would be used to evaluate their private conduct. Of course, some legal rules can be directed only to the arbiter himself dealing with purely remedial problems. We draw our standards from the legal order which regulates private conduct because a primary objective of the use of adjudication is to preserve the viability of this legal order by settling authoritatively the disputes arising within it. Successful adjudication requires that there be a shared consensus about these rules, especially insofar as they can be utilized to evaluate the conduct of the parties which gives rise to the dispute.

In order that adjudicative decisions be characterized by the quality of rationality which is a prerequisite for their moral force and acceptability, the arbiter must have some principles which he can utilize in explaining to himself and to the parties his reasons for deciding one way or the other. The arbiter is under a duty to articulate a reasoned basis for his decision (whether or not he writes an opinion), because he is not conceded the power of *enactment*. He is not considered to have a *legitimate* power to exercise a discretion to settle a matter just because it needs settling, and without giving reasons for deciding on the particular disposition he selects. Hence, he cannot merely confront an undifferentiated factual situation and decide by an intuitive "leap in the dark." He needs a set of ordering principles which enable him to make sense of the situation and abstract those relevent facets of it which can be organized into a reasoned argument.

Second, the adjudicative process can have the enhanced quality of rationality, which derives from its focusing on a specific, concrete dispute for decision, only if there are standards or principles which enable the adjudicator to single out the relevant, problematic facets of the situation on which he is going to concentrate his attention. If there is no framework of settled principles within which he can operate, and every aspect of every situation is always open to question, then the adjudicator will not be able to focus his attention on unresolved problems. Thus, he will not be able to attain a significantly higher quality of rationality in the solution which he produces for the problem.

Thirdly, to the extent that adjudication entails adversary participation, the presentation of proofs and arguments to the arbiter, the process is meaningless unless the parties can know before their preparation and presentation of the case the principles and standards which the arbiter is likely to find relevant to his disposition of the dispute. It is impossible to make an intelligent argument "in the air" and without any idea of which factors are considered relevant by the person whom one's argument is attempting to persuade. If a relatively passive attitude is necessarily conducive to impartiality (although this does not exclude some reciprocal clarification of views), and a high degree of rationality in result thus depends directly on the quality of the preparations and representation by each side, then a consensus of standards is needed in order that intelligent alternative positions are established and that an adequate "joinder of issue" results. . . .

III.   The Judicial Policy-Maker Model: The Judge as Political Actor

A second distinctive model of the judicial process has been developed in recent years, largely by American political scientists. Of course, it is not original in recognizing the inescapable fact that judicial decisions must involve the creative exercise of a court's judgment. It builds on the work of American Legal Realism, which showed that the mechanical application of rigid, automatic rules does not and cannot dispose of individual cases. Men, as judges, decide cases and this activity is one for which they are personally responsible.

However, as we have see, the "adjudication" model also begins with this assumption. Judges must collaborate with other bodies in society in the development and elaboration of the law "as it ought to be." Yet this collaborative role is institutionally distinctive. The creative articulation of new legal rules is limited and incremental; it is based on a moving background of established legal principles; it is related to the dispute-settling focus of courts because the new rule must be appropriate for retrospective application to the facts giving rise to the instant case; finally, the adoption of the new rule must be justified in a reasoned opinion which establishes the probable "rightness" of the new rule. This whole set of limitations on judicial law-making is necessary in order to *legitimate* the final product. However, this legitimacy does not require a mechanical deduction of the rule from legal premises in which it somehow pre-exists, as in a "brooding omnipresence in the sky." The reasoning in the opinion is not of a logical-deductive type. Yet, it is supposed to be sufficiently communicable that it is open, in principle at least, to prior vicarious participation by the parties in the adversary process.

Many political scientists, by contrast, believe that judges should be perceived as political actors, continuously engaged in the formulation of policy for society. To say that judges are political actors is not simply to assert the truism that they are part of the governmental system, "authoritatively allocating values in society." Nor is it characteristic of only this model that judges exercise personal judgment in each decision they make and that no conclusions are automatic. What is distinctive is the thesis that judges make policy, or legislate, through essentially the same mode of reasoning as other actors in the governmental system. Moreover, at least for some courts, such political action is becoming, and is seen to be becoming, their primary concern, and adjudication of disputes is growing secondary.

Legislators have traditionally been contrasted with courts by the fact that society considers it acceptable for them to justify authoritative policy-making by reference to their own value preferences, or the interests of those who support or have access to them. Legislators do not feel institutionally committed to the formulation of new legal rules only if they can be justified by a reasoned opinion relating the development to accepted doctrinal premises. This model suggests that some courts also are not, and should not be, so institutionally committed.

The quality of political decision-making both influences and reflects the make-up of the institution within which it is carried on. If, as, and when judges become candid policy-makers, courts will take on a "political" character, and judges will be subjected to "political" pressures. The new orientation of the "policy-making" model should render appropriate for judges the same analysis that is applied to other political actors, as regards the recruitment of the men who make these decisions, the timing of their policy pronouncements, the influences brought to bear on the court, both internally and externally, and the success which attends its policy promulgation. The new model explains, in an illuminating way, many recent judicial phenomena that have followed the proposal and adoption of the new political role by some courts in some legal system. Moreover, it shows the linkage of the various components in the judicial systems, as it becomes redesigned for its new institutional function. I shall compare the new model with the old, showing the changes we may expect in the existing system if and when judges turn from adjudication to concentrate on policy-making. I will not be interested in empirical proof, by scalogram analysis or otherwise, that courts do or do not make decisions based on "policy," rather than "law." Assuming that judges may internalize the role of "political actor" rather than "adjudicator," I hope to make clear the institutional significance of this fact. . . .

IV.   Conclusion

I do not believe it is possible yet to decide which of these models expresses a more appropriate role for judges in our society. Nor does either version furnish a type of litmus test for discovering the nature of our present system. Probably, the various judiciaries in the common law are based on different mixtures of each role, however contradictory they may appear in the abstract. Our models are "ideal types," furnishing us with distinctive angles of vision on the same judicial reality, thus allowing us a more profound understanding and evaluation of tendencies within the existing system. Moreover, these two artificial constructs of the judicial process show us the practical significance of two as yet unresolved problems in legal philosophy. Is rational and communicable decision-making possible in choosing between social values? Is judicial choice about values that favour one interest over another a fair institution within a democracy?

In conclusion, I should emphasize my belief that the judicial process in Canada fits neither model as regards the appropriate mode of reasoning, although it is organized more or less along adjudicative lines. In fact, common law judging in Canada has truly been a wasteland of arid legalism, one that is only beginning to be relieved by a profounder vision of the scope of judicial action. For this reason alone, I am just as dubious about the desirability of judicial review of legislative action as about the present review of administrative action. Perhaps the proposal for a Canadian Bill of Rights should await the advent of judges who are products of a different legal education. It seems safe to predict that they will have been schooled in some version of the philosophies of judicial decision-making which I have sketched.

2.2

WILL WOMEN JUDGES REALLY MAKE A DIFFERENCE?
Bertha Wilson

This article is reprinted as Reading 4.3.

2.3

HARRISON v. CARSWELL
Supreme Court of Canada (1976)

In this case the Supreme Court was faced with a dispute between Harrison, the manager of a shopping centre in Winnipeg, and Carswell, a striking employee of one of the stores in the shopping centre. Carswell was participating in a lawful strike and was picketing on the sidewalk in front of her employer's store. Harrison informed her that picketing was not permitted in any area of the shopping centre, and asked her to leave. Carswell refused, and was arrested and convicted of petty trespass. The legal issue at stake in this case was the conflict between the traditional rights of private property (protected by the law of trepass) and the right to strike.

The judgment of Laskin C.J. and Spence and Beetz J.J. was delivered by THE CHIEF JUSTICE (dissenting): I would be content to adopt the reasons of Freedman C.J.M. and, accordingly, to dismiss this appeal without more if I did not feel compelled, in view of the course of argument, to add some observations bearing on the decision of this Court in *Peters v. The Queen* dismissing an appeal from the judgment of the Ontario Court of Appeal. The observations I am about to make about the *Peters* case carry into two areas of concern respecting the role of this Court as the final Court in this country in both civil and criminal causes. Those areas are, first, whether this Court must pay mechanical deference to *stare decisis* and, second, whether this Court has a balancing role to play, without yielding place to the Legislature, where an ancient doctrine, in this case trespass, is invoked in a new setting to suppress a lawful activity supported both by legislation and by a well-understood legislative policy. . . .

. . . This Court, above all others in this country, cannot be simply mechanistic about previous decisions, whatever be the respect it would pay to such decisions. What we would be doing here, if we were to say that the *Peters* case, because it was so recently decided, has concluded the present case for us, would be to take merely one side of a debatable issue and say that it concludes the debate without the need to hear the other side.

I do not have to call upon pronouncements of members of this Court that we are free to depart from previous decisions in order to support the pressing need to examine the present case on its merits.

The judgment of Martland, Judson, Ritchie, Pigeon, Dickson, and de Grandpré, J.J. was delivered by Dickson J.

. . . The submission that this Court should weigh and determine the respective values to society of the right to property and the right to picket raises important and difficult political and socio-economic issues, the resolution of which must, by their very nature, be arbitrary and embody personal economic and social beliefs. It raises also fundamental questions as to the role of this Court under the Canadian constitution. The duty of the Court, as I envisage it, is to proceed in the discharge of its adjudicative function in a reasoned way from principled decision and established concepts. I do not for a moment doubt the power of the Court to act creatively — it has done so on countless occasions; but manifestly one must ask — what are the limits of the judicial function? There are many and varied answers to this question. Holmes J. said in *Southern Pacific Co. v. Jensen*, at p. 221: "I recognize without hesitation that judges do and must legislate, but they can do it only interstitially; they are confined from molar to molecular actions." Cardozo, *The Nature of the Judicial Process* (1921), p. 141, recognized that the freedom of the judge is not absolute in this expression of his review:

> This judge, even when he is free, is still not wholly free. He is not to innovate at pleasure. He is not a knight-errant, roaming at will in pursuit of his own ideal of beauty or of goodness. He is to draw his inspiration from consecrated principles.

The former Chief Justice of the Australian High Court, Sir Owen Dixon, in an address delivered at Yale University in September 1955, "Concerning Judicial Method," had this to say:

> But in our Australian High Court we have had as yet no deliberate innovators bent on express change of acknowledged doctrine. It is one thing for a court to seek to extend the

application of accepted principles to new cases or to reason from the more fundamental of settled legal principles to new conclusions or to decide that a category is not closed against unforeseen instances which in reason might be subsumed thereunder. It is an entirely different thing for a judge, who is discontented with a result held to flow from a long accepted legal principle, deliberately to abandon the principle in the name of justice or of social necessity or of social convenience. The former accords with the technique of the common law and amounts to no more than an enlightened application of modes of reasoning traditionally respected in the courts. It is a process by the repeated use of which the law is developed, is adapted to new conditions, and is improved in content. The latter means an abrupt and almost arbitrary change.

Society has long since acknowledged that a public interest is served by permitting union members to bring economic pressure to bear upon their respective employers through peaceful picketing, but the right has been exercisable in some locations and not in others and to the extent that picketing has been permitted on private property the right hitherto has been accorded by statute. For example, s. 87 of the Labour Code of British Columbia Act, 1973 (B.C.) (2nd Sess.), c. 122, provides that no action lies in respect of picketing permitted under the Act for trespass to real property to which a member of the public ordinarily has access.

Anglo-Canadian jurisprudence has traditionally recognized, as a fundamental freedom, the right of the individual to the enjoyment of property and the right not to be deprived thereof, or any interest therein, save by due process of law. The Legislature of Manitoba has declared in The Petty Trespasses Act that any person who trespasses upon land, the property of another, upon or through which he has been requested by the owner not to enter, is guilty of an offence. If there is to be any change in this statute law, if A is to be given the right to enter and remain on the land of B against the will of B, it would seem to me that such a change must be made by the enacting institution, the Legislature, which is representative of the people and designed to manifest the political will, and not by the Court.

2.4

RE CONSTITUTION OF CANADA, 1981: THE *PATRIATION REFERENCE*
Michael Mandel

[The constitutional reference cases of 1981 were] the third and by far most important aspect of the provincial counterattack. Three of the opposing provincial governments, Manitoba, Quebec, and Newfoundland, referred the question of the constitutionality of the federal proposal to their provincial supreme courts. But this was "constitutionality" with a difference. For in addition to the ordinary questions governments ask courts concerning matters of constitutional *legality*, each government asked a separate question about whether it was consistent with constitutional *convention* (understood as meaning, roughly, a historically recognized norm of political behaviour) for the federal government to approach the UK Parliament over such substantial provincial opposition.

Of course, everyone knew that the government's plan was *not* consistent with constitutional convention. What was extraordinary was to ask the courts to say so. Courts had sometimes ruled on conventions where doing so was necessary to resolve a question of law, but they had *never* done so where, as in this case, the supposed convention was completely detached from any legal question. Why?

The technical distinction between conventions and laws is that conventions are *unenforceable* in the courts. This means that the courts will not authorize the use of force to obtain obedience to conventions. But they will with laws. Why is this important? Because this regulation or authorization of the use of official force, this law *enforcement*, is the not merely one of the functions of courts among many. It is their defining characteristic. Courts do not distinguish between the legal and the illegal in a vacuum or as an end in itself. Their determinations are a crucial part of the legitimate use of force in the modern state. The practical activity of the use of force by the state requires an institution capable of finally, efficiently, and authoritatively determining its legitimacy in any given case. The very idea of legality requires such an institution. That institution is the courts. Their word is law. But we do not need only one institution authorized to determine right and wrong or historical practice. Quite the contrary. We can do without "official" moralities and "official" histories. For a court to

The Charter of Rights and the Legalization of Politics in Canada (Toronto, ON: Wall and Thompson, 1989), from pages 24–34. Reprinted with permission.

recognize a convention that by definition it will nevertheless not enforce is to do something that *anyone* has the authority to do. A court's opinion on the matter has no more formal, judicial, legal, or whatever-you-choose-to-call-it, authority than yours, mine, Pierre Trudeau's or René Lévesque's. If it is more persuasive, this is a political fact, not a legal one.

So when the courts were asked a separate question on constitutional convention, they were asked something outside of the realm of law and judging. Nevertheless, there was little reluctance on their part to answer it. Only one judge out of 22 refused out of a sense of judicial propriety . [Ed. note: the figure of 22 judges includes those who initially heard the reference in the Courts of Appeal.] As for the answers to the various questions, the three appellate courts were hopelessly divided, with Manitoba and Quebec (over dissents) in favour, and Newfoundland (unanimously) opposed. Of the 13 appellate judges who heard the cases, seven found in favour of the federal government and six against it. There was no avoiding referring the whole matter to the Supreme Court of Canada. . . .

The arguments before the Supreme Court of Canada by a battery of constitutional lawyers in *Re Constitution of Canada* took only five days of late April 1981, amid what court historians claim was the most concentrated public attention in its history. However, the Court took the entire summer to prepare its decision, which was ready for release on September 28. Far from being reticent about its new role, the Court seemed eager for it, even too eager. It broke yet another tradition by allowing TV cameras into the courtroom for the first time, but the effect was ruined when one of the judges tripped a sound cable rendering the Chief Justice's reading of the judgment inaudible. What he had to say was hardly the stuff of high television ratings anyway. It was a dry recitation of the various questions put to the Court and their technical answers, confusing even for lawyers. The Supreme Court had many lessons to learn in public relations. What the decision would mean in political terms was also unclear at first. It was interpreted differently according to which side of the issue and which side of the Quebec border one was on. Quebec's *Le Devoir* headline was one way of looking at it: "Legal but unconstitutional," while Ontario's *Globe and Mail* headline was another: "PM's bid 'offends' but is legal." Both were technically correct: the legality of the plan was affirmed by a vote of seven judges to two, and its inconsistency with constitutional convention by a vote of six to three. A lot of the confusion came from the shifting alignments on the Court with some judges dissenting on one question yet joining the majority on the other. But closer examination shows the political logic of the decision. The Court voted almost perfectly along political and regional lines:

Judge	Province	Appointed	Legal?	Conventional
Laskin	Ont.	Trudeau	Yes	Yes
Estey	Ont.	Trudeau	Yes	Yes
MacIntyre	B.C.	Trudeau	Yes	Yes
Dickson	Man.	Trudeau	Yes	No
Beetz	Que.	Trudeau	Yes	No
Lamer	Que.	Trudeau	Yes	No
Chouinard	Que.	Clark	Yes	No
Martland	Alta.	Diefenbaker	No	No
Ritchie	N.S.	Diefenbaker	No	No

This was a transparently political decision and gave us a good idea, if we were paying attention, of what Canada could expect with the Charter.

The reasoning of the judges was as revealing as their voting pattern. Of the two questions, the legality question was probably the easiest. As we have seen, for a court to hold an act of government illegal is, at least implicitly, to prohibit it. The majority argued that, however unconventional the federal government's action might be, there was nothing in the decided cases or the statutes authorizing a court actually to interfere with what was, after all, a mere request made by the Canadian Parliament to the UK Parliament. Whatever impact such a request might in fact have, it had no legal effect without a law being passed by the sovereign UK Parliament. Where could a court get the authority to *prohibit* a *request*? Furthermore, given the fact that the entire legal structure of Canada depended on a British enactment, what legal authority could a Canadian court have to refuse to recognize an amendment to the BNA Act by the Parliament that enacted it in the first place, however that amendment came to be proposed? The minority's answer was that the Court should, in effect, make up the authority so as to protect the fundamental federal structure of Canada. Courts had made things up before.

There was logic on both sides and certainly a lack of precedent had become increasingly unimportant to this court—that very day it would do a most unprecedented act. But to hold this action illegal, even if technically possible, would have been reckless on the part of the Court. What if Parliament were unable to achieve an agreement through patently unreasonable provincial intransigence? The Court would then have set up an insuperable legal obstacle to a constitutional amendment and would have found itself confronting an already popular plan (the Charter) as well as what could turn into a popular strategy (unilateralism). If, in such an event, Parliament went ahead despite the illegality, the Court would have had its *order* ignored with a consequent loss of prestige. And what then? Could it actually refuse to enforce the law once it returned? Shades of Roosevelt and 1937! Besides, it was unnecessary to go this far in light of the Court's answer on the convention question.

That there was a convention requiring more provincial consent than the federal government had obtained could not really be challenged. In fact, the historical record was that no amendments had been passed without the consent of *all* of the provinces affected, and this record strongly implied that this was indeed recognized as binding on the federal government. Indeed, the only legitimate questions concerned the requirement of unanimity and the Quebec veto. There was in fact no dissent from anyone on the Court that constitutional convention required more provincial support than had been obtained. What is intriguing about the convention question has nothing to do with the answers given to it nor the arguments offered by majority and minority for their respective conclusions. What is intriguing is the way the convention question was interpreted by each side, the way the answers of each side were presented, and, most intriguing of all, *that it was even answered.*

First, the way the question was interpreted. When it asked whether the "the consent of the provinces" was necessary, did it mean *all* of the provinces or merely *some* of them? Each side interpreted this differently, but in the way that best suited its point of view on the outcome. It was as obvious to the majority that the question did *not* mean to refer to *all* of the provinces as it was to the minority that it *did.*

> Majority:
> It would have been easy to insert the words "all" into the question had it been intended to narrow its meaning. But we do not think it was so intended.
> Minority:
> From the wording of the questions and from the course of argument it is clear that the questions meant the consent of all the Provinces. . . . There is no ambiguity in the questions before the Court.

The only thing that was really clear, of course, was that if the majority wanted to cast doubt on the plan and the minority to approve it, interpreting the question in their respective ways made it easier for each side to achieve its respective goal. If they were only interested in the truth, each side would have given answers to each possible interpretation of the question. If this is not coincidence enough, there are the very obvious attempts by each side to give maximum impact to its respective position. The minority, which found the plan not contrary to constitutional convention, but nevertheless knew itself to have lost this issue, *minimized* the general importance of conventions:

> We cannot . . . agree with any suggestion that the non-observance of a convention can properly be termed unconstitutional in any strict or legal sense. . . . In a federal State . . . constitutionality and legality must be synonymous, and conventional rules will be accorded less significance than they may have in a unitary State such as the United Kingdom.

> With conventions or understandings he [the lawyer and law teacher] has no direct concern. They vary from generation to generation, almost from year to year. . . . The subject

... is not one of law but of politics, and need trouble no lawyer or the class of any professor of law.

The majority, on the other hand, went to great lengths to *maximize* the significance of its holding that the federal resolution, though legal, was contrary to convention: "[W]hile they are not laws, some conventions may be more important than some laws." Indeed, the majority went about as far as it could in this direction when it declared that conventions "form an integral part of the constitution and the constitutional system":

> That is why it is perfectly appropriate to say that to violate a convention is to do something which is unconstitutional although it entails no direct legal consequences. But the words "constitutional" and "unconstitutional" may also be used in strict legal sense, for instance with respect to a statute which is found *ultra vires* or unconstitutional. The foregoing may perhaps be summarized in an equation: constitutional conventions plus constitutional law equal the total Constitution of the country.

But one does not have to look any further for proof of the political nature of the case than to the fact that the Court agreed to answer the convention question at all. And this is the only point upon which it was unanimous! Remember that there was no precedent for the Court ruling on a convention question divorced from any legal question. Indeed, according to the Court's own definition, conventions "are not enforced by the courts." So, answering the convention question at all was out of line with the role of courts as ordinarily conceived. In answering the convention question, the Supreme Court of Canada acted "outside its legal function and [attempted] to facilitate a political outcome." It "intervened as another political actor, not as a court of law." What was the Court's defence of this action? The majority devoted a separate section of its reasons to the issue, but nothing it said really answered the question. We were told that the question was important (though "not confined to an issue of pure legality. . . . it has to do with a fundamental issue of constitutionality and legitimacy") and that courts should not "shrink" from answering a question "on account of the political aspects." But these are reasons for answering a *legal* question with political implications, not for answering a political question that has nothing to do with law. The minority argued that they had to answer because the majority answered, but also because the case was "unusual" and there had been extensive argument on the convention question. Perhaps the judge who came the closest to the truth was the Chief Justice of Manitoba, quoted by the majority in the Supreme Court, who said that the question "calls for an answer, and I propose to answer it." Put another way, the reasons given by the various judges to justify their willingness to answer the convention question, and characterized by one commentator as "inadequate" as, no doubt, technically they were, amounted to no more and no less than that they were answering it because they were *expected* to answer it.

Can anyone doubt that they were right about this? Outside of scholarly criticism of the legal credentials of the decision and the dangers such political behaviour might cause the Supreme Court, not a peep of political criticism was heard of the decision to answer to question. And, while it is impossible to say what would have happened had the convention question not been answered or had it been answered differently, it is clear that with the Court decision as it was, the federal government had no political hope of going ahead without at least another round of negotiations. For one thing, the NDP informed the government that it would now vote against the resolution without a new conference. In Britain, too, the decision was regarded as decisive. . . . The *Guardian* reported that even with strenuous Thatcher sponsorship, the Bill would now have a tough time. Though the outcome would obviously have been impossible to predict with certainty, it is clear that there would have been a serious battle in the British Commons and House of Lords had the federal government tried to go ahead with its original plan after the judgment.

But most important of all was that the whole Charter enterprise depended for its success on reverence for the Court. The reason Trudeau wanted the Charter in the first place was to use it against the unilingual tendencies of provincial governments in areas beyond federal control. He needed it now to use against the popular language legislation of the PQ government of Quebec. The idea was to entrench English language rights which directly contradicted the PQ's Bill 101 so that the courts, ultimately the Supreme Court, would strike down the law as violating the Charter of Rights. Trudeau was going to trump democracy by claiming a greater legitimacy for the Supreme Court of Canada than for any mere government. How could he criticize the Court for going too far today when he needed it to go all the way tomorrow?

So the Supreme Court's decision all but forced the First Ministers' conference that began on November 2, 1981. In fact, it practically determined its outcome. This was due partly to the holding on legality, because the knowledge that a unilateral federal gambit would be legal and enforceable gave the provinces an extra incentive to be conciliatory and even to break ranks to achieve individual objectives. But most important of all to the final outcome was the clear indication given by both majority and minority on the convention question that constitutional convention did not require the unanimous, or even near unanimous, assent of the provinces. Both sides let everyone know that they would approve of much less. For the minority judges, the denial of a unanimity requirement was part and parcel with their dissent, but this would have been a fragile predictor without some expression on the question by the majority judges, and express themselves they did, once again completely without judicial excuse:

It was submitted by counsel for Manitoba, Newfoundland, Quebec, Nova Scotia, British Columbia, Prince Edward Island and Alberta that the convention does exist [and] that it requires the agreement of all the Provinces . . .

Counsel for Saskatchewan . . . submitted that the convention does exist and requires a measure of provincial agreement . . .

We wish to indicate at the outset that we find ourselves in agreement with the submissions made on this issue by counsel for Saskatchewan. . . .

It seems clear that while the precedents taken alone point at unanimity, the unanimity principle cannot be said to have been accepted by all the actors in the precedents. . . .

It would not be appropriate for the Court to devise in the abstract a specific formula which would indicate in positive terms what measure of provincial agreement is required . . .

It is sufficient for the Court to decide that at least a substantial measure of provincial consent is required. . . . Nothing more should be said about this.

The Court had said more than enough already. It had introduced a completely "new element" into the equation, an element that was emphasized by the Premiers of both British Columbia and Saskatchewan (two *opposing* provinces) in their televised opening speeches to the First Ministers' conference on November 2. It was this element that made possible the ultimate exclusion of Quebec, the only province with truly irreconcilable differences with Ottawa, differences over entrenched minority language rights, not only Trudeau's bottom line but actually his *raison d'être*. It is clear that these specific rights, which in their precision and prolixity read more like a tax statute than a constitution, were the only non-negotiables for Trudeau. The grand rights and freedoms of "conscience," "association," "fundamental justice," "equality," and so on, which granted a purely general supervisory jurisdiction over legislation to the courts, were expendable. Trudeau said as much after the referendum. And he proved it in the resulting constitution where none of these grand individualistic rights would be so precious as to be immune from legislative veto by use of s.33, the "notwithstanding" clause. By contrast, language rights would be immune, and at the same time, they would automatically render null and void the language of education provisions of the PQ's "Bill 101," the centrepiece of its program to make the French language *the* language of Quebec.

In other words, unanimity among provinces and the federal government was simply not achievable so long as Trudeau and Lévesque had to sign the same document. The freedom from unanimity which the Supreme Court presumed to grant made possible the only conceivable agreement, one that would exclude Quebec. Furthermore, the "deliberate vagueness" of the Court's formula gave the other provinces more than enough incentive to jump on the federal bandwagon lest they be isolated with English Canada's anathema. This seems in fact to have been what determined Manitoba's capitulation. It was the only other province with a real interest in opposing entrenched language rights (because of its relatively large and linguistically mistreated French minority) and, because of this, the only other province firmly opposed to a Charter at the time of the conference (Alberta had made its deal with the federal government on energy prices in September). An accord excluding Quebec did not necessarily entail the sneakiness of the night of November 4–5, 1981, during which, with all parties but Quebec involved, the compromise that was to be Canada's constitution was worked out and then presented as a *fait accompli* to a shocked René Lévesque the next morning at breakfast. That there would be an accord, however, and that it would exclude Quebec was as about as inevitable as these things ever get.

The Court's role in the ultimate making of the deal and in its general contours was, therefore, a rather large one. Furthermore, the script required it consciously to stride outside of its judicial confines and directly into the political arena. But this, as we have tried to show, was not a random occurrence. For most of the century, everything, and more and more nearly everyone, had been grooming the Court for this part. In fact, the most obvious thing about the decision to answer the convention question was that this thoroughly nontraditional decision of the Court concerned the adoption of a law—a constitutionally entrenched Charter of Rights and Freedoms—that would invest the judiciary with essentially the same thoroughly non-traditional function, namely judging the *legitimacy* of jurisdictionally valid legislation. The Charter of Rights and Freedoms in fact transformed the Court into an institution charged with making the very sort of judgments which it made on the convention issue—though such judgments would henceforth be made under the formally satisfying umbrella of constitutional authority. So if we want to know why the Court would accept such a non-traditional role in determining the outcome of a major political crisis and why its acceptance of this role would in turn be accepted by all the other actors, the answer is that it would have been strange indeed for the Court, standing on the threshold of its new era, to have been too prudish to engage in the very kind of activity that would characterize that era, or to have been criticized for doing so. The decision on the convention should be regarded as the inauguration of a new era in which the judiciary is to play a central role in the political life of this country. The triumph of the legalization of politics can be dated, then, not from the formal entrenchment of the Charter of Rights and Freedoms on April 17, 1982, but from the decision on the convention question in *Re Constitution of Canada* some seven months earlier.

2.5

KEY TERMS

Concepts

declaratory model of judging
legal positivism
legal realism
judicial nationalism
adjudication of disputes model of judging
policy-making model of judging
adversary process
power vs. authority
constitutional law
constitutional convention
"unconstitutional but legal"

Institutions, Events and Documents

Judicial Committee of the Privy Council (JCPC)
O'Connor Report (1939)
Abolition of Appeals to JCPC (1949)
Harrison v. Carswell (1976)
Re Constitution of Canada, 1981 (*Patriation Reference*)

3
The Canadian Judicial System

A distinctive feature of the Canadian judicial system is its unitary character. This distinguishes it from other federal nations such as the United States, which has a "dual court system." A dual court system parallels the division of legislative powers along federal lines, by creating federal courts for federal law, and state courts for state law. While the Canadian Founders adopted the logic of federalism for the distribution of legislative authority, they did not apply it to the judiciary. They created a single judicial system to interpret and to apply both federal and provincial laws. The unitary character of the Canadian judicial system is illustrated by the judicial flowchart (Figure 2) in Reading 3.3. This diagram shows how both civil law, which is mainly provincial in origin, and criminal law, which is almost exclusively federal in origin, move from trial to appeal through the same system of courts. This unitary character of the Canadian judicial system is politically significant, because it can mitigate the centrifugal forces of federal-provincial politics. Rather than accentuating regional differences, it promotes a continuity and uniformity of legal policy across the nation.

The unitary character of the Canadian judicial system is reinforced by the fact that it is the shared responsibility of both levels of government. The legal framework for this joint-responsibility is laid out in sections 92(14) and 96 to 101 of the Constitution Act, 1867. (See Reading 3.2) Section 92 allocates to the provinces the powers to make laws that provide for the "constitution, maintenance, and organization of provincial courts." Section 96 provides that the federal government "shall appoint the judges of the superior, district, and county courts in each province." These provisions create a joint federal-provincial responsibility for the "section 96" courts, which are created and maintained by the provinces but whose judges are appointed by the federal government.

In the judicial hierarchy there are two additional tiers of courts beside the "section 96" or superior courts. "Below" are the "section 92 courts," so-called because they are created, maintained, and staffed wholly by the provincial governments, pursuant to section 92(14) of the Constitution Act. In most provinces these courts are entitled "provincial Courts," and are the modern day successors of the old Magistrates or Police courts. "Above" the "section 96" courts is the Supreme Court of Canada, which, pursuant to section 101 of the Constitution Act, is created, maintained, and staffed wholly by the federal government. This allocation of responsibility for the different tiers of the judicial system is illustrated in the diagram in Figure 1 of Reading 3.3.

Section 92 Courts

The "section 92 courts" can be described as both the least important and the most important courts in Canada. Their lack of status stems from their position as the lowest rung in the Canadian judicial hierarchy. They serve principally as trial courts for less serious offenses and as courts of preliminary inquiry for more serious offenses. Their decisions are always subject to review and reversal by "higher" courts. On the other hand, these courts are critically important because of the high volume of litigation that they process each year. Described as the "workhorse" of the Canadian judicial system, the provincial courts handle over 90 percent of all criminal litigation. For most Canadians, "a day in court" means a day in provincial court. The quality of justice in Canada is thus directly affected by the quality of the provincial court system. As a result of the somewhat belated recognition of their importance, there has been a conscious effort in the past several decades to improve the salaries and training of provincial court judges, the efficiency of court administration, and even the physical setting of court rooms and court houses. The criminal law jurisdiction of the provincial courts is illustrated in the flowchart in Reading 3.4 (Figure 4). Provincial courts hear all provincial offenses and summary conviction offenses, and conduct all preliminary inquiries. In addition they hear indictable offenses under section 483 of the Criminal Code, some indictable offenses of election, and cases under the Young Offenders Act. Their civil law jurisdiction includes issues of minor civil claims and family law.

The "Section 96" Superior, County, and District Courts

Each province has a two-tier system of superior courts: a trial court of general criminal and civil jurisdiction and a corresponding appeal court.[1] The names of these courts vary from province to province, but their constitutional status is the same. In Alberta, Manitoba, and Saskatchewan these courts are the Court of Queen's Bench and the Court of Appeal. In Quebec they are called the Superior Court and the Court of Appeal. In most of the other provinces they are distinguished as the trial division and

---

[1] While Ontario still has County and District Courts, most provinces have amalgamated them with the trial division of the superior court, the Court of Queen's Bench in Alberta.

appellate division of the province's Supreme Court. The judges in both courts are appointed by the federal government.[2]

The Court of Queen's Bench (or Trial Division of the Supreme Court) is generally regarded as "the key to the Canadian court system."[3] Its prestige flows from its very broad criminal and civil jurisdiction, and the fact that it is derived from the English superior courts of common law and equity. W.R. Lederman argues that the independence of these courts is part of the "unwritten constitution" inherited from Great Britain, and that they could not be abolished or significantly altered without doing violence to the fundamental order of Canadian government.[4]

The criminal jurisdiction of the Court of Queen's Bench includes the trial of all indictable offenses under section 427 of the Criminal Code and indictable offenses by election. It also hears appeals from all summary conviction offenses. (See figure 4 in Reading 3.4). The Court of Queen's Bench is clearly the most important civil law court. It hears divorces, separations, and guardianship disputes, and all civil disputes whose monetary claims are too large for small claims courts. It also hears appeals from juvenile and family courts, and from some provincial administrative boards and tribunals.

The Court of Appeal of the province (or Appellate Division of the Supreme Court) is the highest court in the province. It sits principally to hear appeals from the Court of Queen's Bench on questions of law, and its decisions are binding on all other courts within the province (unless overturned on appeal to the Supreme Court of Canada). The Court of Appeal of each province also hears references from the provincial government. The chief justice of the Court of Appeal serves as the chief justice of the province.

Supreme Court of Canada

At the summit of the judicial pyramid sits the Supreme Court of Canada. Since appeals to the Judicial Committee of the Privy Council were abolished in 1949, the Supreme Court has served as the final court of appeal for all matters of Canadian law. Its creation was authorized but not required by section 101 of the Constitution Act, 1867. Parliament, after considerable debate, exercised that power and enacted the Supreme Court Act in 1875.[5]

---

[2] Prince Edward Island does not have a separate appeal court. Appeals are heard by the Chief Justice, and two judges who did not participate in the trial.

[3] S.M. Waddams, *Introduction to the Study of Law* (Toronto, ON: Carswell-Methuen, 1979), p. 157.

[4] See W.R. Lederman, "The Independence of the Judiciary," Reading 5.1.

[5] See Jennifer Smith, "The Origins of Judicial Review in Canada," Reading 10.1.

The Supreme Court has jurisdiction to hear appeals on all questions of criminal and civil law from the provincial courts of appeal, and also accepts appeals from the Federal Court. Since 1975 the Court grants "leave to appeal" in a civil case only if it raises an issue of national concern or public importance, so that the Court now has considerably more control over the content and size of its docket than before. In Reading 3.1, the late Chief Justice Bora Laskin argues that the increasingly discretionary character of the Supreme Court's appellate jurisdiction changes the nature of the Court's function from that of traditional appellate review to one of "supervisory control." This represents a change of emphasis from concern for the individual case to overseeing the consistent development of Canadian law, especially in issues of public importance and national concern. As Ian Bushnell has observed, "In the role of simply another review court, it is the litigant who is afforded access, and he brings the legal issue with him; when the court fulfills a law-making function, it is the legal problem that determines access, and the litigant is brought along with it."[6]

An important exception to this trend is the reference procedure, by which the federal government can ask the Court for an "advisory opinion" on any question of constitutional or statutory law. While the number of references has decreased as a proportion of the total number of cases heard annually by the Court, they frequently represent the most important cases.[7]

The original Supreme Court Act authorized the appointment of six judges, and required that two of the six be from Quebec. This was deemed necessary to accommodate civil law appeals from Quebec. Not to be outdone by her provincial rival, Ontario demanded equal treatment, and eventually a custom of having two Ontario judges on the Court came into being. In 1927 the size of the Court was increased to seven judges, and again in 1949 to nine. The number of Quebec and Ontario judges was increased to three, Quebec's by law and Ontario's by custom. Again by custom, the three remaining vacancies are normally filled by one judge from the Maritime provinces and two from the Western provinces. This *de facto* practice of regional representation on the Supreme Court attests to its perception as an important "political" institution in the process of national government.

The Supreme Court is presided over by a Chief Justice, the highest judicial officer of Canada. Over time, customs developed to govern the appointment of the Chief Justice. A pattern of alternating the position between English-Canadian and French-Canadian judges developed, and also of appointing the most senior judge in terms of service within each of these groups. Both of these customs have been broken by the last two

---

6 S.I. Bushnell, "Leave to Appeal Applications to the Supreme Court of Canada: A Matter of Public Importance," *Supreme Court Law Review* 3 (1982), p. 488.

7 See Barry Strayer, "Constitutional References," Reading 6.1.

appointments of Chief Justices, both by Prime Minister Trudeau. In 1973 he appointed Bora Laskin, who had served considerably less time on the court than several other anglophone members. In April of 1984, Trudeau again broke with tradition by appointing another anglophone, Brian Dickson, to succeed Laskin. These appointments cast doubt on the continued validity of either of these traditions. However, in 1989, upon Dickson's retirement, Prime Minister Mulroney elevated puisne justice Antonio Lamer, the senior Quebec francophone on the Court, to the Chief Justiceship. Lamer's appointment suggests that there is still vitality in the convention.

Because the Supreme Court was not constitutionally entrenched, Parliament could technically have abolished it at any time. Many commentators argued that this impugned the independence and thus the status of the Court. It was illogical, they argued, that the institution responsible for enforcing the constitution protections against governments was not itself constitutionally protected. There was an attempt to change this situation in 1982. The Constitution Act, 1982, section 41(d), declares that the composition of the Supreme Court (nine judges with three from Quebec) can only be changed by the unanimous consent of all the provinces and the federal government. Section 42 requires that any changes to the Supreme Court other than its composition be done according to the new amending formula. These changes were intended to eliminate the Court's potential vulnerability to Parliament, but confused the situation by "constitutionalizing" an arrangement that existed only by statute, the Supreme Court Act. These provisions thus "put the cart before the horse." Some scholars argued that the effect of the 1982 amendments was to constitutionally entrench the entire Supreme Court Act, while others argued that the amendments could have no effect until or unless the Supreme Court itself was made part of the formal constitution.

The 1987 Meech Lake Accord proposed to resolve this confusion by explicitly constitutionalizing the existence of the Supreme Court. Sections 101(a) to (e) of the Meech Lake Accord would have constitutionally entrenched the existence of the Supreme Court and its basic function; the number of judges (a chief justice plus eight others); the requirement that three of the judges come from Quebec; the qualifications, tenure and mode of payment (the same as section 96 court judges, as protected by sections 99 and 100 of the Constitution Act, 1867); and the method of appointment.[8] With the exception of appointments, the proposed changes were largely symbolic, providing formal constitutional status for what had previously existed as a matter of constitutional convention. The appointment procedure proposed under the Meech Lake Accord was both novel and controversial. It would have left the appointment power with the Federal

---

[8] See Peter H. Russell, "The Supreme Court Proposals in the Meech Lake Accord," *Canadian Public Policy* 14 (Sept. 1988), pp. 93–106.

government, but required that all new appointments to the Supreme Court be made from nomination lists submitted by the provinces. This issue is discussed further in the introduction to Chapter 4. In the end, however, the Meech Lake Accord failed to be ratified, so none of these amendments took effect. The ambiguities created by the 1982 amendments remain unresolved.

Federal Court of Canada

In addition to authorizing the creation of the Supreme Court, section 101 of the Constitution Act, 1867, also allows "for the establishment of any additional courts for the better administration of the laws of Canada." If it chose to, Parliament could use this authority to create an entirely new tier of federal courts, similar to those of the United States. In practice it has not done so, creating instead only two federal courts of specialized jurisdiction. In 1875 Parliament created the Exchequer Court. In 1970 it was renamed the Federal Court and given an expanded jurisdiction. The original jurisdiction of the Exchequer Court consisted of a collection of specialized areas of federal law — admiralty law, copyright and trademark law, income and estate tax law, and citizenship and immigration law. It also heard civil claims against the Crown.

In 1970, the new Federal Court inherited this jurisdiction, and in addition was given the function of supervising federal administrative law. The Federal Court has both a trial and an appellate division. The top "wedge" of the flow chart in Figure 2 illustrates how the federal administrative law area has been hived-off from the rest of the judicial system, and made the special responsibility of the Federal Court. There is the possibility of leave to appeal to the Supreme Court from all Federal Court decisions. In 1983, Parliament created a new section 101 court, the Tax Court of Canada. It hears appeals from Revenue Canada, and its decisions may be appealed to the Federal Court.

Judicial Committee of the Privy Council

Prior to Confederation, the Judicial Committee of the Privy Council (JCPC) served as the final court of appeal for the courts of all the British colonies, including Canada. It continued in this capacity under section 129 of the Constitution Act, 1867. The Privy Council served as final court of appeal for the entire British Empire. It was not a part of the regular English court system, and did not hear appeals from English courts. It consisted of five judges drawn mainly from the law lords of the House of Lords.

Even after the Supreme Court was created in 1875, appeals to the Privy Council remained. In addition to appeals from Supreme Court decisions, there were also appeals from the Court of Appeal of each province. This latter possibility, known as a *per saltum* appeal, allowed parties to effectively bypass the Supreme Court of Canada, and reduced its prestige and influence. The decisions of the Privy Council played a major role in shaping the constitutional development of Canada. Its interpretations of the federal division of powers significantly diminished the authority of the federal government while expanding that of the provinces. As discussed in the preceding chapter, this trend reached a climax during the 1930s, and provoked a reaction against the continued role of the Privy Council in Canadian public affairs. This "judicial nationalism" movement culminated in the abolition of appeals to the Privy Council in 1949. However, its pre-1949 decisions remain an important part of Canadian law, especially in the areas of federalism.

3.1

THE ROLE AND FUNCTIONS OF FINAL APPELLATE COURTS: THE SUPREME COURT OF CANADA
Bora Laskin

I

. . . I look upon the functions of the Supreme Court of Canada as those that arise out of its jurisdiction; the definition of its role depends on how that jurisdiction is exercised, how it uses its final appellate authority having regard to the kind and range of cases that come before it. The interaction between jurisdiction and role is obvious; and, inevitably, the judges' view of their role is bound to undergo definition and redefinition in the day-to-day grind of the court's business and in the periodic changes of its membership. One can envisage judges of the Supreme Court having some differences of opinion, probably slight ones, on the court's functions; any differences about its role are likely to be more serious.

II

The starting point for any consideration of the Supreme Court's functions and its role is that fact, a surprising one I am sure to foreign students of federalism, that the Supreme Court of Canada has no constitutional base. This marks it off immediately from such kindred courts as the Supreme Court of the United States and the High Court of Australia. The Supreme Court of Canada is a statutory creation of the Parliament of Canada under

Canadian Bar Review 53 (1975), from pages 469–481. Reprinted with permission.

the power given that Parliament by section 101 of the British North America Act to constitute, maintain and organize "a general Court of Appeal for Canada." The size of the court, its jurisdiction, its procedure, indeed all questions touching its operation as a general court of appeal, an appellate court in short without any declared right to original jurisdiction, were left to the Government and Parliament of Canada to prescribe.

The size of the court, originally composed of six judges, with a seventh added in 1927 and two more added in 1949 upon the abolition of all appeals to the Privy Council from any appellate court in Canada, testifies both to population and regional growth in Canada, to the expansion of the business of the court and to its ultimate grave responsibility as a final appellate court. Of significance in its structure and operations was the provision of a quorum for sittings of the court, the number being fixed at five upon the creation of the court and remaining constant despite increase in its overall size. There could not, and even today there cannot be more than one Bench for the hearing of appeals; and I am thankful that this precludes having two Supreme Courts of Canada. Perhaps the only power a Chief Justice has is to assign the Bench for the hearing of appeals. Since my personal preference is to have the full court sit, and since the recent change in our jurisdiction enables the court to be selective in the cases that it will hear, I will not view with any regret the surrender of the power of assignment which, in any event, has been exercised with regard to the opinions of the other members of the court as to whether a panel of five or the full court should be assigned in any particular appeal.

The jurisdiction of the court, the scope of its appellate authority, was undoubtedly the most important matter that faced the Government and Parliament of Canada in creating the court in 1875. A number of models were available for consideration. There was the model of a national appellate court, functioning like an English appellate court, or like the House of Lords, with general jurisdiction (be it as of right or by leave) not limited to any class or classes of cases. There was, second, the model of a purely federal court, with an appellate jurisdiction limited to matters within or arising out of the exercise of federal legislative powers, including the validity of that exercise, but excluding constitutional issues arising under provincial legislation in view of the fact that appeals then lay directly to the Privy Council from provincial courts of appeal. There was, third, the model of a federal appellate court having also comprehensive appellate jurisdiction in all constitutional matters as ultimate Canadian expositor of the constitution, albeit there was a further appeal to the Privy Council. This was the model offered by the Supreme Court of the United States. There was, fourth, the model of a purely constitutional court and, fifth, the model of a federal and a constitutional court, with separate chambers for each of these functions, in adaptation of the chamber system found today in the *Cour de Cassation* of France.

Happily, in my view, the first model was chosen, thus adapting to federal Canada a system of appellate adjudication operative in unitary Great Britain but familiar to Canadians of Bench and Bar. To have adopted the federal model represented by the Supreme Court of the United States or some other such model, would have required at least consideration of, if not actual establishment of a system of federal courts of original jurisdiction. A dual court system such as obtains in the United States was resisted in Canada, save for the establishment of an Exchequer Court with a limited jurisdiction, and of Admiralty Courts. It was in the character of concurrent appointment as Exchequer Court judges that the judges of the Supreme Court of Canada were invested with original jurisdiction but this ceased when the Exchequer Court was set up on a separate base in 1887, ending a short first life and beginning a second one with a judge wholly its own, but with more added over the succeeding years.

Although the jurisdiction of the Exchequer Court was extended considerably when it was translated into the Federal Court of Canada in 1970, the latter is still a court of limited jurisdiction in federal matters. A serious and, in my view, unfortunate as well as an unnecessary upheaval in our Canadian system of judicature would result if the Government and Parliament of Canada moved now to federalize it at the level of original and intermediate appellate jurisdiction by withdrawing such jurisdiction in all federal matters from the provincial courts and reposing it in a federal court structure.

The Parliament of Canada has power to that end under section 101 of the British North America Act, the same section which authorized the creation of the Supreme Court of Canada. In authorizing as well (in its words) "the establishment of any additional Courts for the better administration of the laws of Canada," the section may be said to reflect some incongruity. On the one hand, it enabled Parliament to establish a "general," a truly national court of appeal whose authority was not limited to federal matters — the telling word is "general" — and, on the other hand to establish federal courts limited to jurisdiction in federal matters. To have exercised both grants of authority to the full, in the light of the fact that at Confederation in 1867 there were developed provincial courts habituated to adjudicate on matters that after Confederation were in terms of legislative power distributed between the central and provincial legislatures, would have created, and would now certainly create great tensions in federal-provincial relations. We can do without adding to those that already exist, although I am bound to add that tension to some degree is a by-product of federalism.

Parliament did exercise its authority to the full in establishing the Supreme Court of Canada in 1875 and in reconstituting the court in 1949 upon the abolition of all appeals in Canadian causes to the Privy Council. This makes good sense to me so long as the provincial courts are left, as they now are, to administer federal law as well as provincial law, indeed federal common law as well as provincial common law, save to the limited extent that judicial jurisdiction in federal matters has been reposed in the Federal Court of Canada, which has both a trial division and an appeal division in respect of those matters.

If there was any thought-out rationale for investing the Supreme Court of Canada with appellate authority from all provincial appellate courts, and in respect of provincial as well as federal matters cognizable in those courts, it was posited and, in my view, may be said to rest today on the following factors. First, there was and is the fact that particular litigation frequently involves issues that engage both federal and provincial matters which provincial courts have continued to handle without difficulty, and forum problems are, in general, avoided notwithstanding the hived-off jurisdiction of the Federal Court. Its jurisdiction is, on the whole, fairly distinct and has hitherto not created any intractable difficulties in forum selection, although some such questions have arisen. Second, there was and is the fact that the common law is largely the same in all the provinces outside of Quebec and that, subject to legislative changes, it ought to have an uniform operation in all those provinces, thus avoiding some possible conflict of laws problems; and, moreover, even in Quebec there are branches of the common law, as for example in the field of public law, that were and are common to it and to the other provinces of Canada. Third, there was and is the fact that many important branches of law, such as the criminal law, the law of negotiable instruments, the law of bankruptcy, the law of shipping, railway law, the law of patents and copyright have a national operation because they fall within exclusive federal competence; and even though they may interact in some respects with some aspects of the common law their interpretation and application must necessarily be uniform, and perhaps all the more so because of the interaction. Fourth, constitutional adjudication, involving the resolution of disputes as to the scope and reach of federal and provincial legislative powers must necessarily end in a court that can speak authoritatively for the whole of Canada, and I may add here that there is equally a case to be made for final uniform resolution of questions touching the operation of public authorities.

Thus it was that upon the establishment of the Supreme Court of Canada we had in the main a one-stream two-tier system of appeals like that in Great Britain, although that country did not have to contend with federalism as we know it in Canada. To some extent, there is a three-tier system in respect of Ontario cases by reason of the recent establishment there of an intermediate appellate court, with a limited jurisdiction, operating between courts of first instance and the Ontario Court of Appeal. Should this innovation spread to other provinces it would not alter the force of the considerations which led to the establishment of the Supreme Court of Canada as a national court. Its character does not depend on the system of appeals within the judicial structure of any one or more provinces but, rather on how far beyond adjudication on federal matters and on constitutional matters its jurisdiction should extend.

The Government and the Parliament of Canada saw no need to water down the broad authority given to establish "a general Court of appeal for Canada"; and Parliament emphasized the breadth of its power by generous scope, especially in civil cases, for appeals as of right, appeals which the Supreme Court of Canada was obliged to hear, however local or private were the issues that they raised. This was appellate review in a traditional sense as distinguished from what I would term supervisory control.

Until the beginning of this year when appellate review was replaced by supervisory control (leave now being required in all non-criminal cases and in most criminal cases before an appeal will be entertained on the merits), appeals as of right in civil cases formed a large part of the Supreme Court's case load. I think this was one of the factors that led some scholarly students of the Supreme Court's work to urge federalization of its jurisdiction. Other factors were also raised in support of this position, such as the virtue of allocating judicial power along the same lines as legislative power, and the merit of leaving to final adjudication in the provincial courts legal issues reflecting local conditions and those based on provincial or municipal legislation.

I think that the amendments recently made to the Supreme Court's jurisdiction, making a previous requirement of leave (whether from the Supreme Court or the provincial appellate court) the general rule, have blunted the case that could formerly have been made and was made for limiting the Supreme Court of Canada to federal and constitutional issues. The four-pronged rationale which I mentioned earlier in this address as supporting a final appellate court with a general national jurisdiction is not, in my opinion, cogently answered by those who would reduce the court to a federal and constitutional institution. Still less is it answerable now that the Supreme Court is a supervisory tribunal rather than an appellate tribunal in the traditional sense. As a supervisory tribunal, it is fully able and would be expected to resist interference in purely local or private issues, and it is in fact enjoined to do so by the statutory formula which prescribes the requirements that must be met in order to obtain leave. The case for leave must be one with respect to which "the Supreme Court is of the opinion that any question involved therein is, by reason of its public importance or the importance of any issue of law or any issue of mixed law and fact involved in such question, one that ought to be decided by the Supreme Court or is, for any other reason, of such a nature or significance as to warrant decision by it."

The discretion given to the court under the foregoing formula is obvious, but it is a necessary control over the flow of cases that have already been before two courts. Now, even more in its supervisory role than in its heretofore more traditional appellate role, the Supreme Court's main function is to oversee the development of the law in the courts of Canada, to give guidance in articulate reasons and, indeed, direction to the provincial courts and to the Federal Court of Canada on issues of national concern or of common concern to several provinces, issues that may obtrude even though arising under different legislative regimes in different provinces. This is surely the paramount obligation of an ultimate appellate court with national authority. It is only under this umbrella that it can, in general, be expected to be sensitive to the correctness of the decisions in particular cases, whether they be between private litigants only or involve some government as a party.

I think I can risk saying that the mere fact that any level of government or any government agency is involved in a particular case is no more telling in favour of leave to appeal than the fact that litigation is private necessarily tells against the granting of leave. The issues in contention and, indeed, the issues which will be determinative of the appeal, however there may be others of importance in the case, and not the character of the parties, will guide the court in the exercise of its power to grant or refuse leave. Even where the court may be disposed to grant leave, it may do so, not at large, but by defining the specific question or questions on which it is prepared to have the case come forward.

III

I turn now to more debatable questions respecting the Supreme Court's exercise of its jurisdiction, questions going to its role as Canada's highest and final court on all justiciable matters. Two considerations affect any assessment of that role. One has to do with the kind of business that comes and will come before the court; the second has to do with the collegiality of the court, with the blend of individual independence of the judges *inter se* and their institutional responsibility. The bulk of the court's business is, and is likely to continue to be, the interpretation and application of statutes, some of which, as for example, parts of the Criminal Code and of the Quebec Civil Code, to take two illustrations, have long ago taken on what I may term a common law appearance. Two statutes, one, the British North America Act (and its amendments), only formally of that character (since it is Canada's chief written constitution), and the second, the Canadian Bill of Rights, a quasi-constitutional enactment are not, for interpretative purposes "statutes like other statutes" (to adopt well-known phraseology); and there is little doubt, certainly none in my mind, that the judicial approach to them, compelled by their character, has been different from that taken with respect to ordinary legislation. The generality of their language and their operative effect compel an approach from a wider perspective than is the case with ordinary legislation, especially legislation that is more precisely formulated.

The collegiality of the court touches a matter that may have a greater interest for the academic component of this assembly than for the practising Bar or members of the judiciary. It is theoretically open to each member of the Supreme Court of Canada, as it is theoretically open to each member of any appellate court, to write reasons in every case in which the member sits. Practical and institutional considerations militate against this; and so it is that when bare concurrences are filed with reasons proposed by a colleague, they may suggest some shift of position by the concurring judge who does not choose to write separate reasons, a shift on some matter subsidiary to or connected with the disposition of the main issue to which the concurrence was given.

Bare concurrences ought not to be taken as representing unqualified endorsement of every sentence of the reasons concurred in. Contextual approval, yes; and approval of the result, of course. After all the scrutiny and conferring on a set of proposed reasons are over, and after changes have been made in language and organization by the writer so far as he is willing to accommodate himself to the views of his colleagues, there may still remain in some colleague some questions about some parts of the reasons. However, he may decide on balance that there is no point in writing his own. In short, it is far safer and surer, if one would assess how a judge discharges his duties and how he regards his role and the role of the court, to assess him on what he himself writes and not on all of what is written by a colleague with whom he concurs in some particular case or cases.

There is no question that seems to have been as continuously and as strenuously considered, in relation to all courts and judges, and more particularly in relation to judges and courts of ultimate authority, as their law-making role. The Supreme Court of Canada began life at about the time Langdell and his case-law approach to the discovery of the "true legal rule" revolutionized legal studies in the United States. On the English side, before the nineteenth century was out the House of Lords had sanctified its own position as the expositor of the one true rule which, once declared, was alterable only by legislation. A quarter of a century later Cardozo was to tell us that at its highest reaches the role of the judge lay in creation and not in mere discovery. In this country, and perhaps in England too, we were inclined to think that creativity applied to what had not been previously considered and determined but, that accomplished in the highest court, creativity was spent and change was only for the legislature or for the constitutional amending process, as the case might be. . . .

. . . Controversy has now ceased on the law-making role of judges, especially of judges of a final appellate court. Laymen may beg the question by consoling the dissenting judges of a divided court with the remark, "too bad the law was against you," but judges and lawyers know better. The late Lord Reid helped to bury the declaratory theory by remarking in a speech delivered in 1971 that law is not some known and defined entity secreted in Aladdin's cave and revealed if one uses the right password. We do not believe in fairy tales any more, said Lord Reid, and Lord Diplock did not doubt, when speaking for the Privy Council in an Australian appeal in 1974, that "when for the first time a court of final instance interprets [a statute] as bearing one of two or more possible meanings . . . the effect of the exercise of its interpretative role is to make law." Such controversy as there is today in judicial law-making in a final court concerns the appropriateness of the occasion or of the case for enunicating a new rule of law and, even more important, the appropriateness of the occasion or of the case for upsetting an existing rule and substituting a different one in its place.

Neither here nor in any of the countries whence come our distinguished guests is *stare decisis* now an inexorable rule for our respective final courts. In this country, what appeared to be at times an obsessiveness about it came partly at least from our link with English law which also involved the ascendancy of English courts, so that *stare decisis* amounted to a form of ancestor worship. We are now able to view it as simply an important element of the judicial process, a necessary consideration which should give pause to any but the most sober conclusion that a previous decision or line of authority is wrong and ought to be changed. Such a conclusion is not likely to be arrived at by any judge or number of judges without serious reflection on its conformity or consistency with other principles that are part of the institutional history or the institutional patterns of the court. None of us operates without constraints that are both personal and institutional, born of both training and experience and of traditions of the legal system of which the court is a part.

When everything considered relevant has been weighed and an over-ruling decision commends itself to a judge, he ought not at that stage to stay his opinion and call upon the legislature to implement it. This is particularly true in respect of those areas of the law which are judge-made, and to a degree true in respect of those areas where legislation is involved which is susceptible of a number of meanings. A final court must accept a superintending responsibility for what it or its predecessors have wrought, especially when it knows how little time legislatures today have (and also, perhaps, little inclination) to intrude into fields of law fashioned by the courts alone, although legislatures may, of course, under the prodding of law reform agencies and of other public influences, from time to time do.

The role of the courts, the role of a final court, in the interpretation of legislation, bringing into play the relation between the legislative and the judicial arms of government, is of a different dimension, in my view, than the role played in the promulgation of judge-made law. The dimension comes from the dominant political and legal principle under which our courts operate, which is that, constitutional issues apart, Parliament and the provincial legislatures are the supreme, certainly the superior law-making bodies. On constitutional issues, issues concerning the division of distribution of legislative power, the courts, and ultimately the Supreme Court of Canada, have the final word (subject to constitutional amendment). This is a critical role, so critical for exercises of legislative and governmental power at both the central and provincial level as to put every Supreme Court decision in this field, whatever it be, into the political mill. Yet it is a role which the court cannot eschew if we believe in constitutional order, any more than can any final court with constitutional jurisdiction in a federal state. There is no other instrument with final authority available for this role. It is of course possible (and indeed there are known examples) for the central and provincial governments to avoid constitutional determinations in the Supreme Court of Canada by entering into co-operative arrangements which do not call for any test of constitutional competence. In this way they may hold some of the tensions in their relations in equilibrium, so long as those arrangements last. The fact that such arrangements exist at all underlines the delicate nature of the Supreme Court's constitutional jurisdiction. Of course, it must proceed with caution in that field but, that having been said, it brings the same independent judgment to bear on constitutional questions as on other matters that are brought before it, fully conscious, however, that there are no more important public issues submitted to its adjudication than those that arise out alleged conflicts of legislative authority.

The stakes in interpretation and application of ordinary legislation may not be as high because here the courts play not an ascendant role but rather more of a complementary one. The judges, no less than others in society, owe obedience to legislation which they may be called upon to interpret and apply; they have a duty to respect the legislative purpose or policy whatever be their view of its merit. Judges subscribe to this proposition, and then may be seen to proceed to differ on what the purpose or policy is, or to differ on whether the legislation or some part of it is apt to realize the purpose. This is not the time nor the place to enlarge on the variety of approaches to legislative interpretation which in close cases can lead to different results in respect of the same piece of legislation. In the majority of cases where legislation is a factor in the litigation, there is no such difficulty in interpretation as to require the particular expertise of a lawyer or a judge. Where that special competence is necessary, the judges owe it to the enacting legislature as well as to the litigants to expose the legal reasoning which underlies their decisions.

The public expectation is, I suspect, of a somewhat different order. Since so much of the legislation that comes before the courts and before the Supreme Court of Canada involves controls or limitation of the social conduct or business behaviour of persons or classes of persons or corporations, either by direct penal sanction or by supervision of administrative agencies, those affected may look to the courts for some wider exposition than a strict regard for legal issues would warrant. Is the policy a desirable or a workable one? Is the administrative structure fair? Is the procedure fair, are the decisions supported by reasons that are disclosed to the affected persons? There is no invariable stance that a court takes on these questions. Where it has deemed it proper to pronounce on policy (as it has on occasion) it has done so with prudence, and, generally, when prompted by difficulties that reside in the interpretation and application of the legislation. Fairness of administrative procedure is more confidently dealt with by the courts because what is compendiously called "natural justice" has long been regarded as involving legal issues for their consideration.

Natural justice, embracing the right to notice of possibly adverse action, the right to be heard or to make representations before being adversely affected, and the right to be judged by an impartial tribunal, is a central feature of an evolved political and legal tradition which sees the courts as wielders of protective authority against an invasion of the liberty of the individual by government or its agencies. Text books, periodical literature and the everyday press reinforce this tradition, and thus strengthen the public expectation that the courts, and especially the Supreme Court of Canada, will speak out on the matter. The enactment of the Canadian Bill of Rights as a federal measure, and operative only at that level, has fed that expectation. It is well to recall that judges of Supreme Court spoke strongly on aspects of individual liberty in the *Alberta Press* case, the *Switzman* case, the *Roncarelli* case, and in other cases too, without the back-up or the direction of the Canadian Bill of Rights, which became effective only in 1960. It was able to do so because the avenues for recognizing individual rights or civil liberties had not been closed by competent legislation, nor did any relevant legislation as interpreted by the judges of the Supreme Court preclude them. Legislation may however appear to be preclusive in some areas of civil liberties, and if interpreted with that result the judicial duty of fidelity to legislation as superior law must be acknowledged whatever be the consequences, although the acknowledgment may be accompanied by an expression of regret or even of remonstrance that the legislation went so far.

The Canadian Bill of Rights has now provided a legislative measure and standard of protection of civil liberties but, in the generality of some of its language, it adds to the dilemmas of interpretation which are so often evident in civil liberties cases. Its direction may be clearer in some cases than it is in others, or clearer to some judges in some cases than to others. Each charts his own course here, as in the other roles that he is called upon to play in the discharge of his judicial duties and, indeed, in determining what roles he should take on.

This, however, is simply another aspect of the side discretion opens to a judge of a final appellate court. There may be differences about the scope of the discretion, but there cannot be any dispute about its existence. As I said at the beginning of my remarks, each judge puts his own questions and supplies his own answers and, in yielding ground to institutional considerations, he does so according to his own assessment of what they demand.

3.2

CONSTITUTION ACT, 1867, SECTIONS 96–101

VII.—Judicature.

96. The Governor General shall appoint the Judges of the Superior, District, and County Courts in each Province, except those of the Courts of Probate in Nova Scotia and New Brunswick.

97. Until the laws relative to Property and Civil Rights in Ontario, Nova Scotia, and New Brunswick, and the Procedure of the Courts in those Provinces, are made uniform, the Judges of the Courts of those Provinces appointed by the Governor General shall be selected from the respective Bars of those Provinces.

98. The Judges of the Courts of Quebec shall be selected from the Bar of that Province.

99. (1) Subject to subsection two of this section, the Judges of the Superior Courts shall hold office during good behavior, but shall be removable by the Governor General on Address of the Senate and House of Commons.

(2) A Judge of a Superior Court, whether appointed before or after the coming into force of this section, shall cease to hold office upon attaining the age of 75 years, or upon the coming into force of this section if at that time he has already attained that age. (44A)

100. The Salaries, Allowances, and Pensions of the Judges of the Superior, District, and County Courts (except the Courts of Probate in Nova Scotia and New Brunswick), and of the Admiralty Courts in Cases where the Judges thereof are for the Time being paid by Salary, shall be fixed and provided by the Parliament of Canada. (45)

101. The Parliament of Canada may, notwithstanding anything in this Act, from Time to Time provide for the Constitution, Maintenance, and Organization of a General Court of Appeal for Canada, and for the Establishment of any additional Courts for the better Administration of the Laws of Canada. (46)

3.3

THE CANADIAN JUDICIAL SYSTEM

Figure 1 represents the Canadian judicial system as it exists in Alberta. The names of the "section 92" and "section 96" courts vary from province to province. In Alberta they are called the Provincial Court and the Court of Queen's Bench, respectively. In Ontario, by contrast, the same courts are known as the High Court of Justice and the Court of Appeal. Together they constitute the trial and appellate divisions of the Supreme Court of Ontario. Also, note that in Alberta there no longer are county and district courts, as they were amalgamated with the Court of Queen's Bench in 1979. The vertical arrows indicate the paths of appeal. The left-diagonal and right-diagonal hatch-marks indicate section 92 and section 101 courts, respectively. The cross-hatched area represents the section 96 courts and the joint responsibility of the two levels of government.

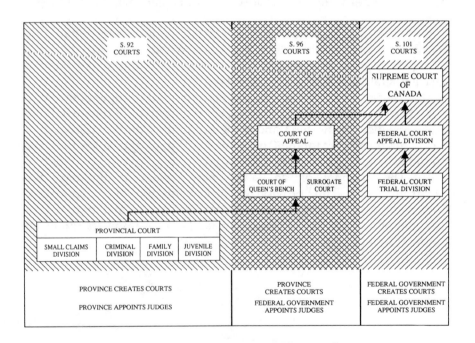

FIGURE 1

THE CANADIAN JUDICIAL SYSTEM

Figure 2 also represents the Canadian judicial system, but emphasizes the case flow pattern for the three principal areas of law: criminal, civil, and administrative.

While each jurisdiction has its own courts, there are certain principles which apply to all jurisdictions. The figure on the following page illustrates several of these principles.

First, there is a structure which applies to each jurisdiction's court system. This is shown by the rings of the model focusing on the Supreme Court of Canada. Not all jurisdictions have a court in each of the rings (for example, some jurisdictions do not have a county or district court). The outside ring contains the courts that hear the less serious cases, and therefore these courts handle the higher volumes of cases. Appeals from a court decision always go to a court farther inwards, though not necessarily to a court in an adjacent ring. As one moves inward on the model, the trials and appeals heard generally increase in seriousness and complexity.

Secondly, Figure 2 reflects the distinction between courts with provincially appointed judges and those superior courts with federally appointed judges.

Thirdly, there are often special authorities, boards or tribunals set up to handle certain kinds of cases.

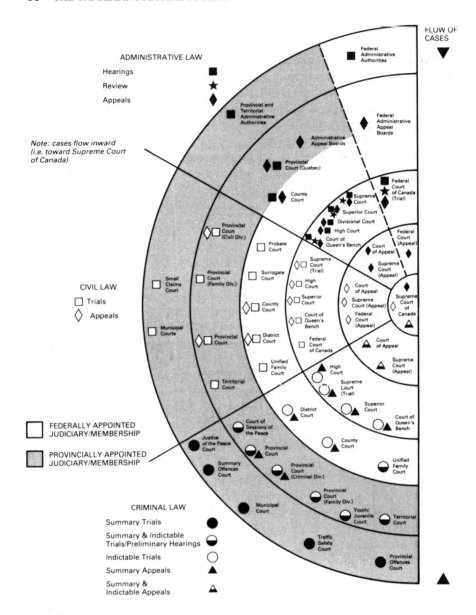

FIGURE 2

**A GENERAL OVERVIEW OF THE HIERARCHY, PROCEDURAL FLOW
AND JURISDICTION OF THE COURTS OF CANADA, 1982**

Statistics Canada. *Manpower, Resources and Costs of Criminal Prosecution in Canada 1980–82.*
1st ed. June 1983. Cat. No. 85–212E (Ottawa: Minister of Supply and Services). Reproduced
with the permission of the Minister of Supply and Services Canada, 1992.

3.4

THE CRIMINAL AND CIVIL COURT PROCESSES

THE CRIMINAL COURT PROCESS

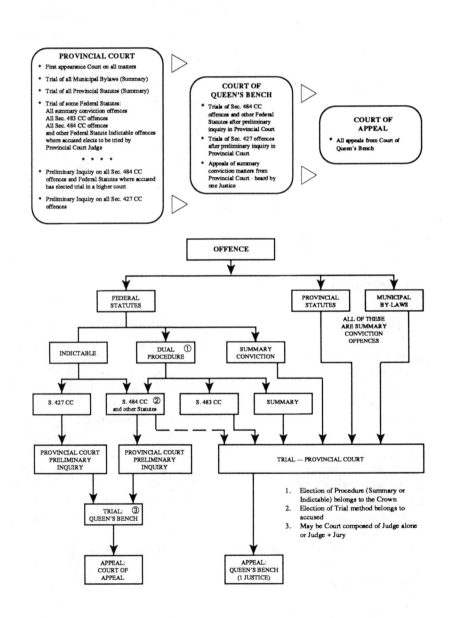

PROVINCIAL COURT

* First appearance Court on all matters
* Trial of all Municipal Bylaws (Summary)
* Trial of all Provincial Statutes (Summary)
* Trial of some Federal Statutes:
  All summary conviction offences
  All Sec. 483 CC offences
  All Sec. 484 CC offences
  and other Federal Statute Indictable offences
  where accused elects to be tried by
  Provincial Court Judge
  • • • •
* Preliminary Inquiry on all Sec. 484 CC
  offences and Federal Statutes where accused
  has elected trial in a higher court
* Preliminary Inquiry on all Sec. 427 CC
  offences

COURT OF QUEEN'S BENCH

* Trials of Sec. 484 CC offences and other Federal Statutes after preliminary inquiry in Provincial Court
* Trials of Sec. 427 offences after preliminary inquiry in Provincial Court
* Appeals of summary conviction matters from Provincial Court - heard by one Justice

COURT OF APPEAL

* All appeals from Court of Queen's Bench

OFFENCE

FEDERAL STATUTES | PROVINCIAL STATUTES | MUNICIPAL BY-LAWS

ALL OF THESE ARE SUMMARY CONVICTION OFFENCES

INDICTABLE | DUAL ① PROCEDURE | SUMMARY CONVICTION

S. 427 CC | S. 484 CC ② and other Statutes | S. 483 CC | SUMMARY

PROVINCIAL COURT PRELIMINARY INQUIRY | PROVINCIAL COURT PRELIMINARY INQUIRY | TRIAL — PROVINCIAL COURT

1. Election of Procedure (Summary or Indictable) belongs to the Crown
2. Election of Trial method belongs to accused
3. May be Court composed of Judge alone or Judge + Jury

TRIAL: ③ QUEEN'S BENCH

APPEAL: COURT OF APPEAL

APPEAL: QUEEN'S BENCH (1 JUSTICE)

THE CIVIL COURT PROCESS

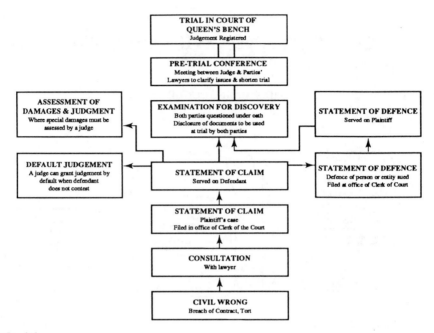

3.5

KEY TERMS

Concepts

unitary court system
dual court system
section 92 courts
section 96 courts
civil law
criminal law
administrative law
Common Law system
Civil Law system (Quebec)
indictable offense
summary conviction offense
preliminary inquiry
discretionary appellate jurisdiction
supervisory vs. appellate function
"per saltum appeal"

Institutions, Events, and Documents

Provincial Court
Court of Queen's Bench
Court of Appeal
Supreme Court of Canada (1875)
Federal Court of Canada (1970)
Exchequer Court (1875–1970)
Judicial Committee of the Privy Council
Constitution Act, 1982 (provision relating to Supreme Court of Canada)
Meech Lake Accord (provision relating to Supreme Court of Canada)

4
Judicial Recruitment and Selection

Under the Constitution Act, 1867, judicial appointments are made by the two different levels of government to three different levels of courts. Pursuant to section 101, the federal government is responsible for appointing all judges of the Supreme Court of Canada (nine), the Federal Court (twenty-five judges), and the Tax Court (ten judges). In addition, the federal government appoints all the judges of the "section 96 courts" (about 750) even though the latter are created and maintained by the provinces. This is one of the distinctive features of Canada's unitary judicial system, and was originally intended to ensure the independence of the provincial superior courts from local politics or prejudice. Finally, the provincial governments appoint all the judges (about 1,250) of the provincial courts created pursuant to section 92 of the Constitution Act, 1867. Altogether, there are just over 2,000 judges in Canada.

Appointment Procedures

Federal judicial appointments are made by the Cabinet on the advice of the Minister of Justice, except for chief justices,[1] who are recommended by the Prime Minister. While final responsibility for appointments remains with the Minister of Justice, under the reforms adopted in 1988, an ongoing search for appropriate candidates is carried on by the Commissioner for Federal Judicial Affairs. The Commissioner solicits suggestions from a nationwide network of contacts. Judges, bar associations, law schools, members of Parliament, and provincial office-holders are all encouraged to recommend individuals for judicial appointment. The Commissioner conducts a preliminary investigation to insure that candidates possess the required technical qualifications[2] and then refers their

---

[1] In addition to the Chief Justice of the Supreme Court of Canada and the Federal Court, the Prime Minister appoints a separate Chief Justice for the Court of Appeal and the superior trial court of each province except PEI, which has only one chief justice.

[2] That the person is a member of a provincial or territorial bar association and has a minimum of ten years experience as a practicing lawyer and/or judge.

names to the appropriate provincial or territorial committee for screening. Each provincial (and territorial) committee consists of five persons (including at least one non-lawyer), and is responsible for assessing whether the candidate possesses the required qualifications for appointment. The Committee can give only two assessments: "qualified" or "not qualified," and must be prepared to give reasons for any negative assessments. It should be noted that this procedure applies only to new appointments to the federal bench. The government's decision to elevate a sitting judge to a higher judicial office is not subject to review by a provincial screening committee.

The procedures for judicial appointments to "section 92 courts" vary from province to province. In the three Maritime provinces, there are no judicial councils and the appointment of provincial judges is left completely to the discretion of the attorney-general. Most of the other provinces have some form of judicial council based on one of two basic models: a screening committee or a nominating commission. The difference is the stage at which the government uses an independent, non-political body to assess potential candidates. In the first, the Attorney-General conducts the initial recruitment and then refers his or her candidate to an independent body for assessment. If approved, the government then proceeds with the appointment. The 1988 federal practice is basically a modified version of this model, since the provincial committees are basically limited to a screening function.

The alternative model is the nominating commission, which actually conducts the initial recruitment as well as screening, and then presents the government with a list of approved nominees from which it must choose. This is the practice in British Columbia and Alberta, where each province's Judicial Council receives applications for provincial court judgeships. After reviewing the credentials of the applicants, the Judicial Council recommends individuals to the provincial Attorney-General. If the Attorney-General disagrees with the Council's recommendation, he or she is free to request another. The difference between these two approaches lies in the extent to which they allow political influence. The Alberta and B.C. governments can only make appointments from a pool of candidates who have already been selected by an independent body, while under the screening model, the government is initially unrestricted, and only uses the independent committees to confirm choices that the Attorney-General has already made. This latter procedure gives the party which forms the government a much freer hand to favour party members and supporters when making appointments to the bench.

Politics versus Professionalism

The judicial selection process in all common law nations manifests a tension between judicial expertise and political influence. With the exception of certain final courts of appeal, the trend in recent decades has been to institute reforms that favour judicial expertise and reduce the degree of political influence. The most obvious manifestation of this is the long-established practice of appointing rather than electing judges. The potential for undue political influence is also limited by review of nominations by independent screening commissions, and reduced still further by merit selection nominating committees.

This emphasis on insulating judicial selection from partisan politics is premised on the assumption that judges and judging are not "political" in the way legislators and legislating are, and therefore that judges need not be politically accountable. (Judges, of course, are political in the sense that they usually accept (and enforce) the underlying political principles and beliefs of a society.) Impartiality is an essential ingredient of judicial authority, and the selection process must be carefully structured to preserve the perception of the judges as impartial arbiters. A non-political selection process assumes a non-political court. According to Weiler's "two models" theory, if the function of a judge is limited to adjudicating disputes, the only prerequisite for appointment is the necessary legal training, accompanied by good moral character and steady work habits.

While the assumptions associated with an adjudicative court were generally true of the common law tradition out of which Canada's legal system has evolved, they became strained with the introduction of written constitutional law and its corollary, judicial review. For reasons discussed in chapters one and two, appellate courts charged with interpreting constitutionally entrenched restrictions on democratic legislatures affect public policy more directly than courts whose functions are limited to resolving disputes arising under common law and statutes. To the extent that this occurs, the original rationale for excluding political considerations from the selection process is weakened. At the extreme is Weiler's "policy-making court." "Rather than focusing on legal ability and training as the key elements in judicial qualifications," writes Weiler,

> the policy-making model holds that a person's political programme and abilities should be most important. In fact, the logic of the system demands that these be evaluated in some manner other than an apolitical appointment process. Instead, judges should either be directly elected, or the various groups whose interests are affected by the judges' decisions should have some more formalized and legitimized form of participation in the making of the selection.[3]

While Weiler's model is theoretical, it reflects a fundamental norm of liberal democracy: that the governors should be accountable to the governed. This normative principle has had practical consequences: courts that act politically will come to be treated politically when it comes to the judicial selection process. Not surprisingly, the politicization of judicial

---

[3] Paul Weiler, "Two Models of Judicial Decision-Making," *Canadian Bar Review* 46 (1968), p. 406.

selection has developed the furthest in the United States, where judicial review first arose and where the fact of judicial "law-making" has long been acknowledged. Under many state constitutions in the U.S., judges are selected through public elections. In California, the judges of the state's Supreme Court are initially appointed by the governor, but after nine years must face a "confirmation vote" in a general election. In 1986, three judges, including the Chief Justice, were rejected by the California voters because they were perceived as blocking the majority will on capital punishment. Even though American federal judges are still appointed, strong political forces shape these appointments, especially appointments to the Supreme Court. (See Reading 4.6) While these practices may seem unacceptable and even shocking by traditional Canadian standards, they are consistent with a more "political" judicial function.

"Politics" can enter the judicial appointment process in four distinct (albeit sometimes overlapping) forms: patronage, regional representation, ethnic or group representation, and ideological compatibility. Such political appointments tend to reflect the contours of political division and the distribution of influence in the larger society. As such, they vary from country to country, and within the same country over time. In Canada, for example, patronage has declined as a major factor in Supreme Court appointments, while group representation has become more important. Note also that a single judicial appointment can encompass several of these political factors simultaneously. American President George Bush's 1991 appointment of Clarence Thomas to the U.S. Supreme Court, for example, represented considerations of both ideology (Thomas was a judicial conservative) and group representation (Thomas, a black, replaced Justice Thurgood Marshall, the first and only black to serve on the U.S. Supreme Court). Similarly, Brian Mulroney's 1987 appointment of Claire L'Heureux-Dubé to the Supreme Court of Canada provided symbolic representation for both francophones and women.

Patronage—appointment as a reward for past service to or support of a party—is the oldest, most common and best known form of political influence in judicial appointments in all common law nations. Patronage has been a dominant factor in both federal and provincial judicial appointments in Canada since before Confederation. Since the 1960s, the Canadian Bar Association has lobbied both levels of government to curb the influence of patronage.

At the "section 92 court" level, patronage was once the dominant criterion for appointment. As recently as 1971, a study of Ontario found that after 25 years of Progressive Conservative rule, most "section 92" provincial court magistrates were past or present supporters of the Progressive Conservative party. The institution of provincial judicial councils has reduced the practice of judicial patronage, especially in provinces such as British Columbia and Alberta where the council is a true "nominating commission."

Patronage has been equally pronounced in federal government's appointment of judges to section 96 courts. Depending on whether "political" was defined strongly (holding office) or weakly (running for office), studies have found that prior to World War II, anywhere from 50 percent to 80 percent of federally appointed judges had "political careers" prior to their appointment, and that appointments followed party lines 80 to 90 percent of the time. The same studies show that patronage declined significantly after World War II, but did not disappear.[4]

In 1966, dissatisfaction with the continuing effects of patronage on the quality of federal judicial appointments led the Canadian Bar Association to create the "Committee on the Judiciary" to provide a non-partisan source of advice to the federal government on judicial appointments. The CBA Committee would receive the names of potential nominees from the Minister of Justice, review the candidate's record, and then rate the candidate as "well qualified, qualified, or not qualified." Under this program, which operated from 1967 until 1988, no candidates receiving an unqualified rating were appointed. The CBA Committee on Judiciary was replaced by the 1988 reforms (described above) by provincial screening committees.

A succession of Liberal Ministers of Justice during the 1970s is generally credited with improving the quality of federal judicial appointments. John Turner initiated the practice of systematically collecting names and background information of potential judicial nominees before openings occurred, and this practice was formalized by his successor, Otto Lang, through the creation of a Special Advisor on Judicial Affairs. By consulting widely and constantly updating the list of potential nominees, the office of the Special Advisor was credited with further improving the quality of federally appointed judges.

Notwithstanding this progress in the quality of appointments, the Trudeau government continued to use its judicial appointments to "section 96 courts" to reward its members and supporters. In 1982 this practice provoked an angry reaction by the newly elected Progressive Conservative party of Premier Grant Devine in Saskatchewan. Devine's Attorney-General, Gary Lane, accused Ottawa of "stacking the courts with partisan appointees," and declared that he "wants more consultation on appointments, not just a phone call after the fact."[5] To protest the Liberals' alleged abuse of patronage in judicial appointments in Saskatchewan, the Devine government began reducing the number of section 96 judgeships by eliminating positions as they became vacant through death or retirement, thereby denying Ottawa the opportunity to make appointments. As recounted by Jeffrey Simpson (Reading 4.1), this stalemate, known as

---

[4] These studies are discussed in greater detail in Peter H. Russell, *The Judiciary in Canada: The Third Branch of Government* (Scarborough, ON: McGraw-Hill Ryerson, 1987), pp. 114–15.

[5] *Calgary Herald*, April 11, 1984, p. A5.

the "Saskatchewan Judges Affair," was not resolved until the defeat of the Liberals in the federal elections in 1984. The newly elected Conservative government informally agreed to consult more closely with the provinces before making superior court appointments. Because of these kinds of tensions, there have been recurrent suggestions that the constitution be amended to return "section 96" appointments to the provinces. However, no one gives these proposals any serious chance of being adopted. The patronage benefits of "section 96 court" appointments are too valuable a political asset for the federal government to give up.

The patronage issue again became the focus of public attention following a series of judicial appointments occasioned by Pierre Trudeau's resignation as Leader of the Liberal Party and Prime Minister in 1984. Before leaving, Trudeau appointed three of his former cabinet ministers to the Federal Court: Mark MacGuigan, Bud Cullen and Yvon Pinard, the last without any prior review by the CBA Committee on the Judiciary. Several other Liberal politicians were also appointed to provincial superior courts.

The 1984 Trudeau appointments were widely criticized in the press. Brian Mulroney, the new leader of the Progressive Conservative party, exploited the judicial patronage issue in the 1984 federal election and promised change if elected. The incident also led to new studies by the Canadian Association of Law Teachers (CALT) and the Canadian Bar Association. In 1985 both the CALT and CBA issued reports recommending reform. While the details varied, both reports recommended a process in which an independent nominating commission would recruit and screen potential candidates and then create lists from which the Minister of Justice would be expected to make appointments. The Mulroney government took these reports under consideration.

In 1988, when the Mulroney government announced its new judicial appointments procedures, it paid lip service to the CALT and CBA Reports. Close scrutiny, however, reveals that the 1988 reforms represented only a half-step in the direction of reform. The novel element was the transfer of the recruitment function from the Judicial Affairs Advisor, who worked within the Justice Minister's personal office, to the Judicial Affairs Commissioner. The latter has the rank and status of a deputy head of a government department, and is thus more independent than the now defunct judicial affairs advisor. The new provincial and territorial committees, however, are not true nominating commissions. Their function remains essentially that of screening names of candidates provided to them by the Commissioner, who, when all is said and done, remains an employee of the federal government. To date, there has been no systematic study to assess the impact of the 1988 reforms.

The 1989 study of Peter Russell and Jacob Ziegel (see Reading 4.2) suggests why the Mulroney government did not rush to embrace the recommendations of the CBA and CALT. Contrary to their promises of reform during the 1984 campaign, it turned out that the Mulroney government did not practice what it preached. Of the 228 federal judges appointed during the first Mulroney government (1984–88), 48 percent were found to have associations with the Progressive Conservative party. While 86 percent received a good or better rating from the CBA Committee on the Judiciary, of the thirteen who did not, ten had Tory political connections. Russell and Ziegel conclude that there was only "marginal improvement" in the judicial selection process during the Mulroney government's first term, that political patronage remained "pervasive," and that the 1988 reforms did "little to address the basic flaws in the appointing system."

Other forms of political influence in judicial appointments—such as regional or ethnic group representation—tend to reflect the the political sociology of a nation. Canada has a long tradition of ethnic and regional representation in the judicial appointments to the Supreme Court. The legal guarantee of three justices from Quebec is technically justified by the Court's appellate jurisdiction over Quebec's civil law, but it also symbolizes the "distinct" status of Quebec and the French people in Canadian politics. The French-English dualism of Canadian political experience has also manifested itself in the tradition of alternating the appointment of the Chief Justice between an anglophone and a francophone. Prime Minister Trudeau's appointment of Brian Dickson as Chief Justice in March, 1984 violated this tradition, and appeared to mark its end. But Prime Minister Mulroney followed the tradition in his 1990 appointment of Antonio Lamer, a Quebec francophone, to succeed Dickson as Chief Justice.

Similarly, the convention of *de facto* geographical representation on the Supreme Court testifies to the strong influence of regionalism in Canadian politics. Significantly, this is not a Canadian idiosyncrasy. For the first century of the United States, geographical representation in appointments was considered essential for maintaining the legitimacy of the Supreme Court and the national government. By tradition, there was a "Southern seat," a "New England seat," and later a "Western seat" on the Court. In nineteenth century American politics, as in contemporary Canadian politics, this practice was a symptom of the relative weakness of the central government and its attempt to reassure the provinces/states that their "special circumstances" could receive a sympathetic "hearing" in a national court of appeal.

This comparative perspective may illuminate a new dimension of the politics of judicial appointments in Canada. The American convention of geographic representation fell into disuse as regionalism ceased to be a dominant factor in American politics. It was replaced, in part, by a new practice of ethnic or "group" representation. Twentieth-century American politics has witnessed the development of the traditions of a Catholic seat (1894), a Jewish seat (1916), a black seat (1967), and more recently a woman's seat (1981). While none of these practices has been treated as absolutely binding, they reflect the emergence of the various groups as potentially powerful voting blocs within the American electorate. Presidents seeking re-election have sought to improve their chances by making judicial appointments that demonstrate solidarity or sympathy with these groups.

There is recent evidence to suggest that this dynamic of group representation (based on political calculation) may be taking hold in Canada. Of course, French Canadians have always been represented. More recently, in 1982, Prime Minister Trudeau set a precedent by appointing Bertha Wilson, the first woman ever to serve on the Supreme Court of Canada. Not to be outdone, Prime Minister Mulroney subsequently appointed two more women to the highest Court: Claire L'Heureux-Dubé (1987) and Beverly McLachlin (1989). Given the high profile of the sexual equality issue in contemporary Canadian politics, it seems that the convention of having at least two women justices is here to stay. Mulroney has also appointed the first Ukrainian-Canadian, John Sopinka (1988), and the first Italian-Canadian, Frank Iacobucci (1991). While it seems unlikely that these appointments will lead to a convention of a Ukrainian- or Italian-Canadian seat, they symbolically reinforce the policy of multiculturalism. They also suggest that the Tories are hoping to garner more votes among these constituencies in the next federal election.

The fourth form of political influence in judicial appointments is political programme or ideology. The influence of ideology is usually limited to final courts of appeal exercising judicial review over written constitutions. It is generally recognized that political compatibility has been the dominant factor in presidential appointments to the American Supreme Court since its origins. The ideological dimension of American Supreme Court appointments is most obvious in the years following a "watershed" or critical election,[6] during which a newly elected president and his party in Congress face a Supreme Court still dominated by the appointments of the preceding regime. Recognizing that their policy agenda is or may be threatened by a hostile Court, these presidents have exercised their power of appointment to "pack the court" with judges who support their political programme. The Reagan-Bush appointments since 1980 are the most recent example of this tendency. (See Reading 4.6)

While "court packing" in its more dramatic form is mainly an American phenomenon, appointments to the constitutional courts in Europe tend to follow party lines very closely. Canada has been different in this regard, at least until recently. Patronage, not ideology, was the dominant factor in appointments to the Supreme Court of Canada through 1949. (See Reading 4.1) Since the Victoria Charter of 1971, a majority of the

---

6 The most important watershed elections were the election of Jefferson and the Democrats in 1800; Lincoln and the Republicans in 1860; Franklin Delano Roosevelt and the Democrats in 1932; and Ronald Reagan and the Republicans in 1980. In each of these general elections, what had been the dominant national party lost the White House and one or both houses of Congress to what had been the minority national party.

provinces have lobbied for increased provincial participation in the appointment process and constitutional entrenchment of the convention of regional representation.[7] While their advocates argued that these changes would guarantee a more "representative" court, critics protested that a provincial veto over Supreme Court appointments would amount to the rejection of "the basic principle of the judicial process: that judges are judges of the issue, not partisans of the parties to the issue."[8]

Such criticisms notwithstanding, the federal government finally accepted these reforms in the hope that they would increase the legitimacy and authority of the Supreme Court, thus making it a more effective vehicle of "intrastate federalism"—the representation of regional interests within the institutions of the national government. The 1987 Meech Lake Accord proposed that the federal government be required to appoint Supreme Court judges from lists submitted by the provinces. Since the Meech Lake Accord would have also required three judges from Quebec, this provision would have forced Ottawa and Quebec to reach an agreement on appointments. With the other provinces, Ottawa would have had more flexibility. If the list submitted by one province was unacceptable, the federal government could turn to a different province from the same region. (This possibility would in turn encourage a provincial government to submit candidates whose credentials were acceptable.)

This proposal for the provincial nomination of Supreme Court appointments was one of the more controversial elements of the Meech Lake Accord. Critics alleged that it would allow provincial governments to mould the political orientation of the Court's decision-making in a decentralist direction, thereby weakening the country and also subverting the potential for an expansive interpretation of the Charter of Rights. Defenders of this proposal argued that it was consistent with the spirit of equality of the two levels of government in Canadian federalism, and that provincially-nominated judges were likely to be as ideologically diverse on Charter-related issues as any other set of nominees.[9]

In the end, the Meech Lake Accord was defeated by an odd alliance that consisted mainly of small-c conservatives—anti-Quebeckers and supporters of Senate reform—and small l-liberals—human rights, native rights, feminist, civil libertarian, and environmental groups. Most of these latter groups considered themselves beneficiaries of the Charter and the new politics of rights that it has generated. They feared that a Supreme Court

[7] See Peter H. Russell, "Constitutional Reform of the Judicial Branch," *Canadian Journal of Political Science* 17:2 (1984), pp. 227–252. Reprinted in the first edition of this book.

[8] E.D. Fulton, as reported in G.M. Stirling, "A Symposium of the Appointment of Judges," *Alberta Law Review* 2 (1973), p. 301. Reprinted in the first edition of this book.

[9] See Peter H. Russell, "The Supreme Court Proposals in the Meech Lake Accord," *Canadian Public Policy* 14 (Sept. 1988), pp. 93, 99.

that was provincially nominated would also be provincially dominated, and generally unreceptive to their expansive vision of the meaning of Charter rights, rights that cut across provincial boundaries and require uniform enforcement in every region of the country.

Allan Cairns aptly characterized the conflict over the Meech Lake Accord as the conflict of two competing constitutional visions of Canada.[10] One is the old constitution, dating from Confederation, the constitution of governments, federalism and French-English dualism. The other is the constitution of the Charter and rights of the various ethnic, multicultural, aboriginal, handicapped and feminist groups who have worked to shape both its original wording and subsequent development through judicial interpretation. (See Reading 7.3) The defeat of the Meech Lake Accord may be seen as the defeat—perhaps temporary—of the politics of federalism by the politics of rights.

The beginning of the influence of the "politics of rights" on appointments to the Supreme Court can be traced back to the appointment of Bora Laskin as Chief Justice in 1973. At this time the Supreme Court was being sharply criticized by civil libertarian lawyers and law professors for its traditional and cautious interpretation of the 1960 Bill of Rights. Laskin had proven himself as the Court's leading civil libertarian and judicial activist since his appointment in 1970, but tradition dictated that the most senior judge in terms of service on the Court be chosen Chief Justice. Prime Minister Trudeau broke with this tradition and chose Laskin, much to the delight of the Court's civil libertarian critics. There were rumours that several of the more senior judges who had been passed over might resign in protest, but this never materialized.

The enactment of the Charter of Rights in 1982 clearly enhanced the potential for Supreme Court judges to influence public policy and has elicited growing interest in the ideological orientation of appointments to the Court, especially from interest groups with a policy stake in Charter interpretation. For example, during 1981–1982, in anticipation of the enactment of the Charter, the National Action Committee on the Status of Women (NAC) began to lobby for the appointment of a woman "acceptable to our purposes" to the Supreme Court of Canada.[11] This campaign bore fruit in March, 1982, when Prime Minister Trudeau appointed Bertha Wilson to the Supreme Court. Several months later NAC honoured Justice Wilson by awarding her with a special medallion commemorating the fiftieth anniversary of the "Persons Case." (See Reading 10.2) Justice Wilson went on to become the Supreme Court's leading practitioner of judicial

---

10   Allan Cairns, "Citizens (Outsiders) and Governments (Insiders) in Constitution-Making: The Case of Meech Lake, " in *Canadian Public Policy* 14 (Sept. 1988), p. 121.

11   "NAC Memo," Committee Report, September, 1981, Justice Committee, p. 5; "NAC Memo," March, 1981, Justice Committee Report, p. 4.

activism during the first decade of the Charter. (See Reading 12.4) Justice Wilson's activism was best exemplified by her outspoken defence of the right of a woman to choose an abortion in her concurring opinion in the Court's 1988 *Morgentaler* decision, which struck down the *Criminal Code* restrictions on abortion.

The *Morgentaler* decision caught Canadians by surprise and alerted them to the new power exercised by judges under the Charter. As Peter Russell observed at the time, "Filling Supreme Court vacancies . . . has always been a little bit political in a subterranean way, and now it will be right at the surface [with] the political interest groups lobbying and pressing the appointing authorities to put people on the court of their persuasion."[12] Russell's prediction was fulfilled almost before he finished making it. The *Morgentaler* decision was criticized by Angela Costigan, counsel for Choose Life Canada, a national pro-life lobby group, as "the expression of personal opinion by the judges." Costigan allowed that in the future her group would try to influence the appointment of judges who shared its position. Norma Scarborough, president of the Canadian Abortion Rights League (CARAL), responded by declaring that while her group had never tried to influence judicial appointments in the past, it would if necessary in the future. "We are going to protect our position as much as possible," she declared.[13] When Justice Estey announced his intention to retire several months later, Member of Parliament James Jepson, an outspoken pro-life Tory backbencher, declared, "We now have a chance to put men and women on the bench with a more conservative point of view." While emphasizing that he had never lobbied for a judicial appointment before, Jepson continued:

> But this one seems to have caught the people's attention. Unfortunately, with the Charter that Trudeau left us, we legislators do not have final power. It rests with the courts. . . . You have seen the battling in the United States for the [most recent] Supreme Court nominee. Well, it doesn't take a rocket scientist to see we have the same situation here now.[14]

In the end, the pro-life lobbying had no apparent effect on the government's appointment of Toronto lawyer John Sopinka to fill Estey's seat on the Court. But Jepson's comments represented a sharp break with past Canadian practice, and were not an isolated incident. Demands for public screening of judicial candidates is not likely to disappear. Interest groups that regularly use Charter litigation as a political tactic tend to explain their choice as an effective "minority strategy" because success does not require forging "a consensus of public opinion," but only "the right

---

[12] "Public to Demand Say in Court Appointments," *Lawyers' Weekly*, February 12, 1988, p. 1.

[13] Ibid.

[14] "Reduced Role for Politicians Urged in Naming of Judges," *Globe and Mail*, May 16, 1988, p. A1.

argument." (See Reading 7.2) The catch is that what constitutes a "right argument" to one judge may not to another. As interest groups and politicians become more sophisticated in their understanding of the connection between the "right argument" and the "right judge," the debate over opening up the process of Supreme Court appointments is likely to grow. (See Reading 4.7)

On April 17, 1992, the tenth anniversary of the Charter, Chief Justice Antonio Lamer waded into this debate by observing that, "I don't think the America process is a good one." While he did not rule out the possibility of change, he stressed that:

> What we must be very careful not to do is to politicize the process. That's what the Americans have done. We've worked very hard to depoliticize the process. We started 25 or 30 years ago, and I think we have succeeded. You know, I was appointed to this court by Mr. Trudeau. I was appointed Chief Justice by Mr. Mulroney. I don't think there is any love lost between the two of them.[15]

This argument was hard to square with the Chief Justice's earlier remark in the same interview that "the Charter has changed our job descriptions." Prior to the Charter, Lamer observed, judges were trained and expected just "to apply" and, if necessary, "to interpret" laws. "But with the Charter," he continued:

> we are commanded to sometimes judge the laws themselves. It is [a] very different activity, especially when one has to look at Section 1 of the Charter [the reasonable limitations clause], which is asking us to make what is essentially what used to be a political call.[16]

Lamer went on to say that this "drastic change in the judicial approach to the law" has required judges to adapt, "to change our libraries, and start reading a lot of American stuff that we weren't used to. . . ." The Chief Justice seemed to admit that under the Charter his Court is now engaged in making "political [judgment] calls," a function similar to that of the U.S. Supreme Court, yet to cling to a British-style appointment process associated with an adjudicatory court. The danger of this hybrid approach is that rather than preventing the politicization of the appointment process, it will just drive the politics underground, beyond public knowledge or scrutiny.

A related development is the push for the appointment of more women judges to all levels of the Canadian judiciary. At the beginning of the decade of the 1980s, only three percent of the federally appointed judges were women. By 1990, women constituted 10 percent of the federal judiciary in Canada. Since 1982 there have been three women appointed to the Supreme Court of Canada (to fill nine vacancies). The Russell and Ziegel study found that 17.5 percent of the Mulroney judicial appointments (1984–

---

[15]   *Globe and Mail*, April 17, 1992, p. A17.

[16]   Ibid.

1988) were women. While there is certainly no longer any controversy over an "equal opportunity" appointments policy, there are critics of "employment equity" measures who argue merit—not gender—should be the only relevant criterion of appointment. (Reading 4.4)

A related controversy has developed over whether "women judges will make a difference." (See Reading 4.3) In a widely publicized speech in 1990, Justice Bertha Wilson argued that certain areas of judge-made law reflect the gender bias of a male judiciary and that women judges will bring a "uniquely feminine perspective" to bear on certain issues of legal interpretation. She also suggested that "some aspects of criminal law, in particular, cry out for change since they are based on presuppositions about the nature of women and women's sexuality that in this day and age are little short of ludicrous." While Justice Wilson did not specify what these aspects were, many assumed, based on her own votes and written opinions, that she was referring to abortion and prostitution.

Justice Wilson's speech provoked a strong protest by REAL (Realistic, Equal and Active for Life) Women, a conservative women's group, that subsequently filed a complaint with the Canadian Judicial Council. REAL Women's complaint argued that there is no necessary connection between gender and political views, and that Justice Wilson was in fact advancing feminist teachings and policy under the guise of gender equality:

> Women in Canada do not all think alike. The views of vocal feminists (scholars or otherwise) do not represent the views of all Canadian women. The failure of Madame Justice Wilson to either understand this point or alternatively, fail to accept the fact that all women (not to mention men) do not agree with the feminist interpretation of law, is in itself deeply disturbing and indicative of her inability to properly carry out her duties to impartially and objectively interpret the law.[17]

There was some truth on both sides of this controversy. One does not have to be a feminist to recognize that in only two generations, Western technology has radically transformed both the means of industrial production and the means of human reproduction, and thereby eliminated most (if not all) of the effects of physical differences that previously imposed very different life experiences on men and women. Unlike their grandparents' generation, young men and women today share similar life expectations. Since all law is more or less a reflection of social mores [or "moeurs," see Reading 1.4], it is not surprising that many laws embodying archaic assumptions about the sexes have failed to keep pace with changing social attitudes. The subject of sexual equality and the law has been the subject of much academic research and debate. Surely it is not inappropriate for a judge addressing a law school audience to explore and expound on such a topic.

---

[17] Letter to the Canadian Judicial Council from Lettie Morse, President, REAL Women, February 13, 1990.

On the other hand, Justice Wilson did indulge in an overbroad generalization if she was asserting the existence of a single "women's position" or "unique feminine perspective" on issues such as abortion or prostitution. The very existence of groups such as REAL Women (and there are analogous groups in the U.S. and elsewhere) is proof of broad differences of opinions among women on gender-related issues. (Indeed, some public opinion polls show that men are more likely than women to support unrestricted access to abortion services.)

Nor are judges necessarily different. Justice Sandra O'Connor, the first woman on the U.S. Supreme Court, has consistently voted to uphold state restrictions on abortion in the post-*Roe v. Wade* era. In Canada, feminists protested loudly when the Supreme Court struck down the "rape-shield" section of the Criminal Code, which prohibited cross-examination of rape victims about their sexual history.[18] Yet the majority judgment in this decision was written by Justice Beverly McLachlin. After a year of listening to this criticism, Justice McLachlin publicly stated that she was still comfortable with her decision. Earlier, the Alberta Court of Appeal had reached the same decision in a judgment written by Justice Mary Heatherington.

These examples make it clear that if there is a semi-official feminist position on gender-related issues, it is not shared by all women. The corollary, of course, is that there are many men who are "feminist" in their views. In short, the broad cluster of issues that defines the current sexual equality agenda transcends gender. Justice Wilson was wrong if she intended to suggest otherwise, but this was hardly grounds for discipline. The Canadian Judicial Council found that the complaint did not even justify a formal investigation, and rejected it.

This incident is indicative of a growing controversy between feminists and their critics over the judiciary. The same dispute has arisen over the recent practice of "education seminars" on gender bias issues for judges, a policy that Justice Wilson also endorsed in her 1990 speech. The Canadian Judicial Centre, established in 1988 to provide continuing education courses for judges, has begun to include seminars on gender bias in judging. Most of the materials used for these seminars have been prepared by law professors associated directly or indirectly with the Legal Education and Action Fund (LEAF), a feminist legal action organization. (See Readings 7.3) This connection has fueled allegations from conservative groups that the Canadian Judicial Centre has become "an indoctrination centre for feminist thought."[19] Gwen Landolt, president of REAL Women, said she respects the right of feminists to use the Charter to advance their policy objectives but objects to what she maintains is their privileged access to judges: "We're

---

18 *Seaboyer and Gayme v. The Queen*, Supreme Court of Canada, Aug. 22, 1991.

19 "Political Correctness Undermines Judicial System: Reader." Letter to the editor from C. Gwendolyn Landolt, *Lawyers' Weekly*, August 2, 1991, p. 5.

saying, if you've got an argument to make, line up like everyone else and make your case in court."[20] Kathleen Mahoney, a law professor at the University of Calgary who has contributed to the development of the gender bias seminars, defends them: "The historical patriarchal ideology in the law is perpetuated by men who perceive women as inferior to men. . . . I really wish REAL Women would define feminist to me. To me it is someone who seeks justice and humanity for all human beings."[21]

While the Centre has defended the utility of gender bias seminars and continues to offer them, the federal Minister of Justice, Kim Campbell, recently rejected the recommendation of the National Action Committee on the Status of Women (NAC) to make them mandatory. To require attendance at any such seminar, the Justice Minister explained, would infringe the principle of judicial independence.[22]

From a political science/judicial process perspective, feminist support for gender-bias seminars for judges is analogous to the efforts of American feminists to prevent judges like Robert Bork from being appointed, except that this "lobbying" occurs after the appointment and is directed at the appointee rather than the appointers. The common denominator of both tactics is the perception that judges can and do use their discretion in interpreting constitutional rights to alter public policy. Since there is no opportunity to exert influence prior to the appointment, such as the hearings of the Senate Judiciary Committee in the U.S., Canadian interest groups are forced to seek access after the appointment. These "special education" seminars for judges provide just such a forum. Nor is it surprising that conservative groups have protested this "privileged audience" with the judges. Since presumably other Canadian interest groups would also welcome the opportunity to educate judges on their views of "the public interest," it will be interesting to see whether this practice is expanded or eliminated.

To conclude, there have been somewhat contradictory trends in judicial selection in Canada during recent decades. Based on the proven decline in patronage appointments, Sir Robert Megarry has predicted further depoliticization of judicial selection in Canada along the lines of the British experience that he describes. (See Reading 4.5) But then British judges have never exercised judicial review of a federal constitution nor interpreted an entrenched Charter of Rights. British judges have thus never become embroiled in the "constitutional politics" or "politics of rights" that result from judicial review. These considerations were reflected in

---

20 "Justice and Gender," *Alberta Report*, February 26, 1990, p. 35.

21 Ibid.

22 "Mandatory Training of Judges Rejected by Justice Minister, " *Globe and Mail*, April 11, 1992, p. A6.

Peter Russell's 1982 prediction that a principal effect of the Charter would be "its tendency to judicialize politics and to politicize the judiciary."[23] The jockeying for position by feminists and conservatives on judicial appointments in the wake of the 1988 Morgentaler decision support Russell's prediction. Political patronage considerations might well be replaced by political considerations of a more ideological nature.

On the other hand, the availability of the section 33 legislative override may neutralize the "court packing" tendencies of unhappy politicians and interest groups. If a government finds a judicial interpretation of the Charter legally wrong , politically unacceptable or both, it can always invoke the section 33 "notwithstanding" power to overrule the judges' "mistake." This is a much more direct and precise way of dealing with such decisions than the blunt (and uncertain) method of "court packing." Presumably, American President Franklin D. Roosevelt would have felt no need to "pack" the American Supreme Court during the 1930s if he had a power like the section 33 legislative override. With this consideration in mind, it remains to be seen whether the Charter of Rights will produce a more ideologically charged appointment process to the Supreme Court of Canada.

---

[23] See Peter H. Russell, "The Effect of the Charter of Rights on the Policy-Making Role of Canadian Courts," *Canadian Public Administration* 25 (1982), p. 1. Reprinted in the first edition of this book.

4.1

PATRONAGE IN JUDICIAL APPOINTMENTS
Jeffrey Simpson

. . . Broadly speaking, the further down the judicial hierarchy, the more obvious the evidence of patronage. The Supreme Court of Canada, for example, is now completely devoid of patronage, or even of the tinge of partisan appointments. . . . Supreme Court appointments were not always so pure. A scholarly history of the Supreme Court makes clear that partisanship joined religion and region—and merit, when available—as indispensable criteria for Supreme Court appointments until the immediate post-war years. When Louis St. Laurent became prime minister in

---

The Spoils of Power: The Politics of Patronage (Toronto, ON: Collins, 1988), from pages 300–310. Reprinted with permission.

1949, the court contained seven justices, four of whom had had extensive political ties to the Liberal party. St. Laurent himself appointed justices from a mixture of non-political and political backgrounds, the most obvious being long-time Liberal cabinet minister Douglas Abbott. But partisanship appeared to wane throughout subsequent years as prime ministers increasingly sought advice from the legal fraternity before making Supreme Court appointments. Twenty-two of forty Supreme Court judges appointed before 1949 had previously been politicians; since then, only two of twenty-two justices had entered politics.

That sharp decline in previous political experience of Supreme Court justices is partly—but only partly—reflected further down the hierarchy. The Canadian Bar Association said as recently as 1985 that "there is ample scope for the functioning of a political patronage system without applying it to judicial appointments." The association declared itself satisfied that patronage had been rooted out of the Supreme Court, but it worried about patronage elsewhere in the judiciary, especially in the Federal Court, whose members are appointed by Ottawa. Writing after Prime Minister Pierre Trudeau sent three former ministers (Mark MacGuigan, Bud Cullen and Yvon Pinard) to the Federal Court as part of his 1984 orgy of patronage appointments, the association remarked, "at present, this court is perceived by many, rightly or wrongly, as a government-oriented court because so many former politicians and federal officials have been appointed to it." The association added, "as to appointments to the Federal Court of Canada, political favouritism has been a dominant, though not sole, consideration; many appointees have been active supporters of the party in power."

Trudeau's parting gesture also featured the appointment of two other Liberal MPs and a defeated Liberal candidate to lower courts. These appointments fitted a familiar Trudeau pattern for patronage. A professor of law before entering politics, Trudeau took considerable care in his early years in office to temper patronage in making senior judicial appointments. This was consistent with other intermittent efforts to change traditional assumptions about patronage. But such efforts declined in intensity as his years in office wore on, so that by the end of his sixteen years as prime minister Trudeau was practising patronage as relentlessly as his predecessors.

The association also analysed federal appointments to higher courts in the provinces—so-called section 96 courts—and concluded that political favouritism still existed in Alberta, Manitoba, Newfoundland, and Ontario, and that it remained a "dominant" but not exclusive consideration in New Brunswick, Nova Scotia, Prince Edward Island, and Saskatchewan. That the three Maritime provinces appeared on the association's list was not surprising; there the traditions of political patronage have persisted longer than almost anywhere else in Canada. But Saskatchewan's inclusion might raise a few eyebrows, until one remembers that Saskatchewan was the fiefdom of Otto Lang, Trudeau's minister of justice and a former dean of the University of Saskatchewan law school.

Lang and his successor Mark MacGuigan scattered prominent or low-profile Liberals throughout the Saskatchewan judiciary, including former party leaders, MLAs, defeated candidates and loyal party workers. This propensity for appointing Liberals to Saskatchewan courts led directly to a *contretemps* with the Conservative government of Premier Grant Devine. The provincial Conservatives, eager dispensers of patronage themselves, became sufficiently riled by Liberal appointments to the bench, and by Ottawa's refusal to consult the provincial government before making appointments, that they tried to restrict Liberal opportunities for patronage. In 1982 the provincial government passed an order-in-council reducing the number of judges on the Saskatchewan Court of Appeal from seven to five.

For the next two years, open warfare raged between the provincial Conservative government and the Trudeau Liberals. The provincial cabinet passed another order-in-council closing down each vacancy on the Court of Queen's Bench, so that its strength fell from thirty to twenty-four. Only the election of the Mulroney Conservatives ended the impasse. With Conservatives in Regina and Ottawa, the provincial party quickly restored the judicial positions, and filled some of them with prominent supporters such as George Hill and Irving Goldenberg, former presidents of the Saskatchewan Conservative party. The Saskatchewan experience of the 1980s mirrored that of Newfoundland in 1960 when Liberal premier Joey Smallwood, rebuffed by the federal Conservatives in his demand for control of judicial appointments, refused to proclaim legislation creating a new position on the provincial Supreme Court.

The Bar Association's 1985 review of judicial appointments gave provincial governments better marks than it gave the federal government. In five provinces—Alberta, British Columbia, Newfoundland, Quebec, and Saskatchewan—the association thought "political favouritism has played no part in appointments." In Manitoba, favouritism played "some part" in appointments, whereas in those hardy patronage perennials—New Brunswick, Prince Edward Island and Nova Scotia—the association found that "most appointees have been active supporters of the party in power."

That 1985 review, sparked by Trudeau's parting orgy of patronage and his failure to consult the bar before making Yvon Pinard's appointment, flowed from the association's decades-long campaign to squeeze patronage from the process of selecting judges. Moral suasion was about the association's only weapon for many years, although it helped the association's case when its president, R.B. Bennett, became prime minister in 1930 and tried to set a better example in selecting Supreme Court justices. But the concept of formal consultation with the legal community had to await the arrival of Trudeau as minister of justice in 1967.

Trudeau became the first minister of justice to seek an opinion of the Canadian Bar Association's National Council on the Judiciary before appointing a judge. This practice continued when John Turner became minister of justice in the first Trudeau government, and Turner is fairly credited with having improved the quality of judicial appointments across the country. In 1972, a special adviser on judicial appointments was named in the minister's office. These reforms sprang both from Trudeau's own convictions as a professor of law and from intermittent attempts to change some traditional conventions of patronage in his early years in office. In five provinces—Alberta, British Columbia, Newfoundland, Ontario, and Saskatchewan—attorneys-general now formally consult provincial judicial councils before making appointments, while in Quebec the attorney-general consults a nominating committee. British Columbia's Provincial Court Act even requires the cabinet to appoint only persons recommended by the judicial council.

Pressure from the bar, then, has been among those restricting the incidence of political patronage on judicial appointments. Some numbers illustrate the point. Will Klein studied federally appointed judges in Manitoba, Ontario, and Quebec from 1905 to 1970. He found that nearly 95 percent of former politicians appointed to Ontario courts by Liberal governments were Liberals, and 81 percent appointed by Conservative governments were Conservatives. But he also discovered that although 43 percent of all Laurier's appointments had contested elections, only 21 percent of Trudeau's (up to 1970) had done so. Klein concluded that "political activities prior to appointment to the bench have been common to about a third of the judges appointed in Manitoba, Ontario, and Quebec between 1905 and 1970 but that . . . proportion of judges with electoral experience has diminished through these years."

What Klein could not measure was the partisanship of appointees who had participated in politics other than by running in elections or serving in legislatures. It was a key omission, since many judicial appointees have been active party supporters without ever having entered electoral politics. His general conclusion that political considerations in judicial appointments have waned over this century was supported by Guy Bouthillier, who examined the careers of appointees to the Quebec Court of Appeal from 1867 to 1972. Bouthillier found that the proportion involved in politics had dropped from over 78 percent between Confederation and World War I to 22 percent since World War II. But remember that these sorts of studies undoubtedly underestimate, often considerably, the partisan factor in appointments. They trace only electoral careers, and forget that many judges with the proper political credentials never ran for office. For example, one study in the early 1950s found that in six provinces all judges were supporters of the party in power at the time of their appointment. In the four other provinces, the percentage of party supporters ranged from 70 percent to 87 percent. And a survey for the Association of Canadian Law Teachers in 1966 concluded, "All but a few of the judges appointed during the period were affiliated with the party in power at the time of their appointment, and most were actively engaged in politics."

The practice still continues. For example, Prime Minister Joe Clark appointed five judges to the Superior Court for the Montreal district. All had Conservative credentials: Claude Gérin, who ran unsuccessfully against Liberal kingpin Marc Lalonde; Gérard Trudel, a Conservative organizer; Maurice Mercure, a former Union Nationale candidate and Conservative organizer; Bernard Flynn, who worked for Clark and his predecessor Robert Stanfield; and Claude Nolin, former president of the Conservative party in Quebec.

4.2

MULRONEY'S JUDICIAL APPOINTMENTS AND THE NEW JUDICIAL ADVISORY COMMITTEES
Peter H. Russell and Jacob S. Ziegel

The data we have collected on the Mulroney government's first-term judicial appointments [1984–1988] are presented in [this section]. . . .

First, we should note the distribution of the 228 judicial appointments. . . . By far the bulk of these appointments, over 90 percent, is to the section 96 courts, that is, the provincial and territorial courts presided over by federally appointed judges. . . .

. . . Of the 228 appointments, 67 were promotions within the judicial system. . . . [T]here is a promotional ladder from the highest provincial trial court (the General Jurisdiction Trial Court) to the Court of Appeal, and then to the Supreme Court of Canada. Indeed, over half of the appointments to the provincial courts of appeal were "elevations" from the superior trial court. It is pleasantly surprising to find that as many as 13 judges were promoted from the lower provincial courts and that these were spread across the country. In the past such promotions have been very rare. Perhaps their increased frequency reflects the improvements many of the provinces have made in their method of selecting judges. . . .

University of Toronto Law Journal 41 (1991), from pages 4–37. Reprinted with permission.

... [Women comprised 17.5 percent of the appointees, and these appointments were spread] proportionately among the various positions and levels. Certainly this is a clear improvement over the situation at the beginning of the decade, when Pauline Jewett reported to the House of Commons that only three percent of the federally appointed judiciary were women. . . . [this] suggest[s] a conscious effort at affirmative action to redress the gender imbalance on the bench.

It would appear that this move towards appointing more women judges has not been at the expense of merit. All but one of the 13 appointees whose professional reputation were in the lower of categories—"fair" or "weak"—were men. It is indeed an "old boys network" that enables less qualified lawyers to obtain appointments. . . .

. . . We turn now to information about the political background of the appointees. We organized this information . . . by placing each appointee in one of five categories: those with a major involvement with the Conservative party, those with a minor involvement or association with that party, those with no known political affiliation, those with a minor involvement or association with an opposition party, and those with a major involvement with an opposition party. A major involvement with a party includes running for elected office under the party's banner, serving as a party official or "bagman," and active involvement in election or leadership campaigns. [Lesser partisan associations include] minor constituency work, financial contributions, and close personal or professional associations with party leaders. . . .

. . . The appointment of a lawyer associated with an opposition party may well be politically motivated. There are well-known incidents in Canadian history where a political opponent received an appointment in order to make it easier to elect a government member in the appointee's constituency. . . .

. . . [What our "political background" data do] show is that patronage, or "political favouritism," to use the CBA's phrase, continued to have a major influence on judicial appointments during the first Mulroney government. One hundred and eight of the appointees, just under half of the total number (47.4 percent), had a known political association with the Conservative party. For just under a quarter (24.1 percent), the involvement was considered strong. Mr. Mulroney's government, it would appear, so far as judicial appointments are concerned, did not exercise its options much differently from the Trudeau/Turner Liberal government. . . .

. . . In five provinces—Manitoba, New Brunswick, Nova Scotia, Prince Edward Island, and Saskatchewan . . . the percentage of appointees with a known connection to the Conservative party ranges from P.E.I's 71.5 percent to Manitoba's 87.5 percent. These findings closely resemble the CBA committee's findings on judicial appointments from 1978 to 1985. [It] reported that in New Brunswick, Nova Scotia, Prince Edward Island, and Saskatchewan "political favouritism has been a dominant, though not the sole, consideration; most appointees have been active supporters of the party in power." . . . [P]olitical favouritism has not been concentrated on appointments to the lowest level. On the contrary, the percentage of appointees with ties to the Conservative party was greater—over half—among those appointed to the provincial courts of appeal and the superior courts than to the county or district courts, where it was 39.6 percent. In this respect our results differ from those of the CBA committee, which found that under the Trudeau and Clark governments the influence of political favouritism was generally greater at the county and district court level.

. . . While the influence of political favouritism is less marked [in regard to promotion], it is still strong: 29 of the 66 judges and one court administrator who were promoted by the Mulroney government were known to have had an involvement or association with the Conservative party, while 11 had opposition party affiliations. . . .

This observation is disturbing. Judicial promotions have always been a delicate issue. In the common law world some observers have expressed concern that the desire for promotion may colour an appointee's conduct on the bench so that he or she will be well thought of by the appointing authority. . . . Our data show, however, that promotions are frequent and not necessarily based on merit, and that some may well have a political flavour. In the next section, we note that promotions have been excluded from the reformed judicial appointing process. . . .

. . . On the whole, the persons appointed by the Mulroney government in its first term appear to be well regarded within the profession. Nearly a quarter of them are considered outstanding, and 86.3 percent are considered no less than good. [Interestingly,] appointees with a strong political profile, at either end of the spectrum, were not rated as highly as those with weak political connections: for example, only 19.2 percent of appointees with strong Conservative party connections were rated as outstanding, compared with 30.9 percent with weak Conservative party linkages, and 41.7 percent for appointees with slight opposition party linkages. However, these differences become much smaller when the percentages for outstanding and outstanding/good reputations are combined in each of the categories. Only 13 appointees, 6.1 percent of those appraised, were considered by both assessors to be either fair or weak.

On the basis of this part of our research, some might question the need to reform the traditional appointing system. . . . But we think there are at least three reasons for dissatisfaction. . . .

First, it should be noted that among the most poorly regarded appointees—those considered fair or weak—there is a disproportionately large number with political connections to the government—10 out of 13, or 76.9 percent. . . .

Second, we believe Canadians should strive for a system that is designed so far as possible to appoint not simply persons who will make acceptable judges but those who are best qualified for judicial service. . . .

Third, . . . [t]here is also the danger of producing a judiciary which is ideologically imbalanced. Canadians have reasons to be especially sensitive to this danger, now that their judges are playing such a significant policy-making role in interpreting the Charter of Rights and Freedoms. We should be looking for a reasonable balance in the political and philosophical perspectives represented on the bench. . . .

Finally, but not least, . . . there is a highly subjective component in assessing the merits of appointees, a difficulty that argues strongly in favour of using committees to assess candidates for judicial office. With the benefit of hindsight we now also recognize that our categories were too broad, and that there is a large gap between an "outstanding" appointee and a "good" one. . . .

. . . Based on the analysis of the data and other developments described in this report, our conclusions are that only marginal improvements were made in the system of selection of judges by the Mulroney government during its first term of office. Political patronage in judicial appointments was still pervasive. . . .

The federal government's much delayed response to the CALT and CBA recommendations was deeply disappointing and does little to address the basic flaws in the judicial appointing system. . . . The fact remains that the new committees are essentially toothless. They are not authorized to rank candidates, they have no staff to assist them to do well the limited task assigned to them, and they are not even required (nor for the most part do they have the resources) to interview candidates before determining whether or not they are qualified for judicial office. . . .

The committees face the further invidious task of being asked to give five reasons for not deeming a candidate suitably qualified and of having their assessments reversed on appeal by the minister of justice. Most disturbing of all, the new screening process will not prevent the federal government from continuing to promote candidates on political and personal grounds or to appoint even highly qualified candidates for the wrong reasons. There is an almost irresistible inference that the wish to cling to political patronage power, if not for the sake of the patronage then for the power itself, is the federal government's primary reason for refusing to allow the advisory committees the right to rank candidates. . . .

4.3

WILL WOMEN JUDGES REALLY MAKE A DIFFERENCE?
Bertha Wilson

. . . Many have criticised as totally unreal the concept that judges are somehow super-human, neutral, above politics and unbiased, and are able to completely separate themselves from their personal opinions and predispositions when exercising their judicial function. . . .

In his text, *The Politics of the Judiciary*, Professor Griffith caused a furor in legal and judicial circles in the United Kingdom when he questioned whether the English judiciary were capable of impartiality. He stated that for a judge to be completely impartial he or she would have to be like a political, economic and social eunuch and have no interests in the world outside the court. Because this is impossible, Griffith concludes that impartiality is an ideal incapable of realization. He says of the English judiciary: "These judges have by their education and training and the pursuit of their profession as barristers acquired a strikingly homogeneous collection of attitudes, beliefs, and principles which to them represents the public interest."

The public interest, in other words, is perceived from the viewpoint of their own class. Chief Justice Nemetz has suggested that Professor Griffith's views may have some validity in Canada too, more particularly, Professor Griffith's view that judicial attitudes towards political and social issues reflect the lack of a proper understanding of the view of labour unions, minorities and the under-privileged.

Judge Rosalie Abella (Chair of the Ontario Law Reform Commission) also doubts that judicial impartiality is a realistic requirement. In her article "The Dynamic Nature of Equality," she emphasizes that "[e]very decisionmaker who walks into a courtroom to hear a case is armed not only with the relevant legal texts but with a set of values, experiences and assumptions that are thoroughly embedded." [Ed. note: In March, 1992 Justice Minister Kim Campbell announced Judge Abella's appointment to the Ontario Court of Appeal.]

Judge Shientag refers to the fact that many judges believe that they have acted with the cold neutrality of an impartial judge when, in fact, they have completely failed to examine their prejudices and biases. He points out that the partiality and prejudice with which we are concerned is not overt, not something tangible on which the judge can put his or her

Osgoode Hall Law Journal 28, no. 3 (1990), from pages 507–522. Reprinted with permission.

finger. Yet by failing to appreciate this, many judges are lulled into a false sense of security. Judge Shientag emphasizes that progress will only be made when judges recognise this condition as part of the weakness of human nature. Then, "[h]aving admitted the liability to prejudice, unconscious for the most part, subtle and nebulous at times, the next step is to determine what the judge, with his trained mind, can do to neutralize the incessant play of these obscure yet potent influences." Judge Shientag concludes that "the judge who realizes, before listening to a case, that all men have a natural bias of mind and that thought is apt to be colored by predilection, is more likely to make a conscientious effort at impartiality and dispassionateness than one who believes that his elevation to the bench makes him at once the dehumanized instrument of infallible logical truth."

But what has all this got to do with my subject: "Will women judges really make a difference?" It has a great deal to do with it and whether you agree or not will probably depend on your perception of the degree to which the existing law reflects the judicial neutrality or impartiality we have been discussing. If the existing law can be viewed as the product of judicial neutrality or impartiality, even though the judiciary has been very substantially male, then you may conclude that the advent of increased numbers of women judges should make no difference, assuming, that is, that these women judges will bring to bear the same neutrality and impartiality. However, if you conclude that the existing law, in some areas at least, cannot be viewed as the product of judicial neutrality, then your answer may be very different.

Two law professors at New York University, Professor John Johnston and Professor Charles Knapp, have concluded, as a result of their studies of judicial attitudes reflected in the decisions of judges in the United States, that United States judges have succeeded in their conscious efforts to free themselves from habits of stereotypical thought with regard to discrimination based on colour. However, they were unable to reach a similar conclusion with respect to discrimination based on sex and found that American judges had failed to bring to sex discrimination the judicial virtues of detachment, reflection and critical analysis which had served them so well with respect to other areas of discrimination. They state: "'Sexism'—the making of unjustified (or at least unsupported) assumptions about individual capabilities, interests, goals and social roles solely on the basis of sex differences—is as easily discernable in contemporary judicial opinions as racism ever was."

Professor Norma Wikler, a sociologist at the University of California, has reviewed a number of other studies of judicial attitudes by legal researchers and social scientists. These studies confirm that male judges tend to adhere to traditional values and beliefs about the "natures" of men and women and their proper roles in society. The studies show overwhelming evidence that gender-based myths, biases and stereotypes are deeply embedded in the attitudes of many male judges as well as in the law itself. Researchers have concluded that gender difference has been a significant factor in judicial decision-making, particularly in areas of tort law, criminal law and family law. Further, many have concluded that sexism is the unarticulated underlying premise of many judgments in these areas and that this is not really surprising having regard to the nature of the society in which the judges themselves have been socialized.

. . . So, where do we stand in Canada on this matter? As might be expected, feminist scholars in Canada have over the past two decades produced a vast quantity of literature on the subject, some of it very insightful, very balanced and very useful, and some of it very radical, quite provocative and probably less useful as a result. But all of it, it seems, is premised, at least as far as judicial decision-making is concerned, on two basic propositions: one, that women view the world and what goes on in it from a different perspective from men, and two, that women judges, by bringing that perspective to bear on the cases they hear, can play a major role in introducing judicial neutrality and impartiality into the justice system.

Taking from my own personal experience as a judge of fourteen years' standing, working closely with my male colleagues on the bench, there are probably whole areas of the law on which there is no uniquely feminine perspective. This is not to say that the development of the law in these areas has not been influenced by the fact that the lawyers and the judges have all been men. Rather, the principles and the underlying premises are so firmly entrenched and so fundamentally sound that no good would be achieved by attempting to re-invent the wheel, even if the revised version did have a few more spokes in it. I have in mind areas such as the law of contract, the law of real property and the law applicable to corporations. In some other areas of the law, however, I think that a distinctly male perspective is clearly discernable. It has resulted in legal principles that are not fundamentally sound and that should be revisited when the opportunity presents itself. Canadian feminist scholarship has done an excellent job of identifying those areas and making suggestions for reform. Some aspects of the criminal law in particular cry out for change; they are based on presuppositions about the nature of women and women's sexuality that, in this day and age, are little short of ludicrous.

But how do we handle the problem that women judges, just as much as their male counterparts, are subject to the duty of impartiality? As was said at the outset, judges must not approach their task with pre-conceived notions about law and policy. They must approach it with detachment and, as Lord MacMillan said, purge their minds "not only of partiality to persons, but of partiality to arguments." Does this then foreclose any kind of "judicial affirmative action" to counteract the influence of the dominant male perspective of the past and establish judicial neutrality through a countervailing female perspective? Is Karen Selick, writing recently in the

Lawyers' Weekly, correct when she argues that offsetting male bias with female bias would only be compounding the injustice? Does the nature of the judicial process itself present an insuperable hurdle so that the legislatures rather than the courts must be looked to for any significant legal change?

In part this may be so. Certainly, the legislature is the more effective instrument for rapid or radical change. But there is no reason why the judiciary cannot exercise some modest degree of creativity in areas where modern insights and life's experience have indicated that the law has gone awry. However, and this is extremely important, it will be a Pyrrhic victory for women and for the justice system as a whole if changes in the law come only through the efforts of women lawyers and women judges. The Americans were smart to realize that courses and workshops on gender bias for judges, male and female, are an essential follow-up to scholarly research and learned writing. In Canada, we are just beginning to touch the fringes.

. . . The Canadian Judicial Council and the Canadian Judicial Centre have both recognized the need for judicial education in this area and will include gender issues in their summer seminars for judges this year. I understand that the Centre hopes to subsequently present the program in a number of locations across the country, and the course materials will be available to all Canadian judges. I heartily endorse this initiative. It is a significant first step towards the achievement of true judicial neutrality. But it is only a first step and there is a long way to go.

I return, then, to the question whether the appointment of more women judges will make a difference. Because the entry of women into the judiciary is so recent, few studies have been done on the subject. Current statistics, however, show that just over 9 percent of federally appointed judges are women; it is reasonable to assume that more and more women will be appointed to the Bench as more and more women become licensed to practice law. Will this growing number of women judges by itself make a difference?

The expectation is that it will, that the mere presence of women on the bench will make a difference. In her article "The Gender of Judges," Suzanna Sherry (an Associate Law Professor at the University of Minnesota) suggests that the mere fact that women are judges serves an educative function; it helps to shatter stereotypes about the role of women in society that are held by male judges and lawyers, as well as by litigants, jurors and witnesses.

. . . Some feminist writers are persuaded that the appointment of more women judges will have an impact on the process of judicial decision-making itself and on the development of the substantive law. As was mentioned earlier, this flows from the belief that women view the world and what goes on in it from a different perspective from men. Some define the difference in perspective solely in terms that women do not accept male perceptions and interpretations of events as the norm or as objective reality. Carol Gilligan (a Professor of Education at Harvard University) sees the difference as going much deeper than that. In her view, women think differently from men, particularly in responding to moral dilemmas. They have, she says, different ways of thinking about themselves and their relationships to others.

In her book, *In a Different Voice*, Gilligan analyses data she collected, in the form of responses from male and female participants in a number of different studies. These responses, she submits, support her central thesis that women see themselves as essentially connected to others and as members of a community; men see themselves as essentially autonomous and independent of others. Gilligan makes no claim about the origins of the differences she describes. She does, however, use the psychoanalytical work of Dr. Nancy Chodorow as a starting point. Chodorow postulates that gender differences arise from the fact that women do the mothering of children. Because the gender identity of male children is not the same as their mothers, they tend to distance and separate themselves from their mothers' female characteristics in order to develop their masculinity. Female children, on the other hand, define themselves through attachment to their mothers. Masculinity is therefore, according to Gilligan, defined through separation and individualism; femininity is defined through attachment and the formation of relationships. The gender identity of the male, she submits, is threatened by relationships while the gender identity of the female is threatened by separation.

Gilligan's work on conceptions of morality among adults suggests that women's ethical sense is significantly different from men's. Men see moral problems as arising from competing rights; the adversarial process comes easily to them. Women see moral problems as arising from competing obligations, the one to the other; the important thing is to preserve relationships, to develop an ethic of caring. The goal, according to women's ethical sense, is not seen in terms of winning or losing but, rather, in terms of achieving an optimum outcome for all individuals involved in the moral dilemma. It is not difficult to see how this contrast in thinking might form the basis of different perceptions of justice.

There is merit in Gilligan's analysis. In part, it may explain the traditional reluctance of courts to get too deeply into the circumstances of a case, their anxiety to reduce the context of the dispute to its bare bones through a complex system of exclusionary evidentiary rules. This is, one of the characteristic features of the adversarial process. We are all familiar with the witness on cross-examination who wants to explain his or her answer, who feels that a simple yes or no is not an adequate response, and who is frustrated and angry at being cut off with a half-truth. It is so much easier to come up with a black and white answer if you are unencumbered by a broader context which might prompt you, in Lord

MacMillan's words, to temper the cold light of reason with the warmer tints of imagination and sympathy.

Gilligan's analysis may explain also the hostility of some male judges to permitting intervenors in human rights cases. The main purpose of having intervenors is to broaden the context of the dispute, to show the issue in a larger perspective or as impacting on other groups not directly involved in the litigation at all. But it certainly does complicate the issues to have them presented in polycentric terms.

. . . One of the important conclusions emerging from the Council of Europe's Seminar on Equality between Men and Women held in Strasbourg last November is that the universalist doctrine of human rights must include a realistic concept of masculine and feminine humanity regarded as a whole, that human kind *is* dual and must be represented in its dual form if the trap of an asexual abstraction in which *human being* is always declined in the masculine is to be avoided. If women lawyers and women judges through their differing perspectives on life can bring a new humanity to bear on the decision-making process, perhaps they *will* make a difference. Perhaps they will succeed in infusing the law with an understanding of what it means to be fully human.

4.4

A "GENDER PATRONAGE" FOR JUDGES?
Rob Martin

Nothing ever really seems to change. To be sure, we are constantly presented with the illusion of change, especially in an economy based on consumption. But it is mostly illusion, appearance. The substance of things tends to remain the same. Take judicial appointments. The Canadian way has been to use patronage as the main—not the only, but the main—basis for appointing people to the Bench. Loyal service to the party in power has been the most important qualification for a judgeship. The tradition of patronage appointments is a long, if not particularly honourable, one. It predates Confederation.

Lawyers' Weekly, March 29, 1991, p. 5. Reprinted with permission.

The Canadian Bar Association, to take but one example, has been criticizing patronage since 1916. In 1985 it even produced a report about the whole business. The report observed:

> There has been a long history of patronage appointments by both major parties in Canada. Although there have been some commendable exceptions, the practice of appointing the party faithful to the Bench has been all too common.

From time to time various political leaders have denounced patronage and promised to put the bad old days behind us. Success has been limited. Pierre Trudeau first gained national prominence in 1966 as Minister of Justice in the government of Lester Pearson. He announced his determination to end patronage and make judicial appointments on merit. The determination didn't last long. Trudeau resigned as prime minister in 1984. His departure was accompanied by an orgy of patronage appointments which was shocking, even by Canadian standards. A small horde of Cabinet ministers, terrified at the prospect of their party's impending electoral debacle, went to their reward on the Bench. [Ed. note: see Reading 4.1]

Brian Mulroney promised to do better. He didn't. A 1989 study of judicial appointees during Mulroney's first four years in office concluded that 48 percent were known supporters of the Progressive Conservative party. [Ed. note: See Reading 4.2] An ostensibly new system for making federal judicial appointments was instituted in 1988. But its newness is more apparent than real. The final authority over appointments remains in political hands.

Well, what's the problem with patronage appointments? Obviously, not all are, or have been, bad. Long service to a political party should not disqualify someone from holding judicial office. But should it be the most important consideration? The real problem lies in the failure of patronage appointments to address, or even raise, the question of an individual's fitness to be a judge. Politics, not merit, determines the decision.

The problem is compounded because we don't really know what we are looking for in judges. We have never, probably because we are inured to patronage appointments, determined what qualities make people fit to be judges and how we might go about assessing those qualities. But if we regard judging as important, we should concede that patronage is not the ideal basis for electing judges. Merit, however we eventually decide to define it, should take precedence over politics.

All of which brings me to the new Ontario government's approach to appointing judges. Once again, we have the illusion of change. The reality is business as usual. Upon taking office as attorney-general, Howard Hampton announced his determination to have more women judges in Ontario. He went to the point of saying he was prepared to look outside the province if enough women who were members of the Ontario Bar could not be found. These statements were followed up with letters to many women lawyers inviting them to apply for judgeships. And Hampton has been true, more or less, to his word. At my count he has made 18 judicial appointments since taking office. Eleven of these have been women.

So what's my problem? I'm certainly not opposed to women judges. And I'm definitely not worried about lowering the quality of the Provincial Court Bench in Ontario—a virtually impossible task, I would think. And I'm even prepared to accept some of Hampton's appointees may turn out to be competent judges. No, the point is that Hampton is continuing the dismal Canadian tradition of politics over merit. The announced basis for his appointments is the gender of the people chosen, not their ability or qualifications. I don't believe it's much of a step forward to replace party loyalty with gender as the basis for choosing judges. Gender is as much a political consideration as is party loyalty. Neither relates directly to an individual's fitness to be a judge.

In our federal and provincial public services we go through an elaborate ritual of assessing people's ability and qualifications before they can be appointed. Might we not devote the same care to picking judges?

4.5

JUDICIAL APPOINTMENTS IN GREAT BRITAIN
Sir Robert Megarry

. . . First, I must make a brief disclaimer. Naturally I shall say nothing that comes from any confidential source; I merely recount what is generally known or believed by the English Bar, or is the public domain. That said, I may begin with the formal details of appointment to the Bench in England. It is briefly told. There are three main categories of judges, and I give the figures in round numbers. First, there is the High Court and above (Court of Appeal and House of Lords), with a total of 100. Second, there are 125 county court judges; and third, there are 50 stipendiary magistrates. That makes a total of 275. All are appointed by the Crown on the Advice of the Lord Chancellor or, in the case of the Court of Appeal and House of Lords, the Prime Minister. The responsibility for this advice is individual and not collective; it is not a Cabinet matter. The Prime Minister is generally believed to consult closely with the Lord Chancellor before

From G.M. Stirling, "A Symposium of the Appointment of Judges," *Alberta Law Review* 2 (1973), from pages 279–309. Reprinted with permission.

making his recommendations, and so it is the Lord Chancellor who in substance is the great appointer to the Bench.

The Judicature Act, 1925, s.12, replacing provisions in the Judicature Act, 1873, and the Act of Settlement, 1700, provides that judges of the Supreme Court (that is, the High Court and Court of Appeal) hold office "during good behaviour, subject to a power of removal by the Crown" on an address presented to His Majesty by both Houses of Parliament. No English judge has ever been removed under these provisions, but in 1830 Sir Jonah Barrington, a judge of the Court of Admiralty in Ireland, was removed for misconduct and malversation in office. That is all. County court judges and stipendiary magistrates are in effect removable by the Lord Chancellor for inability or misbehaviour. I know of only one such removal. In 1851 Judge Ramshay had become very eccentric indeed, and after a hearing he was removed from office. From his chambers in the Temple he continued to send letters to court officials asserting that he was still the judge, and adjourning the court, but all to no avail; and quo warranto proceedings against his successor failed. . . . So we have little experience in this field that would assist you. At the same time, it is said that there have been some instances—a very few—in which the Lord Chancellor and others have encouraged a resignation; but that is a little different. Other and more subtle forces, and not least, association with the Bar, and the influence of the Inns of Court, do much to sustain the judge in England on the difficulties of his office.

Retirement? This is now mandatory at 75 for High Court judges and above, at 72 for county court judges, and at 70 for stipendiary magistrates. Machinery for discipline? Nil. Training? Nil. And so on that I seem to be of very little use to you. Yet I think that we have been merely looking at the tip of the iceberg. We must look a little below the surface if we want to get a balanced picture. Let me mention, as briefly as may be, seven factors which help to show the realities.

1. There are relatively few appointments to be made. With a population for England and Wales approaching 50 million, there are a little less than 100 judges of High Court level and above to do all the trial and appellate work; and that comes to two judges per million of population. At the same level, Canada had roughly five and half times as many judges per million population, and about three times as many at the county court level; if one ignores the size of the population and takes absolute figures, yours are of the order of 250 and 160 as compared with our 100 and 125. . . .

2. The field from which appointments are made is much smaller in England than in Canada. Three main factors play their part: specialization of function, specialization of subject-matter, and age. The first lead primarily refers to the division of our legal profession into barristers and solicitors. Of a total legal profession of some 28,000 or 29,000, less than about 2,600 are practising barristers. With certain exceptions at the lower levels, all appointments are made from the Bar, the branch of the profession that

lives out its professional life in the courts. There is then the further division of barristers into Q. C.'s and juniors. Of the 2,600 practising barristers, rather less than 300 are Q.C.'s; and appointments to the High Court are nearly always made from among practising Q.C.'s. In fact, the field of choice is smaller than that, because after discounting those who are approaching retirement or have not been very successful, probably there are some 150 or 200 who do the great bulk of the work; and it is from them that the appointments will be made.

In England, of course, silk is a reality and not merely an honour. A junior who takes silk takes his professional life in his hands, for he has to give up all his smaller work, including settling pleadings, and, being unable to appear in court without a junior, must confine himself to the bigger cases; and the number of these is limited. A junior does not lightly apply for silk, and silk is not to be had for the asking. It is believed that something like four out of five applications fail. Solicitors play an important part in this field. Nobody will be appointed a Q.C. unless many solicitors, on a basis of trial and error, have acquired a faith in his abilities as an advocate; and no Q.C. will get much work unless many more solicitors have faith in his forensic abilities at the higher level of silk. The collective judgment of solicitors thus plays a large part in selecting the field of possible candidates for the Bench. Solicitors judge from knowledge and experience, too; unlike the lay client, they will not confuse a flashy but incompetent display with a restrained but skilled performance.

I need say little about specialization of subject-matter. Barristers tend to specialize in work which usually finds its way into one or other of the three Divisions of the High Court, Chancery, Queen's Bench, and Probate, Divorce and Admiralty (soon to become the Family Division); and within those broad divisions there are often specialist sub-divisions. This, of course, narrows the field. A Queen's Bench judge dies; who will be appointed in his place? You may be sure that it will not be a Q.C. who normally practises in the Chancery Division.

As for age, there is in practice a limited range for appointment. Looking at recent years, the average age for appointment to the High Court comes out at about 52 for the Probate, Divorce and Admiralty Division, 53 or 54 for the Queen's Bench Division, and 55 or 56 for the Chancery Division. The youngest age at which anyone has been appointed to the High Court this century is 42 and the oldest 65 (though I cannot forbear from mentioning that Sir Salathiel Lovell began his five years in the Court of Exchequer when he was 89; but that was in 1708). The normal effective range of ages is from the late forties to the late fifties. Again, this restricts the field of choice.

Let me take a melancholy but practical example. Suppose that, overwhelmed by the hospitality that I have been receiving here (and that is far from a remote possibility), I keel over and die before your eyes. A successor to my seat in the Chancery Division will then have to be appointed.

Well, this does not look very difficult. In the *Law List* there is a list of the
Q.C.'s who practise specially in the Chancery Division. There are 28 names
there. Some of the more senior are over the age at which appointment is
probable; others are too young or too inexperienced. There are other considerations, too, and in the end probably most lawyers who have any
familiarity with the Chancery Division would agree upon the handful of
names, perhaps two, three or even four, from which the appointment
would almost certainly be made. The Chancery Division is small, with
only ten judges, and the field is more open in the Queen's Bench Division,
with some 45 judges. But even so, in most cases the question must come
down to one of choosing from a very small number of possibilities; and
this must usually make the process of appointment far less complex than
it must be in some other jurisdictions.

3. Most judges have had some trial runs on the Bench before being
appointed. Your chairman touched on this a short while ago when he
mentioned what Henry Cecil had said in his book. It is common for a
potential judge to be appointed a Commissioner of Assize for a period of
four, six or eight weeks at a time; and during this period he has the temporary status of a High Court judge. Again, many a barrister sits three or four
times a year as a Recorder, or Chairman or Deputy Chairman of Quarter
Sessions, spending perhaps some twenty days a year as a judge in criminal cases too serious for the magistrates and not serious enough for a High
Court judge. Although the prime purpose of these activities is to get the
work done, there is great value in the incidental result that it becomes
known what sort of a judge the barrister is likely to make if he is appointed
to the Bench. Nobody can really tell how anyone will behave as judge until
he has been seen performing as a judge. Being a judge is so different from
being an advocate, not least in that the advocate knows which side he is
on. There have been many instances of Commissioners of Assize demonstrating their suitability for judicial office, and in other instances
demonstrating just the opposite, for a wide variety of reasons. Men react
to the stresses of the Bench in remarkably different ways. Like the el-
ephant, the judicial quality is easily recognizable but very difficult to define;
and so this is one of the fields in which "Try it and see" becomes an important adage. By way of footnote, I may add that until 1933 Scotland even
had a trial run for each newly appointed judge of the Court of Session *after*
his appointment; but this had become a mere formality.

I would attach very little value to any formal training for judicial office.
I do not see how you can effectually train a man to be a judge. You can, of
course, teach a man the technique of driving a car; but it is the man and not
his training that predominantly determines whether he uses wisely and
tolerantly the skills that he has acquired, or whether he is a foolish and
aggressive driver. The judicial quality is something that the man has or
has not got; and whatever training may do to improve the native quality,
it cannot graft a judicial temperament on to barren stock.

4. The Lord Chancellor, the great appointer of judges, is an active judge himself. He is a Cabinet Minister, of course, but he is far from being that alone. He is necessarily someone of a sufficient judicial stature to enable him to preside over the House of Lords, and command the respect of the other law lords. He does not merely sit in an office and in Parliament, but lives and moves in the world of law. He has long known many of the senior members of the Bar, and of course in the House of Lords he listens to many arguments. There is, therefore, much that he can decide upon his own first-hand knowledge, and not merely upon report.

5. Judges live and work with the Bar. If you are near the Inns of Court in London at lunch-time on any day during term, you will see that at about one p.m. most of the judges of the High Court and Court of Appeal and many of the practising members of the Bar are on their way to the halls of their Inns of Court for lunch. Each judge will be a bencher of his Inn, and the senior Q.C.'s and some of the senior juniors (you will know what I mean) will also be benchers. All lunch together on a basis of equality, whether judge, silk or junior. Seniority as a bencher depends on seniority of election, and is unaffected by judicial office. The atmosphere is one of ease and friendliness; and informal though this is, it has a constitutional importance. It is in these regular and informal contacts that we find so much of value rubbing off on each other. It tends to prevent the judges from becoming pompous and overbearing; and not only is the judge constantly reminded of his own days at the Bar, but also the silk or junior find himself absorbing overtones of the Bench. A civilizing atmosphere spills over into the courts, and sweetens the acerbities of the contest. This association contributes towards a firmness of moral tone throughout the administration of the law, and provides a nursery for the future judge.

6. It is rare for an appointment to the High Court to be refused. The prevailing tone is that it is of paramount importance to the country that the standard of the Bench should be maintained at the highest possible level, and that if a barrister is offered an appointment to the Bench, this shows that the Lord Chancellor thinks him the most suitable person to be appointed. Whatever the individual feelings may be, the need to maintain the standard of the Bench impels acceptance.

7. Last, and in some ways the most important, is the fact that 25 years ago politics dropped almost completely out of appointment to the English Bench. The effect of political considerations in making judicial appointments is certainly not something to be exclusively attributed to Lord Halsbury while he was Lord Chancellor, interesting though some of his appointments were. Long before his time, and for many years after it, the general belief was that a career in Parliament was a powerful aid to appointment to the Bench; and there were many appointments that gave colour to this belief. The normal road to many of the highest offices in the law, too, was not by successful service as a puisne judge but by becoming Attorney-General or Solicitor-General. The Attorney-General of the day

was regarded as having something of a right to the Chief Justiceship of the Common Pleas when it fell vacant. It was his "pillow," and when in 1880 that office in effect became merged in the Chief Justiceship of the Queen's Bench as the Lord Chief Justiceship of England, some regarded that office as having become the pillow. Later events tended to support that view; and although the emphasis on politics was probably lessening, down to the war of 1939–45 the position was substantially unaltered.

The change can almost be pinpointed. On January 21, 1946, Viscount Caldecote, C.J., a former Solicitor-General, Attorney-General and Lord Chancellor, resigned, and Lord Goddard, a law lord, was appointed Chief Justice in his place. Lord Goddard was a lawyer through and through, with no more than a faint brush with politics in his youth; and he had moved steadily up from the King's Bench to the Court of Appeal and then to the House of Lords. Within a fortnight, on February 1, 1946, Sir Donald Somervell, a former Tory Attorney-General, was appointed to a seat in the Court of Appeal, even though the Government in power from 1945 to 1951 was a Labour government. These two appointments seem to have set the seal on the change. Politics were out, and such politics as were in were bi-partisan. During the six years of the Labour government, Lord Jowitt, as Lord Chancellor, was responsible for the appointment of over half the entire Bench; and yet not until towards the end of the time did he make any appointment to the High Court from the M.P.'s supporting his own party, and then only one. In 1958 Lord Goddard retired as Chief Justice, and despite political contenders, the appointment made was of Lord Parker, a Lord Justice with no political career. When Lord Parker retired this year, again the appointment as Chief Justice went to a non-political member of the Court of Appeal, Lord Widgery; and each of these appointments was made while a Tory government was in power. With that unanimity of performance, there is good reason to believe that each of the two major political parties is at least agreed on the proper approach to judicial appointment today.

I am not saying that to have been in politics is today an actual disqualification for appointment to the Bench; but I do say that to be an active supporter of the party in power no longer seems to be an asset of any real weight. Experience in public affairs, especially in Parliament, may be a factor of great value in moulding a man's character and giving him breadth of vision; the Bench would be the poorer without some who have this background. But it has ceased to matter much whether the candidate for appointment is a supporter or opponent of the party in power. With the withering of partisan claims to appointment has come another change. For over twenty years nearly all appointments to the Court of Appeal and House of Lords have been by way of promotion from the High Court, and not per saltum from the Bar. A vacancy in the Court of Appeal will be filled from the ranks of the High Court judges whose judicial abilities are known. No longer is there the problem of trying to guess the probable performance of a giant of the Bar as a Lord Justice of Appeal, and trying to compare that guess with a reasoned estimate, based on experience of how a High Court judge of, say, five years standing would do in the Court of Appeal.

Those, then, are the seven factors that I wanted to put before you. Perhaps I may add some comments on two final matters. First, there is the actual process of appointment to the Bench. On this, I speak with no certain knowledge, but on guesses which I hope are intelligent. The Lord Chancellor's Office is in effect a small government department, with a staff of some two dozen lawyers. By a mysterious system of osmosis and grape-vines, I would expect the Lord Chancellor and his staff to have a pretty good idea about all that is going on in the legal world. If at any given moment you were to ask the Lord Chancellor whether X or Y or Z is likely to be appointed a judge when a vacancy occurs, and he were willing to answer, I should expect him to be able to say, then and there, that X is a strong candidate, that Y is a possible, and that Z is a nonstarter. You will remember how small the English Bar is, how few English silks there are, and how small the country is. Only a very small part of the population lives more than 250 miles from London.

Despite the background of knowledge of the Bar, the Lord Chancellor may be expected to consult the Chief Justice and the Master of The Rolls (who presides over the Court of Appeal) when a vacancy occurs; and if it is in the Chancery Division or the Probate, Divorce and Admiralty Division, he may well consult the head of that Division as well. Whether those consulted ever have or take the initiative, suggesting that A or B is better than X and Y who are under consideration, I cannot say. I should doubt if there are rules or even conventions; I should expect everything to be highly informal or, if you like, very English. When the Courts Act, 1971, comes into force there will be many changes, some of them important; but I do not think that they will alter the essence of what I have been saying.

Secondly, perhaps I may be mildly historical. On at least some views it is possible to discern four stages in the part played by politics in appointments to the Bench, each stage merging into the next. In the first stage, party politics may play so large a part that some of those appointed fall short of the standards that the office demands. In the second stage, political claims do no more than give some preference among those who are fully qualified for appointment; of three candidates with not much to choose between them, the supporter of the party in power will be preferred to the political opponent or the politically inert. Without being unduly cynical, it is possible to observe that there are times when a government may prefer the sight of a political opponent sitting non-politically on the Bench to the sight of him in vigorous opposition in the legislature. The third stage comes when the political opponent has prospects of appointment which, other things being equal, are on a par with those of a political supporter, or nearly so. At the fourth stage politics have ceased to play any real part.

Appointments are made very largely from the ranks of those who have made law and not politics their life.

As I indicated, England seems to have reached this fourth stage in 1946. Where Canada is I must leave you to say; if I had to guess, from what I have read and heard recently my surmise would be that it is somewhere about the third stage, or not far short of it. I repeat that I would not suggest that politics should disqualify. In considering suitability for the Bench a strong case can be made for the wide-ranging span of a statesman's career as against the restricted vision of a technically superb lawyer; the old jibe is that law sharpens the mind by narrowing it. But not all politicians are statesmen, nor do all fine lawyers have minds that are closed to the wider issues of life—not by a long chalk. In the end, the question, as in so many fields, is one of balance, within the national genius. . . .

4.6

JUDICIAL APPOINTMENTS IN THE UNITED STATES: THE JUDGE BORK AFFAIR

F.L. Morton

The Bork Affair was one of the important political events of the Reagan Presidency (1981–1988). On July 1, 1987, President Reagan nominated Federal Appeals Court Judge Robert H. Bork to become the 104th justice of the United States Supreme Court. The Bork nomination marked the culmination of a seven-year Reagan Administration policy of appointing "judicial conservatives" to the federal courts. The appointment of federal judges had been a central policy plank of the 1980 and 1984 Republican Party platforms. It was one of the "social issues" that had mobilized formerly Democratic voters into the Reagan-led Republican coalition of the 1980s.

Judge Bork was widely known in legal and political circles as one of the most articulate and outspoken critics of the the liberal judicial activism pioneered by the Warren Court. His appointment to the Court of Appeal for the District of Columbia in 1982 was widely seen as a stepping stone to an eventual appointment to the Supreme Court. The Bork nomination would have been Reagan's fourth appointment to the Supreme Court, and was widely perceived as adding the fifth and potentially decisive vote to the conservative wing of the Court. A consistent conservative ma-

"The Bork Affair: Politics as Usual or Constitutional Crisis?" Paper presented at the 1988 Annual Meeting of the American Political Science Association, Washington, D.C. Sept. 1–4, 1988.

jority would threaten the liberal constitutional legacy of the Warren Court era. This prospect was greeted with enthusiasm by conservatives and with alarm by liberals. The latter mounted an unprecedented national political campaign to defeat the Bork nomination, culminating in the Senate Judiciary Committee's rejection of the Bork nomination in October, 1987.

This defeat was a serious loss for the Reagan Administration and conservatives, and an equally important victory for American liberals. The Reagan nominee eventually approved by the Senate, Judge Anthony Kennedy, was perceived as a "pragmatic" (as opposed to an "ideological") conservative, and thus less likely to challenge the Court's liberal precedents. But beyond the short-term political stakes looms a larger issue. Was the Bork affair simply politics as usual? Or was it symptomatic of deeper problems in American constitutional law and a changing role for the Supreme Court?

The Courts and the Conservative Counter-Revolution of the Eighties

In 1983, Vincent Blasi edited a widely cited book entitled *The Burger Court: The Counter-Revolution That Wasn't*. A series of articles by leading constitutional scholars chronicled the failure of the Burger Court to alter significantly the liberal constitutional legacy inherited from the preceding Warren Court. The book is instructive in several respects. First, it tacitly recognizes that there was a *prior* "revolution" in American constitutional law—the triumph of a result-oriented approach to constitutional interpretation in support of civil rights and then other liberal policy objectives. Second, Blasi's title serves to remind us that President Richard Nixon's appointments to the Supreme Court were intended to reverse or at least halt this "revolution." Finally, it tells us very explicitly that the "Burger (or Nixon) Court" failed to achieve this objective. The Bork affair can only be fully understood against this background.

The Bork nomination represented the proverbial "tip of the iceberg." It was not an isolated incident, but the culmination of growing partisan conflict over the appointment of federal judges dating back to the late 1960s. In 1968, then Republican presidential candidate Richard Nixon tried to exploit the unpopularity of some Warren Court decisions—especially in the South—by promising to appoint Supreme Court judges who were "strict constructionists . . . who saw their duty as interpreting law and not making law." While his "Southern strategy" succeeded in helping him get elected president, Nixon saw it partly defeated by a Democrat-controlled Senate, which rejected two of his nominations from the South. While Nixon eventually made four new appointments to the Court—including Warren Burger as the new Chief Justice—they did not reverse the liberal activist legacy of the Warren Court.

The Supreme Court and judicial appointments reemerged as an important issue in the 1980 presidential elections. The "counter-revolution" that conservatives had hoped for in the Nixon Court had failed to materialize. Affirmative action, court-ordered busing, and the exclusionary rule had all been upheld. Moreover, it was the Burger Court's 1973 decision in *Roe v. Wade* that had overturned 47 state laws and created, in effect, a national "abortion on demand" policy.

The 1980 Republican party platform called for the appointment of federal judges who believed in "the decentralization of the federal government and efforts to return decision-making power to states and local elected officials." In a not-so-covert criticism of *Roe v. Wade*, the platform also supported the appointment of judges "who respect the traditional family values and the sanctity of innocent human life." The Republicans' anti-*Roe* stance was countered by the Democrats, whose platform explicitly supported "the right of women to choose whether and when to have a child" and denounced any attempt to abridge this right through constitutional amendment.

The sweeping Republican electoral victories in November, 1980 led to more direct attempts at "court curbing." In the first six months of the Ninety-Seventh Congress, 27 bills were introduced to restrict or to remove Supreme Court or lower federal court jurisdiction to hear cases dealing with abortion, school prayer, and court-ordered busing of school children. While several of these bills were adopted by the now Republican-controlled Senate, none were passed by the House, in part because Peter Rodino, Democratic chairman of the House Judiciary Committee, refused to report them out of his committee.

Conservative dissatisfaction with the Supreme Court's performance was voiced from the White House as well as the Hill. At the end of the Court's 1984–85 term, Reagan's Attorney-General, Edwin Meese, used a high-profile address to the American Bar Association to publicly criticize the Court for its "inaccurate" and "incoherent" interpretations of the Constitution. The justices, declared the Attorney-General, had abandoned their "intended role . . . as the 'faithful guardians of the Constitution' . . . by departing from the literal provisions of the Constitution." As a result, the Court's decisions were said to be "more policy choices than articulations of constitutional principle." "A Constitution that is viewed as only what the judges say it is," Meese continued, "is no longer a constitution in the true sense." The solution, Meese concluded, "was a jurisprudence of original intention" . . . [an approach] that would not be tainted by ideological predilection" of judges.

This unusual public attack on the Court by the highest law-enforcement officer of the nation provoked an equally vituperative response from some of its liberal members. In an address at Georgetown University, Justice William Brennan labeled Meese's call for judicial fidelity to the intention of the framers as "little more than arrogance cloaked as humility" and "facile historicism." It is often impossible to "gauge accurately the intent of the Framers," declared Brennan. The Court must not ignore "social progress." "The ultimate question," Brennan emphasized, "must be what the words of the text mean in our time."

The Meese-Brennan exchange is anecdotal evidence of a much more systematic attempt by the Reagan White House to reshape the political orientation of the federal judiciary through the appointment process. In his first seven years in office, Reagan was able to appoint 322 federal judges—over 40 percent of both the district and fulltime appeals court judges. By the end of his second term, Goldman projected that Reagan will have appointed more than half of all lower federal judges, a record equalled by only two other modern presidents—Roosevelt and Eisenhower.

More important than the quantitative aspect is the qualitative impact of the Reagan appointees. Goldman's (1985) study of the demographic and attribute profiles of Reagan's first-term judicial appointments found that they differ from other presidents' in important ways. At the district court level 97 percent of his appointees have been from his own political party, a higher percentage than for any president since Woodrow Wilson. At the appeal court level he is the first president since Warren Harding not to appoint a single member from the other party. Reagan has also appointed a higher percentage of Catholics to the district courts than any Republican president, and even more than Democratic presidents Johnson and Carter. This choice reflects the importance of the Catholic vote in the Reagan coalition and the administration's conservative views on the "social issues." Reagan's subsequent choice of Antonin Scalia, the first Italian-American ever appointed to the Supreme Court, and a devout Roman Catholic and father of nine, is further evidence of this development.

Under the banner of "affirmative action," the Carter administration appointed unprecedented numbers of women and minorities to federal judgeships. This trend has been abruptly reversed. Reagan has appointed fewer black judges to the federal district courts than any president since Eisenhower, who appointed none. Reagan's court of appeal appointees have included only three female and minority judges (out of 31), while Carter appointed 23 (out of 56). The Reagan administration's explanation for the small percentage of minority appointments is its inability to find candidates who "share the President's philosophy."

Concern with the "right" judicial philosophy also explains the unusually high percentage of Reagan appointees who have prior judicial experience. The existence of a prior "track record" has allowed the Reagan administration to be more certain that a candidate subscribes to the principles of judicial self-restraint. The concern with judicial philosophy also explains one final anomaly in the Reagan appointment record. Five of his 31 appeal court appointees were former law professors. This was the highest percentage of any recent president. Like Robert Bork (Yale) and Antonin Scalia (Chicago), all were "well known as conservative thinkers and advocates of judicial self-restraint." It was hoped that they would provide conservative intellectual leadership on their respective judicial circuits as well as serving as a pool of candidates for Reagan's next Supreme Court appointments. Scalia's appointment was the first fruit of this strategy. Bork's was supposed to have been the second.

To maximize its impact on the federal judiciary, the Reagan Administration centralized the recruitment process in the White House to a far greater extent than any of its predecessors. Recruitment processes that in past administrations were more "informal and fluid" were institutionalized in a new "Presidential Selection Committee" that bridged the White House and the Justice Department, but was tilted toward the former. According to Goldman's 1985 study, this committee "has resulted in the most consistent ideological or policy-oriented screening of judicial candidates since the first term of Franklin Roosevelt."

The conventional wisdom holds that in the long run presidents are usually disappointed in the decisions of those they have appointed to the Supreme Court. Several recent studies of the Reagan appointees, however, suggest that they have indeed exercised the kind of judicial self-restraint called for in the Republican platform. In Stern's 1984 qualitative study of 62 Reagan judges, 31 were found to "exercise restraint in all of their significant cases without exception"; 16 exercised restraint in "nearly all of their significant cases"; while nine did so in less than half. (Six published no opinions.) John Gottschall's (1985) more quantitative study of the same decisions disclosed a number of conservative trends. In non-unanimous cases in which both Carter- and Reagan-appointed judges were involved, the Carter appointees voted for the "liberal outcome" in 95 percent of the cases, while the Reagan appointees did so in only five percent. Even when compared to the Nixon-Ford appointees, the Reagan judges' voting profiles were slightly more conservative. Goldman's 1987 study confirmed the continuation of this trend into Reagan's second term.

Constitutional law is made from the top down but administered from the bottom up. The precedent-setting influence of the Supreme Court's decisions in landmark cases is obvious. But these number less than 150 a year, while lower federal court decisions number in the thousands. The quantity of federal litigation is so great and the time of the Supreme Court so limited that the lower federal courts operate with substantial autonomy and independence. To consolidate a national political realignment in the federal judiciary a president must substantially alter the composition of both the tip and the base of the federal judicial "pyramid." Reagan may well be the first president since Franklin Roosevelt to do so.

During his first term as president, Reagan's influence on the composition of the Supreme Court was limited to one appointment—that of Sandra Day O'Connor. The O'Connor appointment illustrated the legendary Reagan good fortune. Reagan was able to silence his liberal and feminist critics by appointing the first woman ever to serve on the Supreme Court. Since her appointment, however, O'Connor has consistently voted with the conservative wing of the Court. In the Court's 1987 term, O'Connor's support for conservative outcomes was second only to Chief Justice Rehnquist's, her old law school friend and a fellow Arizonan.

By 1984, it was apparent that Reagan was likely to have the opportunity to make several appointments if he were re-elected. The three most liberal members of the Court—Brennan, Marshall, and Blackmun—were all over 75 and two were in poor health. Democratic presidential candidate Walter Mondale tried to make Supreme Court appointments an issue in the Fall election. Mondale claimed that if Reagan were re-elected, Jerry Falwell would choose the next Supreme Court justice. The issue never caught on, and Reagan subsequently swept to victory in November.

While the appointments issue flopped with the American public, pro-grammatic liberals had a keener sense of the political stakes and continued to develop the issue. In an article published in the *New York Review of Books* the week after Reagan was re-elected, constitutional scholar Ronald Dworkin (1984) sounded the alarms for fellow liberals. Cleverly entitled, "Reagan's Justice," and accompanied by a Kafkaesque pen-and-ink sketch of the bearded Bork, the article savagely attacked then Appeals Judge Robert Bork for his decision in a homosexual rights case—*Dronenberg v. Zech*. Judge Bork had not only rejected the proposition that consensual homosexual activity is protected by a constitutional "right to privacy," but questioned the very existence of the "right to privacy" doctrine. Since the "right to privacy" was the foundation of the Supreme Court's 1973 abortion decision, Bork's opinion was viewed with alarm and outrage by feminists and civil libertarians as well as homosexual rights groups. Dworkin skillfully sketched in the connections between Bork's decision, Attorney-General Meese's "jurisprudence of original intention," and the Reagan appointment strategy. Dworkin concluded with a dire prediction for American liberals.

> If justices with that view of their work colonize the Supreme Court, earning their places through decisions like Bork's, the Court will no longer be what our traditions celebrate, a forum of principle where unpopular minorities can argue for liberty on grounds of right. It will become the Moral Majority's clubhouse, where the prejudices of the day are called constitutional law.

Six weeks later Laurence Tribe, another leading liberal constitutional scholar, published his subsequently much quoted book, *God Save This Honorable Court* (1985). Tribe's stated purpose was to debunk "two myths" about Supreme Court appointments: first, that presidents could not "pack the Court" because they could not accurately predict how their appoint-ees would vote in future cases; second, that the Senate should limit itself to inquiring into only the legal competence of the president's nominees. Tribe's book was a thinly veiled justification for the Senate to reject any future Reagan nominees to the Supreme Court for "political reasons." The battle lines were clearly drawn.

The first test came in the summer of 1986 when Chief Justice Warren Burger unexpectedly announced his intention to retire. Reagan seized this opportunity to elevate Associate Justice William Rehnquist to Chief Justice and then fill this opening with Judge Antonin Scalia. Scalia was one of the outspoken conservative legal scholars that Reagan had earlier appointed to an appeals court judgeship to groom him for precisely such an opening on the Supreme Court. Senate liberals, however, concentrated their energy on defeating the Rehnquist nomination.

Led by Edward Kennedy, a small band of Senate liberals used four days of televised hearings to publicize obscure events from Rehnquist's past in hope of tarnishing his reputation and discrediting his nomination. While some of these charges gave cause for concern, the real reason for the liberals' opposition to Rehnquist was not at all obscure. In the 15 years since Richard Nixon had appointed him, Rehnquist had established himself as the most conservative member of the Court. On every constitutional issue that divides conservatives and liberals—from abortion to court-ordered busing to the exclusionary rule—Rehnquist had taken the conservative position. Kennedy expressed the true liberal view when he declared that Rehnquist was "too extreme on race, too extreme on women's rights, too extreme on freedom of speech, too extreme on separation of church and state, too extreme to be Chief Justice."

Rehnquist was eventually recommended by the Judiciary Committee and confirmed by the full Senate, notwithstanding a record-breaking thirty-three negative votes. Exhausted by their unsuccessful campaign against Rehnquist, Senate liberals mounted only token opposition to Scalia, who was also approved.

Choosing Judges by National Plebiscite: The Bork Nomination

In 1983, American liberals had taken a certain pleasure from the message that the conservatives' constitutional "counter-revolution" had failed. This satisfaction turned out to be premature. Within a year the Court reversed or restricted a series of liberal precedents dealing with affirmative action, prisoners' rights, the Miranda rule, the exclusionary rule, and separation of church and state. By 1986, the conservative wing of the Court had been expanded by the Scalia appointment, and its leader, Justice Rehnquist, had become the Chief Justice. When President Reagan nominated Robert Bork to replace retiring Justice Lewis Powell, it appeared that the conservatives' constitutional counter-revolution—pronounced dead by Blasi only four years earlier—was on the verge of success.

Senate liberals were much better prepared for Bork than Rehnquist. There were two important differences from the previous year. First, the Democrats had regained control of the Senate in the November, 1986 elections, and thus the chairmanship of the Judiciary Committee. Second, they had learned that the tactics used against Rehnquist were not sufficient.

Simply producing a litany of the nominee's "political sins" was unlikely to persuade moderate Senate colleagues. This led to a new, much more ambitious strategy. To defeat Bork, Senate liberals decided to go over the heads of their Senate colleagues and to appeal directly to their constituents. In cooperation with liberal interest groups, they would mobilize national public opinion against the Bork nomination, and then use it to pressure undecided and politically vulnerable colleagues.

The new Chairman of the Judiciary Committee, Sen. Joseph Biden (Dem.-Delaware), played a pivotal role in the campaign against Robert Bork. In consultation with Kennedy and other Senate liberals, Biden took the very unusual step of delaying his committee's hearings. As Kennedy commented later, "The first point was to gain time to organize against the nomination, and so a decision was reached that there be no hearings until after the August recess." This strategic delay of two months created the time to try to mobilize public opinion against Bork. Kennedy hired Anthony Podesta, a liberal lobbyist, to organize the opposition.

Podesta helped to coordinate the efforts of the anti-Bork Senators with liberal interest groups. Even before the Bork nomination had been announced, the Leadership Conference on Civil Rights had convened a meeting with the representatives of more than forty civil rights, black, feminist, and organized labour groups. Assisted by Senators Biden, Kennedy, Cranston, and Metzenbaum, these interest groups spent the summer campaigning against the Bork nomination. The anti-Bork coalition included the American Civil Liberties Union, the National Association for the Advancement of Colored People, the Southern Christian Leadership Conference, the National Association of Women, National Abortion Rights Action League, Planned Parenthood, Common Cause, the National Education Association, the National Association of Law Teachers, People for the American Way, the American Federation of State, County, and Municipal Employees, and the AFL-CIO.

The mobilization of interest groups was reinforced by a media campaign worthy of a presidential election. The anti-Bork forces used sophisticated polling techniques to identify "which themes would affect people the most, which Senators were most vulnerable, and where advertising should be targeted." As the Senate Judiciary Committee hearings approached, the anti-Bork forces ran full-page advertisements in newspapers, and took the unprecedented step of purchasing radio and television spots on the national networks.

Most of the advertising was the "hard-negative" variety characteristic of recent American political campaigns. It presented harsh caricatures of Bork designed to provoke visceral responses. Typical was a People for the American Way's (PFAW) full-page advertisement in the New York Times. Boldly entitled, "Robert Bork vs. The People," it told its readers that Bork had "consistently taken positions against the Constitutional rights of average Americans." It then invited the reader to "judge" for himself, and summarized the "evidence" under five bold banners:

Sterilizing Workers . . . Billing consumers for power they never got . . . Turn back the clock on civil rights . . . No day in court . . . Big business is always right. . . .

Perhaps the most effective anti-Bork television spot was PFAW's Gregory Peck commercial. Against the background of an "all-American family" staring reverently at the Supreme Court building, Peck solemnly tells the audience about Judge Bork:

> He defended poll taxes and literacy tests, which kept many Americans from voting. He opposed the civil-rights law that ended "whites only" signs at lunch counters. He doesn't believe the Constitution protects your right to privacy. And he thinks freedom of speech does not apply to literature and art and music.

The anti-Bork media made use of the "false innuendo" technique of deducing misleading (if not false) statements from actual events or words. While this type of "negative media" tactic has become standard fare in American electoral politics, it was unprecedented in the context of judicial appointments. Also unprecedented was its cost. Because it has never occurred before, there were no regulations and reporting requirements, but estimates run into the millions.

The perceived unfairness of the paid media attacks on Bork provoked angry protests from his supporters, but in the end the negative media had its intended effect. Prior to the Senate hearings, polls indicated that 73 percent of Americans were undecided on the Bork nomination, with the remainder evenly divided. By October, a large plurality of voters opposed the Bork nomination. The extensive use of media had turned the Senate Judiciary Committee hearings into "an emotional public referendum over the direction of the Supreme Court." Against this background, Bork's measured and carefully reasoned responses to the marathon questioning of the Judiciary Committee seemed cold and academic. His opponents exploited weekly polls that indicated public opinion shifting against him as the hearings wore on into October.

Central to a Reagan-Bork victory was the support of the Southern Democrats on the Senate Judiciary Committee. One by one, they abandoned the Bork nomination, citing intense constituency pressure and fears of voter backlash in their next election. As syndicated columnist George Will protested, summer fund-raising campaigns had financed a fall media blitz that shaped opinion-poll results that now were determining how Senators voted. The Bork hearings had been transformed into a national plebiscite.

The Reagan administration and their conservative supporters belatedly realized this, and tried to fight back with their own media campaign, but it was too little, too late. On October 6, the Judiciary Committee recommended against his nomination by a 9–5 vote. Dismayed by the way the Committee had handled his nomination, Bork refused to withdraw and forced a recorded Senate vote. The final tally (58–42) was not the end of the Bork controversy.

An angry President Reagan then nominated Appeals Court Judge Douglas Ginsburg. Less known than Bork but an equally ardent advocate of judicial self-restraint, Ginsburg was immediately opposed by the liberal lobby. As it turned out, Ginsburg was much easier to defeat. Within days, his former colleagues at Harvard Law School leaked to the media that Ginsburg had smoked marijuana while a professor. Within days Ginsburg withdrew his name. Smarting from two defeats, the Reagan White House retreated, and on November 11 nominated Judge Anthony Kennedy. Satisfied with Kennedy's reputation as a "pragmatic conservative," Senate liberals relented and approved Kennedy.

Politics as Usual or Constitutional Crisis?

Much ink has been spilled over whether the Bork affair was simply "politics as usual" or a constitutional crisis. This issue mainly turns on the proper role of the Senate in the confirmation of judges. Should the scope of the Senate's inquiry be limited to certifying the requisite professional expertise and moral character of the nominee? Or can the Senate also reject a nominee for "political reasons"? Most contemporary commentators have argued that the Senate can and has rejected nominees for "political reasons," and therefore there was nothing unusual in the Democratic Senate's rejection of the Bork nomination. Indeed, the successful propagation of this view was instrumental in the Bork defeat. Bork's defenders in the Senate repeatedly urged their colleagues that the Senate's scrutinizing function was limited to legal expertise and moral character, not political orientation. A senator could in good conscience vote against Bork only after he had first been persuaded that it is constitutionally proper to cast a vote for "political" reasons.

Probably no one was more influential in promoting this view than Harvard law professor Laurence Tribe, whose book, *God Save this Honorable Court*, was published just weeks after Reagan's 1984 reelection. Tribe's announced purpose was to encourage the Senate to scrutinize a candidate's "constitutional and judicial philosophies . . . substantive views of what the law should be, and the candidate's institutional views of what role the Supreme Court should play." Tribe reviews past American practice and concludes that this is both how it has been and how it should be. The only slightly less explicit purpose of the book was to give American liberals the intellectual ammunition they would need to defeat the anticipated second term Reagan appointments to the Supreme Court.

While Professor Tribe's book may have had the distinction of contributing to the defeat of Judge Bork, it cannot support the verdict of "politics as usual" with respect to that defeat. It is, of course, true that ever since John Adams' hurried appointment of John Marshall, politics have always played a role in Supreme Court appointments. Especially during times of national political realignment, these politics have been partisan indeed. A new president and his Congressional majority find their agenda frustrated by the constitutional decisions of judges appointed by the "old regime." As soon as the opportunity presents itself, the president exercises his appointment power to put judges with the "right" constitutional views on the Court. Presidents Thomas Jefferson, Andrew Jackson, Abraham Lincoln, and Franklin Roosevelt all used the appointment power to bring the Supreme Court back into step with the dominant national political coalitions they led. And, while invariably controversial at the time, it is generally agreed that the appointment power so used secures some measure of democratic accountability to the Court's power of judicial review.

There are strong elements of continuity between the Bork affair and these previous periods of *de facto* "court packing." As previously noted, the Bork nomination culminated a sustained attempt by the Reagan-led Republican coalition of the Eighties to displace liberal judges and liberal precedents. A "politics as usual" reading would interpret the Bork defeat as a simple reflection of the political weakness of the Reagan coalition: its inability to translate presidential majorities into Congressional majorities, and specifically its loss of the Senate to the Democrats in the 1986 elections.

These parallels notwithstanding, there are three novel and distinguishing characteristics of the Bork affair that augur against understanding it as just "politics as usual." First, both the scale and the scope of the Bork affair are unprecedented. Second, the current conflict over judicial appointments occurs against the backdrop—and is in part caused by—an unprecedented crisis in constitutional interpretation. Third, the de facto "election" of Supreme Court justices through national plebiscites fits into an older and stronger trend of dismantling the "republican" (non-majoritarian) institutions of American politics. [Ed. note: Only the first of these arguments is reprinted here.]

The politics of the Bork affair represent a qualitative not just a quantitative change from past judicial politics. This is evident in several ways. First, the Bork affair was not an isolated incident, but the culmination of two decades of growing political struggle for control of the federal judiciary, as documented in the preceding section. The second consideration is the unprecedented scale and scope of the anti-Bork effort. The Senate did not simply vote on the "constitutional and legal philosophy" of Robert Bork. Had they done so *in July*, Bork would have been approved in the same fashion as the Rehnquist nomination a year earlier—with significant opposition but still approved. Precisely because they understood this, the anti-Bork liberals in the Senate delayed the Bork hearings to give them time to crank up the anti-Bork juggernaut. The subsequent "campaign" to mobilize (or create) public opinion—replete with fundraising, survey-directed media blitz, and opinion polls—is clearly unprecedented. No other nominee for the Supreme Court has ever been rejected or accepted through a de facto national plebiscite.

More importantly, there is every reason to believe that the current politicization of federal judicial appointments will persist. President Bush, who defended the Bork nomination during his campaign, is not likely to forsake the Reagan approach to systematic judicial recruitment. Success begets itself. The same holds true for the Senate and the tactics of mobilizing mass opinion through interest group activism and paid media campaigns. Would Senate liberals hesitate to use it again if presented with a nomination such as Judge Richard Posner? As for the Republicans, some conservatives have charged that the nasty anti-intellectualism that characterized the anti-Bork campaign has become a monopoly of the Left. But the successful media-campaign to unseat California's Chief Justice Rose Bird and two other liberal appointees of former Governor Jerry Brown show that conservatives are willing and able to play the same game. Considering Senator Jake Garn's (Republican-Utah), bitter comment after the Bork defeat—"There will never be another liberal judge as long as I'm in the Senate"—it seems to be a safe bet that Senate conservatives would "rise above principle" to try to defeat Bork's counterparts on the constitutional left, a Laurence Tribe or an Alan Dershowitz, for example.

Activists in both political parties now see the political stakes of judicial appointments as sufficiently high to justify almost any means. While these means may seem unduly partisan and even constitutionally suspect—as undermining the independence of the judiciary— it is unrealistic to expect politicians to put long-term constitutional good ahead of short-term political gain. They would not be politicians if they did.

4.7

DEBATE: SHOULD THERE BE CONFIRMATION HEARINGS FOR SUPREME COURT JUDGES?

AFFIRMATIVE:
F.L. Morton

Mr. Justice William McIntyre's retirement again focuses attention on the Supreme Court and how little we know about Canada's new constitutional guardians. McIntyre's replacement will be the fourth new appointment to the court in less than 12 months and the sixth by the

"Charter changed Judges' Role; Their Selection needs Review." *The Financial Post*, Feb. 20, 1989, p. 16. Reprinted with permission.

Mulroney government. Like the other five, he or she will be chosen privately, behind closed doors without any public scrutiny or review. As in the selection of a Pope, the public will simply be informed once the choice has been made. This method may be fine for the Catholic Church, but it is hardly appropriate for a modern democracy.

The Charter of Rights has changed the practice of politics in Canada. It has conferred new power on judges and new limitations on legislators. Indeed, 1988 may well be remembered as the "year of the court"—the year that began with *Morgentaler* and abortion and ended with Bill 101 and Quebec. These and other decisions make it clear that the Charter has altered the balance of power between the Supreme Court and Parliament. The justices have moved onto the the centre stage of Canadian politics, and are now the constitutional equals of parliamentarians.

Yet the Mulroney government persists in selecting justices as if nothing has changed, as if the only criteria are legal expertise, personal integrity and a willingness to work long hours. These, of course, remain essential prerequisites, but under the new Charter regime they are not enough. If legal expertise and political neutrality were the essential components of the ideal court of appeal, then Canada should never have abolished appeals to the JCPC.

The case for a judicial selection process based solely on "professional merit" rests on the mistaken view that the Supreme Court's job is simply to "discover the true meaning" of the Charter and to follow the proper precedents. In truth, the role of the Supreme Court under the Charter is not so much to follow precedents as to make them. As for "discovering the true meaning" of the Charter, this truth is often in the eye of the beholder. Different judges give different answers to such key Charter issues as "what is consistent with 'the principles of fundamental justice' " (section 7); or "what constitutes 'a reasonable limitation' on a right" (section 1). These differences flow from the judicial philosophy and political orientation of the judges, not from the text of the Charter.

Those who understand constitutional law primarily as law do not understand constitutional law. Its form is legal but its content is political. It is political in the double sense that the judges have considerable freedom to choose between equally plausible interpretations and, secondly, that these different interpretations carry very different policy consequences.

The two Charter abortion cases provide a telling example. Both Henry Morgentaler and Joe Borowski based their challenges to Canada's abortion law on the same section of the charter—section 7. Morgentaler argued the "principles of fundamental justice" include a woman's absolute right to abortion. Borowski argued the same words protect the right to life of the unborn. Which version was right? Strictly speaking—based on the text and legislative history—neither was correct. But which ever can garner the support of at least five justices becomes the new law of the land.

The adoption of the Charter has shifted primary (but not final) responsibility for the rights and freedoms of Canadians from legislatures to the courts. But taking constitutional law out of politics has not taken the politics out of constitutional law. In the law of federalism everyone takes this truth for granted. The new appointment process proposed in the Meech Lake Accord—under which the federal government must choose Supreme Court judges from lists provided by the provincial governments—reflects a realistic assessment of the power that constitutional interpretation confers on judges. The Charter is no different.

In the next several years, the Supreme Court will make authoritative if not final judgments on such diverse policy issues as abortion, mandatory retirement, immigration, the political activities of unions, censorship of pornography, anti-hate literature laws, bilingual education services, and a mind-boggling host of section 15 equality issues. These are important issues and they will directly affect the quality of life in Canadian society for the rest of our lifetimes. Does it really make sense that we know absolutely nothing about the judges who will make these decisions until after they are appointed?

The irony of our present situation is readily apparent. Canadians know more about Judge Robert Bork—a failed nomination to the American Supreme Court—than we do about Justices L'Heureux-Dubé, Sopinka, Cory, Gonthier, and "Justice X." Yet these five otherwise anonymous Canadians could determine such major policies as abortion until they reach mandatory retirement at age 75. (Of course, they will soon have the opportunity to strike down mandatory retirement as unconstitutional age discrimination, in which case they can stay as long as they choose!)

It is time to change the selection process to reflect the new power of individual Supreme Court justices. Our tradition of "responsible government" dictates that the governors be accountable to the governed. Political institutions that fail this litmus test of democracy wither and decline—the Canadian Senate being a leading example. By the same logic, as the Supreme Court becomes more influential in the governing process, it should become more accountable. This need not mean going to the American extremes of electing judges or subjecting them to recall elections. It does mean that prior to final appointment, a nominee for the Supreme Court should be expected to field responsible questions about his or her final philosophy from a multiparty parliamentary committee.

The Mulroney government would have us believe that in giving us a British-style judicial selection process with an American-style judicial review of constitutional rights, Canadians have the best of both worlds. In fact, this combination can just as easily produce the worst of both worlds—judicial law-making without any accountability.

NEGATIVE:
Ian Hunter

In his article, Professor Morton reasons from what is a true and significant fact to what is, I submit, a misguided and dangerous conclusion. The truth is the Charter of Rights and Freedoms has transformed Canada from a system of parliamentary supremacy, derived from the British model, to a system of constitutional supremacy, derived from the U.S. model. The misguided conclusion is that therefore we should import U.S.-style confirmation hearings for prospective Supreme Court appointees.

With much of Professor Morton's analysis I concur. The Charter has made of our judges modern "philosopher kings," arbiters of social, political and even moral issues that were once the preserve of politicians and priests. The traditional function of common law courts was to "discover" not to "make" law (albeit with some limited scope for judicial creativity); now the Supreme Court fashions the law like a draper from whole cloth, measuring, cutting and assembling it to its pleasure. Constitutional law, once confined to disputes over the division of legislative powers, is now concerned almost exclusively with "fundamental rights and freedoms," highly political in nature.

The Chief Justice of Canada acknowledged this: "The judiciary now plays a pivotal role in defining our rights and freedoms, and limiting the powers of government to pass laws which impinge upon these rights. The Charter has elevated the judiciary to a new plateau of legal, and, I daresay, political prominence." And this was said before the Court ventured forth upon that most dangerous and political of seas: Equality (s.15). Several of the Court's Charter judgments, particularly the long-winded, unctuous liberalism that characterizes the majority of opinions in *R. v. Morgentaler*, almost make one nostalgic for the brisk professionalism and detached neutrality of the Judicial Committee of the Privy Council. So yes, Professor Morton, yes, yes and yes.

But the cure you propose—confirmation hearings—is worse than the malady. They would prove ineffective, unseemly, and antithetical to the common purpose of appointing the best and most qualified men and women as judges. Such hearings will prove ineffective because only two kinds of questions may be put to a prospective nominee: irrelevant questions, which will be answered but are a waste of time, and relevant questions, which any prospective judge worth his salt will decline to answer.

The irrelevant questions (age, education, employment history, etc.) will be apparent to anyone from a résumé. The relevant questions ("What is

"Confirmation Hearings for Judges would lower Quality of Court." *The Financial Post*, March 27, 1989, p. 16. Reprinted with permission.

your view on mandatory retirement; reverse discrimination; abortion?") will be declined with the polite answer that, if appointed, those issues may have to be judicially examined. By and large, this has been the history of most American confirmation hearings. Either an excellent candidate is rejected (as was Robert Bork) for political and ideological reasons masquerading as objective inquiry, or a prospective judge parries the question with the stock reply: "Should that issue come before me, I shall endeavor to decide it, to the best of my ability, in accordance with my oath and the law." What else can properly be said?

Confirmation hearings will prove unseemly because they are offensive to a cardinal principle of the British parliamentary system of government: division of powers. Division of powers means more than simply three branches of government: executive, legislative and judicial. It means as well that each branch should mind its own business. Because elected members of Parliament are also (at least nominally) heads of government departments, there is a fusion at the top of the executive and legislative branches. Separation of powers is still zealously preserved between the legislative and judicial branches of government (as any politician who has tried to influence the outcome of litigation has learned to his chagrin).

The Charter of Rights has compelled some judicial intrusion on legislative turf, though not nearly so exhaustive a trespass as the activists on the Supreme Court, particularly Madam Justice Wilson and Chief Justice Dickson, have wrought. Even so, the cure is not for the legislative branch to trespass back on the judiciary. If there is any doubt that confirmation hearings can prove unseemly, consider the spectacle of John Tower promising, like a naughty schoolboy, never to have another drink if only the Senate will make him Secretary of Defence.

Finally, confirmation hearings will prove antithetical to what Professor Morton, and I, and all Canadians want: namely the appointment of the best-qualified people as judges. What judge of a provincial superior or appellate court, what prominent barrister, will be anxious to become the Robert Bork of Canada?

It is easy to forget that a judicial appointment, even to the Supreme Court of Canada, is not a particularly attractive plum. The hours are long. The work load is crushing. The incumbent must cut himself off from past associations and circles. The right to speak publicly is severely curtailed. And the pay, while handsome in the abstract, is little more than provincial appellate judges are already earning, while for a barrister of John Sopinka's eminence the cut in pay is staggering. Add in confirmation hearings and some candidates may well say: "Forget it."

Before he became Chief Justice of the U.S. Supreme Court, Charles Evan Hughes said: "We are under a Constitution, but the Constitution is what the judges say it is." Thanks to the Charter of Rights (Pierre Trudeau's most enduring legacy to Canadians) this has become true for us as well. We are no longer a government of laws but of judges. Before we go any

further down the U.S. road, we might pause and reflect upon this conclusion of a 1985 Canadian Bar Association study on the independence of the
judiciary:

> One final concern of this committee is that the appointment process not be too public.
> Unnecessarily detailed public scrutiny will naturally tend to discourage some excellent
> candidates from accepting positions on the bench and thereby decrease the quality of our
> judges.

4.8

KEY TERMS

Concepts

group representation
ideological judicial appointments
impartiality
judicial independence
merit nominating commission
merit screening committee
political patronage
politics of rights
regional representation

Institutions, Events, and Documents

National Committee on the Judiciary (1966)
Office of Special Advisor to the Minister of Justice (1973)
Alberta Judicial Council
Saskatchewan Judges Affair
Commissioner for Federal Judicial Affairs (1977)
Meech Lake Accord (1987)
Judge Bork Affair (1987)
1988 Reforms of Federal Judicial Appointments Procedure
Russell-Ziegel Study (1989)
gender bias seminars for judges

5
Judicial Independence, Ethics, and Discipline

Disputes are a fact of life in political communities. In the course of their personal and commercial interactions, individuals become involved in disputes over what happened (questions of fact) and what the rule is that governs their situation (questions of law). Typically, neither party is willing to allow the other to unilaterally answer these questions, for fear that an adversary will exploit any ambiguity of fact or law to his or her own advantage. The self-interest of both parties prevents either from serving as arbiter of the dispute. What is needed is an outside third party who is independent of both disputants, and thus can be expected to render an impartial inquiry and resolution of the dispute.

While the need for a mechanism of dispute resolution is common to all societies, different cultures have met this need in different ways. In the Western European tradition, the institutions that have evolved to perform this function are what we know today as courts. Historically speaking, Canada is a very recent part of the Western European tradition, and our legal system (like the rest of our culture) is in large part inherited and adapted from this tradition. The authority of contemporary Canadian courts still rests on the ancient requirement of impartiality. We are willing to submit our disputes to judges and to obey their decisions voluntarily, even if we lose, because we believe that they provide an unbiased and reasoned application of the laws to the facts of our particular dispute. In order to insure impartiality, we expect a judge to be independent of our adversary. In the area of criminal law and other types of disputes between individuals and the state, this means that judicial independence from the Crown is an essential prerequisite for the proper functioning of our legal system.

Canada's legal system did not evolve from the Western European tradition at large, but rather from the distinctive British common law tradition.[1] This means that Canada has been fortunate enough to inherit

---

[1] Except for Quebec, whose Civil Law originated in France. Note, however, that since criminal law and procedure are matters of federal jurisdiction, the criminal law process in Quebec is based on the same common law practices as the rest of Canada.

the British institutional practices and safeguards of judicial independence that for centuries have made Great Britain an exemplary model for the protection of individual freedom.[2]

While the tradition of judicial independence is much older, it became an official part of Britain's "unwritten constitution" as part of the Act of Settlement in 1701. During the seventeenth century, the Stuart Kings had flagrantly violated the independence of the British courts. After James II was deposed in the "Glorious Revolution of 1688," Parliament and the English bar were eager to provide more certain guarantees for judicial independence in the future. As part of the Act of Settlement, they forced the new king, William III, to agree to legal provisions securing the independence of the judiciary. Judicial tenure of office was established on the principle of *quamdiu se bene gesserint*—"during good behaviour"—and henceforth judges could be removed only by address of both houses of Parliament. In addition, judicial salaries had to be ascertained and established by law, and were no longer set by royal decree.[3]

Having established judicial independence at home, the British Parliament was somewhat reluctant to introduce it in British North America. Originally, colonial judges served only "at pleasure." This practice inevitably led to abuses by colonial governors, and these abuses were one of the grievances enumerated in the Declaration of Independence by the American revolutionaries in 1776. Significantly, no sooner had the Americans successfully thrown off British political rule, than they entrenched the British provisions for judicial independence in their new state and federal constitutions.[4] It was not until the 1830s and 1840s that similar provisions for judicial independence were made for the rest of British North America.

At Confederation in 1867, the now familiar terms of judicial independence were written into the Constitution Act. Section 99 provides that "judges of the superior courts shall hold office during good behaviour, but shall be removable by the Governor General on address of the Senate and House of Commons." In 1960 this was amended to require mandatory retirement at the age of 75. Section 100 requires that the "salaries, allowances and pensions of the judges of the Superior, District, and County Courts.... be fixed and provided by the Parliament of Canada."

---

[2] See the admiration of the nineteenth century French political thinker, Alexis de Tocqueville, quoted by A.V. Dicey in Reading 1.4.

[3] "He has made judges dependent on his will alone, for the tenure of their offices, and the amount and payment of their salaries."

[4] Note that there was no national judiciary under the first American constitution, The Articles of Confederation. The more centralist Constitution of 1788 created a national Supreme Court, and provided for judicial independence in essentially the same terms as the Act of Settlement. The practice of electing judges in some American states, referred to in chapter four, dates from a later period in American history.

It should be noted that the tenure provisions apply explicitly only to the superior courts created pursuant to section 96. This has raised the question of whether the judges of the Supreme Court and Federal Court of Canada, County and District Court judges, and the judges of the "section 92" provincial courts enjoy less independence than their superior court brethren. Lederman argues that although the independence of these courts is not constitutionally entrenched in explicit, written provisions, it remains part of Canada's "unwritten constitution." While tenure of office in these courts is provided for only by ordinary statute, Lederman declares that these provisions are "'ordinary' in form only, because they are declaratory of basic constitutional principles and traditions." (See Reading 5.1) The constitutional reforms of 1982 appear to further reinforce the independence of the Supreme Court of Canada by entrenching its present size and composition. As noted earlier, the unsuccessful 1987 Meech Lake Accord would have formally extended the written guarantees of sections 99 and 100 to the Supreme Court of Canada.[5]

Historically, the concept of judicial independence extends beyond these formal, institutional guarantees. It also stands for the convention of non-interference in the judicial process by members of the executive and legislative branches of government, as well as the non-interference of judges in the political process. The former branch of the non-interference doctrine was illustrated in the "1976 Judges Affair," when it came to light that several different members of the Trudeau Cabinet had personally telephoned judges to inquire about cases they were in the process of deciding. While none of the Cabinet ministers ultimately resigned, the government issued a policy guideline stating that:[6]

> In the future no member of the Cabinet may communicate with members of the judiciary concerning any matter which they have before them in their judicial capacities, except through the Minister of Justice, his duly authorized officials, or counsel acting for him, nor may any member of the Cabinet communicate with quasi-official bodies which are constituted as courts of record concerning any matter which they have before them in their judicial capacities except through the minister responsible, his duly authorized officials, or counsel acting for him.

This policy has been strictly observed. Two years later, when it was discovered that MP John Munro had telephoned a judge who was hearing a case involving one of Munro's constituents, Munro was forced to resign as Minister of Labour. The change in government in 1984 has not affected the strict enforcement of this policy. In 1989, the Conservative Minister of

---

[5] See Introduction to Chapter 3.

[6] A more detailed account of this matter may be found in Peter H. Russell, *The Judiciary in Canada: The Third Branch of Government* (Scarborough, ON: McGraw-Hill Ryerson, 1987), pp. 78–81.

Fitness and Amateur Sport, Jean Charest, resigned following revelations that he had telephoned a judge concering a case then under consideration.

A different but related aspect of judicial independence arose in the wake of the Donald Marshall scandal in the 1980s: Can a duly constituted royal commission compel a judge to testify about the reasons for a decision or the composition of the panel of judges that heard a case? (See Reading 5.2) While judges normally enjoy an old and well-established immunity from being compelled to explain their judicial decisions (other than in their written judgments), the facts in the Marshall affair were anything but normal.

In 1971, Donald Marshall, a young Native man, was convicted of murder in Halifax. Marshall steadfastly maintained his innocence, and in 1982, after eleven years in prison, his lawyer introduced new evidence that persuaded the Federal minister of justice to order the Nova Scotia Court of Appeal to review the case. While the Court of Appeal subsequently found Marshall innocent and ordered him freed, at the end of their judgment the court wrote that Marshall's "untruthfulness . . . [had] contributed in large measure to his conviction" and that "any miscarriage of justice is . . . more apparent than real."

The disclosure that an innocent young person had spent eleven years in prison, combined with the Appeal Court's apparent attempt to "blame the victim," caused a public outcry. The scandal was further heightened by the revelation that 10 days after Marshall's conviction, police had failed to take any action after receiving credible new evidence that someone other than Marshall had committed the murder. There was widespread belief that a similar disregard for fairness would not have shown toward a white man, and led to allegations that Marshall's mistreatment was symptomatic of a more general racial prejudice against natives in the criminal justice system in Nova Scotia.

To clear the air, in 1986, the government of Nova Scotia appointed a royal commission to investigate the Marshall prosecution from start to finish. When the Royal Commission subsequently received testimony that the new evidence supporting Marshall's innocence had been communicated to the then Attorney-General, Leonard Pace, they became concerned why Pace, who had since been appointed to the court of appeal, had been assigned to the panel of judges who reviewed the Marshall conviction in 1982. The Commission asked Pace and the other judges to appear before it to answer questions, but they refused on the grounds of judicial independence.

When the case arrived at the Supreme Court, the Court cited precedents and practice dating back to the 1692 case of *Knowles' Trial* that judges cannot be forced to testify about the reasons for decisions that they have rendered. While the Court was unanimous on this issue, they divided on whether judges had the right to refuse to testify as to the composition of a panel, that is, an administrative matter. The majority judgment, written by Justice McLachlin, held that while judges did not enjoy a general immunity from answering questions about all aspects of judicial administration, there was such immunity on the critical issue of the assignment of judges. Justices Cory and Wilson dissented. While agreeing that judges enjoy a qualified immunity from testifying about administrative decisions, the facts in the Marshall case made it one of those rare exceptions where the judges should be compelled to testify in order "to reaffirm public confidence in the administration of justice."

As a result of this decision, neither Chief Justice MacKeigan nor Justice Pace had to testify before the Royal Commission. Nonetheless, the Commission's final Report was so critical of the judges that the Attorney-General of Nova Scotia lodged a complaint with the Canadian Judicial Council. (A summary of Commission's findings appears at the beginning of Reading 5.5.) The Judicial Council responded by striking a Committee of Inquiry to determine if there had been judicial misconduct serious enough to warrant removal from office. The Committee of Inquiry's report (Reading 5.5) found that while the Court of Appeal may have used "grossly inappropriate language" and that its "mischaracterization" of the evidence was so serious as to constitute a "legal error," neither of these faults constituted grounds for removal from office.

In recent years increasing attention has been given to a new dimension of the old issue of judicial independence: the administrative independence of the judges collectively from the executive branch of government. Historically, the departments of justice, at both the federal and provincial levels, have been responsible for administering their respective judicial systems. This has resulted in multiple roles for the respective attorney-generals and ministers of justice, who are also responsible for arguing the Crown's position in cases before these same courts. An increased sense of the potential for conflict of interest in this situation has resulted in a series of reforms. In 1977, the federal government created the Commissioner for Federal Judicial Affairs to administer federal judicial business independently of the Minister of Justice. This Commissioner has the rank and status of a deputy head of a government department, and can be best described as "the personnel office of the federally appointed judiciary." Under the 1977 amendments to the Judges Act, the Commissioner is responsible for the administration of the salaries, benefits and programs of all federally appointed judges. In 1988, the Commissioner was given the additional responsibility for most of the judicial recruitment process, which was previously carried out by an advisor within the Justice Minister's personal office. Several provinces, including British Columbia, Manitoba, New Brunswick, and Ontario, also have created professional court administrators.

In 1981, Justice Jules Deschenes and Professor Carl Baar completed a study commissioned by the Canadian Judicial Council investigating the problem of the administrative independence of the courts. (See Reading 5.6) They concluded that the problem was sufficiently serious to merit complete judicial control of court administration. However, in September, 1982, the Canadian Judicial Council rejected complete administrative autonomy, at least for the present, and called instead for more and better consultation and decision-sharing between court administrators and judges.

No matter is more critical to the maintenance of judicial independence than the procedure for removing judges guilty of serious misconduct or gross incompetence. While such exigencies must be provided for, the removal procedure must be structured so as to minimize the potential for political abuse. While requiring address by both houses of Parliament is a solid guarantee of judicial independence, in 1971 the federal government took additional steps to further reform the removal process.

In 1971, the Judges Act was amended to authorize the creation of the Canadian Judicial Council, consisting of the chief justices and associate chief justices of all the superior courts, and chaired by the Chief Justice of the Supreme Court of Canada. The Judicial Council is authorized to supervise judicial conduct and to investigate allegations of judicial misconduct. If the Council discovers sufficiently serious misconduct on the part of a judge, it can direct the removal of county and district court judges, and recommend to Parliament the removal of superior court judges. By transferring the responsibility for investigating allegations of judicial misconduct from the executive branch to the judges themselves, the potential for political abuse is reduced, and the independence of the judiciary enhanced.

The Canadian Judicial Council came close to exercising its new powers in 1982 at the conclusion of its investigation into allegations of misconduct by then Justice Thomas Berger of the British Columbia Court of Appeal. On November 5, 1981, the federal government and all the provinces except Quebec reached a compromise agreement on the proposed constitutional reforms of the Trudeau government. One of the compromises was the federal government's agreement to delete those sections that dealt with the protection of the "aboriginal rights" of Native peoples. In the weeks following, Justice Berger publicly criticized Canadian political leaders for this action on at least two occasions. These criticisms were reported in the press, and a justice of the Federal Court, upon reading these reports, lodged a complaint of judicial misconduct with the Canadian Judicial Council. (See Reading 5.3) The Judicial Council appointed a committee of investigation, and invited Justice Berger to testify in his own defence. He refused, but sent two letters defending his actions as a matter of conscience and a question of principle. (See Reading 5.3) The Committee of Investigation's final report concluded that Justice Berger was guilty of judicial misconduct, and stated that they would have recommended removal from office, had it not been for the unique circumstances of the incident. (See Reading 5.3) The Judicial Council modified the Investigation Committee's report. Its final report to the Minister of Justice declared that Justice Berger's actions had been "indiscreet," but that they did not constitute grounds for removal from office. Meanwhile, Justice Berger announced his intention to resign anyhow, and did so several months later.

The Canadian press gave the "Berger affair" considerable publicity, and some editorials criticized the Canadian Judicial Council for trying to censor or punish Justice Berger for exercising his "freedom of speech." The late Chief Justice Bora Laskin, was sufficiently upset with what he considered to be a gross misunderstanding of these events to publicly address the issue in a speech to the Canadian Bar Association in September, 1982. (See Reading 5.4) The late Chief Justice's remarks are important because they demonstrate that judicial independence cuts both ways. Not only does it prohibit politicians from interfering in the judicial process, but it also prohibits judges from interfering in the political process. In response to Berger's appeal to individual conscience, Laskin argued that a judge's "abstention from political involvement is one of the guarantees of his impartiality, his integrity, his independence."

The Canadian Judicial Council itself has become entangled in the ongoing battle between feminists and conservatives over the role of judges and the courts. As noted earlier, in 1990, REAL Women filed an unsuccessful complaint with the Judicial Council over a speech by then Justice Bertha Wilson. This episode was repeated in 1991, when Justice Beverly McLachlin, in a speech to the Elizabeth Fry Society in Calgary, explicitly criticized Canada's traditional laws on abortion and prostitution as denying women equality and reflecting the bias of male legislators. REAL Women again accused a member of the Supreme Court of advancing "a feminist analysis of the law" that was not shared by all women and represented a violation of her judicial oath of impartiality. Again the Judicial Council rejected the complaint outright, replying that Justice McLachlin's remarks were an "informative and thoughtful historical analysis" of the issues she addressed.

This response prompted an angry reply from REAL Women, which compared McLachlin's 1991 speech to Justice Berger's 1981 speech and alleged that the Council was not evenly enforcing Chief Justice Laskin's principle that speaking on political issues of the day is "forbidden territory" for judges. The Council's refusal to take action against Justice McLachlin, said REAL Women, "indicates that there has either been a very significant change in the role of judges in Canada," or an inconsistent application of the old rule:

> Either Canadian judges are now permitted by the Canadian Judicial Council to engage in political debate or, in the alternative, only those judges supporting the feminist ideology and analysis of the law are permitted to do so.

While REAL Women no doubt thought that the Council was playing favourites, the truth may be closer to the alternative explanation: that with the expanded political involvement of judges under the Charter of Rights, the Council should adopt (or has adopted) a more lenient policy for off-the-bench speeches by sitting judges. This possiblity, however, appears to be contradicted by a publication recently released by the Canadian Judicial Council, *Commentaries on Judicial Conduct*. This work was the product of a two-year study by the Council's Judicial Independence Committee to "formulate a statement of practical ethics to help judges and the public alike." On the subject of "When the Judge makes a Speech," the *Commentaries* state: "We agree that the Charter has tended to blur the distinction between political and legal issues. Almost any issue may now become the subject of litigation. We see that as a reason for judges to become more, rather than less, circumspect than in the past."[7]

This new controversy and confusion over what constitutes the proper limits of judicial comment on political issues is just one reflection of the rapid change in the role of judges since the adoption of the Charter in 1982. Traditional assumptions are being challenged by new forms of judicial conduct. This controversy may be illuminated by Paul Weiler's discussion of relationship between greater judicial involvement in politics and "judicial accountability." Weiler reminds us that the reason judges are purposely made "unaccountable," unlike other high ranking officials of the state, is that the judges' function is perceived as non-political. To the extent that courts openly and explicitly engage in policy-making, the justification of judicial independence is eroded. Weiler argues that a court that actually resembled his hypothetical "policy-making model" could not logically lay claim to judicial independence. The "judges" of such a court would be much more like administrative executives, who would serve "at the pleasure" of the executive, and could be changed with the change of political party control of the House of Commons. Note that this analysis is completely at odds with the view advanced by former Chief Justice Dickson in the *Beauregard* (1986) decision, and quoted by Justice McLachlin in the *Hickman* case, that the need for judicial independence becomes even greater when the courts assume the additional role of "protector of the Constitution."

While Dickson and McLachlin's position is correct as a matter of abstract constitutional theory, the accuracy of Weiler's political or democratic logic is reflected in the real world experience of other countries with more experience with a powerful constitutional court. The sporadic periods of "court packing" in American history are only the most dramatic evidence of the generally accepted fact of American politics that, "policy views dominant on the Court are never for long out of line with the policy views dominant among the lawmaking majorities of the United States."[8] Keeping the court "in tune with the times" need not take such traumatic and conflictual forms. It can be insti-

---

[7] Canadian Judicial Council, *Commentaries on Judicial Conduct* (Cowansville, PQ: Les Editions Yvon Blais, Inc., 1991), p. 42.

[8] Robert Dahl, "Decision-Making in a Democracy: The Supreme Court as National Policy-Maker," *Journal of Public Law* 6 (1958), pp. 279–295.

tutionalized through constitutional procedures such as that used by the state of California, whereby a judge appointed to the state supreme court must, after his or her first nine years of service, undergo a confirmation vote in a general election.[9] France accomplishes the same objective by limiting the term of each judge on its *Conseil Constitutionnel* to a non-renewable nine-year term, staggering the terms so that one-third of its nine-person membership is replaced every three years. This guarantee of a constant flow of "new blood" onto the court means that it is unlikely to stay out of step for long with the governing majority coalition.

These examples may indeed seem foreign and repugnant to Canadians long accustomed to Professor Lederman's assumption that judicial independence is a prerequisite of the "rule of law." But they help us to "think the unthinkable," in Weiler's words; that is, the institutional implications of increasing the policy-making role of courts for the tradition of judicial independence. These examples encourage us to assess the potential costs (and not just the potential benefits) of the greater policy-making role for Canadian courts made possible by the Charter of Rights. They also may cast a more positive light on the controversial section 33 legislative override of the Charter, which, as was suggested earlier, may provide a more salutory alternative to ideological judicial appointments or "court packing."[10]

---

[9] See Introduction, Chapter 4.

[10] See Introduction to Chapter 4 and also Reading 13.4.

5.1

THE INDEPENDENCE OF THE JUDICIARY
W.R. Lederman

Introduction

An independent judiciary has long been an established feature of our Constitution in Canada, coming to us as a primary part of our great inheritance of English public law and governmental institutions. My purpose here is an ambitious one—to explain the essential *positive* functions of an

---

In A.M. Linden, *The Canadian Judiciary* (Toronto, ON: Osgoode Hall, 1976,) from pages 1–12. Reprinted with permission.

independent judiciary as an integral part of our total constitutional system. This involves examining the relations between the judiciary on the one hand, and parliaments and cabinets on the other, as they play their respective parts in making and applying laws for our country, at both the provincial and the federal levels. Also, of course, this task requires some examination of the institutional arrangements that are the basis of judicial independence, and some assessment of the relevance of such independence to the needs of our time for good government under law. . . . What I have to say falls under three main headings:

1.   Our English Constitutional Inheritance,
2.   Essential Operational Elements of Judicial Independence, and
3.   Judicial Independence, Democracy, and The Rule of Law.

1. Our English Constitutional Inheritance

Sir Arthur Goodhart has told us, in his distinguished lectures on "English Law and the Moral Law," that the English are not as much without a constitution as they frequently profess to be. He gives four principles which he maintains are equally basic as first or original principles of the English constitution. They are briefly as follows: (1) "That no man is above the law" (among other things, this means that all official persons, the Queen, the judges and members of Parliament included, must look to the law for the definition of their respective positions and powers). (2) "That those who govern Great Britain do so in a representative capacity and are subject to change. . . . The Free election of the members of the House of Commons is a basic principle of English constitutional law."(3) That there shall be freedom of speech, of thought and of assembly. (4) That there shall be an independent judiciary.

> The fourth and final principle which is a basic part of the English constitution is the independence of the judiciary. It would be inconceivable that Parliament should today regard itself as free to abolish the principle which has been accepted as a cornerstone of freedom ever since the Act of Settlement in 1701. It has been recognized as axiomatic that if the judiciary are placed under the authority of either the legislative or the executive branches of the Government then the administration of the law might no longer have that impartiality which is essential if justice is to prevail.

Sir William Holdsworth expressed a very similar view on the status of the judiciary. He said:

> The judges hold an office to which is annexed the function of guarding the supremacy of the law. It is because they are the holders of an office to which the guardianship of this fundamental constitutional principle is entrusted, that the judiciary forms one of the three great divisions into which the power of the State is divided. The Judiciary has separate and autonomous powers just as truly as the King or Parliament; and, in the exercise of those powers, its members are no more in the position of servants than the King or Parliament in the exercise of their powers. . . it is quite beside the mark to say that

modern legislation often bestows undivided executive, legislative and judicial powers on the same person or body of persons. The separation of powers in the British Constitution has never been complete. But some of the powers in the constitution were, and still are, so separated that their holders have autonomous powers, that is, powers which they can exercise independently, subject only to the law enacted or unenacted. The judges have powers of this nature because, being entrusted with the maintenance of the supremacy of the law, they are and always have been regarded as a separate and independent part of the constitution. It is true that this view of the law was contested by the Stuart kings; but the result of the Great Rebellion and the Revolution was to affirm it.

. . . For present purposes, two things are noteworthy about the Canadian judicial system. First, while it is true that the guarantee of removal from office only by joint address of the Parliament of Canada is explicitly specified by the B.N.A. Act just for the Superior courts of the Provinces, this most emphatically does not mean that there is no constitutional protection for the security of tenure in office of other judges in the total judicial system just described. The same point applies concerning the explicit guarantee of salaries in the B.N.A. Act, which mentions only the Superior, District and County courts of the Provinces. The position in my view is that the Superior Courts, by virtue of the explicit provisions for them in the B.N.A. Act afford the prototype—the model—which should be followed for all other Canadian courts.

In other words, I am saying that security of tenure and salary for judges in Canada, as a matter of basic constitutional law and tradition, is not limited to the strictly literal reach of sections 99 and 100 of the B.N.A. Act. I remind you of the words of Goodhart and Holdsworth. They make it clear that essential provision for the independence of the judiciary generally has long been deeply rooted as an original principle in the basic customary law of the constitution. In Britain herself, the explicit provisions about judicial security are in the ordinary statutes—but these ordinary statutes, including the Act of Settlement itself, manifest the more fundamental unwritten constitutional principle I have described, as Goodhart and Holdsworth insist. The same point can and should be made about the status of Canadian judges. In Canadian Federal statutes we have provisions ensuring the independence of the County and District Court judges, the judges of the Federal Court of Canada and the judges of the Supreme Court of Canada itself. In various Provincial statutes, security is likewise provided for provincially-appointed judges, for example, the Provincial Criminal Court judges in Ontario. My point is that though these are ordinary statutory provisions, they are "ordinary" in form only because they are declaratory of basic constitutional principles and traditions.

Now of course, for the judges who depend on ordinary statute in this respect, there is room for variations in just how their basic constitutional independence is to be implemented. But, provided they are guaranteed security of tenure in office until a reasonable retirement age, subject only to earlier removal for grave misconduct or infirmity, after full due process by way of enquiry, then the basic constitutional mandate for their independence is satisfied. I am not arguing that all judges are, or have to be, under the parliamentary joint address procedure in order to be secure and independent. Adequate due process leading to removal for cause may take several forms. In this respect, we should note the recent advent of the Canadian Judicial Council, under which the federally-appointed judges as a group themselves apply due process and self-discipline concerning any of their own members against whom complaints may have been entered. This is a progressive step in safeguarding the independence of the judiciary that is quite in harmony with the concept of independence. . . .

2. Essential Operational Elements of Judicial Independence

What I have said so far implies that the elements of judicial independence fall into two groups, individual elements and collective ones.

The individual elements may be stated in these terms. A judge is not a civil servant, rather he is a primary autonomous officer of state in the judicial realm, just as cabinet ministers and members of parliament are the primary official persons in the executive and legislative realms respectively. No minister of the Crown, federal or provincial, and no parliament, federal or provincial, has any power to instruct a judge how to decide any one of the cases that comes before him. If a parliamentary body does not like the judicial interpretation of one of its statutes in a particular case, then it can amend the statute, use different words, and hope that this will cause a different judicial interpretation when next the statute is before a court. But that is all a parliamentary body can do or should attempt to do under the constitution. As for ministers of the Crown, when the government is an interested party in litigation or prosecution before the courts, then the minister can instruct counsel to appear and argue in court for the result the executive government would prefer, but that is all a minister can do or should attempt to do under the constitution. The judge remains autonomous, both as to his determinations of fact and his interpretations of the applicable law. As Chief Justice Laskin said recently, the judge must supply his own answers from his own resources, and thus there is something of the loneliness of the long distance runner in every judge. Long term security of tenure in office with the corresponding guarantee of salary ensures that the judge can maintain this position, especially as he is not allowed to hold any other office concurrently with his judicial office.

The reason for this individual independence of judges is best explained in the words of the late Robert MacGregor Dawson, as follows:

> The judge must be made independent of most of the restraints, checks and punishments which are usually called into play against other public officials. . . . He is thus protected against some of the most potent weapons which a democracy has at its command: he

receives almost complete protection against criticism; he is given civil and criminal immunity for acts committed in the discharge of his duties; he cannot be removed from office for any ordinary offence, but only for misbehaviour of a flagrant kind; and he can never be removed simply because his decisions happen to he disliked by the Cabinet, the Parliament, or the people. Such independence is unquestionably dangerous, and if this freedom and power were indiscriminately granted the results would certainly prove to be disastrous. The desired protection is found by picking with especial care the men who are to be entrusted with these responsibilities, and then paradoxically heaping more privileges upon them to stimulate their sense of moral responsibility, which is called in as a substitute for the political responsibility which has been removed. The judge is placed in a position where he has nothing to lose by doing what is right and little to gain by doing what is wrong; and there is therefore every reason to hope that his best efforts will he devoted to the conscientious performance of his duty. . . .

. . . But, assuming the appointment of able people to judicial office, this is not in itself enough to ensure that the judicial system functions well as a whole and in all its parts. There are problems of the whole system of courts that have an important bearing on the independence of the judiciary. . . .

. . . First, my outline of the many parts that make up the unitary Canadian judicial system shows that responsibility for necessary appointments and legislation is shared between the federal and provincial levels of government. Accordingly, for the solution of these system problems, there must be a great deal of federal-provincial consultation and collaboration at the cabinet and parliamentary levels. This applies also to the provision of adequate financial support for the judicial system. Generally speaking, the administration of justice in Canada has been seriously under-financed, and both levels of government are to blame for this.

In the second place, in certain vital respects, collective responsibility for the effective operation of the judicial system should be invested in the judges themselves. Here the role of the Chief Justices and the Chief Judges is very important, as spokesmen for themselves and their brother judges. This refers particularly to the assignment of judges to case lists, and to determination of priorities for the grouping and hearing of cases. In my view, to safeguard the basic independence of the judiciary, the Chief Justices and the Chief Judges should be in operational control of these matters for their respective courts, with adequate administrative staff responding to their directions.

I have now spoken of the individual and the collective elements that go to make up an independent judiciary. But there is a final question that remains to be answered. What, in the end, is the main purpose of maintaining an independent judiciary? Sir William Holdsworth said, "The judges hold an office to which is annexed the function of guarding the supremacy of the law." My third and final topic is an attempt to explain why he said this.

3. Judicial Independence, Democracy, and the Rule of Law

At this point I return with particular emphasis to the special importance of our superior courts of general jurisdiction. We say that we have the rule of laws rather than of men, but this has a special dependence on the men who are the superior court judges. Constitutionally they have the last word on what the laws mean, so, does this not really mean the personal supremacy of superior court judges? I deny this for the following reasons. It is basic to the rule of law that doctrines, ideas and and principles are supreme, not persons. The great case of *Roncarelli v. Duplessis* confirmed this as the position in Canada. In aid of this supremacy, we find that the superior courts possess under the constitution a final supervisory review function over lesser courts, and over officials, boards and tribunals of all kinds, to ensure that they stay within the limits of the powers respectively given them by the constitution, or by statute, or by common law. The superior courts have power to nullify decisions of other officials and tribunals for excess of jurisdiction or breach of natural justice in procedure. But here we encounter that basic constitutional dilemma—Who watches the watchman? Who checks the superior courts themselves for excess of jurisdiction or breach of natural justice in procedure? The answer is that, at this primary level of constitutional responsibility, the superior court judges must be trusted to obey the laws defining their own functions, and to check themselves. Believing in the supremacy of law, they must themselves scrupulously obey it. They must be all the more careful about this precisely because there is no one to review their powers, as they review the powers of others. Judicial restraint on these terms at the superior court level is the ultimate safeguard of the supremacy of the law, enacted and unenacted, to use Holdsworth's terms. Remember too that at the intermediate and final levels of judicial appeal you have a plural bench, so that a majority of several judges is necessary to reach a decision. Several heads are better than one, and in the process purely personal peculiarities are likely to be cancelled out. It seems to me that this is as close as we can get to the rule of laws rather than of men.

There are further reasons for confidence in the independent judiciary, and I am speaking now of all judges, both provincially-appointed and federally-appointed. The conditions on which they hold office mean that they have a personal career interest to be served by the way they go in deciding cases that come before them. The laws to be interpreted and applied must be expressed in words, and words are not perfect vehicles of meaning. Hence there is frequently room for partisan interpretation, and that is precisely what you would get if one of the interested parties was in a position to make his interpretation prevail. At least the judges have no such personal interest in biased interpretation one way or the other, hence, in the words of Sir Arthur Goodhart, they are able to bring to the administration of the law that impartiality which is essential if justice is to prevail.

Finally, I assert that the power of the independent appointed judiciary is neither undemocratic nor anti-democratic. The statutes of our popularly elected legislatures do have priority, and will be made to prevail by the courts, if the parliamentarians speak plainly enough. [Ed. note: This was written in 1976, before the adoption of the Charter of Rights and Freedoms in 1982. The Charter now has higher priority than ordinary statutes.] But often their statutes speak only in general terms that must be further particularized by someone else, or they speak in ambiguities that must be resolved by someone else. These tasks fall to interpretative tribunals, especially the courts at all levels of the judicial system. Judicial procedure respects the individual by giving him a fair hearing and allowing him and his counsel to argue that the reason of the law is in their favour. This is as much a feature of democracy as it is to give the same citizen a vote, as a means of influencing his own fate. As for judicial law making, the judicial tasks just referred to do involve discretions that are at times legislative in character. But I must stop here, for the judge as lawmaker is another large subject, with its own place later in this book.

5.2

HICKMAN v. MACKEIGAN
[1989] 2 S.C.R. 796

[Ed. note: MacKeigan was the Chief Justice of the Nova Scotia Court of Appeal. He and four of his associate justices had refused to testify before the Royal Commission investigating the Donald Marshall affair. Hickman represented the Royal Commission.]

McLACHLIN J.: [L'Heureux-Dubé and Gonthier JJ., concurring]
These appeals raise the question of whether an investigative commission of inquiry can compel judges involved in the matters being investigated to testify as to the reasons for their judicial decision and the composition of the panel that heard the case. . . .

On November 5, 1971, Donald Marshall, Jr., a 17 year-old native adolescent boy around whom most of these appeals turn, was convicted of the murder of Sandford William Seale. Marshall consistently maintained his innocence from the day he was first arrested, throughout his trial and subsequent imprisonment. He had been in prison some 11 years before his claim of innocence was finally upheld. The failure of the Nova Scotian justice system in Donald Marshall, Jr.'s case led the Attorney-General of Nova Scotia in October, 1986 to establish a Royal Commission pursuant to the Public Inquiries Act, R.S.N.S. 1967, c. 250, with a mandate to inquire into the prosecution of, and subsequent handling of, Donald Marshall, Jr.'s case. . . .

Donald Marshall, Jr. was wrongly convicted of a murder he did not commit. During his trial, two "eye witnesses," Maynard Chant and John Pratico, testified that they saw Marshall stab Seale. Another witness, Patricia Harriss, testified that she had seen Seale and Marshall together in the area where the stabbing of Seale occurred just prior to the time of that incident. Marshall testified in his own defence that he and Seale had a conversation with two people who were dressed like priests and that one of these people had stabbed Seale.

Ten days after Marshall's conviction, James MacNeil went to the Sydney police and advised that on the night of the stabbing, he and Roy Ebsary were attacked by Seale and Marshall and that Seale had been stabbed by Ebsary during the robbery attempt. MacNeil and Ebsary were the two individuals who matched the description given at the trial by Marshall and given to the Sydney police by Marshall the day following the stabbing. Neither MacNeil nor Ebsary had been located during the investigation or prior to the trial.

The RCMP conducted polygraph tests of MacNeil and Ebsary and concluded that Ebsary was telling the truth when he said that he had not stabbed Seale and that MacNeil's evidence was inconclusive. The results of these tests were relayed to the Crown Prosecutor and, according to evidence now before the Commission, from the Crown Prosecutor to the Attorney-General's office, possibly to Attorney-General Pace himself. The Crown Prosecutor is now dead and, therefore, unavailable to testify as to this possible conversation with Attorney-General Pace.

In 1982, Marshall's lawyer provided the Sydney police with new information. They asked the RCMP and Crown Prosecutor of Cape Breton to carry out a second investigation of the Marshall affair. During this investigation, former witnesses Chant, Pratico and Harriss all recanted their evidence at trial and stated that they had been under pressure by certain members of the Sydney Police Department to tell the stories they had told at trial. On the basis of this fresh evidence, the federal Minister of Justice . . . referred the conviction to the Appeal Division of the Supreme Court of Nova Scotia, pursuant to s. 617(b) of the Criminal Code, for a redetermination. . . .

The Court then heard evidence on December 1 and 2, 1982. The Bench consisted of the Chief Justice [MacKeigan] and Hart, Jones, Macdonald and Pace JJ.A. [Ed. note: Pace was the Attorney-General at the time of Marshall's original conviction.]

On May 10, 1983, the Court of Appeal rendered its judgment. It quashed Marshall's conviction and directed an acquittal. At the end of its judgment, the Court makes the following comments:

Donald Marshall, Jr. was convicted of murder and served a lengthy period of incarceration. That conviction is now to be set aside. Any miscarriage of justice is, however, more apparent than real.

In attempting to defend himself against the charge of murder Mr. Marshall admittedly committed perjury for which he still could be charged.

By lying he helped secure his own conviction. He misled his lawyers and presented to the jury a version of the facts he now says is false, a version that was so farfetched as to be incapable of belief.

By planning a robbery with the aid of Mr. Seale he triggered a series of events which unfortunately ended in the death of Mr. Seale.

By hiding the facts from his lawyers and the police Mr. Marshall effectively prevented development of the only defence available to him, namely, that during a robbery Seale was stabbed by one of the intended victims. He now says that he knew approximately where the man lived who stabbed Seale and had a pretty good description of him. With this information the truth of the matter might well have been uncovered by the police.

Even at the time of taking the fresh evidence, although he had little more to lose and much to gain if he could obtain his acquittal, Mr. Marshall was far from being straightforward on the stand. He continued to be evasive about the robbery and assault and even refused to answer questions until the court ordered him to do so.

There can be no doubt but that Donald Marshall's untruthfulness through this whole affair contributed in large measure to his conviction.

We accordingly allow the appeal, quash the conviction and direct that a verdict of acquittal be entered.

After his acquittal, Marshall's solicitors sought compensation from federal and provincial authorities for the time that Marshall had spent in prison. Marshall was eventually paid approximately $250,000 by the provincial government and executed a complete release of all claims he might have against that government. It is evident from the materials before the Court, however, that the comments of the Court of Appeal had an impact on the quantum of that payment.

On October 28, 1986, the Governor in Council instituted the present Royal Commission. [The Commission's mandate was to investigate] the murder investigation, the charging of Mr. Marshall, the conduct of the trial and the appeal, Mr. Marshall's years in prison, the eventual acquittal by the Nova Scotia Court of Appeal and the process through which compensation was granted to him in 1984. . . .

Since the opening of the Commission's Inquiry, it has heard from numerous witnesses, including the witness who believes that he overheard the Crown Prosecutor (now deceased) discuss over the telephone with the then Attorney-General Pace, the information provided to the police by MacNeil ten days after Marshall's conviction.

As a result of this and other testimony before it, the Commission sought to question the justices who had sat on the Reference. . . .

The five justices declined to appear and Orders to Attend were accordingly issued by the Commission. The justices targeted by these Orders to Attend applied for a declaration that the Commission had no authority to compel their attendance by virtue of judicial immunity and for orders quashing the Orders to Attend and prohibiting the Commission from inquiring into their operations, deliberations, decisions and orders in respect of the Reference. . . .

[Ed note: Both the courts below ruled in favor of the five justices and against the Commission.]

The Issues

These appeals raise two issues. The first issue is whether ss. 3 and 4 of the Public Inquiries Act may be used to compel superior court judges to testify before the Commission, either with respect to how and why they reached their decision or with respect to the composition of the panel that heard the case.

The second question is whether the direction to the Commission to inquire into a reference by the Minister of Justice is ultra vires the Province because it is a matter of criminal law and procedure reserved exclusively to the federal Parliament under s. 91(27) of the Constitution Act, 1867. . . . [Ed. note: On this second issue, the Court unanimously ruled that the Commission did not invade the s.91(27) powers of the federal government.]

Whether the Public Inquiries Act Authorizes the Commission to Compel Judges to Testify

The appellants submit that the judges who sat on the Marshall appeal are required to testify before the Commission by reason of ss. 3 and 4 of the Public Inquiries Act. The respondents maintain that judges are immune from testifying at common law and as a matter of constitutional principle.

The differences between the parties lie in the interpretation they adopt of ss. 3 and 4 of the Act, and in their different views of the nature of judicial immunity. The appellants contend that s. 3 of the Act, which entitles the Commission to summon "any person" to testify, encompasses judges. While they do not deny that judges may in some circumstances be immune from testifying, they contend that the privilege is not absolute, but relative, subject to override where the public interest demands, as they submit it does in this case.

The respondents, on the other hand, assert that s. 3, read in the context of the Act, and particularly in the context of s. 4, which confines the powers of the Commission to compel testimony to those enjoyed by a judge of the Supreme Court, does not empower the commission to compel judges to testify, given the long-standing and fundamental principle of judicial immunity. Alternatively, they contend that if s. 3 did have this effect, it would be unconstitutional on the ground that it infringes the fundamental constitutional principle of judicial independence. . . .

It is my opinion that these sections, interpreted in accordance with the governing rules of construction, do not empower the Commission to compel the judges to testify on the matters at issue in this case.

I start from the fundamental principle of construction that provisions of a statute dealing with the same subject should be read together, where possible, so as to avoid conflict. . . .

This raises the question of whether a Supreme Court judge sitting on a civil case can compel another judge to testify: (a) on how and why he or she arrived at a particular judicial decision; and (b) on why a certain judge sat on a particular panel of the court. The answer to these questions depends on the nature and character of the principle of judicial independence, to which I now turn.

The Principle of Judicial Independence

This Court has spoken of this cardinal principle, albeit in the context of s. 11(d) of the Charter, in two recent decisions, *Valente v. The Queen*, [1985] 2 S.C.R. 673, and *R. v. Beauregard*, [1986] 2 S.C.R. 56. In *Valente v. The Queen*, *supra*, LeDain J., . . . observes that the "constitutional" principle of judicial independence has two major elements, an individual element and an institutional element:

> It is generally agreed that judicial independence involves both individual and institutional relationships: the individual independence of a judge, as reflected in such matters as security of tenure, and the institutional independence of the court or tribunal over which he or she presides, as reflected in its institutional or administrative relationships to the executive and legislative branches of government.

In *Valente v. The Queen*, LeDain trains his mind upon the function of the judiciary as the impartial adjudicator. The discussion turns on the relationship between judicial impartiality—a state of mind—and judicial independence—the relationship between judges and others, particularly others in the executive branch of government. LeDain J., for the Court, enunciates three "essential conditions" for judicial independence: (1) security of tenure; (2) financial security; and (3) the institutional independence of judicial tribunals regarding matters affecting adjudication. . . .

It should be noted that the independence of the judiciary must not be confused with impartiality of the judiciary. As LeDain J. points out in *Valente v. The Queen*, impartiality relates to the mental state possessed by a judge; judicial independence, in contrast, denotes the underlying relationship between the judiciary and other branches of government which serves to ensure that the court will function and be perceived to function impartially. Thus the question in a case such as this is not whether the government action in question would in fact affect a judge's impartiality, but rather whether it threatens the independence which is the underlying condition of judicial impartiality in the particular case.

In *R. v. Beauregard, supra,* the present Chief Justice (Estey and Lamer JJ. concurring; Beetz and McIntyre JJ. dissenting in part) quotes LeDain J. in *Valente v. The Queen,* as above, and explains . . . why the principle of judicial independence is so important in the liberal democratic society that is Canada:

> The rationale for this two-pronged modern understanding of judicial independence is recognition that the courts are not charged solely with the adjudication of individual cases. That is, of course, one role. It is also the context for a second, different and equally important role, namely as protector of the Constitution and the fundamental values embodied in it—rule of law, fundamental justice, equality, preservation of the democratic process, to name perhaps the most important. In other words, judicial independence is essential for fair and just dispute-resolution in individual cases. It is also the lifeblood of constitutionalism in democratic societies.

In *R. v. Beauregard,* the discussion of the concept of judicial function is broadened to encompass not only the idea of impartial adjudication, but also the notion of the Court as protector of the Constitution. Both these functions must be borne in mind when determining the "reasonable ambit of judicial independence." The test, according to Dickson C.J., is stringent; the courts' function "as resolver of disputes, interpreter of the law and defender of the Constitution" requires that they be completely separate in "authority and function" from all other branches of government. It is important to note that what is proposed in *Beauregard* is not the absolute separation of the judiciary, in the sense of total absence of relations from the other branches of government, but separation of its authority and function. It is impossible to conceive of a judiciary devoid of any relationship to the legislative and executive branches of government. Statutes govern the appointment and retirement of judges; laws dictate the terms upon which they sit and are remunerated. Parliament retains the power to impeach federally-appointed judges for cause, and enactments such as the Supreme Court Act, R.S.C. 1970, c. S19, stipulate on such matters as the number of judges required for a quorum. It is inevitable and necessary that relations of this sort exist between the judicial and legislative branches of government. The critical requirement for the maintenance of judicial independence is that the relations between the judiciary and other branches of government not impinge on the essential "authority and function," to borrow Dickson C.J.'s term, of the court. What is required, as I read *R. v. Beauregard,* is avoidance of incidents and relationships which could affect the independence of the judiciary in relation to the two critical judicial functions—judicial impartiality in adjudication and the judiciary's role as arbiter and protector of the Constitution.

To summarize, judicial independence as a constitutional principle fundamental to the Canadian system of government possesses both individual and institutional elements. Actions by other branches of government which undermine the independence of the judiciary therefore attack the integrity of our Constitution. As protectors of our Constitution, the Courts will not consider such intrusions lightly.

. . . The immunity of judges from testifying on the grounds for their decisions is established by the authorities and by the general principles of judicial independence summarized in *Valente v. The Queen* and *R. v. Beauregard*.

I turn first to the cases where the question has arisen. One of the earliest assertions of this immunity dates to *Knowles' Trial* (1692), 12 How. St. Tr. 1167. Two justices were called before a committee of the House of Lords to explain why they had quashed an indictment for murder. In reply to this request, Holt L.C.J. stated at p. 1179:

I gave judgment as it appears on the record.

It would be a submitting to an arraignment for having given judgment if I should give any reasons here. I gave my reasons in another place at large.

If your lordships report this to the House, I desire to know when you do so, that I may then desire to be heard in point of law.

The judgment is questionable in a proper method, but I am not to be questioned for my judgment.

Mr. Justice Eyres (who then sat on the bench with me, and concurred with me and the other judges) is living. I am not any way to be arraigned for what I do judicially. The judgment may be arraigned in a proper method by writ of error. I might answer if I would, but I think it safest for me to keep myself under the protection the law has given me; I look upon this as an arraignment; I insist upon it, if I am arraigned, I ought not to answer.

Eyres J. also was asked to testify before the Committee and stated at p. 1180:

I remember we adjudged the earl of Banbury's plea to be good in law; he was indicted by the name of Charles Knowles, esq. he pleaded a patent to his grandfather from king Charles the first, and claimed by descent from him; we all held it a good plea, and I was of that opinion, I own it, it was according to my judgment and conscience.

The king intrusts me with the administration of justice. I have ever given my opinion upon the greatest consideration and upon my conscience.

I humbly beg pardon if I say I ought not by the law to be called to account for the reasons of my opinion. If we err, the judgment may be rectified by writ of error, but the law acquits us.

> I humbly beg pardon as to the reasons for my opinion; if the matter comes before the lords by writ of error I shall give my reasons as well as my opinion, being called by writ ad consulendum. I humbly beg your pardon for giving no reasons at present.

The two justices were later called before the House of Lords "to give . . . an account why [they] had so done" (at p. 1181). Holt L.C.J. repeated what he had said to the Committee and later, on being forced to attend again, he stated at p. 1182:

> I never heard of any such thing demanded of any judge as to give reasons for his judgment. I did think myself not obliged by law to give that answer.

> What a judge does in open court he can never be arraigned for it as a judge.

In the end, the justices' assertions of immunity were heeded (p. 1204).

I observe that the principle of judicial immunity in *Knowles Trial* was maintained on a constitutional basis, the King having entrusted the justices with the administration of the law. Subsequent cases have affirmed the immunity of judges from compulsion to testify about judicial proceedings in which they have been included. . . .

The judge's right to refuse to answer to the executive or legislative branches of government or their appointees as to how and why the judge arrived at a particular judicial conclusion is essential to the personal independence of the judge, one of the two main aspects of judicial independence: *Valente v. The Queen, supra; R. v. Beauregard, supra.* The judge must not fear that after issuance of his or her decision, he or she may be called upon to justify it to another branch of government. The analysis in Beauregard supports the conclusion that judicial immunity is central to the concept of judicial independence. As stated by Dickson C.J. in *R. v. Beauregard*, the judiciary, if it is to play the proper constitutional role, must be completely separate in authority and function from the other arms of government. It is implicit in that separation that a judge cannot be required by the executive or legislative branches of government to explain and account for his or her judgment. To entertain the demand that a judge testify before a civil body, an emanation of the legislature or executive, on how and why he or she made his or her decision would be to strike at the most sacrosanct core of judicial independence.

I return to ss. 3 and 4 of the Public Inquiries Act. Nothing in the language of those sections suggests that the legislators intended to clothe the Commission with power to abrogate the fundamental principle that judges cannot be compelled to testify as to how and why they arrived at their decisions. I note in this connection the principle that vague and general statutory language should not be read as displacing fundamental rights: *Eccles v. Bourque*, [1975] 2 S.C.R. 739. Reading ss. 3 and 4 together in accordance with the established principles of statutory construction, I conclude that the Act does not empower the Commission to compel the justices who sat on the Marshall appeal to testify as to the grounds for their decision, including the record relied on.

The next question is whether the general words of ss. 3 and 4 empower the Commission to compel a judge to testify as to why a particular judge sat on a particular case? I note that subsequent to the decisions under appeal, the judge in question, Pace J.A., has been questioned and has advised that he had not had any conversations which might have disqualified him. Nevertheless, the Commission presumably wishes to question the Chief Justice as to why he placed Pace J.A. on the panel, given that Pace J.A. had served as Attorney-General during critical aspects of the Marshall case. This question goes to the administrative or institutional aspect of judicial independence. . . . In *Valente v. The Queen* and *R. v. Beauregard* this Court affirmed in the strongest terms the necessity that the courts control administrative matters related to adjudication without interference from the Legislature or executive. In *Valente v. The Queen* the importance of the courts having exclusive control over the assignment of judges was considered central to the institutional independence of the judiciary. In *R. v. Beauregard*, the Chief Justice stated in this respect, at p. 73, that the very role of the courts "as resolver of disputes, interpreter of the law and defender of the Constitution requires that they be completely separate in authority and function from all other participants in the justice system."

I do not say that the power in the courts to control their own administration is absolute, if by absolute what is meant is that in no circumstances can the Legislature or Parliament enact laws relating to the functioning of the courts or enquire into the conduct of particular judges. As noted earlier, Parliament and the Legislatures have long enacted legislation establishing courts and setting general guide lines as to how they function. Nor is there any doubt that Parliament may impeach a federally appointed judge for dereliction of duty. To this extent the fundamental principle of judicial independence must leave scope for another cardinal doctrine—the principle of Parliamentary supremacy. But at the same time, it is clear that Parliament and the Legislatures cannot act so as to trammel what Dickson C.J. in *R. v. Beauregard* refers to as the authority and function of the courts. As LeDain J. puts it in *Valente v. The Queen*, at p. 709, the third essential condition for judicial independence, the collective independence of tribunals, extends to matters directly affecting adjudication—"assignment of judges, sittings of the court, and court lists—as well as the related matters of allocation of court rooms and direction of the administrative staff engaged in carrying out these functions."

It thus appears clear beyond doubt that the assignment of judges is a matter exclusively within the purview of the court. It would be unthinkable for the Minister of Justice or Attorney-General to instruct the Chief Justice as to who should or should not sit on a particular case; that prerogative belongs exclusively to the Chief Justice as the head of the Court. To allow the executive a role in selecting what judges hear what cases would constitute an unacceptable interference with the independence of the judiciary. Inquiries after the fact must be similarly barred, in my view. A Chief Justice who knows that he or she may be examined and cross-examined by the executive or its emanation on why he or she assigned a particular judge to a particular case may feel, consciously or unconsciously, pressure to select someone pleasing to the executive. Even if the Chief Justice did not permit himself or herself to be influenced by such a prospect, the public perception that he or she might have been influenced could harm the esteem in which our system of justice is held. In short, the principle of judicial independence which underlies judicial impartiality and the proper functioning of the courts would be threatened by the possibility of public inquiries as to the reason for the assignment of particular judges to particular cases.

In view of these principles, I conclude that ss. 3 and 4 of the Public Inquiries Act should not be read as empowering the Commission to tramel on the exclusive right of the judiciary, through its chief justices, to control the assignment of judges, free from constraint, whether before or after the event, from other agencies. I should not, however, be taken as suggesting that a judge could never be called to answer in any forum for the process by which the judge reached a decision or the composition of the court on a particular case. I leave to other cases the determination of whether judges might be called on matters such as these before other bodies which have express powers to compel such testimony and which possess sufficient safeguards to protect the integrity of the principle of judicial independence. . . .

I would dismiss the appeals.

LAMER J.:

. . . While I agree with the principles set out in my brother Cory's judgment, when applying them to this case, I reach the same conclusion as my colleague McLachlin J. and, accordingly, would dismiss this appeal.

LAFOREST J.: [J. LaForest concurs with the judgment of J. McLachlin.]

CORY J.: [dissenting in part]

I have read with great interest the reasons of my colleague Justice McLachlin. Although I am in almost complete agreement, I differ in part from the conclusions which she has reached. In the special circumstances of this case I would allow the appeal to the extent necessary to permit interrogation on two of the three questions sought to be posed on behalf of the Commission of Inquiry. Namely, the two questions are those concerning first, the make-up of the appellate panel, particularly the inclusion of Pace J.A. who was Attorney-General at the time of Mr. Marshall's conviction, and secondly, the composition of the record before the court at the time of the reference, specifically directed at determining which affidavits formed part of that record. . . .

The qualified privilege of judges on administrative matters will clearly apply in most situations. However, there are exceptional cases such as this one where the qualified privilege of immunity from testifying must give way; this will occur when it is necessary to reaffirm public confidence in the administration of justice. . . .

In this case it is appropriate to review some of the administrative decisions. The wrongful conviction of Marshall of the crime of murder in itself called for a public inquiry. Later the composition of the panel which heard his appeal could have been the subject of public criticism. The lack of any certainty as to what material comprised the record on the appeal was disquieting. Like the wrongful conviction, these last two matters are of grave concern. They can probably be readily and completely answered, but answered they should be. . . .

The aim and goal of all aspects of judicial independence is to preserve and foster public confidence in the administration of justice. Without public confidence the courts cannot effectively fulfil their role in society. Where as here the public confidence in the administration of justice has been called into question then in the interest of that public confidence which is essential to the functioning of the courts the qualified privilege should give way.

It follows that in the case at bar where public confidence in the administration of justice is at stake, questions as to the composition of the panel and of the record would not violate the constitutional principle of judicial independence. These questions pertain primarily to the manner in which justice was administered in this case, a matter of public concern and they are within the jurisdiction of the province and of the Commission.

WILSON J.: [Justice Wilson wrote a short dissenting opinion in which she agreed with Justice Cory.]

5.3

THE BERGER AFFAIR

BERGER BLASTS "MEAN-SPIRITED" MINISTERS
Ottawa *Advocate Citizen*

Justice Tom Berger said Monday the decision of all Canadian first ministers to abandon native rights as one of the prices for agreement on the constitution was "mean-spirited and unbelievable."

The B.C. Supreme Court justice also said the compromise provincial override clauses on major parts of the charter of rights is a cause for grave concern in the light of the treatment of minorities by all Canadian governments.

Ottawa *Advocate Citizen*. November 10, 1981, p. A4. Reprinted with permission.

Berger was head of the Royal commission on the MacKenzie Valley pipeline, which heard the concerns of native people about industrial development in the North.

"Last week our leaders felt it was in the national interest to sacrifice the rights because they felt they were serving the greater good in reaching an agreement."

"It was mean-spirited. There are a million and more natives in Canada: Indians, Inuit and Metis and for the most part they are poor and powerless. They were the people who were sacrificed in this deal."

"That is the whole point of minority rights, that they should not be taken away for any reason."

Berger said "I can still hardly believe that it has happened. We have had 10 years of increasing consciousness of native rights and land claims."

"It has had an impact on many people but not on Canadian statesmen. It passed right by them."

Berger said the blame lies with all first ministers including René Lévesque since he did not point to the denial of native rights as a reason for his refusal to sign the agreement.

Berger said Canadians, concerned about the protection of unpopular minorities, can take little comfort from the fact that the federal government insisted on a five-year renewal of every action to override the fundamental, legal and equality rights in the Charter of Rights.

Berger said the problem is always "the first time when an inflamed majority wants to strike at a defenceless minority, not five years later when it is irrelevant."

REPORT OF THE COMMITTEE OF INVESTIGATION TO THE CANADIAN JUDICIAL COUNCIL
May 31, 1982

From the material annexed it can be seen that Mr. Justice Berger intervened in a matter of serious political concern and division when that division or controversy was at its height. His office and his experience as a Royal Commissioner (appointments made because of his office and his competence), obviously made his comments newsworthy. He described the decision of the first ministers to "abandon" native rights to be "mean-spirited and unbelievable." In his article he criticized the loss of Quebec's veto and argued for one amending formula in preference to another. He again attacked the first ministers for "repudiating" native rights and argued for the restoration of s. 34 "for the recognition and confirmation of aboriginal and treaty rights of Indians, Inuit and Metis."

Justice Berger, while agreeing that what he did may be unconventional, argues that the issues he discussed transcended partisan politics. Because the resolution of the issues in his opinion bore directly on how we were to be governed for the next 100 years, he felt obliged to speak out publicly. He refers to the late Mr. Justice Thorson and Chief Justice Freedman speaking on public issues. We do not have the facts with relation to those matters and are not in a position to comment on them.

Justice Berger also notes that no complaint was made to the Judicial Council about his address to the Canadian Bar Association. It is true that it appears that judges, in speaking to legal bodies, are accorded somewhat greater leeway in expressing their views than they are in speaking to the general public. However, it should be noted that a great part of the address seems to be a thoughtful philosophical discussion of the nature of Canada and its parts and the importance of its preservation. It may be, on reflection, that some of the statements made in this address, although not of as strident a nature as the material complained of, were inappropriate for a judge. It may also be that because he was speaking to an audience of lawyers and judges, the media and others took no notice of his remarks.

Justice Berger's views, which he eloquently defends in his letter to Chief Justice Laskin, are not in issue. What is in issue is his use of his office as a platform from which to express those views publicly on a matter of great political sensitivity. It is possible that other members of the judiciary held opposing views, as obviously elected representatives did, with equal conviction. Justice Berger makes reference to the Honourable Mr. Martland's statements with regard to the Charter of Rights after he retired from the bench. The analogy is not a helpful one except to underline the principle that judges do not speak out on political issues while holding office. Mr. Martland at the time he gave his interview was no longer a judge. His franchise had been restored and there was no longer any possibility that he would be called on to determine issues as an impartial judge. In our view, Justice Berger completely misses the mark when he says "does it make all the difference that nothing was said until he (Mr. Martland) retired?" It makes the greatest of difference. Politically controversial statements by a citizen who is no longer a judge and who can never again be called on to be a judge, do not destroy the necessary public confidence in the impartiality of judges.

Not only must judges be impartial, the appearance of impartiality, as Lord Devlin pointed out, must be maintained for the fair and proper administration of justice. If a judge feels compelled by his conscience to enter the political arena, he has, of course, the option of removing himself from office. By doing so, he is no longer in a position to abuse that office by using it as a political platform. One would not have expected Justice Berger's views to have been given the media attention they were given if he had not been a judge but merely a politician expressing his views in opposition to other politicians.

Judges, of necessity, must be divorced from all politics. That does not prevent them from holding strong views on matters of great national importance but they are gagged by the very nature of their independent office, difficult as that may seem. It can be argued that the separation of powers is even more emphatic here than in England. In England, High Court judges have the right to vote. Here, federally appointed judges are denied the right to vote in federal elections and in a number of provinces they have been deprived by statute of a right to vote in provincial elections, and in some cases, even in municipal elections.

It is apparent that some of the native peoples are unhappy with s. 35 of the Canadian Charter of Rights and Freedoms. If Justice Berger should be called on to interpret that section, for example, the meaning to be given to the word "existing" in the phrase "the existing aboriginal and treaty rights of the aboriginal peoples of Canada," would the general public have confidence now in his impartiality? After Justice Berger spoke publicly on the necessity for Quebec retaining a veto, his brother judges in Quebec were called on to determine whether such a right existed.

Conclusion

In our view it was unwise and inappropriate for Justice Berger to embroil himself in a matter of great political controversy in the manner and at the time he did. We are prepared to accept that he had the best interests of Canada in mind when he spoke, but a judge's conscience is not an acceptable excuse for contravening a fundamental rule so important to the existence of a parliamentary democracy and judicial independence. To say that not all judges are cast in the same mold, as does Justice Berger, is only to state the obvious. On every great matter of political concern it would be probable that judges would hold opposing views privately and, if Justice Berger's view is acceptable, it would be possible to have judges speaking out in conflict one with the other because they hold those opposing views from a sense of deep conviction.

We say again if a judge becomes so moved by conscience to speak out on a matter of great importance, on which there are opposing and conflicting political views, then he should not speak with the trappings and from the platform of a judge but rather resign and enter the arena where he, and not the judiciary, becomes not only the exponent of those views but also the target of those who oppose them.

This is not a question, as Mr. Justice Berger suggests, which each judge must decide for himself. That question has been answered for him from the moment he accepts the Queen's Patent as a judge.

So far as the material before us reveals, Justice Berger's impropriety has been an isolated instance. Chief Justice McEachern also advised us in his Submission that Justice Berger had disengaged himself from the constitutional debate as soon as the Chief Justice spoke to him. Nevertheless, we view his conduct seriously and are of the view that it would support a recommendation for removal from office. There are, however, in addition to those already noted, special circumstances which make this case unique. As far as we are aware, this is the first time this issue has arisen for determination in Canada. It is certainly the first time the Council has been called on to deal with it. It is possible that Justice Berger, and other judges too, have been under a misapprehension as to the nature of the constraints imposed upon judges. That should not be so in the future. We do not, however, think it would be fair to set standards *ex post facto* to support a recommendation for removal in this case.

The judicial office is one which confers important privileges, obligations and protections necessary to the carrying out of the duties of one of Her Majesty's judges. A judge must accept the duty to protect that office, his fellow judges and the public from political controversy as the best way of maintaining "the historic personal independence" of judges.

We conclude that the complaint *non se bene gesserit* is well founded but, for the reasons stated, we do not make a recommendation that Justice Berger be removed from office.

A MATTER OF CONSCIENCE
Justice Thomas R. Berger Letter to Canadian Judicial Council, December 3, 1981

CONFIDENTIAL   3rd December, 1981.
The Honourable Chief Justice Bora Laskin,
c/o Canadian Judicial Council
130 Albert Street
Ottawa, Ontario, K1A 0W8

Dear Chief Justice:
I understand that you and your colleagues on the Judicial Council are concerned by my intervention in the constitutional debate. I spoke at Guelph University on November 10th. The following week the Globe and Mail published an article of mine on the constitutional accord of November 5th. I enclose copies of both the speech and the article. The Prime Minister has accused me of making a foray into politics.

What I have done may be unconventional. But it was not a venture into politics in any ordinary sense. It is not as if I had discussed the ordinary stuff of political debate—inflation, interest rates, the budget, or the nationalization of the Asbestos Corporation. The issues which I discussed transcended partisan politics. In fact, when the vote on the constitutional resolution was taken this week, there were dissenting votes by members of all parties in the House.

This was, after all, a moment of constitutional renewal, unique in our country's history. The First Ministers (except Premier Lévesque) had signed a constitutional accord. I felt a sense of great dismay about the accord. My remarks were directed not to the Prime Minister or any one of the premiers, nor to any political party, but to our leaders collectively.

While these are questions that rise above narrow partisanship, they are nevertheless political questions in the broad sense. Indeed, they bear directly on the question of how we are to be governed for the next 100 years. It was for this reason that I felt obliged to speak out publicly.

What I did is not without precedent. Mr. Justice Thorson used to participate in the campaign for nuclear disarmament. Chief Justice Freedman went on television in October, 1970, to declare his support for the invoking of the War Measures Act. On the occasion of his visit to Vancouver to open the new Court House in September, 1979, Lord Denning told us that the trade unions in England were a threat to the freedom of that country. No doubt each of these judges felt compelled to speak out. It may be said that it would undermine the independence of the judiciary if judges were constantly engaged in such activity. But they are not. These interventions by judges are infrequent, even rare.

I enclose a copy of the Prime Minister's remarks made here in B.C. He taxes me for not supporting him at an earlier stage of the debate (he had also done this at a press conference a week earlier) and then goes on to urge that my conduct has been offensive. In fact, I did support his Charter before he abandoned it. I enclose a speech I made to the annual meeting of the Canadian Bar Association in Vancouver in September, to an audience of 1,000 or more lawyers and judges, presenting the case for the Charter. (I remind you that Lord Scarman is one of the leading figures in England who has publicly urged the adoption of a Charter of Rights in that country.) I was, I am afraid, outspoken. Yet none of the lawyers, judges or politicians there present complained. I do not understand why what was opportune before November 5th became "inopportune" after November 5th. The views I expressed had not changed (though couched, perhaps, in more forceful language after November 5th).

What I did was done after considering carefully what I should do, and with the best interests of my country in mind. I do not believe that anything I have done has impaired the independence of the judiciary.

The Prime Minister has, with respect to my intervention, urged the judges to "do something about it." I believe it is a mistake to think it is possible to place fences around a judge's conscience. These are matters that no tidy scheme of rules and regulations can encompass, for all judges are not cast from the same mould.

Mr. Justice Addy's letters have arrived. I do not think anything that he has said calls for a reply beyond what I have already written in this letter. It is a question of principle. Should the Judicial Council issue edicts on matters of conscience? If you and your colleagues agree with Mr. Justice Addy, there is nothing more to be said. I believe, however, that these are matters that individual judges must decide for themselves.

Yours sincerely,

Thomas R. Berger

cc: The Hon. Chief Justice McEachern

OUTSPOKEN B.C. JUDGE RESIGNING
Calgary Herald

VANCOUVER (CP)—Justice Thomas Berger, an outspoken champion of minority rights who refused to accept that his judicial robes include a gag, will be stepping down from the B.C. Supreme Court this summer.

And when he departs on August 27, he will leave an imprint that, flouting tradition, endorses the concept of judges defending minorities against parliamentary incursions.

"I believe a judge has the right, a duty, in fact, to speak out on an appropriate occasion on questions of human rights and fundamental freedoms," Berger said last year.

On Wednesday, Berger resigned from the bench, citing differences between himself and Supreme Court of Canada Chief Justice Bora Laskin and the Canadian Judicial Council over constraints imposed on public speaking by judges.

Starting in September, Berger will teach constitutional law and civil liberties at the University of B.C. two days a week and resume a limited law practice. . . .

. . . In a letter addressed to Justice Minister Mark MacGuigan, he said his differences with Laskin and the Judicial Council are well known.

He said this extended beyond the dispute over his intervention in a constitutional debate in November, 1981, when he said that on rare occasions a judge may have an obligation to speak out on human rights. Berger said his departure also concerns Laskin's views on judicial involvement in royal commissions.

MacGuigan said Thursday he has no qualms about accepting Berger's resignation, but he was unhappy that Berger made public his letter of resignation now when he plans to remain a judge until August 27.

MacGuigan said judges should avoid public controversies.

Calgary Herald, April 29, 1983, p. A3. Reprinted with permission.

5.4

THE MEANING AND SCOPE OF JUDICIAL INDEPENDENCE

Bora Laskin

. . . I hope I do not abuse this privilege if I strike a serious note in this address. It would please me better if I could banter and amuse, which I may assure you is not beyond my capacity. But special reasons, to which I will come shortly, impel me to speak more soberly on a subject of fundamental importance to the judicial office. That subject is the meaning and scope of judicial independence. I would have thought that its meaning would have been well understood over the years in which the Judges have exercised their judicial roles. I would have thought that there was a clear public understanding that Judges cannot be measured in the same way as other holders of public office or any members of the public. In my understanding, and in that of most of the members of the legal profession and members of the Bench, Judges are expected to abstain from participation in political controversy. Obviously, considering the storm that has brewed early this year on the Berger affair, I was somewhat mistaken. The limited public role of the Judge, one perfectly clear to me, seems to have been misunderstood or forgotten, even by lawyers, let alone by members of the press and of the public.

A fundamental principle has pervaded the judicial role since it took root in the reign of Queen Anne. It was established—not without fits and starts—that Judges would no longer hold office at the pleasure of the Crown, at the pleasure of the government. They would have security of tenure, once assigned to their position, and would hold office during good behaviour to the age of retirement. Their duration in judicial office would no longer depend on governmental whim, and they could be removed only for judicial misbehaviour.

What this imported, as it evolved over the years, was the separation of the executive and the judiciary; no admixture of the one with the other; no mixture of the judiciary in politics or political controversy; correspondingly, no intermeddling of the executive with the judiciary; each branch was to be independent of the other, left alone to carry on its separate duties. For the Judges, they had utmost freedom of speech in the discharge of their judicial functions. Unbelievably, some members of the press and some in public office in this country, seem to think that freedom of

From an address to the Annual Meeting of the Canadian Bar Association, September 2, 1982. Reprinted with permission.

speech for the Judges gave them the full scope of participation and comment on current political controversies, on current social and political issues. Was there ever such ignorance of history and of principle?

A Judge, upon appointment—and I am speaking here of appointments which cover all members of our provincial and federal superior courts as well as the Supreme Court of Canada—takes a prescribed oath of office. It is a short oath which is common to all superior court Judges, being as follows:

> I do solemnly and sincerely promise and swear that I will duly and faithfully, and to the best of my skill and knowledge, execute the powers and trust reposed in me as. . . .
>
> So help me God.

But it is invested with all the authority and surrounded by all the limitations that are imported by the principle of judicial independence and that are spelled out in the Judges Act, the federal statute which defines the judicial office.

What does the Judges Act say about the judicial office? It says quite clearly that a Judge may not, directly or indirectly, engage in any occupation or business other than his judicial duties. There is a limited exception for him or her to act as commissioner or arbitrator or adjudicator or referee or conciliator or mediator, if so appointed in respect of a federal matter by the federal Government; and similarly, if so appointed by the provincial government in respect of a provincial matter. These are short-term, temporary assignments not intended to give a Judge a regular assignment to carry out a non-judicial role. Two recent illustrations of the distinction may be mentioned. A few years ago, the Government of Canada wished to appoint a Judge as a Deputy Minister of an executive department. He was unwilling to accept the position unless he retained his security as Judge. The Government was prepared to go along. I felt it my duty as Chief Justice to protest and did so vigorously, pointing out that it was either the one position or the other, but not both.

A Judge who wishes to accept an executive appointment could not remain Judge at the same time. In the case I mentioned, the Judge put more store on his judicial position than on the proposed executive position. The matter was accordingly dropped. The same thing happened a little later in Ontario when the provincial government wished to appoint an Ontario Supreme Court Judge as Chairman of the provincial Workmen's Compensation Board. Again, I protested; if the Judge wished to accept the provincial appointment, he should resign from the Bench; he could not be both Judge and non-judicial or executive functionary. The principle was accepted and the matter was abandoned.

These instances concerned permanent appointments to governmental positions. The authorized exceptions to allow governments to appoint Judges to special assignments as, for example, by order-in-council or by a limited inquiry, do not involve Judges in executive government or in governmental operations. They are asked to perform a particular service, with generally a short-term duration, although some inquiries like the MacKenzie Valley Pipeline and the McDonald Inquiry into the RCMP did go on for some years.

I am myself not a great supporter of the use of Judges to carry out short term assignments at the behest of a government, federal or provincial. Apart from anything else, it is not always convenient to spare a particular Judge, given the ever increasing workload of all Courts. Moreover, there is always the likelihood that the Judge will be required to pass on policy, which is not within the scope of the regular judicial function. But I recognize that governments will continue to ask Judges (generally with the consent of their Chief Justice) to perform these limited tasks. The important thing to remember is that these short-term assignments are not intended to establish a career for the Judge in the work he or she carried out. The Judge is expected to make his or her report to the particular government and to regard the assignment as completed without any supplementary comment. Any comment or action is for the government; the Judge himself or herself is *functus*, done with the matter. This has been the general behaviour of Judges who have accepted and carried out special or particular governmental assignments. Whatever has been the value of the inquiry must rest in what it says—the Judge is certainly not intended to be a protagonist, however enamored he or she may become of the work. Nor is the Judge intended to make a career of the special assignment.

There has been a large increase in the number of federally-appointed Judges in the last decade. Indeed, there are now 466 superior court Judges throughout Canada and 232 county and district court Judges. I do not take account of provincial court Judges who are appointed by provincial governments. The increase in the number of federally-appointed Judges increased the burden of judicial administration, the need to monitor complaints (which are inevitable, even if in most cases misconceived) and the need also to provide outlets for judicial conferences. It was beyond the capacity of Parliament to provide for these matters and they also raised sensitive matters engaging the independent position of the Judges.

In 1971, a new policy was introduced by Parliament to govern supervision of judicial behaviour or, I should say, alleged misbehaviour. . . .

. . . The Canadian Judicial Council came into being in October, 1971 and has had a considerable amount of business in the past decade. It has exercised its powers of inquiry and investigation with great care, seeking on the one hand to satisfy complaints against alleged judicial misbehaviour and on the other hand to protect the reputation of the Judge against unfounded allegations. The most common type of complaint received against Judges has to do with objections to their judgments. Laymen have misconceived the role of the Council: it is not a court of appeal to rectify decisions alleged to be in error; for that there are established appeal courts, and the

Council repeatedly has to tell complainants that the recourse is an appeal, not an invocation of the powers of the Canadian Judicial Council.

Since the Canadian Judicial Council has a statutory mandate to conduct inquiries into alleged judicial misbehaviour, it can hardly ignore a responsible complaint. In the Berger case, the complaint was made by a long-serving superior court Judge. Was the Canadian Judicial Council to ignore it? At least, it had the obligation to consider whether the complaint merited investigation, that it was not merely frivolous. Those members of the press who became engaged with the complaint in Justice Berger's support seemed entirely ignorant of the mandate of the Canadian Judicial Council. They appeared to be of the view that a Judge's behaviour was for him to measure, that it was not open to the Canadian Judicial Council to investigate, let alone admonish a Judge in respect of a complaint against objectionable behaviour. This was clearly wrong and could have been established by some modest inquiry.

My mention of the Berger case is not to reopen an issue which is closed. It is only to set the record straight on the statutory function and duty of the Canadian Judicial Council, whoever be the subject of a complaint to it. In view of the obvious misunderstanding to which the Berger incident gave rise, it seemed important to me that I, as Chairman, should underline the role and duty of the Canadian Judicial Council, however distasteful it may be to assess the behaviour of a fellow Judge. I would have welcomed, as I always do, the balance provided by the media, by the press, and I regret that it was unfortunate that they did not discharge that responsibility on this occasion.

There was one respect in which members of the press, and indeed some public "bodies" and members of Parliament, showed their ignorance of judicial propriety. It was said that pursuit of the complaint against Justice Berger was an interference with his freedom of speech. Plain nonsense! A Judge has no freedom of speech to address political issues which have nothing to do with his judicial duties. His abstention from political involvement is one of the guarantees of his impartiality, his integrity, his independence. Does it matter that his political intervention supports what many, including the press, think is a desirable stance? Would the same support be offered to a Judge who intervenes in a political matter in an opposite way? Surely there must be one standard, and that is absolute abstention, except possibly where the role of a Court is itself brought into question. Otherwise, a Judge who feels so strongly on political issues that he must speak out is best advised to resign from the Bench. He cannot be allowed to speak from the shelter of a Judgeship.

In the Berger case, the Judge's intervention was on critical political and constitutional issues then under examination by the entire Canadian ministerial establishment. No Judge had a warrant to interfere, in a public way, and his conviction, however well intended, could not justify political intervention simply because he felt himself impelled to speak. To a large degree, Judge Berger was reactivating his MacKenzie Valley Pipeline inquiry, a matter which was years behind him and should properly be left dormant for a political decision, if any, and not for his initiative in the midst of a sensitive political controversy.

The Canadian Judicial Council—one member of Parliament accused us of being engaged in a witch hunt—was badly served by those who, obviously, did no homework on the Council's role and on its obligation. There was another matter which seemed rather shabby, also the result of failure to do any homework. It was indicated, quite explicitly in some news quarters, that the Canadian Judicial Council acted because the Prime Minister had complained of the Judge's intrusion into the political sphere when the Prime Minister was giving a press interview in Vancouver. The record on this matter is quite clear. The written complaint against Justice Berger was addressed to me under dates of November 18 and 19, 1981 and delivered to me, from Ottawa, on those days. The next day, November 20, 1981, I sent a memorandum to the Executive Secretary of Council asking that the complaints—there were two successive ones—be referred for consideration by the Executive Committee. So far as the Canadian Judicial Council was concerned, the complaint had become part of our agenda. The interview of the Prime Minister did not take place until November 24, 1981. It is therefore mere mischief making to suggest that the Canadian Judicial Council was moved to action by the Prime Minister.

The Berger inquiry, as I have said, is behind us, and I regret that I found it necessary to say as much as I did about it. However, the Canadian Judicial Council, which does not and cannot reach out publicly to the media, deserves to have its record cleared. This would not have been necessary if we had been better served by the press throughout the whole affair. A matter like the Berger case is not likely to recur; the Canadian Judicial Council has signaled the danger of recommended removal from office if it should recur. As it was, the Council took a placating view and administered an admonishment in the following terms:

1. The Judicial Council is of the opinion that it was an indiscretion on the part of Mr. Justice Berger to express his views as to matters of a political nature, when such matters were in controversy.

2. While the Judicial Council is of the opinion that Mr. Justice Berger's actions were indiscreet, they constitute no basis for a recommendation that he be removed from office.

3. The Judicial Council is of the opinion that members of the judiciary should avoid taking part in controversial political discussions except only in respect of matters that directly affect the operation of the Courts.

In view of the obfuscation that surrounded the Berger case, there are a number of propositions that must be plainly stated. First, however personally compelled a Judge may feel to speak on a political issue, however knowledgeable the Judge may be or think he or she may be on such an issue, it is forbidden territory. The Judge must remain and be seen to remain impartial. Compromise which would impair judicial independence and integrity is out, if the Judge is to remain in judicial office. Second, no federally-appointed Judge can claim immunity from the examination by the Canadian Judicial Council of complaints (unless obviously frivolous) lodged against the Judge; nor against the decision of the Canadian Judicial Council to investigate the complaints through a formal inquiry. Third, the Canadian Judicial Council is not limited to recommending removal or dismissal; it may attach a reprimand or admonishment without either recommending removal or abandoning the complaint. Only if it gets to removal does it become necessary, in the case of a superior court Judge, to engage the Minister of Justice and Parliament, whose approval on a recommended removal must be sought. Fourth, Judges who are objects or subjects of a complaint are entitled to a fair hearing, to appear before the Council or before an appointed committee or to refuse to appear (as Justice Berger did refuse). Refusal to appear does not paralyze the Council, and did not in the Case under discussion. . . .

5.5

REPORT TO THE CANADIAN JUDICIAL COUNCIL RE THE CONDUCT OF JUDGES INVOLVED IN THE DONALD MARSHALL PROSECUTION

[Ed. note: For a summary of the facts in the Marshall case, see Reading 5.2.]
    . . . The comments of the Royal Commission respecting the setting up of the Reference and the Reference decision appear at pages 113 to 127 of volume one of its report [The Royal Commission on the Donald Marshall, Jr. Prosecution, Digest of Findings and Recommendations 1989]. The findings in respect of the Reference decision are reported at page 116 where the Commissioners say:

We find:

1.   that the Court of Appeal made a serious and fundamental error when it concluded
      that Donald Marshall, Jr. was to blame for his wrongful conviction.

Reprinted in the *UNB Law Journal* 40 (1991), from pages 212–222. Reprinted with permission.

2.   That the Court selectively used the evidence before it   as well as information that had not been admitted in evidence—in order to reach its conclusions.

3.   that the Court took it upon itself to 'convict' Marshall of a robbery with which he was never charged.

4.   that the Court was in error when it stated the Marshall 'admittedly' committed perjury.

5.   that the Court did not deal with the significant failure of the Crown to disclose evidence, including the conflicting statements by witnesses, to defence counsel.

6.   that the Court's suggestion that Marshall's 'untruthfulness . . . contributed in large measure to his conviction' was not supported by an available evidence and was contrary to evidence before the Court.

7.   that the Court did not deal with the errors by the trial judge in limiting the cross-examination of [John] Pratico.

8.   that Mr. Justice Leonard Pace should not have sat as a member of the panel hearing the Reference.

9.   that the Court's decision amounted to a defence of the criminal justice system at Marshall's expense, notwithstanding overwhelming evidence to the contrary.

10.   that the Court's gratuitous comments in the last pages of its decision created serious difficulties for Donald Marshall, Jr., both in terms of his ability to negotiate compensation for his wrongful conviction and also in terms of public acceptance of his acquittal.

. . . In view of the way the issues were argued before us, we find it unnecessary to discuss the Commission's specific criticisms of the judgment of the Reference Court. We say this because, in our view, the serious criticisms of the Reference Court by the Commission may be merged into a single, comprehensive question which may be stated as follows:

> Was it misconduct justifying removal from office for the Court to characterize the conduct of Mr. Marshall as it did having regard to all the circumstances it knew from the record which it had before it?

*   *   *

It seems to us that during the course of argument in this case, the emphasis shifted from error demonstrating bias to allegations of a lack of fairness in the way the Court characterized the conduct of Mr. Marshall.

We wish at the outset to state our strong disapproval of some of the language used by the Reference Court in its comments about Mr. Marshall. In reviewing the record before the Reference Court, we cannot help but be struck by the incongruity between the Court's legal conclusion that Mr.

Marshall's conviction in 1971 was "unreasonable" and "not now supported by the evidence" and its *obiter* observations that nonetheless "any miscarriage of justice" was "more apparent than real." Surely it cannot be seriously argued that the conviction of an innocent person, let alone one who was at the time an adolescent, who was then unfairly incarcerated for more than ten years, was anything but a blatant miscarriage of justice.

The wrongful conviction and imprisonment of any person constitutes a real miscarriage of justice; it cannot be termed "more apparent than real." This is especially so when the conviction is based upon perjured evidence obtained with the complicity of the agencies of the crown. The miscarriage is greater still when crown agencies, subsequent to conviction but while an appeal is pending, receive conclusive or practically conclusive evidence of innocence but do not move promptly, or at all, to have the conviction reviewed. The miscarriage of justice, of course, becomes worse each day the innocent person remains imprisoned. There is no formula that it is possible to suggest that can be applied to redress completely more than ten years of wrongful imprisonment or which will accurately reflect the horror of what happened to Mr. Marshall. We have no difficulty in assuming that any reasonable person, knowing the circumstances adduced in evidence before the Reference Court, would regard some of its language to be at least inappropriate.

Nevertheless, in making findings of credibility, the Court was within its jurisdiction. It was entitled to believe or disbelieve any of the witnesses before it, including Mr. Marshall. Accepting part of Mr. MacNeil's evidence, the Court concluded that an attempted robbery had been in progress. There was evidence before the Court from which this finding could honestly be made. We do not say that this is what happened, or that another court would have so concluded.

In disbelieving part of Mr. Marshall's testimony, the Court concluded, from the evidence, that his "evasions" had unleashed the tragic consequences he experienced and that he had thwarted his own defence. The Court also apparently concluded that Mr. Marshall would probably not have been convicted if he told his lawyers, as he did not, where the real murderer could be found. And the Court concluded that Mr. Marshall was at least an unsatisfactory witness who did not tell the truth. It is not for us to substitute our own opinion about the findings of credibility made by the Reference Court. We are left to conclude that those findings led the Court to the impression which found expression in the *obiter* paragraphs.

The real question, however, is whether inappropriate language, even grossly inappropriate language, constitutes judicial misconduct in the circumstances of this case, keeping in mind that the Reference Court was entitled in the performance of its judicial duty to analyze the evidence and to comment upon it.

What we must observe is that in the six *obiter* paragraphs the Court focused upon Mr. Marshall to the exclusion of the other destructive factors which had a role in the wrongful conviction. A Court is entitled to comment on the evidence before it and upon the conduct of the parties or witnesses. Nevertheless, by referring exclusively to Mr. Marshall, the six paragraphs give the impression that the Court was ignoring the grossly incorrect conduct of other persons and concentrating on the victim of the tragedy.

The Court may have been reluctant to criticize those who were not before it, but it had the choice of noting that fact. Any criticism, if at all, due Mr. Marshall would be mild indeed compared to that due to those who had given perjured evidence, to those who had induced the witnesses to give it, to those who had failed to disclose prior inconsistent statements of witnesses and to those who suppressed the evidence of an eyewitness to the murder.

Whatever its intention in choosing to refer only to the person it acquitted, there can be no doubt that the impact of the Court's derogatory *obiter* statements created the strong impression that it was not responsive to the injustice of an innocent person spending more than ten years in jail. Although the Court's mandate was to determine whether or not Mr. Marshall's conviction was sustainable and not to investigate all of the circumstances surrounding it, as it would have been obliged to under paragraph 613(c) of the Criminal Code (now paragraph 690(c)), in taking it upon itself to comment in *obiter* on these surrounding circumstances, the Court ought to have referred to the other factors apparent in the material before it.

We would go so far as to suggest that the Court, in seeming to attribute to Marshall exclusive responsibility for the wrongful conviction, and thereby inferentially exculpating the other persons and factors demonstrated in the record to have played a key role in that conviction, so seriously mischaracterized the evidence before it as to commit legal error. . . .

We take it as a presumption, however, that judges ought not to be removed from office for legal error. Having found that the five judges in the collegial decision-making capacity were inappropriately harsh in their condemnation of the victim of an injustice they were mandated to correct, we nonetheless accept the submissions of all counsel that their removal from office is not warranted. While their remarks in *obiter* were, in our view, in error, and inappropriate in failing to give recognition to manifest injustice, we do not feel that they are reflective of conduct so destructive that it renders the judges incapable of executing their office impartially and independently with continued public confidence. The three remaining judges collectively had 58 years of judicial experience prior to deciding the Reference and have each served since for seven more years. Moreover, the Court did in fact acquit Mr. Marshall and find his conviction unsustainable.

We do not make our criticisms lightly. We are deeply conscious that criticism can itself undermine public confidence in the judiciary, but on balance conclude in this case that confidence would more severely be impaired by our failure to criticize inappropriate conduct than it would by our failure to acknowledge it.

While we cannot condone or excuse the severity of the Reference Court's condemnation of Donald Marshall, Jr., and in particular its extraordinary observation that any miscarriage of justice was "more apparent than real," we do not find that the comments can lead to the conclusion that the judges cannot execute their office with the impartiality, integrity and independence the public rightly expects from the judiciary. We therefore, do not recommend their removal from office.

5.6

ADMINISTRATIVE INDEPENDENCE: CONCERNS OF THE CANADIAN JUDICIARY

Jules Deschenes and Carl Baar

Although, at least by tradition, the Canadian judiciary is independent in the exercise of its judicial prerogatives, it does not enjoy, generally speaking, the same independence in the administration of the Courts.

Everywhere across Canada, it is basically the provincial Ministers of Justice who are responsible for this administration and in turn they call upon various other departments: Public Works, Supply, Public Service, Social Affairs, Communications, the Treasury Board, and so on.

This administrative subordination of the judicial to the executive causes a great deal of friction. However, as might be expected, the friction has not attained a uniform level throughout the country.

On the contrary, judges of all jurisdictions in Alberta and Manitoba, and judges of the Ontario and British Columbia courts of superior jurisdiction seemed generally satisfied with their relations with the executive.

But as I was told over and over again, whether relations between the judicial and the executive are good or poor depends very often on the personalities of the parties involved; no system can be based on such a flimsy and unstable foundation.

Indeed, it would seem that this factor is responsible for the surprising turnover of the judicial personnel in the Territorial Court of the Yukon: five of its judges in succession have resigned since 1968, while the Deputy Minister of Justice remains.

Masters In Their Own House: A Study of the Independent Judicial Administration of the Courts (Ottawa: The Canadian Judicial Council, 1981), pp. 19–24. Reprinted with permission.

Leaving aside these differences between regions, there are two questions which profoundly disturb the judiciary at all jurisdictional levels from one end of the country to the other.

The first general cause for concern results from the multiple role played by Ministers of Justice or Attorneys-General. Everywhere except in the Northwest Territories, where the federal Minister of Justice sees to public prosecution, the same minister:

a.   acts daily before the courts personally or, more often, through his substitutes, as attorney for public prosecution;

b.   provides the courts with the support staff and services needed for them to operate; and

c.   defends the budgets of the courts in Parliament.

This means that the courts hear the minister submit the conclusions which he feels are necessary in the public interest, and they must impartially adjudicate in the light of the law.

But it is on this same minister that the courts must rely for their financial support; and it is to this same minister that the courts must apply for the staff and services they need. The conflict is obvious and the dangers it conceals are ever present. Both the British and the Americans clearly understood this point.

Forty years ago, when the question of the administrative independence of the courts was being discussed in the United States, Attorney-General Homer S. Cummings himself sharply criticized a situation which he described in these terms:

> The Attorney-General presently fixes the numbers and salaries of the court clerks, the deputies, the judges' secretaries, and the amount and character of equipment for judges and clerks. It controls the travel arrangements, the accommodation in federal buildings, the payment of salaries of judges, clerks, and deputies, and the travel expenses for judges and clerks. It controls even the power of judges and their law clerks and the secretaries to travel on official business. It prepares and presents to the Bureau of the Budget the estimates for the expenses of the courts, and it is with all of this power over the affairs of the court, the principle (*sic*) litigant before them.

In 1971, Lord Hailsham, Lord Chancellor of England, expressed the same point of view during the debate on the reform of the British Courts:

> Many Ministers of Justice not merely appoint judges, but also look after prisons, and start prosecutions. To my mind, this would be something altogether dreadful in the British system and I would fight that in the last ditch.

Consequently it is not surprising that in 1976 Professor Watson concluded:

> Yet in Canada, the current trend is for provincial departments which are heavily involved in litigation before the courts to assume increasing and broad roles in court administration. This would appear to be an unsatisfactory state of affairs.

This problem falls outside the competence of the courts: it can only be solved politically.

Now, while in certain provinces such as Quebec, the difficulty is recognized, in others such as Ontario or Nova Scotia many officials are satisfied with a system which "may not be logical, but it works," and seem to fear that the cure might be worse than the disease. There are even other provinces where it is considered offensive merely to raise the question at all!

One thing is certain: it is the unanimous wish of the Canadian judiciary to see this ambiguity eliminated and the functions of attorney for public prosecution and provider of court services separated. Therefore, I recommend that:

4. *The political authorities should realize the ambiguity in the present position of Minister of Justice or Attorney-General and separate the function of attorney for public prosecution from that of provider of court services.*

The second general cause for concern within the judiciary has to do with the ambivalent relations existing between court staff and judiciary.

The staff is composed of people who are appointed under different provincial statutes and who are answerable to the Minister of Justice. Essentially, their training, job descriptions, annual evaluations, promotions and salaries depend on the minister. Therefore, it is from him that they will expect to receive their instructions. As well, except for management, they are usually members of a union within the public service and thereby have still another allegiance.

At the same time, however, by the very nature of their duties, members of any court support staff are called upon to cooperate daily with the judiciary; and by the very nature of the institution, Chief Justices are required to give the staff directions which they expect to be respected.

Thus, the support staff may well find itself torn between conflicting loyalties: one to the minister and the other to the courts. Some have tried to alleviate the problem, or to ignore it, or even to dispute that it exists; but I saw it in various regions of the country: in Prince Edward Island as in Quebec, in Ontario as in Alberta. For example:

a) a judge gave employees of a registry instructions that they found difficult to reconcile with directions from the Attorney-General's Department; they decided to give priority to the departmental directions;

b) a registrar stated that he didn't have to take orders from Chief Justices and didn't have to answer to them either;

c) a clerk refused in open court to make certain entries the judge dictated to him in the minutes of the hearing; the clerk justified his refusal by citing instructions to the contrary that he had been given by the registrar in order to save time;

d) a registrar agreed to a request from a Chief Justice, although he
knew it would be refused; then he did not forward the request to
the department so as to avoid the negative reply he anticipated; a
futile attempt to curry favour with both parties;

e) another registrar stated that he works in a world full of mental
reservations where nothing is ever straightforward.

Therefore, there is nothing surprising in the avowal of one Chief Justice: he is always concerned that his directions will be interfered with by
people who have a hierarchical authority over those to whom he gives
directions.

It is obvious that this unhealthy situation cannot be allowed to continue, even among those who seem able to adapt to it. This implies a
reorganization of the line of authority within the court administration
system. I will study how this reorganization may be achieved in theoretical and practical terms later. For the moment, I recommend that:

5. *The Executive should adopt suitable measures to ensure that the support staff give faithful*
allegiance to the courts which it is engaged to assist.

Over and above these two general causes for concern, the administrative subordination of the judicial to the executive—bad in
principle—spawns a host of difficulties, as the list below, which is by no
means complete, will show:

a) difficulty in obtaining the necessary staff (throughout the country
and on all jurisdictional levels);

b) inadequate premises (in many places);

c) problems with office supplies, photocopies;

d) inadequate security;

e) problems related to transportation and travelling expenses;

f) no prior consultation concerning
   i) changes in registry office hours;
   ii) changes in forms prescribed in the rules of practice;
   iii) legislation affecting the judiciary;

g) indirect or covert amassing of statistics on judges;

h) budgetary subordination of various judicial councils;

i) fear on the part of certain judges that the administration will transfer them to a remote region.

In Quebec, the Courts of Justice Act even goes so far as to make the
Code of Ethics of the judiciary subject to Government approval (sec. 261)
and to make it the Government's prerogative to decide whether the Judicial Council's head office is to be in Quebec City or in Montreal (sec. 252)!

All these worries, great and small, of the Canadian judiciary result from
its administrative subordination to the executive power. In turn, this subordination is rooted in the executive's overt intention to take, exercise and

keep total control—except for a few recent timid innovations—of the management, particularly the financial management, of the courts.

Now the public's perception of justice cannot help but be adversely affected by this situation where judges must entreat permission and beg for resources from the executive. One Chief Justice avowed frankly: "There is no longer even a resemblance of independence."

One incident will help convey more clearly the breadth of the gulf separating the political and judicial positions. I had just pointed out to an Attorney-General that the judicial is subordinated to the executive: "What you call the weakness of the system," he replied, "is precisely what constitutes its strength."

We must therefore study appropriate measures to loosen the grasp of the executive on the judicial: the public interest would be all the better protected.

5.7

ARE CANADIAN JUDGES INDEPENDENT ENOUGH?
Ian Greene

Although judicial independence is accepted as one of the most important principles in the Canadian constitution, its implications for judges and those having dealings with them are far from clear. The incidents related below illustrate this point.

- In 1975, Mr. Justice Marc Beauregard of the Quebec superior court brought a suit against the federal government for allegedly violating judicial independence by forcing judges to pay into a pension fund.
- In 1979, the Deputy Attorney-General of British Columbia telephoned a judge to ask whether he would transfer himself to another court to avoid having to decide on a constitutional issue. A subsequent inquiry confirmed a violation of judicial independence.
- In 1981, Mr. Justice Thomas Berger of the British Columbia Supreme Court publicly criticized the constitutional accord worked out by Prime Minister Pierre Trudeau and nine provincial premiers for disregarding the rights of native peoples and Quebeckers. Another judge complained to the Canadian Judicial Council—a body composed of approximately 40 Chief Justices which is responsible for investigating complaints about federally-appointed judges—that Berger had

Written for the second edition of this book.

violated judicial independence. This complaint led to a full investigation by the Council.

- In 1982, the lawyer for Walter Valente, who had been charged with dangerous driving, claimed that the judges of Ontario Provincial Courts are not independent, and the Provincial Court judge hearing the case disqualified himself until the issue could be determined by a higher court.
- In 1983, five Nova Scotia Court of Appeal judges acquitted Donald Marshall, Jr. of murder, but he had already spent 11 years in jail. The Court blamed Marshall for having "contributed in large measure" to his original wrongful conviction. A 1988 royal commission into the Marshall affair criticized the appeal judges for blaming Marshall. The Attorney-General of Nova Scotia then requested the Canadian Judicial Council to inquire into the conduct of the judges. As a result of the inquiry, in 1990, the Council established guidelines as to when judicial misconduct is so serious as to warrant removal and "justify interference with the sanctity of judicial independence."
- In 1986, the Chief Justice of the Quebec Superior Court brought a suit against the government to prevent the provincial Justice Minister from firing some of the judges' support staff. The Chief Justice felt that the staff reductions, if carried out, would violate judicial independence.
- In 1989, the Minister of Fitness and Amateur Sport, Jean Charest, telephoned a judge about a case involving the eligibility of a Canadian athlete in the Seoul Olympics. Charest was criticized for violating judicial independence, and resigned.
- In 1989, Ontario's Attorney-General, Ian Scott, decided to proceed with major reforms of the system of court administration in the province. These reforms included a number of changes in the case management procedures which previous Ontario governments had been unwilling to proceed with for fear of violating judicial independence.

Some would argue that these incidents show that Canadian judges do not yet have enough independence; others, that they have too much. To understand this controversy, some background commentary about judicial independence is useful. As noted above, judicial independence is one of the cornerstones of the Canadian constitution. First, it is a convention inherited from the United Kingdom constitution, thanks to the preamble of the Constitution Act, 1867, which states that Canada will have a constitution "similar in principle" to that of the United Kingdom. Judicial independence became established in England with the Glorious Revolution in 1688, and was officially recognized by Parliament in 1700. At its base, judicial independence implies that because judges should try to be as impartial as possible in applying the law, they should be free from interference in making their decisions. By 1688 it was accepted that neither Parliament nor the executive could any longer tamper with judicial salaries in an attempt to influence judges. As well, it became established that judges could not be removed or in any way punished for making a "wrong" decision, but would have life appointments subject only to removal for engaging in behaviour inappropriate for a judge such neglecting court-related duties or accepting a bribe. Eventually, it also became accepted that judicial participation in partisan politics violated judicial independence because politicians cannot be expected to act independently from their political associates.

Second, sections 96, 99 and 100 of the Constitution Act, 1867 are usually considered to be safeguards of judicial independence for the federally appointed judges in the provincial courts. Section 96 gives the federal government the power to appoint the 800 or so provincial superior and district court judges (currently only Nova Scotia retains a District Court separate from the provincial superior trial court). This division of responsibility for the superior and district courts—giving the provincial governments the responsibility to establish and administer these courts while the federal government appoints the judges—is regarded as a safeguard for judicial independence because some deliberate violations of judicial independence by politicians would require the federal and provincial governments to act together, not a frequent occurrence. Section 99 stipulates that provincial superior court judges have appointments until the retirement age of 75, and may only be removed through a joint address of both houses of Parliament. Section 100 states that the salaries and pensions of the s.96 judges will be "fixed and provided" by Parliament, rather than by the cabinet. As a result, the federal Judges Act contains a complex set of formulas which set the salaries and pensions of s.96 judges. It would therefore be impossible for a cabinet quietly to reduce the salary of an uncooperative judge.

Section 11(d) of the Canadian Charter of Rights and Freedoms is the third and newest facet of the cornerstone of judicial independence. It guarantees that anyone charged with an offence has the right to "a fair and public hearing by an independent and impartial tribunal."

In spite of these safeguards, there are some who would argue that Canadian judges do not have as much independence as they ought to, as testified to by five of the incidents mentioned above. The first of these is the case of Mr. Justice Beauregard. Soon after Beauregard's appointment to the Quebec Superior Court in 1975, Parliament changed the provisions relating to the pensions of s.96 judges. For the first time in Canadian history, judges would have to contribute a portion of their incomes to their pension fund; in return, judicial pensions were handsomely increased. The legislation was made retroactive to its date of introduction, which was before Beauregard's appointment. Beauregard claimed not to have known about the impending pension legislation when he accepted his appointment. He objected to his forced pension contribution (about $3,000 per year) on constitutional grounds. He sued the government for breach of s.100 of the Constitution Act, 1867—in other words, for violation of judicial independence. Although successful in the Federal Court, Beauregard lost his case in the Supreme Court of Canada. The Supreme Court considered that the pension legislation was in no way intended to manipulate judicial decision-making; thus, it could not be considered a violation of judicial independence.

Not uncommonly, a Supreme Court decision will be more important for its *obiter dicta*, or "words in passing," than for the actual narrow holding of the decision. The *Beauregard* decision may be such a case. Chief Justice Dickson, the writer of the majority decision in *Beauregard*, claimed in *obiter* that judicial independence has two functions in the Canadian context: to allow judges to decide individual cases without improper interference, and to allow the courts to act as independent umpires with regard to federalism and Charter of Rights issues. He said that the second purpose of judicial independence implies that the courts must be "completely independent from government." Even though Beauregard lost his case, this *obiter* may be useful as a jumping-off point for future litigants who wish to see the scope of judicial independence expanded through court decisions.

The 1979 incident involving the Deputy Attorney-General of British Columbia provides grist for the mill of those who propose that judges should have greater control over court administration. At present, the provincial superior and lower court systems are administered by public servants responsible to a provincial Attorney-General or Justice Minister. (As well, the much smaller system of federal courts, consisting of the Supreme Court of Canada, the Federal Court and the Tax Court, is administered by officials responsible to the federal Minister of Justice.) Some judges object to this executive-centred approach to courts administration, arguing that it would be better for judicial independence if courts were administered by a committee of judges, as in the United States federal courts system, or by the Chief Justice, as in some state court systems south of the border. One such critic is Mr. Justice Jules Deschenes, the former Chief Justice of the Quebec Superior Court. In 1981, the Canadian Judicial Council commissioned Deschenes to investigate the relation between judicial independence and court administration. In a report with the provocative title of *Masters in Their Own House*, Deschenes recommended that responsibility for all court administration activities should gradually be transferred to the judiciary in order to protect judicial independence; he cited the 1979 incident in B.C. as an example of what could happen to judicial independence if judges do not control court administration. This recommendation became controversial, even among Canadian judges. The Canadian Judicial Council eventually endorsed a position that the judiciary should be consulted with regard to court administration decisions, but it declined to adopt the principle of full judicial control over court administration. One reason for the Council failing to adopt the Deschenes position is that if judges have control over court administration, then they would also have to be accountable for their administrative and financial decisions and would have to become involved in politics, to some extent, to obtain an adequate budget for the courts from the legislature. The United States experience has shown that because of the accountability and budget obligations, judge-centred court administration systems do not necessarily promote greater judicial independence.

The *Valente* case has drawn attention to the fact that lower court judges in Canada—the nearly 1000 judges appointed by the provincial governments—do not enjoy the same formal safeguards for judicial independence as provincial superior court judges. In 1982, Valente was in an accident in Ontario in which three young pedestrians were killed. Appearing before a Provincial Court Judge, he was charged with dangerous driving, a criminal code offence which could result in a jail sentence. In an effort to keep his client out of jail, Valente's lawyer challenged the dangerous driving charge on constitutional grounds. He invoked s.11(d) of the Charter of Rights, and claimed that a Provincial Court Judge does not possess the independence which that section required. Valente's lawyer realized that the judicial independence issue would take some time to resolve, considering all the appeals which would be possible; in the meantime, Valente would stay out of jail. In the trial court, Valente's counsel described a number of alleged violations of judicial independence. He pointed out that Provincial Court Judges have neither the authority to direct the staff in the courthouse, nor the same constitutional guarantees of their independence as superior court judges. The Provincial Court judge before whom these arguments were put decided that they had sufficient merit to be heard by a higher court. Thus, the judicial independence issue was brought to the Ontario Court of Appeal in 1983, and then on appeal to the Supreme Court of Canada, in 1985. The Supreme Court's decision in *Valente* is a landmark concerning the meaning of judicial independence.

The Court viewed the principles behind ss. 99 and 100 as essential to judicial independence for any Canadian judge. In other words, judicial independence requires that no government could fire a judge, or manipulate his or her salary, in order to influence the judge's decision. The Court concluded that although constitutional protection of the independence of all judges might be desirable (for example, Sections 99 and 100 of the Constitution Act, 1867) safeguards in the form of ordinary statutes are sufficient. Similarly, although it might be desirable for judges to supervise court staff, this measure is not essential to judicial independence. Thus, Valente was ordered to stand trial, and Provincial Court judges across Canada were assured that they, along with their superior court colleagues, were independent so long as provincial statutes protected their right to salaries and their tenure in office.

Even if judges are left alone by governments to decide cases, their ability to decide independently and impartially may be hindered if they are provided with an inadequate complement of support staff. Of what use, for example, is a judge's independent decision if there is no secretary available to type up the decision for distribution to the litigants and the law reporters? Moreover, some judges may feel pressured to decide critical constitutional cases in favour of the government's position in the hope that they will be provided with adequate support staff in return. The potential connection between judicial independence and adequate court support staff was highlighted in the court action taken against the Quebec Justice Minister, Herbert Marx, by the Chief Justice of the Superior Court, Mr. Justice Alan Gold, in 1986. In the spring of that year, Quebec's Liberal government implemented a programme of budget cuts which affected every government department. The Ministry of Justice, which has responsibility for court administration, was hit with a 10 percent budget cut. To meet this goal, Marx decided to let go about half of the Superior Court judges' secretaries, and most of the judges' ushers. The decision was taken without consulting the judges. The Chief Justice felt that the support staff for the Superior Court was already at a bare bones state, and that further staff reductions would substantially impair the ability of judges to judge cases fairly. As a result, the Chief Justice launched a suit against the government to stave off the staff reductions. The case was based in large measure on the position that the staff reductions would erode judicial independence.

When the hearing began, counsel for the Justice Minister requested the abandonment of the hearing because of the lack of the appearance of impartiality on the part of the judge. (How could a judge of the Superior Court be impartial regarding a suit launched by his own Chief Justice?) The Judge dismissed this objection on the grounds that there was no better alternative. The hearing was then adjourned to give counsel for the judiciary and for the Justice Minister time to prepare their arguments. In the meantime, the Chief Justice requested an injunction from the judge who was seized with the suit, to prevent the firing of the secretaries and ushers until the outcome of the suit was known. This injunction was granted, and the hearing appears to have been adjourned indefinitely. The result, however, is that it is unlikely that a future Justice Minister would attempt to reduce judicial support staff without at least consulting first with the Chief Justice.

The fact that Jean Charest, federal Minister of Fitness and Amateur Sport in 1989, telephoned a judge about a case that Charest had an interest in, and other incidents like this one, could be taken as evidence that Canadian judges need more protection for their independence. The violation of judicial independence by cabinet ministers who contact a judge about a particular case is from one perspective which is rare in Canada—only three other examples during two decades come to mind—and from another perspective far too common in a country in which cabinet ministers are supposed to realize that to intervene with a judge about a case represents a flagrant violation of judicial independence. The other three examples all came to light in 1976, when it was disclosed that Marc Lalonde had telephoned a judge in 1969, Jean Chretien in 1971, and Bud Drury in 1976. In none of these cases did the intervention of the cabinet minister have the desired effect. However, one wonders whether there are more such cases which have never been revealed.

On the other hand, the Berger and Marshall cases, together with the history of attempts to reform the Ontario court system, support the proposition that at least occasionally judges exercise autonomy beyond what is required by the constitutional principle of judicial independence. Berger's troubles began when he spoke to a university convocation in November 1981, and in his address, was critical of the recently-adopted constitutional accord. His views may have gone unnoticed by those who might think them inappropriate for a judge, except that they were subsequently published in the *Globe and Mail*. As a result, Mr. Justice Addy of the Federal Court wrote to the Canadian Judicial Council and complained that Berger had violated judicial independence. The Council reprimanded Berger for his political remarks, noting that statements such as Berger's might make a judge appear to be biased. As well, the Council's committee of investigation pointed out that if a judge attacks a politician, the politician may not reply without in turn violating judicial independence. Thus, by refraining from political commentary, a judge is actually protecting judicial independence, although accepting a limitation on his or her personal autonomy.

The royal commission which was set up to inquire into the wrongful conviction of Donald Marshall, Jr. concluded that the Nova Scotia Court of Appeal, in its decision blaming Marshall for his wrongful conviction, "was not sustained by the evidence before the Court . . . [and] amounted to a defence of the criminal justice system at the expense of Donald Marshall, Jr. in spite of overwhelming evidence that the system itself had failed." The Inquiry Committee subsequently established by the Canadian Judicial Council found that the judges in question had committed a legal error; as well, the Committee registered its disapproval of some of the language employed by the judges in referring to Marshall. Because the formal power of the Council is limited to recommending for or against a judge's removal from the bench, the Committee devised a test as to whether a judge should be removed. According to the 1991 Annual Report of the Canadian Judicial Council, the test is the following:

> Is the conduct alleged so manifestly and profoundly destructive of the concept of the impartiality, integrity and independence of the judicial role, that public confidence would be sufficiently undermined to make the judge incapable of executing the judicial office?

In this case, the Council concluded that the removal of the judges was not warranted. Even so, it is clear that the judges wrote more than they needed to in order to acquit Marshall; the question remains whether they slid into legal error because judicial independence is too well-protected.

The fact that Ian Scott's court reform package of 1989 was the first major reform of the system of administering Ontario's courts for a century can be attributed largely to uncertainty about the implications of judicial independence for the administration of the courts. Until backlogs in urban courts in Ontario created a "caseload crisis" in the early 1970s, the lack of an overall court administration policy in the province—and for that matter, in any other province—was not a serious concern. But in 1973, in an effort to respond to increasing delays in some courts, the Ontario Attorney-General announced that professionally trained court administrators would be hired and given a mandate to clean up the backlog. A number of judges objected to this plan as violating judicial independence because the professional administrators would take over case management responsibilities which some of the judges had heretofore assumed. Anxious to do something—anything—to respond to the caseload crisis, the government took a new tack: a committee of judges would be given responsibility for overseeing how the professional administrators tackled the backlog. This scheme failed when a number of justice system personnel and trial lawyers, as well as some judges, objected to a major role for judges in court administration. Not only did they claim that court administration had little to do with judicial independence, the critics of the new policy also pointed to the constitutional principle of responsible government. They claimed that according to this principle, it is the government, not the judiciary, which has to account for the proper administration of the courts.

In 1987, Ontario's Liberal government commissioned Mr. Thomas Zuber of the Ontario Court of Appeal to undertake an inquiry into court administration. After a year of study, Zuber drew up recommendations designed to bring the management of Ontario's courts into the twentieth century. He concluded that judicial independence gives the judges complete control only over matters directly related to the deciding of cases—procedure in the courtroom, the assigning of cases to judges, and judicial workload. Through court management advisory committees, judges would have a say in court administration policy-making, along with other affected parties (trial lawyers, court administrative staff and the lay public). This judicial role in policy-making would be regarded as a reflection of sound management principles, not judicial independence. In 1989, the courts were re-organized according to this general blueprint, and the new NDP government has continued in the same direction. So far, complaints have not been heard from the judges that the new system violates their independence, and this may be because of the consultative mechanisms.

Returning to our original question, do Canadian judges have too much or too little independence? My own inclination is to answer, "in some respects too little, and in others, too much." Judicial independence is key to promoting impartial decision-making by judges, and therefore to making the rule of law work. It is unacceptable for cabinet ministers, or for anyone else, to try to influence a judge outside of court concerning a case, and these kinds of violations of judicial independence may not have been taken seriously enough in the past. In general, judges should be consulted more than they currently are with regard to court administration issues because the way in which courts are administered can affect not only the ability of judges to decide independently and impartially, but also the quality of their decisions. However, complete judicial control over court administration may impose as many impediments for judicial independence as benefits. The continued treatment of Provincial Court judges in many parts of Canada as second-class judges may not affect their ability to decide individual cases independently, but it may make an independent and impartial state of mind more difficult to achieve. On the other hand, a judge who objects to paying into a contributory pension fund, or to administrative reforms in general, on judicial independence grounds, may have confused judicial independence with a desire for greater personal autonomy. And judges who are tempted to take advantage of their security of tenure to make inappropriate remarks in court or to participate in a debate in the arena of partisan politics are stretching their independence beyond what is required to make impartial decisions. Clearly, more emphasis on the protection of judicial independence is required, but at the same time there may be a need for more effective accountability mechanisms to discourage the potential misuse of judicial independence.

5.8

KEY TERMS

Concepts

accountability
administrative independence
impartiality
judicial independence
non-interference (convention of)
"tenure for good behaviour"

Institutions, Events, and Documents

Knowles Trial (1692)
Act of Settlement (1701)
Constitution Act, 1867, ss.99–100
Canadian Judicial Council (1971)
1976 Judges Affair
Commissioner for Federal Judicial Affairs (1978)
Berger Affair (1981)
Charter of Rights and Freedoms, s.11(d)
Donald Marshall, Jr. Affair
Valente v. The Queen (1985)
Beauregard v. The Queen (1986)
Meech Lake Accord (1987)
Hickman v. MacKeigan (1989)

6
Access to Judicial Power

Traditionally, access to the courts has been limited to individuals who meet the threshold requirements of "standing," the right to bring a case before a court. In order to establish standing, a would-be litigant must usually prove the existence of a *lis*, or legal dispute. Not all disputes raise legal issues, and not all legal issues arise in the context of real life disputes. In the realm of constitutional law, mere distaste for or opposition to a particular statute or government policy does not constitute a dispute. A legally recognizable dispute requires the existence of a specific legal interest and an injury or a demonstrable threat of injury to that interest. In addition, a case must not become "moot" during the course of litigation. If the original dispute that gave rise to the case ceases to exist, a judge will normally deem the case moot and refuse to answer the legal issues raised.

Like other aspects of the judicial process, these restrictions on access to the courts can be traced back to the original common law purpose of courts as adjudicators of real life disputes between individuals. These restrictions ably serve the adjudicatory purposes of the courts, but are subject to criticism in modern public law cases, which often have a policy dimension that transcends the immediate dispute. As Weiler has pointed out, other policy-making institutions are not restricted in these ways. If final appeal courts are essentially policy-makers, why should an interest group have to wait for a dispute involving one of its members in order to bring its policy issue into court? Not only do these traditional rules frustrate the ability of groups to get their cause into court, but they also restrict the freedom of judges to intervene in a timely fashion.

Given the historical attachment of Canadian judges to the more British, adjudicatory view of the judicial process, it was not surprising that the rules governing standing and mootness in Canadian constitutional law were stricter than their American counterparts until quite recently. For example, in 1953 in the celebrated *Saumur* case, the Supreme Court struck down the Quebec City bylaw used to prosecute Jehovah's Witnesses for distributing their pamphlets. The fifth and deciding vote for the Supreme Court majority ruled that the bylaw violated Quebec's own Freedom of Worship Act. The government of Quebec Premier Maurice Duplessis promptly responded to this decision by amending the Act to exclude the Jehovah's Witnesses' pamphleteering from its protection. When Saumur initiated a new legal action to have this amendment declared invalid, the Supreme Court (affirming the judgment of the

Quebec courts) ruled that since the amended legislation had not actually been applied against any Witnesses, there was no real *lis* (dispute). Thus the Court refused to rule on the validity of the amended Act.

The rules on standing remained restrictive until the mid-1970s. The governing precedent was a 1924 ruling that, "An individual . . . has no status to maintain an action restraining a wrongful violation of a public right unless he is exceptionally prejudiced by the wrongful act."[1] In 1975, the Supreme Court overruled this precedent by granting standing to a civil servant seeking a declaratory judgment that the Trudeau government's new bilingualism legislation was invalid even though he was not personally affected by it. Three judges, led by Justice Judson dissented, arguing that, "the action was an attempt to get an opinion which the Court had no right to give."[2] But the other six judges granted Thorson standing, based on what Chief Justice Laskin declared was "the right of the citizenry to constitutional behaviour by Parliament."[3] Justice Judson's dissent shows that Laskin's decision to eliminate the requirement of a *lis* served not just to broaden access for litigants, but also expanded the Court's jurisdiction and thus its ability to intervene in the policy process.

The rules governing standing were further relaxed the following year in *Nova Scotia Board of Censors v. McNeil.*[4] Even though the Censor Board's ruling applied only to theatre owners not the viewing public, the Court granted standing to a reporter to challenge the Board's ruling to ban the film, *Last Tango in Paris.* This trend reached its peak in the Court's 1981 ruling in *Minister of Justice of Canada v. Borowski.*[5] (Reading 6.3) The Court ruled that even though pro-life crusader Joe Borowski was not personally harmed or even affected by the abortion law, he could still challenge its constitutional validity. The majority ignored Chief Justice Laskin's dissent, which warned that "the result would be to set up a battle between parties who do not have a direct interest [and] to wage it in a judicial arena." The *Borowski* decision seemed to remove the traditional requirement that a would-be litigant demonstrate a concrete personal interest that is affected by the legal issue raised, and created instead a very broad right for all citizens to go to the courts and demand that the judges force the government to "behave constitutionally."

In 1992, the Court finally placed some restrictions on standing when it ruled that an interest group (the Canadian Council of Churches) did not have standing to challenge new amendments to the Immigration Act because the

---

[1] *Smith v. Attorney-General of Ontario,* [1924] S.C.R. 331, at pp.337–38.

[2] *Thorson v. Attorney-General of Canada,* (1975) 1 S.C.R. 138.

[3] Ibid., p. 163.

[4] (1976) 2 S.C.R. 265.

[5] (1981) 2 S.C.R. 575.

same challenge could have been brought by a private individual.[6] But while the Court was saying "no" to the Canadian Council of Churches, it reaffirmed its very broad discretion to grant standing in Charter cases:

> By its terms the Charter indicates that a generous and liberal approach should be taken to the issue of standing. If that were not done, Charter rights might be unenforced and Charter freedoms shackled. The Constitution Act, 1982 does not of course affect the discretion Courts possess to grant standing to public litigants. What it does is entrench the fundamental right of the public to government in accordance with the law.

The Supreme Court has also weakened the doctrine of mootness as a barrier to engaging the courts in constitutional politics. In October, 1988, Borowski returned to the Supreme Court, this time to challenge the abortion law on its merits. However, eight months earlier in its *Morgentaler* decision, the Supreme Court had struck down the abortion law, although for the very opposite reasons argued by Borowski. The Court now ruled that with no law left to challenge, Borowski's case had become moot and dismissed it, again without ruling on the merits. But even as it dismissed Borowski's claim as moot, the Supreme Court elaborated a new mootness doctrine that allows otherwise moot cases to be decided if they can meet certain criteria. (See Reading 6.3) In fact, in its other Charter cases found to be moot, the Court went ahead and ruled on the merits. *Borowski* has turned out to be the exception not the rule, and is a good example of a Charter "loss" that will actually broaden access for future Charter litigants.

In its 1985 decision in *Operation Dismantle*, the Supreme Court rejected a "political questions" doctrine from precluding judicial review of government decisions involving foreign policy or national defence. (See Reading 6.4) Operation Dismantle, a coalition of anti-nuclear "peace groups," had petitioned the courts to declare illegal the government's decision to allow the American testing of unarmed cruise missiles over western Canada. They alleged that the development of the cruise missile would make nuclear war more likely by stimulating the arms race. This was said to infringe section 7 of the Charter, which protects the rights to life and security of the person. The government responded by arguing that the courts lacked jurisdiction to even hear the case because the Charter did not apply to foreign policy decisions based on "crown prerogative" and because the case presented a "political question."

The political questions doctrine is a convention developed by the American Supreme Court that prevents courts from hearing constitutional challenges to foreign policy or national defence decisions of the government. It is based on the judges' view of the proper role of courts: that responsibility for such decisions are explicitly allocated to other branches of government (i.e., separation of powers); that judges lack the expertise and facts necessary to make

---

[6] *Canadian Council of Churches v. Minister of Employment and Immigration*, Supreme Court of Canada, January 23, 1982, unreported.

such decisions; and that foreign policy decisions are based on practical judgment and thus are not susceptible to judicial decision based on "neutral principles." While foreign precedents have only "persuasive" value for Canadian courts, there was reason to believe that the Supreme Court would be reluctant to involve itself in reviewing foreign policy and defence decisions for the same reasons as its American counterpart. There were also Canadian precedents suggesting that judicial deference was the appropriate policy in these circumstances."[7]

The Supreme Court of Canada, in a decision written by then Chief Justice Dickson, avoided dealing with the political questions doctrine and dismissed Operation Dismantle's claim because it was based on alleged facts that could not be proven. In a concurring opinion, however, Justice Wilson boldly stated that crown prerogative did not shield the government's foreign policy decisions from Charter challenge nor did any political questions doctrine. The issue, declared Wilson was "whether the the courts *should* or *must* rather than . . . whether they can deal with such matters." For her, the answer was clear: "The question before us is not whether the government's defence policy is sound but whether or not it violates the appellants' rights under s.7 of the Charter. This is a totally different question."

Justice Wilson's reasoning has been greeted skeptically. Professor Monahan identified the problem when he wrote that Justice Wilson's

> statement is only meaningful if the issue of legality can be determined without recourse to questions of 'wisdom.' Madame Justice Wilson's confident assertion that the issues are 'totally different' seems based on the fact that the Court is being called on to interpret and to apply a specific 'legal' standard, in this case s.7. But the mere fact that statutory language is involved does not, in itself, provide a distinction between legal and political questions. The issue is whether it is possible to apply the statutory language without an inquiry into the 'wisdom' of the legislation under review.[8]

Many agree with Monahan that *Operation Dismantle* is a good example of a case where the legal question is inseparable from the policy question. These criticisms notwithstanding, *Operation Dismantle* appears to have preempted the development of a political questions doctrine that would restrict the scope of the Charter's applicability.

The *Thorson, McNeil, Operation Dismantle* and the two *Borowski* decisions, combined with the Charter of Rights, have had the net effect of significantly increasing the potential for judicial policy-making. There would appear to be

---

[7] Cf. the JCPC's discussion of whether a wartime emergency still existed in *Fort Frances Pulp and Power Co. v. Manitoba Free Press*, [1923] A.C. 695: "The question of the extent to which provisions for circumstances such as these may have to be maintained is one on which a Court of law is loath to enter. No authority other than the central Government is in a position to deal with a problem which is essentially one of statesmanship."

[8] Patrick Monahan, *Politics and the Constitution: The Charter, Federalism, and the Supreme Court of Canada* (Toronto, ON: Carswell-Methuen, 1987), pp.52–53.

few remaining legal barriers to prevent the litigation of the constitutionality of most government decisions or policies. If American practice is any guide, the "losers" in the legislative arenas will try to take advantage of this new forum to challenge government policy that they oppose. If a majority of the judges on the Supreme Court decide that they want to become involved, they are no longer restrained by the doctrines of mootness, standing or political questions.

An important exception to the traditional requirement of a *lis* is the reference procedure. (See Reading 6.1) Starting with the original Supreme Court Act of 1875, the federal government has given itself the authority to "refer" questions of law to the Supreme Court of Canada for answering. A reference procedure is not a case in the true sense, as there is no real dispute and no real litigants, but only a request for an advisory opinion on a hypothetical legal issue. This distinctive characteristic of the Canadian judicial process is not found in American jurisprudence. Article III of the American Constitution spells out the requirement of a *lis* by limiting the federal courts to hearing only "cases or controversies." At a very early stage this "case or controversy" requirement was interpreted as preventing the Supreme Court from providing "advisory opinions" to the federal government.

The fact that reference cases are technically "advisory opinions" on hypothetical questions of law should not lead one to underestimate their importance in Canadian law and politics. Approximately one quarter of all final appellate court decisions involving constitutional law have been references. Since 1949, this figure has declined to 16 percent. Among these are many of Canada's most important and politically influential constitutional law decisions. Predictably, governments almost never refer questions to the courts in a political vacuum. References tend to be very timely politically, either anticipating a political problem that is on the horizon or, in some cases, already being litigated in a lower court. The 1977 *Anti-Inflation Reference* (Reading 10.4) and the 1981 *Patriation Reference* (Reading 2.4) both illustrate the political potential of the reference procedure. Finally, even though judicial decisions in references are not technically binding on anyone (since there are no real parties), they have been regarded as authoritative nonetheless.

The reference procedure has generated ongoing controversy in Canadian jurisprudence. In the original Supreme Court Act of 1875, some provincial leaders perceived it as suspiciously resembling the much disliked disallowance power of the federal government, and opposed the entire Supreme Court Act for this reason. (See Reading 10.1) This suspicion was nurtured by the rather non-judicial characteristics of the original reference procedure. Only the federal government could refer questions of law to the Supreme Court, but these could be questions concerning the validity of provincial laws. Once the question was referred, there was no opportunity for affected parties—including provincial governments—to present oral or written arguments in defence of their interests. When the Supreme Court decided a reference, it did not provide any written opinion to support or explain its decision.

In response to continued provincial criticism of the reference procedure, it was substantially reformed in 1891 to make it more closely resemble a normal judicial proceeding. The 1891 amendments require that interested parties be given the opportunity to submit oral and written arguments to the Court, and that the Court hand down a written opinion with its final decision. While the federal government did not give provinces the authority to refer questions to the Supreme Court, during the next decade most provinces gave themselves a reference power to their own courts of appeal. Even after these reforms, the question remained whether answering reference questions from the executive branch was a proper judicial function. This question was put to rest in 1912, when the Judicial Committee of the Privy Council decided a provincial challenge to the constitutionality of the federal government's reference procedure. The JCPC ruled that although answering references was a "non-judicial function," it could nonetheless be imposed on the courts by statute. It also noted in passing that similar provincial practices implicitly supported the legitimacy of the federal reference procedure.

The advantages and disadvantages of the reference procedure are discussed by Justice Barry Strayer in Reading 6.1. One of the alleged advantages, however, deserves further comment. The reference procedure, Strayer and others have argued, is a practical device for each level of government to police the constitutional excesses of the other. While no doubt this is true in theory, in practice there has been a strong tendency for both levels of government to abuse the reference device as a political weapon to attack policies of the other. The federal government's *Off-Shore Mineral Rights Reference* in 1967 is commonly cited as an example of a bad-faith effort by the federal government to seize through the reference procedure what it could not get through political negotiation. The Supreme Court's decision in favour of the federal government in this case seriously harmed the Court's image as an impartial arbiter of federal-provincial disputes. A more recent example was Brian Peckford's (at that time, Newfoundland's Premier) use of the reference procedure to try to improve his bargaining position on the issue of who has the legal authority to control the development of the Hibernia oil reserves. Although Peckford's gamble backfired miserably,[9] he had made it clear from the start that he would not accept the "moral authority" of a Supreme Court decision that went against him. This type of political maneuvering places the Supreme Court in an almost "no win" situation, where the justices are "damned if they do, and damned if they don't." This sort of political abuse of the reference procedure threatens to erode the authority of the courts.

---

[9] *Reference re Newfoundland Continental Shelf*, [1984] 1 S.C.R. 86. The federal government referred the same issue to the Supreme Court of Canada before the Newfoundland Court of Appeal made a decision, and the Supreme Court ruled in favour of the federal government. This decision effectively destroyed any legal support for Newfoundland's position on Hibernia development.

For both governments and interest groups there is an alternative to participating directly as a party in public law litigation: the legal device of intervenor or *amicus curiae* ("friend of the court"). Under this form of "third-party" participation, a court may grant permission to an individual, group or government to present a written factum, participate in oral argument, or both. Historically there was considerable reluctance to allow such third party participation, because it violates the logic of the adversarial process. If the principal function of the court is to resolve the dispute before it, the judges can and should rely on the self-interest of the disputants to develop the legal arguments and facts. If one party fails to do this adequately, only the individual litigant suffers the consequences. However, this argument is less persuasive in public law cases, where the policy dimension of the dispute means that parties beyond the disputants will also be affected. If a constitutional ruling is going to affect other governments or groups, why shouldn't they also be allowed to present legal arguments and facts to the court?

In response to the logic of this argument, the practice of allowing governments to intervene in federalism cases developed very early (1880s). In a federal state, a loss or gain of jurisdiction for one government has implications for all governments. Currently, when a constitutional issue (division of powers or Charter) is before the Supreme Court, all governments are notified and requests to participate as intervenors are automatically accepted. Intervenors are especially common in references, both because of their long-term constitutional implications and the absence of any concrete factual context within which to judge the legal issues. For example in the 1976 *Anti-Inflation Reference*, the Supreme Court granted intervenor status to five provincial governments and five labour unions. (See Reading 10.4) In 158 federalism cases between 1970 and 1989, there were only 28 without any governmental intervenors.[10]

With the exception of references, Canadian courts have not been receptive to allowing non-government parties to intervene. This policy reflected the traditional British, adjudicatory view of the judicial function and the desire not to encourage interest groups to look to the courts as agents of social change.[11] This policy seemed to be changing in the 1970s, when, under the leadership of Chief Justice Laskin, non-government parties were allowed to participate as intervenors in cases involving the controversial issues of sex discrimination against Indian women and abortion.[12] With the adoption of the Constitution Act, 1982, there was a widespread expectation amongst the interest groups who had lobbied for the Charter that the Court would

---

[10] See Katherine E. Swinton, *The Supreme Court and Canadian Federalism: The Laskin-Dickson Years* (Toronto, ON: Carswell, 1990), pp.68–75.

[11] See the discussion of Kenneth McNaught's thesis in the introduction to chapter 7.

[12] Swinton, *The Supreme Court and Canadian Federalism*, p. 70.

continue to welcome non-government intervenors. To their chagrin, this did not happen. From 1983 to 1986, the Supreme Court rejected more than half the interest group requests for intervenor status.

The Supreme Court's "closed-door" policy provoked a chorus of protests from groups counting on participating in the judicial development of "their" new constitutional rights by intervening in Charter litigation. One of the most influential actors in the campaign to persuade the Court to change its ways was Alan Borovoy, General Counsel of the CCLA. In an unusual "open letter" to the Supreme Court of Canada (Reading 6.5), Borovoy forcefully argued that it was both unfair and unwise to allow governments but not interest groups to intervene in the scores of Charter appeals that were beginning to filter their way up to the Court. In such a novel document as the Charter, the Court was essentially working on a "blank slate." The Court's first interpretation of each right would become an instant "landmark" precedent, shaping the course of subsequent development. Borovoy predicted (correctly) that most governments would instinctively oppose broad interpretations of rights, because this would mean more limitations on governments' choice of policy goals and means. It was important for the country, Borovoy argued, for the Court to hear "countervailing long-term theories for interpreting the Charter." Allowing non-government intervenors would mean a better informed Court, which in turn would produce a better Charter jurisprudence.

The protest worked. In 1987, the Supreme Court issued new rules for intervenors (factums limited to 20 pages; no oral argument except for special circumstances) and also began a new "open door" policy. Brodie's study (Reading 6.6) found that since 1987, the Court has accepted more than 90 percent of requests to intervene. Encouraged by the Court's new policy, the number of group requests to participate as intervenors also soared, from an average 19 requests per year between 1983 and 1986, to an annual average of 35 after 1987. Brodie's study found that the Supreme Court now hears intervenors in more than half of its Charter decisions, a radical departure from the pre-Charter era.

While there are persuasive legal reasons for allowing non-government intervenors, the policy also encourages and supports interest group litigation as a political tactic. What Borovoy did not state in his open letter to the Court was that the CCLA and other Charter groups also have a vested interest in "theories for interpreting the Charter." Most Charter-oriented groups want to encourage judges to give a broad judicial reading of the rights that most directly concern them. This is what Alan Cairns has described as the process of "constitutional imperialism," a process in which political actors—a group previously limited to governments but that now includes the various "Charter Canadian" groups—"works the constitution" to advance their short- and long-term jurisdictional/jurisprudential objectives. This process of "influencing the influencers" can take different forms, such as writing law review articles that support a preferred interpretation or influencing the appointment of judges. But the most direct way to "lobby the Court" is to participate in constitutional litigation, if not as a litigant then as an intervenor. Their presence as intervenors allows interest groups to provide appellate judges with legal arguments and favourable facts to support preferred interpretations of the right in question. It also serves as a political "cue" to signal interest group support or opposition to the policy issues before the court. Interest group use of litigation is the subject of the next chapter.

6.1

CONSTITUTIONAL REFERENCES
Barry Strayer

One of the most distinctive features of Canadian judicial review is its frequent resort to the constitutional reference. This frequency can be demonstrated by a survey of the leading cases: those reaching the Privy Council up to 1949, the Supreme Court of Canada thereafter, decided from 1867 to 1981. Of 352 cases involving the constitutional issues, 91 had their origins in a constitutional reference while 261 involved concrete cases. Nor does the fact that over a quarter of the leading decisions were given in such proceedings reveal the full significance of constitutional references. In terms of impact on the political, social, and economic affairs of the country the decisions in these cases have had an effect far beyond their numerical proportion. It is therefore essential in any study of judicial review of legislation in Canada to give some particular attention to this device. . . .

Advantages

To the extent that problems of standing can still prevent judicial review on constitutional grounds, references provide a means whereby constitutional issues may be placed before the courts.

. . . [R]ules of standing in constitutional cases have largely depended in the past on the requirements of particular remedies and . . . as a result certain remedies were available for judicial review only to persons with an "interest" distinct from that of the general public. At best the applicant for a declaration, injunction, *certiorari* or prohibition, who does not have such a specific interest, will be subject to the discretionary power of the

The Canadian Constitution and the Courts: The Function and Scope of Judicial Review. 3rd ed. (Toronto, ON: Butterworths, 1988), from pages 311–334. Reprinted with permission.

court to grant or withhold standing, and in the case of *mandamus* he will not be able to proceed. There may be certain constitutional norms, such as the requirements for distribution of constituencies or of periodic elections, in which no individual would be regarded as having a sufficient interest in such judicial review. There may be issues, such as the validity of the federal spending power when used in areas of provincial legislative juris-diction, or the propriety of constitutional amending procedures, where no individual could persuade a court to grant him standing.

It must be recognized, however, that if the recent trend continues with respect to the discretionary grant of standing in declaratory actions for judicial review, the resort to references to overcome standing problems in constitutional cases may be of marginal importance.

As well as permitting initial judicial review where it would not other-wise be available, a reference may be used to obtain the opinion of a higher court where an appeal would not lie. It is improbable that this precise type of situation would arise now with respect to an appeal from the highest court of a province to the Supreme Court of Canada. Since 1949 the Su-preme Court Act has permitted appeals without limitation in any matter where either the provincial appellate court or the Supreme Court gives leave. In a constitutional case, leave would no doubt be forthcoming from either court. Yet the reference will still be a good substitute for an appeal in some cases. In some provinces there may be situations where an appeal to the highest court is not available, and a reference may be used. Or the parties to the original litigation may not wish to carry a case to the Court of Appeal or the Supreme Court and the provincial or federal Attorney-General may be powerless to do so. There is also the possibility that the courts may refuse leave to appeal a case which the Government feels should be appealed. While the Government's power should not be used lightly in such circumstances, the court could be forced by a reference to deal with the issue on which they had refused leave to appeal. Or a reference could be used instead of an appeal to raise related issues not involved in the lower court.

In cases where judicial review will be ultimately possible through pri-vate litigation, a reference may nevertheless be desirable to hasten the process. To facilitate public or private planning it may be very valuable to have a judicial opinion in advance with respect to the legality of a particu-lar course of action. For example, the Government may wish to have clarified the constitutionality of a nation-wide unemployment insurance scheme or a marketing scheme before establishing elaborate machinery for its operation. A vivid example of this kind of situation may be found in *Reference re Anti-Inflation Act.* In order to move swiftly to combat a high rate of inflation, Parliament had passed this Act on December 15, 1975, effective October 14, 1975, directly imposing wage and price controls in the federal public and private sectors, and providing for the imposition of similar controls in the provincial sector where any province entered into an agreement to have those controls apply along with federal administration thereof. All provinces except Quebec entered into such agreements and Quebec established parallel controls. Questions were soon raised as to the validity of the federal law, and its application by agreement to the Ontario provincial domain was being challenged in an action commenced in the courts of that province. Other cases were contemplated elsewhere in Canada. Since the application of the law would disrupt a myriad of transactions throughout the country, it was urgent that the constitutional position be clarified. It was referred to the Supreme Court on March 11, 1976, argued on May 31–June 4, 1976, and judgment was given on July 12, 1976, generally upholding the validity of these arrangements. Thus within seven months of the passage of the Act a definitive ruling of the highest court had been obtained as to its validity. The disruptive effect of continuing uncertainty, and the probability of much longer delays before all the issues would otherwise have reached the Supreme Court by ordinary appeal, made the reference device a valuable means of clarifying the situation.

It may be important to businessmen to know under which level of Government they are to operate, and speed of clarification of this issue may be useful in encouraging economic development. This justification has been used, for example, in connection with references to the courts to seek judicial opinions on questions of jurisdiction and ownership over offshore resources.

There will also be situations where speedy determination is more of a necessity than a convenience. Emergency conditions such as war make it imperative that the Government be assured at once of the validity of proposed action. For example, if it wishes to create a regulatory system to ensure the maintenance of vital supplies and the prevention of waste, it cannot afford the luxury of waiting for chance litigation to uphold or strike down the scheme.

A reference may also provide relief where a private citizen would not find it convenient to take a constitutional case to the higher courts. A litigant may have grave doubts about the validity of a statute applied against him, but it may be less expensive for him to drop his objection than to carry the case to an appeal. Yet such a statute applied similarly to dozens or hundreds of people may collectively cause great expense or injustice. In addition, various lower courts may hold conflicting views as to the validity of the law, some upholding it and others deeming it invalid. If no affected individual is prepared to undertake the expense and trouble of appeal, the enforcement of the statute will fall into chaos and the law itself into discredit. A reference to an appellate court may provide the authoritative decision required to restore order. If the statute is held invalid, numerous citizens will be relieved from compliance with legislation which it was not practical for them to contest individually.

With respect to issues which the courts usually regard as non-justiciable, a reference might be used to permit a judicial determination. There are obviously many non-justiciable issues where the decision ought not to be made by the judiciary, in any form of procedure, because a policy determination is required and there are no objective criteria for guidance. But there are other areas, such as the propriety of parliamentary procedure, where pre-established norms are available for application. It is not certain that a court would review a federal statute on the basis that it was passed by a procedure not in accordance with the Constitution Act. Yet the directions of the Act in this regard are as clear as those of sections 91 and 92 which the courts constantly apply.

Finally, references provide a flexible means for each level of Government to challenge the constitutional authority of the other level of Government. The federal Government was given this power in another form through the disallowance procedure. But federal disallowance of provincial legislation on the sole grounds that it was *ultra vires* fell into disfavour and by 1935 was expressly abandoned. Even where the power was exercised on this ground, it was common for the Federal Government first to refer the question of validity to the Supreme Court and be guided by its advice. The reference is now the principal means for the Government of Canada to challenge the validity of provincial legislation. It may of course refer such legislation on its own initiative or at the request of the province concerned. Equally, the provinces may challenge the validity of federal legislation or even a parliamentary resolution by referring it to a provincial court, in this way ensuring that it will ultimately reach the highest tribunals. In Ontario, the Attorney-General may, in the alternative, seek a declaration that an Act of Parliament is invalid, but presumably the reference procedure would be speedier.

The essential advantage of the reference system thus appears to be facilitation of judicial review. In some cases it makes the impossible possible, in others it speeds the process where time is of the essence. To those for whom enforced judicial activism poses no threat, the constitutional reference may appear as an unmixed benefit. But it is also essential to consider some of the problems which arise out of its use.

Disadvantages

Two principal disadvantages of references can be identified: they may foster abstract jurisprudence because they require an opinion from the court without the benefit of an adequate factual context; and they may cause the court to decide issues which are not really justiciable because Governments are seemingly unlimited in the questions they can refer. These difficulties flow from the very nature of references: that is, they do not arise out of a specific controversy between parties where legal rights are in issue.

The first problem mentioned, the lack of an adequate factual basis, has been thought not only to hinder sound characterization of laws, but also to lead more frequently to a finding of invalidity.

The suspicion that they favour findings of invalidity cannot be clearly confirmed on a statistical basis. A survey of leading constitutional cases from

1867 through 1986, those reaching the highest tribunal available, either the Privy Council or the Supreme Court, shows that the results in the courts for each level of Government were not dramatically different as between references and ordinary litigation. Of cases involving provincial competence, in 51 references provincial authority was upheld in 24 cases and found lacking in 27 cases—a failure rate of about 53 percent. In ordinary litigation, in 164 cases the provinces succeeded in 102 and lost in 61, a failure rate of about 37 percent. For the federal authority, in 42 references there was a finding of invalidity in 13 cases, a loss rate of about 31 percent whereas the loss rate in ordinary litigation was 18 of 82 cases, or about 22 percent. So the contrasts are far from marked as between results achieved in references and ordinary litigation. The statistical results are unreliable because of the relatively small numbers and the probable existence of other factors involved as between references and litigation and as between federal and provincial results.

It is interesting, however, to look at some of the most abstract and influential reference decisions in our constitutional history to understand the nature of this problem. One need only look at a few examples. In the 1916 *Reference re Insurance Act* the Supreme Court was asked for an opinion as to the validity of certain sections of the federal Insurance Act, 1910. This legislation required the federal registration of insurance companies before they could carry on business. It was broad enough to cover provincially incorporated companies carrying on business in Canada outside the province of incorporation. A majority of the Supreme Court confined itself to an exercise in semantics, holding that the federal power to regulate "trade and commerce" could not include "a trade." The insurance business was regarded as "a trade," hence not susceptible to federal control. One of the dissenting judges, Davies J., took a more functional approach. He took judicial notice of the national significance of the insurance business, the mobility of insured persons, and the possible national repercussions of the failure of a major company. This enabled him to find that the business of insurance was clearly a matter of national trade and commerce. But the Privy Council on appeal sided with the majority below, Viscount Haldane at his dogmatic best holding that

> ... it must now be taken that the authority to legislate for the regulation of trade and commerce does not extend to the regulation by a licensing system of a particular trade in which Canadians would otherwise be free to engage in the provinces.

Here was a reference involving the bare question, "Are sections 40 and 70 of the 'Insurance Act, 1910,' or any or what part or parts of the said sections, *ultra vires* of the Parliament of Canada?" No factual information was included with the reference, nor apparently was any otherwise presented to the court. Without consideration of the factual context in which the legislation would operate, the majority of the Supreme Court and the Privy Council set aside the legislation on a conceptual analysis of the word "trade." The net result was to bar the Parliament of Canada from regulating businesses which were interprovincial in scope, because their operations could be analytically dismembered into a collection of "particular trades" carried on in particular provinces. . . .

. . . This examination of a few major reference decisions of historic importance illustrates their potential for creating abstract jurisprudence. There are, however, several mitigating factors which should be recognized in assessing the merits of the reference system by this standard.

First it should be recognized that while such decisions were conceptual rather than functional, this was also true of contemporary decisions in normal litigation. There were many concrete cases where facts were probably available but not relied on. In defence of the Privy Council decisions of this period, whether on references or in litigation, it has been argued that, whatever their economic validity, they were politically realistic.

Second, there are situations where there is arguably no need for a factual study of legislative effect or administrative action. This arises where the issue is solely that of an interpretation of a section of the constitution where no legislation is involved and no official action is being questioned, and where the court is prepared to make a decision based on the text and its history without resort to policy considerations. These cases will be rare, and the decision therein may be of limited use. But occasionally they will be valuable, where the issue in question is sufficiently narrow. For example in *Edwards v. A.G. Can.* the question was whether the word "persons" in section 24 of the B.N.A. Act included women, thus making the latter eligible for appointment to the Senate. The answer turned completely on internal evidence in the Act. The effect of each possible interpretation was readily apparent. . . .

. . . Third, the remedy for abstract reference decisions should not be total abandonment of this sometimes useful device, but rather a more selective use of it accompanied by adequate fact-introduction. . . . It has been demonstrated that the Supreme Court has led the way in emphasizing the importance of facts in references and the trend appears to be for counsel to meet these judicial expectations. What we are seeing in reality is a rather unsteady movement from the conceptual jurisprudence so beloved by the Judicial Committee and its followers to a more functional jurisprudence in which facts are all important. Therefore much of this particular problem traditionally associated with the reference process may disappear, although the inherent nature of the device is a reminder that constant care must be exercised in its use. There should be a careful framing of the questions so that issues may be raised as precisely as possible. Courts should refuse to answer questions which are too general or which require a factual context if none is provided. They should also avoid answering questions not clearly included in the reference order. If these principles are faithfully applied in reference cases, there will be far less complaint of abstractness.

The second major problem with references noted above is that they may call upon a court to answer questions that are not justiciable. Reference statutes at both the federal and provincial level allow Governments to refer any "matter" to the courts. This would appear on its face to include any question not only of law, but also of politics, science, or taste. It was held, however, by a majority of seven in the Supreme Court in the *Re Resolution to Amend the Constitution* that such a provincial statute

> . . . is wide enough to saddle the respective courts with the determination of questions which may not be justiciable and there is no doubt that those courts, and this Court on appeal, have a discretion to refuse to answer such questions.

Given the lack of a clear separation of powers in our system it is perhaps not surprising that the court did not on that occasion deny itself the right to decide non-justiciable questions but only asserted a power to decline to do so at its discretion. It is encouraging to know that the courts should not feel obliged to decide questions which functionally belong elsewhere. But at the same time it must be noted that, having asserted the right to refuse to answer, the court in this same case proceeded to answer questions posed by provincial Governments to their courts and appealed to the Supreme Court as to the existence and nature of a political convention concerning the use of legal powers.

While Legislatures have thus authorized Governments to refer non-justiciable questions to the courts, normally they do not do so nor, it is submitted, should they do so if they wish to protect the courts from undue political controversy and resulting hazards to their legitimacy. The federal Government has in fact articulated such a principle in the course of resisting pressures for references to the Supreme Court.

When governments do not exercise self-restraint in this respect, it is open to the courts to do so and to decline to decide such issues. When these safeguards are not employed, the reference system does thrust the courts into the decision of non-justiciable issues that may in the long term impair their effectiveness.

Lesser criticisms of the reference system include that of possible interference with private rights. Judges have occasionally hesitated to answer a referred question because, though worded generally, it may include issues on which the rights of specific individuals may turn. It is thought unfair to render such decisions where individuals who may be seriously affected are not represented before the court. As previously noted, this criticism appears specious for the same may be said of almost any decision. . . .

The real fault lies, not in the initial reference decision having possible implications for private individuals, but rather in the misplaced fidelity with which such decisions are subsequently followed. This is part of the broader complaint that reference decisions have generally been given undue precedential value. In other words, what were originally intended to be opinions only have been treated as judgments.

When the Supreme Court Act was amended in 1891, reference opinions were described as "advisory only." This was soon ignored and the Privy Council and Supreme Court expressly followed the decisions in earlier federal references with undiscriminating zeal. Not until 1957, after the "advisory only" provision had actually been dropped from the Supreme Court Act did the Supreme Court suggest the possibility that it would ignore earlier reference decisions, even those of the Judicial Committee. It then stated that it was not bound by a decision of the Judicial Committee rendered in a reference involving some of the same issues and parties now before it in a concrete case. It may be noted, however, that this was *obiter dicta*, for the Supreme Court accepted the opinion of the Privy Council.

It is to be hoped nevertheless that this judicial declaration of independence will not be forgotten. Uncritical following of reference decisions brings discredit on the whole reference system. The rendering of opinions on hypothetical questions or on issues affecting private rights would create few problems if they were not subsequently treated as conclusive. An opinion on an abstract question should be regarded as of limited value, valid only in relation to the assumptions and facts on which it was rendered. . . .

Combined with the abandonment of *stare decisis* with respect to reference opinions, there should be a more discriminating use of such opinions when invoked for persuasive purposes. In analyzing what a reference actually "decided," the opinion should be carefully examined in relation to the precise hypotheses put to the court and the facts, if any, before it. Such analysis may reveal that the opinion decided very little, in which case it ought not to be an embarrassment in subsequent cases.

In sum, it is suggested that if references have created premature or overly broad precedents, the fault lies more in judicial practice than in the reference system. Judicial reform would remove the substance of this complaint.

Conclusion

The controversy over references is really an aspect of the larger controversy with respect to the role of the judiciary in interpreting and applying the constitution. Judicial activists will generally approve of a system which overcomes obstacles to judicial review. Those who take a more restricted view of the role of the judiciary will see it as a hazardous procedure, burdening the courts with hypothetical questions and producing premature decisions with mischievous consequences.

On balance the case for the use of references seems more supportable. If one accepts the courts as the best arbiters of constitutional rules, one should favour a system which facilitates judicial review. There are some situations where a reference will be justified in the interests of speed, clarification for the benefit of many individuals who would not readily be able to seek judicial review, or the elimination of technical barriers to bringing actions or taking appeals.

Several caveats must be entered, however. In the first place, some of the justifications for the use of references have been attenuated by developments of the last decade. The obstacles to standing for individuals to seek declarations on constitutional issues, the nearest substitute for a reference, have largely disappeared. With almost universal legal aid for the needy and numerous special interest groups able to undertake or support litigation, Government initiatives by way of a constitutional reference are now not as necessary to ensure judicial review. At the same time the development of a more functional jurisprudence with greater emphasis on the factual context tends to militate against the use of the reference which often lacks factual substance. So although there is still a role for the reference, it has been somewhat reduced by events.

Where there are reasons for resorting to a reference, Governments should still avoid doing so if the issue to be referred is not justiciable in the sense that it is one better left to another branch of Government or one which lacks objective criteria for its determination. The principal danger to be avoided here is the reference of essentially a political issue to the courts: where there are few, if any, genuinely legal criteria to which courts can resort for a rationale for their decision, they may be perceived as making a political judgment which may impair their long-term credibility.

Once the decision is taken to refer a constitutional question, then care should be taken in its framing so that the issues are precisely defined. The referring Government and counsel on all sides should make every effort to ensure that all relevant facts are placed before the court.

As for the courts, they should be prepared to refuse answers to questions that are non-justiciable, or too vague to be effectively answered. They should have regard to gleaning all relevant evidence, including an active resort to judicial notice. They should also examine critically earlier opinions and be prepared to disregard or distinguish those which were too general, too vague, or too abstract.

Even a carefully constructed reference system must play a secondary role in judicial review, however. A decision based on complete facts and real issues is to be preferred to one based on incomplete facts, or hypothetical problems, and a binding authority is likely to be more reliable than an advisory opinion. Thus, if other circumstances are equal and judicial review through a concrete case is feasible, it should be preferred. The reference should be seen as a useful supplement to our judicial review system, but one to be resorted to with caution and perhaps, in the future, with diminishing frequency. The second century of Confederation has so far seen a sharply reduced rate of references in comparison to the volume of ordinary constitutional litigation, and this trend is likely to continue.

6.2

MINISTER OF JUSTICE OF CANADA v. BOROWSKI
Supreme Court of Canada (1981)

LASKIN, C.J C.(dissenting): This appeal, which is here by leave of this Court given on terms as to costs, arises out of a taxpayer's action brought in the Court of Queen's Bench of Saskatchewan. The purpose of the action was to obtain a declaration against the appellants, the Minister of Justice of Canada and the Minister of Finance of Canada, that the so-called abortion provisions of Criminal Code, s. 251(4), (5) and (6) are inoperative as offending ss. 1(a) and 2(e) and (g) of the Canadian Bill of Rights and that any expenditure of public money to support therapeutic abortions under the aforesaid provisions of the Criminal Code is consequently illegal. Issue was taken by the defendants appellants as to the jurisdiction of the Court of Queen's Bench to entertain the action. . . . In their statement of defence, the defendants also challenged the standing of the plaintiff to maintain the action, regardless, apparently, of the appropriateness of the forum.

I start with the proposition that, as a general rule, it is not open to a person, simply because he is a citizen and a taxpayer or is either the one or the other, to invoke the jurisdiction of a competent Court to obtain a ruling on the interpretation or application of legislation or on its validity, when that person is not either directly affected by the legislation or is not threatened by sanction for an alleged violation of the legislation. Mere distaste has never been a ground upon which to seek the assistance of a Court. Unless the legislation itself provides for a challenge to its meaning or application or validity by any citizen or taxpayer, the prevailing policy is that a challenger must show some special interest in the operation of the legislation beyond the general interest that is common to all members of the relevant society. This is especially true of the criminal law. For example, however passionately a person may believe that it is wrong to provide for compulsory breathalyzer tests or wrong to make mere possession of marijuana an offence against the criminal law, the Courts are not open to such a believer, not himself or herself charged or even threatened with a charge, to seek a declaration against the enforcement of such criminal laws.

The *rationale* of this policy is based on the purpose served by Courts. They are dispute-resolving tribunals, established to determine contested rights or claims between or against persons or to determine their penal or criminal liability when charged with offences prosecuted by agents of the Crown. Courts do not normally deal with purely hypothetical matters where no concrete legal issues are involved, where there is no *lis* that engages their processes or where they are asked to answer questions in the abstract merely to satisfy a person's curiosity or perhaps his or her obsessiveness with a perceived injustice in the existing law. Special legislative provisions for references to the Courts to answer particular questions (which may be of a hypothetical nature) give that authority to Governments alone and not to citizens or taxpayers. Merely because a Government may refuse a citizen's or taxpayer's request to refer to the Courts a question of interest to the taxpayer does not *per se* create a right in the citizen or taxpayer to invoke the Court's process on his or her own, or by way of a class action on behalf of all citizens or taxpayers with the same interest.

There are exceptions to the general rule and to the policy. One of the earliest recognized has been a municipal taxpayer action to restrain an allegedly illegal municipal expenditure. . . . An explanation of this exception is that it involved a public right to see that municipal expenditures were lawfully made, being expenditures which were limited by considerations that do not apply to a Province or to Canada. No municipal taxpayer could raise a *lis* in the ordinary sense or court a penalty or other sanction in respect of an allegedly illegal municipal expenditure and, hence, unless a taxpayer action was permitted, the illegality would go unchallenged and unchallengeable.

In the provincial and federal field, the issue of an illegal, or perhaps unconstitutional, expenditure would not likely arise *per se* but, in the main, only (as is alleged in this case) in connection with the operation of challenged legislation: the challenge to the expenditure would thus depend on the outcome of the challenge to the legislation.

Another exception (but a more limited one in view of the discretion associated with it) is shown in the judgment of this Court in *Thorson* v. *A.G. Can. et al. (No. 2)* (1974). . . . That case involved a taxpayer's class action to obtain a declaration of the invalidity of the Official Languages Act, now R.S.C. 1970, c. 0-2, and of the illegality of the appropriation of money to administer it. It was clear that a justiciable question was raised to the claim of invalidity, namely, whether Parliament had respected the limits of its legislative authority under the British North America Act, 1867. Again, the Official Languages Act was not a regulatory type of statute nor a penal one but rather, uniquely, a declaratory and directory statute, a statute which created no offences and imposed no penalties. Unless, therefore, a citizen or taxpayer action was permitted to question its validity, there would be no way in which its validity could be tested unless the federal Attorney-General did so through a reference and a request to this end had been denied. . . .

. . . There is, in this respect, in the permissive provisions of s. 251(4), (5) and (6), some similarity perhaps to the directory features of the legislation in the *Thorson* case. However, these provisions are part of a scheme which embraces sanctions as well, and I do not find the similarity to be sufficient to put the legislation here on the same level as the statute involved in the

Thorson case. Indeed, to borrow from the words of this Court in the *Thorson* case, the present case is not one where all members of the public are affected alike. This, in my view, is a central consideration in the exercise of the Court's discretion against giving standing here to the plaintiff respondent.

It is contended on the plaintiff's behalf that if he cannot bring himself within the Thorson case, his position as to standing is as strong as that of the respondent in this Court's follow-up decision to *Thorson* in *Nova Scotia Board of Censors* v. *McNeil* (1975). . . . That was also a case where a taxpayer action challenging the validity of legislation, provincial legislation in that case, was held to be maintainable. . . . The Theatres and Amusements Act of Nova Scotia, whose validity was challenged in the *McNeil* case, was a regulatory statute directed to film exchanges, theatre owners and cinematograph operators and apprentices. It also provided for the appointment of a Board, empowered to permit or prohibit the use or exhibition in Nova Scotia, for public entertainment, of any film or any performance in any theatre. Licensing regulations were provided for in respect of theatres and film exchanges, in respect of cinematograph operators and apprentices and in respect of theatre performances. Unfettered discretion to suspend or revoke any licence was vested in the Board. It had, to put it shortly, complete control over the exhibition of films and over theatres in the Province. Although there was a statutory right of appeal to the Lieutenant-Governor in Council, it was not open to a member of the public.

The Nova Scotia Courts, before whom the question of standing came, and this Court on appeal construed the challenged statute as involving members of the public in so far as the Board had the power to determine what members of the public were entitled to view in theatres and other places of public entertainment. This Court assessed the matter as follows:

> Since the issue of validity does not fall for determination here and, indeed, has not even been argued in relation to the question of standing I would not, in this case, go beyond the tentative conclusion that there is an arguable case under the terms of the challenged legislation that members of the Nova Scotia public are directly affected in what they may view in a Nova Scotia theatre, albeit there is a more direct effect on the business enterprises which are regulated by the legislation. The challenged legislation does not appear to me to be legislation directed only to the regulation of operators and film distributors. It strikes at the members of the public in one of its central aspects.

> In my view, this is enough, in the light of the fact that there appears to be no other way, practically speaking, to subject the challenged Act to judicial review, to support the claim of the respondent to have the discretion of the Court exercised in his favour to give him standing.

This passage underlines at least one important difference between the situation in *McNeil* and the present case. In *McNeil*, the plaintiff could legitimately complain (on this Court's construction of the challenged statute) that he was a person within its terms who was being deprived of a right to view a film because of an allegedly unconstitutional exercise of legislative and administrative power. In the present case, there is no deprivation under or by reason of the challenged legislation of which the plaintiff can complain. In short, the plaintiff here is not in the same position under the legislation which he challenges as was McNeil in his case. There he was a person within the compass of the enactment that he was challenging; the plaintiff is outside the Criminal Code provisions that he is attacking.

I am of the opinion that the plaintiff in this case cannot bring himself within the *McNeil* case nor within the *Thorson* case, so far as concerns the character of the legislation involved here as compared with the legislation in those cases. . . . My reason for distinguishing the legislative situation is that here there are persons with an interest in the operation of s.251(4), (5) and (6) who might challenge it as offending the Canadian Bill of Rights. I refer to doctors and to hospitals, both having a clearer interest in the operation of s.251(4), (5) and (6) than does the plaintiff. Husbands who might object to their pregnant wives seeking therapeutic abortions also have a clearer interest. It may be that in their case there would be a dilemma, having regard to the inexorable progress of a pregnancy. . . . In principle, however, this should not be preclusive; the point will have been decided at the instance of a person having an interest and not at that of a person having no interest other than as a citizen and taxpayer.

. . . The present case lacks concreteness despite the fact that it raises a highly charged issue. Moreover, it appears to me that to permit the issue to be litigated in as abstract a manner as would be the case in having the plaintiff alone carry it against two Ministers of the Crown would hardly do justice to it, absent even any intervenors who might, with the same obsessiveness on the opposite side of the issue, argue for the valid operation of the challenged provisions. Even accepting, as is probable, that if standing was accorded to the plaintiff, other persons with an opposite point of view might seek to intervene and would be allowed to do so, the result would be to set up a battle between parties who do not have a direct interest, [and] to wage it in a judicial arena.

I would hold, therefore, that not only has the plaintiff failed to establish any judicially cognizable interest in the matter he raises but, on any view of this case, the discretion of the Court should be exercised to deny him standing. It follows that his action should be dismissed. . . .

MARTLAND, J. (for the Court):

. . . The issue raised is a difficult and important one, involving the question as to whether the human rights declared in the Canadian Bill of Rights protect a human foetus.

In his statement of claim, the respondent states that he is a citizen of Canada and a taxpayer to the Government of Canada. He goes on to state in the following paragraphs of the statement of claim:

3. On February 20, 1969 the Plaintiff was elected by the voters of the provincial constituency of Thompson, Manitoba to represent them in the Legislative Assembly of Manitoba, a position he maintained until June 28, 1973. In his capacity as taxpayer, elected representative of the people in the Legislative Assembly, a member of the governing party in the legislative Assembly of Manitoba and Minister of and adviser to Her Majesty the Queen in Right of the Province of Manitoba, the Plaintiff has continuously promoted and defended the rights of individual human foetuses, including their right to life.

4. The Plaintiff has canvassed all practicable means to invoke action on the part of both Provincial and Federal Governments to repeal or to impugn the validity of the abortion sections of the *Criminal Law Amendment Act*, Statutes of Canada, 1968-69, chapter 38, section 18, (now section 251, subsections (4), (5) and (6), of the *Criminal Code of Canada*, hereinafter referred to as "the abortion section of the *Criminal Code*") and to cease and desist from spending public funds to abort and destroy individual human foetuses.

5. The steps taken by the Plaintiff included:

    (a) His resignation, on or about September 5, 1971, *inter alia*, because as Minister of and adviser to Her Majesty the Queen, he "could not be a party to, or accept, child-destroying legislation in which we (are) involved";

    (b) His address in the Legislative Assembly of Manitoba, on May 4, 1973, opposing adoption of the budget presented by the Provincial Treasurer that proposed to finance the abortion and destruction of individual human foetuses by the expenditure of public funds;

    (c) His continuous objection over a term of years to payment of his personal income tax to the Federal Government to protest its expenditures of public moneys collected by personal income taxes, to finance and to promote the abortion and destruction of individual human foetuses, and his conviction and sentence to terms in jail for his stand;

    (d) His personal correspondence with the Premier and Cabinet of the Province of Manitoba, with the Prime Minister of Canada and with Members of his Cabinet including the Minister of Justice, the Minister of Finance, and the Solicitor-General of Canada requesting that they take appropriate legal action to protect the rights of individual human foetuses;

    (e) His request addressed to the Official Guardian of Manitoba in the year 1977, to take legal proceedings on behalf of individual human foetuses to prevent their abortion and destruction, and to protect their right to life.

In every instance, the efforts of the Plaintiff to move public officials to impugn the validity of the abortion provisions referred to in paragraph 4 hereof by judicial proceedings met with negative response. No one undertook to subject these provisions, of great public importance, to judicial review.

For the purpose of these proceedings, all of these statements must be accepted as being true. . . .

In both the *Thorson* and *McNeil* cases, the challenge to the legislation in question was founded upon their alleged constitutional invalidity. In the present case, the challenge is based upon the operation of the Canadian Bill of Rights. I agree with the view expressed by the Chief Justice that no distinction should be made between a declaratory action to obtain a decision on validity under the British North America Act, 1867 and a declaratory action to obtain a decision on the operative effect in the face of the Canadian Bill of Rights.

The legislation under attack here is not declaratory or directory as in the case of the Official Languages Act nor is it regulatory as in the case of the Theatres and Amusements Act. It is exculpatory in nature. It provides that in certain specified circumstances conduct which otherwise would be criminal is permissible. It does not impose duties, but instead provides exemption from criminal liability. That being so, it is difficult to find any class of person directly affected or exceptionally prejudiced by it who would have cause to attack the legislation.

Doctors who perform therapeutic abortions are protected by the legislation and would have no reason to attack it. Doctors who do not perform therapeutic abortions have no direct interest to protect by attacking it, and, consequently, an attack by a doctor in that category would be no different from that made by any other concerned citizen. The same thing applies to hospitals. A hospital which appoints a therapeutic abortion committee has no reason to attack the legislation. A hospital which does not appoint such a committee has no direct reason to attack the legislation.

There is no reason why a pregnant woman desirous of obtaining an abortion should challenge the legislation which is for her benefit. The husband of a pregnant wife who desires to prevent an abortion which she desires may be said to be directly affected by the legislation in issue in the sense that by reason of the legislation she might obtain a certificate permitting the abortion if her continued pregnancy would be likely to endanger her life or health and thus prevent the abortion from constituting a crime. However, the possibility of the husband bringing proceedings to attack the legislation is illusory. The progress of the pregnancy would not await the inevitable lengthy lapse of time involved in Court proceedings leading to a final judgment. The abortion would have occurred, or a child would have been born long before the case had been finally terminated, perhaps in this Court.

The legislation proposed to be attacked has direct impact upon the unborn human foetuses whose existences may be terminated by legalized abortions. They obviously cannot be parties to proceedings in Court and yet the issue as to the scope of the Canadian Bill of Rights in the protection of the human right to life is a matter of considerable importance. There is no reasonable way in which that issue can be brought into Court unless proceedings are launched by some interested citizen.

In the light of the *Thorson* and *McNeil* cases, it is my opinion that the respondent should be recognized as having legal standing to continue with his action. In the *Thorson* case, the plaintiff, as an interested citizen, challenged the constitutional validity of the Official Languages Act. The legislation did not directly affect him, save in his position as a taxpayer. He had sought, without avail, to have the constitutional issue raised by other means. He was recognized to have status. The position is the same in the present case. The respondent is a concerned citizen and a taxpayer. He has sought unsuccessfully to have the issue determined by other means.

In the *McNeil* case, the plaintiff was concerned about censorship of films in Nova Scotia. He had sought by other means to have the validity of the Theatres and Amusements Act tested, but without success. In that case there were other classes of persons directly affected by the legislation who might have challenged it. None the less, he was recognized as having legal standing because it also affected the rights of the public. The position of the respondent in this case is at least as strong. There are in this case no persons directly affected who could effectively challenge the legislation.

I interpret these cases as deciding that to establish status as a plaintiff in a suit seeking a declaration that legislation is invalid, if there is a serious issue as to its invalidity, a person need only to show that he is affected by it directly or that he has a genuine interest as a citizen in the validity of the legislation and that there is no other reasonable and effective manner in which the issue may be brought before the Court. In my opinion, the respondent has met this test and should be permitted to proceed with his action.

6.3

BOROWSKI v. ATTORNEY-GENERAL OF CANADA

Supreme Court of Canada (1989)
[Intervenors: Interfaith Coalition on the Rights and Wellbeing of Women and Children, REAL Women of Canada, and Women's Legal Education and Action Fund (LEAF)]

The judgment of the Court was delivered by SOPINKA J.: This appeal by leave of this Court is from the Saskatchewan Court of Appeal, [1987] which affirmed the judgment at trial of Matheson J. of the Saskatchewan Court of Queen's Bench, [1984] dismissing the action of the plaintiff (appellant in this Court). In the courts below, the plaintiff attacked the validity of subss. (4), (5) and (6) of s. 251 of the Criminal Code, relating to abortion, on the ground that they contravened protected rights of the foetus. Subsequent to the decision of the Saskatchewan Court of Appeal but by the time the appeal reached this Court, s. 251, including the subsections under attack in this action, had been struck down in *R. v. Morgentaler* [1988].

From this state of the proceedings it was apparent at the commencement of this appeal that a serious issue existed as to whether the appeal was moot. As well, it appeared questionable whether the appellant had lost his standing and, indeed, whether the matter was justiciable. The Court therefore called upon counsel to address these issues as a preliminary matter. Upon completion of these submissions, we reserved decision on these issues and heard the argument of the merits of the appeal so that we could dispose of the whole appeal without recalling the parties for argument should we decide that, notwithstanding the preliminary issues, the appeal should proceed.

In view of the conclusion that I have reached, it is necessary to deal with the issues of mootness and standing only. Since it is a change in the nature of these proceedings which gives rise to these issues, a review of the history of the action is necessary. . . .

[Ed. note: Justice Sopinka recounts Borowski's first trip to the Supreme Court, culminating in the 1981 decision granting standing. (See Reading 6.2) Sopinka notes that Borowski's claim was amended in 1983 to include claims based on the 1982 Charter of Rights. Borowski's Charter challenge to section 251 was rejected by the Saskatchewan Court of Queen's Bench (1983) and the Saskatchewan Court of Appeal (1987).]

On January 28, 1988, after leave to appeal was granted, this Court decided *R. v. Morgentaler (No. 2), supra*, in which all of s. 251 was found to violate s. 7 of the Charter. Accordingly, s. 251 in its entirety was struck down.

In July of 1988 in light of this Court's judgment in *R. v. Morgentaler (No. 2), supra*, counsel on behalf of the Attorney-General of Canada applied to adjourn the hearing of the appeal. The respondent argued that the issue was now moot as s. 251 of the Criminal Code had been nullified and that the two remaining constitutional questions (numbers 1 and 3), which simply ask whether a child *en ventre sa mère* is entitled to the protection of ss. 7 and 15 of the Charter respectively, are not severable from the other, now moot, constitutional questions. Although the respondent claimed the matter was moot, no application to quash the appeal was made. The application to adjourn the hearing of the appeal was denied by Chief Justice Dickson on July 19, 1988, leaving it to the Court to address the mootness issue.

I am of the opinion that the appeal should be dismissed on the grounds that: (1) Mr. Borowski's case has been rendered moot and (2) he has lost his standing. When s. 251 was struck down, the basis of the action disappeared. The initial prayer for relief was no longer applicable. The foundation for standing upon which the previous decision of this Court was based also disappeared.

Mootness

The doctrine of mootness is an aspect of a general policy or practice that a court may decline to decide a case which raises merely a hypothetical or abstract question. The general principle applies when the decision of the court will not have the effect of resolving some controversy which affects or may affect the rights of the parties. If the decision of the court will have no practical effect on such rights, the court will decline to decide the case. This essential ingredient must be present not only when the action or proceeding is commenced but at the time when the court is called upon to reach a decision. Accordingly if, subsequent to the initiation of the action or proceeding, events occur which affect the relationship of the parties so that no present live controversy exists which affects the rights of the parties, the case is said to be moot. The general policy or practice is enforced in moot cases unless the court exercises its discretion to depart from its policy or practice. The relevant factors relating to the exercise of the court's discretion are discussed hereinafter.

The approach in recent cases involves a two-step analysis. First, it is necessary to determine whether the required tangible and concrete dispute has disappeared and the issues have become academic. Second, if the response to the first question is affirmative, it is necessary to decide if the court should exercise its discretion to hear the case. The cases do not always make it clear whether the term "moot" applies to cases that do not present a concrete controversy or whether the term applies only to such of those cases as the court declines to hear. In the interest of clarity, I consider that a case is moot if it fails to meet the "live controversy" test. A court may nonetheless elect to address a moot issue if the circumstances warrant.

When is an Appeal Moot?—The Authorities

The first stage in the analysis requires a consideration of whether there remains a live controversy. The controversy may disappear rendering an issue moot due to a variety of reasons, some of which are discussed below.

In *The King ex rel. Tolfree v. Clark,* [1944] this Court refused to grant leave to appeal to applicants seeking a judgment excluding the respondents from sitting and exercising their functions as Members of the Ontario Legislative Assembly. However, the Legislative Assembly had been dissolved prior to the hearing before this Court. As a result, Duff C.J., on behalf of the Court, held at p. 72:

> It is one of those cases where, the state of facts to which the proceedings in the lower Courts related and upon which they were founded having ceased to exist, the sub-stratum of the litigation has disappeared. In accordance with well-settled principle, therefore, the appeal could not properly be entertained.

A challenged municipal by-law was repealed prior to a hearing in *Moir v. The Corporation of the Village of Huntingdon* (1891), leading to a conclusion that the appealing party had no actual interest and that a decision could have no effect on the parties except as to costs. Similarly, in a fact situation analogous to this appeal, the Privy Council refused to address the constitutionality of challenged legislation where two statutes in question were repealed prior to the hearing: *Attorney-General for Alberta v. Attorney-General for Canada*, [1939] A.C. 117 (P.C.). . . .

The particular circumstances of the parties to an action may also eliminate the tangible nature of a dispute. The death of parties challenging the validity of a parole revocation hearing (*Re Cadeddu and The Queen* (1983)) and a speeding ticket (*R. v. Mercure*, [1988]) ended any concrete controversy between the parties.

As well, the inapplicability of a statute to the party challenging the legislation renders a dispute moot: *Law Society of Upper Canada v. Skapinker*, [1984]. This is similar to those situations in which an appeal from a criminal conviction is seen as moot where the accused has fulfilled his sentence prior to an appeal: *Re Maltby v. Attorney-General of Saskatchewan* (1984).

The issue of mootness has arisen more frequently in American jurisprudence, and there, the doctrine is more fully developed. This may be due in part to the constitutional requirement, contained in s. 2(1) of Article III of the American Constitution, that there exist a "case or controversy." . . .

However, despite the constitutional enshrinement of the principle, the mootness doctrine has its roots in common law principles similar to those in Canada. . . .

The American jurisprudence indicates a similar willingness to consider the merits of an action in some circumstances even when the controversy is no longer concrete and tangible. The rule that abstract, hypothetical or contingent questions will not be heard is not absolute. . . .

Is This Appeal Moot?

In my opinion, there is no longer a live controversy or concrete dispute as the substratum of Mr. Borowski's appeal has disappeared. The basis for the action was a challenge relating to the constitutionality of subss. (4), (5) and (6) of s. 251. That section of the Criminal Code having been struck down in *R. v. Morgentaler (No. 2)*, the raison d'être of the action has disappeared. None of the relief claimed in the statement of claim is relevant. Three of the five constitutional questions that were set explicitly concern s. 251 and are no longer applicable. The remaining two questions addressing the scope of ss. 7 and 15 Charter rights are not severable from the context of the original challenge to s. 251. These questions were only ancillary to the central issue of the alleged unconstitutionality of the abortion provisions of the Criminal Code. They were a mere step in the process of measuring the impugned provision against the Charter.

In any event, this Court is not bound by the wording of any constitutional question which is stated. Nor may the question be used to transform an appeal into a reference. . . .

By reason of the foregoing, I conclude that this appeal is moot. It is necessary, therefore, to move to the second stage of the analysis by examining the basis upon which this Court should exercise its discretion either to hear or to decline to hear this appeal.

The Exercise of Discretion: Relevant Criteria

Since the discretion which is exercised relates to the enforcement of a policy or practice of the Court, it is not surprising that a neat set of criteria does not emerge from an examination of the cases. This same problem in the United States led commentators there to remark that "the law is a morass of inconsistent or unrelated theories, and cogent judicial generalization is sorely needed." I would add that more than a cogent generalization is probably undesirable because an exhaustive list would unduly fetter the court's discretion in future cases. It is, however, a discretion to be judicially exercised with due regard for established principles.

In formulating guidelines for the exercise of discretion in departing from a usual practice, it is instructive to examine its underlying rationalia. To the extent that a particular foundation for the practice is either absent or its presence tenuous, the reason for its enforcement disappears or diminishes.

The first rationale for the policy and practice referred to above is that a court's competence to resolve legal disputes is rooted in the adversary system. The requirement of an adversarial context is a fundamental tenet of our legal system and helps guarantee that issues are well and fully argued by parties who have a stake in the outcome. It is apparent that this requirement may be satisfied if, despite the cessation of a live controversy, the necessary adversarial relationships will nevertheless prevail. For example, although the litigant bringing the proceeding may no longer have a direct interest in the outcome, there may be collateral consequences of the outcome that will provide the necessary adversarial context. . . .

In the United States, the role of collateral consequences in the exercise of discretion to hear a case is well recognized. . . . The principle that collateral consequences of an already completed cause of action warrant appellate review was most clearly stated in *Sibron v. New York*. The appellant in that case appealed his conviction although his sentence had already been completed. At p. 55, Warren C.J. stated:

> . . . most criminal convictions do in fact entail adverse collateral legal consequences. The mere "possibility" that this will be the case is enough to preserve a criminal case from ending "ignominiously in the limbo of mootness."

In Canada, the cases of *Law Society of Upper Canada v. Skapinker, supra,* and *R. v. Mercure, supra,* illustrate the workings of this principle. In those cases, the presence of intervenors who had a stake in the outcome supplied the necessary adversarial context to enable the Court to hear the cases.

The second broad rationale on which the mootness doctrine is based is the concern for judicial economy. It is an unfortunate reality that there is a need to ration scarce judicial resources among competing claimants. The fact that in this Court the number of live controversies in respect of which leave is granted is a small percentage of those that are refused is sufficient to highlight this observation. The concern for judicial economy as a factor in the decision not to hear moot cases will be answered if the special circumstances of the case make it worthwhile to apply scarce judicial resources to resolve it.

The concern for conserving judicial resources is partially answered in cases that have become moot if the court's decision will have some practical effect on the rights of the parties notwithstanding that it will not have the effect of determining the controversy which gave rise to the action. . . .

Similarly an expenditure of judicial resources is considered warranted in cases which although moot are of a recurring nature but brief duration. In order to ensure that an important question which might independently evade review be heard by the court, the mootness doctrine is not applied strictly. This was the situation in *International Brotherhood of Electrical Workers, Local Union 2085 v. Winnipeg Builders' Exchange, supra*. The issue was the validity of an interlocutory injunction prohibiting certain strike action. By the time the case reached this Court the strike had been settled. This is the usual result of the operation of a temporary injunction in labour cases. If the point was ever to be tested, it almost had to be in a case that was moot. Accordingly, this Court exercised its discretion to hear the case. . . .

There also exists a rather ill-defined basis for justifying the deployment of judicial resources in cases which raise an issue of public importance of which a resolution is in the public interest. The economics of judicial involvement are weighed against the social cost of continued uncertainty in the law. See *Minister of Manpower and Immigration v. Hardayal* [1978]. Locke J. alluded to this in *Vic Restaurants Inc. v. City of Montreal, supra*, at p. 91: "The question, as I have said, is one of general public interest to municipal institutions throughout Canada."

This was the basis for the exercise of this Court's discretion in the *Re Opposition by Quebec to a Resolution to amend the Constitution*, [1982] 2 S.C.R. 793. The question of the constitutionality of the patriation of the Constitution had, in effect, been rendered moot by the occurrence of the event. The Court stated at p. 806:

> While this Court retains its discretion to entertain or not to entertain an appeal as of right where the issue has become moot, it may, in the exercise of its discretion, take into consideration the importance of the constitutional issue determined by a court of appeal judgment which would remain unreviewed by this Court.

> In the circumstances of this case, it appears desirable that the constitutional question be answered in order to dispel any doubt over it and it accordingly will be answered.

Patently, the mere presence of an issue of national importance in an appeal which is otherwise moot is insufficient. National importance is a requirement for all cases before this Court except with respect to appeals as of right; the latter, Parliament has apparently deemed to be in a category of sufficient importance to be heard here. There must, therefore, be the additional ingredient of social cost in leaving the matter undecided. This factor appears to have weighed heavily in the decision of the majority of this Court in *Forget v. Quebec (Attorney-General)* [1988].

The third underlying rationale of the mootness doctrine is the need for the Court to demonstrate a measure of awareness of its proper law-making function. The Court must be sensitive to its role as the adjudicative branch in our political framework. Pronouncing judgments in the absence of a dispute affecting the rights of the parties may be viewed as intruding into the role of the legislative branch. This need to maintain some flexibility in this regard has been more clearly identified in the United States where mootness is one aspect of a larger concept of justiciability. . . .

In my opinion, it is also one of the three basic purposes of the mootness doctrine in Canada and a most important factor in this case. I generally agree with the following statement in P. Macklem and E. Gertner: "Re Skapinker and Mootness Doctrine" (1984), 6 *Supreme Court L. Rev.* 369, at p. 373:

> The latter function of the mootness doctrine—political flexibility—can be understood as the added degree of flexibility, in an allegedly moot dispute, in the law-making function of the Court. The mootness doctrine permits the Court not to hear a case on the ground that there no longer exists a dispute between the parties, notwithstanding the fact that it is of the opinion that it is a matter of public importance. Though related to the factor of judicial economy, insofar as it implies a determination of whether deciding the case will lead to unnecessary precedent, political flexibility enables the Court to be sensitive to its role within the Canadian constitutional framework, and at the same time reflects the degree to which the Court can control the development of the law.

I prefer, however, not to use the term "political flexibility" in order to avoid confusion with the political questions doctrine. In considering the exercise of its discretion to hear a moot case, the Court should be sensitive to the extent that it may be departing from its traditional role.

In exercising its discretion in an appeal which is moot, the Court should consider the extent to which each of the three basic rationalia for enforcement of the mootness doctrine is present. This is not to suggest that it is a mechanical process. The principles identified above may not all support the same conclusion. The presence of one or two of the factors may be overborne by the absence of the third, and vice versa.

Exercise of Discretion: Application of Criteria

Applying these criteria to this appeal, I have little or no concern about the absence of an adversarial relationship. The appeal was fully argued with as much zeal and dedication on both sides as if the matter were not moot.

The second factor to be considered is the need to promote judicial economy. Counsel for the appellant argued that an extensive record had been developed in the courts below which would be wasted if the case were not decided on the merits. Although there is some merit in this position, the same can be said for most cases that come to this Court. . . .

None of the other factors that I have canvassed which justify the application of judicial resources is applicable. This is not a case where a decision will have practical side effects on the rights of the parties. Nor is it a case that is capable of repetition, yet evasive of review. It will almost certainly be possible to bring the case before the Court within a specific legislative context or possibly in review of specific governmental action. In addition, an abstract pronouncement on foetal rights in this case would not necessarily promote judicial economy as it is very conceivable that the courts will be asked to examine specific legislation or governmental action in any event. Therefore, while I express no opinion as to foetal rights, it is far from clear that a decision on the merits will obviate the necessity for future repetitious litigation.

Moreover, while it raises a question of great public importance, this is not a case in which it is in the public interest to address the merits in order to settle the state of the law. The appellant is asking for an interpretation of ss. 7 and 15 of the Canadian Charter of Rights and Freedoms at large. In a legislative context any rights of the foetus could be considered or at least balanced against the rights of women guaranteed by s. 7. See *R. v. Morgentaler (No. 2), supra, per* Dickson C.J.C., at p. 75; *per* Beetz J. at pp. 122-23; *per* Wilson J. at pp. 181-82. A pronouncement in favour of the appellant's position that a foetus is protected by s. 7 from the date of conception would decide the issue out of its proper context. Doctors and hospitals would be left to speculate as to how to apply such a ruling consistently with a woman's rights under s. 7. During argument the question was posed to counsel for REAL Women as to what a hospital would do with a pregnant woman who required an abortion to save her life in the face of a ruling in favour of the appellant's position. The answer was that doctors and legislators would have to stay up at night to decide how to deal with the situation. This state of uncertainty would clearly not be in the public interest. Instead of rendering the law certain, a decision favourable to the appellant would have the opposite effect.

Even if I were disposed in favour of the appellant in respect to the first two factors which I have canvassed, I would decline to exercise a discretion in favour of deciding this appeal on the basis of the third. One element of this third factor is the need to demonstrate some sensitivity to the effectiveness or efficacy of judicial intervention. The need for courts to exercise some flexibility in the application of the mootness doctrine requires more than a consideration of the importance of the subject matter. The appellant is requesting a legal opinion on the interpretation of the Canadian Charter of Rights and Freedoms in the absence of legislation or other governmental action which would otherwise bring the Charter into play. This is something only the government may do. What the appellant seeks is to turn this appeal into a private reference. Indeed, he is not seeking to have decided the same question that was the subject of his action. That question related to the validity of s. 251 of the Criminal Code. He now wishes to ask a question that relates to the Canadian Charter of Rights and Freedoms alone. This is not a request to decide a moot question but to decide a different, abstract question. To accede to this request would intrude on the right of the executive to order a reference and pre-empt a possible decision of Parliament by dictating the form of legislation it should enact. To do so would be a marked departure from the traditional role of the Court.

Having decided that this appeal is moot, I would decline to exercise the Court's discretion to decide it on the merits.

Standing

. . . There have been two significant changes in the nature of this action since this Court granted Mr. Borowski standing in 1981. The claim is now premised primarily upon an alleged right of a foetus to life and equality pursuant to ss. 7 and 15 of the Canadian Charter of Rights and Freedoms. Secondly, by holding s. 251 to be of no force and effect in *R. v. Morgentaler (No. 2), supra*, the legislative context of this claim has disappeared.

By virtue of ss. 24(1) of the Charter and 52(1) of the Constitution Act, 1982, there are two possible means of gaining standing under the Charter. Section 24(1) provides:

24. (1) Anyone whose rights or freedoms as guaranteed by this *Charter*, have been infringed or denied may apply to a court of competent jurisdiction to obtain such remedy as the court considers appropriate and just in the circumstances.

In my opinion s. 24(1) cannot be relied upon here as a basis for standing. Section 24(1) clearly requires an infringement or denial of a Charter-based right. The appellant's claim does not meet this requirement as he alleges that the rights of a foetus, not his own rights, have been violated.

Nor can s. 52(1) of the Constitution Act, 1982 be invoked to extend standing to Mr. Borowski. Section 52(1) reads:

52. (1) The Constitution of Canada is the supreme law of Canada, and any law that is inconsistent with the provisions of the Constitution is, to the extent of the inconsistency, of no force or effect.

This section offers an alternative means of securing standing based on the *Thorson, McNeil, Borowski* trilogy expansion of the doctrine.

Nevertheless, in the same manner that the "standing trilogy" referred to above was based on a challenge to specific legislation, so too a challenge based on s. 52(1) of the Constitution Act, 1982 is restricted to litigants who challenge a law or governmental action pursuant to power granted by law. The appellant in this appeal challenges neither "a law" nor any governmental action so as to engage the provisions of the Charter. What the appellant now seeks is a naked interpretation of two provisions of the Charter. This would require the Court to answer a purely abstract question which would in effect sanction a private reference. In my opinion, the original basis for the appellant's standing is gone and the appellant lacks standing to pursue this appeal.

Accordingly, the appeal is dismissed on both the grounds that it is moot and that the appellant lacks standing to continue the appeal. . . .

6.4

OPERATION DISMANTLE v. THE QUEEN
Supreme Court of Canada (1985)

DICKSON J.: [Estey, McIntyre, Chouinard and Lamer JJ. concurring] This case arises out of the appellants' challenge under s. 7 of the Canadian Charter of Rights and Freedoms to the decision of the Federal Cabinet to permit the testing of the cruise missile by the United State of America in Canadian territory. The issue that must be addressed is whether the appellants' Statement of Claim should be struck out, before the trial, as disclosing no reasonable cause of action. In their Statement of Claim, the appellants seek: (i) a declaration that the decision to permit the testing of the cruise missile is unconstitutional; (ii) injunctive relief to prohibit the testing; and (iii) damages. Cattanach J. of the Federal Court, Trial Division, refused the respondents' motion to strike. The Federal Court of Appeal unanimously allowed the respondents' appeal, struck out the Statement of Claim and dismissed the appellants' action.

The facts and procedural history of this case are fully set out and discussed in the reasons for judgment of Madame Justice Wilson. I agree with Madame Justice Wilson that the appellants' Statement of Claim should be struck out and this appeal dismissed. I have reach this conclusion, however, on the basis of reasons which differ somewhat from those of Madame Justice Wilson.

In my opinion, if the appellants are to be entitled to proceed to trial, their Statement of Claim must disclose facts, which, if taken as true, would show that the action of the Canadian Government could cause an infringement of their rights under s. 7 of the Charter. I have concluded that the causal link between the actions of the Canadian Government, and the alleged violation of appellants' rights under the Charter is simply too uncertain, speculative and hypothetical to sustain a cause of action. Thus, although decisions of the Federal Cabinet are reviewable by the courts under the Charter, and the government bears a general duty to act in accordance with the Charter's dictates, no duty is imposed on the Canadian Government by s. 7 of the Charter to refrain from permitting the testing of the cruise missile. . . .

(a) Application of the Charter to Cabinet Decisions

I agree with Madame Justice Wilson that Cabinet decisions fall under s. 32(1)(a) of the Charter and are therefore reviewable in the courts and subject to judicial scrutiny for compatability with the Constitution. I have no doubt that the executive branch of the Canadian Government is duty bound to act in accordance with the dictates of the Charter. Specifically, the Cabinet has a duty to act in a manner consistent with the right to life, liberty and security of the person and the right not to be deprived thereof except in accordance with the principles of fundamental justice.

(b) The Absence of a Duty on the Government to Refrain from Allowing Testing

I do not believe the action impugned in the present case can be characterized as contrary to the duties of the executive under the *Charter*. Section 7 of the Charter cannot reasonably be read as imposing a duty on the government to refrain from those acts which *might* lead to consequences that deprive or threaten to deprive individuals of their life and security of the person. A duty of the Federal Cabinet cannot arise on the basis of speculation and hypothesis about possible effects of government action. Such a duty only arises, in my view, where it can be said that a deprivation of life and security of the person could be proven to result from the impugned government act.

Justiciability

The approach which I have taken is not based on the concept of justiciability. I agree in substance with Madame Justice Wilson's discussion of justiciability and her conclusion that the doctrine is founded upon a concern with the appropriate role of the courts as the forum for the resolution of different types of disputes. I have no doubt that disputes of a political or foreign policy nature may be properly cognizable by the courts. My concerns in the present case focus on the impossibility of the Court finding, on the basis of evidence, the connection, alleged by the appellants, between the duty of the government to act in accordance with the Charter of Rights and Freedoms and the violation of their rights under s. 7. As stated above, I do not believe the alleged violation—namely, the increased threat of nuclear war—could ever be sufficiently linked as a factual matter to the acknowledged duty of the Government to respect s. 7 of the Charter.

Section 52 of the Constitution Act, 1982 and Section 1 of the Charter

I would like to note that nothing in these reasons should be taken as the adoption of the view that the reference to "laws" in s. 52 of the Charter is confined to statutes, regulations and the common law. It may well be that if the supremacy of the Constitution expressed in s. 52 is to be meaningful, then all acts taken pursuant to powers granted by law will fall within s. 52. . . .

I would accordingly dismiss the appeal with costs.

WILSON J.: [Concurring with reasons]
. . .

Is the Government's Decision Reviewable?

(a) The royal prerogative

The respondents submit that at common law the authority to make international agreements (such as the one made with the United States to permit the testing) is a matter which falls within the prerogative power of the Crown and that both at common law and by s. 15 of the Constitution Act, 1867 the same is true of decisions relating to national defence. They further submit that since by s. 32(1)(a) the Charter applies "to the Parliament and government of Canada in respect of all matters within the authority of Parliament," the Charter's application must, so far as the government is concerned, be restricted to the exercise of powers which derive directly from statute. It cannot, therefore, apply to an exercise of the royal prerogative which is a source of power existing independently of Parliament. . . . Since there is no reason in principle to distinguish between Cabinet decisions made pursuant to statutory authority and those made in the exercise of the royal prerogative, and since the former clearly fall within the ambit of the Charter, I conclude that the latter do so also.

(b) Non-Justiciability

LeDain and Ryan JJ. in the Federal Court of Appeal were of the opinion that the issues involved in this case are inherently non-justiciable, either because the question whether testing the cruise missile increases the risk of nuclear war is not susceptible of proof and hence is not triable (*per* Ryan

J.) or because answering that question involves factors which are either inaccessible to a court or are of a nature which a court is incapable of evaluating (*per* LeDain J.). To the extent that this objection to the appellants' case rests on the inherent evidentiary difficulties which would obviously confront any attempt to prove the appellants' allegations of fact, I do not think it can be sustained. It might well be that, if the issues were allowed to go to trial, the appellants would lose simply by reason of their not having been able to establish the factual basis of their claim but that does not seem to me to be a reason for striking the case out at this preliminary stage. It is trite law that on a motion to strike out a Statement of Claim, the plaintiff's allegations of fact are to be taken as having been proved. Accordingly, it is arguable that by dealing with the case as they have done LeDain and Ryan JJ. have, in effect, made a presumption against the appellants which they are not entitled, on a preliminary motion of this kind, to make.

I am not convinced, however, that LeDain and Ryan JJ. were restricting the concept of non-justiciability to difficulties of evidence and proof. Both rely on Lord Radcliffe's judgment in *Chandler v. Director of Public Prosecutions* [1962] 3. All E.R. 142 (H.L.), and especially on the following passage at p. 151:

> The disposition and equipment of the forces and the facilities afforded to allied forces for defence purposes constitute a given fact and it cannot be a matter of proof or finding that the decisions of policy on which they rest are or are not in the country's best interests. I may add that I can think of few issues which represent themselves in less triable form. It would be ingenuous to suppose that the kind of evidence that the appellants wanted to call could make more than a small contribution to its final solution. The facts which they wished to establish might well be admitted: even so, throughout history men have had to run great risk for themselves and others in the hope of attaining objectives which they prize for all. *The more one looks at it, the plainer it becomes, I think, that the question whether it is in the true interests of this country to acquire, retain or house nuclear armaments depends on an infinity of considerations, military and diplomatic, technical, psychological and moral, and of decisions, tentative or final, which are themselves part assessments of fact and part expectations and hopes.* I do not think that there is anything amiss with a legal ruling that does not make this issue a matter for judge or jury. (Emphasis added)

In my opinion, this passage makes clear that in Lord Radcliffe's view these kinds of issues are to be treated as non-justiciable not simply because of evidentiary difficulties but because they involve moral and political considerations which it is not within the province of the courts to assess. ...

I cannot accept the proposition that difficulties of evidence or proof absolve the Court from making a certain kind of decision if it can be established on other grounds that it has a duty to do so. I think we should focus our attention on whether the courts *should* or *must* rather than on whether they *can* deal with such matters. We should put difficulties of evidence and proof aside and consider whether as a constitutional matter it is appropriate or obligatory for the courts to decide the issue before us. I will return to this question later.

(c) The Political Question Doctrine

It is a well established principle of American constitutional law that there are certain kinds of "political questions" that a court ought to refuse to decide. In *Baker v. Carr* 369 U.S. 186 (1962) at pp. 210–11 Brennan J. discussed the nature of the doctrine in the following terms:

> We have said that "In determining whether a question falls within [the political question] category, the appropriateness under our system of government of attributing finality to the action of the political departments and also the lack of satisfactory criteria for a judicial determination are dominant considerations." *Coleman v. Miller*, 307 U.S. 433, 454–455. The non-justiciability of a political question is primarily a function of the separation of powers. Much confusion results from the capacity of the "political question" label to obscure the need for case-by-case inquiry. Deciding whether a matter has in any measure been committed by the Constitution to another branch of government, or whether the action of that branch exceeds whatever authority has been committed, is itself a delicate exercise in constitutional interpretation, and is a responsibility of this Court as ultimate interpreter of a Constitution.

At p. 217 he said:

> It is apparent that several formulations which vary slightly according to the settings in which the questions arise may describe a political question, although each has one or more elements which identify it as essentially a function of the separation of powers. Prominent on the surface of any case held to involve a political question is found a textually demonstrable constitutional commitment of the issue to a coordinate political department; or a lack of judicially discoverable and manageable standards for resolving it; or the impossibility of deciding without an initial policy determination of a kind clearly for nonjudicial discretion; or the impossibility of a court's undertaking independent resolution without expressing lack of the respect due coordinate branches of government; or an unusual need for unquestioning adherence to a political decision already made; or the potentiality of embarrassment from multifarious pronouncements by various departments on one question.

While one or two of the categories of political question referred to by Brennan J. raise the issue of judicial or institutional competence already referred to, the underlying theme is the separation of powers in the sense of the proper role of the courts vis-à-vis the other branches of government. In this regard it is perhaps noteworthy that a distinction is drawn in the American case law between matters internal to the United States on the one hand and foreign affairs on the other. In the area of foreign affairs the courts are especially deferential to the executive branch of government. . . .

While Brennan J.'s statement, in my view, accurately sums up the reasoning American courts have used in deciding that specific cases did not present questions which were judicially cognizable, I do not think it is particularly helpful in determining when American courts will find that those factors come into play. In cases from *Marbury v. Madison*, 5 U.S. (1 Cranch) 137 (1803) to *United States v. Nixon*, 418 U.S. 683 (1974) the Court has not allowed the "respect due coordinate branches of government" to prevent it from rendering decisions highly embarrassing to those holding executive or legislative office. . . . More recently, commentators such as Tigar ("Judicial Power, the 'Political Question Doctrine' and Foreign Relations," 17 *U.C.L.A. L.R.* 1135 (1970)) and Henkin ("Is there a 'Political Question' Doctrine?", 85 *Yale L.J.* 597 (1976)) have doubted the need for a political questions doctrine at all, arguing that all the cases which were correctly decided can be accounted for in terms of orthodox separation of powers doctrine.

Professor Tigar in his article suggests that the political questions doctrine is not really a doctrine at all but simply "a group of quite different legal rules and principles, each resting in part upon deference to the political branches of government" (p. 1163). He sees Justice Brennan's formulation of the doctrine in *Baker v. Carr* (*supra*) as an "unsatisfactionary effort to rationalize a collection of disparate precedent" (p. 1163).

In the House of Lords in *Chandler* (*supra*), Lord Devlin expressed a similiar reluctance to retreat from traditional techniques in the interpretation of the phrase "purpose prejudicial to the safety or interest of the State . . ." in the Official Secrets Act, 1911. . . .

It seems to me that the point being made by Lord Devlin, as well as by Tigar and Henkin in their writings, is that the courts should not be too eager to relinquish their judicial review function simply because they are called upon to exercise it in relation to weighty matters of state. Equally, however, it is important to realize that judicial review is not the same thing as substitution of the court's opinion on the merits for the opinion of the person or the body to whom discretionary decision-making power has been committed. . . The question before us is not whether the government's defence policy is sound but whether or not it violates the appellants' rights under s. 7 of the Charter of Rights and Freedoms. This is a totally different question. I do not think there can be any doubt that this is a question for the courts. Indeed, s. 24(1) of the Charter, also part of the Constitution, makes it clear that the adjudication of that question is the responsibility of "a court of competent jurisdiction." While the court is entitled to grant such remedy as it "considers appropriate and just in the circumstances," I do not think it is open to it to relinquish its jurisdiction either on the basis that the issue is inherently non-justiciable or that it raises a so-called "political question": . . .

I would conclude, therefore, that if we are to look at the Constitution for the answer to the question whether it is appropriate for the courts to "second guess" the executive on matters of defence, we would conclude that it is not appropriate. However, if what we are being asked to do is to decide whether any particular act of the executive violates the rights of the citizens, then it is not only appropriate that we answer the question; it is our obligation under the Charter to do so.

One or two hypothetical situations will, I believe, illustrate the point. Let us take the case of a person who is being conscripted for service during wartime and has been ordered into battle overseas, all of this pursuant to appropriate legislative and executive authorization. He wishes to challenge his being conscripted and sent overseas as an infringement of his rights under s. 7. It is apparent that his liberty has been constrained and if he is sent into battle, his security of the person and, indeed, his life are put in jeopardy. It seems to me that it would afford the conscriptee a somewhat illusory protection if the validity of his challenge is to be determined by the executive. On the other hand, it does not follow from these facts that the individual's rights under the Charter have been violated. Even if an individual's rights to life and liberty under s. 7 are interpreted at their broadest, it is clear from s. 1 that they are subject to "such reasonable limits prescribed by law as can be demonstrably justified in a free and democratic society." If the Court were of the opinion that conscription during wartime was a "reasonable limit" within the meaning of s. 1, the conscriptee's challenge on the facts as presented would necessarily fail.

By way of contrast, one can envisage a situation in which the government decided to force a particular group to participate in experimental testing of a deadly nerve gas. Although the government might argue that such experiments were an important part of our defence effort, I find it hard to believe that they would survive judicial review under the Charter. . . .

In What Circumstances May a Statement of Claim Seeking Declaratory Relief be Struck Out?

. . . In my view, several of the allegations contained in the Statement of Claim are statements of intangible fact. Some of them invite inferences; others anticipate probable consequences. They may be susceptible to proof by inference from real facts or by expert testimony or "through the application of common sense principles": see *Leyland Shipping Co. v. Norwich Union Fire Insurance Society* [1918] A.C. 350 at p. 363 *per* Lord Dunedin. We may entertain serious doubts that the plaintiffs will be able to prove them by any of these means. It is not, however, the function of the Court at this stage to prejudice that question. I agree with Cattanach J. that the Statement of Claim contains sufficient allegations to raise a justiciable issue. . . .

The law then would appear to be clear. The facts pleaded are to be taken as proved. When so taken, the question is do they disclose a reasonable cause of action, i.e., a cause of action "with some chance of success." . . .

Could the Facts as Alleged Constitute a Violation of s. 7 of the Charter?

Whether or not the facts that are alleged in the appellants' Statement of Claim could constitute a violation of s. 7 is, of course, the question that lies at the heart of this case. If they could not, then the appellants' Statement of

Claim discloses no reasonable cause of action and the appeal must be dismissed. The appellants submit that on its proper construction, s. 7 gives rise to two separate and presumably independent rights, namely the right to life, liberty and security of the person, and the right not to be deprived of such life, liberty and security of the person except in accordance with the principles of fundamental justice. In their submission, therefore, a violation of the principles of fundamental justice would only have to be alleged in relation to a claim based on a violation of the second right. . . .

The appellants' submission, however, touches upon a number of important issues regarding the proper interpretation of s. 7. Even if the section gives rise to a single unequivocal right not to be deprived of life, liberty or security of the person except in accordance with the principles of fundamental justice, there nonetheless remains the question whether fundamental justice is entirely procedural in nature or whether it has a substantive aspect as well. This, in turn, leads to the related question whether there might not be certain deprivations of life, liberty or personal security which could not be justified no matter what procedure was employed to effect them. These are among the most important and difficult questions of interpretation arising under the Charter, but I do not think it is necessary to deal with them in this case. It can, in my opinion, be disposed of without reaching these issues.

In my view, even an independent, substantive right to life, liberty and security of the person cannot be absolute. For example, the right to liberty, which I take to be the right to pursue one's goals free of governmental constraint, must accommodate the corresponding rights of others. The concept of "right" as used in the Charter postulates the inter-relation of individuals in society all of whom have the same right. The aphorism that "A hermit has no need of rights" makes the point. . . .

The concept of "right" as used in the Charter must also, I believe, recognize and take account of the political reality of the modern state. Action by the state or, conversely, inaction by the state will frequently have the effect of decreasing or increasing the risk to the lives or security of its citizens. It may be argued, for example, that the failure of government to limit significantly the speed of traffic on the highways threatens our right to life and security in that it increases the risk of highway accidents. Such conduct, however, would not, in my view, fall within the scope of the right protected by s. 7 of the Charter.

In the same way, the concept of "right" as used in the Charter must take account of the fact that the self-contained political community which comprises the state is faced with at least the possibility, if not the reality, of external threats to both its collective well-being and to the individual well-being of its citizens. In order to protect the community against such threats, it may well be necessary for the state to take steps which incidentally increase the risk to the lives or personal security of some or all of the state's citizens. Such steps, it seems to me, cannot have been contemplated by the draftsman of the Charter as giving rise to violations of s. 7. As John Rawls states in *A Theory of Justice* (1971) at p. 213:

> The government's right to maintain public order and security is . . . a right which the government must have if it is to carry out its duty of impartially supporting the conditions necessary for everyone's pursuit of his interests and living up to his obligations as he understands them.

The rights under the Charter not being absolute, their content or scope must be discerned quite apart from any limitation sought to be imposed upon them by the government under s. 1. . . .

It is not necessary to accept the restrictive interpretation advanced by Pratte J., which would limit s. 7 to protection against arbitrary arrest or detention, in order to agree that the central concern of the section is direct impingement by government upon the life, liberty and personal security of individual citizens. At the very least, it seems to me, there must be a strong presumption that governmental action which concerns the relations of the state with other states, and which is therefore not directed at any member of the immediate political community, was never intended to be caught by s. 7 even though such action may have the incidental effect of increasing the risk of death or injury that individuals generally have to face.

I agree with LeDain J. that the essence of the appellants' case is the claim that permitting the cruise missile to be tested in Canada will increase the risk of nuclear war. But even accepting this allegation of fact as true, which as I have already said I think we must do on a motion to strike, it is my opinion for the reasons given above that this state of affairs could not constitute a breach of s. 7. Moreover, I do not see how one can distinguish in a principled way between this particular risk and any other danger to which the government's action vis-à-vis other states might incidentally subject its citizens. A declaration of war, for example, almost certainly increases the risk to most citizens of death or injury. Acceptance of the appellants' submissions, it seems to me, would mean that any such declaration would also have to be regarded as a violation of s. 7. I cannot think that that could be a proper interpretation of the Charter.

This is not to say that every governmental action that is purportedly taken in furtherance of national defence would be beyond the reach of s. 7. If, for example, testing the cruise missile posed a direct threat to some specific segment of the populace—as, for example, if it were being tested with live warheads—I think that might well raise different considerations. A court might find that that constituted a violation of s. 7 and it might then be up to the government to try to establish that testing the cruise with live warheads was justified under s. 1 of the Charter. Section 1, in my opinion, is the uniquely Canadian mechanism through which the courts are to determine the justiciability of particular issues that come before it. It embodies through its reference to a free and democratic society the essential features of our constitution including the separation of powers, responsible government and the rule of law. It obviates the need for a "political questions" doctrine and permits the court to deal with what might be termed "prudential" considerations in a principled way without renouncing its constitutional and mandated responsibility for judicial review. It is not, however, called into operation here since the facts alleged in the Statement of Claim, even if they could be shown to be true, could not in my opinion constitute a violation of s. 7. . . .

In summary, it seems to me that the issues raised on the appeal are to be disposed of as follows:

1) The government's decision to permit testing of the cruise missile in Canada cannot escape judicial review on any of the grounds advanced;

2) The Statement of Claim may be struck out if the facts as alleged do not disclose a reasonable cause of action. . . .

3) Taking the facts alleged as proven, they could not constitute a violation of s. 7 of the Charter so as to give rise to a cause of action under s. 24(1);

4) The appellants could not establish their status to sue at common law for declaratory relief for the same reason that they could not establish a cause of action under s. 24(1); and

5) The appellants could not establish a cause of action for declaratory relief under s. 52(1) since the facts as alleged could not constitute a violation of s. 7 and therefore no inconsistency with the provisions of the Constitution could be established.

I would accordingly dismiss the appeal with costs.

6.5

INTERVENTIONS AND THE PUBLIC INTEREST
A. Alan Borovoy

July 17, 1984
TO: Supreme Court of Canada
RE: Interventions in Public Interest Litigation
FROM: Canadian Civil Liberties Association
             per A. Alan Borovoy (General Counsel)

In the era of the Charter of Rights and Freedoms, the issue of participation in the cases before the Supreme Court of Canada has acquired a new significance. It is likely that a great many Charter cases will be determining issues of fundamental principle affecting the very nature of Canadian democracy. Moreover, the impact of the Court's judgments will be far less vulnerable than ever to abridgement or amendment at the hands of the political authorities. It is significant that in the more than 200 years of American history, the political authorities in that country have enacted fewer than 25 amendments to their Constitution. In many ways, the new Canadian Constitution will be even harder than its American counterpart to amend at the political level.

While it is possible, of course, for Parliament and the provincial legislatures to invoke the override in section 33 against the application of key Charter provisions, that is likely to be a relatively rare event outside the Province of Quebec. As a result of the widespread public participation in the Joint Parliamentary hearings and their aftermath, the Charter has acquired enormous prestige throughout much of the country. In every jurisdiction apart from Quebec, the ousting of Charter protections will entail a substantial political price. During all the years that such overrides have existed in both the federal Bill of Rights and a number of its provincial counterparts, they have been invoked in a relatively infinitesimal number of cases—and, so far, not once to overcome the impact of a judicial decision.

The effective transfer of so much power to the judiciary raises issues of fundamental fairness. Since the entire community will be increasingly affected for substantially longer periods by the decisions of the Court, larger sectors of the community should be able to participate in the process which produces those decisions. It is simply not fair to limit such participation on the basis of the coincidence of which parties litigate first. Public respect for both the Charter and the Court will require a more inclusive process.

The peculiar position of government serves to strengthen these considerations. In many cases, government will be a party. In criminal matters, for example, the federal or a provincial government will be prosecuting. But, even when they have not been parties, governments seeking to intervene have usually been allowed to do so. The frequency of such involvement in Charter cases will enable governments in a systematic way to put before the Court their various theories of what the Charter provisions mean. This gives the governments a special advantage over every other interest in the community. The party against which a government is litigating in any particular case might well not have any interest in addressing the long-term implications of whatever interpretation may be at issue. Indeed, the limited interest of a particular party might be better served by making certain tactical concessions to the government's long-term point of view. If no one else but the immediate parties regularly participate, the Court and the community will likely be deprived of countervailing long-term theories for interpreting the Charter.

Suppose, for example, section 7 were to become an issue in the context of a criminal case. It may well be in the interest of the prosecuting government to argue for the narrowest interpretation possible. The accused, on the other hand, might wish to argue that the concluding words in the section must have a substantive as well as a procedural impact. He might consider it tactically wise, therefore, to concede to the government that the word "liberty" is restricted to *physical* freedom. But there may be a number of free enterprise groups which would agree with the substantive interpretation of the concluding words but would argue that 'liberty' includes freedom of contract. There may also be some social democratic groups which would argue that "liberty" means something more than physical freedom and something less than contractual freedom but would urge nevertheless that the concluding words should receive a procedural construction only.

Or, suppose the leaders of a pressure group were charged with a breach of the Election Expenses Act. The accused might believe that it is in their interest to argue that no such restriction on interest group advocacy is compatible with the Charter's protections for "freedom of expression." On the other hand, it might be in the interests of the prosecuting government to argue that its goal of financial equity during election campaigns constitutes a reasonable limit on Charter freedoms and the restriction at issue is the only way to achieve such a goal. But there may be other groups in the community which differ with both litigants. They may believe that the government's goal is legitimate but not its means. They may wish to demonstrate to the Court how a less restrictive means could adequately achieve the same goal.

The examples go on and on. Suffice it, for present purposes, to acknowledge how both the quality of jurisprudence and the appearance of fairness can be undermined by restricting participation in court to the principal litigants.

In this regard, it would be helpful to consult the experience of the common law democracy which has developed the most sophisticated adjudication in the area of constitutional rights—the United States. Both at the appellate level and in the U.S. Supreme Court, there has been a growing receptivity to the participation of third parties. While *amicus* counsel are rarely heard during the course of oral argument, they are frequently permitted to file written briefs. In the Supreme Court, the inclusion of an amicus brief is virtually automatic on the written consent of the principal parties. And, if such consent is not forthcoming, there are special provisions for obtaining leave directly from the Court itself.

What is most significant about the American situation, however, is not simply the rules but also the actual experience. With the passage of time, the rules have been applied in an increasingly liberal fashion. Indeed, in cases of crucial public importance, the principal parties rarely object to amicus participation. There is reason to believe that the attitude of the Court itself paved the way for this development.

As long ago as 1952, the late Mr. Justice Felix Frankfurter criticized the U.S. Solicitor-General for refusing too often to grant such consent.

For the Solicitor-General to withhold consent automatically in order to enable this Court to determine for itself the propriety of each application is to throw upon the Court a responsibility that the Court has put upon all litigants, including the government. . . .

Two years later, a similar observation was made by the late Mr. Justice Hugo Black.

Most of the cases before this Court involve matters that affect far more people than the immediate record parties. I think the public interest and judicial administration would be better served by relaxing rather than tightening the rule against *amicus curiae* briefs.

A recent survey illustrates the growing liberalism of the American practice. During the period from 1941 until 1952, fewer than 19 percent of the cases in the U.S. Supreme Court involved the participation of *amicus curiae*. From 1953 until 1966, this participation rose to 23.8 percent. And, during the period 1970 until 1980, *amicus* involvement had increased to more than 53 percent of all cases in the U.S. Supreme Court. These statistics produced the following remark in a journal of legal scholarship.

It seems fair enough to conclude . . . that *amicus curiae* participation by private groups is now the norm rather than the exception.

When the kind of cases is examined, the statistics acquire an even greater significance, During the period between 1970 and 1980, there was *amicus* participation in more than 62 percent of the cases involving church-state issues. The free press cases recorded more than 66 percent *amicus* participation and in race discrimination matters, such involvement had climbed to more than 67 percent. Union cases revealed a remarkable 87.2 percent participation by *amicus curiae*. Moreover, there is also a growing number of cases in which there is *multiple amicus* participation. In those cases during the 1970–1980 period which featured the involvement of at least one *amicus* brief, as many as 26.7 percent included the participation of four or more such interventions. In the famous *Bakke* case involving affirmative action for blacks in university enrolment, there were more than 50 *amicus* briefs.

The American experience suggests also that these *amicus* briefs have played a vital role in a number of important cases. Consider, for example, the brief of the American Civil Liberties Union in the famous case of *Miranda v. Arizona*. Samuel Dash, counsel to the Senate Watergate Committee and Director of the Institute of Criminal Law and Procedure at Georgetown University Law Centre, made the following comment.

Perhaps the most striking lesson to learn from these materials is the role an *amicus* brief can play in shaping a majority opinion, even without oral argument. Undoubtedly, the most effective presentation to the Court was the *amicus* brief of the American Civil Liberties Union. . . . It is clear that it presented a conceptual legal and structural formulation that is practically identical to the majority opinion—even as to use of language in various passages of the opinion. Also, it is from this brief and its appendix that the Court apparently draws its lengthy discussion of the contents of leading and popular police interrogation manuals. Both the ACLU brief and the Court explain that resort to the manuals is necessary because of the absence of information on what actually goes on in the privacy of police interrogation rooms.

In the case of *Mapp v. Ohio*, the issue was whether unlawfully seized evidence could be introduced against an accused in a state trial. Although such evidence had for some years been rendered inadmissible in federal prosecutions, the 1949 case of *Wolf v. Colorado* had held that this principle did not extend to state prosecutions. Although counsel for the accused in *Mapp* attempted to distinguish the Wolf case, an *amicus* brief filed by the ACLU urged the court to over-rule the earlier case. The majority of the court accepted the ACLU argument and over-ruled *Wolf*. As lawyer Ernest Angel commented in a subsequent law journal article, "the *amicus* scored an important victory."

In *Poe v. Ullman* a majority of the U.S. Supreme Court held that a prohibition on the distribution of birth control information was not justiciable. But the dissent of Mr. Justice Douglas argued that the law was unconstitutional on a ground raised by the *amicus* brief of the ACLU—the right to privacy. Four years later, in *Griswold v. Connecticut*, the Court majority adopted a position closer to that of Justice Douglas and the ACLU. According to Ernest Angel,

The case is noteworthy for the . . . . invalidation of the statute . . . *for the part played by the amicus* and for the formulation of a right of privacy doctrine. (emphasis ours)

There is some suggestion that the *amicus* brief of the National Association for Advancement of Coloured People played an important role in the case of *Furman v. Georgia* where the U.S. Supreme Court held that the death penalty constituted "cruel and unusual punishment" in the circumstances at issue. In the famous *Bakke* case, the Court included as an appendix to its judgment the joint *amicus* brief which had been filed by Columbia, Harvard, Stanford, and Pennsylvania Universities.

While such non-party interventions have not arisen often in Canada, they are nevertheless rooted in our legal history. Apart from those few cases where it may have been considered equitable to accommodate certain private interests, most of the interventions in recent Canadian history have been prompted by broad and fundamental issues of public policy. As far back as 1945, for example, in the case of *Re Drummond Wren*, the Supreme Court of Ontario permitted the Canadian Jewish Congress to argue, *amicus curiae*, that racially restrictive covenants were not legally enforceable. During the last decade, however, the number of such interventions has increased significantly. On at least a dozen occasions during this period, Canadian tribunals have permitted the involvement of strangers to the litigation. In a good number of these cases, the matter at issue concerned an interpretation of our quasi-constitutional statute, the Canadian Bill of Rights. Whatever considerations have motivated this and other courts to permit such interventions in cases involving the Bill of Rights, the argument will be even stronger when the document at issue is the new Canadian Charter.

It is our view, therefore, that the Supreme Court of Canada should develop a rule on interventions which broadens the effective right of constituencies other than the immediate parties to participate in important public interest litigation. We recognize, of course, that these considerations must be balanced against the concerns of efficiency. Among the consequences accompanying the advent of the Charter is an increased workload for the Supreme Court of Canada. Understandably, therefore, the Court will feel obliged to avoid, where possible, the prospect of unduly long and repetitive hearings. We believe, however, that the valid interests of efficiency can coexist with an expanded role for intervenors.

This objective can be accomplished by permitting a wide latitude for partial interventions, i.e., interventions primarily through written briefs rather than oral argument. A liberal rule for the inclusion of such briefs would broaden the right to participate and permit the judges to obtain an ever expanding amount of assistance without in any way increasing the amount of time allocated for the Court's hearings.

While the practice in the U.S. Supreme Court is a possible model, we believe that some reasonable modifications are in order. Instead of foreclosing almost automatically on the oral participation of intervenors, our Court might adopt the practice of selectively inviting their counsel to appear for the purpose of speaking to whatever limited issues would assist in the disposition of the cases at Bar. From their advance reading of the briefs and factums, the judges could decide which, if any, of the intervenors' counsel they may wish to hear and on what issues. Such invitations to counsel could range from involvement on one or more limited points to virtually full-scale participation in certain special cases. Even at that, the presentations of such counsel could be subject to abridgement at the hearing itself to whatever extent it became evident that they were not contributing significantly beyond what had already been advanced on behalf of the parties. In all of these ways, the Court could still control its processes and prevent any undue prolongation of the oral hearings.

The adoption of this approach should also help to overcome some of the concerns that have been expressed about interventions in criminal cases. To whatever extent there were several interventions on the side of the Crown, it has been said that the situation might look like a "ganging up" on the accused. It will be appreciated, however, that such an appearance is rendered far less likely when the interventions are handled primarily through written briefs rather than oral argument. In any event, such interventions would be addressed, not to the guilt or innocence of a particular accused, but rather to the resolution of a question of law or the interpretation of a section of the Charter. All of these considerations should militate against prohibiting interventions in criminal cases.

Moreover, there is no reason why this approach should not apply equally to the proposed interventions of the various attorneys general. Governmental intervenors are no more likely (and may well be less likely) than non-government intervenors to adopt arguments which are significantly different from those of the immediate parties. Upon meeting whatever liberal threshold test is adopted, government intervenors, like their non-government counterparts, should be able to participate. But they too should do so subject to the rules applying to everyone—usually through partial rather than full intervention.

In the submission of the Canadian Civil Liberties Association, it is essential to continue and expand the role of intervenors before the Supreme Court of Canada. The Charter of Rights and Freedoms has launched a new era in the relationship between the judicial and political processes of this country. Ever since the Joint Parliamentary hearings on the Constitution, there has been a heightened public awareness and concern about Charter developments in particular and public interest law in general. Indeed, one of the consequences of the constitutional deliberations has been a raised public consciousness with respect to a wide spectrum of public law issues. Many of the processes of the Court, therefore, will be the subject of increased scrutiny. Thus, it is more important than ever that those processes conform to public perceptions and expectations of fairness. On the basis of all these considerations, the Canadian Civil Liberties Association respectfully urges the adoption of an approach which is hospitable to non-party interventions in public interest litigation.

6.6

INTERVENORS AND THE CHARTER
Ian Brodie

An intervenor is a person, organization or government department that is not a direct party to a case but receives permission from a court to present its own arguments in that case. Sometimes an intervenor is called an *amicus curiae*, the Latin phrase for "friend of the court." Since the entrenchment of

Adapted from author's M.A. Thesis, Department of Political Science, University of Calgary, 1992. Reprinted with permission.

the Charter of Rights, some Canadian interest groups have become frequent intervenors in important Charter cases that could affect their interests. Since 1983, governments enjoy a right to intervene in constitutional cases at the Supreme Court of Canada, but non-government interest groups must first receive the court's permission to do so. After an initial reluctance, the Supreme Court has become quite receptive toward "public interest" intervenors in its Charter cases.

Before the Charter, interest group rarely intervened in Canadian court cases. Although interest groups sometimes got permission to intervene in reference cases, few interest groups bothered intervening in other cases, and the courts were not enthusiastic about hearing their arguments. The first generally recognized case of an interest group intervening in a Canadian court case was in 1945. In that year, the Canadian Jewish Congress intervened in an Ontario case about racially-restrictive housing agreements. Not until 1963 was there a notable interest group intervention in the Supreme Court of Canada, when the Court agreed to hear the Lord's Day Alliance of Canada in the Bill of Rights Sunday-closing case, *Robertson and Rosetanni v. The Queen*. (The Lord's Day Alliance feared that the government would not enforce their Sunday-closing law with sufficient enthusiasm.)

By contrast, interest groups have frequently participated in U.S. Supreme Court cases as *amici curiae* in recent decades. Interest groups have played prominent roles as *amici curiae* in many of the U.S. Supreme Court's leading cases since the famous 1954 school desegregation case, *Brown v. Board of Education*. In fact, groups like the National Association for the Advancement of Colored People (NAACP) and the American Civil Liberties Union (ACLU) became famous in the 1950s and 1960s because of their litigation in the U.S. Supreme Court. By the 1970s, interest groups intervened in over half of the U.S. Supreme Court's cases and in almost two-thirds of its non-criminal cases. *Amicus* activity reached a record in 1978 when 57 *amici* appeared in the "reverse discrimination" case of *Regents of the University of California v. Bakke*. The Court even appended one of the *amicus curiae* briefs to its decision in this case.

After the Charter had been entrenched in the Canadian constitution, some interest groups and lawyers expected the Supreme Court of Canada to follow the U.S. pattern and open its doors to more interest group intervenors. The Court had started to allow some interest group intervenors during the 1970s. After 1982, both commentators and activists thought that the broader policy impact of Charter cases would push the courts toward hearing the groups that could be affected by their decisions. It was also suggested that the courts would need new types of extrinsic evidence and social facts to make Charter decisions, information that was more likely to be provided by the interest groups that intervened in court cases.

Contrary to these expectations, the Supreme Court instead began to turn away would-be interest group intervenors after the adoption of the

Charter. It appears that the Court was struggling with the new workload of the Charter and it was also temporarily short of judges, so to save time, it began to limit the number of groups it heard. When the Court Registrar asked Chief Justice Laskin whether he might be interested in allowing the noted judicial administration expert, Carl Baar, to intervene in the judicial independence case of *Valente*, in 1983 Laskin fired back a curt memorandum declaring that, "I am not going to let this kind of thing [intervenors] get out of hand. The answer is plainly 'no'." Soon after, the CCLA was denied permission to intervene in such high-profile Charter cases as the *Oakes* case, in which the Supreme Court first laid out a comprehensive approach to interpreting the critical Section 1 "reasonable limits" clause. In 1984, the Court decided not to hear the Seventh-day Adventist Church in the Sunday-closing case, *Big M Drug Mart*. The Court also refused to let the Canadian Labour Congress and other unions intervene in three major Charter cases concerning labour law in 1986.

The Court's refusal to grant intervenor status to so many interest groups provoked vigorous protests from the groups planning to intervene in Charter cases to try to influence their outcome. In 1984, Alan Borovoy, longtime general counsel of the Canadian Civil Liberties Association (CCLA), kicked off this campaign by writing an open brief to the Court that demanded that it hear more interest group intervenors. [Ed. note: See Reading 6.5] In 1986, Ken Swan, a CCLA Vice-President publicly complained that, by refusing to hear interest groups, the Court was losing a valuable opportunity to get some help with its new Charter cases. Other legal commentators and interest group litigators also took up the task of criticizing the Court's sudden coolness toward intervenors. The Supreme Court responded by asking the Canadian Bar Association (CBA) to investigate the entire issue of interest group interventions and recommend a new policy for the Court. A CBA committee heard presentations from the CCLA, LEAF and other public interest litigators before meeting with three of the Court's judges in 1986 to recommend that the Court adopt a more open-door policy towards intervenors.

The Court responded to the CBA report by rewriting its rules on interventions in 1987 and letting many more interest groups intervene in its cases. Since 1987, the Supreme Court has done a complete reversal and rarely refused interest-group requests to intervene, particularly in Charter cases. From 1983 through 1986, the rate of acceptance for requests by non-government groups was less than 50 percent. From 1987 through 1990, the success rate soared to over 90 percent. This change in policy encouraged more groups to intervene. During the four years prior to 1987, there was an average of 19 requests per year. In the four following years, the average jumped to 35. Some groups have been especially successful. LEAF made 11 requests and was accepted 11 times. The CCLA was admitted seven out of eight times, while the Canadian Jewish Council was five for five. REAL Women, a conservative women's group, was four for four.

In sum, the Supreme Court now hears intervenors in approximately as many of its Charter cases (58% of Charter cases in 1990 attracted government and non-government intervenors) as the U.S. Supreme Court hears in its cases (53% of its cases during the 1970s attracted government and non-government *amici*). Commenting on this abandonment of pre-Charter practice, Justice Sopinka recently observed: "It is imperative that all legitimate interests are fully represented." This dramatic change of judicial attitude and the growth in interest group intervenors it has encouraged both testify to the new political role of the Court under the Charter.

6.7

KEY TERMS

Concepts

standing
lis
case or controversy requirement
taxpayer's suit
declaratory judgment
intervenor
moot case
reference
advisory opinion
political questions doctrine
justiciable

Institutions, Events, and Documents

The Supreme Court Act (1875)
Minister of Justice of Canada v. Borowski (1981)
Operation Dismantle v. The Queen (1985)
Borowski v. A.-G. Canada (1989)
Canadian Civil Liberties Association (CCLA)
American Civil Liberties Union (ACLU)

7

Interest Groups and Litigation

The difference between traditional litigation and "litigation designed to elicit policy-making" is that the latter "is designed primarily to promote the interests of a class of persons rather than to correct the wrongs done to a particular litigant."[1] Politically motivated litigation also usually involves interest groups, either as litigants, financial sponsors or as intervenors (*amicus curiae* in U.S.). Prior to the adoption of the Charter, there was a sharp contrast between Canadian and American attitudes and practice with regards to interest group litigation.

In the United States this kind of litigation has become commonplace and accepted. One of the important developments in American law and politics during the past 30 years has been the strategic use of constitutional litigation by organized interest groups to achieve public policy objectives. This new form of political action was successfully pioneered by the National Association for the Advancement of Colored People (NAACP), the leading black civil rights group, in its fight against racial segregation in the American South. Politically stymied in both the national Congress and in the Southern state legislatures, the NAACP turned to the federal courts for help. The success of the NAACP inspired other interest groups to adopt similar strategies to change existing public policies on such issues as capital punishment, abortion, censorship of pornography, and women's rights. Almost all of the most important and most controversial decisions of the American Supreme Court since 1954 have been litigated directly or indirectly by organized interest groups.

By contrast in Canada, interest group use of litigation was rare, a tactic of last resort. This pattern reflected a social consensus that discouraged judicial activism and viewed interest group litigation as somewhat illegitimate. In 1975, Kenneth McNaught, one of Canada's leading historians, concluded that his study of Canadian political trials

---

[1] Jeremy Rabkin, "The Charismatic Constitution," *The Public Interest* 73 (Fall, 1983), p. 42, quoting Aryeh Neier, *Only Judgment: The Limits of Litigation in Social Change* (Middletown, CT: Wesleyan University Press, 1983).

strongly suggests that our judges and lawyers, supported by the press and public opinion, reject any concept of the courts as positive instruments in the political process. In Canada the positive aspects of politics seem more clearly to belong to the political parties, the legislatures, and the press. A corollary of this is that political action outside the party-parliamentary structure tends automatically to be suspect—and not least because it smacks of Americanism.[2]

As if to underscore the accuracy of Professor McNaught's assessment, later that same year the Supreme Court of Canada sent Dr. Henry Morgentaler to jail for performing illegal abortions.

Seven years later, the Charter of Rights was adopted. One of the important questions at the time was whether the Charter would act as a catalyst for litigation as an interest group activity in Canada. After 10 years in "Charterland," the answer to this question is clearly "yes." There has been a veritable surge in interest group litigation since 1982. There were two related but distinct factors that accounted for this change. One was the issue of access, and it depended on the Supreme Court. Would the Court adapt the rules governing standing, mootness, political questions and intervenors to allow interest groups access to the judicial process? The readings in Chapter 6 show that the Court did precisely this. The other factor was the response of the interest groups. The Supreme Court could open the courthouse door, but it could not force interest groups to come in.

In fact, interest groups responded immediately to the adoption of the Charter. Within days, for example, a group styling itself the "Ontario Film and Video Appreciation Society" (OFVAS) filed suit in Toronto challenging the authority of the Ontario Board of Censors. Similarly, Dr. Henry Morgentaler announced his second campaign of civil disobedience against Canada's abortion laws the month the Charter was adopted. Joe Borowski, Morgentaler's perennial adversary, was already in the courts with his pro-life challenge to the same laws, and quickly amended his legal claims to Charter-based arguments.[3] That same year a coalition of "peace groups" went to court to challenge the government's policy to permit the testing of American cruise missiles over Canadian territory. (See Reading 7.4) In 1984, the National Citizens' Coalition, a conservative "public interest" group, successfully challenged the Canada Election Act's restrictions on third-party spending in federal elections. (See Reading 7.5)

While some instances of group use of Charter litigation have been "one-shot affairs," other interest groups have pursued Charter litigation in a more sustained and systematic fashion. This is particularly true of those groups

---

[2] Kenneth McNaught, "Political Trials and the Canadian Political Tradition," in M.L. Friedland, *Courts and Trials: A Multidisciplinary Approach* (Toronto, ON: University of Toronto Press, 1975), p. 137. Reprinted in the first edition of this book.

[3] These two men and their cases are the subject of F.L. Morton's book, *Morgentaler v. Borowski: Abortion, The Charter and the Courts* (Toronto, ON: McClelland and Stewart, 1992).

who were active in lobbying for and influencing the wording of the Charter: the Canadian Civil Liberties Association (sections 1, 2 and 7–15); feminist organizations (sections 15 and 28); handicapped and visible-minority groups (section 15); official language minority groups (sections 16–23); multicultural groups (section 27); and aboriginal groups (sections 25 and 35).

The largest, best organized and best financed use of Charter litigation has been mounted by Canadian feminists. Feminists gained a headstart on other interest groups by successfully lobbying Parliament for favourable wording of section 15 equality rights while the Charter was still in draft stage. Soon after the Charter was proclaimed, the Canadian Advisory Council on the Status of Women (CACSW) commissioned a study of the "precedents, resources, and strategies" for feminist use of the Charter. (See Reading 7.1) The study surveyed the experience of feminist and minority group use of constitutional litigation in the United States, and concluded that with the adoption of the Charter, "we find ourselves at the opportune moment to stress litigation as a vehicle for social change." The study recommended the creation of a single, nationwide "legal action fund" to coordinate and pay for a policy of "systematic litigation" of strategic "test cases." During the three-year moratorium before the equality rights provisions took effect, feminist lawyers conducted a massive "statutory audit" to identify potential violations of section 15. The primary purpose of this study was to assist legislatures to purge their statutes of discriminatory laws. But if legislatures failed to take the initiative, the study also provided a list of targets for future section 15 litigation. On April 13, 1985, only days before the equality rights section of the Charter came into effect, the Women's Legal and Education Action Fund (LEAF) was launched. Its purpose was "to assist women with important test cases and to ensure that equality rights litigation for women is undertaken in a planned, responsible, and expert manner."

Sherene Razack's account of LEAF's activities and strategies since 1985 discloses some of the subterranean aspects of Charter politics. (See Reading 7.2) In addition to taking test cases to court as part of a plan of systematic litigation, LEAF has also conducted a behind-the-scenes campaign of "influencing the influencers." This campaign was based on the belief that "Rights on paper mean nothing unless the courts correctly interpret their scope and application." By "correct interpretation," LEAF meant a theory of equality that stressed equality of results or "adverse impact," not just equal application of equal laws. To ensure that the theory of equality adopted by the courts was the right one, LEAF undertook a broad range of activities in addition to the traditional techniques of lobbying legislators and top bureaucrats. These included encouraging and even sponsoring legal scholarship that supported an "adverse impact" interpretation of section 15, participating in judicial training programs, participating in the relevant committees of the Canadian Bar Association and provincial legal societies, encouraging the appointment of feminist judges and cultivating contacts in the media. (See Reading 7.2) This effort went so far as to include a three hour, one-on-one lobbying effort on

Peter Hogg, author of a very influential constitutional law textbook, to try to persuade him of the "correct" interpretation of section 28 of the Charter. The feminist lawyer later ruefully recounted that even after three hours, Professor Hogg "still got it wrong" (i.e., he disagreed).[4]

These out-of-court activities are designed to complement and support the litigation campaign. When LEAF lawyers go into court, they can cite law review articles and books that support their arguments for theories of "adverse impact" on "historically disadvantaged groups." They might even be fortunate enough to appear before judges who have attended one of their judicial education seminars. Razack recounts how much of LEAF's original pro-active strategy of systematic litigation and "occupying the field" has been frustrated by the large number of section 15 cases brought by men. This has sometimes forced LEAF into a reactive mode, and explains its frequent appearance as an intervenor, a strategy that at the outset it hoped to avoid. These setbacks notwithstanding, LEAF did achieve one of its highest priority goals when the Supreme Court of Canada adopted an "adverse impact" on "historically disadvantaged groups" interpretation in its first major section 15 decision, *Andrews v. Law Society of British Columbia*.[5] Not by coincidence, both LEAF and COPOH (Coalition of Provincial Organizations of the Handicapped) participated as intervenors in the *Andrews* appeal.

Interest group use of Charter litigation has been further encouraged by the Court Challenges Program initiated in September 1985 by the federal government. (See Reading 7.3) The government allocated nine million dollars over five years to fund litigation arising under the equality rights, language rights, and multiculturalism provisions of the Charter. Applications for financial support were screened according to the criteria of "substantial importance ... legal merit ... [and] consequences for a number of people." The administrators of the program stated that they would "emphasize the setting of social justice priorities." Selected cases were eligible for $35,000 at each stage of litigation—trial, provincial appeal court, and the Supreme Court of Canada. The Court Challenges Program was renewed in 1990 for another five-year term, but then abruptly cancelled in February, 1992 as part of the Mulroney government's program of financial restraint. While the future of the program is thus in doubt, it shows the extent to which even governments have come to accept the legitimacy of interest group litigation. The provision of government funding to Charter litigants also suggests that it is no longer accurate to conceive of all Charter litigation as a contest between the individual and the state. In many cases it may be a contest between different components of the state (i.e.,

---

[4] Michael Mandel, *The Charter of Rights and the Legalization of Politics in Canada* (Toronto, ON: Wall-Thompson, 1989), p. 40.

[5] [1989] 1 S.C.C. 143

federal versus provincial governments), or certain social interests versus others, with different governments lining up on different sides.

The significance of interest groups' use of the Charter does not just rest on their success in particular cases. Organized interest groups have significantly influenced the Court's agenda during this critical formative period of Charter interpretation. The Supreme Court, like all courts, is essentially a passive institution: it must wait for litigants to come to it with cases. Although it is now free to choose which cases it will hear, it still must choose from cases initiated by others. What Cairns wrote of the JCPC in 1971 is equally true of the Charter: "A comprehensive explanation of judicial decisions . . . must include the actors who employed the courts for their own purposes."[6]

Indeed, Cairns has extended this analysis to interest group use of the Charter. Charter politics, Cairns suggests, is a new variation of the old game of constitutional imperialism.[7]

> The Charter is imperialistic. Its various clientele groups seek to extend its jurisdiction. In a general way, the attitude of Charterphiles to their instrument is analogous to the attitudes of Oliver Mowat, W.A.C. Bennett, and Peter Lougheed to section 92 of the BNA Act, or for Lougheed section 109. These premiers sought, at a minimum, to protect, and more ambitiously, to extend the scope of the powers crucial to their governing capacities. Thus LEAF is to section 28 of the Charter, and the Canadian Ethnocultural Council to section 27, what Oliver Mowat was to section 92 of the BNA Act. The efforts of Charter supporters to eliminate the notwithstanding clause precisely parallels the efforts of provincial premiers to get rid of the federal power of disallowance.

While Cairns appears to be referring primarily to constitutional negotiations and constitutional litigation, the concept of protecting and expanding one's "constitutional turf" extends to the less visible but equally important aspects of interest groups' Charter activities.

Yet another way interest groups can use litigation to achieve policy objectives is through the "class action suit." A class action is a lawsuit brought by an individual on behalf of himself and other similarly situated persons, who have a common interest and a common grievance. It has been used extensively in the United States by environmental and other "citizens' action groups" to force corporate and governmental compliance with regulatory policies. Its use in Canada has been much more limited due to strict judicial interpretation of what constitutes a "common interest" and to other procedural problems affecting expenses. (See Reading 7.6) Recent developments suggest that this too may be changing. Quebec

---

[6] Alan C. Cairns, "The Judicial Committee and its Critics," *Canadian Journal of Political Science* 3 (1971), p. 301.

[7] "The Charter: An Academic (Political Science) Perspective," paper presented at "Roundtable Conference on the Impact of the Charter on the Public Policy Process," Osgoode Hall Law School, Toronto, November 15-16, 1991; p. 2.

recently established a public fund to pay the legal expenses of class action suits, and an Ontario Law Reform Commission report has recommended legislative reforms that would facilitate the bringing of class action suits in that province. These recommendations are controversial, however, as witnessed by the debate presented in Reading 7.7.

7.1

EQUALITY RIGHTS AND LEGAL ACTION
M. Atcheson, M. Eberts, & B. Symes

[Ed. note: all emphasis is from the original document.]

After looking carefully at some of the landmark legal cases involving matters of crucial interest to women in Canada, and after studying how American women's groups have chosen play a role in their legal system, we can now outline a course of action. *We have come to the conclusion that a legal action fund to concentrate on issues of sex-based discrimination is an essential component of an effective strategy to promote the interests of women in the Canadian legal system.*

First of all, we find ourselves at the opportune moment to stress litigation as a vehicle for social change. The Canadian Charter of Rights and Freedoms has brought about a significant change in our legal system, moving us further from a system where the legislatures are the supreme lawmakers to a system where the courts may be asked to review the activities of legislatures and governments in accordance with the rights established in the Charter.

Unlike American women who have fought with mixed results for a constitutional guarantee of equality through the interpretation of the Fourteen Amendment and the proposed Equal Rights Amendment, we have achieved a constitutional guarantee of equality through nation-wide lobbying. Section 28 of the Charter came into force on April 17, 1982, and section 15 comes into force on April 17, 1985. The challenge is to make the application of these equality guarantees meaningful and to ensure that the equality theory which our courts will develop and apply on a case-by-

"Conclusion," *Women and Legal Action: Precedents, Resources and Strategies for the Future* (Ottawa: Canadian Advisory Council on the Status of Women, 1984), from pages 163–172. Reprinted with permission.

case basis is in the best interests of women. Accepting the challenge will necessitate a change in the way Canadian women approach law reform because the role of courts has been enhanced by the Charter. Litigation, more than ever, has been opened up as a strategy to achieve equality.

As we saw in our review of the legal efforts of Canadian women to improve their lives, in the past women have had to take action as individuals and they have had to stand alone. Their cases were isolated ones, not part of an overall scheme to advance equality for Canadian women. The successful cases, such as the *Persons Case*, advanced rights for women and added momentum to subsequent cases and lobbying activities. The losses, such as *Bliss* and *Murdoch*, were devastating to the individual women and also had serious adverse effects on the case law affecting all women in the years immediately following the decisions. However, as symbols of women's inequality those losses triggered persistent and effective lobbying for legislative change. When we see our rich legacy, we also see how much more powerful a unified approach to change can be.

There can be no doubt that women and men will invoke section 28 of the Charter and section 15 when it comes into force, and that many decisions will be made which will influence how quickly, and by what means, Canadian women achieve equality. It makes sense, then, to find ways to increase the number of successful cases, to pursue the development of legal precedents of real value to the greatest number of Canadian women and to distribute the costs of such activity.

A. Why a Fund at All?

In our view, Canadian women should not assume that the existing legal system or existing groups will fill the current vacuum and devote sufficient resources to establishing organizations which will pursue Charter litigation in women's interests. It is difficult, if not impossible, for individual lawyers working in relative isolation to do systematic litigation. Furthermore, although lawyers often do provide some legal services at little or no charge, the reality is that they must bill for most of their services in the same way that any business would. They are not motivated, nor should they be expected, to bear the full cost of taking cases which are in the public's interest.

In addition, legal aid schemes do not fit in with the theory of systematic litigation. Generally, legal aid exists to assist people in paying for regular legal services which are important to the conduct of their day-to-day lives. So while economic support is provided, it is provided only where the person is involved in certain types of legal matters and is unable to pay. The worthwhile goals of legal aid do not always mesh with the need to select strategic cases.

Of the Canadian groups organized to undertake legal advocacy, none has selected women's issues as a priority for activity. In addition, none of the Canadian women's groups organized to focus on various women's issues has undertaken legal advocacy as a priority for activity.

B. One Fund or More?

On the one hand, it would seem better to have one large fund because that fund would have the opportunity to achieve greater control over the development of the law of equality than if a variety of funds were pursuing separate legal actions. A single fund would make better use of scarce financial resources whereas a variety of funds would compete for limited public and private monies. A single fund could speak on behalf of a large number of Canadian women with one voice whereas a variety of funds might be perceived as sectarian, divisive and fragmented. One such fund could more easily coordinate its efforts with groups bringing or sponsoring cases on behalf of those in other categories, like race or handicap, which are protected by section 15.

On the other hand, it would be complicated to organize one national legal action fund because lawyers are admitted to practice on a province-by-province basis and very few lawyers are qualified to practise law in more than one province or in both of Canada's two legal systems. One law fund may have difficulty accommodating the variety of legal issues which women in various regions of the country feel are important. As well, differences in political orientation may militate against a single law fund. In fact, a law fund might have to spend so much time and energy keeping itself together in these circumstances that its capacity to undertake litigation may be diminished.

Similarly, there are arguments for and against a variety of funds. The advantages of multiple funds are: the task facing women is enormous and should be shared; the expertise that is developed can be enriched by cooperation and communication amongst funds; funds have a ripple effect in that they provide a valuable service to a community, whether defined by geography or issue; and they enhance the public profile of women's issues and solutions for those issues.

The clear risks are that funds may operate at cross purposes or waste limited resources. Solving these problems, if they occur, will also detract from litigation activity.

The American experience cautions us that when there are several funds it is crucial that they work cooperatively. Resources can be squandered and efforts duplicated or what is worse, cancelled out, if individual funds do not establish "issue focuses"—in other words, priorities or goals—which mesh and contribute to the overall goal of equality.

Over and above the foregoing considerations, however, is the pending implementation of section 15. It seems to us that some fund with substantial resources is essential to ensure that cases are found and prepared in time to establish a responsible presence in the field of equality after April

1985. Furthermore, cases invoking equality will begin to enter the courts at that time and women will wish to become involved in cases brought by other parties under sections 15 and 28 to protect their interests and to contribute to the clarification of the law. One fund will have a better opportunity of doing this than would a number of funds in their formative stages.

After weighing all of those arguments, we believe that one national fund is the most attractive option for now.

C. What Will the Fund Do?

In our view, a legal action fund concentrating on the litigation of equality under the Charter should take, as the basis of its method of operation, the systematic approach to litigation developed in the United States. As described in this report, that approach would require taking the following four basic steps:

(1) defining a goal in terms of the desired principle of law to be established;

(2) plotting how the principle of law can be established from case to case in incremental, logical and clear steps;

(3) selecting winnable cases suitable for each stage taken to achieve the goal;

(4) consolidating wins at each stage by bringing similar cases to create a cluster of cases in support of the principle established.

Implicit in this theory are two fundamental organizational principles: first, *success is dependent upon direct sponsorship of cases;* second, *cases which will frustrate or complicate the development of the principle should be avoided if possible.*

The importance of these two principles cannot be underestimated. The success or failure of the American women's law funds can be measured, in large part, by the extent to which direct sponsorship of all cases in a given area has been possible. The ACLU Women's Rights Project, which uses direct sponsorship more than most of the other women's groups, has had more impact in achieving equality in areas such as employment than have the NOW Legal Defense and Education Fund and Women's Equity Action League which have relied primarily on an *amicus* strategy. Drawing upon the historical development of public interest litigation in the United States, the specific experience of the women's law funds and the Canadian groups discussed earlier, *we conclude that the direct sponsorship of litigation is the most productive strategy and therefore the strategy of first choice for any Canadian fund.* It is the most expensive option, but it is potentially the most productive. Moreover, in Canada, there may not be another option. It is becoming increasingly difficult for non-parties to intervene in ordinary court proceedings and it is difficult to predict how receptive courts will be to such interventions in Charter cases. [Ed. note: This was written before the Supreme Court's policy reversal in 1987, as described in Reading 6.6.]

In any case, it would not be advisable to use the scarce resources and time of a women's fund to wage a campaign to broaden the law on interventions when the preferred course of action is direct sponsorship of cases either by being the plaintiff itself or by providing the legal services for the individual woman plaintiff. As well, even in direct sponsorship, there may be one more hurdle to face in Canadian law. Unlike the American law of public interest litigation, the right of a fund to sponsor cases is not necessarily assured in Canada.

The merit of systematic litigation is that it is premised on an appreciation of how law develops in the judicial system. Left to its own devices, the development of law on a case-by-case basis tends to be uneven and unpredictable because judges can only decide on the case that is before them and no one plans the order in which the cases arise or the issues they will deal with. The systematic approach to litigation attempts to impose some order on this process by following the four basic steps outlined above. Implicit in this process is the commitment to the development of law in a steady, predictable manner over a long period of time.

There can be no better time than the present for Canadian women to contemplate undertaking such systematic litigation. Largely as a result of energetic lobbying pursued by Canadian women, the wording of the equality rights provision of the Charter makes a clear break with the restrictive interpretation of the equality rights provision of the Canadian Bill of Rights developed in the *Lavell* and *Bliss* cases discussed in Chapter 1. The time is right to begin to develop a theory of equality that will meet the expectations of Canadian women.

D. How Will the Fund Be Structured?

The next consideration is: what should be the structure of the fund? Ideally, a fund should have a membership base. It will take time and effort to establish a large base but our review of the American funds showed us that a large national membership provides the organization with a source of funds, longevity and impact both in lobbying efforts and in the courts.

A fund should start off with *a small working board of directors*; some directors can be chosen for their legal expertise so that they can provide information and assistance to the staff on a regular basis. Directors with stature in the community can attract funds to the undertaking.

A successful fund needs adequate staff. There must be a commitment to a large enough staff to ensure the ongoing existence of the organization. A skilled fund raiser is essential. An administrator is necessary to perform the functions of accounting, personnel, office maintenance, budgets, planning, and reporting to the funding sources and the membership. The fund should have lawyers on staff: they will work with the board to establish legal priorities, to review and select cases and to conduct litigation through trial. As well, the fund should plan to retain more senior lawyers to give advice from time to time and to take charge of the difficult and important cases. Staff members must also have a commitment to the ongoing education of women with respect to their legal rights and be prepared to lobby for legislative change.

E. Where Will the Money Come From?

Once the important decision is made to establish a fund, the next question to deal with is: where will the money come from? Our review of American funds showed us that finding adequate funding is a perennial time-consuming concern. When we look at the prospects for fundraising in Canada, it is clear that there are differences from the American situation. First, there is simply not as much private foundation money available in Canada for any kind of public interest work. Second, foundations in Canada do not appear to have a history of commitment to funding civil rights or human rights projects. This lack of involvement may be because the foundations have not been approached or it may be because the foundations have not perceived these issues to be important. In any event, the foundations may not be as rich a source of seed money as in the United States.

Third, the Canadian women's groups have accepted considerable funds from governments over the past number of years. However, it must be recognized that the principal defendant in Charter cases will be the provincial or federal government. Canadian organizations such as the Consumers' Association of Canada and the Public Interest Advocacy Centre have not faced this problem because they participate in regulatory settings where their target is most often the regulated party, for example, Bell Canada, and not the government itself. The Canadian Civil Liberties Association, whose adversary is often the government, makes it a policy never to accept government funding.

Fourth, there are real benefits in securing money from a broad membership base. The contributors feel that they have a stake in the process and will assist the organization to flourish. With a widespread membership base, the fund can speak with greater authority.

As well, in the United States the normal rule is that each party pays its own legal costs win or lose. In Canada, on the other hand, the normal rule is that the losing party must pay the costs of the winner. Thus, Canadian funds face the possibility of a real financial drain due to the structure of our court system. In litigation under the Charter, this will mean that an individual who loses may have to pay the costs of the government which has successfully opposed her case. She, in turn, will look to the fund for indemnification (compensation) of the costs awarded against her as well as for her own legal costs. These expenses must be built into any litigation scheme.

Several valuable lessons are apparent from the American experience. *Every attempt should be made to obtain funding from a variety of sources—from individuals and corporations as well as foundations—so that failure to have one grant renewed will not jeopardize the life of the organization. The amount of tied funds should be controlled,* or the organization will begin to replace its priorities with those of its funders. Sufficient funds must be raised in order to ensure that staff members are not required to work for insufficient compensation and so that an adequate staff can be hired for the workload; expertise is developed over time and a high staff turnover or rate of burnout can significantly hinder a fund's effectiveness. This is particularly important in Canada because very few lawyers have experience in equality litigation. Finally, *legal action funds should give high priority to developing permanent fundraising skill* and allocate sufficient staff resources to that task.

F. Beyond Litigation

Even though we strongly believe in the necessity to create a women's legal action fund, we also believe that *litigation should not be seen as a replacement for the varied activities of the women's movement.* The long-term goal of equality for women will best be furthered by a strategy which combines public education, lobbying, use of the media, law reform, education of lawyers and the judiciary, as well as litigation. Litigation is time-consuming, expensive, and a risky route for change. A win may be interpreted to affect only the parties who are before the court while the interpretation of a loss may act to limit the progress of all women for years. Litigation is a blunt instrument, with large downside costs and generally does not provide for accommodation or compromise. On the other hand, litigation may be the most effective means of achieving change on an issue. The American and Canadian experience has shown that as a strategy for change, litigation should be used in conjunction with other tools.

A legal action fund or funds would strengthen the general aim of the organized women's movement in Canada—equality. The optimum situation would be to have an overall strategy combining a number of elements.

First, efforts must continue to ensure that the *public is educated to raise its awareness of equality and discrimination issues.* The staff of a fund can contribute to this by establishing and building contacts with the media, by creating media events around issues, by public speaking, and by being a resource for information and materials for other lawyers concerning the issues. It is critical to the long-term success and existence of a fund that it build links to the publics so that the fund is seen as a respected and necessary institution for the community. Judges, too, live in the real world and are not immune to public perceptions.

Second, as have many other women's groups, *the fund must establish a presence at all levels of government* so that it can lobby for legislative change, ensure that new laws do not discriminate against women and monitor the government's enforcement of legislation. It is important that a fund have visibility and credibility in the community so that when it appears before public bodies seeking changes, politicians and government officials will listen, not only because of the content of the presentation, but also because of the constituency or interest group that the fund is seen to represent. Over time, the fund staff will be seen by governments, politicians and civil servants as a valuable information resource and will be consulted before laws are drafted. It must be realized that essential cases will be lost in the courts. It is important then to have built contacts with legislators so that laws can be enacted to reverse such losses.

Third, *it is critical to build a theory of equality which is accepted by academics, lawyers and the judiciary.* Legal writing in respected law journals, presentation of papers at legal seminars or "educationals," and participation in judges' training sessions are all means of disseminating and legitimizing such theories of equality. It will be important to coordinate these endeavours with other organizations such as lawyers' professional groups, or with those who seek equality on the basis of race, age, or mental or physical handicap. An exchange of ideas and resources will benefit all such groups and further the definition of equality.

Finally, *the fund can be a resource centre for other litigants and women's groups.* For example, fund staff might assist in drafting pleadings and act as a clearinghouse for the most recent cases and legal writings in an area of law. The staff might also collect economic and statistical data on the effects of discrimination, including retaining experts who will give evidence in court, and who can predict future trends in society to assist in planning a long-term litigation strategy.

How an organization undertakes these activities, and the extent to which it undertakes these activities, will determine its structure, its size, and its effectiveness. We have learned from the American experience that these combined activities, although expensive and time-consuming, are effective in achieving the goal of equality. We have learned from our own experience that Canadian women can sustain a commitment to litigation, both financially and with other resources, and we suspect that with an organized long-term approach the gains of Canadian women made through litigation could parallel and strengthen those made through legislative lobbying.

The challenge is ours.

7.2

THE WOMEN'S LEGAL EDUCATION AND ACTION FUND
Sherene Razack

Rights on paper mean nothing unless the courts correctly interpret their scope and application. Charter activists began trying to influence judicial interpretation through charterwatching, an all-consuming activity. It entailed having national consultations, planning conferences, writing books and articles, making speeches, doing audits of statutes, offering workshops; in short, attempting to inform the decision-makers, women, and the Canadian public (in that order) exactly what the new equality guarantees should mean in law.

The frenzy of activities began, as though by a starter's gun, when the government included in its constitution bill a three-year moratorium on section 15's equality rights. Ostensibly giving governments sufficient time to bring their legislation into conformity with the law, the delay inspired women to plan for the day when they could take their unresolved equality claims to court, armed with the hard-won guarantees of sections 15 and 28.

Not surprisingly, the women most compelled to plan for litigation and to charterwatch were those legally-trained or connected to the women's organizations active on the lobby. As early as March 1981, Marilou McPhedran recorded in her diary her awareness of the experience of American women's legal defence funds and their possible relevance to the Canadian context. In May 1981, when the long-delayed Canadian Advisory Council on the Status of Women (CACSW) conference on Women and the Constitution took place in Ottawa, Beth Atcheson, later a founder of LEAF, mentioned the idea of a Canadian women's litigation fund in her speech, which she had prepared in collaboration with Beth Symes and Marilou McPhedran. Mary Eberts, the chair of the conference, Beth Symes, and Beth Atcheson were then commissioned by the CACSW to work with the researcher Jennifer Stoddart on a feasibility study of a women's litigation fund. Although the study, *Women and Legal Action*, [See Reading 7.1] was not available until the fall of 1984, its authors relied on its findings to start organizing support for the idea in 1982. ...

Canadian Feminism and the Law: The Women's Legal Education and Action Fund and the Pursuit of Equality (Toronto, ON: Second Story Press, 1991), from pages 36-63. Reprinted with permission.

In May, 1982, . . . several of the women connected to the issue applied for funding and organized a national think tank which was held in Toronto. They invited well-known constitutional experts Peter Hogg and Walter Tarnopolsky because, not only were they trying to secure answers to their questions about what the constitutional equality guarantees meant, they were beginning to adopt what they described as a process of "influencing the influencers," an approach fuelled by their increasing awareness that "things were being written that we didn't exactly agree with." A number of ideas surfaced at this time about how best to promote women's interests in law: the idea of a defence fund was already on the table and to this was added the idea of a legal text book and a symposium, all based on the belief that "it was very important to get in at the academic level."

In their own educational session, billed as a workshop on the Charter and held in the same month as the think tank, the women proceeded to determine what their position was on the new law. . . . Again, the rationale was the same: if women could convey their point of view to those in "responsible positions," they could influence how equality rights were ultimately understood in the courts.

Energetic in their efforts to promote women's constitutional interests, a core of women in Toronto, who were active on constitutional issues, created a trust fund known as the Charter of Rights Educational Fund (CREF), a Charter of Rights Coalition (CORC), and called together 30 women in the area who launched several educational activities. The minutes of the meeting held on November 25, 1982, at the large and prestigious law firm of Tory, Tory (where Mary Eberts worked), indicated a general consensus on the need to publicize the issues and further educate women on the specifics of the equality guarantees. Under the auspices of CREF, two study days were planned and, at a later meeting, a committee was struck to coordinate the massive undertaking of an audit of federal and provincial statutes not in compliance with the Charter. The idea of a legal defence fund, supported very strongly by the group's only independently wealthy member, Nancy Jackman, is described in the minutes as the "least formalized" of all the projects.

The study days, held on January 15 and February 19, 1983, attracted over 170 persons, largely women from the legal community. The papers presented, and which were later published, made clear that the group saw their task as one of shaping the legal community's views, and the judiciary's in particular, on the meaning of equality. . . .

The statute audit project, born "out of the nasty suspicion that their [the government's] idea of equality and ours was not going to be the same," intended to pinpoint for Canadian legislatures exactly what had to be done to avoid subsequent legal battles over equality; but, it was also meant to provide women with a "catalogue" of changes from which they might launch a litigation effort. The Americans, with whom the CACSW'S *Women and Legal Action* team had spoken, had generally concurred that litigation had to be staged and to do so required a clear knowledge of the range of laws that discriminated against women. The 70 women who worked on the audit were organized into teams and coordinated by a CREF member. They began on the premise that equality means "more to women than the equal opportunity to participate in a male-defined world." They then examined 10 areas of women's lives, suggesting where and how the law had contributed to a situation of inequality. Key to their approach was the notion that "the aim is not to sex-neutralize all laws and pretend that one has thereby created equality: the aim is to positively accommodate sex specific situations."

While both the audit and the study days dealt with the complexities of using the equality guarantees in litigation, the activities of the Charter of Rights Coalition were more broad-based in appeal. A key figure behind CORC'S creation was Pat Hacker who, during her lobbying for section 28 and later when she served as chair of NAC'S constitution committee, was concerned that Canadian women had to be made aware of the three-year moratorium and of the need to push governments into action before this time was up. As a result, NAC created CORC as a subcommittee of its constitutional committee. . . .

The CORC group received government funding to plan a national conference on Charter issues that would complement the symposium then being planned "for legal types." Nancy Jackman, who led the CORC team, remembered that they then began to build a series of "mini-coalitions" across the country, using the institutionalized women's groups as a base. The function of these coalitions was to "bug" their governments about the moratorium and educate women about the Charter. CORC prepared a slide tape show and an educational kit which optimistically declared:

> There is potential in the Charter of Rights to support whatever change women want. It's like a magic wand one could wave to bring about things like fair labour legislation, better protection for women in areas such as sexual assault and enactment of affirmative action programs. *Women can get what we want if we lobby now and do our research and help judges understand what equality means.* [Emphasis in original]

The idea of a national conference, however, proved unworkable given the difficulties of Quebec women's groups with the charter issue. The CORC group settled for a series of regional task forces and conferences, thereby facilitating the development of regional bases—in B.C., for example, where CORC women later formed the West Coast LEAF—and providing an opportunity for women from Toronto and Ottawa to travel the country and organize a litigation fund. . . .

The Birth of LEAF

In August of 1984, nine months before Section 15 of the Charter of Rights and Freedoms came into effect, specific planning began for the birth of the

Women's Legal Education and Action Fund. The small group that met at 21 McGill, a private Toronto women's club, on August 9, 1984, began the organizing of the fund with characteristic energy and a shared sense of what needed to be done. Besides the authors of the forthcoming *Women and Legal Action*, the planning group for LEAF initially included Marilou McPhedran, two well-known professional women Shelagh Day and Kathleen O'Neil, and Nancy Jackman whose importance as a potential financial contributor to the fund would become evident over the next few months.

Events moved quickly. In September the group considered who might form the board of LEAF, which was scheduled for birth immediately after section 15 came into force; by October, they had received for their use $100,000 from the Jackman Foundation. The release of *Women and Legal Action* that month made it clear that a litigation fund could not succeed without a great deal of money, a requirement that made funding for LEAF the greatest priority. High profile professional women, typically lawyers and human rights professionals, were drawn into the organizing, and fundraising began in earnest. Kathleen O'Neil was asked to go to her organization, the Federation of Women Teachers of Ontario; endorsements were sought from the YWCA; and every conceivable network was activated in the interest of finding the financial support for LEAF.

Kasia Seydegart was hired to plan the fundraising and suggested that the group cultivate well-known human rights advocates such as the Canadian Human Rights Commission's Gordon Fairweather . . . and Judge Rosalie Abella, who wrote the *Report of the Royal Commission on Equality in Employment* published in October 1984. By November, animated by "the dream . . . to make the promise of equality contained in section 15 a reality for all Canadian women," the group could record in the minutes their finances to date: $117,000 from the Federation of Women Teachers of Ontario ($70,000 in funds and the rest in services); an initial $50,000 from the Jackman Foundation; and $700 in smaller donations. Appeals to wealthy women and grant applications consumed the rest of 1984.

In the frenzy of organizing, LEAF women relied heavily on their traditional networks. Thus, although the minutes of January 11, 1985, contained a passing reference to the need to involve immigrant women and women of colour, and Magda Seydegart recalled pressing for community involvement, the composition of both the working committee and the board remained homogeneous in character. Seventeen professional white women made up the working committee struck on December 18, 1984; eleven of them were either lawyers or human rights professionals. On April 13 and 14, 1984, when LEAF officially came into being with an elected board and an executive committee, the composition did not change.

LEAF embodied the three main features recommended in *Women and Legal Action*: the establishment of a single national fund, the direct sponsorship of (preferably winnable) cases, and a complementary strategy of education and lobbying. As the epicentre of this strategy LEAF, Mary Eberts wrote, had a good chance of occupying the field of equality rights in the courtroom, but

> expertise can be applied in ways other than this case-by-case approach. Counsel and volunteers from the organization can become involved in legal writing, legal education, and continuing education of bench and bar. In this fashion, they may come to influence how decision-makers view the legal issues involved. Just as important, however, they may influence how lawyers prepare and present cases they bring forward.

"Occupying the field" on equality issues in court, doing proactive litigation, influencing the influencers, were components of LEAF's vision. The criteria for selecting cases, as adopted at the founding meeting, reflected their ambitious intent. Cases taken had to concern equality rights; arise under the Charter of Rights and Freedoms or under Quebec's Charter; present strong facts; and be of importance to women. Finally, LEAF declared itself particularly interested in cases in which women were doubly disadvantaged, that is, subjected to sex discrimination as well discrimination on the basis of race, disability, etc.

A decision was made early on to begin immediately in the courtroom. On April 17, 1985, in a blaze of publicity, LEAF announced its first two cases—one concerned the right of married women to keep their own names, and the other attacked the requirement that welfare recipients, the majority of whom are women, live as single persons in order to qualify for assistance. Beth Symes described the day:

> [Counsel] Eloise Spitzer's name change case involved the Yukon, a Francophone [Suzanne Bertrand, a French Canadian living in the Yukon who wished to retain her maiden name because it reflected her French-Canadian ancestry] and a blatant case we could win. The second case, the spouse-in-the-house case, was chosen [because] it was for disadvantaged women and because it was a symbol of the state oppressiveness [toward] women. April 17 was a wonderful spectacle on the hill. We raised $20,000 that day in Ottawa and $25,000 in Toronto.

It was an auspicious beginning, full of hope and confidence and undeterred by the enormity [sic!] of the task at hand. . . .

Equality of Results

Equality of results was clearly the prevailing rhetoric of the 1980s. Federal government reports, while they did little to concretely achieve it, did not quarrel with its major premises: that inequality was a group phenomenon, that white men could no longer be the norm against which everyone was measured, and that equality meant the recognition of both biological and social differences. Even the courts had begun to accept some of these perceptions. In the *O'Malley* case, involving the demotion of a woman whose newly-acquired religious beliefs prevented her from working on Saturdays, the Honourable Mr. Justice McIntyre ruled that "it is the result or the effect of the action complained of which is significant. If it does, in fact, cause discrimination, if its effect is to impose on one person or group of persons obligations, penalties or restrictive conditions not imposed on other members of the community, then it is discriminatory." Thus when Lynn Smith declared, in an article first presented at the symposium on equality rights, that equality is measured by whether it means "equal results for women in light of their reality, as it does for men in light of their reality," she was expressing a results-oriented view of equality advanced by some members of the judiciary, the legal profession, human rights professionals, women's groups, and groups representing Native people, disabled people, and visible minorities. . . .

*   *   *

When the Women's Legal Education and Action Fund officially came into being on April 17, 1985, its founders intended its structure to replicate the best features of American litigation funds and to avoid their worst short-comings. Impressed by the record of the American organization the National Association for the Advancement of Colored People (NAACP), in particular their strategy of pursuing incremental gains in specific areas, LEAF's founders concluded that Canadian women would best secure their legal rights in a similar way. In American terminology, the NAACP approach was to "occupy" a particular area of law and become known as the expert litigators in that field, and by selecting winnable issues and controlling the development of case law, judges could be asked to take small steps at any one time. Such a long-term strategy of staged litigation requires considerable funding, preferably from a broad, non-governmental base. The intention is for the litigating organization to act as the sponsor of a party to the case, financially a more onerous role than that of intervenor where an organization acts as a "friend of the court" and limits its participation to offering a written and oral opinion on how the case affects the interests it promotes. In the United States, the vision of a proactive legal fund usually involves lobbying and public education, activities that mandate a close relationship with feminist communities.

LEAF's founders intended to pursue a proactive strategy involving the building of test cases. Accordingly, they developed five criteria for case selection, and, following Karen O'Connor's recommendations in her book on American women's legal organizations, they erected a structure to complement the strategy of seeking out important cases nationally, researching them, and having the financial resources to shepherd cases through the lengthy and costly court process. O'Connor also emphasized the importance of strong national headquarters and highly-skilled legal volunteers, the value of publicity both for funders and for credibility in the legal community, the value of local affiliates in keeping the organization in touch with its constituency, and the importance of both legal and public education. Conspicuously absent was any mechanism for ensuring the legal fund's accountability to feminist communities.

LEAF's structure acknowledged the importance of the factors O'Connor outlined. Its board of directors included a national chair and vice-chair, a national legal committee made up of representatives from across the country, finance and fundraising chairs, a chair of public education and research, and local affiliates on the prairies, in the Yukon, and on the west and east coasts. . . .

LEAF's first litigation report recognized that "selecting the right test cases for litigation involves a careful process of winnowing, investigation and research." Typically (and LEAF, as I show below, has not been typical in this respect), someone brings a possible test case or, more commonly, a legal problem women have experienced to the organization's attention. The staff then proceeds to research the issue involved, meeting with a variety of legal consultants before it reaches the legal committee for consideration. Unless one or more of the consultants contacted have a strong community orientation, and unless there are sufficient time and a resources to seek consultation further afield, only the legal aspects of the issue are considered. For LEAF, then, as a feminist organization seeking to protect and improve women's legal rights essentially through the telling of women's stories in court, the first challenge is to accommodate a variety of women's voices to a process that fundamentally negates consultation and difference. . . .

Attracting the large sums of money that litigation requires also places a women's legal defence fund under greater than usual pressure to respond to funders' desires. LEAF's founders knew from the beginning that a broad funding base was desirable, but in actively pursuing it those involved in funding gained a keen appreciation of the compromises in image that would be required. To Marilou McPhedran, the group's chief fundraiser at several points in its history, fundraising meant "breaking into those echelons where feminists have never been very comfortable" and presenting an appropriate image for corporate and government funders that spoke of LEAF women's credibility as members of the legal, not the feminist, community. To another LEAF founder, Beth Atcheson, LEAF had to appear to be an elite corps because this was the only way to garner sufficient financial support from those most able to give it. This left LEAF, however, in the position of being attractive to its funders but alienated from the feminist communities it served and needed. When LEAF hosted a $100-a-plate dinner, it raised funds from the middle and upper classes but strengthened its image as an organization with few ties to women in the community. Moreover, as the beneficiaries of relatively large government grants, LEAF was vulnerable to the rancour of some segments of the community who felt that litigation activities attracted more governmental support than grass-roots activities—rape crisis centres, for example.

Perhaps because of who in Canadian society are legally trained and the necessity of attracting large sums of money (and therefore being "credible" to potential corporate and government funders), LEAF's founders and its main activists, as we have seen, were a remarkably homogeneous group who for the most part chose to remain professionally anchored in the corporate legal world. LEAF women themselves have noted that one way of coming to terms with the contradiction of a feminist challenge from within the corporate world is to capitalize on this insider status. LEAF certainly reflected this approach: it used the resources of large law firms, the status of well-known litigators, and its own credibility as a legal organization with elite connections (when lobbying governments, for example) to contribute to its success. In both its internal and external activities, however, an organization that operates in this fashion runs the risk of losing the self-critical edge that comes with diversity of races, classes, and occupations. It might also be argued, as Andrea Nye has argued of women who must work within the language of patriarchal discourse, that "respectability is inevitably self-defeating" because challenge is unlikely to be sustained from within. Those who felt at odds with the style and approach of LEAF women found it hard to participate. Indeed, for many would-be supporters of LEAF it was LEAF'S image as an "intellectual, trail-blazing organization" with a stellar legal cast that was attractive, while others mentioned their early sense of discomfort with the organization's "corporatist-feminist" approach and the priority litigation had, at least in the first two years of LEAF'S operation, over the building of a strong community base. . . .

In what was to become a trend of disturbing significance, men began to use the Charter soon after its promulgation to protest against the few protections women enjoyed in law. In one of these cases, *Seaboyer/Gayme*, two men accused of rape protested that their right to a fair trial as guaranteed in the Charter was infringed upon because of provisions in the Criminal Code that prohibited using as evidence a victim's previous sexual history (except in three specific instances). LEAF applied for and was granted intervenor status whereupon it had 30 days to submit its legal argument concerning why these "rape shield" provisions should continue to stand. In what was intended to be a strategic move, LEAF hired a well-known male criminal lawyer who prepared a somewhat scant brief for the court; it included some examples of possible infringements on the right to a fair trial that might result from the rape shield provisions of the Criminal Code. Further, the approach taken was a rather conservative one where no mention was made of the relationship between these provisions in the Code and women's right to equality under section 15 of the Charter. A group of feminists working on the possibility of civil remedies for women harmed by pornography were highly critical of the LEAF brief, pointing out the lack of equality arguments and noting particularly the ill-advised examples that conceded there may be times when a women's previous sexual history may be relevant to a determination of whether or not she was raped.

For LEAF, the *Seaboyer/Gayme* case was its first reminder of the perils of not seeking consultation within the wider feminist community. To its credit, the organization then responded constructively to criticism and developed a process of "workshopping" cases with working groups of feminists who had specific expertise on the issues under consideration. Indeed, the working group formed to discuss what had gone wrong in *Seaboyer/Gayme* remained active for subsequent cases, and workshopping has continued to be the approach taken, the cost of such consultation notwithstanding. According to Mary Eberts, a working group is formed for cases where there is enough lead time, consisting of a member of the national legal committee and/or LEAF's executive director, volunteer lawyers, and representatives from the local LEAF chapter. Each working group develops its own links with the women's community. As the report on the second year of LEAF litigation commented: "Developing case strategy requires a sure vision about the meaning of equality and how that theory should be made concrete in this particular instance, a vision that cannot be arrived at in isolation." . . .

Damage Control

While the progress made in winning acceptance of the principle of adverse impact was heartening, LEAF had no sooner begun its litigation activities when it became clear that, the favourable judicial climate of the 1980s notwithstanding, it would not be able to maintain the type of control over equality litigation it had originally anticipated. More was at stake than judicial recognition of unintentional discrimination. As Beth Symes ruefully reflected at the round table discussion in 1988, in which LEAF's founders discussed their achievements and common history:

> If you're going to build law with respect to equality, you want to build it your way. So therefore, you flood the courts with your cases and your issues in the order in which you want the court to hear them. We have not occupied the field. Men have. We have been involved in damage control . . . men have been popping up all over Canada in various courts challenging things that we as women fought to get, such as maternity benefits, such as the rape shield provisions. Resources have gone into these interventions.

LEAF's careful building of feminist jurisprudence based on precedent and their planning the court's progress toward acceptance of key concepts fell by the wayside when proactive quickly turned to reactive and LEAF found itself acting as a third party, as an intervenor in cases brought by men. They were thereby forced to abandon their agenda and respond to one set by men's claims for equality. The intervention process poses two major constraints: first, it involves extreme time pressures (only 30 days remain from the time an appeal is filed to the time an intervenor must file its request for intervention); once granted the status to intervene, an intervenor then has a further 30 days from the time the last party's factum (written argument) is filed to file her own. Second, as one American legal advocate has observed, the lawyer representing the (male) party bringing the case to court has a considerable advantage in characterizing the issue. Canadian intervenors are required to speak to the specific interests they claim to defend and are seldom empowered to bring evidence, cross-examine, or expand upon the issue in any way. LEAF women entered the legal fray under these constraints, factors that influenced their success more than the benefits of an otherwise favourable judicial climate.

Overview of LEAF Cases

In its first three years of litigation, LEAF opened over 300 files. Of these, it adopted 64 cases for consideration by the legal committee, pursuing over 30 in some detail. Its caseload far exceeded capacity, and in 1989 LEAF had to limit its acceptance of intake calls to one day of the week. While there were cases where LEAF took a proactive approach, initiating court action and seeking to build on acceptance of such concepts as adverse impact (and these naturally had a longer gestation time than others), most of its cases to date were those in which LEAF acted as an intervenor, defending women's interests in cases brought by men. Thus, at the board's annual meeting in June of 1986, decisions were made to concentrate on proactive work in the two major areas of employment law and income assistance for low-income women (areas where routine policies or practices had an adverse impact on certain groups of women), and to establish a strategy to cope with the epidemic of cases brought by men. As the board concluded, "the strong Charter attacks brought by men against legislative protection for victims of sexual assault were thought to require an appropriate response." . . .

7.3

THE COURT CHALLENGES PROGRAM
Ian Brodie

Launching a court case is always an expensive enterprise, but taking a Charter of Rights case all the way to the Supreme Court of Canada can cost hundreds of thousands of dollars. Between 1985 and 1992, the federal government's Court Challenges Program (CCP) helped to fund certain Charter cases and most constitutional language rights challenges against both the federal and the provincial governments. Most of the CCP's money went to interest groups, some of which the CCP itself helped to create.

Many Canadian interest groups became involved in the process of drafting the Charter in 1981 with the hope that they could use it later to protect or advance their policy objectives through litigation. After the Charter was adopted, however, they quickly discovered how costly Charter cases were

Written for the second edition of this book.

going to be. Many would-be Charter litigators lobbied the federal government to create a program that would help them to defray the costs of expensive Charter litigation. In response, on September 25, 1985, Justice Minister John Crosbie and Secretary of State Benoit Bouchard announced that the federal government had signed a contract with the Canadian Council on Social Development (CCSD) to create a new program that would help to fund court cases under the equality rights provisions of the Charter and various constitutional language rights guarantees. They gave the CCSD $9 million for five years to fund these cases. Under the terms of the contract, the CCP could give up to $35,000 to a case at each level of the court system, so that a single case could receive up to $105,000 if it went all the way to the Supreme Court. By 1989/90, the CCP was spending $1.2 million per year and committing $2 million to cases just entering the court system.

This new Court Challenges Program was, in fact, an extension of an earlier Court Challenges Program. The Trudeau government established the first CCP in 1977 as part of its battle against Quebec's language law, Bill 101. When the separatist Parti Quebecois government was elected in 1976, it passed a wide-ranging language law, known as Bill 101, to promote the French language in Quebec, in many cases by restricting the use of English. Bill 101 contradicted every aspect of Trudeau's own policies to promote bilingualism as a means of achieving national unity. The Trudeau government was so outraged by the PQ legislation that it briefly considered using the reference procedure to ask the Supreme Court to overturn Bill 101. However, some of Trudeau's ministers thought that a federal reference would be too controversial and might look like the federal government was "ganging up" on Quebec just before the PQ was going to hold a provincial referendum on gaining a form of sovereignty for the province. Instead, the government decided to create a small Court Challenges Program that would pay the legal costs of minority language interest groups and individuals using the various language rights guarantees in the constitution to challenge Bill 101 and other provincial language laws in the courts. The recipients of these monies were anglophone groups in Quebec and francophone groups outside Quebec that were sponsored by the federal government in the wake of the 1969 Official Languages Act.

The old Court Challenges Program was run "in-house" by the federal justice department because the federal government wanted to keep a close eye on the cases that it was funding. When the Mulroney government expanded the CCP in 1985, it agreed to give the CCP a bit more independence from the government of the day, so its contract with the CCSD allowed the CCP to operate at "arms length" from the federal government.

Under the contract, CCSD created two panels of experts to determine which cases would get CCP funding—one panel for language rights cases and another for equality rights cases. The two panels operated quite differently. The language rights panel could fund any case that involved constitutional language guarantees, even if the case challenged a provincial law. Indeed, the new language rights sections of the Charter were specifically created to "target" restrictive provincial laws. Most of the language panel's grants funded challenges to provincial laws brought by groups like l'Association culturelle francaise-canadienne de la Saskatchewan and Alliance Quebec. In turn, these language groups were also funded by the federal Secretary of State Department's official languages program. For example, l'Association canadienne-francaise de l'Ontario received $8.7 million between 1983 and 1990 from the Secretary of State and also got a grant to intervene in the language rights case of *Mahé v. Alberta* at the Supreme Court.

The equality rights panel, on the other hand, was only authorized to fund cases that challenged federal laws, and then only cases that involved section 15, 27 and 28 of the Charter of Rights. Apparently the Mulroney government, elected on a promise to bring harmony to federal-provincial relations, thought that it would be too controversial for the federal government to fund challenges to provincial laws generally. Despite these restrictions, the equality rights side of the CCP spent more than twice as much money as the language rights panel in 1989/90 and committed more than four times as much to new cases entering the court system. As with the language rights panel, much of the equality rights funding went to groups that also received substantial operating grants from the federal Secretary of State.

For example, the Supreme Court's first case to interpret the equality rights provisions of the Charter's section 15 involved a provincial law. Despite the restriction of the CCSD contract with the federal government, the Court Challenges Program paid the research costs for two of the interest group intervenors in the case—$15,400 to the Women's Legal Education and Action Fund (LEAF) and $35,000 to the Coalition of Provincial Organizations of the Handicapped (COPOH). Both of these groups used CCP money to argue that section 15 was primarily intended to improve the position of historically disadvantaged groups, the position that the Supreme Court eventually adapted. Both LEAF and COPOH also received regular grants from the Secretary of State in the years leading up to the Andrews case.

The CCP also had a long-standing involvement in *Mahé v. Alberta*, the leading case under the Charter's guarantee of minority-language education rights, section 23. The old Court Challenges Program had funded some of the litigants in *Mahé* to help launch the case, and subsequently also funded several intervenors like the Quebec Association of Protestant School Boards and l'Association canadienne-francaise de l'Ontario in the case when it reached the Supreme Court. In *Mahé*, the Supreme Court not just confirmed that the Charter allowed French-language parents outside Quebec access to French-language schools, it began the process of giving them control over their children's schools as well. The *Mahé* precedent, of course, applies equally to all 10 provinces.

Some of the CCP's funding decisions stirred political controversy. The saga of abortion cases in the courts provides one example. When anti-abortion crusader Joe Borowski appeared before the Supreme Court to argue that

Canada's abortion law violated the section 7 right to life of the unborn, the CCP provided the maximum $35,000 grant to LEAF so that it could oppose Borowski's claims. When LEAF's conservative counterparts, REAL Women, applied for money to enable it to support Borowski's side, it was turned down. In its written decision on the application, the equality rights panel claimed that REAL Women's case would reduce the control that women exercised over their own lives and was therefore inimical to the equality rights of women. This decision was strongly criticized by REAL Women, who charged the CCP was being run by and for radical feminists. As a result, the CCP was charged with taking sides in the abortion debate, at the very time when the Mulroney government was drafting a new abortion law in response to the *Morgentaler* decision.

The appearance of partisan bias was also fed by the CCP's activities in encouraging the creation of new groups that would in turn qualify for CCP funding. For example, the CCP organized a meeting of prisoners' rights advocates in 1989 that led to the creation of the Canadian Prisoners' Rights Network. Similar meetings sponsored by the CCP led to a Working Group on Aboriginal and Treaty Rights and the Canadian Ethnocultural Council's Equality Rights Committee. Most of these groups in turn began litigation that was funded by the CCP. By taking an active role in creating groups who were in turn given funding, the CCP has invited criticism from conservatives that it has used public money to promote a partisan policy agenda of left-liberal causes.

When the CCP's first five-year mandate ended in 1990, the Mulroney government asked the House of Commons Standing on Human Rights to hold public hearings on the Court Challenges Program's track record and to recommend whether or not it should be renewed. Almost all of the groups that appeared before the Committee have received CCP funding, and these groups were predictably uniform in their praise. They applauded the CCP's contribution to their public interest litigation on behalf of historically disadvantaged groups. The sole dissenting voice was that of REAL Women, which used the Committee's hearing to attack the CCP for its ideological bias. They argued that groups like LEAF were not disadvantaged at all. REAL Women also claimed that, by deciding which cases made appropriate equality rights arguments and which did not, the CCP had usurped the function of the Supreme Court. By rejecting funding applications from groups with whose objective it disagreed, the CCP was controlling access to the Canadian courts on the basis of political belief, argued REAL Women.

In the end, the Commons committee ignored REAL Women's criticisms. The committee recommended that the CCP not only be renewed, but expanded to fund aboriginal rights cases and equality rights challenges to provincial laws. While the federal government did not extend the scope of the CCP, it did renew the CCP until 1995 and increased its budget to $12 million over five years. When the CCP was renewed, it was also transferred from CCSD to the University of Ottawa's Human Rights Centre.

In its February, 1992 spending estimates, the Mulroney government unexpectedly cancelled the CCP. The decision to cancel the CCP was part of a broader cost-cutting program that saw several other programs wound-up. The cancellation was also defended on the grounds that the CCP's initial purpose of bringing the first-generation of landmark Charter cases involving equality rights and minority language rights had been achieved. The cancellation was greeted with universal condemnation by the groups that had received money from the CCP. CCP staff and its clientele groups immediately launched a campaign to have its funding restored. This campaign was soon endorsed by the House of Commons Committee on Human Rights, the Canadian Human Rights Commission and retired Supreme Court Justice Bertha Wilson. At the time of writing, it remains uncertain whether this campaign will persuade the Mulroney government to restore the CCP.

7.4

OPERATION DISMANTLE v. THE QUEEN
Supreme Court of Canada (1985)

This case is reprinted as Reading 6.4.

7.5

THE NCC CHALLENGES THE CANADA ELECTIONS ACT
Janet Hiebert

The establishment of a formal system of rights in the Canadian Constitution has increased the judiciary's responsibility for resolving conflicts that arise between individual and collective values. The Charter of Rights and Freedoms is replete with unqualified phrases requiring content and scope to determine what circumstances are actually protected by its open-ended guarantees. Further, the inclusion of the limitation clause in section 1 requires

"Fair Elections and Freedom of Expression under the Charter," *Journal of Canadian Studies* 24, no. 4 (Hiver 1989–90 Winter), from pages 72–86. Reprinted with permission.

that courts assess the justification of legislation which conflicts with the protected rights to determine whether the legislative decision to limit a right was the constitutionally correct one. When making this determination, courts will have to consider whether the policy being pursued warrants constitutional recognition and if the means chosen to administer that objective are acceptable. There is nothing particularly legal about this task; rather it is inherently policy-oriented. The process of "balancing" a litigant's protected right with the public good involves the kinds of considerations presumably made already by legislators when enacting the legislation. The concerns which are part of these policy decisions involve not only competing philosophical principles about which interests should take precedent but also different conceptions how best to achieve the desired goal.

This enhanced policy role will be particularly evident in decisions from the Supreme Court. Although the hierarchical nature of the Canadian judicial system ensures that the most significant policy impact of Charter review will occur in decisions at the Supreme Court level, this paper will argue that one particular lower court outcome has had a profound impact on a vital aspect of federal elections policy. The decision is *National Citizens' Coalition Inc. and Brown v. Attorney-General of Canada,* in which legislation regulating interest groups' campaign-spending activities was declared unconstitutional for violating freedom of expression. While other lower court decisions have had a potential effect on public policy, what makes this case atypical is both the extent of the policy implications and the political decision not to contest the outcome.

The judicial declaration that regulations on interest-group spending are invalid is significant because the contentious sections of the Canada Elections Act represented the culmination of many years' efforts to prevent interest groups from negating the effect of financial regulations governing what candidates and parties can spend during elections. Despite the fact that the invalidation occurred in a lower court and involved legislation characterized as an integral part of the financial regulatory scheme to improve the accountability of electoral participants, the case has neither been appealed nor has [it] encouraged the enactment of alternative legislation. The reasons for silence that now pervades Ottawa on the issue of interest-group spending are complex and involve the timing of the decision, a change in government and a weakened political resolve to acknowledge, never mind redress, the potential impact of unregulated campaign spending by interest groups. The fact that there has been no political remedy is as important in explaining the significance of this lower court decision as the actual judgment itself.

History of the Legislation

The intention of the legislation was to ensure that financial ceilings on parties and candidates during elections would not be rendered meaningless by the unregulated campaign spending of interest groups. . . .

Chief Electoral Officer Jean-Marc Hamel . . . informed Parliament that the financial regulations on candidates and parties would become meaningless without effective limits on interest-group spending. The Elections Act was amended in 1983 and the "good faith" defence was repealed. The amendments effectively prohibited all opportunity for interest groups to financially oppose candidates or parties during an election and it allowed for their financial promotion only when authorized. Although, in parliamentary debate, members from both opposition parties remarked on the likelihood that the legislation impinged on individual rights, the Act was supported by both the Conservatives and NDP.

The amendments were challenged by the National Citizens' Coalition in Alberta Queen's Bench, January 16, 1984. The Coalition's principal criticism of the legislation was that the assumptions underlying the policy objective are flawed: the regulations attempt to reduce the inequities among the three principal parties but do little to facilitate the chances of new parties or independent candidates. Moreover, the regulations do not encourage or enhance public participation in the electoral process; by regulating the election expenses of interest groups a vital aspect of public participation is unlawful. . . .

Judgment

Mr. Justice Medhurst declared that the legislation violates freedom of expression and can be considered valid only if it satisfies section 1, the reasonable limits clause. That clause reads as follows: "The Canadian Charter of Rights and Freedoms guarantees the rights and freedoms set out in it subject only to such reasonable limits prescribed by law as can be demonstrably in a free and democratic society."

In deciding whether the legislation could be "saved" by section 1, Medhurst held that this involves an objective test: can the government empirically prove that the limitations are justified? Medhurst argued that, in order for the legislation to be upheld, the government must satisfy him of the likelihood that the mischief or the harm perceived will occur. A limitation on freedom of expression cannot be justified, he indicated, unless the government has demonstrated that harm will be caused to other values in society. . . .

Medhurst evidently concurred with the suggestion by the National Citizens' Coalition that the record of mischief caused by interest groups was meager. He held that the government had not established, to the degree required, that freedom of expression need be limited. The fact that the government's submissions fell short of the requirement that it demonstrate the lesser test of "a real likelihood of harm" suggests that nothing short of proving the more rigid test, "actual demonstration of harm," would have satisfied Medhurst that the limitation was necessary.

Although Medhurst did not directly address the government's claim that spending regulations foster, rather than curtail, freedom of expression by providing for equality among registered participants and allowing for an informed and meaningful political debate, what is implied in his judgment is that freedom of expression does not embrace qualitative considerations of access and opportunity. Rather, it is a negative value which requires only the absence of restraints on individuals or organizations to exercise free speech.

It is important to note that this decision was rendered before the Supreme Court had articulated principles for determining whether legislation which has been found to encroach upon a Charter right is, nevertheless, a reasonable limit within the meaning of section 1. . . .

While the *Oakes* test is not an easy one for governments to satisfy, the requirements are far less rigid than Medhurst's empirical proof of harm. . . .

[Ed. note: Hiebert reviews the section 1 text articulated by the Supreme Court in 1986 decision in *R. v. Oakes*.]

Implications of the Judgment

The policy implications of the decision are significant. The outcome means that it will be difficult to maintain effective limits on the election expenses of candidates and parties. Interest groups are free either to financially support the candidate of their choice and augment that candidate's legal limit or to mount a negative campaign against an ideological opponent whose own financial abilities to respond are limited. The only limit on what interest groups can spend will be the amount of money they can raise.

The judicial declaration that the spending restrictions were unconstitutional is only part of the explanation for why the case has had such a profound impact on federal elections policy. As important as the judgment itself is the fact that there has been no political attempt to address the impact of the decision. None of the options available to the federal government, which have included appealing the decision, passing new legislation, or enacting the legislative override of section 33, have been employed. . . .

Despite the media backlash and declining support from the Conservative Opposition, the decision not to appeal seems more the result of the timing of the judgment than a weakening of the Liberal government's resolve. The release of the decision coincided with the change in leadership of the Liberal government and, more significantly, with the call for the 1984 federal election. The decision on interest-group spending was handed down June 27, 1984. Three days later John Turner was sworn in as Prime Minister. The government had until the end of July to appeal the judgment, but the election call on July 9 precipitated the decision to let the outcome stand. A justice official suggests that the federal government did not contest the ruling because, in light of the election call, an appeal would create more confusion than it would solve. Despite the decision not to appeal, federal officials advised interest groups to abide by the spending restrictions and warned them that all election spending would be closely monitored. Justice Minister Donald Johnston indicated that while the election call had influenced the decision not to appeal, the government was "reserving its prerogative to tackle the spending limits after the election" and if re-elected might revive the legislation in another form if interest groups abused the lack of enforcement.

The 1984 election resulted in the replacement of the Liberal government, which had introduced the legislation, by an overwhelming Progressive Conservative majority government. During its four-year term the Conservative government did not introduce alternative legislation and ignored the advice of the Chief Electoral Office that a fair electoral process requires the regulation of interest-group spending.

The most plausible explanation of why the Mulroney government did not introduce new legislation to regulate interest-group spending in its first four-year term is that the political costs of redressing the issue were likely perceived to be higher than the probable benefits. The introduction of spending regulations would have subjected the government to the kinds of criticisms made before, that the legislation was motivated by self-interest and worked to undermine, rather than enhance, participation in the electoral process. Moreover, to enact spending regulations for interest groups would be to contradict a widely publicized judicial pronouncement, albeit from a lower court, that these restrictions are an unconstitutional violation of freedom of expression.

Another reason why the Conservative government might not have felt that the benefits of introducing new legislation were worth the costs is that Conservative MPs are not likely to feel threatened by interest-group campaign spending. . . .

A third reason why the issue of interest-group spending has not been redressed is that the threat interest groups were thought to pose did not materialize in the 1984 election. . . .

Whatever the reasons for the lack of such activity in the 1984 election, interest-group spending reached unprecedented levels in the 1988 general election. Estimates of campaign expenses by the three largest spending groups other than political parties are about $3.5 million, and this figure does not include the more modest spending by dozens of smaller organizations. Current Federal Election Commissioner George Allen is particularly disturbed by the extent of the unauthorized spending. His concern is that it is undermining the significance of financial restrictions on candidates and parties. Allen is also bothered by the flurry of last-minute advertising campaigns on the eve of the election when candidates and parties, because of legal blackouts, are incapable of responding. Despite his concerns, Allen has decided to uphold the policy not to prosecute interest-group spending. Although the legislation remains on the books, he argues it would be unconscionable to have people in one part of the country subject to some aspect of the federal law and its penalties while in another part they are not.

The majority of the unauthorized spending in the 1988 election was directly related to the free trade issue. Pro-free trade expenditures far outstripped the amount spent opposing free trade. The largest expenditures came from the Canadian Alliance for Trade and Job Opportunities, a coalition of business organizations, which spent $2 million promoting free trade. That coalition ran a series of four-page newspaper advertisements entitled "Straight Talk on Free Trade," which appeared many times in Toronto and at least twice in 40 other cities across the country. Two other organizations made large expenditures—the National Citizens' Coalition spent $720,000, mostly to promote free trade, and the Alberta government embarked on an extensive pro-free trade campaign within the province. The principal anti-free trade group was the Pro-Canada Network which estimated its spending at $750,000.

Free-trade advertising appeared in two forms. Some of the advertisements actually named a candidate or party while others confined their message to information on the issue. Of those which did name a candidate or party, the interest groups relied on both positive and negative advertising. Many organizations preferred to advise Canadians to vote for a specific candidate or party, while others warned voters against a particular candidate.

Pro-life organizations were also financially active during the campaign. Many of the pro-life advertisements were in the form of negative advertising often intended to shock the reader. One particularly disturbing example was the pamphlet distributed to Toronto homes on the eve of the election—when, legally, candidates are unable to respond—displaying signs supporting NDP candidate Dan Heap. On one side the pamphlet carried the message: "Guess who believes it's okay for some children to go to the Dung Heap?" On the other side was a graphically disturbing picture of an advanced fetus that had been grossly mutilated and the answer to the previous question, with Heap's name in large type. . . .

Conclusions

The Charter of Rights and Freedoms has enhanced the policy impact of judicial review. While the most significant effect will be the result of Supreme Court decisions, the *National Citizens' Coalition* case is an example of a lower court decision which has had a profound impact on public policy. What makes this particular case atypical is both the extent of the policy implications and the political circumstances responsible for the decision not to contest the outcome.

The ruling that regulations on interest-group spending are not justified and that freedom of expression during an election does not embrace qualitative considerations of access and opportunity has significant implications for the electoral process. The 1988 election experience suggests that, without legislative redress, there is no way of guarding against the impact of unaccountable and unregulated campaign spending by wealthy interest groups. The fact that three separate organizations spent in excess of $700,000, all beyond the legal bounds of candidates and parties, raises the question of whether the Canada Elections Act is capable of ensuring that the impact of unaccountable money does not undermine a fair electoral process or unduly distort its outcome.

The decision is also important for what it reveals about some of the problems of subjecting important policy decisions to judicial review. The case, which is a good example of how the Charter can be used by a wealthy interest group to secure interests denied it in the political process, reinforces concerns that, when discourse about political choices is transferred from the political arena to the judiciary, the terms of debate change from political and social to narrow legal consideration. In this instance, questions in the public interest of how to attain a more equitable election outcome were deemed irrelevant to legal requirements of freedom of expression which were confined to the consideration of formal access.

But the significance of the *National Citizens' Coalition* decision is not only that it has declared restrictions on interest-group spending unconstitutional. As important as the actual decision itself is the fact that the situation has not been redressed. While it is not clear how the impact of judicial review will generally affect the level of political debate and discourse about competing and contested values in Canada, this case is one example in which the judicial invalidation of legislation and the publicity generated by the decision have weakened the political will to reenact beneficial, although controversial, legislation.

7.6

CLASS ACTIONS AS A REGULATORY INSTRUMENT
D.N. Dewees, J.R.S. Prichard, & M.J. Trebilcock

Regulation may take many forms, but it is usually a means by which society, through government agencies, alters the behaviour of individuals, groups, or organizations. There are other ways to alter behaviour than direct regulation. Private lawsuits are a means of both redressing some grievances and controlling behaviour—deterring behaviour that might subject one to a lawsuit. The private lawsuit can therefore substitute in some ways for direct regulation. . . . One special form of private lawsuit, the class action, is examined in this paper as, among other things, a means of affecting behaviour in place of direct regulation. . . .

. . . A class action is a lawsuit brought by an individual, the class representative, on behalf of himself and all other persons similarly situated,

From the Monograph. (Toronto, ON: Ontario Economic Council, 1980). Reprinted with permission.

who constitute the class. The class members must have a common interest and a common grievance. . . .

. . . In many areas of law we rely upon both public enforcement and private litigation to limit in the public interest wrongful activity that falls short of traditionally criminal acts. The laws governing these areas may be classified as public welfare legislation or "social regulation," since they deal with acts that are prohibited for the improvement of social welfare generally but are not inherently criminal. For example, the Ontario Environmental Protection Act prohibits the discharge of certain pollutants in excess of specified amounts, and the Crown can prosecute violators of this Act. In addition, a private citizen who is harmed by a pollution discharge can in some cases bring a civil action seeking compensation for the damage he has suffered and perhaps an injunction against further harmful emissions. If a firm produces a sufficiently hazardous product it may be in violation of laws governing product safety and subject to public prosecution for this activity. It may also be liable in a civil suit to those injured as a result of the product's hazardous design. The threats of both public prosecution and private civil litigation act as deterrents to wrongful activity in a wide variety of fields, such as environmental protection, product safety and quality, occupational health, restrictive trade practices, and securities regulation.

Thus there are two procedures for attacking wrongful activity. The first is public prosecution, in which the Crown prosecutes the wrongdoer for violation of a specific statute or regulation. If the prosecution is successful a fine is imposed on the wrongdoer to be paid to the state, and further wrongdoing may be prohibited. The second procedure is a private civil suit in which the victim of the wrongful activity sues the wrongdoer for the damages he suffered and perhaps for an injunction against further wrongdoing. A variation of the civil suit is a class action in which a private citizen brings a suit against the wrongdoer on behalf of himself and all other victims similarly situated. A successful class action results in damages paid by the wrongdoer and distributed to the members of the class who can be identified and contacted. An injunction prohibiting further wrongful activity may also be granted. . . .

Barriers to Suit

The major economic disincentives facing a class representative in deciding whether to lend his name to a potential suit all involve some form of transaction cost, just as in the case of non-class litigation. If litigation were truly costless for any plaintiff, he would in theory bring a suit in respect of a 10-cent claim with only a 10 percent probability of success. But of course litigating is not costless, and apart from the personal time and effort entailed in lending one's name to a suit as a class representative, other costs or potential costs are incurred. Some of these are out-of-pocket expenses or disbursements associated with meeting procedural requirements, such as providing notice to other class members of the pendency of the suit and the right to opt out. Individual class members may also face distribution costs in proving a right to a share in a common class recovery. Other possible costs faced by the class representative relate to the expense entailed in hiring a lawyer for the class and the risk of having to pay his legal costs if the suit fails.

1. Notice costs

   Perhaps surprisingly, present Anglo-Canadian law on class actions does not require a class representative to give notice to other class members of the pendency of the suit on their behalf and their right to opt out if they wish. . . . In contrast to the Anglo-Canadian notice rule, U.S. class action law requires notice to class members, although there has been debate over the appropriate scope and financing of this requirement. The notice issue is clearly one of the major design issues to be resolved in the reform of class action procedures. . . .

2. Distribution costs

   Assuming that a class action has been successful and a judgment for compensation given in favour of a class, class members will still face the costs of coming forward individually to prove a claim to a share in the common recovery. Present Canadian class action rules regard this as the only permissible form of distribution of a common class recovery.

   The existing rules prevent class actions being brought in many cases because of the difficulty of proving individual claims to a share in the common recovery. . . .

3. Legal fees

   Legal costs use special problems for class actions. Existing Anglo-Canadian rules produce the following results. If a class action succeeds, the class representative, while of course not liable for the other side's legal costs, remains liable for that portion of the legal costs of the class not indemnified by the defendant (i.e., the difference between solicitor and client costs and party and party costs) and is not entitled to a contribution from other members of the class. If his own claim is relatively small it will not be worth pursuing in the face of this prospect. If the class action fails the class representative will become liable for two sets of costs: the legal costs incurred by the class and the legal costs of the defendant. These rules operate as daunting disincentives to the bringing of class actions. . . .

Two alternative "private" (non-subsidized) solutions, both involving contingent fee components, might be considered. The first would be to retain the traditional two-way costs rule, which is economically sound because it ensures that the losing party bears the full costs inflicted by his conduct on the other party, but with the following modifications. If a class action succeeded, the class would recover its damages and its lawyer his costs from the defendant, those costs reflecting the value of his time invested in the suit multiplied by a factor to compensate him for the risk of non-compensation in the event of the suit's having failed. If the suit instead failed, the lawyer for the class would have no claim for costs against the class or its representative, and he might be made personally liable for the defendant's costs (to discourage unmeritorious suits), thus freeing the class or its representatives from any such liability. The compensation received by the lawyer for the class in successful suits must of course reflect the risk of this liability.

The second alternative would be to adopt the no-way costs rule proposed in Bill C-13 but provide for compensation to the lawyer from the class fund in successful suits on a basis which reflects the risk of non-compensation in the event of an unsuccessful suit, where no costs would be recoverable (to discourage unmeritorious suits). This is essentially the present American rule. . . .

. . . It has been shown that both of the alternatives just described can significantly lower a barrier to class litigation without unleashing a flood of non-meritorious claims.

Contingent fee arrangements are at present prohibited in Ontario. The subject arouses strong passions. On one hand it can be argued that throughout our economy there exist specialized risk-bearers, such as insurance companies, mutual funds, and manufacturers through product warranties, offering to assume risks—at a price—that other people would prefer not to bear. By specializing in risk-bearing these firms are able to diversify away some of the risks assumed in a way that the individual risk-bearer is commonly unable to do. The lawyer under a contingent fee arrangement is performing much the same function. In return for the prospect of a higher fee in the event of a successful suit, he agrees to absorb all his own costs (and possibly the defendant's cost and notice costs) in a losing suit and absolve his client from them. On the other hand it is argued that contingent fee arrangements are open to abuse. For example, lawyers may have stronger incentives to settle suits so undertaken on terms very favourable to themselves but highly disadvantageous to their clients. Also, lawyers will typically be much better placed than their clients to assess the risks entailed in bringing suit and to take advantage of their clients' relative ignorance in entering a contingent fee arrangement. Judicial supervision of settlements or fee levels may be at best an imperfect check on such abuse. However, the weak incentives for class representatives and class members to monitor their lawyers' performance pose problems not peculiar to contingent fee arrangements.

If a contingent fee approach to the problem of overcoming legal cost disincentives to bringing class actions were unacceptable, the broad alternative approach would be a "public," subsidized, response to the cost barriers. This is the direction followed in the Quebec Class Action Bill (Bill 39, 1978), where a special public fund is set up out of which class actions may be subsidized. While this approach might be an improvement over the current system, it does present difficulties. First, the funding agency is given a very poorly chartered discretion, the exercise of which is likely to involve it in considerable controversy (the spectre of a trial within a trial), because very often its decisions will mean life or death to a proposed class action. Second, there is no clearly articulated theory of why public subsidization of this class of non-means-tested litigant can be socially justified.

Class Actions as "Legalized Blackmail"

One of the most persistent and trenchant criticisms of class actions is that they are a form of "legalized blackmail" allowing class representatives and class lawyers to exact unjustified settlements from class defendants.

Though the charge has typically been loosely made, there appears to be some substance to it. First, to the extent that class actions promoted purely deterrent and not compensatory objectives (i .e., non-viable suits), critics who believe such an objective is inappropriate for a private law suit may view such actions as an illegitimate form of private coercion. Second, to the extent that class members or class lawyers are able to manipulate the selection of a class representative to ensure that he is judgment-proof in the event of a losing suit and an adverse costs award, parties bringing an unmeritorious class action may have an ability to inflict, or threaten to inflict, substantial and non-recoverable legal costs on the defendant, the desire to avoid which may induce unjustified settlements. Third, the combination of the large amounts of money involved and the large number of allegedly aggrieved parties entailed in many class actions may generate false signals to the public by inducing unjustified identification or association with the grievances asserted by the class. In view of the extensive coverage the media are often likely to attach to large lawsuits, corporate defendants will often feel under pressure to settle in order to foreclose flow of adverse publicity that may well continue throughout the typically lengthy course of most class action litigation. Fourth, all other things equal, class actions may be more likely to involve claims with a lower probability of success than individual suits for the same aggregate amount. In the latter case, litigants will often tend to be business or institutional parties engaged in continuous dealings, where litigation is invoked only as a last resort in dispute resolution. The constraint of continuous dealing will apply less frequently to most types of class actions. . . .

. . . The concern over class actions as blackmail has arisen primarily under the U.S. rules allowing contingent percentage fees. It has been shown that under certain circumstances this fee arrangement may lead both the class representative and his lawyer to be willing to sue even though they have a very small chance of winning: sometimes less than 10 percent. . . .

The Lawyer as an Entrepreneur of Law Enforcement

The traditional model of the lawyer-client relationship depicts the lawyer as an agent sought out, retained, instructed, and monitored by a client who has recognized for himself that he faces an existing or potential legal problem. However, this model is not an accurate description of the relationship between a lawyer and his client in a class action involving a large number of relatively small claims. It is not plausible that an individual with a claim of $100 will hire a lawyer and bring a $2 million class action simply to recover his $100. The lawyer, not the class representative, has the real economic interest here.

A change to an entrepreneurial role for lawyers is inherent in a private enforcement mechanism for cases in which the potential recovery of individual plaintiffs or class members is small in relation to the legal costs. If policy seeks to promote class actions of this kind, the incentive structure facing a prospective lawyer for the class becomes a critical issue. In many class action situations the class lawyer can only realistically expect to be paid if the suit succeeds. It is unlikely that he will be able to look to the class representative for payment if the suit fails, and he has no right at present to seek payment from the class members at large. Moreover, such a right would often be of little value because of the transaction costs entailed in enforcing a costs claim against individual members of a large class. Thus, for better or worse, class actions in many cases must be undertaken if at all, on a contingent fee basis, giving the lawyer a direct stake in the outcome of the action.

Beyond fee arrangements, the entrepreneurial role played by lawyers in much class action litigation has other implications. In particular, present prohibitions against maintenance and champerty ("fomenting" or financing litigation) would need to be abrogated in situations where this form of private enforcement was desired. Also, current prohibitions against advertising and other forms of solicitation of clients by lawyers would require modification in a class action context. If law enforcement policy contemplates a positive role for private law enforcement through the class action mechanism, those persons most capable of identifying violations of the law should be encouraged to do so and to take action to prevent the offensive conduct. . . .

Private versus Public Enforcement

. . . Besides seeing the class action as an instrument of regulation, this paper analyzes it as an alternative to public enforcement of regulatory standards. That is, even when a collective decision sets appropriate rules of conduct, the issue whether these rules should be enforced by public or private prosecutions remains. In this context the private class action is a variant of private prosecution that merits consideration as an alternative to public enforcement actions. . . .

... 1. An assessment of private and public enforcement reveals that the primary advantages of private enforcement are the sometimes superior ability to detect offences, the change from criminal to civil liability with a consequent lessening of the standard of proof, the potential compensatory contributions of a civil action in cases involving significant individual losses whether they are recovered in individual or class form, a check, though not a costless one, on abuses of the public prosecutor's discretion, the possibility of relief from systematic public underenforcement of regulatory statutes.

2. Private prosecution should not be looked to as a panacea for achieving optimal levels of enforcement, because it faces a number of difficulties. The determination of the damages payable in a civil suit is likely to be more complex than the assessment of a fine. The "perverse incentive" problem limits the desirability of using multiple levels of damages to reflect the fact that the probability of enforcement is often less than certain. Fluid class recovery schemes may cause inequities and inefficiency. Finally, cases of both underenforcement and overenforcement may rise where the incentive structure facing private enforcers is relied on to achieve optimal levels of enforcement. . . .

7.7

DEBATE: SHOULD ACCESS TO CLASS ACTIONS BE EXPANDED?

AFFIRMATIVE:
Allan C. Hutchinson and Kent Roach

The possibility of class-action reform hovers in the penumbra of the legislative spotlight.

An apparently arcane piece of lawyers' law, it arouses bitter political controversy and forebodes significant changes in corporate accountability. While there is general acceptance of the need for change in Ontario's antiquated existing procedure, there is profound disagreement over the nature and extent of that change.

"Legislation needed to increase access to class action suits," *Financial Post*, February 26, 1990, p.15. Reprinted with permission.

Toronto lawyers William Macdonald and William Rowley wrote forcefully on this page (Jan. 20–22) about the need for a conservative and cautious approach to class-action reform. They contend that any expanded approach is to be shunned as infringing notions of "democratic justice" and dislodging the present equitable balance between plaintiffs and defendants. Moreover, it would be unpatriotic—prompting a crass Americanization of Canada's justice system.

This defence of the status quo is strong on rhetoric but weak on facts. By any "fair and balanced" standard, an expanded class-action procedure is essential to ensure the Canadian justice system is responsive to the realities of litigation between individual plaintiffs and corporate defendants. Democracy is about substantive justice for real people, not simply its formal and often deceptive appearance. A typical situation involves an individual consumer with a potentially valid claim against a manufacturer—a claim that cannot be brought because of the expense with legal costs often far exceeding the amount of the claim. A class action would make it economical for one consumer to bring a representative action on behalf of a group of consumers. Existing rules deter all but the profligate or quixotic plaintiff.

Under the present regime, limited class-action opportunities frustrate the expectations of consumers who must absorb any losses: manufacturers receive a windfall. The suggestion that "normal litigation rules today are widely regarded as balanced and equitable" would be laughable, if it were not so blatantly false. The natural advantages of large and wealthy corporations over individual consumers are enhanced, not neutralized, by the litigation rules. One well-publicized case illustrates the problem.

Four people wanted to sue General Motors on behalf of almost 5,000 buyers of 1971 and 1972 Firenzas. They claimed General Motors was in breach of certain warranties on the cars' durability. This had cut the resale value of the cars by about $1,000. The prospect of each owner bringing a separate action was unlikely because of the cost. In Canada, unlike the U.S., the loser has to pay the winner's legal costs; this, of course, discourages people from suing. As the total claim amounted to $5 million, a class action seemed appropriate and necessary to enforce the owners' rights.

Upholding a century of precedents, the Supreme Court of Canada held that a class action was not possible under existing procedures. In a strong judgment, Justice Estey stressed the entirely inadequate nature of the rules and urged quick and effective legislative intervention. Unfortunately, Estey's suggestion has yet to be acted upon.

The Ontario Law Reform Commission Report of 1982, revealing the deficiences of present procedural rules providing group redress for common wrongs, still remains the best blueprint for legislative action. A combination of corporate pressure and political foot-dragging has worked to prevent successful change. Last June, Attorney-General Ian Scott established an advisory committee to examine class actions and provided some simple guidelines. Representative plaintiffs would have to be certified before they could sue on the behalf of a commonly situated groups. Unless it was not feasible, notice would be given to the members of the class so that they would could opt out of a class action and preserve their rights to sue as individuals. If they did not exercise their right to opt out, plaintiffs would be included in the group whose rights would be decided in the class actions. To ensure that representative plaintiffs and their lawyers were not faced with financial disincentives when they brought suit on the behalf of diffuse groups, court-controlled contingency fee arrangements would be allowed.

These propositions clearly point in the direction of the introduction of class actions. It would be wrong for the committee to sidestep the need for class actions by minor revisions to present rules. The time for such tinkering is well passed and ill-serves Ontario citizens. The proposed opting-out principle sets the burden in the proper place. Class actions are most needed where it is not economical for individuals to sue for what lawyers would unfortunately dismiss as trivial amounts. If individuals believe their interests can be better represented through an individual claim, they can manifest their competence and concern by taking the initiative to opt out.

If, however, the individuals cannot economically bring a claim, it is difficult to see them being worse off—even if, despite judicial certification, the representative plaintiff botches the case and loses it. Being bound by such a judgment is not qualitatively different from "lumping the claim" as one more unremedied consumer grievance. As the song says, nothing from nothing leaves nothing.

Class actions offer benefits not only to aggrieved individuals but also to society at large and even defendants. One alternative to class action is for courts to allow a defendant's loss in a civil action to be held against it in subsequent suits launched by similarly situated plaintiffs. Canadian courts are close to following British and American courts in doing so. If this judicial doctrine is accepted, defendants will be faced with the uncertainty of not knowing how many "wait and see" plaintiffs are hovering around a lawsuit ready to capitalize on the defendant's loss. It is arguably fairer for the defendant to know up front through a formalized procedure for class certification what its total exposure will be in any one lawsuit. Similarly, public resources will obviously be saved by avoiding a multiplicity of suits by "wait-and-see" plaintiffs.

Many who oppose class actions are involved in an ideological defence of present litigation rules at the expense of would-be plaintiffs who cannot afford to pursue a remedy in court. They prey on fears that Canada will become more like the U.S., beset by litigation explosions and money-grubbing lawyers. Ironically, the same lawyers opposing the modest increase in litigation that will accompany class-action reform defend automobile-accident litigation as a fundamental right and freedom. What we face in Ontario today is a lack of class-action litigation because lawyers are too expensive for most individuals. If anything is unCanadian, it is not the prospect of legislation to regulate class actions. It is the continuing reality of corporate defendants remaining unaccountable for significant wrongs that must be borne by many uncompensated individuals.

NEGATIVE:
William Macdonald and William Rowley

Ontario Attorney-General Ian Scott appears determined to introduce an expanded class action procedure in Ontario some time in 1990. He believes this is necessary to provide greater access to the justice system for those who have suffered losses from a common wrong. The key issue is whether this enhanced class access for plaintiffs can be achieved without reduced fairness for defendants. The outcome is not only important to a wide range of potential defendants, it is also important to the kind of society we live in. Moreover, what Ontario does will probably affect the rest of the country, except Quebec, where an expanded class procedure was introduced in 1978.

Class actions are highly controversial proceedings. Now, after several abortive attempts to expand class actions over the past decade, a broadly acceptable expanded class procedure may be achievable in Ontario. The attractive idea behind a class procedure is that where numerous individuals have suffered a common wrong, they are able to assert a common cause of action in one lawsuit as a group, rather than in numerous lawsuits as individuals. The trick is to provide access to justice for such individuals in a manner which really does economize on limited court resources and remains fair and balanced between plaintiffs and defendants. It has not been easy to perform this trick. This is why Scott established a consultative process with a broadly representative Advisory Committee on Class Actions. Its members will attempt to prepare an expanded class action procedure which is acceptable to all of them and thus presumably to a wide spectrum of the affected community.

A class procedure already exists where all members of the class base their claims on a completely common set of facts and law. Even this limited procedure is not free from problems, as it allows one claimant to appoint himself as the representative of the whole class without either class approval or court supervision. Nonetheless, where it applies, the existing procedure has proven reasonably easy for the courts to administer with no insuperable practical or fairness problems. The only concerns

---

"Reforming Ontario class action procedures," *Financial Post*, January 22, 1990, p. 21. Reprinted with permission.

have been about the limited practical availability of the procedure. The courts do not permit the procedure to be used where the claims of class members differ even slightly in respect of an essential element of their case (each may have different damages as the result of a common fault).

While this may seem unduly stringent, there are real problems of both procedure and balance in any attempt to move beyond the existing limited class action model, which is why many hold there should be no expansion of class procedures. The present rules have prevailed for a long time. There is nothing to stop individuals from starting separate actions and having them consolidated or tried together. Staying with what we have is a realistic alternative: option one.

This position does not respond to two issues which others feel a properly designed expanded class procedure should address: improved access to civil justice and improved court efficiency. It is argued both could be achieved by modest changes to allow common facts and law to be established in a single case, rather than requiring multiple court proceedings on the common elements simply because some factual or legal aspect may be different for different claimants. Legislative changes to the rules along these lines would be the second option.

There is a third, more extreme, option for a broadly expanded class procedure, the principal objective of which is behavior modification. The central purposes of the present legal justice system are to provide for private actions to redress private wrongs and public actions to redress public wrongs. However, the proponents of the third option seem obsessed by a concept which is foreign to both private and public law in Canada. They see a need for self-appointed private sheriffs to remedy so-called "mass wrongs" through multi-plaintiff proceedings. That such suits could be brought on behalf of people who have never agreed to sue, and may not even know about the suit, is not considered to be a problem.

This was the perspective which underlay the Ontario Law Reform Commission's Class Actions Report of 1982. Five elements of the commission's majority recommendations (there was substantial dissent) ran counter to longstanding fundamentals and would have removed class procedures from their private remedy mooring. These were:
   (1) Forced inclusion of individuals in class proceedings who might not even know about them;
   (2) The right of the court to estimate global damages without normal proof of individual damage:
   (3) The forfeiture to the Crown of estimated damages that had not been collected by class members;
   (4) Special cost rules favoring class plaintiffs; and
   (5) Contingent fees for class action lawyers which were not otherwise available in normal civil actions.

The Attorney-General, by announcing the consultative process on June 29, 1989, effectively rejected both the first and the third options. He made it clear the consultative process was to be carried out within the constraints that the class action remedy "will treat plaintiffs and defendants in a fair and equitable manner, and will impose no unnecessary burdens on the courts" and "that balanced court rules and procedures should apply to this unique remedy."

It will not be easy to craft an acceptable procedure. Some on the committee will be concerned about even a limited expansion of the present class procedure, given the experience in the U.S. They might prefer the first option of retaining the present restrictions on class actions. Others will be tugged toward accepting the distortions necessarily involved in the "unremedied mass wrong" concept. Option two is thus the only one which has any real prospect of achieving a consensus among those engaged in the consultative process, let alone in the broader institutional community.

The attorney general was clearly aware of these three broad options and his first step was to limit the parameters within which a consensus was to be sought by acceptance of six principles:

- A structured judicial certification process before a class action could be commenced;
- Inclusion of all class members who do not opt out;
- So as to permit opting out, notice to all class members following certification unless the court directs otherwise;
- Introduction of hitherto prohibited, court-controlled contingency fee arrangements;
- No special role for the Attorney-General in class actions; and
- Generally no distribution to third parties of any unclaimed recoveries in a successful class action.

These are intended to ensure that class actions are effective; that plaintiffs and defendants are treated fairly and equitably; and that they impose no unnecessary burdens on the courts.

The normal litigation rules today are widely regarded as balanced and equitable. Therefore fair treatment between plaintiffs and defendants requires that an expanded class procedure not improve the basic legal position of either over the position they would have in separate individual actions. One of the disadvantages of option two is that this cannot be wholly achieved.

The right position in principle is that only those who state a positive wish to become plaintiffs are included (an opt-in approach). However, because it was felt this would not be practical, an opt-out procedure after some kind of attempted notice is stipulated instead. This is troublesome to a democratic society that rests on some kind of majority principle before individuals can be bound by the actions of others. The opt-out concept means even a class procedure based on the second option will necessarily be tilted toward the plaintiffs. The ability of one plaintiff to appoint himself as representative of all class members enables that one person and his lawyer to wield a very big club. The consequences could be so great that the class plaintiff and his lawyer (especially if there are also contingent fees and no legal cost risks if you lose) gain disproportionate power to force settlements in cases not having real merit.

This significant tilt in favor of plaintiffs means all the other provisions must be scrupulously balanced. First, if there are to be contingent fees, those applicable to class actions must be strictly controlled by the courts and must relate to actual professional work done. There must be no massive incentive to trial lawyers to instigate class actions for monetary gains. Second, the key source of balance in the civil dispute resolution system is that losing parties pay the legal costs of the successful parties. This reflects the long recognized need to balance the two crude motivators of greed and fear. An expanded class procedure, no matter how carefully constructed, unavoidably tilts the economic incentives to bring litigation by greatly increasing the pot of gold at the end of the rainbow. The only effective compensating disincentive is the risk of costs. To remove or significantly reduce that risk, contrary to the long-standing norm in Canada, is to introduce a largely one-way bet for class plaintiffs and their lawyers.

Those who understand the economic dynamics that have come to dominate U.S. litigation believe that the interaction in the past of largely unregulated contingency fees (now in the process of changing) and the no cost rule (each side bears its own costs, win or lose) have been the fuel for the litigation and insurance cost explosion in the U.S. reinforced by class litigation.

This discussion has been exclusively concerned with legal system impacts, but the issue goes a good deal further. Many Canadians have visited the U.S. and been subjected to a barrage of television ads which promote litigation. The amount of litigation and the role of litigation lawyers is one of the defining characteristics of a society. At the extremes, the differences between American and Japanese society are striking in this respect and reflect and reinforce profound societal differences. It will be ironic if the province which fought the alleged Americanizing influence of the free trade agreement most strongly should be the unilateral importer of one of the most powerful mechanisms for Americanization. It has been the American way to commercialize just about everything, including even justice. It has not yet been the Canadian way.

7.8

KEY TERMS

Concepts

litigation as a form of interest group activity
"influencing the influencers"
constitutional imperialism
political disadvantage theory
systematic litigation
test case
amicus curiae
intervenor
political trial
class action suit
contingency fee
incentives to litigate
disincentives to litigate

Institutions, Events, and Documents

Court Challenges Program (CCP)
National Association for the Advancement of Colored People (NAACP)
Legal Education and Action Fund (LEAF)
Alliance Quebec
Mahé v. Alberta (1990)
National Citizens Coalition v. A.-G. Canada (1984)

8

Fact Finding in the Courts

All informed decisions must be based on an adequate knowledge of relevant facts, and different kinds of decisions require different kinds of facts. Accordingly, decision-making institutions have developed different fact-finding procedures designed to suit their distinctive needs.

The original adjudicatory function of courts has strongly influenced the procedures and rules governing judicial fact-finding. In order to determine guilt or innocence—"what really happened" (or "historical facts")—common law courts developed special rules to guard against biased or false evidence. The judge assumed a neutral and passive role. The parties to the dispute were responsible for developing all the relevant facts and legal arguments. Hearsay evidence was excluded altogether, and first-hand testimony had to be given under oath, subject to cross-examination and the introduction of contradictory evidence by one's adversary. The giving of false information under these circumstances, perjury, was itself made criminal. These rules and procedures are known collectively as the adversary process, and they constitute the core of the judicial process in all common law countries.

Precisely because it is well suited to its original purpose, the adversary process is much less adept at collecting the kind of facts relevant to public policy-making decisions. Policy-makers want to know about general patterns of human behaviour—what Horowitz calls "social facts"—in order to formulate public policy. (See Reading 8.1) To get these facts, legislators and administrators may consult past studies of the problem, commission new studies to provide current socio-economic information, and conduct extensive hearings to gather additional information, including indications of political support and opposition. Under the traditional rules of the adversary process, judges can do none of this.

The advent of written constitutional law and judicial review placed serious strains on the common law courts' fact-finding procedures. While the inevitable policy impact of constitutional law decisions created a felt need among judges for additional factual information, their procedures were inadequate and even hostile toward such information. There was also a strong sense that it was inconsistent with the adjudicatory function of courts to base a decision on "social facts." This was perceived as more a legislative than a judicial activity. As Weiler points out, this perception was not, and is not, simply an old-fashioned attachment to traditional ways. If a judge makes unanticipated use of non-traditional factual materials, is this fair to unsuspecting litigants who presented facts and arguments along traditional lines? In some cases the relevant "historical facts" and the "social facts" may actually suggest conflicting solutions. Should judges ignore the plight of the individual plaintiff in the name of making policy for the many? In short, when it comes to collecting and using facts, there are serious and real tensions between the adjudicatory and policy-making functions of courts.

Historically, Canadian judges have used "extrinsic evidence" (the Canadian legal term for social facts) very sparingly. The adjudicatory view of the judicial function, the influence of the decisions and style of the British Privy Council, and a deference to the tradition of parliamentary supremacy have all led Canadian judges to use a textually-oriented form of judicial reasoning. The written opinions accompanying the Court's decisions have tended to be highly conceptual and not grounded in the socio-economic contexts that gave rise to the cases. This problem is further aggravated in reference procedures, where there are not even any "historical facts" to guide the judges' reasoning.[1]

This textual approach has been especially criticized in the area of constitutional law as too legalistic. There have been calls for a more sociological jurisprudence, a kind of judicial reasoning "which insists that constitutional words and statutory words must be carefully linked by judicially noticed knowledge and by evidence to the ongoing life of society."[2] This type of jurisprudence requires a more extensive use of extrinsic evidence than Canadian judges have been willing to accept until quite recently.

For similar reasons, American judges also refused to allow social facts into court until 1908. In that year a young lawyer (later to become a Supreme Court justice) named Louis Brandeis successfully defended the state of Oregon's maximum hour labour laws by submitting studies showing a higher incidence of serious maternal health problems for women working long hours in certain occupations. He asked the judges to accept these studies as proof that the legislators had a "reasonable basis" for enacting the mandatory restrictions on freedom of contract. The Supreme Court agreed, and thus began the American practice of the "Brandeis brief," or judicial use of pertinent

---

[1] See Paul Weiler's discussion of the *Chicken and Egg Reference* for a notorious example of what can happen in these circumstances: *In the Last Resort: A Critical Study of the Supreme Court of Canada* (Toronto, ON: Carswell-Methuen, 1974), pp.156–164. Reprinted in the first edition of this book.

[2] W.R. Lederman, "Thoughts on Reform of the Supreme Court of Canada," *The Confederation Challenge*, Ontario Advisory Committee on Confederation, Vol. II (Toronto, ON: Queen's Printer, 1970), p. 295.

socio-economic facts.[3] This practice is consistent with the greater policy-making role of the American Supreme Court, and distinguishes it from other final appellate courts.[4]

The Canadian Supreme Court's 1976 decision in the *Anti-Inflation Reference* suggested that the Canadian aversion to extrinsic evidence was waning, and has since come to be recognized as a turning point in Canadian practice.[5] (See Reading 8.2) The question of the validity of the federal government's wage and price control legislation was referred to the Supreme Court. The mandatory restraint policies clearly were being applied to sectors of the economy that were normally under provincial jurisdiction, and could not be supported by the federal government's normal section 91 power to regulate "trade and commerce." Based on existing precedents, the mandatory wage and price controls could only be justified as an exercise of the federal residual power to make laws for the "peace, order, and good government" of Canada. There were, however, only two possible legal justifications for the exercise of the POGG power: the "national emergency" test or the "inherent national importance" test. Both of these tests seemed to pose an essentially empirical question: Had inflation become so serious in Canada by the mid-1970s as to constitute a "national emergency" or an issue of "inherent national importance"?

Recognizing the inadequacy of the traditional factum and oral argument procedures to deal with this dimension of the case, the then Chief Justice Bora Laskin summoned the counsel for the various governments and private intervenors involved in the case. After several private meetings, the late Chief Justice announced a two-stage procedure for the submission of factual evidence and an opportunity to rebut evidence prior to oral argument. The result was a new chapter in Canadian judicial process.

The federal government submitted its "white paper" on inflation, the documentary basis of its legislative policy, and also a Statistics Canada bulletin showing changes in the monthly consumer price index. The Canadian Labour Congress, one of the intervenors opposed to the wage and price controls, submitted a 64-page economic study of inflation in Canada, which had been especially commissioned for the occasion. It was later supported by telegrams from 38 Canadian economists. On the "rebuttal date," the federal government and Ontario made additional submissions responding to the economic arguments advanced in the CLC's original submission.

---

[3] *Muller* v. *Oregon*, 208 U.S. 412 (1908).

[4] The High Court of Australia does not even receive a written factum or brief before oral argument, thus precluding any "Brandeis brief" presentation of "social facts." The same is true of courts in Great Britain and New Zealand. The refusal to use written factums in these courts is an implicit commentary on their self-perception as adjudicators not policy-makers.

[5] See Katherine E. Swinton, *The Supreme Court and Canadian Federalism: The Laskin-Dickson Years* (Toronto, ON: Carswell, 1990), pp.75–85.

In the end, the Supreme Court made minimal use of the extrinsic evidence that had been submitted. Laskin's opinion noted that the extrinsic material supported the contention that the government had a "rational basis for the legislation," while Ritchie's opinion cited the "white paper" as proof of the existence of an "emergency." More importantly, the *Anti-Inflation Reference* set a new precedent for the use of "social science" briefs in Canadian constitutional law. Henceforth, the Supreme Court may resurrect the procedures elaborated by Laskin whenever it deems it appropriate.

There are other less dramatic devices that judges can use to import social facts into a judicial proceeding. One is the traditional practice of "judicial notice," which is a technique through which a judge may unilaterally take notice of factual matters that he or she deems relevant to the legal questions that must be answered. A good example was the late Chief Justice Laskin's opinion for the majority in a 1972 "breathalyzer" case brought under the 1960 Bill of Rights. In finding that the breathalyzer requirement did not violate "due process of law," Laskin declared,

> I am, moreover, of the opinion that it is within the scope of judicial notice to recognize that Parliament has acted in a matter that is of great social concern, that is the human and economic costs of highway accidents arising from drunk driving, in enacting s. 223 and related provisions of the Criminal Code.[6]

A judge may not "take notice" of extrinsic facts that are highly technical or not well-known. As the preceding example illustrates, "judicial notice" is limited to facts that are generally known and accepted, or at least easily demonstrated. While it is thus an effective vehicle for introducing common sense into judicial proceedings, it has much more limited value in cases involving complex policy issues.

Yet another device for the introduction of social facts into judicial proceedings is the use of the "expert witness." Under the Canada Evidence Act each party can call up to five "expert witnesses" to testify on a subject at issue before the court. One restriction is that the subject must be sufficiently complex that specialized study is required to become an "expert" on it. For this reason an Ontario judge refused to allow Father Philip Berrigan, an American "peace activist," to testify at the trial of the 63 persons charged with trespassing during an anti-nuclear demonstration at a Litton Systems Canada plant in November, 1983. The judge ruled that Berrigan's testimony was not relevant to the trespassing charge.

By contrast, several months later a Charter of Rights case in Calgary saw a total of four expert witnesses called to testify on the issue of whether Canada's election law violates the "freedom of speech" provision of the Charter. These included a Canadian and an American political scientist, a

---

6 *Curr v. the Queen*, (1972) S.C.R. 889.

Canadian constitutional historian, and Canada's Chief Electoral Officer. (See Reading 7.5) The use of such "experts," both as *viva voce* witnesses and as authors of specially commissioned studies, has since become quite common in politically important Charter cases. The use of experts, however, has the disadvantages pointed out by Horowitz. They are hired and paid by the parties to the case, so they are inevitably partisan. Nor is there any guarantee that the "experts" definition of the relevant facts and issues is adequate.

A related matter is the judicial use of "legislative history" in determining the constitutional validity of a statute. While legislative history is not the same as social facts, it can serve a similar purpose of situating a case in the real-world context from which it comes. Historically, common law courts did not go beyond the actual text of a statute in interpreting its meaning. With the advent of ever increasing government social and economic regulation, courts have felt the need to go beyond the texts of statutes to discover their legislative purposes. American courts began to use legislative history in constitutional cases during the 1920s, and now do so extensively. Legislative history has usually been held inadmissable in Canada, but again the 1976 *Anti-Inflation Reference*, and the use of the government "white paper," marks a departure from past practice. Since then, the Supreme Court has made more frequent use of Hansard and other historical sources in constitutional cases.

While historically Canadian courts were reluctant to admit, much less use social facts, the changes that began in the 1970s have accelerated since 1982 under the Charter of Rights. As noted by Justice Bertha Wilson in 1986, several Charter sections seem to require some presentation of social facts. (See Reading 8.3) Section 1, for example, declares that the subsequently enumerated rights are not absolute, but subject to "such reasonable limitations prescribed by law as can be demonstrably justified in a free and democratic society." The last element of this test suggests comparisons between challenged Canadian practices and practices of other "free and democratic societies." This occurred in the series of "one person, one vote" cases decided in B.C., Saskatchewan, the Supreme Court, and Alberta between 1988 and 1991. Both litigants and judges made extensive comparisons of Canadian electoral distribution practices with those of England, Australia and the United States.[7]

The Supreme Court further encouraged the presentation of social facts by embracing the so-called "Charter two-step" approach to interpreting section 1.[8] In its landmark 1986 decision in *R. v. Oakes*, the Court ruled that

---

[7] See chapter 12, "Fair and Effective Representation," in Rainer Knopff and F.L. Morton, *Charter Politics* (Toronto, ON: Nelson Canada, 1992), pp. 332–373.

[8] For a fuller exposition of the section 1 "Charter two-step," see Knopff and Morton, *Charter Politics*, pp. 38–57.

once a violation of a Charter right has been identified, the burden then shifts to the government to prove that the challenged statute or policy serves a "pressing and substantial objective"; that the means used are "rationally connected" to that objective; that the law impairs the rights involved as little as is reasonably possible (i.e., there is no "alternative means" of achieving the same end with less impairment of rights); and that on balance the public good achieved outweighs the private harm to individual rights. Needless to say, government lawyers cannot meet this burden of proof by assertion alone. They need social facts to document their claims. Perhaps this also explains Chief Justice Lamer's remark that when judges interpret section 1, they are making "essentially what used to be a political call."[9]

A similar need for social facts seems implicit in the section 15 right to "equal benefit of the law" and the section 23 right to minority language education "where numbers merit." In its leading section 15 decision, *Andrews v. Law Society of British Columbia* (1988), the Supreme Court emphasized that section 15 requires laws not just to provide "equal treatment" but to have "equal effects," especially for historically disadvantaged groups. The effect or impact of a public policy can only be determined by reference to social science studies. There is thus increasing pressure on Canadian judges to allow and to use extrinsic evidence and social facts more than in the past.

Former Justice Bertha Wilson has expressed optimism that the courts, with the help of intervenors, will be up to this challenge and will not fall victim to the problems of institutional capacity described by Horowitz. Weiler points out, however, that getting relevant social facts into the courts does not guarantee that they will be understood or properly used. He argues that there is a qualitative difference between the judicial use of social facts to determine whether there is a "reasonable basis" for government legislation (the original purpose of the Brandeis brief and also the role played by social facts in the *Anti-Inflation Reference*), and the judges' use of social science data to craft a new judicially created policy.[10]

Carl Baar's account (See Reading 8.4) of the Supreme Court's attempt to craft a policy implementing the section 11(b) right to trial within a reasonable time bears out Weiler's scepticism. In trying to determine how much delay is too much, the Supreme Court erred twice in its use of social facts. In its 1990 decision in *R. v. Askov*, the Court laid down a maximum permissible delay of six to eight months for "institutional delay," delay caused by overcrowded court calendars and facilities. To the dismay of the Court, law-enforcement agencies and many of the general public, this new policy led to the dismissal of tens of thousands of criminal cases for

---

9   "How the Charter changes Justice," *Globe and Mail*, April 17, 1992, p. A17.

10   "Two Models of Judicial Decision-Making," *Canadian Bar Review* 46 (1968) pp. 406–471.

failure to meet the new limit. The source of the problem was subsequently traced to Justice Corey's erroneous use of data from Montreal, data that the Court had obtained on its own initiative *after* oral argument; and his failure to carefully read (or understand) the statistics on court delay submitted by Askov's lawyer. These statistics, taken from a study by Professor Baar, indicated that a six to eight month rule would negatively affect about 25 percent of the criminal cases studied in the Toronto area.

In response to the negative impact of *Askov* and the criticism it generated, the Supreme Court moved quickly to "fix" its alleged mistake. In March, 1992, with Justice Corey conspicuously absent from the panel of seven judges who heard the appeal, the Supreme Court issued an opinion in *R. v. Morin*, which was intended to clarify the "*Askov* rule." Justice Sopinka's majority opinion blamed the "large number of stays and withdrawals" on the "interpretation and administration" of the *Askov* rule by lower court judges. *Askov* was intended as "an adminstrative guideline," wrote Sopinka, and was "not intended to be applied in a purely mechanical fashion." It was "neither a limitation period nor a fixed ceiling," and should be reasonably interpreted in light of the different facts of each case. Sopinka recognized the relevance of statitical evidence from other jurisdictions, but cautioned "care must be taken that a comparison of jurisdictions is indeed a comparative analysis." He then acknowledged that the use of the Montreal data in *Askov* had been inappropriate, but blamed Professor Baar—incorrectly—for providing the Court with the Quebec data!

The *Morin* case, unlike *Askov*, dealt with delay in a section 92 provincial court hearing a summary conviction offence. Sopinka went on to propose a longer period of permissible delay for trials conducted in provincial courts— eight to ten months—on the grounds that the section 92 courts are busier than the superior courts and that statistics show that, on average, it takes longer to dispose of cases in provincial courts than in superior courts. Once again, the source of the Court's data was Professor Baar's affidavit in *Askov*, and once again the Court got it wrong. Indeed, the Court misinterpreted Baar's data not once but twice: first, by confusing "median total time" for the trial of indictable offences (in s. 92 and s. 96 courts combined), with the median delay for provincial court stage of the same cases; and second, by treating the latter as if it were the median delay for provincial court disposal of summary conviction offences (trials that start and finish in section 92 courts).

Such problems should not come as a surprise for a judiciary that has plunged so quickly into a greater policy-making role. Horowitz, Weiler and others have shown there is an inherent tension between the fact-finding procedures and judicial expertise associated with adjudicating disputes and the data-gathering and analysis required by a policy-making role. At a minimum, the public embarassment of *Askov* and *Morin* should stimulate both the justices and their clerks to circulate draft opinions more widely and proof read more critically. Perhaps it will also induce more caution in judges who are inclined to use social facts to craft new policies.

8.1

FACT FINDING IN ADJUDICATION
Donald C. Horowitz

The fact that judges function at some distance from the social milieu from which their cases spring puts them at an initial disadvantage in understanding the dimensions of social policy problems. The focused, piecemeal quality of adjudication implies that judicial decisions tend to be abstracted from social contexts broader than the immediate setting in which the litigation arises, and, as already indicated, the potentially unrepresentative character of the litigants makes it hazardous to generalize from their situation to the wider context.

The judicial fact-finding process carries forward this abstraction of the case from its more general social context. To make this clear, it is necessary to distinguish between two kinds of facts: historical facts and social facts. Historical facts are the events that have transpired between the parties to a lawsuit. Social facts are the recurrent patterns of behavior on which policy must be based. Historical facts, as I use the term, have occasionally been called "adjudicative facts" by lawyers, and social facts have also been called "legislative facts." I avoid these terms because of the preconceptions they carry and the division of labor they imply. Nonetheless, by whatever designation they are known, these are two distinct kinds of facts, and a process set up to establish the one is not necessarily adequate to ascertain the other.

Social facts are nothing new in litigation. Courts have always had to make assumptions or inferences about general conditions that would guide their decisions. The broader the issue, the more such imponderables there are. The breadth of the issues in constitutional law has always made it a fertile field for empirical speculation. Does a civil service law barring alleged subversives from public employment have a "chilling effect" on free speech? Is the use of third-degree methods by the police sufficiently widespread to justify a prophylactic rule that would exclude from evidence even some confessions that are not coerced? Does pornography stimulate the commission of sex crimes, or does it provide cathartic release for those who might otherwise commit such crimes?

Constitutional law is a fertile field, but it is not the only field in which such questions arise. If a court refuses to enforce against a bankrupt corporation an "unconscionable contract" for the repayment of borrowed

The Courts and Social Policy (Washington, DC: The Brookings Institute, 1977), from pages 45–51. Reprinted with permission.

money, will that make it more difficult for firms needing credit to obtain it and perhaps precipitate more such bankruptcies? Does it encourage carelessness and thus undercut a prime purpose of the law of negligence if an automobile driver, a shopkeeper, or a theater owner is permitted to insure himself against liability inflicted as a result of his own fault?

These are, all of them, behavioral questions. They share an important characteristic: no amount of proof about the conduct of the individual litigants involved in a civil service, confession, obscenity, bankruptcy, or negligence case can provide answers to these probabilistic questions about the behavior of whole categories of people. As a matter of fact, proof of one kind of fact can be misleading about the other. What is true in the individual case may be false in the generality of cases, and vice versa. The judicial process, however, makes it much easier to learn reliably about the individual case than about the run of cases.

The increasing involvement of the courts in social policy questions has increased the number and importance of social fact questions in litigation. As the courts move into new, specialized, unfamiliar policy areas, they are confronted by a plethora of questions about human behavior that are beyond their ability to answer on the basis of common experience or the usual modicum of expert testimony. A few examples, drawn from a social science manual for lawyers, will make the point:

> Do the attrition rates for different racial groups applying for admission to a union apprenticeship program suggest a pattern of racial discrimination?

> How would the elimination of a local bus system through bankruptcy affect low income people and the elderly poor in particular?

> How are different income groups and communities of varying sizes differentially affected by the formula allocation of General Revenue Sharing funds?

Obtaining answers to such behavioral questions has become exigent, and not only because the interstices in which courts make fresh policy keep expanding. If a judge or a jury makes a mistake of fact relating only to the case before it, "the effects of the mistake are quarantined." But if the factual materials form the foundation for a general policy, the consequences cannot be so confined.

Traditionally, the courts have been modest about their competence to ascertain social facts and have tried to leave this function primarily to other agencies. They have shielded themselves by applying doctrines that have the effect of deferring to the fact-finding abilities of legislatures and administrative bodies, to avoid having to establish social facts in the course of litigation.

The reasons for this general modesty are well grounded. There is tension between two different judicial responsibilities: deciding the particular case and formulating a general policy. Two different kinds of fact-finding processes are required for these two different functions. The adversary system of presentation and the rules of evidence were both developed for the former, and they leave much to be desired for the latter.

In general, the parties can be depended upon to elicit all of the relevant historical facts, through the ordinary use of testimony and documentary evidence, and the judge or jury can be presumed competent to evaluate that evidence. Social facts, on the other hand, may not be elicited at all by the parties, almost surely not fully, and the competence of the decision-maker in this field cannot be taken for granted.

These deficiencies of the adversary process have led to proposals for the employment of outside experts as consultants to the courts. So far, relatively few impartial experts have been appointed, and the proof of social facts has largely been left to the traditional adversary method.

Expert testimony is the conventional way for the litigants to prove social facts, but its deficiencies are considerable. The experts are usually partisans, employed by the parties, and their conclusions tend to reflect that status. If the parties provide a skewed picture of the problem they purport to represent, their expert witness may do the same. Finally, reliance on expert witnesses hired by the parties makes the judge the prisoner of the parties' definition of the issues of social facts that are involved.

The rules of evidence are equally inapt for the verification of social facts. They are geared to the search for truth between the parties, not to the search for truth in general. Understandably, there is a prohibition on the introduction of hearsay evidence. Courts must act on what happened, not on what someone said happened. The emphasis in judicial fact-finding on choosing between conflicting versions of events by assessing the credibility of witnesses also places a premium on requiring witness to have firsthand knowledge of the events about which they testify. Sensible though the hearsay rule may be, however, it makes the ascertainment of scientific facts of all kinds including social science, very difficult. Books and articles constitute inadmissible hearsay; they are not alive and cannot be cross-examined. Consequently, when behavioral materials are introduced into evidence, it is usually pursuant to some exception to the hearsay rule. . . .

. . . The use of expert testimony involves another kind of exception. Duly qualified experts, unlike ordinary witnesses, need not confine themselves to testifying about facts. They may also state their opinion, which may be nothing more than a guess or a bias. Yet the studies on which their opinion may be based remain inadmissible as hearsay (though they may be introduced to impeach an expert's opinion).

All of these cumbersome devices tend to make the judge dependent on secondary interpretations of the relevant empirical material and to discourage him from going directly to the material itself. As we shall see in later chapters, filtered knowledge has its problems.

If new rules and mechanisms do develop to aid in informing the courts about social facts, further problems will arise. The courts may have to administer a dual system of evidence—one part for historical facts, another for social facts—and there is the problem of what might be called contamination. Evidence introduced for one purpose may, as it often does, spill over to infect the other set of issues. Compartmentalization to prevent contamination is one of the hardest jobs a judge must perform. This particular problem suggests again the underlying tension between deciding the litigants' case and making general policy.

How have social fact issues been handled by the courts in practice? They have been handled in much the same way that the rules of evidence and the adversary system have been adapted to accommodate social facts: by neglect or by improvisation.

A first, quite common way is to ignore them or to assume, sometimes rightly, sometimes wrongly, that the litigants' case is representative. This is patently inadequate. . . .

. . . A third way of dealing with social facts is to go outside the record of the case in search of information. This is what Mr. Justice Murphy did when he sent questionnaires to police forces in thirty-eight cities in order to determine the relationship between the admissibility of illegally obtained evidence and police training in the law of search and seizure. The same impulse has sometimes moved other judges, restless in their ignorance of behavioral fact, to consult experts of their acquaintance, as Judge Charles Clark, then former Dean of the Yale Law School, consulted the Yale University organist about a music copyright case that was pending before him. These attempts, primitive as they are, show the existence of a deeply felt need rather than a method of satisfying it.

What these examples also suggest is that the need for empirical data is often not even sensed until the case is on appeal. The traditional formulation of causes of action rarely incorporates social facts as an element of proof. When behavioral facts are implicitly incorporated (for example, "reasonable care of a prudent man under the circumstances"), these standards are often not met by evidence but left to the decision-maker to judge from his own experience.

The law thus tends to slight the need for behavioral material in a number of ways. In practice, this means that the option of utilizing such material falls on counsel. Generally, public-interest lawyers have been much more assiduous about introducing evidence of social facts than have other lawyers, and it is they who have often compiled voluminous records of expert testimony and memoranda. . . .

That the process of adjudication places the emphasis heavily on the accurate ascertainment of historical facts, while it neglects and renders it difficult to prove social facts, is, of course, exactly what might be expected from its traditional responsibilities. This is to say, the fact-finding capability of the courts is likely to lag behind the functions they are increasingly required to perform.

To argue that this problem of capability exists is still to say nothing of the materials on which proof of social facts might be based. The problems here are considerable. There may be no studies that cast light on the issue in litigation. If there are, the behavioral issue may be framed in a way quite inappropriate for litigation. Studies may, of course, be specially commissioned for the purposes of the lawsuit. Even if the potential bias of such studies is overcome, the constraints of time and resources may dictate research methods much less than satisfying. On large issues, existing data are likely to be fragmentary. Then the question becomes one of generalization from partial or tentative findings, or one of drawing inferences from proxies. This is no place for a full-scale consideration of the imperfect fit between law and social science. It is enough to say here that the problems of social science do not disappear in litigation, but are instead compounded by the litigation setting, the different ways in which lawyers and social scientists ask questions, and the time constraint.

This last point needs to be underscored. As I have said earlier, litigation is, for the most part, a mandatory decision process. Courts do not choose their cases; cases choose their courts. With certain exceptions, a case properly brought must be decided. Whereas a legislator or administrator has some freedom to shy away from issues on which his quantum of ignorance is too great to give him confidence that he can act sensibly, courts are not afforded quite the same latitude. Courts have difficulty finding and absorbing social facts in the context of a largely mandatory decision process that puts them at a comparative disadvantage in social policymaking.

8.2

THE *ANTI-INFLATION* CASE: THE ANATOMY OF A CONSTITUTIONAL DECISION
Peter H. Russell

This article is reprinted as Reading 10.4.

8.3

THE INSTITUTIONAL CAPACITY OF THE COURT
Bertha Wilson

Let us look more closely at the Court's new role to see whether or not the Court has the institutional capacity to discharge it. Are we equipped to do the job? And will the process be any different from the one we were engaging in before the Charter?

The starting point for this enquiry is the Charter itself. It sets out a number of guaranteed rights and freedoms which by virtue of section 52 are declared to be the "supreme law" of Canada. Any laws or any conduct on the part of government which violates these fundamental rights and freedoms must be declared unconstitutional by the courts, subject, of course to section 1 of the Charter. This section contemplates that even though these enumerated rights and freedoms are fundamental, they may be limited or curtailed if the limits are prescribed by law, are reasonable, and can be justified in a free and democratic society. This section reveals why these particular rights and freedoms were selected for special protection under the Constitution. It is because they represent the fundamental values of a free and democratic society and, if any limits are to be put upon them, then the government must establish to the satisfaction of the courts that those limits can be justified in that kind of society. The courts, in other words, have been given the responsibility for developing some kind of balance between the fundamental rights of the citizens on the one hand and the right and obligation of democratically elected governments to govern on the other. The challenge for the courts is to develop norms against which the reasonableness of the impairment of a person's rights can be measured in a vast variety of different contexts. But not only that. These norms must reflect to the maximum extent possible the political ideal of a free and democratic society.

Some say that the courts are not suited to this kind of role because of the broad range of competing interests involved in the policy choices that will have to be made. The courts, they say, are well adapted to purely adversarial decision-making but are not equipped to conduct enquiries into the operation of public policy. Nor, they say, are judges trained to do that. They have not in the past displayed any awareness of the breadth of the judicial

"Decision-making in the Supreme Court," *University of Toronto Law Journal* 36 (1986), pp. 241–244. Reprinted with permission.

function in society. Can they be expected now to abandon their narrow legalistic habits and "think large" about the kind of society Canadians want to live in?

I accept this as a valid criticism, but I wish that our critics did not stop there. Judges are the products of their legal training and of the disciplines of the adjudicative process by which their skills have traditionally been honed. So also are the counsel to whom the courts are now going to have to look for assistance in their new role. What proposals has Professor Weiler, for example, put forward for a new approach to legal training in order to produce the kind of counsel we now desperately need? In 1968, when the Canadian Bill of Rights was proposed, he expressed great reservations about the desirability of judicial review of legislative action and concluded with this comment: "Perhaps the proposal for a Canadian Bill of Rights should await the advent of judges who are products of a different legal education." That was 17 years ago, and counsels' way of thinking about the law has changed but little in the interval. Nowhere is this more apparent than on applications to our Court for leave to appeal, where counsel is asked "What is the issue of national public importance raised by this appeal?" This question requires them to raise their sights, to put the law into a larger social perspective, and to relate it to the reality of everyday life—still the hardest thing for them to do!

I agree with our critics that we have to start from the ground floor, and that the traditional approach to legal education might benefit from some review. In the meantime, however, I think there are some fairly straightforward procedural accommodations that we can make to our new role. The most important one, in my view, is to alter the traditional two-party structure of public law litigation by giving a generous interpretation to the Court's rules governing interventions. If constitutional decisions have ramifications for a broad range of interests and involve distinct choices between conflicting social policies, then we must devise some way of bringing those interests before the Court. While many judges shy away from this solution on the basis that it will add considerably to the time expended on hearings when time has become our rarest commodity, it seems to me that it is the most direct and immediate way to respond to what the commentators refer to as the polycentricity of Charter issues. The burden on the process could, of course, be minimized by a more rigid control on the oral presentations of intervenors by the presiding judge or by limiting the participation of intervenors to submissions in writing. Because of the presence of divergent views on this matter in our own Court, it has been referred by the members of the Court to their Joint Committee of the Bench and Bar for input from the profession.

Liberalized intervention, in my view, would have another important advantage. It would assist in legitimizing the Court's new role through a more open and accessible court process, and it would go part way to solving the counter-majoritarian problem which some see as inherent in judicial power. Some commentators have argued that the removal of what are essentially political disputes from the political to the judicial arena diminishes the capacity of Canadians as a people to take responsibility for problems which should be resolved through political compromise and negotiation. I expressed the view earlier that section 33 of the Charter— the opting-out provision—is not really an adequate answer to that problem. Perhaps a more accessible court process is a pragmatic alternative.

The other accommodation we can make is to broaden the base of the admissible evidence in Charter cases. The courts, of course, were already moving in this direction in constitutional cases pre-Charter by admitting evidence of "legislative facts," that is, the facts which would portray the context in which the legislation was passed. This occurred typically in cases where the legislative power that had been exercised was properly exercisable only if some factual pre-condition was present. We see it in cases dealing with the federal legislature's "peace, order and good government" power, the exercise of which had to be premised on the existence of some kind of national emergency. For example, in the *Board of Commerce* case the Privy Council had to consider whether the economic turmoil that followed in the wake of the first world war amounted to the type of "exceptional" circumstances required for federal intervention in otherwise provincial regulatory spheres. Similarly, the *Unemployment Insurance Reference* in the mid-1930s raised a question as to whether the unemployment experienced during the great depression was of sufficient dimension that it could be said to touch on the life of the nation as a whole. And more recently, in the *Anti-Inflation Reference* the Court had to decide whether double-digit inflation could constitute a national emergency justifying the use of the "peace, order and good government" power. Although these questions were essentially questions of fact, their very magnitude and intrinsic character seemed to demand a significantly different approach to the rules of evidence from that utilized in the fact-finding process at an ordinary trial.

It seems to me that the Court may now have to expand the evidentiary base even further. Indeed, problems of proof under the Charter are going to be among the more interesting and difficult ones. The provisions in the Charter are replete with words such as "reasonable," "unreasonable," "promptly," "arbitrarily," "fair"—all of which seem to call for some comparison with an accepted standard which is presumably subject to proof. Likewise, phrases like "cruel and unusual punishment," "where numbers warrant," and "bring the administration of justice into disrepute" all seem to require solid factual underpinnings. Otherwise the judges will be unable, as Judge Cardozo put it, to "transcend the limitations of their own egos" and will tend to rely upon their own personal systems in interpreting and applying the Charter. As you know, the inclusion of relevant social science information in the record presented to U.S. courts is firmly entrenched in American constitutional practice. For example, in the well-known desegregation case of *Brown v. Board of Education*, the question arose as to whether the separate educational facilities afforded to black children in some states effectively denied them the equal protection of the law as entrenched in the Fourteenth Amendment. Crucial to the analysis, it would seem, was a statement filed by the appellant and signed by some 30 eminent psychologists and sociologists dealing with the effects of segregated education on minority group children. It was this knowledge placed at the Court's disposal which laid the groundwork for the Court's overturning of the "separate but equal" doctrine which until then had upheld racial segregation. The factual inquiry established to the Court's satisfaction that separate facilities simply could not provide the equality which the Constitution required. Although it is somewhat unclear as to whether the Court took an extremely liberalized view of the judicial notice rules based on the social science data, or whether these data were seen as factual proof of the detrimental effects of segregation on a balance of probabilities, it is clear that the expanded record greatly facilitated the judicial analysis, which would otherwise have entailed a great deal of guesswork.

I believe that the same kind of development will take place in Canada. The extent to which it occurs may, however, depend on what approach the courts take to the interpretation of the Charter.

8.4

SOCIAL FACTS, COURT DELAY AND THE CHARTER

Carl Baar

The case of *Regina v. Askov*, decided by the Supreme Court of Canada on October 18, 1990, became one of the most important and controversial Supreme Court judgments interpreting legal rights under the Canadian Charter of Rights and Freedoms. It was the Supreme Court's fifth judgment on section 11(b) of the Charter, guaranteeing accused persons a "trial within a reasonable time." It was, however, the Court's first section 11(b) case to address the question of whether excessive "institutional delay" violates the Charter. Institutional delay is the time that elapses not because the crown is proceeding too slowly or a particular case is very complex, but because resources and practices make it impossible for a court to deliver an earlier trial date.

Written for the second edition of this book.

As a direct result of the decision in *Askov*, more than 40,000 criminal charges, largely but not exclusively within the province of Ontario, were dismissed for failure to bring accused persons to trial within a reasonable time. Yet the reasons given by the majority in *Askov* concluded by saying that there would be little difficulty complying with the decision in "most regions" of the country. The surprising result was acknowledged publicly in July, 1991 by Justice Cory, the author of the majority judgment, and by March, 1992, the Supreme Court used its next section 11(b) case, *Regina v. Morin*, to limit the possibility for accused persons to cite *Askov* to gain dismissal of pending criminal charges.

What made the *Askov* controversy both frustrating and ironic was that the Supreme Court had in fact made social science data—"social facts" in Donald Horowitz's terms—more central to its judgment than in any previous constitutional case. For many years, Canadian court watchers had urged the Court to consider social facts, following the American practice of the "Brandeis brief." In *Askov*, the Court accepted and used an affidavit reporting systematic data on elapsed time of criminal cases in 10 Canadian cities in three provinces, but still failed to anticipate the results of its judgment.

This failure can be attributed to a number of characteristics of the judicial process in Canada which, taken together, make it difficult for the courts to deal effectively with social facts. *Askov* itself shows in key respects a fundamentally sound understanding of section 11(b) of the Charter, and is likely to be beneficial in its long-term impact on Canadian criminal justice. But its immediate shortcomings illustrated one of the most troubling aspects of Charter adjudication.

The Historical Facts

The particular facts of the *Askov* case are straightforward. Askov and three co-accused were charged with a number of offences arising from the use of threats and violence to corner the market on exotic dancers in the Metropolitan Toronto area. Following their arrests in November, 1983, they were brought to Provincial Court, the starting point for any criminal court proceeding in Canada. They elected to be tried by a judge and jury, which required that their case be moved to a section 96 court (one staffed by federally appointed judges), because only federally appointed judges can preside over jury trials in Canada. Before the accused could proceed to trial in the section 96 court, they had to be committed to trial by a Provincial Court judge, and were entitled to a preliminary hearing before committal.

The preliminary hearing for Askov and his co-accused began on July 4, 1984, in the Provincial Court in Brampton, Ontario. Following a postponement, the preliminary hearing was completed on September 21 and the accused were committed to trial in the District Court, which had jurisdiction over most criminal jury cases in Ontario at that time (it was replaced in 1990 following a province-wide reorganization). The 10-month period from arrest to committal, while longer than most cases, was not unusual, and was not challenged by the accused, since it was a result in part of an effort to find a convenient time for the lawyers for all four accused to be present together in court.

However, when the accused appeared in the District Court on October 1, 1984, to set a date for trial, the earliest available date was October 15, 1985. When the accuseds' trial date arrived a year later, and their place on the list was still not reached by October 25, the case was put over for trial on September 2, 1986. When that date arrived, more than 23 months after the case left Provincial Court, the accused successfully argued that the delay in District Court violated their right to be tried within a reasonable time.

Askov's case was different from cases that arose before the Charter. Prior to 1982, accused persons could only contest excessive delays if they could show that the delay resulted from the crown abusing its discretion in prosecuting the case (for example, by refusing to bring a case to trial for a long period of time while pursuing related charges against another person). In *Askov*, no allegations were made about the crown's conduct of the case. Both sides agreed that the delay was entirely a result of the unavailability of any earlier trial date. But prior to the Charter, the unavailability of a trial date was not grounds for dismissal of charges.

The Supreme Court was thus faced in *Askov* with a new and important question. Should delay not attributable to the crown or the accused be covered by section 11(b)? If the lack of a trial date counts against the crown, an accused could go free through no fault of the prosecution. If, on the other hand, the lack of a trial date does not count against the crown, an accused could wait years for trial and have no remedy.

The Court ruled unanimously that these "institutional delays" must count against the crown. The Court declared that to do otherwise would be to negate section 11(b). The Court further reasoned that the provincial government, which was responsible for prosecuting criminal cases, was also responsible for providing the institutional resources that would allow trial courts to offer trial dates within a reasonable time.

Defining Reasonable Time

Once the Supreme Court agreed on the principle that institutional delay could count as a factor in determining whether section 11(b) had been violated, the next question was the practical and more difficult one: how long is too long?

The first task of Askov's counsel was to argue that 23 months from committal to the beginning of trial was too long. But no standard existed in Canadian law to draw that conclusion. Unlike a number of jurisdictions outside Canada, we have no statutes or court rules that indicate the number of days or months within which a criminal case must be completed. The federal government introduced Criminal Code amendments in 1984 that would have set a standard of six months from first appearance to trial or committal in the Provincial Court, and an additional six months from committal to trial in the section 96 court, with certain important exceptions as well. The proposal died when the Liberal government called the election in 1984, and no other proposal to set a time standard has been introduced by subsequent Conservative governments.

Earlier decisions under section 11(b) provided some clues about how Askov's counsel could approach the task of enunciating a standard in the absence of legislation. Particularly relevant was the extensive set of reasons presented by the then Justice Lamer (speaking for himself but not for the Court) in *Regina v. Mills*, the first section 11(b) case decided by the Supreme Court of Canada. Lamer argued that allowable time should be based on comparative jurisdictional analysis, so that the "appropriate models" are those courts with "greater degrees of promptness" or "lesser amounts of systemic delay."

Quite apart from the *Askov* case, in 1988 political scientist Carl Baar had obtained funding from the Social Sciences and Humanities Research Council to conduct empirical research on the Canadian judicial system. One of his chief objectives was to obtain data on the pace of litigation in Canadian trial courts that would allow comparison with the pace of litigation in the United States. He adapted measuring instruments first used in an influential study of 21 American state trial courts (Thomas Church's *Justice Delayed*, 1978), and focused on Ontario criminal cases that had their final dispositions in section 96 trial courts. By the time data gathering was completed in 1989, a sample of close to 3,000 criminal cases, primarily from 1987, had been collected from five Ontario court centres, as well as three in New Brunswick and two in British Columbia. Among the five Ontario courts was Brampton, chosen because of its reputation as one of the province's slowest courts, and London, chosen because of its reputation as one of the most expeditious. New Brunswick was also chosen because it was usually considered very expeditious.

While the data were being gathered during 1988–89, a casual conversation between Baar and University of Toronto law professor Lorraine Weinrib prompted her to mention the then pending *Askov* appeal. As it turned out, one of her students was working on the case as a class project with Askov's lawyer, Michael Code. Baar met with the student and provided background literature and studies on court delay. When Code realized that Baar's data base included over 400 criminal cases from the Brampton District Court (all 1987 dispositions), as well as data from other urban centres comparable to Brampton (London and Ottawa in Ontario, as well as Vancouver and the Vancouver suburbs covered by the New Westminster court), he sought an affidavit from Baar presenting a summary of the data and relevant findings on court delay that could be presented to the Supreme Court of Canada.

By the spring and fall of 1989, analysis of the elapsed time in the various court centres confirmed the informed judgment of those familiar with criminal litigation in Ontario. Brampton was indeed the slowest of five Ontario courts, both in terms of the total time from first appearance in Provincial Court until disposition in the section 96 court, and in terms of the "upper court time" alone, counting only from the time the indictment was lodged in the section 96 court (following committal) until disposition in that court. London was the most expeditious of the other four Ontario courts, and the two British Columbia courts had a pace comparable to or faster than those Ontario courts. In turn, New Brunswick's Court of Queen's Bench was faster than any of the B.C. and Ontario courts.

What was more revealing was that when compared with courts in the United States, no Canadian court was particularly fast. The pace of criminal litigation in Toronto and Ottawa, for example, was well behind large American urban centres like Detroit, Oakland and New Orleans. By this comparison, in the much-quoted words of Justice Cory in *Askov*, Brampton was the slowest court "anywhere north of the Rio Grande."

Baar's affidavit summarizing these findings was submitted to the Supreme Court early in 1990. The findings were accepted by the crown, and incorporated in Code's oral argument in March. The affidavit focused on where the elapsed time in Askov fit into the overall pattern of criminal litigation in Canada, concluding that the *Askov* case took longer than over 90 percent of the criminal cases concluded in Brampton in 1987, while Brampton itself was slower than all other locations for which data were available. By any analysis of comparable jurisdictions, Code could conclude, delay in Askov's case was unusually long.

Going Beyond the Facts of *Askov*

How then could a decision in an apparently exceptional case lead to the dismissal of thousands of cases, not only those facing trial in section 96 courts, but also those pending in Provincial Courts? Stated most simply, this happened because the Supreme Court not only held that 23 months from committal to trial was too long, but also suggested that six to eight months from committal to trial (i.e., "upper court time") "might be deemed to be the outside limit of what is reasonable" for normal and uncomplicated cases. This stricter standard was then applied by Ontario judges and crown attorneys to Provincial Court cases as well, since the principles underlying the Court's recommendation of a six to eight month standard appeared to apply with equally persuasive force to the period from first appearance to trial or preliminary hearing in the Provincial Court.

The Supreme Court arrived at the six to eight month standard by doubling the amount of time it took an average case to proceed from committal to trial in the Montreal area, which the Court chose as a comparable jurisdiction that was performing well. Unfortunately, this reasoning had two fundamental flaws:

First, there was no evidence before the court on the pace of criminal cases in Montreal. Baar gathered no data from Quebec in his 1988–89 study, and the crown submitted no data from Quebec. In an appendix to his affidavit, Baar even indicated that Quebec data might not be comparable because the division of criminal jurisdiction between the Quebec Superior Court and the Cour du Québec (that province's equivalent to the Provincial and Territorial Courts elsewhere in Canada) was unique.

In fact, the Supreme Court of Canada had obtained the Montreal data on its own initiative after oral argument, without the knowledge of either party to the appeal. Also, it is not clear whether the Montreal times cited by the court were median times, as used by Baar, or mean times, or some other measure of expected time to trial.

Thus the "social facts" most important to the Supreme Court's reasoning were not subject to examination and assessment through the adversary process. While critics of the judicial process, including Horowitz, see the adversary process as preventing courts from considering social facts, the Supreme Court in *Askov* ran into difficulties when it made insufficient use of the adversary process, doing its own research that led to a constitutional standard based on information not reviewed or questioned by counsel.

Second, there was no empirical basis for the Supreme Court to conclude that multiplying the average time in a good jurisdiction (i.e., Montreal) by two would yield a constitutionally reasonable maximum in a normal and uncomplicated case. In fact, a more careful reading of the empirical data submitted to the Court should have engendered great caution. The median time in various Canadian courts (the time it takes 50 percent of the cases to be completed) is, by definition, faster than the time it takes for 75 percent or 90 percent of the cases to be completed. Exhibit E to Baar's affidavit, a collection of tables derived from his data, showed how much longer those cases to take. The first table in Exhibit E indicated that while it took 133 days for the median case in the Toronto District Court to go from committal to disposition ("upper court time"), it took 251 days for 75 percent of the Toronto cases to proceed from committal to disposition. Since 251 days is over eight months, this means that over 25 percent of the cases disposed of in Toronto in 1987 could have potentially been in jeopardy under the *Askov* standard. Since Justice Cory indicated his belief that Toronto was operating within an acceptable time period, one can conclude either that the six to eight month standard was more flexible than lawyers and judges realized, or that the standard was established without an adequate understanding of available empirical evidence on the pace of criminal litigation.

The possibility that the Supreme Court of Canada did not fully understand a dense set of tables and explanatory notes should not be seen as a

criticism of a lack of statistical knowledge on the part of any individual justice. We demand exceptional backgrounds and abilities of the nine men and
women who serve on our highest court, and they have developed their skills
through many years of law practice and experience on the bench. Where the
difficulties arose in *Askov* was in the process by which the Court obtained and
applied empirical data. Yet there are at least three alternatives the Court could
have pursued, in keeping with existing procedures, that would have facilitated more effective consideration of social facts.

The Court could have held, as it did, that the 23-month delay in *Askov*
violated the Charter, and that institutional delay must count against the
crown. At that point, rather than state how much delay is too much, it
could have waited for later cases with shorter delays and evolved a standard incrementally, in keeping with the case-by-case approach associated
with traditional common law decision making.

Alternatively, if the Court wished to avoid an incremental approach
that would have created uncertainty over a period of years, it could have
scheduled the Askov case for reargument, informing counsel that it wished
to hear further argument on the length and nature of a standard for reasonable time. Counsel could have focused their submissions on that issue,
other provinces might have chosen to intervene and present additional
data, and the Court could have sought clarification of its interpretation of
previously submitted social facts. The most famous use of this two-step
approach in American constitutional law was in the school desegregation
cases, *Brown v. Board of Education*. The United States Supreme Court decided in 1954 that *de jure* school segregation was unconstitutional, but set
for reargument the question of what remedy and standard it would prescribe for ending segregation. [Ed. note: In the 1976 *AIB Reference*, Chief
Justice Laskin created special procedures for the introduction of extrinsic
evidence. See Reading 10.4.]

A third possibility would have been for the Court to render the same
judgment that it made in *Askov*, but then state that its six to eight month
standard would be phased in. For example, the Court could have given
the provinces a period of time to implement the standard, as it did in 1985
when it gave the province of Manitoba five years to translate its statutes
into the French language even after holding that English-only statutes
were invalid. At the very least, the Court could have applied the standard
only to new cases, not those already in the courts, since provincial governments and crown attorneys had no inkling that a numerical standard was
likely to emerge from *Askov*.

From *Askov* to *Morin*

Since the decision in *Askov* was applied retroactively, the six to eight month
time standard led to tens of thousands of charges being dismissed. While
the impact of the case was felt largely in Ontario, by August, 1991, even

normally reticent members of the judiciary were describing Askov as a "public relations disaster." (*Lawyers' Weekly*, September 6, 1991, p. 1)

In an effort to clarify and if appropriate modify its holding in *Askov*, the Supreme Court of Canada scheduled oral argument in two pending section 11(b) cases arising out of pre-*Askov* dismissals in the Provincial Court in Ontario. The two cases, *Morin* and *Sharma*, involved impaired driving charges that awaited trial in Provincial Court for periods of 14 and 12 months. Both cases were uncomplicated, and impaired driving is the most frequent charge in Ontario's Provincial Court. Nonetheless, in March, 1992, the Supreme Court of Canada ruled in favour of the crown and held that no violation of section 11(b) had taken place.

Speaking for the Court, Mr Justice Sopinka declared that the six to eight month standard should be enforced flexibly, and that an eight to ten month guideline was more appropriate for the high-volume Provincial Courts. Sopinka's reasons made less reference to empirical data than Cory's in *Askov*, although the affidavits submitted by defence and crown in *Askov* were both resubmitted in *Morin* along with supplementary information. However, on the two occasions in which Sopinka referred to social facts, his references were erroneous.

First, Sopinka correctly noted that elapsed times in Montreal were not necessarily comparable to those in Ontario or other provinces, a point that had been stressed by the crown in oral argument (and in the public criticism of *Askov*). But in so doing, he incorrectly attributed the Montreal data to Baar's affidavit, rather than to the subsequent data gathering efforts of the Supreme Court itself.

The second error was more serious, as it lies at the core of the Court's decison. Part of Sopinka's justification for the additional time allowed in the Provincial Courts was his conclusion that the elapsed times in Provincial Courts are longer than elapsed times in section 96 courts. He supported this statement by reference to data derived originally from a paragraph in Baar's *Askov* affidavit. Unfortunately, he misinterpreted Baar's data, confusing the total times that elapsed in both the Provincial Courts and section 96 courts combined (Baar's *Askov* data) with the elapsed times for Provincial Courts alone.

This error may have derived from the use of the same numbers by Justice Cory in his judgment in *Askov*. Cory's language suggests the possibility of a misinterpretation, but neither the "total time" nor the Provincial Court elapsed time were relevant to that case, so Cory's paragraph went unnoticed at the time. The crown in *Morin* was never asked during oral argument to discuss those figures. Thus the Supreme Court of Canada, while using the *Morin* case in an effort to clarify the constitutional rule and reasoning in *Askov*, compounded its difficulties in interpreting the relevant social facts. In theory, the use of social facts should have enhanced the Supreme Court's ability to implement an important Charter right. In practice, the gains were mitigated by the criticism that resulted from the Court's intervention.

The Lessons of *Askov* and *Morin*

In *Askov*, the Supreme Court of Canada showed justifiable impatience with the failure of governments to act to ensure that Charter guarantees of trial within a reasonable time were respected. Cory's judgment also showed an understanding of criminal court delay as a condition that not only jeopardizes rights under the Charter, but also harms the public and the victims of crime. In the process, the Court enunciated a standard where Parliament had not acted.

When courts set general policy, however, they need the background information necessary to assess the impact of their action. *Askov* was a rare case in that directly relevant empirical data were available to the Court. But questions inevitably arise about whether and how the available data apply. The Supreme Court must develop a process to identify and answer those questions and test the social facts before it, or risk the kinds of misunderstandings that found their way into the *Askov* and *Morin* decisions.

*   *   *

[Ed. note: A comparison on the two relevant paragraphs may reveal more clearly Justice Sopinka's error:]

Affidavit of Carl Baar in the case of *Askov v. The Queen*: (Supreme Court of Canada, sworn 16 January, 1990, pp. 6–7):

> The tables found in Exhibit "E" show that New Brunswick is more expeditious than either British Columbia or Ontario, measuring both total time from first appearance in Provincial Court to final disposition in s.96 Court, as well as measuring total time in s.96 Court after the lodging of the indictment in the court. *The median total time in New Brunswick was 152 days and the median upper court time was 72 days.* (emphasis added) Within Ontario, London was consistently the most expeditious of the five locations studied. It had a median total time of 239 days and median upper court time of 105 days. Toronto, Ottawa and St. Catharines were clustered close together with median total times between 315 and 349 days and median upper court times between 133 and 144 days. Median times in Vancouver, British Columbia, were somewhat faster than London, Ontario, while New Westminster, British Columbia, was comparable to Toronto, Ottawa and St. Catharines. By all measures used in the study, Brampton District Court was significantly slower than any other location studied: median total time was 607 days and median upper court time was 423 days. . . .

Judgment of Justice Sopinka in *R. v. Morin* (March 26, 1992):

> A longer period of institutional delay for Provincial Courts is justified on the basis that not only do these courts dispose of the vast majority of cases, but that on average it takes more time to dispose of cases by reason of the demands placed on these courts. *Statistics for 1987 submitted by the respondent show a median delay in New Brunswick of 152 days for Provincial Court and 72 days for upper courts.* (emphasis added) Delay in London, Ontario was shown to be 239 days in Provincial Court and 105 in upper courts; Toronto, St.

Catharines and Ottawa showed delays of 315 to 349 days in Provincial Court and 133 to 144 days in upper courts; median delays in Brampton were 607 days for Provincial Court and 423 for upper courts. Figures for Vancouver were similar to London and for New Westminster comparable to Toronto, St. Catharines and Ottawa.

[Ed. note: Sopinka's error was in fact two-fold. First, he mistook figures involving the preliminary hearing, provincial court stage of indictable offences (such as *Askov*, which are eventually "disposed of" in section 96 "upper courts") for figures about summary conviction proceedings (cases such as *Morin*, which are "disposed of" entirely in provincial courts. Secondly, Sopinka did not even correctly identify the figures for the provincial court stage of indictable offences. He mistook figures for total elapsed time in indictable offence cases (the italicized figures in Baar's affidavit, above) for figures about total provincial court time for the same cases. Exhibit E of Baar's Askov affadavit showed that median times for lower courts (from first appearance to committal) were usually about the same, and in some instances much lower, than median upper court time. But no lower court time was anywhere near twice as long as upper court time, the ratio suggested by Sopinka's figures. Thus, even if the time spent at the provincial court stage of an indictable offence proceeding was relevant to the question of how long it takes to dispose of summary offences in provincial courts (which it is not), the figure is nowhere as high as Sopinka suggests and would not support the longer periods of institutional delay that he allows. The data in Professor Baar's affidavit simply did not address the issue before the Court in *Morin*: how long it takes provincial courts to schedule and decide cases involving summary conviction offences.]

8.5

KEY TERMS

Concepts

historical/adjudicative facts
social/legislative facts
adversary process
rule of hearsay evidence
perjury
extrinsic evidence
"Brandeis brief"
judicial notice
expert witness
legislative history

Institutions, Events, and Documents

The *Anti-Inflation Reference* (1976)
R. v. Askov (1990)
R. v. Morin (1992)

9

Precedents, Statutes, and Legal Reasoning

One of the most distinctive characteristics of the judicial process is its formalized method of reasoning. Because their authority flows from the public perception that they are "merely" applying pre-existing rules to resolve new disputes, judges are not permitted the broad prerogative enjoyed by the legislative and the executive branches. Unlike the latter, courts are not supposed to create new policies to deal with new problems. In their oral or written judgments, judges must explain where and how they derived the "rule" used to settle a case. There are three principal sources for these "rules": a written constitution, legislative statutes (including administrative regulations), and prior judicial decisions, known as precedents. Constitutional interpretation is the subject of the following two chapters. This chapter is concerned with the role of precedent and statutory interpretation in judicial reasoning.

Until the middle of the nineteenth century, most internal or domestic law in English-speaking societies was common law. Common law originated in the judicial recognition and enforcement of traditional usages and customs of the Anglo-Saxon and later Norman peoples in the British Isles. As these judicial decisions were made, they in turn became part of the common law. The common law in contemporary Canadian society consists of all previous judicial decisions by Canadian and British courts, as they are recorded in the case reports of these nations. The common law system is distinguished from the civil law system by its basis in precedent rather than legislative enactment. The civil law system originated in ancient Roman law, developed on the European continent, and was imported into Quebec by the French. It is based on comprehensive codes, enacted by the legislature.

The law of precedent, or *stare decisis*, is a self-imposed judicial rule that "like cases be decided alike." As Gordon Post explains, the law of precedent is essentially a formalization of the common sense use of past experience as a guide to present conduct. (See Reading 9.1) The value of judicial adherence to *stare decisis* is two-fold. First, continuity and certainty in the law is a prerequisite of civilized human activity. If there is no reasonable guarantee that what is valid law today will still be valid law

tomorrow, personal, economic, and political intercourse would grind to a
halt. In each of these spheres of human activity, present-day decisions and
activities are predicated on expectations about the future. Ensuring a high
degree of predictability and continuity between the present and the future
is one of the primary purposes of a political regime. As the institutions
charged with interpreting and adapting the laws over time, the courts are
responsible for maintaining continuity and certainty. As Dicey said, "a
law which was not certain would in reality be no law at all." (See Reading
9.2) Adherence to the rule of precedent—"deciding like cases alike"—is
the mechanism that provides this certainty.

The rule of precedent also contributes to promoting the "rule of law,
not of men." One of the ideals of the Western traditions conception of
justice is that the laws be applied equally and impartially to all persons.
This ideal precludes *ad hoc* application of the laws, and demands instead
that laws be applied uniformly, or that any deviation from the rule be
justified on principle that is, by another rule. The idiosyncrasies or personal preferences of a judge are not permissible grounds for judicial
decisions. This would reintroduce the "rule of men" rather than the "rule
of law." By minimizing the discretion or freedom of individual judges,
stare decisis preserves the "rule of law."

Stare decisis minimizes but does not eliminate the element of judicial
discretion or creativity. While legal reasoning presents itself as a deductive process, the reality is a more subtle blend of both inductive and
deductive reasoning. Legal reasoning is accurately described as "reasoning by example."[1] The judges are essentially asking, "Whether the present
case resembles the plain case 'sufficiently' and in the 'relevant' aspects."[2]
In determining what is "sufficient" and what is "relevant," the judge must
ultimately make certain choices. Because of this element of choice, a judge
is responsible for striking the balance between continuity and innovation.
The central thrust of the theory of legal realism (discussed in Chapter two)
has been to emphasize this element of choice and judicial discretion, and
the ensuing responsibility of the judge for his choice.

Weiler's analysis of the Supreme Court's responsibility for the development of tort law is based on this legal realist perspective. (See Reading 9.3)
Weiler argues that judges can no longer claim that precedent "dictates" non-
sensical or patently unfair legal conclusions. Judges must be critical in their
use of precedent, and go beyond the surface "rule" to discover the animating
"principle." The proper function of the common law judge, according to
Weiler, is to derive specific rules from more general principles, as the situation demands. Since situations change, rules must change also. While the

---

[1] Edward H. Levi, *An Introduction to Legal Reasoning* (Chicago: University of Chicago Press,
1949), p. 1.

[2] H.L.A. Hart, *The Concept of Law* (Oxford: Oxford University Press, 1961), p. 124.

"cattle trespass" exemption to normal tort law responsibility may have been appropriate to the rural, agricultural society of eighteenth-century England, it had become a dangerous anachronism in twentieth-century Canada. (See Reading 9.3) Similarly, in *Boucher v. the King*, the Court was faced with a conflict between the definition of "seditious libel" developed in nineteenth-century, homogeneous, protestant Britain, and the norms of freedom of religion and speech in twentieth-century, pluralistic Canada. (See Reading 9.4) Appeal court judges have a duty, says Weiler, to adapt the common law to the changing needs and circumstances of contemporary society.

Strict adherence to *stare decisis* is yet another aspect of the "adjudication of disputes" function of courts that poses problems for judicial policy-making. Refusal to disavow or change past decisions plays no constructive role in a policy-making institution, as the examples of legislative and executive practice make clear. While certainty and continuity are legal virtues, adaptability and innovation are more important in the policy-making process. The case for abandoning a strict adherence to precedent is especially strong in constitutional law. Not only is policy-impact more probable, but constitutional law lacks the flexibility of common law and statutes. If the courts make a "mistake" in the latter areas, it can be corrected by remedial legislation. But if the Supreme Court makes a constitutional decision with undesirable policy consequences, the only direct way to correct the damage is through formal constitutional amendment, an extremely cumbersome and difficult process.[3] Predictably, the U.S. Supreme Court was the first court of appeal in a common law nation to abandon *stare decisis* as an absolute requirement. The demotion of *stare decisis* from a binding rule to a guiding principle is another index of a court's evolution toward a greater policy-making role.

The recent advent of judicial realism in Canadian jurisprudence has brought with it a decline in the status of the rule of *stare decisis*. Long after the American Supreme Court had abandoned absolute adherence to precedent, the Canadian Supreme Court continued to perceive itself as bound to adhere not only to its own previous decisions but those of the British House of Lords as well. (Ironically, the Judicial Committee of the Privy Council, which served as Canada's final court of appeal until 1949, did not consider itself bound by its previous decisions, since, technically, it was not a court of law but an advisory board to the Imperial Crown.) Ten years after the abolition of that role, the Supreme Court declared its independence from British precedents as well. (See Reading 9.3) In 1966, the British House of Lords officially declared that, when appropriate, it would no longer follow its own prior decisions. However, the Supreme Court of Canada continued to profess strict adherence to its prior decisions until the 1970s. Under the leadership of Bora Laskin, the Canadian Supreme Court began to move in the same direction. In 1972, before his appoint-

---

[3] This is not true of judicial decisions based on sections 2 and 7 through 15 of the Charter of Rights, which are subject to the section 33 "legislative override" provision.

ment as chief justice, Laskin had written that *stare decisis* was "no longer an article of faith in the Supreme Court of Canada, but it still remains a cogent principle."[4] Speaking as the new Chief Justice at the Centennial Symposium of the Supreme Court in 1975, Laskin repeated that *stare decisis* was no longer "an inexorable rule," but rather,

> simply an important element of the judicial process, a necessary consideration which should give pause to any but the most sober conclusion that a previous decision or line of authority is wrong and ought to be changed.[5]

Practicing what he preached, Laskin led the Supreme Court to overturn three precedents during the next three years, including an old Privy Council decision dealing with the federal division of powers.[6] This abandoning of strict adherence to *stare decisis* is yet another indicator of the Supreme Court's institutional evolution toward more of a policy-making court.

The second principal source of law is legislative statutes. Beginning in the nineteenth century, legislatures in Great Britain, Canada, and the United States began to codify large portions of the common law. In large part this was a democratic reaction against the perceived elitism of the "judge-made" character of the common law. By reducing the confusing maze of common law precedent to clearly worded, legislative statutes, it was thought that the law would be made easier for "the people" to understand, and that the democratic authority of "government by consent" would be enhanced.

In 1892 the Canadian Parliament abolished all criminal offenses at common law, and replaced them, with a comprehensive statute, the Criminal Code. In so doing, Parliament hoped to reap the alleged advantages of codification mentioned above, including restricting judicial discretion in the criminal law. Since crimes were now clearly and authoritatively defined, judges would simply apply the law as Parliament had written it. It would no longer be necessary to refer to a vast and confusing system of precedent to apply the criminal law, or so it was hoped.

In fact, precedent and *stare decisis* quickly found their way back into the criminal law. Perhaps, as Parker has suggested, it was (and still is) impossible for judges and lawyers trained in the common law tradition to properly construe a code of law.[7] More likely, the common law "habit" simply

---

[4] "The Institutional Character of the Judge," *Israel Law Review*, 7 (1972), p. 341.

[5] Bora Laskin, "The Role and Functions of Final Appellate Courts: The Supreme Court of Canada," *Canadian Bar Review*, 53 (1975), p. 478. See also Reading 3.1.

[6] *R. v. Paquette*, [1977] 2 S.C.R. 189; *McNamara Const. Western Ltd. The Queen*, [1977] 2 S.C.R. 654; and *Reference re Agricultural Products Marketing Act*, [1978] 2 S.C.R. 1198.

[7] Graham Parker, *An Introduction to Criminal Law*. 2nd ed. (Toronto, ON: Methuen, 1983), p. 43.

compounds a more serious problem—the ultimate ambiguity of statutory terminology itself. Try as they might, legislators will never be able to draft statutes that anticipate and encompass all possible future situations. This is due in part to the inherent tension between the generality of words and the specificity of reality, and in part to human ignorance of the future. As new situations inevitably arise, the applicability of the original wording of statutes becomes increasingly questionable. *Regina v. Ojibway* is a clever satire on the inadequacies of statutory language, and the occasional tendency of judges to exacerbate the problem. (See Reading 9.5) The comical example of "BLUE, J." notwithstanding, the only practical way to bridge this gap is through judicial discretion; and the traditional (if not the only) way to discipline the exercise of judicial discretion is through adherence to *stare decisis* —to decide like cases alike. In the final analysis, judicial interpretation of statutes is similar to the "reasoning by example" method of the common law.

The preceding argument notwithstanding, judicial discretion in interpreting statutes, including the Criminal Code, is still more circumscribed than in interpreting the common law. As Weiler says, judges can develop new torts, but not new crimes, and there are sound reasons for preferring this arrangement. As issues of tort law are rarely the subject of partisan political controversy, an innovative court cannot be accused of usurping the legislative function. The controversies over capital punishment and abortion show that the same is not true of the criminal law. In the area of tort law, judicial expertise is very high, relative to other policy-making institutions. Finally, judicial initiatives in substantive criminal law would pose the threat of punishing innocent persons. No comparable problem of "due process" arises in tort law.

While codification and statutes circumscribe the limits of judicial law-making, there remains the element of judicial "choice" and its accompanying responsibility. In Reading 9.6, Thomas Flanagan illustrates just how extensive such "policy-making by exegesis" (by interpretation of written text) can be. When the government of Manitoba introduced a prohibition on age discrimination to its human rights act in 1974, it had no intention of abolishing "fixed age" retirement policies in the province. Notwithstanding such intentions, within a decade a series of judicial decisions had effectively abolished the policy of "mandatory retirement." Flanagan's case study illustrates how the persistence of a handful of activist lawyers can persuade a few similarly inclined judges to "find" new and unintended meaning/policies in a broadly worded statute. In the case of fixed age retirement, this new judicially-mandated, "one-size-fits-all" policy was not without problems. Drawing comparisons to similarly broadly worded guarantees in the 1982 Charter of Rights, Flanagan concludes by cautioning against similar "policy-making by exegesis."

9.1

STARE DECISIS: THE USE OF PRECEDENTS
G. Gordon Post

In the resolution of conflicts a court invokes and applies rules of law to proven facts. A question arises: Just where does a court find these rules?

There are two *chief* sources of law: *statutes* and *precedents*. The former, of course, come from the legislature which consists of the elected representatives of the people. The latter come from the courts; precedents are the products of earlier decisions. To the latter, we should add the decisions of an increasing number of administrative bodies and the precedents established thereby, but of this matter we shall speak later.

Most everybody knows what a statute is, but what is a precedent? In a general, non-legal way, precedent plays an important role in our lives. Often, we do things as our parents did them and cite their experience as precedent for what we do now; out of some continuing or repetitive situation there comes a rough rule of thumb. When a father is questioned as to why he spanked his son for some infraction of the household rules, he might reply that as a boy in like circumstances he had been spanked as had his father before him. He might go on to explain that such treatment was an application of the rule of experience, "Spare the rod and spoil the child."...

... In all of these instances, there is the application of a rule of experience to a given situation. These are homely examples. Clubs, business organizations, boards of trustees, student groups all have their rules, some written, some unwritten, which are often invoked as precedent for doing, or not doing, one thing or another. And a precedent here is defined by Webster as "something done or said that may serve as an example or rule to authorize or justify a subsequent act of the same or analogous kind."

Judicial Precedent

A judicial precedent is defined in the same dictionary as "a judicial decision, a form of proceeding, or course of action that serves as a rule for future determinations in similar or analogous cases."

The driver of a wagon loaded with buckskin goods stopped for the night at a certain inn. He was received as a guest and the innkeeper took

---

Introduction to Law (Englewood Cliffs, NJ: Prentice Hall, 1963), from pages 80–83. Reprinted with permission.

charge of his property. During the night a fire broke out which resulted in the destruction of horses, wagon and goods. The owner of the property thus destroyed sued the innkeeper for damages.

Let us suppose that this was a case of first impression, that is, a situation which is before a [Canadian] court for the first time. After hearing the evidence from both sides, the judge does not simply say "I decide for the plaintiff," or "I decide for the defendant." He decides for one or the other and gives his reasons. He will speak as follows: "An innkeeper is responsible for the safe keeping of property committed to his custody by a guest. He is an insurer against loss, unless caused by the negligence or fraud of the guest, or by the act of God or the public enemy." The judge looks to the English common law and finds that the liability of innkeepers was expressed tersely in *Cross v. Andrews*: "The defendant, if he will keep an inn, ought, *at his peril*, to keep safely his guests' goods," and at greater length by Coke in *Calye's Case*: "If one brings a bag or chest, etc., of evidences into the inn as obligations, deeds, or other specialties, and by default of the innkeeper they are taken away, the innkeeper shall answer for them."

The judge will go on to explain the reason for the rule. He will say that the rule has its origins in public policy.

> Every facility should be furnished for secure and convenient intercourse between different portions of the kingdom. The safeguards, of which the law gave assurance to the wayfarer, were akin to those which invested each English home with the legal security of a castle. The traveller was peculiarly exposed to depredation and fraud. . . .

Stare Decisis

Let us suppose that a year or so later, another driver with a wagon load of hides spends the night at an inn. Again, the horses, the wagon, and the hides, are turned over to the innkeeper; and again, a fire occurs during the night and the property of the guest is burned up. The owner of the property then sues the innkeeper for damages. The situation here is exactly the same as in the earlier case.

The judge in the second case, according to the theory, will apply the rule or principle (which is the precedent) and decide in favor of the plaintiff. The precedent or authority of the first case is precise and fits the facts of the second case very nicely. This application by courts of rules announced in earlier decisions is spoken of as *stare decisis*, which means "let the decision stand." This has been, and is, a fundamental characteristic of the common law, although . . . it is the practice upon occasion for a high court to overrule its own precedents.

Obviously, a legal system in which judges could decide cases any which way, manifesting prejudice, whimsy, ignorance and venality, each decision being a entity in itself unconnected with the theory, practices and precedents of the whole, would be a sorry system, or, one might say, no system at all, and a source of little comfort either to attorneys or litigants. Speaking of *stare decisis* many years ago, Judge Maxwell said: "In the application of the principles of the common law, where the precedents are unanimous in the support of a proposition, there is no safety but in a strict adherence to such precedents. If the court will not follow established rules, rights are sacrificed, and lawyers and litigants are left in doubt and uncertainty, while there is no certainty in regard to what, upon a given state of facts, the decision of the court will be."

One concludes, after a little thought, that *stare decisis* is "the instrument of *stability* in a legal system," that it "furnishes a legal system with *certainty* and *predictability*," and "clothes a legal system with reliability"; in addition, it "assures all persons of *equality and uniformity of treatment*" and judges with "an instrument of *convenience and expediency*." In short, "*Stare decisis* preserves the judicial experience of the past."

After a little more thought, however, one also sees that *stare decisis* is an instrument of conservatism, of immobility, of eyes-in-the-back-of-the-head, of stultification. The application of the same rule, decade after decade, long after changed conditions have robbed the rule of its validity, makes the rule a troublesome fiction.

But, American high courts do not hesitate to overrule their own precedents when social, economic, or political change demand a corresponding change in the law. Cardozo has said that

> If we figure stability and progress as opposite poles, then at one pole we have the maxim of *stare decisis* and the method of decision by the tool of a deductive logic; at the other we have the method which subordinates origins to ends. The one emphasizes considerations of uniformity and symmetry, and follows fundamental conceptions to ultimate conclusions. The other gives freer play to considerations of equity and justice, and the value to society of the interests affected. The one searches for the analogy that is nearest in point of similarity, and adheres to it inflexibly. The other, in its choice of the analogy that shall govern, finds community of spirit more significant than resemblance in externals.

"Much of the administration of justice," says Pound, "is a compromise between the tendency to treat each case as one of a generalized type of case, and the tendency to treat each case as unique." "Each method," concludes Cardozo, "has its value, and for each in the changes of litigation there will come the hour for use. A wise eclecticism employs them both."

9.2

THE DUTY OF A COURT
A.V. Dicey

The duty of the court . . . is not to remedy a particular grievance but to determine whether an alleged grievance is one for which the law supplies a remedy. . . . If Parliament changes the law, the action of Parliament is known to every man and Parliament tries in general to respect acquired rights. If the Courts were to apply to the decision of substantially the same case, one principle today and another principle tomorrow, men would lose rights which they already possessed; a law which was not certain would in reality be no law at all.

Lectures on the Relation between Law and Public Opinion in England during the Nineteenth Century. 2nd ed. (London: MacMillan, 1914), pp. 365, 367. Reprinted with permission.

9.3

ARCHITECT OF THE COMMON LAW
Paul Weiler

I shall begin my analysis of the role and performance of the Supreme Court of Canada by reviewing some of its decisions in the area of tort liability for personal injuries. Perhaps some students of the judicial process will ask why bother with these rather insignificant cases? Let's get on to the attention-getting constitutional or civil liberties decisions. However, there are several reasons why I think tort law is a good starting point. First, we can fully understand much of the contemporary character of the judicial process only if we see how it is directed at the adjudication of private law disputes between one individual and another. Moreover, most of this area of law is almost totally judge-made, the *common law*. Our Supreme Court is a useful vehicle for reflecting on the true range and

---

In the Last Resort: A Critical Study of the Supreme Court of Canada (Toronto, ON: Carswell-Methuen, 1979), pp. 57–65. Reprinted with permission.

complexity of the judicial function precisely because of the breadth of its jurisdiction. The Court regularly handles the garden variety tort case as well as the newsworthy public law dispute. We must not miss the opportunity to appraise the exercise of judicial creativity in a private law area where the Court is not distracted by the involvement of other institutions, whether legislative or administrative. Finally, as I shall try to demonstrate, these attitudes concerning the private law role of the Supreme Court of Canada are wrong. Tort cases do raise important issues of public policy, and it is critical that they be settled intelligently. Let us start with a typical motor vehicles action which reached the Court, and produced a not-so-typical response.

The Curious Doctrine of Cattle Trespass

One sunny summer afternoon, Floyd Atkinson was driving a jeep along a gravelled country road in a farming district in Ontario. Suddenly, upon reaching the brow of a hill, he was confronted with a herd of cows belonging to a farmer named Leo Fleming. Although he applied his brakes and steered past some of the cows, Atkinson's jeep eventually struck three of the animals, killing two, and causing serious injuries to his own knee. The driver sued the farmer for his personal injuries and the latter responded with a claim for his two dead cows. Apparently Fleming took the attitude that he could let his cows wander where they wanted and they customarily pastured on the highway, strolling back and forth across the road. The trial judge found this to be negligence on his part and, given a certain lack of due care on the driver's part also, apportioned the relative responsibility 60 percent to the farmer and 40 percent to Atkinson.

This would seem to be a relatively straightforward case and easy to resolve in terms of the ordinary doctrines of negligence law. Unfortunately, hidden away in the nooks and crannies of the common law was a legal rule which absolved the farmer of any duty to prevent his cattle from straying on the highway and endangering its users. This rule owed its origin to two factors: (1) when highways were first created at the end of the medieval period in England, land was dedicated by the adjoining landowners subject to their own right of passage for their animals; (2) for a very long time this created no risk of danger from domestic animals such as cattle because traffic was so slow moving that the animals could easily be avoided. With the advent of automobiles, this factual situation was radically changed. However, the House of Lords, in its 1947 decision in *Searle v. Wallbank*, declined an invitation to revise the legal duties of the farmer to bring them into line with modern needs, and the Ontario Court of Appeal felt compelled to respect the authority of this common law precedent in its 1952 decision in *Nobel v. Calder*. The true wishes of the Ontario judges were expressed in these concluding passages from their own opinion in *Fleming v. Atkinson*.

I do not want to part with this case without expressing the hope that it may draw attention to the present unsatisfactory state of the law in this province as to civil liability for injuries sustained due to the presence on our public highways of straying domestic animals. *The Courts cannot change the law; the legislation can.* The common law as applied by the House of Lords in England to the highways there is not adequate here, and yet the Courts of this province must follow those decisions. . . . [emphasis added].

. . . When the case reached the Supreme Court of Canada, one judge, Mr. Justice Cartwright, agreed that the English common law, as reflected in *Searle,* defined the duties of the cattle owner until and unless they were changed by legislation. In his view it was not the function of the judges to alter a legal doctrine when it no longer reflected reasonable social policies. Fortunately for Canadian law, and for Floyd Atkinson, Mr. Justice Judson for the majority took a wider view of the judicial mission. He did not consider himself bound by an English doctrine which originated in features which are not part of Canadian society and which was reiterated in a heavily-criticized House of Lords decision. The decision of the Supreme Court in *Fleming v. Atkinson* is important because it clearly expressed our judicial independence of the House of Lords, especially when that body adheres to such an irrational legal anomaly. It is even more important as a example of the style of legal reasoning which a truly independent Supreme Court, at the top of our judicial hierarchy, must exhibit.

A rule of law has, therefore been stated in *Searle v. Wallbank* and followed in *Noble v. Calder* which has little or no relation to the facts or needs of the situation and which ignores any theory of responsibility to the public for conduct which involves foreseeable consequences of harm. I can think of no logical basis for this immunity and it can only be based upon a rigid determination to adhere to the rules of the past in spite of changed conditions which call for the application of rules of responsibility which have been worked out to meet modern needs. It has always been assumed that one of the virtues of the common law system is its flexibility, that it is capable of changing with the times and adapting its principles to new conditions. There has been conspicuous failure to do this in this branch of the law and the failure has not passed unnoticed. It has been criticized in judicial decisions (including the one under appeal), in the texts and by the commentators. . . . My conclusion is that it is open to this Court to apply the ordinary rules of negligence to the case of straying animals and that principles enunciated in *Searle v. Wallbank,* dependent as they are upon historical reasons, which have no relevancy here, and upon a refusal to recognize a duty now because there had been previously no need of one, offer no obstacle.

Judson's opinion is almost a textbook illustration of the conception of legal reasoning I proposed in the preceding chapter. Judges should not just blindly follow a legal rule because it has been recognized in the law for a long time. If the rule appears to require unjust results in the immediate situation, the judge must ask why. He should have a sense of unease when asked to use a rule that does not fit comfortably into the basic principles of tort responsibility which condition a lawyer's perception of the area. Perhaps there will be good reasons for this exceptional doctrine: on investigation of the cattle trespass rule, its only support turns out to be ancient history. In such a situation the legal obligation of a judge is clearly the forthright elimination of the legal anomaly which produces that kind of injustice.

The Need For Judicial Renovation

What are the lessons we can draw from *Fleming v. Atkinson* about when and how the Court should respond in the common law? The case is certainly an unprepossessing factual situation with which to lead off a detailed assessment of the work of the Supreme Court across the spectrum of Canadian law. The question of whether the farmer or the motorist should bear the losses caused by a cow does seem to be of a somewhat lesser order of importance than constitutional disputes, issues of civil liberties and due process, problems of administrative regulation of the economy, and other such issues which regularly appear before the Supreme Court. The legal situation in the *Fleming* case is typical of the private law disputes which still constitute the bulk of the Court's work and which many now advocate deleting from its jurisdiction. [Ed. note: This is no longer true, as right of appeal in civil cases was abolished in 1975.] I will leave my assessment of these proposals for later when we have a more detailed view of the kinds of problems involved in these cases. For the moment we must recognize that there was an issue of general law to be resolved in the case and that the Supreme Court of Canada still has final judicial authority in this area. As is typical of a great many private law doctrines, tort liability for escaping cattle will not affect very many people but when it does arise, the question of whether damages can be collected will be of vital importance to the person involved. There are many legal doctrines with precisely this impact and the cumulative quality of their policies tells a lot about the justice afforded to the individual in our society. Up to now, the judiciary has been primarily responsible for their development in Canada. It behooves us then to enquire into the Court's performance in this area and to suggest the standards by which it should govern itself.

As Mr. Justice Judson stated in *Fleming v. Atkinson*, there is a general *principle* of law firmly established in this area. A person is required to take reasonable care in his behaviour when it creates the risk of physical injuries to another. If he does not take care and his faulty behaviour causes losses to another, the law requires that he assume responsibility for payment of damages to make whole the innocent victim. This legal principle had been clearly and authoritatively established in the general law of torts in the case of *Donoghue v. Stevenson*, but had become embedded in the motor vehicle area some time earlier. Appraised in the light of this theory of liability, the special immunity for "cattle trespass" was an historical anomaly. As Judson J. showed in his opinion, there may have been some rationale for its original adoption in England several hundred years ago but there certainly was no valid argument which could be made for its retention in contemporary Canada.

Mr. Justice Cartwright's dissent did raise some doubt whether the Court should leave it to the legislature to administer the *coup de grace* to the doctrine. To adopt the framework of analysis I sketched earlier, assuming there are good policy reasons for tort liability in this situation, are there countervailing legal values which should make a court wary of itself abolishing the immunity? In my view, the *Fleming* case is significant because when we assess in a realistic way the arguments against judicial innovation, they seem largely inapplicable here. In this respect *Fleming* is typical of tort law and, indeed, of much of the private law area.

What about the argument of predictability in the law and the possibility that judicial elimination of the immunity will defeat the expectations of those who relied on it being the law? Did the farmer rely on his immunity from tort liability when he failed to take reasonable care to control his cattle? If he did, is this the kind of expectation the legal system should be concerned to satisfy? Simply to ask these questions is to answer them. In tort law, at least as regards accidental injuries, the reliance on interest of possible defendants enters primarily at the point of insurance planning against liability for the risk. Studies have indicated that special rules of tort immunity such as this one, especially when they are hedged in by equally anomalous exceptions, are irrelevant to insurance decisions. Indeed, if there are any reasonable expectations which will be frustrated in a situation similar to that of the *Fleming* case they will be those of the injured motorist when he consults his lawyer and finds that the farmer is protected by a special rule dating back to medieval England. If the farmer's lawyer (or that of his insurer) has any understanding of this whole area of tort law and the rationale for its evolution, he can estimate the shakiness of the farmer's immunity and anticipate its probable removal. For these reasons, the Supreme Court in *Fleming v. Atkinson* could quite confidently ignore the argument about the damage to the predictability of the law.

What about the competence of the Court to make an intelligent change in the law? The possible defects in judicial law reform seem irrelevant to this actual problem. There is no need for lengthy investigations, social science research, expert testimony, and so on, to decide about change. The issue is basically one of esoteric "lawyer's law" which can be resolved by careful analysis of the implications of the basic legal principles underlying the area. If the legislature were moved to reform in this area, it would have to rely on the same sort of appraisal and it would find it in the textbooks and law review articles which are equally available to the courts.

In fact, the "cattle trespass" rule is one in which the resources of the judicial forum are especially valuable. The issue is narrow in compass, occurs infrequently, and is only one of a very large number of such relatively independent tort problems. Yet there are a lot of judges in a lot of courts hearing such cases all the time. Each judge sees the human implications of the issue vividly portrayed in the concrete dispute before him. On the basis of the research and arguments prepared for him by opposing counsel, he can work out the solution which seems most rational in the light of the basic policies in the area. This proposed rule, when reported, can become a piecemeal addition to the evolving common law of torts. The legislature seems much too bulky and unwieldy an instrument to solve the problem of cattle trespass. It operates at the wholesale level while so much of our private law requires retail treatment.

But at least the legislature is elected, one may suggest. Should not changes in the law be made by a representative body, rather than the appointed and tenured court? We must turn to the reasons for our qualms about judicial innovation and take a realistic view of their relevance to particular cases. The problem in *Fleming v. Atkinson* is not one which will figure in an election campaign. It is inconsistent with democratic values (though not always illegitimate for this reason) for a court to intervene and impose its own policies in an area where the popular will has been expressed in the political arena. If the legislature were moved to reform in this esoteric problem area, it would merely be ratifying a proposal worked out by an equally unrepresentative Law Reform Commission at as invisible a level as would be a judicial innovation.

Once more we find that not only is there no real argument against a judicial initiative, but there are positive reasons in favour of such an active role. Private law doctrines such as this often lead to a distortion of the legislative process. Pressure for reform is very diffuse and unorganized. There is no lobby of accident victims petitioning the government. Instead, there is usually only an academic who has shown how some legal relic is working a real injustice on the very few people who run afoul of it. However, there is often a narrow interest group which might be somewhat harmed by the change. The farmer's insurance premiums will go up a bit and he may have to answer for his negligence in a lawsuit. A politician might be a little worried about the farmers' votes if their organizations object, especially if there is no countervailing lobby pressing for the reform. It is extremely unlikely he would be moved to *create* the cattle trespass immunity, but he might be loath to come out in the open and remove it entirely. The safest course in his eyes is to "let sleeping dogs lie," allow the proposal to die on the legislative order paper, and rationalize this inaction on the grounds (often valid) that he is busy on too many other problems.

By contrast, the Supreme Court was duty-bound to reach a positive conclusion about this legal problem in order to resolve the concrete dispute between Fleming and Atkinson. It had to hear the arguments from both sides, decide which position was most persuasive, and justify its conclusion in a written opinion which is reported for others to see and criticize. If judges within such an institution are willing to exercise their power to develop our law in a rational way, then we can provide the individual litigant who has been hurt with a forum to which he can come as a one-man lobby looking for legal justice. There is something to be said in a democracy of an institution which will resolve such disputes on the basis of the quality of the arguments presented, rather than the number of votes represented.

On just about every dimension then, these legal or institutional values seem to favour *judicial* initiative in this area, and they certainly do not warn against it. In order to complete this picture, let me give an example of a tort law reform I do not think a court is entitled to make, even though the judges may be convinced of its substantive desirability. The basic principle underlying our current law of torts, the one appealed to in *Fleming v. Atkinson*, is that negligent fault is the basis of liability. More and more voices contend that this is too narrow a criterion. Especially in the motor vehicle accident area, we hear proposals for a market deterrence, etc. I think we are going to see some such doctrine adopted in Canada shortly but this reform should be the work of the legislature, not the court. Why is this so?

In the first place, this will introduce a very substantial change in the incidence of legal liability and it may require substantial increases in the premium level. To the extent that insurance companies have charged lower premiums in reliance on the fault doctrine, they can claim that this justifiable expectation should not be frustrated by retrospective judicial alteration of the law. I am not sure myself how compelling this argument is. It depends on the degree of increased recovery in the new system and the ability of the insurance industry to finance the extra payments for past losses out of future premiums.

The real point is that the court could not likely estimate this either, which brings us to a second and major objection against judicial adoption of strict liability. The court simply is not competent to set up a complete new scheme for compensating automobile accident victims. This is not a simple matter of eliminating an irrational anomaly like the cattle trespass doctrine and applying the established principle of fault. The objectives of a strict liability scheme require a complex series of adjustments in the kinds and level of damages recoverable, the relationship of tort liability to various other forms of liability compensation, the nature of the insurance which is to be used, and even the forum in which claims are to be made. To perform this job, we want royal commissions, legislative committees and research by a battery of experts. We cannot rely on the efforts of a few Supreme Court judges sitting in their chambers in Ottawa.

Finally, the Court does not have the authority to adopt such a scheme into law. Let us suppose that a Royal Commission had been appointed, had laboured for several years examining the issues and the various alternatives, and then worked out a detailed scheme. The expert work has been done but the legislature, for various reasons, has not gotten around to acting on it. Should the Court decide to implement this new scheme in substitution for the common law of fault-based tort liability on the assumption that it is indeed a better system? In my view, the answer is still no! As anyone who reads Canadian newspapers will realize, the desirability of compensation without fault is a matter of sharp political controversy in several Canadian provinces. It has figured prominently in several election campaigns and governments have teetered on the edge of defeat in trying to get schemes enacted. The various plans present important and ambiguous value judgments about such matters as social welfare, compulsory government insurance, administrative agencies, and the responsibility of the dangerous driver. The place where these controversial issues should be aired and inevitable compromises worked out is the public legislative arena where the participants can be held responsible for their judgments. The last place in which we would want the decision made is the sheltered, closed world of the judges who are in the process of resolving a private lawsuit. . . .

9.4

BOUCHER v. THE KING
Supreme Court of Canada (1951)

RAND J.: For the reasons given by me following the first argument, I would allow the appeal, set aside the verdict and conviction and enter judgment of not guilty.

[Ed. note: The reasons given by Mr. Justice Rand, following the first argument, read as follows.]

This appeal arises out of features of what, in substance, is religious controversy, and it is necessary that the facts be clearly appreciated. The appellant, a farmer, living near the town of St. Joseph de Beauce, Quebec, was convicted of uttering a seditious libel. The libel was contained in a four page document published apparently at Toronto by the Watch Tower Bible & Tract Society, which I take to be the name of the official publishers of the religious group known as The Witnesses of Jehovah. The document was headed "Quebec's Burning Hate for God and Christ and Freedom Is the Shame of all Canada": it consisted first of an invocation to calmness and reason in appraising the matters to be dealt with in support of the heading; then of general references to vindictive persecution accorded in Quebec to the Witnesses as brethren in Christ; a detailed narrative of specific incidents of persecution; and a concluding appeal to the people of the province, in protest against mob rule and Gestapo tactics, that through the study of God's Word and obedience to its commands, there might be brought about a "bounteous crop of the good fruits of love for Him and Christ and human freedom." At the foot of the document is an advertisement of two books entitled "Let God be True" and "Be Glad, Ye Nations," the former revealing, in the light of God's Word, the truth concerning the Trinity, Sabbath, prayer, etc., and the latter, the facts of the endurance of Witnesses in the crucible of "fiery persecution."

The incidents, as described, are of peaceable Canadians who seem not to be lacking in meekness, but who, for distributing apparently without permits, bibles and tracts on Christian doctrine; for conducting religious services in private homes or on private lands in Christian fellowship; for holding public lecture meetings to teach religious truth as they believe it of the Christian religion; who, for this exercise of what has been taken for granted to be the unchallengeable rights of Canadians, have been assaulted and beaten and their bibles and publications torn up and destroyed, by individuals and by mobs; who have had their homes invaded and their property taken; and in hundreds have been charged with public offences and held to exorbitant bail. The police are declared to have exhibited an attitude of animosity toward them and to have treated them as criminals in provoking, by their action of Christian profession and teaching, the violence to which they have been subjected; and public officials and members of the Roman Catholic clergy are said not only to have witnessed these outrages but to have been privy to some of the prosecutions. The document charged that the Roman Catholic Church in Quebec was in some objectionable relation to the administration of justice and that the force behind the prosecutions was that of the priests of that Church.

The conduct of the accused appears to have been unexceptionable; so far as disclosed, he is an exemplary citizen who is at least sympathetic to doctrines of the Christian religion which are, evidently, different from either the Protestant or the Roman Catholic versions: but the foundation in all is the same, Christ and his relation to God and humanity.

The crime of seditious libel is well known to the Common Law. Its history has been thoroughly examined and traced by Stephen, Holdsworth and other eminent legal scholars and they are in agreement both in what it originally consisted and in the social assumptions underlying it. Up to the end of the 18th century it was, in essence, a contempt in words of political authority or the action of authority. If we conceive of the governors of society as superior beings, exercising a divine mandate, by whom laws, institutions and administrations are given to men to be obeyed, who are, in short, beyond criticism, reflection or censor upon them or what they do implies either an equality with them or an accountability by them, both equally offensive. In that lay sedition by words and the libel was its written form.

But constitutional conceptions of a different order making rapid progress in the 19th century have necessitated a modification of the legal view of public criticism; and the administrators of what we call democratic government have come to be looked upon as servants, bound to carry out their duties accountably to the public. The basic nature of the Common

Law lies in its flexible process of traditional reasoning upon significant social and political matter; and just as in the 17th century the crime of seditious libel was a deduction from fundamental conceptions of government, the substitution of new conceptions, under the same principle of reasoning, called for new jural conclusions. . . .

. . . The definition of seditious intention as formulated by Stephen, summarised, is, (1) to bring into hatred or contempt, or to excite disaffection against, the King or the Government and Constitution of the United Kingdom, or either House of Parliament, or the administration of justice; or (2) to excite the King's subjects to attempt, otherwise than by lawful means, the alteration of any matter in Church or State by law established; or (3) to incite persons to commit any crime in general disturbance of the peace; or (4) to raise discontent or disaffection amongst His Majesty's subjects; or (5) to promote feelings of ill-will and hostility between different classes of such subjects. The only items of this definition that could be drawn into question here are that relating to the administration of justice in (1) and those of (4) and (5). It was the latter which were brought most prominently to the notice of the jury, and it is with an examination of what in these days their language must be taken to mean that I will chiefly concern myself.

There is no modern authority which holds that the mere effect of tending to create discontent or disaffection among His Majesty's subjects or ill-will or hostility between groups of them but not tending to issue in illegal conduct, constitutes the crime, and this for obvious reasons. Freedom in thought and speech and disagreement in ideas and beliefs, on every conceivable subject, are of the essence of our life. The clash of critical discussion on political, social and religious subjects has too deeply become the stuff of daily experience to suggest that mere ill-will as a product of controversy can strike down the latter with illegality. A superficial examination of the word shows its insufficiency: what is the degree necessary to criminality? Can it ever, as mere subjective condition, be so? Controversial fury is aroused constantly by differences in abstract conceptions; heresy in some fields is again a mortal sin; there can be fanatical puritanism in ideas as well as in mortals; but our compact of free society accepts and absorbs these differences and they are exercised at large within the framework of freedom and order on broader and deeper uniformities as bases of social stability. Similarly in discontent, affection and hostility: as subjective incidents of controversy, they and the ideas which arouse them are part of our living which ultimately serve us in stimulation, in the clarification of thought and, as we believe, in the search for the constitution and truth of things generally.

Although Stephen's definition was adopted substantially as it is by the Criminal Code Commission of England in 1880, the latter's report, in this respect, was not acted on by the Imperial Parliament, and the Criminal Code of this country, enacted in 1891, did not incorporate its provisions. The latter omits any reference to definition except in section 133 to declare that the intention includes the advocacy of the use of force as a means of bringing about a change of government and by section 133A, that certain actions are not included. What the words in (4) and (5) must in the present day be taken to signify is the use of language which, by inflaming the minds of people into hatred, ill-will, discontent, disaffection, is intended, or is so likely to do so as to be deemed to be intended, to disorder community life, but directly or indirectly in relation to government in the broadest sense: Phillimore, J. in *R. v. Antonelli* "seditious libels are such as tend to disturb the government of this country. . . ." That may be through tumult or violence, in resistance to public authority, in defiance of law. The conception lies behind the association which the word is given in section 1 of chapter 10, C.S. Lower Canada (1860) dealing with illegal oaths:

"To engage in any seditious, rebellious or treasonable purpose;" and the corresponding section 130 of the Criminal Code: "To engage in any mutinous or seditious purpose."

The baiting or denouncing of one group by another or others, without an aim directly or indirectly at government, is in the nature of public mischief: *R. v. Leese & Whitehead*; and incitement to unlawful acts is itself an offence.

This result must be distinguished from an undesired reaction provoked by the exercise of common rights, such as the violent opposition to the early services of the Salvation Army. In that situation it was the hoodlums who were held to be the lawless and not the members of the Army: *Beatty v. Gillbanks*. On the allegations in the document here, had the Salvationists been arrested for bringing about by unlawful assembly a breach of the peace and fined, had they then made an impassioned protest against such treatment of law abiding citizens, and had they thereupon been charged with seditious words, their plight would have been that of the accused in this case.

These considerations are confirmed by section 133A of the Code, which is as follows:

WHAT IS NOT SEDITION — No one shall be deemed to have a seditious intention only because he intends in good faith,—

(a) to show that His Majesty has been misled or mistaken in his measures; or

(b) to point out errors or defects in the government or constitution of the United Kingdom, or of any part of it, or of Canada or any province thereof, or in either House of Parliament of the United Kingdom or of Canada, or in any legislature, or in the administration of justice; or to excite His Majesty's subjects to attempt to procure, by lawful means, the alteration of any matters in the state; or,

(c) to point out, in order to their removal, matters which are producing or have a tendency to produce feelings of hatred and ill-will between different classes of His Majesty's subjects.

This, as is seen, is a fundamental provision which, with its background of free criticism as a constituent of modern democratic government, protects the widest range of public discussion and controversy, so long as it is done in good faith and for the purposes mentioned. Its effect is to eviscerate the older concept of its anachronistic elements. But a motive or ultimate purpose, whether good or believed to be good, is unavailing if the means employed is bad; disturbance or corrosion may be ends in themselves, but whether means or ends, their character stamps them and intention behind them as illegal.

The condemned intention lies then in a residue of criticism of government, the negative touchstone of which is the test of good faith by legitimate means toward legitimate ends. That claim was the real defence in the proceedings here but it was virtually ignored by the trial judge. On that failure, as well as others, the Chief Justice of the King's Bench and Galipeault, J. have rested their dissent, and with them I am in agreement.

9.5

REGINA v. OJIBWAY

BLUE, J.: This is an appeal by the Crown by way of a stated case from a decision of the magistrate acquitting the accused of a charge under the Small Birds Act. R.S.O., 1960. c. 724, s. 2. The facts are not in dispute. Fred Ojibway, an Indian, was riding his pony through Queen's Park on January 2, 1965. Being impoverished, and having been forced to pledge his saddle, he substituted a downy pillow in lieu of the said saddle. On this particular day the accused's misfortune was further heightened by the circumstance of his pony breaking its right foreleg. In accord with current Indian custom, the accused then shot the pony to relieve it of its awkwardness.

The accused was then charged with having breached the Small Birds Act, s. 2 of which states:

> 2. Anyone maiming, injuring or killing small birds is guilty of an offence and subject to a fine not in excess of two hundred dollars.

The learned magistrate acquitted the accused, holding in fact, that he had killed his horse and not a small bird. With respect, I cannot agree.

In light of the definition section, my course is quite clear. Section 1 defines "bird" as "a two-legged animal covered with feathers." There can be no doubt that this case is covered by this section.

Counsel for the accused made several ingenious arguments to which, in fairness, I must address myself. He submitted that the evidence of the expert clearly concluded that the animal in question was a pony and not a bird, but this is not the issue. We are not interested in whether the animal in question is a bird or not in fact, but whether it is one in law. Statutory interpretation has forced many a horse to eat birdseed for the rest of its life.

Counsel also contended that the neighing noise emitted by the animal could not possibly be produced by a bird. With respect, the sounds emitted by an animal are irrelevant to its nature, for a bird is no less a bird because it is silent.

Counsel for the accused also argued that since there was evidence to show that the accused had ridden the animal, this pointed to the fact that it could not be a bird but was actually a pony. Obviously, this avoids the issue. This issue is not whether the animal was ridden or not, but whether it was shot or not, for to ride a pony or a bird is of no offense at all. I believe that counsel now sees his mistake.

Counsel contends that the iron shoes found on the animal decisively disqualify it from being a bird. I must inform counsel, however, that how an animal dresses is of no concern to this court.

Counsel relied on the decision in *Re Chicadee*, where he contends that in similar circumstances the accused was acquitted. However, this is a horse of a different color. A close reading of the case indicates that the animal in question there was not a small bird, but, in fact, a midget of a much larger species. Therefore, that case is inapplicable to our facts.

Counsel finally submits that the word "small" in the title Small Birds Act refers not to "Birds" but to "Act," making it The Small Act relating to Birds. With respect, counsel did not do his homework very well, for the Large Birds Act, R.S.O., 1960, c. 725, is just as small. If pressed, I need only refer to the Small Loans Act, R.S.O., 1960, c. 727, which is twice as large as the Large Birds Act.

It remains then to state my reason for judgment which, simply, is as follows: Different things may take on the same meaning for different purposes. For the purpose of the Small Birds Act, all two-legged, feather-covered animals are birds. This, of course, does not imply that only two-legged animals qualify, for the legislative intent is to make two legs merely the minimum requirement. The statute therefore contemplated multilegged animals with feathers as well. Counsel submits that having regard to the purpose of the statute, only small animals "naturally covered" with feathers could have been contemplated. However, had this been the intention of the legislature, I am certain that the phrase "naturally covered" would have been expressly inserted just as "Long" was inserted in the Longshoreman's Act.

Therefore, a horse with feathers on its back must be deemed for the purposes of this Act to be a bird, and *a fortiori*, a pony with feathers on its back is a small bird.

Counsel posed the following rhetorical question: If the pillow had been removed prior to the shooting would the animal still be a bird? To this let me answer rhetorically: Is a bird any less of a bird without its feathers?

Appeal allowed.

9.6

POLICY-MAKING BY EXEGESIS: THE ABOLITION OF "MANDATORY RETIREMENT" IN MANITOBA
Thomas Flanagan

Peter Russell predicted even before its adoption that the Charter would "expand the policy-making role of the Canadian courts." Or, to be more precise, "a constitutional charter of rights guarantees not rights but a particular way of making decisions about rights in which the judicial branch of government has a much more systematic and authoritative role." This prediction has already been confirmed by a recent quantitative study of the first year of the Charter's life. . . . The main effect up to now has been in the field of criminal law with many Charter-based challenges in matters such as search and seizure. When s.15 takes effect, the courts will be thrust more deeply into social and economic questions than they have ever before been in Canada, and dozens of federal and provincial statutes will be challenged because of alleged discriminatory effect. . . .

This paper provides some observations about the policy process based on a single case study: the step-by-step abolition of fixed-age retirement in Manitoba. The Manitoba case was chosen because it is a particularly striking example of how the process of judicial interpretation can produce a policy which is demonstrably different from the historical intent of the legislature. The observations derived from the Manitoba experience are, I believe, broadly applicable to the policy-making process whenever it is affected by human rights or anti-discrimination guarantees. . . .

The Rise of Age Discrimination

The concept of "age discrimination" is a child of the American civil rights movement. The success of blacks in attaining political objectives by pre-

---

Canadian Public Policy 11, no. 1 (1985), from pages 40–53. Reprinted with permission.

senting themselves as victims of discrimination led other groups to begin conceptualizing themselves in the same way. The analogy between race and age is tenuous at best. Age, like race, is not within the individual's control, but there the resemblance ends. Race is an invariant characteristic, whereas age varies throughout the life cycle. Racial groups perpetuate themselves through heredity, whereas age groups are not segmented within society. The family ties together individuals of different ages in a way that has no counterpart for race. Additionally, there are ideologies of racial dominance and superiority which have supported movements of racial oppression; there are no counterparts to these phenomena with respect to age. But these profound differences have not prevented political acceptance of the concept of "age discrimination."

Although numerous states had previously legislated on the subject, "age discrimination" became a national issue in 1964, when attempts were made to introduce age, along with race and sex, as a prohibited ground of discrimination in the Civil Rights Act. Congress, while not accepting the amendment, directed the Secretary of Labor to study "older people." The Labor Department study led to the Age Discrimination in Employment Act (ADEA) of 1967, which applied to private sector employers with more than 25 employees. . . . Most importantly, it applied only to workers between the ages of 40 and 65. . . .

The movement against "age discrimination" quickly spilled over into Canada. Even before the passage of ADEA, British Columbia (1964) and Ontario (1966) had passed age legislation in the employment field. After ADEA, Canadian provinces began to put age provisions into their human rights acts. The pioneers were British Columbia (1969), Newfoundland (1970), Ontario (1972) and Alberta (1972). In all cases, ADEA's emphasis on the older worker was the model for Canadian legislation, with corresponding avoidance of the retirement issue. All four provinces imitated ADEA's age cap of 65 as well as the exemption for *bona fide* occupational qualifications (bfoq), i.e., job qualifications deemed reasonable by human rights authorities. All except Ontario also incorporated clauses, modelled on the language of ADEA, exempting retirement and pension plans. In 1973 New Brunswick broke with the ADEA model in a different direction by defining age as "nineteen years of age and over" without a ceiling—but the likely impact on retirement practices was blunted by a bfoq exemption and a clear, ADEA type statement that the prohibition of age discrimination did not apply to "the termination of employment or a refusal to employ because of the terms or conditions of any *bona fide* retirement or pension plan."

While these carefully worded provisions on age discrimination were being inserted into provincial human rights codes, attempts were being made to attack fixed retirement practices in labour arbitration cases. After some years of confusion, the Supreme Court of Canada held in 1973 that "retirement" and "discharge" were separate concepts, and that an employer did not have to justify a retirement policy in any special way, unless a collective agreement supervened. Subsequent labour relations cases have followed this doctrine, albeit with occasional aberrations. Thus it is a fair statement that as of 1973, fixed retirement was legal in Canada and had not been disturbed by provincial anti-discrimination legislation.

Manitoba dealt with age discrimination in a package of amendments to its Human Rights Act in 1974. By comparison with Canadian precedents, there were some important changes. Like New Brunswick, Manitoba put no ceiling on age, but went farther by omitting an age floor in the definition. The concept of bfoq was redefined as "a reasonable occupational qualification and requirement for the position or employment." The substitution of "reasonable" for "*bona fide*" emphasized that the age qualification must be persuasive to external observers, no matter how sincere the employer's belief in it might be. Finally, the clause relating to retirement plans was somewhat weakened.

> 7. (2) No provision of section 6 or of this section relating to age prohibits the operation of any term of a *bona fide* retirement, superannuation, or pension plan, or the terms or conditions of any *bona fide* group or employee insurance plan or of any *bona fide* scheme based upon seniority.

The language of this section was similar to that of the Alberta Act in referring to the "operation" of retirement or pension plans. It was weaker than that of similar clauses in the British Columbia, Newfoundland, and New Brunswick legislation which allowed "termination of employment" in connection with a retirement plan.

Events would soon show that the cumulative effect of the innovations in the Manitoba Human Rights Act was to enable a plausible legal challenge to fixed retirement to be made. I could not establish whether this was apparent at the time to the anonymous draftsmen of the amendments, but it certainly does not seem to have been the intention of the politicians who took responsibility for the legislation. The then Attorney-General, Howard Pawley, referred only to the employment problems of older workers when he introduced the amendments into the Legislative Assembly on June 1, 1974; he did not mention retirement at all. The same was true of the government's press release describing the bill. Two members of the cabinet later made public statements that they had not intended the law to have an impact on retirement practices. Sydney Green said: "I know of no legislator at the time who felt that that was the result of the legislation." Ben Hanuschak said: "I was party to the initial draftsmanship of it . . . we were not so much concerned, in fact I don't think that we gave any attention to or any thought, to the issue of retirement." If actions speak louder than words, it is also relevant that the same government continued to operate its civil service with a normal retirement age of 65 and subsequently passed a bill allowing school boards to establish a fixed retirement age for teachers. I have found no informed person in Manitoba who believes the legislature intended to abolish fixed retirement in 1974.

Once proclaimed, however, legislation escapes the control of its creators and its "intent" becomes a legal artifact of statutory construction, perhaps having little to do with the historical intent of the legislators. This happened very quickly in the case of *Derksen v. Flyer Industries* (unreported).

Peter Derksen was a lathe operator who had worked for Flyer Industries 13 years when he turned 65 in January, 1975. After another month on the job, he was asked to retire. Retirement was not mentioned in the collective agreement, although the union had been trying to negotiate a retirement age of 60. The company had a policy of retirement at 65 which, although documented and made known to the union, was not rigorously implemented in every case. Many employees seem to have been unclear about the policy. There was a voluntary pension plan in which Derksen did not participate; only six employees did.

Derksen first grieved through his union. A labour arbitration board was convened which ruled that the new amendments to the Human Rights Act had not made fixed retirement discriminatory. With the support of his union, Derksen then complained to the Human Rights Commission. After investigation, Jack London, Professor and later Dean of Law at the University of Manitoba, was appointed to a board of inquiry, which rendered its decision in June 1977.

London had no special familiarity with age issues, but he had spent a sabbatical in the United States where he had heard much about racial and sexual discrimination. When he began to think about the *Derksen* case, it struck him that "ageism" was just like racism or sexism. In his own words, the *Derksen* Case "radicalized" his position on age discrimination. He has subsequently become something of a spokesman for the abolition of "mandatory retirement."

The issue in *Derksen* was how Flyer, in the absence of an age cap in the Human Rights Act, could defend its policy of retirement at 65. Claiming that age was a "reasonable occupational qualification and requirement" was a hypothetical possibility, but not a very serious one, for Derksen was plainly able to continue the physical work of operating a lathe. Flyer therefore chose to rest its case on s.7(2), that the Act did not prohibit "the operation of any term of a *bona fide* retirement, superannuation, or pension plan.". . .

Counsel for Derksen and the Commission was Roland Penner, later New Democratic MLA and Attorney-General. He offered to London several ways of reinstating Derksen without giving a sweeping decision against fixed retirement in general. His strategy was to argue that the Flyer retirement plan was not *bona fide* because it had been unilaterally proclaimed, ineffectively communicated to the workforce, inconsistently enforced, and did not necessarily involve a pension. Surprisingly, London did not accept any of these proffered grounds for a narrow decision. Instead, he rendered a sweeping decision that s.7(2) referred only to contributions paid into and benefits paid out by a retirement plan, not to the actual practice of retirement, i.e., pension contribution and annuity payments, as well as other fringe benefits, could be proportioned to age; but age could not be a factor in requiring an employee to retire.

This decision was questionable first of all because it was more far-reaching than required under the circumstance. Furthermore, the language of s.7(2) was plainly traceable to s.4(f)(2) of ADEA, and that section was interpreted by the Supreme Court of the United States in 1977 in a sense opposite to London's view, i.e., that it applied not just to retirement benefits but to the retirement decision. An American precedent is not binding in Canada, but it is persuasive, particularly where the Canadian statute is modelled on an American one. However, London's decision did not mention the American cases, perhaps because they were not brought to his attention by counsel for either side.

Curiously, the radical decision in *Derksen* did not have the impact one might have forecast. To judge from its annual reports, the Human Rights Commission, even before *Derksen*, had developed the cautious policy of using its powers to conciliate retirement cases only where the complainant did not have a pension and so retirement might mean financial hardship. This was only nibbling at the fringes of fixed retirement, for the large employers with formal retirement policies always have pension plans. Small employers may have a retirement policy but are usually much less insistent about adhering to it. After *Derksen*, the Commission simply ignored the implications of the decision and continued its previous policy. There may have been an element of bureaucratic inertia in this, but there was also important political pressure. The Cabinet was not pleased with *Derksen*, and the Minister of Labour privately threatened the Commission that he would "cap" the definition of age in the Act if the Commission started accepting complaints about retirement in general. The underlying motives of each side in this *de facto* co-operation are clear: the Commission did not want the Act weakened, and the government did not want the status quo in the labour market upset. The government also would not have wanted the embarrassment of having to admit it had not foreseen the consequences of its own legislation; and the Commission, composed largely of NDP supporters, would not have wanted to embarrass the government gratuitously.

This *ad hoc* compromise between the government and the Commission ran counter not only to *Derksen* but also to one possible reading of a recent amendment to the Human Rights Act. In 1976 s.7(2), which London had explained away, had been amended to remove the explicit mention of retirement, superannuation, and pension plans. The new wording referred only to employee benefit plans. Although London had had to interpret the *old* s.7(2) because Derksen's complaint had arisen under it, he had effectively imported into it one interpretation of the *new* s.7(2). Thus, after the decision in *Derksen* was rendered in June, 1977, both precedent and statute seemed to agree in depriving fixed retirement of any claim to legitimacy. Ironically, it seems that neither the Commission nor the government had foreseen this consequence of the amendment to s. 7(2), which had been conceived as a purely technical measure without independent effect. Thus the Commission, with the government's tacit approval, continued its policy of rejecting most retirement complaints.

On July 18, 1978, John Finlayson, a Winnipeg police officer recently retired at age 60 pursuant to a collective agreement, lodged a complaint with the MHRC [Manitoba Human Rights Commission]. His situation raised not only the general problem of fixed retirement but the special problem of whether age could be a bfoq for occupations like police work where public safety was involved.

Before much could be done in his case, the entire MHRC was replaced on August 15. Premier Sterling Lyon, who had led the provincial Tories to victory in the election of 1977, replaced a Commission widely (and accurately) considered to be sympathetic to the NDP with an entirely new Commission just as obviously Conservative in complexion. The new Chairman was Sig Enns, a former Conservative MP. From the course of events, it can be deduced that the new MHRC and the government decided to continue their policy of deflecting retirement cases. Finlayson's complaint, which was already on record, was put on a bureaucratic merry-go-round, so that it took almost three years to come to a board of adjudication.

On October 31, 1978, Aubry Newport, a Manitoba civil servant, was retired at 65 pursuant to the Civil Service Act. He tried to complain to the MHRC, which at first refused even to receive his complaint. This was probably illegal, as the Human Rights Act stated, "The Commission *shall*, as soon as is reasonably possible, investigate and endeavour to effect a settlement of any complaint of an alleged contravention of the Act." The Commission was finally forced to accept the complaint when Newport's counsel, one of whom was Jack London, now Dean of the Manitoba Law Faculty, threatened to obtain a writ of mandamus. Once it accepted the complaint, the Commission conducted a perfunctory investigation and then called upon the Attorney-General to appoint a board of adjudication. Whereas the Commission legally has "carriage of the complaint" and normally appears with the complainant and pays legal expenses, in this instance it removed itself from the proceedings, leaving Newport's counsel to act *pro bono publico*.

These delays led to an end run around the Commission by Imogene McIntire, a Professor of Education at the University of Manitoba. She was due for retirement June 30, 1980, at age 65, according to the University's collective agreement with academic staff. She obtained the services of Mel Myers, who had been Chairman of the MHRC under the NDP and who was now acting for the Winnipeg Senior Officers Association against Finlayson. Knowing that McIntire would find only delay if she complained to the Commission, Myers took her complaint directly to the Court of Queen's Bench, as was allowed by s.34 of the Manitoba Human Rights

Act. He asked for a declaratory judgment that the collective agreement was void with respect to setting an age for retirement because it conflicted with the Human Rights Act. The Court agreed, ruling that, since the Act contained no upper limit on age, "no employer may refuse to continue to employ a person solely on the basis of the age." The collective agreement made no difference because "parties may not contract out of the provisions of the human rights legislation."

This decision was quickly followed by a board of adjudication in the grievance of Stewart Thexton, a non-academic employee of the University of Manitoba. The legal issue was identical, namely the validity of retirement at 65 under a collective agreement. More importantly, the *McIntire* decision was upheld in an appeal to the Manitoba Court of Appeal in early 1981. By a vote of 3–2, the Court held that "in passing legislation without any limitations by way of definition of the word 'age,' the Manitoba legislature intended to prohibit discrimination in employment against its adult citizens of whatever age." In dissent, Justice Monnin observed that this issue "should be resolved by the elected representatives of the people and not left to the courts to struggle with, unaware of all social, actuarial, and other implications involved." Retirement at 65 was widespread in both public and private sectors, and the government had continued to follow that practice even after introducing age into the Human Rights Act in 1974. Monnin reasoned that the legislature would not have brought about such a drastic change in existing practice without some explicit statement. He was undoubtedly correct about the historical intent of the legislation, but on weaker ground as far as pure statutory construction was concerned.

Meanwhile the complaints of Finlayson and Newport were grinding ponderously ahead. In the fall of 1980, the Attorney-General appointed Winnipeg lawyer Marshall Rothstein to adjudicate both cases. Rothstein was connected to the Conservative party, highly respected in legal circles, sympathetic to individual rights, but not a human rights crusader.

Newport differed importantly from *McIntire*. In the latter case, retirement rested upon a collective agreement; in the former, the age of 65 was explicitly established by two provincial statutes, the Civil Service Act and the Civil Service Superannuation Act. The legal question was whether the Human Rights Act, passed after these two, had impliedly repealed provisions which were inconsistent with itself. Rothstein ruled that implied repeal had not taken place, chiefly because the Civil Service Act stated that it applied "unless explicitly provided to the contrary in another Act." Rothstein reasoned, therefore, that the Human Rights Act did not repeal the retirement provision of the Civil Service Act because it did not explicitly say so.

This victory against the abolition of fixed retirement proved to be short-lived. In two levels of appeal, both the Court of Queen's Bench and the Court of Appeal disagreed with Rothstein. The *ratio decidendi* was that the *Human Rights Act* was later in time than the early statutes and that it contained a statement explicitly binding the Crown. In the words of Justice Monnin:

... the old law and the new law cannot stand together, and one must give way. The Human Rights Act was passed later in time, and in view of the fact that it contains a specific provision declaring the Crown to be bound—thereby necessarily making it applicable to member of the Civil Service—this is a case where the later enactment prevails over the earlier one.

While the *McIntire* and *Newport* appeals were decisive in giving an authoritative interpretation of the law, other cases extended the law to various situtations. *Bedrich* (unreported) covered the by-laws of the City of Winnipeg, *Parkinson* the by-laws of the government-funded Health Science Centre. *Paterson v. Price* applied to employer policy in the private sector where "retirement age was not specified in a collective agreement."

The abolition of fixed retirement has thus been effectuated except for three minor limitations. First, Adjudicator Rothstein ruled, and was upheld in two appeals, that Finlayson could be required to retire at 60. Age could be a *bona fide* occupational qualification for a police officer, particularly because public safety was involved and no satisfactory tests existed, capable of measuring each officer's physical and mental abilities in individual terms. Second, in *Galbraith and Lylyk*, the Manitoba courts refused to make the impact of *Newport* retroactive, thus staving off a reinstatement of civil servants retired before *Newport*. Third, after adding age to the Human Rights Act, the Manitoba legislature in 1980 revised and repassed the Public Schools Act. Section 50 of the new statute allowed public school divisions to establish a retirement age for teachers, leading to the involuntary retirement of Doreen Craton at 65. The Court of Queen's Bench and the Court of Appeal have both held that the Human Rights Act takes precedence over the Public Schools Act. A statute such as the Public Schools Act would have to contain an explicit statement exempting it from the Human Rights Act before it could legitimate fixed retirement. However, one judge in dissent has argued that, according to the logic of *Newport*, the later statute should take precedence. The Winnipeg School Division No. 1 has received leave to appeal from the Supreme Court of Canada. Craton's counsel, Mel Myers, believes that this will be a chance to establish the quasi-constitutional status of human rights acts.

Even if *Craton* is reversed by the Supreme Court, it will constitute only a very limited exception to the abolition of fixed retirement, as does *Finlayson*. The reality is that fixed retirement in Manitoba has been effectively abolished by judicial interpretation of the Human Rights Act, even though that interpretation was almost certainly contrary to the historical intention of the legislature which had passed the Act in 1974 and amended it in 1976. Of course, as the judges often remarked in these cases, if the legislature did not like the judiciary's view of the law, it was at all times free to "cap" the Act or in some other way to provide for the continuation of fixed retirement.

That the Lyon government considered this possibility is shown by its appointment, on March 11, 1981, of a Commission on Compulsory Retirement. The Commissioner was Marshall Rothstein, who at that point had already rendered his decision in *Newport* and was still seized of the protracted *Finlayson* case. Given his ruling in *Newport* that the Human Rights Act had not repealed the retirement provisions of the Civil Service Act, his appointment by the government may have looked like a prelude to the reestablishment of fixed retirement. But again there was a surprise. Rothstein's long report, presented after a year of studying legal and economic evidence, recommended continuation of the *status quo*, which by that time had become "abolitionist." While Rothstein worked, his ruling in *Newport* had been reversed by the courts and further decisions had overturned fixed retirement in other sectors of the Manitoba economy. Rothsteins's report ratified these developments, albeit with a strong statement in favour of retaining the bfoq exemption for certain exceptional situations. This result would have made it difficult for any government to restore fixed retirement by amending the Human Rights Act, but in any case the Lyon cabinet was replaced by a new NDP government even before the report was delivered.

Analysis

This slice of Manitoba history illustrates how a policy-making process can emerge from the adjudication of private rights. By 1982, the result was effectively the same as if the legislature had decided to abolish fixed age retirement; yet the legislature never made such a decision, and it is questionable whether such a proposition could have been passed at any time between 1974 and 1982. Rather than making a clear decision of its own, the legislature, by including age in the Human Rights Act in 1974, set in motion a policy process involving a complex interaction of legislative, administrative, and judicial institutions.

The most striking feature of the process was the attainment within a very few years of a result clearly divergent from the intent of the legislature. The historical evidence makes clear that the cabinet and legislature were primarily concerned about the employment opportunities of older workers, men and women in the 40–65 range who were required by circumstances to change jobs. Ironically, it is unknown whether this group was helped at all by the legislation. Human Rights Commission conciliation files are confidential, but no complaint in this category has gone as far as a board of adjudication. Whatever the impact on the original target group, the legislation's most visible consequences were clearly unintended ones. No one seems to have realized that drafting the age provision in sweeping language without the customary upper limit or "cap" would lead to the abolition of fixed retirement. Later statements by government officials as well as a consistent pattern of government actions show that this outcome was neither intended nor desired.

The outcome was a victory for the literal word. The Manitoba courts followed the British model of precluding themselves from examining historical evidence of legislative intent. Statutory construction depended upon the reading of the legal text, aided by certain canons of construction. This style of interpretation may be appropriate for the adjudication of private rights, but it leads to a peculiar form of policy process which I shall call "policy-making by exegesis." The exegetical approach to policy proceeds by deductive logic to unpack the possible meanings of legislative words. No notice is taken of "social facts," i.e., of recurrent patterns of behaviour or of historically established practices. Public policy is thus produced syllogistically rather than empirically. This approach, long typical of Canadian courts, is beginning to change in favour of certain American practices. The Supreme Court of Canada, at least, will now look at historical evidence of legislative intent in interpreting a constitutional text and will examine social facts, as shown in the *Anti-Inflation Reference* case. But the older positivistic traditions of statutory construction are still overwhelmingly dominant in the lower courts.

To say this is not to criticize the Manitoba courts for "judicial activism." The courts did not at all seek out the policy-making role that was thrust upon them by the expansive wording of the 1974 amendments to the Human Rights Act. "In the beginning was the word. . ." The courts were bound by the legislative word and had to deliver an exegesis on demand. Responsibility for the situation rests with the government of the day for introducing into the legislature a statute so broadly worded that it amounted to a delegation to the courts of legislative authority over a broad area of public policy.

Policy-making by exegesis leads to the domination of the policy process by exegetical specialists, usually lawyers. In the events described here, a small number of Winnipeg lawyers interested in "human rights" questions repeatedly played key roles. Mel Myers, Chairman of the MHRC at the time of *Derksen*, was later counsel for the complainant in *McIntire* and *Craton*, and counsel for the defendant in *Finlayson*. Jack London, the adjudicator in *Derksen*, represented the complainant in *Newport*. Marshall Rothstein, the adjudicator in *Bedrich*, *Newport* and *Finlayson*, was also appointed commissioner to study the whole question. The judges of the Manitoba courts made the ultimate decisions on appeal, of course, but the activities of counsel and adjudicators were vital in formulating the issues. Rothstein's report was also crucial in legitimating what the judiciary had wrought. Thus it is not an overstatement to say that provincial public policy on this issue was made by a small number of unelected lawyers and judges in Winnipeg. The government and legislature, which could legally have reversed the outcome, were politically paralyzed by the mystique of human rights.

Another noteworthy fact is that the abolition of fixed retirement was achieved against remarkable opposition. Neither the NDP nor the Conservatives, who controlled the government and legislature at different times, favoured it. Pliant human rights commissions, heeding the voice of the cabinet, did their best to hold up abolition. City governments, school districts, and police commissions fought the trend as did the University of Manitoba, which made vigorous public statements. Large private sector employers were almost universally opposed to abolition; the insurance industry, which is particularly important in Winnipeg, made a submission to Rothstein. Small employers were more or less unconcerned about the issue since they do not normally rely on a fixed age of retirement. The labour movement was badly split on the issue. McIntire, Newport, Finlayson, and Craton all had to act without or even against their unions. The Manitoba Government Employee Association and the Manitoba Federation of Labour publicly advocated leaving such matters to collective bargaining. The University of Manitoba Faculty Association, after sitting on the sidelines in *McIntire*, did recommend abolition to the Rothstein Commission, but only for a five-year trial period.

Throughout this period, no large or powerful organization in Manitoba was pushing for an end to fixed retirement; complaints were all brought by isolated individuals without institutional support. Their objectives were opposed by public sector employers, big business, and at least a large part of organized labour. Almost incredibly, this imposing array of political power could find no way to influence or reverse the outcome of the judicial policy-making process. Again, the mystique of human rights was triumphant.

One reason for the power of the word is that there was little institutional control over complaints. The MHRC by statute had to receive and investigate complaints. It did not have to request the Attorney-General to appoint a board of adjudication; but if it did so, the Attorney-General had to comply. Additionally, complainants could go directly to the Court of Queen's Bench for an injunction, as McIntire did. Once the legislation had been passed, neither the government nor the MHRC could control the resultant process of adjudication.

Such circumstances make it likely that sooner or later all logical possibilities of a statutory text will be exhausted. As complainants come forward with their grievances, counsel will develop arguments as necessary. There is a high probability that a wide variety of complaints will actually be made, for the costs of complaining have been deliberately made low. The Commission's "carriage of the complaint" means it pays expenses when it supports the complainant before the board of adjudication and in court appeals. Litigation without the Commission's support, as in *McIntire* and *Newport*, imposes a cost on the complainant for legal fees, which may however be reduced or erased if counsel acts *pro bono publico*, as London did in *Newport*. Even if the complainant loses his case and has to pay legal fees, he is very unlikely to be assessed costs and/or damages for the defendant; at least, this has not yet happened in Canada in human rights proceedings. All of this means that it is only a matter of time before all logically possible interpretations of broadly worded human rights codes are tested. Policy-making by exegesis will not fail to thrive for lack of disputes.

The incremental nature of the process is not by itself open to objection. The common law is a valuable incremental process of law-making, in which the law emerges as an unintended consequence of adjudicating particular disputes. The virtues of the common law, as of all incremental decision-making processes, are many: gradualism, incorporation of practical experience, avoidance of catastrophic error, possibility of correction, responsiveness to changing conditions. However, there is an essential difference between the common law and human rights law. The common law method of reasoning by analogy is a method of formulating rules of law to settle particular cases. Undergirding the process is the people's real but largely inarticulate sense of justice. Common law adjudication "discovers" the law by articulating these principles of justice as they apply to particular cases. Once articulated, a principle stands until it is modified or specified by another principle brought to light in a different case. Thus the common law is a gradual process of discovery and articulation of principles which are already implicit in the morality of the people. Because discovery and articulation are based on existing patterns of behaviour, the tendency is to confirm rather than upset expectations.

In contrast, human rights law begins with a legislated statement of an abstract principle: that there shall be no "age discrimination." This is not an articulation of existing practice but a radical innovation. Prior to 1974, "age discrimination" was part of life in Manitoba as everywhere else in the Western world. Age was routinely considered as a relevant factor in decisions about school entry, apprenticeship, hiring, retirement, and innumerable other aspects of daily life. To suddenly declare such reliance on age to be a form of discrimination is not an expression of popular *mores* but an attempt to change them. It is an effort to reform reality according to intellectually conceived norms. "In the beginning was the word. . ." The human rights complaint machinery now sets up a discovery process which, unlike the common law, is unguided by actual behaviour. The major constraint on adjudication is the wording of the statute. The formulation of legal principles becomes a kind of textual exegesis rather than an articulation of tacitly observed patterns of behaviour.

Although the incremental process of common law adjudication is oriented toward the resolution of particular conflicts, as general principles emerge they will have an impact on public policy. For example, the rise in the nineteenth century of the doctrine of negligence in torts had the effect of removing from employers most liability for industrial accidents suffered by their employees. Ultimately legislatures intervened to reintroduce, in various forms, the notion of strict liability. But the policy impact of common law is qualitatively different from that of human rights adjudication because of the greater dependence on existing behaviour as opposed to intellectually conceived standards of reform. An abstract idea such as the prohibition of age discrimination is bound to have policy consequences in many unexpected directions.

At this point should be mentioned the well-known weaknesses of adjudication as a method of making policy. These apply almost equally to courts and to quasi-judicial tribunals such as the boards of adjudication established under the Manitoba Human Rights Act. Courts and tribunals do not control their own agendas; they must react to cases brought before them. Their methods of inquiry focus on the history of particular cases, not on recurrent patterns of behaviour. The necessity to declare individual rights precludes compromise and turns bargaining situations into contests of principle. Courts must declare individual rights under the law regardless of social consequences; they would be rightly reproached if they denied justice to a complainant because of a view of the policy consequences. And in any event, they have no machinery to allow them to study the policy consequences of their decisions and to change direction if the consequences are undesirable. The precedential method encourages a straight-ahead movement towards the logical limits that a doctrine will bear.

All these characteristics of judicial policy-making were evident in the abolition of fixed retirement in Manitoba. Individual complaints forced the issue to the fore, even though it was not on the agenda of government or of any well-organized interest in the province. The tribunals and courts had to deal with individual cases in the absence of general information. Ironically, an excellent study was done, but only after the legal decisions had been made. Research served the function of retrospective legitimation, not prospective definition of policy choices. The rights format required a decision of principle—fixed retirement, yes or no—whereas the matter might also have been handled by legislative compromise, as it was in the United States. A legislative increase of the retirement age to 70 would have dealt with practically all realistic complaints without introducing the sweeping principle that *no* fixed age for retirement may be established by collective bargaining or employer policy. Similarly, the legislature could have made special provision for certain categories of employment, as was done in ADEA.

This does not mean that courts are inferior institutions. The peculiar characteristics of their decision-making processes are all beneficial features for the resolution of particular disputes, and courts which were not of this type would soon lose their legitimacy in adjudication. But what is a strength for adjudication of disputes can be a weakness for general policy-making The appropriate conclusion is that the legislature should not force the courts to play a role for which they are poorly equipped.

Alternatively, if the Canadian courts are to be thrust by legislatures into policy-making role, they will have to adopt new procedures to cope as best they can with their new responsibilities. Two innovations with which the Supreme Court of Canada has already experimented are suggested by this case study. First, it would have been useful if the courts could have examined historical evidence about legislative intent instead of deducing intent through exegesis. Second, the courts would have been assisted by taking judicial notice of the "social facts" concerning retirement practices. This might have been accomplished by submission of "Brandeis briefs" by the litigants or by intervention of informed parties. Such changes in judicial procedure create new difficulties of their own to the extent that they transfer the court's focus from a particular conflict to a general question of policy, but the costs may have to be accepted if courts are compelled to be policy-makers.

Abolition of fixed retirement is a *fait accompli* in Manitoba. It has been legislated in Quebec, and may ensue in New Brunswick from human rights cases now being heard. The unqualified use of the term "age" in s.15 of the Canadian Charter of Rights and Freedoms may produce the same result in all of Canada, at least in the public sector. [Ed. note: In 1990, the Supreme Court rejected a section 15 challenge to mandatory retirement policies at universities. The majority argued that universities are not part of government and thus not restricted by the Charter; and even if they were, mandatory retirement would be a "reasonable limitation" (per section 1 of the Charter) on the right against age discrimination.] I am not necessarily opposed to the substance of these developments. I believe that expansion of individual choice is normally desirable. However, there are also many situations where fixed retirement seems to be a useful part of a package of employment arrangements: in the judiciary, so that the government will not get into the dangerous habit of forcing the resignation of aging judges whose competence is declining; in military and quasi-military hierarchies, where "up or out" promotion prevails; in the university, where tenure becomes a guarantee of lifetime employment in the absence of a retirement age; for high corporate executives, who otherwise might be retired only at the cost of a disastrous fight within the board of directors; for pilots, bus drivers, and other occupations where public safety is involved. Only a few of these situations are adequately covered by the concept of bfoq.

Apart from the substance of the outcome, the way in which it was reached has alarming implications. Since employment conditions in a market economy are so diverse, retirement provisions should be left to the flexibility of individual or collective bargaining. If government regulation is necessary, it should be done through specific legislation passed after debate by elected legislators, so that compromises can be struck and exceptions provided for. The path taken in Manitoba seems the least desirable policy process for a liberal democracy: the legislature passes a statute of unknown meaning, the exegesis of which leads unelected lawyers and judges to impose a sweeping policy change on all employers and unions.

Transforming such important policy matters into "rights" questions takes them out of the conventional political process where they belong, short-circuits debate on the broad issues, and makes it extraordinarily difficult for the legislature to regain control of events. This is hardly the substance of representative government.

The considerations developed in this section apply with equal or even greater force to the coming era of Charter jurisprudence. Consider again the wording of s.15(1) of the Charter:

> 15. (1) Every individual is equal before and under the law and has the right to the equal protection and equal benefit of the law without discrimination and, in particular, without discrimination based on race, national or ethnic origin, colour, religion, sex, age or mental or physical disability.

Even more than human rights legislation, this language is a triumph of abstract principle. Words like "sex" or "age" are wholly undefined. Will "sex" apply to such difficult practical issues as maternity leave or fringe benefits to homosexual partners? What impact will "age" have on school entry, on retirement practices, on government-regulated automobile insurance rates? Existing human rights legislation is filled with provisions to cover such practical problems: bfoq clauses, age floors and ceilings, specific exemptions, etc. The Charter leaves all such questions to the courts to determine as best they can.

One important difference between human rights and Charter litigation is worth noting. Human rights legislation facilitates access to adjudication by allowing a Minister to appoint boards of inquiry and by giving the Commission "carriage of the complaint" before such boards and before the courts on appeal. This access is so generous that it allows individuals to affect the policy process without being part of a larger organized group, as happened in this case study. Access under the Charter, although generous by any usual standard, is not so wide. There are no quasi-judicial tribunals to hear Charter cases, so litigants will have to go directly to court under s.24(1): "Anyone whose rights or freedoms, as guaranteed by this Charter, have been infringed or denied may apply to a court of competent jurisdiction to obtain such remedy as the court considers appropriate and just in the circumstances." This section makes it easy to get into court, but litigants will have to find their own lawyers and pay expenses, obligations which Commissions undertake in human rights cases. This difference means that the Charter will be less useful to random individuals than to organized groups providing money and legal advice in support of a strategy of litigation. Canadian feminists are already on this path, preparing lawsuits to be filed April 17, 1985. Other interest groups will doubtless imitate the feminists if the latter are successful.

Section 15 of the Charter thus promises to make the courts an arena for the combat of organized groups pursuing deliberate strategies. In such an environment, policy-making by exegesis will be satisfactory to no one's interest, least of all the public interest. Legislatures will have to take steps to regain control over some of the power which they have devolved upon the courts, while the courts will have to adjust their procedures to deal with their more prominent role in the policy process. The inevitable politicization of courts will be an epochal development in Canadian government. With such a broad policy-making role, the political neutrality of the judiciary will be increasingly transformed from a half-truth to a fiction, with incalculable long-range consequences for the legitimacy of the courts.

9.7

KEY TERMS

Concepts

common law system
stare decisis
ratio decidendi
obiter dicta
precedent
"distinguishing a precedent"
"limiting a precedent"
"ignoring a precedent"
"overruling a precedent"
"prospective overruling"
statute
administrative rules and regulations
civil law system
codification
policy-making by exegesis

Institutions, Events, and Documents

James Fitzjames Stephen, Draft Code of 1879
Criminal Code (1892)
Fleming v. Atkinson (Cattle Trespass Case) (1959)

10

Judicial Review and Federalism

Constitutional Origins

The Constitution Act, 1867 united on a federal basis the separate colonies that had until that time constituted British North America. The federal form was essential to the act of union. None of the provinces, particularly Quebec, was willing to relinquish the degree of political autonomy and self-government to which they aspired, and to be subsumed under a single unitary state. At the same time the most influential leaders of the confederation movement, men like John A. Macdonald and George Brown, desired a strong central government based on "legislative union," in order to avoid what they considered to have been the near fatal weakness of the central government in American federalism.[1]

The Constitution Act, 1867 represented an uneasy compromise between these conflicting goals. Provincial demands for preserving local autonomy and self-government were accommodated through a distribution of legislative powers between the newly created federal government and the provinces, primarily in sections 91 and 92 of the Act. The centralists' goals were recognized by a very broad wording of the federal government's section 91 law-making powers, and by the unilateral power to strike down provincial laws through the devices of disallowance (s. 56) and reservation (s. 90). The result was a written constitutional document establishing a highly centralized form of federalism. As it turned out, this original design was modified considerably by subsequent political developments in which judicial review played a major role.

It is now accepted that judicial review is a very frequent corollary to a federal form of government based on a written distribution of powers between two levels of government. For a federal division of legislative powers to be effective, there must be a mutually acceptable process for

---

[1] This scepticism toward federalism appeared quite justified at the time. The Confederation process took place during and after the bloody American Civil War, which had pitted the "states' rights" advocates of the Southern slave-holding states against the national government.

settling the inevitable disputes over where one government's jurisdiction ends and the other's begins. Neither level of government can be permitted to define unilaterally (and thus to redefine) the boundaries of federal-provincial jurisdiction, as this would violate the equal status of both levels of government, a central principle of federalism.[2] In practice, the need for a "neutral umpire" of federal systems has been met through judicial review by a final court of appeal. Of the six federal democracies studied by Lijphart in 1984, only one—Switzerland—did not have judicial review. Those federations with judicial review included Australia, Canada, Germany, Austria and the United States.[3]

Historical Origins

Originally, judicial review of the constitution came easily and without controversy in Canada. The Constitution Act, 1867 took the form of an Imperial statute, and section 129 mandated the continuation of the existing legal regime. This meant that the Constitution Act was subject to the already existing Colonial Laws Validity Act, which required consistency of colonial law with British Imperial statutes. The Judicial Committee of the Privy Council (JCPC) was charged with the responsibility of enforcing this policy. The JCPC had served as the final court of appeal for British North America prior to Confederation, and simply continued in this capacity after 1867. Any alleged violation of the federal division of powers set out in the Constitution Act could be challenged in the existing superior courts of the provinces, and appealed from a provincial court of appeal directly to the Judicial Committee in London.

This explained the Founders' lack of urgency in creating the Supreme Court of Canada. The absence of a national court of appeal also made the introduction of judicial review in Canada easier. When the federal government did move to exercise its section 101 authority to create such a court, controversy quickly erupted. As Professor Smith explains, the attempt to create the Supreme Court of Canada became entangled in the

---

[2] The disallowance and reservation powers violate the principle of parity, and for that reason it has been argued that Canada is not a "true" federal state. However, neither power has been exercised by Ottawa for over 40 years. Although both powers still exist *legally*, it is generally accepted that a convention of non-use has been established, and that it is politically unacceptable for the federal government to re-activate either of these powers. For example, in 1989 when the Quebec government invoked the section 33 legislative override to reinstate its "French-only" public signs law (which had been struck down by the Supreme Court a month earlier), some MPs called on Prime Minister Mulroney to use disallowance to protect the rights of the Anglophone minority in Quebec. With much of his Cabinet from Quebec and Alberta, two of the most vocal advocates of provincial rights, it was not surprising that the Prime Minister did not consider disallowance a viable option.

[3] Arend Lijphart, *Democracies: Patterns of Majoritarian and Consensus Government in Twenty-One Countries* (New Haven, CT: Yale University Press, 1984), p. 195.

already robust politics of federal-provincial competition. (See Reading 10.1) This controversy was engendered in large part by the inclusion of the reference procedure as part of the Supreme Court Act. Some "provincial rights" advocates perceived the simultaneous creation of a "federal" court of appeal and a reference authority vested exclusively with the federal government as an ill-disguised attempt to refurbish the already controversial disallowance power by cloaking it with judicial legitimacy. This suspicion of "disallowance is disguise" was supported by the original form of the reference procedure and the comments of centralists such as John A. Macdonald.

Provincial fears of a centralizing Supreme Court notwithstanding, the Supreme Court Act was finally adopted in 1875. The newly created Supreme Court of Canada immediately began to exercise the power of judicial review, and did so without controversy. However, its decisions could be appealed to the Privy Council, and it could be avoided altogether by *per saltum* appeals directly from a provincial court of appeal to the Privy Council. Both of these routes of appeal were abolished by amendments to the Supreme Court Act in 1949, which established the Supreme Court of Canada as the final and exclusive court of appeal. Until 1949, however, the Supreme Court was decidedly the junior partner in overseeing the judicial aspects of Canada's constitutional development. Its early decisions were frequently overturned by the JCPC, and the doctrine of *stare decisis* meant that it was bound to follow the Privy Council's lead. This meant that the Supreme Court of Canada was functionally more like a middle-tier British appeal court until 1949, and the habits and procedures associated with such a court lingered for almost another generation.

The student should note the shifting basis of authority for the Canadian courts' exercise of judicial review. Initially, the legal authority for the judicial enforcement of the Constitution Act, 1867 was the Colonial Laws Validity Act. This remained true until 1931, when federalism replaced imperialism as the basis for judicial review. After World War I, mounting discontent with the inferior status implied by the Colonial Laws Validity Act led to demands for its abolition by Canada and other British dominions. Canada, however, requested and received an exemption for the Constitution Act, 1867. Canadian leaders feared that without the Colonial Laws Validity Act, the federal division of powers could be altered unilaterally by either level of government. The preservation of Canadian federalism, they believed, required the continuation of the legal paramountcy of the Constitution Act, 1867. Unable to agree upon an amending formula of their own, Canadian leaders requested that the Constitution Act, 1867 remain under the legal regime of the Colonial Laws Validity Act. This anomolous condition was finally brought to a close in 1982 with the patriation of the constitution. Sections 38–42 of the Constitution Act, 1982 set out a "made-in-Canada" amending formula and section 52 clearly established constitutional supremacy as the legal basis for judicial review.

Constitutional Interpretation

Constitutional interpretation raises problems that do not occur in common law or statutory interpretation. Because constitutional law regulates the powers of governments (rather than the private rights of individuals and corporations) it inevitably affects the making of public policy. Judicial review thus injects into the judicial process a political dimension that previously did not exist. Common law judges have been reluctant to acknowledge the policy-making function conferred on them by judicial review, as it seems to contradict and undermine so many of the traditional aspects of the judicial process. As a result, Canadian, British, and Australian judges have tended simply to transfer the techniques of statutory interpretation to constitutional interpretation.

This was especially true of the Privy Council's approach to the Constitution Act. While this is easily explained by the unfamiliarity of British judges with the practice of a "written constitution" (indeed, to them it was just another Imperial statute!), it had the unfortunate effect of establishing this mode of constitutional interpretation as the standard for Canadian judges to follow. Discontent with the substance of the Privy Council's constitutional decisions (discussed below) led in turn to criticisms of its technique of interpretation. These critics called for an approach to constitutional interpretation that acknowledged the inherent policy dimensions of constitutional law, and reflected the need to adapt a written constitution to the changing needs and circumstances of the society it governs. William Lederman has summarized this issue as follows:

> There are principally two types of interpretation—literal or grammatical emphasizing of the words found in statutes and constitutional documents; and sociological, which insists that constitutional words and statutory words must be carefully linked by judicially noticed knowledge and by evidence to the ongoing life of society.[4]

Examples of these two different approaches to constitutional interpretation are found in the excerpts from the JCPC opinions of Lord Sankey (See Reading 10.2) and Lord Atkin (See Reading 10.3). Lord Sankey articulated his now famous "living tree" approach in his opinion in the well-known "Persons Case."[5] Henrietta Muir Edwards, a leader of the women's suffrage movement in the West, had been proposed for an appointment to the Senate from Alberta. At issue was whether any woman could be appointed to the Senate. Legally the case boiled down to whether the term used in section 24 of the Constitution Act, "qualified persons,"

---

[4] W.R. Lederman, "Thoughts on Reform of the Supreme Court of Canada," *The Confederation Challenge*, Ontario Advisory Committee on Confederation, Vol. II (Toronto, ON: Queen's Printer, 1970), p. 295.

[5] *Re Meaning of the Word "Persons" in Section 24 of the B.N.A. Act* [1928], S.C.R. 276.

included women. The Supreme Court of Canada ruled that it did not, basing its decision on internal evidence of the Constitution Act itself and the fact that at the time of Confederation, women did not have the right to vote, much less to hold public office. While this decision was arguably correct in a technical, legal sense, it was overturned on appeal by the JCPC. Lord Sankey stressed the necessity of interpreting constitutional language in light of society's changing beliefs and needs, and not just internal grammatical constructions or original understanding.

Lord Atkin's very different approach to constitutional interpretation occurred in the 1937 *Labour Conventions Case*.[6] This case raised the issue of Parliament's authority to enact legislation implementing Canada's treaty obligations when the legislation involved matters that would normally have fallen under the provinces' section 92 jurisdiction. Despite the recent Statute of Westminster (1931), which had affirmed the sovereignty of Canada in the conduct of her foreign affairs, Lord Atkin ruled that the federal government's treaty-making power did not allow it to encroach upon matters of provincial jurisdiction when implementing a treaty. This decision was widely perceived as a serious blow to the effective conduct of Canadian foreign policy, and was blamed on Lord Atkin's "watertight compartments" view of Canadian federalism. This view was widely condemned as being out of touch with the economic and political realities of twentieth-century Canada.

Constitutional Politics

The Privy Council's decision in the *Labour Conventions Case* was only one in a series of constitutional cases that progressively narrowed the scope of the federal government's section 91 powers while expanding the section 92 jurisdiction of the provinces. The federal government's broad residual power to make laws for the "Peace, Order, and good Government of Canada" was whittled away to almost nothing by the Privy Council's "emergency doctrine" test. The unrestricted power to make laws for the "Regulation of Trade and Commerce" was soon reduced to the narrower ambit of "international and interprovincial trade" by judicial interpretation. At the same time, the JCPC's decisions expanded what originally appeared to be the rather meagre provincial powers to make laws in relation to "Property and Civil Rights in the Province" and "all matters of a merely local or private Nature in the Province." Throughout all of these decisions, the JCPC appeared to adhere to the textually oriented, legalistic method of interpretation described above.

Mounting dissatisfaction with the Privy Council's performance as final constitutional arbiter for Canada manifested itself in the "judicial nationalism" discussed in Chapter One. Following the recommendations of the

---

[6] [1937] A.C. 327; III Olmstead 180.

1939 O'Connor Report, Parliament abolished all appeals to the Privy Council in 1949. While English Canadian jurists were unanimous in condemning the provincial bias of the Judicial Committee's federalism decisions, they were far from agreed upon a diagnosis of the problem or a prescription for an acceptable "made in Canada" jurisprudence after 1949. One school of thought criticized the JCPC for being too textual and literal in its interpretation of the constitution, and thereby failing to make it a "living constitution" that accorded with the changing times. The other principal group of critics accused the Judicial Committee of not following the clear centralist bias of the text closely enough.[7] The inability of Canadian scholars, judges, and political leaders to agree on an appropriate constitutional jurisprudence has carried over into the post-1949 era. The latent pro-Ottawa attitudes of the old JCPC critics have not been acceptable to Quebec leaders or more recent "provincial rights" advocates. The result has been a continuing credibility problem for the Supreme Court whenever it acts as final arbiter of Canadian federalism.

The most important post-1949 division of powers case was the 1976 *Anti-Inflation Reference*.[8] (See Reading 10.4) As Peter Russell recounts, this case seemed to present a perfect opportunity for the Supreme Court, led by its new chief justice, Bora Laskin, a known centralist and veteran critic of the JCPC, to repudiate once and for all the moribund "emergency doctrine." Several post-1949 decisions of the Supreme Court had silently ignored the old "emergency doctrine," and spoke instead of an "inherent national importance" test. Centralists anticipated that the time was ripe to articulate forcefully this new and broader basis for the exercise of the federal government's residual powers. The public policy significance of the case was underscored by the large number of intervenors, consisting of both provincial governments and private groups. The Supreme Court itself tacitly acknowledged the policy dimensions of the case by devising new procedures to allow for the introduction of untraditional, socio-economic evidence by both sides. While the Supreme Court's final decision mildly increased the "Peace, Order, and good Government" authority of the federal government, it did not repudiate the work of the Privy Council. The "emergency doctrine" was preserved, although it now can be invoked in peace-time situations. This compromise result may appear anticlimactic, but it illustrates the Supreme Court's sensitivity to conflicting elite views of federalism, and its instict for the middle ground when this occurs.

As it turned out, the *Anti-Inflation Reference* marked the beginning of a new flood of federalism cases and an escalation in conflict over the role of

---

[7] See Alan C. Cairns, "The Judicial Committee and its Critics," *Canadian Journal of Political Science*, 4 (September, 1971), p. 301.

[8] [1976] 2 S.C.R. 373.

the Supreme Court. From 1970 to 1975 the Supreme Court heard only nine cases disputing the federal division of powers. During the next four years, this number jumped to 36. An objective bottom-line analysis of these decisions discloses a rough balance of wins and losses for both levels of government. But politics is not played objectively, and provincial leaders viewed their losses—especially several dealing with taxation of natural resources[9] and telecommunications[10]—as much more damaging. These decisions contributed to federal-provincial tensions on other fronts, and led to growing provincial suspicions about the dependence of the Supreme Court on the Liberal government in Ottawa. Shortly following several of these cases, an article appeared in the press suggesting that "the image of Chief Justice Laskin and his eight 'sober, grey men' acting as spear-carriers for the federal prime minister fails to add anything to one's hopes for improved national unity."[11]

The implications of these remarks so upset Chief Justice Laskin that he went out of his way to respond publicly. At a hastily arranged "Seminar for Journalists" the same month, the late Chief Justice declared:

> I have to be more sad than angry to read of an insinuation that we are "acting as spear carriers for the federal prime minister" or to read of a statement attributed to a highly respected member of the academic community that "the provinces must have a role in the appointment of members of the Supreme Court in order to ensure that they have confidence that it can fairly represent the interests of the provincial governments as well as of any federal government."
>
> ... The allegation is reckless in its implication that we have considerable freedom to give voice to our personal predilections, and thus to political preferences.... We have no such freedom, and it is a disservice to this Court and to the work of those who have gone before us to suggest a federal bias because of federal appointment.[12]

There is no doubting the sincerity of the late Chief Justice's remarks, and he was subsequently supported by Professor Peter Hogg in an article that argued persuasively against a federal bias in recent Supreme Court decisions.[13]

---

9   *CIGOL v. Government of Saskatchewan* [1978] 2 S.C.R. 545, and *Central Canada Potash v. Government of Saskatchewan*, [1979] 1 S.C.R.42.

10   *Capital Cities Communications v. C.R. T. C.* [1978] 2 S.C.R. 141, and *Public Service Board v. Dionne*, [1978] 2 S.C.R. 191.

11   Edwin R. Black, "Supreme Court Judges as Spear-Carriers for Ottawa: They need Watching," *Report on Confederation* (Feb. 1978), p. 12.

12   Bora Laskin, "Judicial Integrity and the Supreme Court of Canada," *Law Society Gazette* 57 (1978), pp. 118, 120.

13   P.W. Hogg, "Is the Supreme Court of Canada Biased in Constitutional Cases?" *The Canadian Bar Review* 57 (1979), p. 722.

Indeed, Peter Russell has gone even further, arguing that the Supreme Court is so sensitive to maintaining its image as a "neutral umpire" that it is willing to sacrifice the consistent application of legal principle and precedent in order to achieve "politically balanced" results.[14] (Ironically, one effect of a politically balanced but unprincipled federalism jurisprudence is to encourage *more* litigation, since both sides perceive a fair chance of "winning.") David Pond has formalized Russell's insight into a more formal theory of the "strategic" exercise of judicial review. According to this theory, the Court's primary objective in separation of powers adjudication is to maintain its legitimacy and thus authority with both levels of government. Accordingly, the Court shapes its decisions in response to elite consensus and conflict. During periods of consensus (e.g., the 1950s and 1960s), the Court allied itself with dominant elite coalitions by upholding (and thus legitimating) the new cost-sharing and regulatory initiatives of the federal government. In periods of federal-provincial conflict (e.g., the 1970s and 1980s), the Court seeks a strategic middle ground in terms of policy-impact in order to preserve its image as a "neutral arbiter." A corollary is that during periods of consensus, the Court is better able to sustain a "principled" line of jurisprudence, while in periods of dissensus, the Court is prone to sacrifice legal logic for political logic.[15]

The *Anti-Inflation Reference* (Reading 10.4) and the *Patriation Reference* (Reading 2.4) both illustrate the Russell-Pond thesis. In the former, the Court escaped an apparent "no-win" situation by upholding the wage and price restraint legislation but on the very novel—and narrower— grounds of a "peace-time emergency." Similarly, the Court's ruling in the *Patriation Reference* has been described as "bold statecraft . . . questionable jurisprudence."[16] The Court's ruling that federal unilateralism was "legal but unconstitutional" represented a political compromise designed to induce both sides to resume negotiating (which they did). As Mandel and others have noted, however, it took an unprecedented legal ruling on constitutional convention.

The proposition that the Supreme Court has been neutral or balanced in its division of powers jurisprudence has not gone unchallenged. Drawing upon a comparative perspective, André Bzdera has marshalled persuasive evidence that judicial review has had a centralizing effect in

---

[14]   Peter H. Russell, "The Supreme Court and Federal-Provincial Relations: The Political Use of Legal Resources," *Canadian Public Policy* 11 (1985), pp. 161-170.

[15]   David John Pond, "The Supreme Court of Canada and the Politics of Public Law" (Ph.D. thesis, University of Toronto, 1992).

[16]   Peter H. Russell, "The Supreme Court Decision: Bold Statecraft based on Questionable Jurisprudence," *The Court and the Constitution*. Institute for Intergovernmental Relations (Queen's University, Kingston, Ontario; 1982), pp. 1–32.

each of the nine federal states studied.[17] Bzdera explains the "net centralist/ nationalist bias of federal high courts" by their institutional linkages to the central government: creation, administration, budget, internal procedures and especially the appointment of judges. Bzdera's findings are supported by American political scientist Martin Shapiro. Shapiro's comparative study of centralized court systems—those with a final national court of appeal—found that they tend to "serve upper class and nationalizing interests rather than dominant local interests and thus are more satisfactory to persons trying to break through the web of local interests."[18] The Bzdera-Shapiro thesis helps to explain the provincial governments' persistent attempts to gain an agency in the appointment of judges to the Supreme Court of Canada, as witnessed most recently in the 1987 Meech Lake Accord.

The debate over the neutrality or centralist bias of the Supreme Court must also be placed in the real world of Canadian politics. Patrick Monahan's contribution (See Reading 10.5) demonstrates that in Canada's ongoing federal-provincial tug-of-war, a loss in court does not necessarily mean a policy loss. His two case studies show how the availability of alternative policy instruments often permit a government to achieve indirectly what the courts have forbidden it from doing directly. These alternative means include the enactment of the same policy by the other level of government; delegation of the disputed jurisdiction from the "winner" to the "loser"; substitution of an alternative regulatory instrument; and even constitutional amendment. As in the realm of civil liberties, the end of the legal battle does not necessarily mean the end of the "policy war." A judicial ruling becomes one more factor in the battle for elite and/or public opinion. Consensus between governments or sustained determination by one level of government can both lead to alternative means to the same policy objective.

---

[17] André Bzdera, "Comparative Analysis of Federal High Courts: A Political Theory of Judicial Review," *Canadian Journal of Political Science*, forthcoming (December, 1992).

[18] Martin Shapiro, *Courts: A Comparative and Political Analysis* (Chicago: University of Chicago Press, 1981), p. 24.

10.1

THE ORIGINS OF JUDICIAL REVIEW IN CANADA
Jennifer Smith

For many years, students have been taught that the practice of judicial review in Canada is less important than it is in the United States. This is because it has had less scope, and it has had less scope because until recently Canada's written constitution, unlike the American Constitution, included no bill of rights. Whereas in both countries the courts, acting as "umpires" of their respective federal forms of government, have had the power to declare laws beyond the competence of the jurisdiction enacting them, the American courts have had the additional and, to many, fascinating power to enforce against governments the guarantees of the rights of citizens contained in the Bill of Rights. Obviously this line of comparison is outmoded now. After a prolonged and at times bitter debate, the federal government and nine of the ten provincial governments reached agreement last year on a set of amendments to the British North America Act, among them a Charter of Rights and Freedoms. As a result, the breadth of the courts' power of judicial review more closely approximates that possessed by their American counterparts. Is this development consistent with the nature of Canada's constitutional arrangements? Does the Charter provide the basis of the completion of an initially limited power?...

... One of the most thorough studies available is B.L. Strayer's *Judicial Review of Legislation in Canada*. Strayer argues that the BNA Act, 1867 and related acts did not vest explicitly in the courts the power of judicial review. Nor can our common law inheritance be held responsible for it. Instead, judicial review is a product of the British colonial system, "implicit in the royal instructions, charters, or Imperial statutes creating the colonial legislatures." Since these legislatures were bodies of limited power, the colonial charters establishing them typically included clauses prohibiting them from passing laws repugnant to Imperial statutes....

... As early as the fifteenth century, it was customary for the King's Privy Council rather than English domestic courts to hear appeals arising out of colonial matters. This practice was regulated by the Privy Council Acts of 1833 and 1844, which established the Judicial Committee of the Privy Council, specified its membership and authorized it to hear appeals from colonial courts. Thus the Judicial Committee acted as the highest appellate court for the colonies. As Strayer points out, it showed no inclination to question its authority to review the validity of colonial legislation,

Canadian Journal of Political Science, 16 (1983), from pages 115–134. Reprinted with permission.

undoubtedly because the colonies themselves possessed only limited or subordinate legislative powers. He attributes considerable importance to the precedent it set throughout the Empire for the exercise of a similar power by colonial courts. According to Strayer, we must look to the British colonial system, and especially its doctrine of judicial review of colonial legislation, for the origin of judicial review in Canada: "The constitutional law of the Empire in 1867 apparently embraced the convention that where legislative powers were granted subject to limitations the courts would enforce those limitations. The BNA Act was drafted and enacted in this context.". . .

. . . Thus he [Strayer] is faced with the fact that following Confederation, the Canadian courts took up the power of judicial review, and concludes that this was the result of both pre-Confederation practice and the federal character of the new constitution: "There was a continuity of judicial practice because the Imperial structure had not changed basically. . . . Colonial legislatures, whether Dominion or provincial, were limited legislatures, and courts could enforce the limitations." The inner logic of federalism with its distribution of legislative powers pointed to the need for something like the kind of judicial enforcement that pre-Confederation practice had established.

Strayer's search for an explanation of judicial review arises out of his insistence that it is not "absolute," that is, not fully guaranteed in the BNA Act. In his opinion, the relevant clauses of the Act gave Parliament and the local legislatures too much regulatory power over the courts to support such a view, power more in keeping with the principle of parliamentary as opposed to judicial supremacy. Indeed, according to W.R. Lederman, Strayer implies that an "element of judicial usurpation" figures in its establishment, an implication Lederman cannot accept. By contrast, Lederman reads into sections 96 to 100 of the Act an "intention to reproduce superior courts in the image of the English central royal courts." If he can demonstrate that these English courts had acquired a "basic independence" enabling them to withstand even the undoubted supremacy of the British Parliament, then courts deliberately modelled after them in Canada would assume a similar status. In "The Independence of the Judiciary," Lederman undertakes such a demonstration. . . .

. . . Strayer takes note of this argument and dismisses it by observing that the jurisdiction of Lederman's royal courts was subject to the British Parliament's control and that in any event it never included the power to review the validity of Parliament's acts "in spite of the pretensions of Coke and others." Canadian superior courts can hardly claim by inheritance an inviolable right of judicial review their English forebears never possessed. Lederman's rejoinder is that Canadian courts, both before and after 1867, have never faced legislatures equipped with the full supremacy of the British Parliament. Indeed, until 1931 they dealt with subordinate colonial legislatures, and while the Statute of Westminster substituted equality in the place of subordination, the constitution itself remained a British statute. Thus the power to review acts of subordinate bodies undertaken by Canadian courts before 1931 was well established by "history, custom, precedent and the need of federalism" and after 1931 merely continued as a matter of course. . . . Yet a closer examination of the framers' views may throw some light on this debate.

According to the records of the Quebec Conference edited by Joseph Pope, Macdonald alluded to the need for some form of judicial review in his initial argument on the desirability of federal union. Having put the case for a strong central government, he warned the delegates not so much of the importance of provincial governments per se but of the need of the people in each "section" to feel protected, that is, secure from the reach of an overweening central authority. One way of encouraging this feeling was to provide a guarantee of the test of legality against which centralist incursions on sectional matters might be measured. Since the new construction would take the form of a British statute, he continued, British courts could supply an answer to the question, "Is it legal or not?" The availability of some form of judicial arbitration might satisfy local partisans fearful of abandoning local autonomy to the mercies of a strong central power.

The issue was raised once more towards the end of the Quebec Conference, again in connection with the extent of jurisdiction appropriate to local governments. R.B. Dickey of Nova Scotia, expressing some sympathy for the opinion of E.B. Chandler of New Brunswick that the delegates were in danger of establishing a legislative rather than a federal union by insisting on reserving all unspecified subject matters to the central government, proposed a "Supreme Court of Appeal to decide any conflict between general and state rights." He was supported by George Brown, leader of the "Grits" in Upper Canada, who suggested that provincial courts determine jurisdictional disputes, with provision for appeal to a superior court. Both men appeared to contemplate a Canadian court of last resort on constitutional questions. Jonathan McCully of Nova Scotia, however, disputed this proposal. Throughout the Conference, he had made no bones about his preference for a legislative over a federal union, although he was prepared to accept a highly centralized form of federalism. From this perspective, he succinctly stated the difficulty posed by a constitutional court: "Mr. Brown will land us in [the] position of [the] United States by referring [the] matter of conflict of jurisdiction to [the] courts. You thus set them over the General Legislature.". . .

. . . In the Maritime provinces, even less attention was paid to the issue despite the fact that a number of anti-Confederates were sorely exercised by what they deemed the insufficiently federal character of the proposed scheme. . . . Their major concern was the lack of any provision for the scheme's amendment, but in an aside they observed that the "wise framers" of the American Constitution had given the Supreme Court the "power to decide all questions of jurisdiction and authority, between the general

Government and those of the several States." The Quebec scheme, by contrast, did not require the establishment of any such court. Indeed. in their view, it contained no safeguards at all for the provinces in the event of conflict between their legislatures and the central Parliament. Guided by the American example, they recommended establishment of a tribunal authorized to decide disputes arising out of the division of powers. In New Brunswick A.J. Smith, recently defeated by Tilley's pro-union party in a second election over the Confederation issue, similarly advocated "a court for the determination of questions and disputes that may arise between the Federal and Local governments as to the meaning of the Act of Union."

Such clearly worded statements indicated a view of federalism rather more in line with the American example than that set out in the Quebec scheme. Taken together with the views expressed at the Quebec Conference and in the debate in the Parliament of Canada, they also suggest that no one had any illusions about the significance of judicial review, particularly as it related to the distribution of legislative powers between Parliament and the local legislatures. The point at issue was whether the type of federalism set out in the Quebec Resolutions required it. Under the Resolutions, the central government possessed the power to disallow local laws just as the British government retained the power to disallow Parliament's enactments, a parallel feature not unnoticed by critics of the scheme like Christopher Dunkin. Disallowance not only undermined the need for judicial arbitration, whether by the Judicial Committee or a national court, it also suited partisans of parliamentary supremacy like Jonathan McCully, who clearly understood the threat to this supremacy posed by a tribunal patterned after the American Supreme Court.

The question of whether to establish a final appellate court was settled eight years after Confederation when Parliament finally used the power it possessed under section 101 of the BNA Act. The debate at the time is illuminating, since in picking up the threads of the earlier arguments it does so in the light of some years experience of union. It also reveals an attitude towards the new court and its power of judicial review somewhat at variance with that held today. . . .

. . . While the constitutionality of the bill was generally accepted, there remained the question of members' understanding of the Court's position in relation to the central government. Here opinions varied. In introducing the bill, Fournier stressed the need for a court to settle disputes arising out of conflicting jurisdictional claims, particularly when the extent of provincial powers was in question. In this sense he portrayed the proposed court as the completion of the "young construction" established at Confederation, citing earlier remarks by Cartier and Macdonald in support of this view. Along side the notion of the court as an impartial arbiter, however, there is present in his speech the rather different view of it as a substitute for the failing remedy of disallowance. As he explained, the government was required daily to "interfere" with provincial legislation considered *ultra vires* the provinces' jurisdiction, and it was falling behind in the task. The result was that the statute books were filled with an "enormous mass of legislation" of dubious constitutionality, leaving citizens uncertain about what was and was not law. In light of this definition of the problem, namely, the excesses of provincial legislatures, the suggestion that the new court could resolve it more speedily than the central government'spower of disallowance must have struck his listeners as doubtful. Indeed, it quickly became clear he was seeking legitimacy, not speed. The Governor-General, he pointed out, could disallow provincial laws only on the advice of the federal cabinet, in turn advised by law officers of the Department of Justice, and this state of affairs, predictably, was "not satisfactory." What was needed was a tribunal whose decisions — especially those adverse to the provinces — were acceptable to all parties. Apparently Fournier viewed his "independent, neutral and impartial court'" as an instrument of the central government. He contended that Ottawa needed "an institution of its own" in order to ensure proper execution of its laws because, however contrary to the spirit of Confederation, the time might come when "it would not be very safe for the Federal Government to be at the mercy of the tribunals of the provinces."

Some members feared that the powers conferred on the court would conflict with the principle of parliamentary supremacy. An Ontario member, Moss, excused the length of his speech by emphasizing the gravity of establishing a tribunal whose power to determine jurisdictional disputes finally rendered it "paramount" to Parliament itself. Rejecting this view, Macdonald interpreted the Court's role under the "Special Jurisdiction" clauses as one of informing the "conscience" of the government. It would function simply as an adviser to the government in much the same way as the Judicial Committee did when asked for advice by the British Crown. Macdonald's view was consistent with Fournier's exposition of these clauses for, as noted earlier, the Minister of Justice had stated that the Court's decisions in such instances were to have the same effect as its decisions in reference questions, namely, a kind of "moral weight." Since moral weight undoubtedly influences but does not command, it would appear that for both men the supremacy of Parliament remained unimpaired. Their position seemed well grounded for neither the reference case provision nor the special jurisdiction clauses gave the new court's opinions the status of legal judgments. Yet many of their colleagues assumed that it did, especially Robert Haythorne, a Liberal senator from Prince Edward Island, who warned members that "their power of interpretation [on constitutional matters] ceased when the bill passed."

Concern over the precise nature of the Court's advisory function on constitutional questions surfaced again in discussion of the reference case clause. Moss thought it "extreme" that the Governor-General in Council might ask the court for an opinion on any matter, since this would result in the Governor-General relying on others for the advice "he ought under our system of Government to obtain from his responsible advisers." However, he was persuaded that the practice was not incompatible with responsible government on the ground that the British, the greatest authorities on responsible government, used the Judicial Committee in the same manner. Others were not so easily persuaded. Senator Haythorne argued that a ministry under pressure to exercise its power of disallowance might be tempted to refer a provincial act to the court for an opinion on its constitutionality, thus relieving itself of the burden of taking a decision and defending it before Parliament. He also thought it unwisely mixed law and politics because it substituted judicial review for disallowance, that is, a judicial ruling in the place of a political decision. From this flowed his third objection, namely, that judicial review was a greater threat to the small provinces' legislative programme than the power of disallowance since any ministry advising the Crown to exercise the latter power was required to defend publicly its advice in the Commons and, more important, the Senate, the very institution in which the provinces could expect support. The Court's opinion faced no such political test. . . .

. . . Yet while both the constitution and practical necessity apparently pointed in the same direction, members of Parliament clearly entertained two different views of the role of the proposed court in the very area that was thought to stand most in need of its services, namely, jurisdictional conflicts. As is evident from the above, some saw in the court an instrument of the federal government that would enable it to deal more satisfactorily with provincial pretensions. How else to interpret Senator Scott's contention?: "The fact that so many of the Acts in the different Provinces were *ultra vires* showed that a bill of this kind was necessary." The raft of suspect provincial statutes, for Scott, posed a problem for which the central government was inadequately equipped. But why was it ill equipped when it possessed the power of disallowance? As noted earlier, for Fournier the central government's problem was its inescapable partisanship. Only a court and its long-standing reputation of nonpartisanship could tame the aggression of the provinces without provoking bitter controversy. Left unstated was the assumption that the central government, by contrast, was unlikely to experience the embarrassment of an adverse ruling in its exercise of legislative power. Thus the view of the court as a tribunal whose very impartiality would serve the federal cause ignored the obvious tension between that impartiality and the central government's partisanship. The opinion of men like Macdonald that the proposed bill must not and, indeed, did not affect the principle of parliamentary supremacy simply overlooked it in favour of the central government. Had he not said that the special jurisdiction clauses were "principally for the purpose of informing the conscience of the Government"? Despite his interest in setting up the court, he was obviously unwilling to relinquish ultimate determination of the constitution to it.

At the same time, as we have seen, many supposed that the new court did signal a shift from the central government's control over the distribution of legislative powers to judicial determination of disputes arising out of it. It might be objected that this view was as incorrect as Macdonald's on the grounds that the executive's control in this respect was only partial to begin with, limited to supervision of provincial enactments through its power of disallowance, and that Parliament's own enactments in turn were subject to disallowance by the British government. Moreover, the Judicial Committee, representing the judicial mode of constitutional arbitration, had retained its position as the highest court of appeal for the new colony at the outset of Confederation. Nevertheless, it is clear that for many participants in the debate, the Court's institution spelled a retreat from the executive fiat of disallowance in favour of the judicial remedy. And they assumed, contrary to Macdonald's supposition, that its jurisdiction would extend to impugned federal as well as provincial enactments. Indeed, opponents of the court, such as Senator Kaulbach of Nova Scotia, criticized it precisely because it would "take from this Parliament the right to decide constitutional questions.". . .

. . . In the event it appears that those who subscribed to the second view were closer to the mark. Certainly the new Supreme Court agreed with them. As Strayer points out, in its first reported constitutional decision, *Severn v. the Queen* (1878), the court, "without showing any hesitation concerning its right to do so," found an Ontario licensing statute invalid on the ground that it interfered with Parliament's jurisdiction over trade and commerce. The following year, in *Valin v. Langlois*, it reviewed and upheld the Dominion Controverted Elections Act, 1874 as a valid exercise of Parliament's legislative power. In the latter case, Chief Justice Ritchie set out the Court's power of judicial review with unmistakable clarity:

> In view of the great diversity of judicial opinion that has characterized the decisions of the provincial tribunals in some provinces, and the judges in all, while it would seem to justify the wisdom of the Dominion Parliament, in providing for the establishment of a Court of Appeal such as this, where such diversity shall be considered and an authoritative declaration of the law be enunciated, so it enhances the responsibility of those called on in the midst of such conflict of opinion to declare authoritatively the principles by which both federal and local legislation are governed.

Commenting on Ritchies's declaration, Strayer states: "And so the Canadian courts were launched on a course from which they have never swerved. The ease with which they could take up judicial review of legislation after Confederation must have been the result of the situation existing prior to 1867." He nowhere suggests that the Chief Justice might have based his understanding of the Court's role on the terms of the Supreme Court Act or the expectations of many of those who participated in its passage four years earlier. But then, as indicated earlier, Strayer pays little attention to the debate surrounding its passage. Thus he is open to

Lederman's charge, namely, that his argument implies an assumption of judicial review on the part of the court, an assumption possibly unwarranted. Yet Lederman too ignores the very debate in the light of which Ritchie's view is surely intelligible. The Chief Justice clearly favoured the side of those who, like Moss, thought that the proposed court would be able "to determine the [constitutional] controversy finally, virtually therefore, the Supreme Court could overrule the decisions of this legislature."

Although the Chief Justice's generous conception of the court's role in constitutional matters reaffirmed both the hopes and fears of those who supposed its decisions would be as authoritative as he claimed they were, the notion of the court as an instrument of the central government was not wholly eliminated. There remained the reference case provision of the Supreme Court Act, which obliged the court to advise the executive on any question referred to it. To the extent that this obligation is understood as an executive advisory function as opposed to a judicial one, it recalls Macdonald's view of the court as an aid to the government, or the "conscience" of the government. If so, it is hardly surprising that the provinces were uncomfortable with the comprehensiveness of the reference case provision, especially since it enabled the government to refer provincial laws to the courts for a ruling on their validity. In the event, Parliament's competence to enact it was tested before the Judicial Committee in *Attorney-General for Ontario v. Attorney-General for Canada* (1912). The provinces choosing to intervene argued that it imposed an executive function on the court and thereby violated section 101 of the BNA Act, which permitted Parliament to establish a tribunal possessed of judicial powers only. In his judgment delivered on behalf of the Judicial Committee, Earl Loreburn, L.C., appeared to accept their contention that the Court's task in the reference case was in essence merely advisory and therefore nonjudicial, but he did not consider this fatal to its judicial character as a whole.

The competing views of the court apparent at its inception have left their mark on it. For example, those who approve its role as umpire of the federal system are critical of the fact that its establishment was permitted rather than required under the terms of the BNA Act, that its members are appointed formally by one level of government rather than both, and that the reference case procedure remains. On the other hand, partisans of parliamentary supremacy, understandably less enamoured of the American Supreme Court whose example inspired the criticisms just mentioned, prize these very features as symbols of the Court's ultimate dependence on the will of Parliament. This tension between the Court's judicial independence and the claims of the executive figures in the debate between Lederman and Strayer. Lederman, seeking to strengthen and reaffirm its independence, prefers to locate the origins of its power of judicial review in both the tradition of the old English royal courts and the logic of federalism, that is, beyond the reach of Parliament. Thus the intentions of legislators who founded the Court are of little interest to him. By ignoring them, he avoids confronting not only the view of those who supposed they were withholding the full power of judicial review but, more important, the opinion of those who assumed that Parliament could confer it. As a result, he overlooks the possibility that judicial review was deliberately, if tentatively, advanced as a remedy for the failing power of disallowance. In short, since Lederman wishes to secure judicial review, he cannot derive it from anything so precarious as legislators' intentions. This leaves him open to the criticism implied in Strayer's thesis. Strayer, much more sensitive to the claims of the executive, highlights the limitations on the Court's power to review legislative enactments. Yet he is left with the new Court's easy assumption of the power, and since he too disregards the debate surrounding its establishment he looks beyond Parliament to past colonial practice. Thus he does not see the tension between judicial review and executive claims which he ably expands as a reflection of clashing legislative intentions.

Viewed in the light of the older controversy about the Court, the debate culminating in the recent set of amendments contained in the Constitution Act, 1982 took a familiar turn. In the earlier contest, both opponents and partisans of judicial review focussed attention on its implications for the distribution of legislative powers so critical to the shape of the country's federalism. While some saw in it a solution to conflicts arising out of competing jurisdictional claims, others interpreted it as a direct challenge to their presumption in favour of Parliament's control of the constitution. Over a century later, the issue of judicial versus parliamentary supremacy surfaced again in connection with the proposed Charter of Rights and Freedoms. Prime Minister Pierre Trudeau, a determined champion of the notion of a charter, often defended his cause without even referring to the task it necessarily imposes on the courts. Instead, he claimed that it would "confer power on the people of Canada, power to protect themselves from abuses by public authorities." A charter would liberate people by preventing governments from denying specified freedoms. On the other hand, opponents of the idea, like the then Premier of Saskatchewan, Allan Blakeney, attempted to counter the undeniable appeal of this claim by drawing attention to the role of the courts that it implied. According to Blakeney, including rights in a written constitution means transferring responsibility for them from duly elected legislatures, the democratic seat of governments, to nonelected tribunals. It amounts to requiring the courts to make "social judgments" in the course of interpreting a charter's clauses, judgments which, in his view, properly belong to "the voters and their representatives." In the event, a Charter of Rights and Freedoms now forms part of Canada's newly amended constitution. Are we entitled to conclude, then, that acceptance of the Charter, and the increased scope for judicial review that it entails, signals a resolution of the issue of parliamentary versus judicial supremacy in favour of the latter? The answer is not quite.

It is true, as Peter Russell points out, that section 52 of the Constitution Act, 1982, by declaring the Constitution of Canada to be the "supreme law" and any law inconsistent with its provisions to be of "no force or effect," gives the courts' power to invalidate unconstitutional laws an explicit constitutional footing for the first time. Further, under the provisions of the new amending formula, the composition of the Supreme Court is protected from easy change by the stringent requirement of unanimity on the part of the Senate, the House of Commons and provincial legislative assemblies. The Court is also listed under section 42(1) as an item that can be amended only in accordance with the general formula set out in section 38(1). Thus the court is constitutionally entrenched. However, neither the federal government's power to appoint Supreme Court justices nor the nonjudicial advisory task required by the reference mechanism is affected. More important still is the fact that the Charter itself, to the disappointment of its partisans, contains a provision enabling the legislative bodies of both levels of government to override some of its guarantees, namely, those dealing with fundamental freedoms, legal rights and equality rights. The provision is qualified to the extent that legislatures choosing to avail themselves of it are required to declare expressly their intention and reconsider the matter every five years, and there has been speculation about the likely effect of these qualifications on politicians' willingness to resort to the "override." Nevertheless, its very appearance in the the context of the Charter strikes an incongruous note and is testimony to the strength of the lingering tradition of parliamentary supremacy. Finally, there is the first clause of the Charter which subjects its guarantees to "such reasonable limits prescribed by law as can be demonstrably justified in a free and democratic society." Ultimately it is up to the Supreme Court to stake out the "reasonable limits." In the meantime, we do know that they are held to exist, that there is thought to be something higher than, or beyond the Charter's guarantees to which appeal can be made in order to justify their denial or restriction. And the initiative in this regard is secured to governments. While the courts' power of judicial review has undoubtedly surmounted the rather narrow, partisan function envisaged for the new Supreme Court in 1875 by Macdonald, the principle of parliamentary supremacy persists.

10.2

THE "LIVING TREE" APPROACH TO INTERPRETING THE BNA ACT

Lord Sankey, *The "Persons" Case*, Judicial Committee of the Privy Council (1928)

... The British North America Act planted in Canada a living tree capable of growth and expansion within its natural limits. The object of the Act was to grant a Constitution to Canada. "Like all written constitutions it has been subject to development through usage and convention."

Their Lordships do not conceive it to be the duty of this Board — it is certainly not their desire — to cut down the provisions of the Act by a narrow and technical construction, but rather to give it a large and liberal interpretation so that the Dominion to a great extent, but within certain fixed limits, may be mistress in her own house, as the Provinces to a great extent, but within certain fixed limits, are mistresses in theirs.

10.3

THE "WATERTIGHT COMPARTMENTS" APPROACH TO INTERPRETING THE BNA ACT

Lord Atkin, *Labour Conventions Case*, Judicial Committee of the Privy Council (1937)

... It must not be thought that the result of this decision is that Canada is incompetent to legislate in performance of treaty obligations. In totality of legislative powers, Dominion and Provincial together, she is fully equipped. But the legislative powers remain distributed, and if in the exercise of her new functions derived from her new international status Canada incurs obligations they must, so far as legislation be concerned, when they deal with Provincial classes of subjects, be dealt with by the totality of powers, in other words by co-operation between the Dominion and the Provinces. While the ship of state now sails on larger ventures and into foreign waters she still retains the watertight compartments which are an essential part of her original structure. The Supreme Court was equally divided and therefore the formal judgment could only state the opinions of the three judges on either side. Their Lordships are of opinion that the answer to the three questions should be that the Act in each case is *ultra vires* of the Parliament of Canada, and they will humbly advise His Majesty accordingly.

10.4

THE *ANTI-INFLATION* CASE: THE ANATOMY OF A CONSTITUTIONAL DECISION
Peter Russell

The Supreme Court of Canada's decision in July, 1976 on the constitutional validity of the federal Anti-Inflation Act was probably the Court's most heralded decision since it became Canada's final court of appeal in 1949. For the first time since 1949 a major national policy, upon which the federal government placed the highest priority, was challenged before the Court. Also, this was the first clear test of whether the Supreme Court would "liberate" the federal Parliament's general power to make laws for the "peace, order and good government of Canada" from the shackles placed upon it by the Privy Council's jurisprudence and thereby provide the constitutional underpinning for a revolutionary readjustment of the balance of power in Canadian federalism. And it was the first major constitutional case for a Supreme Court headed by Chief Justice Bora Laskin, who during his academic career had earned a reputation as Canada's leading authority on constitutional law and as an articulate critic of the Privy Council. All in all, the case appeared to be a showdown.

The outcome may seem rather anti-climactic. The federal government's wage and price control policy escaped a judicial veto. But the Court's decision gave it only a temporary and conditional constitutional mandate. More importantly, the Court did not endorse the expansive interpretation of Parliament's general power which a generation of central-minded commentators had hoped for as much as a generation of provincially-minded Canadians had feared.

Instead, the Court as a whole could agree only on the Judicial Committee of the Privy Council's "emergency doctrine," while its majority appeared to endorse a novel and unLaskin-like way of interpreting the peace, order and good government clause.

Canadian Public Administration, 20 (1977), from pages 632–665. Reprinted with permission.

To understand the significance of these results, the case must be placed in both its legal and political settings. By so doing we may learn something about the nature of judicial review in Canada. Among other things, the case demonstrates the limited importance of judicial review in the politics of Canadian federalism. The Court's decision may signal that a constitutional revolution is not about to occur, but the decision itself is far from being the major factor in preventing such a centralizing shift in the balance of power. The case also reveals how paradoxically political the process of judicial review can be in Canada even though the end product—the opinions of the judges—is cast in a relatively legalistic style. Above all, the case teaches us a good deal about the interaction of law and politics. The main lesson is clear: politicians and interest groups will risk losses in terms of long-run constitutional doctrine in order to secure important short-run policy objectives, although in the process they may try their best to minimize or obscure their constitutional losses.

The Constitutional Stakes

On October 14, 1975 the federal government unveiled the new anti-inflation program. The program had four main prongs, only one of which was highly controversial and required new legislation. This was a scheme to control prices and wages in certain key sectors of the economy. The Liberal party had vigorously opposed a Conservative party proposal for wage and price controls in the federal election fifteen months earlier. But now Mr. Trudeau's government was apparently convinced that this was a policy whose time had come. Legal authority for the wage and price control policy was contained in the Anti-Inflation Act which became law December 15, 1975 (with retroactive effect to October 14, 1975) and in the detailed regulations or "guidelines" promulgated on December 22, 1975.

It was clear from the start that there was a good deal at stake constitutionally in the enactment of this legislation. The Anti-Inflation Act purported to give the federal government regulatory authority over prices, profit margins and wages in selected areas of the private sector: construction firms with twenty or more employees, other firms with five hundred or more employees, and professionals. The Act applied directly to the federal public sector, and it authorized the government to enter into agreements with the provinces to apply the program to the provincial public sectors. Normally most of the economic relations which the federal Act purported to regulate in the private sector are under exclusive provincial jurisdiction. Since the *Snider* case in 1925, labour relations has been treated as a field of divided jurisdiction, with federal authority confined to the limited number of activities which can be brought under specific heads of federal power. A long series of judicial decisions, beginning with the *Parsons* case in 1881, gave the provinces the lion's share of regulatory power over business and commercial transactions in the province. The only earlier peacetime attempt to control prices and profit levels on a national basis had been ruled unconstitutional by the Judicial Committee of the Privy Council of the *Board of Commerce* case [1922].

On what constitutional basis then could the federal government hope to rest the Anti-Inflation Act? The federal trade and commerce power which would be the basis of federal authority for such legislation in the United States was not a very likely possibility in Canada. "Interprovincial or international" as the main criterion of the trade and commerce which the federal Parliament can regulate has been narrowly interpreted in Canada, and the Act made no gestures toward focusing its impact primarily on activities of an interprovincial or international character. Thus, it was the federal Parliament's general power "to make laws for the peace, order and good government of Canada" which appeared to be the only constitutional basis for the Act, and it was in the possibility of successfully invoking the general power for this purpose that a revolution in constitutional doctrine was in the making.

Constitutional case-law had produced two rival conceptions of what could sufficiently magnify legislative matter normally subject to provincial jurisdiction to bring them under the general or residual power of the national Parliament: the emergency doctrine and the test of inherent national importance. The emergency doctrine was authored by Viscount Haldane of the Judicial Committee of the Privy Council in the 1920s, and, with but one clear exception, consistently followed by that tribunal until the end of its regime as Canada's highest court. The doctrine's only positive application was to justify the virtually unlimited scope of national power in time of war and postwar transition. Beyond war, the Judicial Committee's vision of emergencies serious enough to set aside the normal distribution of powers and invoke the general power had been limited to such possibilities as "famines," "epidemics of pestilence" or a drastic outbreak of the "evil of intemperance." Economic crisis—even the need for a national scheme of unemployment insurance during the Depression— failed to meet the Judicial Committee's standard of necessity. Further, it appeared that the presumption of constitutionality which attached to war-related legislation did not apply to *permanent* peacetime measures. With the former, the onus of proof rested with the opponents of the legislation who would have to adduce "... very clear evidence that an emergency has not arisen, or that the emergency no longer exists ...," whereas, with the latter, the supporters of the legislation would have to provide "evidence that the standard of necessity ... has been reached."

In 1946 Viscount Simon in the *Canada Temperance Federation* case wrote an opinion which offered a much wider conception of peace, order and good government than Haldane's emergency test. In dismissing Ontario's attempt to have the Privy Council overrule *Russell v. The Queen* (the Privy Council's earliest decision finding federal legislation constitutional on the basis of peace, order and good government), Viscount Simon held that the

Dominion Parliament could not legislate in matters which are exclusively within the competence of the provincial legislature "merely because of the existence of an emergency." The "true test" for determining whether the national legislature may assume jurisdiction over matters which are normally provincial ". . . must be found in the real subject matter of the legislation: if it is such that it goes beyond local or provincial concern or interest and must from its inherent nature be the concern of the Dominion as a whole . . ., then it will fall within the competence of the Dominion Parliament as a matter affecting the peace, order and good government of Canada. . . . " This holding seemed to return the interpretation of peace, order and good government to the pre-Haldane formula of national dimensions of concern enunciated by Lord Watson in 1896, namely ". . . that some matters, in their origin local and provincial, might attain such dimensions as to affect the body politic of the Dominion, and to justify the Canadian Parliament in passing laws for their regulation or abolition in the interest of the Dominion." On its face this inherent national importance or national dimensions conception of peace, order and good government appeared to offer the federal government a much wider opportunity to exercise regulatory power in peacetime on more than a temporary basis in areas normally reserved to the provinces.

Court decisions after 1946 were not conclusive as to whether the Haldane emergency doctrine had been superseded by the wider notion of national dimensions. On the two occasions after 1946 when the Privy Council dealt with peace, order and good government it ignored Simon's opinion. The Supreme Court's decision in the *Johannesson* case in 1952 provided the only strong endorsement of Viscount Simon's national importance test. On two subsequent occasions in the 1960s, the Supreme Court employed the vocabulary of "national importance" in upholding federal jurisdiction over the national capital and offshore mineral rights. But in neither case was the Court reviewing a major scheme of federal regulation in an area normally under provincial jurisdiction. Even in *Johannesson*, though the Court sustained the paramountcy of federal control over aeronautics in part on national importance grounds, it was dealing with a regulatory scheme which had been in place for several decades and which could find a large measure of constitutional support in other heads of federal power.

So, coming down to the *Anti-Inflation* case, a large question mark still hung over the peace, order and good government power. That for three decades there had been so little Court action on this issue had much to do with the fact that even during the most centralist years of this period, the federal government had relied primarily on its spending power rather than regulatory schemes for carrying out policy initiatives in areas normally under provincial jurisdiction. But inflationary pressures in the 1970s might force the federal government to shift from spending programs to regulatory schemes. Such a shift, as several political scientists have suggested, would increase the occasions for judicial review. Thus, as the federal government in the fall of 1975 moved toward the implementation of a fairly comprehensive scheme of price and wage controls, the question in constitutional law of whether the peace, order and good government clause would provide a basis for national regulation of broad areas of economic and social activity took on more than academic importance.

Political and Legal Strategies of the Parties

With these constitutional stakes in the background, it is interesting to examine the approach taken by the federal and provincial governments and the major interest groups to the constitutional implications of the anti-inflation program. Turning first to the federal government, we find a significant difference between the political and legal aspects of its behaviour. Politically, Prime Minister Trudeau endeavoured to present the program as an exercise in cooperative federalism. The day before the program was presented to Parliament, the ten provincial premiers came to Ottawa to discuss the program. That night, in his address to the nation on radio and television, Mr. Trudeau said that he had asked the premiers "to join as full partners in the attack upon inflation." During this period Mr. Trudeau tended to be somewhat on the optimistic side in referring to the extent to which the provinces supported federal wage and price controls. Following the first ministers meeting on 13 October, a number of premiers reserved any commitment of support for the program until they had reviewed the matter with their provincial cabinets. Ten days later federal and provincial finance and labour ministers met in Ottawa and following their meeting, Mr. Macdonald, the federal Minister of Finance, announced that "No province declared that it is opposed to the programme or will refuse to cooperate." The next day Mr. Macdonald reported in a more positive vein to the House of Commons: apparently all of the provincial governments were now "prepared to support the programme and cooperate."

While, on the political front, the federal government proceeded on the assumption that provincial co-operation was a political imperative, the Anti-Inflation Act was drafted as if the federal Parliament had full legislative power to proceed with such a program on its own. Section 3 of the Act authorizing the federal government to establish guidelines for the restraint of prices and wages in the private and public sectors made no concessions to any constitutional limitations on the scope of Parliament's regulatory power. It is true that the next section of the Act exempted a province's public sector unless the provincial government entered into an agreement to apply the Act to its public sector. But the implication was that this "opting in" device was entirely dependent on the will of the federal Parliament, and that Parliament, if it had preferred, could have applied the program directly to the provincial public sectors. This implication became explicit later on when the federal government came to defend Ontario's "opting in" Agreement before the Supreme Court. In the absence of any provincial legislation authorizing this Agreement, the only legislative authority for the Agreement was provided by the federal Act and, indeed, federal lawyers asserted the power of the federal Parliament to bind the provincial Crown and regulate the provincial public service.

More important than this is the evidence that the Anti-Inflation Act was drafted so as to preserve the possibility of basing the legislation on a constitutional foundation wider than the emergency doctrine. Nowhere did the Act speak the language of national emergency. Instead, the preamble referred to inflation as "a matter of serious national concern," language clearly suggesting Viscount Simon's approach to peace, order and good government in the *Canada Temperance Federation* case. The only mark of emergency or crisis legislation on the face of the Act was its penultimate section limiting its duration to three years unless Parliament agreed to an extension. Statements by government spokesmen in Parliament made it clear that the omission of any reference to a state of emergency was deliberate. Both Mr. Diefenbaker for the Conservatives and Mr. Brewin for the NDP questioned the government on the constitutional propriety of proceeding without a declaration of an emergency. Mr. Trudeau answered this question with rather vague references to alternative constitutional bases for the Act such as "the banking power" and "the commerce power." Mr. Macdonald gave a much clearer picture of the government's constitutional assumptions in his evidence to the Standing Committee on Finance, Trade and Economic Affairs:

> The opinion of the government on constitutionality is based on some cases that were pleaded before the Judicial Committee on [sic] the Privy Council in 1946, for instance *The Canada Temperance Federation* case, and, since then before the Supreme Court, *Thamieson and St. Paul*, and *Munro* and the *National Capital Commission*. Accordingly, when we have a scheme that goes beyond reasons that are strictly local, provincial or private, when you have a national scheme like this one, there can be a federal jurisdiction under which to legislate on these matters.

Of course, by the *"Thamieson case"* Mr. Macdonald meant *Johannesson v. West St. Paul* in which the Supreme Court had made its most significant application of the "inherent national importance" test of peace, order and good government.

Now, with the federal government playing something of a double game, how did the provinces respond to the constitutional issue? Briefly, because they saw that it was not in their political interests at the time to oppose the federal program, they agreed not to raise the constitutional issue. However, because they wished to avoid conceding constitutional power to Ottawa, they were careful not to commit themselves to any particular view of the Act's constitutional validity. At this stage it was in the interests of both levels of government to suppress the constitutional issue. Apparently the constitutional issue was discussed at the federal-provincial meetings concerning the anti-inflation program, and the federal leaders felt free to declare after these meetings that the provinces would not challenge Parliament's jurisdiction to enact the Anti-Inflation Bill. But, as with so much that happens at meetings of this kind, we do not know in what terms the constitutional issue was discussed. My own guess is that the constitutional discussion was kept at a pretty vague level and that there was just enough reference to the temporary nature of the legislation and the provision of an opting in mechanism for the provinces to set aside, at least for the time being, any reservations of a constitutional nature.

The provinces kept their word. They did not exercise the right which all of them have to refer the question of the Act's constitutionality directly to the courts. All, in varying ways, took steps to bring their public sectors into the program. But, nonetheless, they kept their constitutional options open and, as we shall see, when the constitutional issue was forced before the Supreme Court, a number of them attacked the broad grounds upon which the federal government tried to defend this legislation. In the legal instrument authorizing provincial participation, it is notable that Quebec, of all the provinces, was most careful to concede as little as possible to federal legislative authority. Thus, Quebec's Agreement not only established the province's own Inflation Control Commission to administer guidelines for the public sector "in consultation with" the federal Anti-Inflation Board, but further gave the province's consent to have the guidelines apply to the private sector. Quebec's submission to the Supreme Court subsequently made it clear that in the province's view, even in the context of an emergency, federal regulation of the provincial private sector of the economy could not take effect without provincial consent.

If the federal and provincial governments were the only agencies for initiating judicial review, there would probably not have been an *Anti-Inflation* case. In Canada, only the federal and provincial governments have access to the most direct means of bringing questions before the courts — the reference procedure. Private litigants can raise constitutional issues in the courts only when they are plaintiff or defendant in normal litigation, and Canadian courts have tended to be relatively stringent in granting "standing" to raise such issues. One of the interesting features of the *Anti-Inflation* case is that it was the persistence of private interest groups, namely a number of trade unions, in trying to challenge the constitutional validity of the anti-inflation program through normal litigation which eventually persuaded the federal government to resort to the reference device and bring the issue directly before the Supreme Court.

It is particularly interesting that organized labour rather than business interests were responsible for initiating the constitutional challenge to the anti-inflation program. Traditionally, organized labour has favoured strengthening rather than weakening the capacity of the federal government to deal with national and international economic forces. But once labour representatives perceived what in their view was the unjust character of the federal program, they began to oppose it vigorously, and soon after its introduction officials of the Canadian Labour Congress announced their intention to challenge the program in the courts. There is no indication that union leaders had any qualms about the long-run constitutional consequences if their court action was successful. The attack through the courts was adopted as simply one of the means for conducting the anti-control campaign. However, it should be noted that the grounds upon which the CLC initially proposed to base its challenge were that the controls program was too selective to meet the national dimensions test and that provinces could not turn over their legislative jurisdiction to the federal authority by order-in-council. While these arguments did not so clearly threaten the scope of federal authority, those which union counsel subsequently used before the Supreme Court were much more anti-centralist.

It was not easy for those labour groups who wished to challenge the constitutional validity of the anti-inflation program to gain access to the courts. The most direct means of appealing an order of the Anti-Inflation Administrator to the Appeal Tribunal (and from there to the Federal Court of Canada) was available only to employers. This deficiency in the Act was eventually remedied but not until after the federal government had made the reference to the Supreme Court. The legal actions which eventually provoked the reference all involved unions in Ontario resisting the application of the controls to collective agreements they were in the process of negotiating. The most significant of these, in terms of bringing the constitutional issue before the courts, was that of the Renfrew County branch of the Ontario Secondary School Teachers Federation. In November, 1975, the Renfrew teachers had signed a collective agreement with the Renfrew County Board of Education for an amount considerably in excess of the anti-inflation guidelines. This settlement was made pursuant to the result of binding arbitration under Ontario legislation. The arbitration award had been made two weeks after the introduction of the anti-inflation program. On February 10, 1976, the Anti-Inflation Board notified the teachers and the Board that the settlement should be reduced. Six days later the teachers' federation applied to the Divisional Court of the Supreme Court of Ontario for a declaration that Ontario's Agreement with the federal government bringing its public sector under the anti-inflation program was invalid on the ground that the Order-in-Council authorizing the Agreement had been made without the necessary legislation by the province. It is doubtful whether this legal strategy would have worked because the Federal Court of Canada has exclusive jurisdiction to grant declaratory relief. On the same day that the Renfrew teachers submitted their application to Ontario's Supreme Court, a Board of Arbitration in another Ontario labour dispute (this time involving the University of Toronto and a local of the Canadian Union of Public Employees representing the University's library technicians) ruled that it was not bound by actions of the Anti-Inflation Board.

Apparently it was these two developments which convinced the Attorney-General of Ontario, Mr. Roy McMurtry, that in order to avoid a lengthy and uncertain period of litigation he should ask the federal Minister of Justice to refer the issue to the Supreme Court. There were possibly other factors which influenced Mr. McMurtry. The Ontario government had entered into its Agreement with the federal government without any approval from the provincial legislature. The Agreements of all the other provinces except Newfoundland's had some legislative sanction. The Davis government wished to avoid the legislature because it was in a minority there and both opposition parties indicated they would oppose the government on the controls issue. But by February of 1976, the Ontario Liberals under Mr. Stuart Smith's leadership had shown that they did not want an election in the near future and so for the time being they would not use their balance of power in the legislature to defeat the government. Thus, Mr. McMurtry had some assurance that if the Ontario Agreement was ruled invalid by the Supreme Court he could go back to the legislature and with support from a compliant Mr. Smith obtain the necessary approval for the Agreement. This assurance was important, as the validity of the Ontario Agreement was a much more dubious proposition than was the validity of the federal Act.

On March 12, the federal Minister of Justice, Mr. Basford, announced that the federal cabinet had approved an order-in-council referring the question of the federal Act's constitutional validity and of the Ontario Agreement's validity to the Supreme Court of Canada. It was, he said, the Renfrew teachers' action which prompted this decision,

> Because the whole thing (the anti-inflation programme) is vulnerable to such challenges and because the work of the nation must go on we have decided to avoid time-consuming litigation over issues like this which ultimately would have to be decided by the Supreme Court anyway.

We might also speculate that Mr. Basford's government, with its program well in place and having secured the co-operation of all the provinces, could now contemplate judicial review of the Anti-Inflation Act with a fair degree of confidence.

The Reference: The Parties and Their Submissions

The use of Canada's extraordinary reference procedure in the circumstances outlined above illustrates one of the advantages of this device. Once it was reasonably certain that judicial review would occur through private litigation, it was in the government's interest to remove as quickly as possible the legal clouds surrounding the program — especially a program which was encountering considerable resistance from those whose behaviour it was supposed to regulate. In the alternative, if the unions had found their access to the courts completely blocked, the reference would compensate for the relative disadvantage which citizens or private groups are under in obtaining judicial review in Canada and give the unions an opportunity to establish their constitutional rights before the country's highest tribunal.

But the disadvantages of the reference procedure have been advertised just as much as its advantages. The primary criticism has been that the procedure forces judges to make decisions about the constitutional validity of government policies in a highly abstract and hypothetical manner divorced from any consideration of the factual context which gave rise to the legislation and in which the real effect of the legislation may be revealed. Added to this is the fear that such a procedure, by bringing statutes to court "... in the very flush of enactment, while the feelings that produced them were at their highest pitch ..." may unduly politicize the process of judicial review and force the judges to participate in a political controversy in a way which will ultimately weaken their authority. It is instructive to review the conduct of the *Anti-inflation Reference* in the light of these criticism and concerns.

Certainly, the questions submitted to the court by the Reference Order were presented in the barest possible way:

1. Is the Anti-Inflation Act *ultra vires* the Parliament of Canada either in whole or in part, and, if so, in what particulars and to what extent?

2. If the Anti-Inflation Act is in *ultra vires* the Parliament of Canada, is the Agreement entitled "Between the Government of Canada and the Government of the Province of Ontario," entered into on January 13, 1976 effective under the Anti-Inflation Act to render that Act binding on, and the Anti-Inflation Guidelines made thereunder applicable to, the provincial public sector in Ontario as defined in the Agreement?

The reference itself was not accompanied by any factual material describing the situation which gave rise to the legislation or details concerning the implementation of the Anti-Inflation program. However, procedures were soon set in motion to provide the basic ingredients of a law case — adversaries and their submissions — and make the decision-making process less like an academic seminar and more like the adjudication of a concrete dispute.

There was no difficulty in obtaining parties to argue all sides of both questions. The federal government, of course, would appear in support of the legislation. All the provinces were notified of the hearing but only five decided to participate: Ontario, Quebec, British Columbia and Saskatchewan in support of the legislation (although for the latter three this "support" turned out to be qualified indeed) and Alberta in direct opposition. Alberta would be joined by five unions (or groups of unions) who were considered to have distinct interests at stake in the proceedings. This labour representation included the Ontario teachers and public service unions which had been attempting to litigate the constitutional issues in Ontario courts, the Canadian Labour Congress which had been pressing for judicial review since the introduction of the Act, and one major international union, the United Steel Workers of America. Thus, the reference procedure, compensating for the relatively cautious policy of Canadian courts in granting access to the judicial process, enabled the major political contestants to do battle in the judicial arena. But the Supreme Court was not prepared to go all the way in the "politicization" of its process and drew the line at political parties, declining to give permission to the Ontario NDP to appear as an interested party.

The material submitted by these parties compensated, in part, for the bareness of the reference questions. Some of it also posed a severe challenge to the Supreme Court's jurisprudential style. Non-legal material such as the "Brandeis brief" prepared by social scientists and designed to support propositions about the social or economic background and implications of legislation has not played an important role in the Canadian Supreme Court's decision-making. This is not because there is any rule formally proscribing such material. It has stemmed primarily from the character of jurisprudence favoured by Canadian judges and lawyers. In constitutional interpretation, as in other areas, Canadian jurists have been most comfortable with a highly conceptual approach in which the focus is on applying definitions of legal categories to the words of the statute with little or no reference to the empirical meaning of this exercise. But in the *Anti-Inflation* case some of the counsel came from a younger generation of lawyers imbued with the example of modern American constitutional jurisprudence which has been far more receptive to social science material. The Chief Justice of the Court both as an academic and a judge had stressed the importance of empirical evidence in constitutional interpretation. Also, one of the basic questions in the case — whether inflation in Canada had become a matter of inherent national importance or a national emergency — seemed to be essentially an empirical issue. Thus, it is not surprising that the Court's reception and use of socio-economic material as an "extrinsic aid" to constitutional interpretation became one of the most significant features of the case.

About a month after the Reference Order was issued, Chief Justice Laskin met with counsel for the various parties to consider some of the procedural issues. On April 6, at the conclusion of this hearing, the Chief Justice made a number of rulings: application to join the proceedings as an interested party would be accepted up until April 15; the Attorney-General of Canada was to prepare the "case" (the material submitted by the appellant in an appeal which would normally include full documentation of the proceedings in the lower courts), which here was to include the federal government's White Paper and any other materials the Attorney-General considered appropriate; the parties were to file their factums (the written briefs setting out each party's arguments on the various issues) by May 10, and could "annex supplementary material" to their factums; parties would have a short period (until May 21) in which to submit additional material in reply to material filed by other parties; the oral hearing of the case would begin on May 31, 1976. These rulings gave an opportunity to all the parties to submit whatever empirical argumentation they wished and met one of the traditional complaints against this type of material by giving the parties an opportunity to prepare written replies to their adversaries' submissions. However, the Chief Justice could not make any commitment as to weight which the Court would give any of this material in reaching its final conclusion.

It is interesting to see how the various parties responded to this opportunity. Only the Canadian Labour Congress annexed supplementary material to its factum. This took the form of a 64-page brief written by Richard G. Lipsey, professor of economics at Queen's University. A group of 38 economists who had been attacking the controls program outside of the judicial arena supported the Lipsey brief. Their telegrams of support were added to the CLC material. Professor Lipsey's study advanced the argument that it was very far-fetched to regard the state of the Canadian economy when controls were introduced as an "economic crisis." This argument was supported both by absolute considerations (inflation is primarily redistributive in its effects so that *average* living standards are not lowered) and, perhaps more impressively, by comparative data showing, for instance, that compared both with other periods in Canadian history and with the economic situation of Canada's major trading partners the level of inflation in the fall of 1975 was not extraordinary. Professor Lipsey concluded that:

> It seems hard to believe that the inflation-unemployment problem is unique in its degree of seriousness. . . . If it is held that this problem constitutes an economic crisis, then it is hard to avoid the conclusion that economies are nearly always in states of "economic crises." If this kind of "economic crisis" justified the use of extraordinary measures, these extraordinary measures may be nearly always justified.

In the light of the Supreme Court's final holding, this is a very significant conclusion. Professor Lipsey's study also attacked the efficacy of the controls program in reducing inflation. Given the strict taboo in our legal tradition against courts reviewing the wisdom of legislation, this, I believe, was a serious tactical mistake and made it easier for the judges to discount the Lipsey brief.

The only other material of this kind was submitted by the federal government and the Province of Ontario. The "case" material prepared by the Attorney-General of Canada included, in addition to the White Paper requested by the Chief Justice (which nowhere referred to the existence of a "crisis" or "emergency"), the monthly bulletin of Statistics Canada showing fluctuations in the consumer price index up to September, 1975. In reply to the Lipsey brief, the Attorneys-General of Canada and Ontario

RUSSELL, *THE ANTI-INFLATION CASE*   371

both submitted additional material. The federal submission was a copy of an after-dinner speech delivered by the Governor of the Bank of Canada, Gerald K. Bouey, a month before controls were introduced. The speech stressed the seriousness of inflation but was in no sense a counter-analysis to Professor Lipsey's brief. But Ontario's additional material, prepared by the province's Office of Economic Analysis, did attempt a direct rebuttal of Lipsey's main argument. It challenged neither the accuracy of his data nor his technical economics, but (on Galbraithian grounds) it questioned his judgment that the severity of Canada's existing economic problems could be expected nearly always to prevail from now on. Perhaps most significantly, it argued that the question of whether or not a "crisis" exists cannot be answered by technical economics but by public opinion polls (although it cited no actual poll results on this question).

While empirical considerations were more prominent than is usually the case in constitutional references, the arguments which predominated in both the written factums and the oral hearing were still essentially legal in character. These arguments were put to the Court by as impressive an array of legal talent as has ever been assembled for a constitutional case. Among the group of participating lawyers were the federal government's counsel, Mr. J.J. Robinette, whom many regard as the outstanding advocate currently practising in Canada, a number of constitutional scholars including a dean, an ex-dean, and a dean elect of law, some of the country's ablest labour and civil rights lawyers, perhaps the most dynamic Attorney-General and Deputy Attorney-General in Canada, as well as some of the leading members of the youngest generation of Canadian lawyers. Certainly it would be difficult to contend that the outcome of this case was influenced by the fact that one or the other side was badly argued. This is important because the strictly adversarial dimension of the proceedings is probably more significant in the Canadian Supreme Court than it is, for instance, in the United States Supreme Court, where the time allowed for oral argument is very limited. In typical Canadian fashion our Supreme Court procedure combines the written American brief (called factums in Canada) with the English emphasis on virtually unlimited time for oral argument. In this case the oral hearing ran for a full week and it is likely that the way in which the adversarial exchange in the courtroom structured the issues had more to do with the Court's final decision than would be the case in the United States.

The Ontario Agreement was defended only by counsel for Ontario and the federal government. The other provinces did not make submission on this question. The unions all vigorously attacked the Agreement's validity. The Ontario unions were able to use the concrete situations which had been the original basis for their litigation as illustrations of the extent to which the Agreement altered the basic law regulating collective bargaining in Ontario. This added considerable strength to their proposition that an executive Agreement without any legislative sanction which purported to set aside existing legislation was a clear violation of the principle of responsible government. The main defence of the Agreement did not contend that the federal Act had actually provided the legislative sanction for the Ontario Agreement. Instead it relied primarily on precedents of executive agreements and contracts for which there had been no specific legislative authorization. Nonetheless one of the Canadian Labour Congress counsel, P. W. Hogg, argued that in a federal system of dual sovereignty there must be a basic immunity of the Provincial Crown which would set some limit on federal authority to regulate the remuneration of the provincial civil service directly under ministers of the Crown — even in an emergency, and yes, even during a war. This contention clearly shocked a number of judges, and one was heard to exclaim that "if the argument had any validity it would ultimately deny the existence of a Canadian Nation."

On the issues associated with the first question concerning the Anti-Inflation Act's constitutional validity, the alignment of the parties was revealing. The federal position before the Court was the most predictable. It reflected the double game which the federal government had been playing from the start on the peace, order and good government issue. Ottawa was fairly confident that the Act could at the very least be sustained as emergency legislation and its counsel now put forward the emergency use of the general power as a basis for the legislation — *but only as a fall back position*. The primary argument advanced by federal counsel was that "because inflation is a subject matter going beyond local or provincial concern or interests and is from its inherent nature the concern of Canada as a whole," the Anti-Inflation Act should be upheld as a proper exercise of the peace, order and good government power. To this was added reference to several specific heads of federal power — trade and commerce, taxation, the power to borrow, currency, banking, interest, legal tender — all of which were closely related to the aims and effects of the anti-inflation program and hence, it was argued, provided evidence of the inherently national character of the legislation. Obviously, the primary federal argument was designed to do more than save the Act: if it were accepted by the Court it would consolidate the gains in constitutional law which the federal government hoped would flow from Viscount Simon's decision in the *Canada Temperance Federation* case. Surprisingly, Ontario endorsed the federal position. In fact, Mr. McMurtry in one respect went further in that he did not advance the emergency doctrine even as an alternative argument. For Ontario, Viscount Simon's test of inherent national importance was the only test for invoking peace, order and good government.

But the other provinces and the unions all argued that the only possible way of supporting such legislation was on emergency grounds. The constitutional issue which it had been convenient to suppress in October now came out in the open. The most important constitutional arguments were advanced by Mr. Lysyk, the Deputy Attorney-General of Saskatchewan, and Professor Lederman for the Renfrew teachers. They put forward a new thesis on the meaning of previous decisions dealing with peace, order and good government. The gist of this thesis was that outside of emergencies, peace, order and good government can be used only in a residual sense to support federal legislation in discrete, narrowly defined areas of legislation which clearly fall outside provincial jurisdiction. Legislation in an area defined as broadly as "inflation" and clearly intruding on matters which are normally subject to exclusive provincial jurisdiction fails to meet this test. This interpretation of peace, order and good government was a clear alternative to the views expressed by Chief Justice Laskin in his academic writings — views which his frequent interventions from the bench indicated he might still hold.

Even on emergency grounds the federal position received meager support from the provinces. Alberta along with the unions went all the way and argued (in the CLC's submission on the basis of the Lipsey brief) that the Act should be found unconstitutional as there was no economic emergency. Quebec, British Columbia and Saskatchewan remained on the federal government's side of the courtroom nominally in support of the legislation. But their support, at times, must have reminded federal counsel of the old saying, "With friends like that, who needs enemies?" In their factums, they were at best agnostic as to whether an emergency existed sufficient to justify the use of the general power. Mr. Vickers, the Deputy Attorney-General for British Columbia, concluded his oral presentation by submitting that the burden of proof (on the existence of an emergency) lay with the federal government, and that "on the evidence now before the court I do not feel one could conclude that there was a national emergency." Counsel for the federal government did not try to meet this burden of proof nor parry the economic arguments of the Lipsey brief. Mr. Robinette's position was that the Court had only to find that it was not unreasonable for Parliament to believe that there was an emergency or "a generally apprehended crisis."

The submissions of the parties in the *Anti-Inflation* case contrast in some important ways with those of counsel in the New Deal references of the 1930s — the last occasion on which there was a serious challenge to federal power through judicial review. In those cases a foreign tribunal witnessed a strong provincial attack on federal legislation rather weakly defended by a government whose political opponents had actually introduced the legislation. Here, a Canadian court in the national capital was considering the constitutional validity of what at the time was the federal government'smost important domestic policy initiative. The judges knew that all of the provinces had in fact agreed to co-operate with the federal program. In the courtroom they *saw* on the federal side four provinces (including the three largest) with governments covering the entire Canadian political spectrum supporting the legislation. But they also heard that the only common denominator of constitutional support was the emergency doctrine. In these circumstances it would have taken an exceptionally bold court either to have found the federal Act *ultra vires* or to have based its constitutional validity on a wider footing than the emergency use of peace, order and good government.

The Court's Decision

Five weeks after the conclusion of the hearing the Supreme Court pronounced its judgment. The Court unanimously found that the Ontario Agreement did not render the Anti-Inflation program binding on the provincial public sector. On the question of the Anti-Inflation Act's constitutional validity, the Court split seven to two: seven judges found that it was constitutional on emergency grounds, but Justices Beetz and de Grandpré, both from Quebec and the most recently appointed judges, dissented. That is the bare bones of the decision, but, as is always the case with appellate decisions, the reasons of the judges are more important than their votes.

First, the Court's decision on the validity of the Ontario Agreement, while constituting a small portion of the judgment quantitatively, is not without its constitutional significance. Chief Justice Laskin wrote the Court's opinion on this question. Because the federal Act did not spell out precisely how the guidelines should apply to the provincial public sector, the Chief Justice found that the Act itself did not provide the necessary legislative sanction for the Ontario Agreement. The Agreement could not be regarded as sanctioned by conditional legislation for which action by the provincial government was merely a "triggering device." However, it is significant that in reaching this conclusion he went out of his way to indicate that he did not accept the view that it would have been beyond federal power to regulate the provincial public service. Assertions of immunity for the provincial public service, he wrote, "misconceive the paramount authority of federal legislative power . . . and the all-embracing legislative authority of the Parliament of Canada when validly exercised for the peace, order and good government of Canada." But, in the absence of federal or provincial legislation *clearly* authorizing the Agreement, he ruled that the executive agreement could not make new labour legislation binding on the citizens of the province. The Chief Justice seemed bent on de-emphasizing the constitutional significance of this holding: the issue, he said, did *not* engage "any concern with responsible Government and the political answerability of the Ministers to the Legislative Assembly." Nonetheless, by holding that:

> There is no principle in this country, as there is not in Great Britain. that the Crown may legislate by proclamation or Order in Council to bind citizens where it so acts without the support of a statute of the Legislature; see Dicey, *Law of the Constitution*,

he at least confirms an essential element of our "unwritten constitution." Those concerned about the increasing erosion of the role of the legislature and the trend in Canada toward policy-making within the closed confines of federal-provincial negotiations, should welcome this judicial recognition of an important constitutional principle.

The Court's decision on the primary question concerning the constitutional validity of the Anti-Inflation Act can be analysed by breaking the question into two components: (1) the interpretation of the peace, order and good government clause and (2) the judgment as to whether the Anti-Inflation Act could be upheld as emergency legislation. The court split in quite different ways on these two aspects of the question. Three opinions were written: Chief Justice Laskin's reasons were supported by three Justices, Judson, Spence and Dickson; Mr. Justice Ritchie's were concurred in by Justices Martland and Pigeon; Mr. Justice de Grandpré concurred in Mr. Justice Beetz's opinion. On the second aspect of the question, Chief Justice Laskin's group of four and Justice Ritchie's group of three formed the majority which found the Act *intra vires*. But on the first issue — the fundamental question of constitutional doctrine — the reasoning of Mr. Justice Beetz's dissenting opinion was adopted by the Ritchie threesome and so became, in effect, the majority position of the Court.

The short five-page opinion of Mr. Justice Ritchie at least has the merit of highlighting the Court's division on the meaning of peace, order and good government. Ritchie rejects broad considerations of national concern or inherent national importance as the framework within which to test whether Parliament can exercise its peace, order and good government power in areas normally under provincial jurisdiction. For him the relevant precedent is not Viscount Simon's judgment in the *Canada Temperance Federation* case, but the decisions following it, especially the *Japanese Canadians* case, in which the Privy Council returned to the emergency doctrine. Since then, Justice Ritchie takes it to be established "that unless such concern [i.e., national concern] is made manifest by circumstances amounting to a national emergency, Parliament is not endowed under the cloak of the 'peace, order and good government' clause with the authority to legislate in relation to matters reserved to the Provinces under s. 92." For more elaborate jurisprudential reasons he refers to Mr. Justice Beetz with whose reasons he is "in full agreement."

Justice Beetz provided a re-interpretation of previous judicial decisions on this constitutional issue. This re-interpretation followed the mainline of argument submitted to the Court by Mr. Lysyk and Professor Lederman. The essence of this approach is to draw a radical distinction between the "normal" and the "abnormal" uses of peace, order and good government. The normal use of the clause is as a national residual power to cover ". . . clear instances of distinct subject-matters which do not fall within any of the enumerated heads of s. 92 and which, by nature, are of national concern." Thus, it has been invoked successfully in the past to support such fields as radio, aeronautics, the incorporation of Dominion companies and the national capital, all of which in Justice Beetz's view display the requisite "degree of unity," "distinct identity" or "specificity." But the containment and reduction of inflation fails to meet this test of specificity: "It is so pervasive that it knows no bounds. Its recognition as a federal head of power would render most provincial powers nugatory." The normal application of peace, order and good government has the effect of adding, by judicial process, new subject matters of legislation to the list of exclusive federal powers in Section 91 of the BNA Act. National concern, national dimensions are still relevant in determining whether such unforeseen, discrete, new subject matters should be brought under the federal residual power or under its counterpart on the provincial side, Section 92(16) — "Matters of a merely local or private nature in the province." But the only constitutional basis for federal legislation cast in such broad terms as the Anti-Inflation Act is the abnormal use of peace, order and good government — the emergency doctrine. It is abnormal precisely because it "operates as a partial and temporary alteration of the distribution of power between Parliament and the provincial Legislatures." Once the Court agrees to apply this doctrine no longer is the power of Parliament limited by the identity of subject matters but solely "by the nature of the crisis."

This then was the new constitutional doctrine fashioned by Justice Beetz and supported by a bare majority of the Court. Against it — but by no means in total opposition to it — was Chief Justice Laskin's opinion supported by three other judges. The Chief Justice wrote a long review of all the major cases bearing upon peace, order and good government. While it is not always clear just where this review is going, it contains one basic point of contrast with the majority position. Instead of driving a wedge between the normal and abnormal use of the general power, Chief Justice Laskin tries to weave a single piece of cloth out of all the strands to be found in previous decisions. The key to this approach, the central idea which gives the multi-coloured fabric some shape and pattern, is Lord Watson's proposition in the *Local Prohibition* case that ". . . matters in origin local or provincial . . . might attain national dimensions." Since then Laskin sees the jurisprudence moving in two directions — under Viscount Haldane narrowing to the hint of "studiously ignoring" Lord Watson's "national dimensions," but then returning to it, at first cautiously in judgments written by Lord Atkin and Chief Justice Duff followed by the more expansive views of Viscount Simon. The Chief Justice's response to this legacy of competing emphases is not to pick his own favourite strand and discard the others but to identify the extremes which clearly lie beyond the main body of jurisprudence. Thus, at one extreme, basing the use of peace, order and good government on the mere desirability or convenience of national regulation (a possible interpretation of the first Privy Council decision on this issue, *Russell v. The Queen*) is ruled out. But at the other extreme, a pure Haldane approach which ignores "national dimensions" and confines the use of peace, order and good government to war-related emergencies is equally beyond the pale. In between these extremes there are many possibilities, and the Chief Justice warns against fixing constitutional doctrine so tightly as to prevent the constitution from serving " . . . as a resilient instrument capable of adaptation to changing circumstances."

In the case at hand, because all of the parties accepted as constitutional doctrine the use of peace, order and good government to deal with a national emergency, " . . . it becomes unnecessary to consider the broader ground advanced in its support . . ." So the Chief Justice was willing to rest his decision on the narrow ground of emergency (semantically softened to "crisis"). But unlike the majority he did not rule out the broader ground advanced by the federal government.

For those who have admired the Chief Justice's contribution to Canada's constitutional jurisprudence, the opaque, open-ended quality of his reasoning in this case may be a disappointment. But it is reasonable, I think, to regard his opinion as that of a Chief Justice endeavouring to build a majority around the widest common denominator on his Court without foreclosing jurisprudential possibilities which he personally favoured. That he failed is not too surprising. Since joining the Court in 1970 he has been its most frequent dissenter. The available statistical data (based on the *Supreme Court Reports* from 1970 to 1974 inclusive) reveal that of the 196 dissents recorded during this period more than half (109) were attributed to three justices: Laskin (45), Spence (34) and Hall (30). The relative isolation of these justices is not tied to issues of federalism. Between the time the present Chief Justice joined the Court and the *Anti-Inflation Reference*, the Court rendered 20 decisions on the division of powers in the BNA Act. Fifteen of them were unanimous, and although the Chief Justice was on the dissenting side in three of the split decisions, an examination of these cases does not suggest a division on provincial rights/centralist lines. Chief Justice Laskin's differences with a majority of his colleagues more likely stem from general questions of judicial philosophy and style. If there is a consistent pattern of division on matters of substance, it is more likely to be found in cases dealing with criminal law and the Bill of Rights.

Given the clear consensus both on the Court and among the litigants concerning the power of Parliament in a national emergency (or crisis) to override the normal division of powers, the second dimension of the constitutional question — whether in fact the Anti-Inflation Act was emergency legislation — may become more important than the general doctrinal issue of the meaning of peace, order and good government. The Supreme Court's handling of this issue indicates a significant shift to a more deferential attitude to the exercise of emergency powers in peacetime by the national government.

The Court's split on the issue — Chief Justice Laskin's group of four plus Justice Ritchie's group of three versus Justices Beetz and de Grandpré in dissent — did not turn on the empirical question of whether in fact there was an emergency. It concerned the prior question of whether emergency legislation must be clearly identified as such by Parliament. The dissenters took the position that a necessary but by no means sufficient test of valid emergency legislation is a clear, unambiguous indication by Parliament that it is enacting the legislation on an emergency basis. Justice Beetz emphasized that responsibility for declaring an emergency must lie with the "politically responsible body," not the courts. The court's responsibility begins after the affirmation by Parliament that an emergency exists. In this case not only was there no acknowledgment on the face of the federal Act (as there had been with other recent exercises of the emergency power), but there was clear evidence to show that this was no accidental oversight. Breaking the convention which precludes Canadian judges from considering parliamentary history, Justice Beetz referred to the numerous passages in Hansard where government spokesmen refused to be pinned down on the constitutional basis of the legislation and refused to preface the Bill with a declaration of an emergency. Further, the large gaps in the Act's coverage — the omission of farmers and small businesses, the optional nature of the provincial public sector's inclusion — were, in Justice Beetz's view, not easily reconciled with an emergency characterization of the Act. He was also impressed by the lack of provincial support for the view that it was emergency legislation.

For the majority, Parliament's failure to declare an emergency or stamp "emergency" on the face of the Act was not fatal. The reference in the Act's preamble to a level of inflation "contrary to the interests of all Canadians" which had become "a matter of serious national concern," combined with similar statements in the government's White Paper, were enough to indicate how serious the situation must have appeared to Parliament. The omissions from the Act's coverage and the opting-in approach to the provincial public sector, in Chief Justice Laskin's view, could be accounted for in terms of administrative convenience and need not be regarded as indicating a lack of any sense of crisis. Since there were no formal deficiencies in the federal Act, the only grounds upon which its validity as emergency or crisis legislation could be impugned was the factual question: did an emergency exist? Here, for a least three of the justices, the onus of proof was placed squarely on the Act's opponents. The peacetime exercise of the federal emergency power was put on the same footing as its use in time of war. Justice Ritchie cited Lord Wright's statement in the *Japanese Canadians* case.

> But very clear evidence that an emergency has not arisen, or that the emergency no longer exists, is required to justify the judiciary, even though the question is one of *ultra vires*, in overruling the decision of the Parliament of the Dominion that exceptional measures were required or were still required.

In Justice Ritchie's opinion the evidence presented by the opponents of the legislation failed to meet Lord Wright's test.

Chief Justice Laskin approached the issue in terms of assessing the rationality of Parliament's judgment. The Court would be justified in over-ruling the Act as emergency legislation only if it found that:

> ... The Parliament of Canada did not have a rational basis for regarding the *Anti-Inflation Act* as a measure which, in its judgment, was temporarily necessary to meet a situation of economic crisis imperilling the well-being of the people of Canada as a whole and requiring Parliament's stern intervention in the interests of the country as a whole.

In assessing rationality, the Chief Justice did not place the burden of proof solely on the Act's opponents. He took into consideration statistics showing the rise in the Consumer Price Index submitted by the federal government as well as the arguments advanced in Professor Lipsey's brief. He noted Professor Lipsey's candid admission that whether "a problem is serious enough to be described as a crisis must be partly a matter of judgment," and added that the Court cannot be governed by the judgment of an economist, however distinguished he may be in the opinion of his peers. Positive evidence of the rationality of Parliament's judgment could be found in the connection between rising inflation and Parliament's clear constitutional responsibilities in monetary policy ...

Thus, the Chief Justice concluded that the Court would be unjustified in finding Parliament lacked a rational basis for its judgment that the legislation was needed to meet an urgent crisis. But we should note how in this part of his opinion he attempted to retain as close a link as possible between the emergency use of peace, order and good government and broad consideration of national dimensions or national aspects. With severe inflation impinging so heavily on areas of federal responsibility, the subject matter of the Anti-Inflation Act — the regulation of prices and wages — loses its ordinary parochial or local character and becomes a matter sufficiently urgent for the well-being of all Canadians as to require national action.

The Significance of the Decision

Normally a judicial decision in our system of government "settles" one aspect — the judiciable aspect — of what is usually a larger dispute. In the context of this larger dispute a Court's role is perhaps better described as "dispute processing" rather than "dispute settlement." In assessing the political importance of a judicial decision it is important to see how it affects the political interests involved in the larger area of conflict. The political impact of a constitutional decision by the national court of appeal will usually be felt much more in terms of the long-run significance of the new rules of law it produces than in terms of the immediate outcome of the adjudication.

This is certainly true of the Supreme Court's decision in the *Anti-Inflation* case. For the labour organizations which provoked the case as part of a general anti-controls campaign the immediate outcome was a loss. The controls would continue. Even that part of the decision which invalidated the Ontario Agreement was quickly overcome. The ink was scarcely dry on the Court's judgment when the Ontario government went back to the legislature and obtained retroactive legislative sanction for its participation in the anti-inflation program. The government's minority position in the legislature proved to be no problem, as Mr. Smith, the Liberal leader, was as compliant as predicted. But the "loss" for labour was probably not a very serious one. Labour opposition to the controls program, if anything, intensified rather than diminished after the decision. It is doubtful that the Supreme Court's validation of the Anti-Inflation Act added to the program's political legitimacy. In fact, a judicial veto of the Anti-Inflation Act might have provided the immediate benefit to the Trudeau government of a politically safe exit from a potentially unpopular program. Besides, the ground of the Court's decision meant that the door was far from closed on future constitutional challenges to the program. If the inflationary situation significantly eased, it would always be possible to argue that the circumstances which made it reasonable to regard the Act as an emergency measure no long existed. Indeed, shortly after the Parti Quebecois took over in Quebec City, Mr. Parizeau, Quebec's Finance Minister, announced that he was considering a challenge on precisely those grounds.

The rules of law and the constitutional doctrine which emerge from the decision bear more directly on the interests of the two levels of government in the Canadian federation than upon the labour-capital axis. Indeed, one of the interesting features of the case is the apparent indifference of organized labour to the division of powers question. The federal and provincial governments cannot be indifferent because Supreme Court rulings on the constitution directly increase or diminish their political resources. From this perspective, the Court's judgment on the Ontario Agreement entails a slight decrease in the resources of both levels of government. The decision reduces the freedom of provincial and federal governments to collaborate in making policy through the mechanisms of co-operative federalism without obtaining support from their respective legislatures. This modest restraint on "executive federalism" is a boon for citizens and interest groups (like labour unions), not to mention old-fashioned democrats who believe that major changes in the law should be approved by the legislature. But its significance must not be over-rated. Chief Justice Laskin's decision clearly implies that federal legislation upheld on emergency grounds could, if properly worded, regulate all aspects of a field normally under provincial jurisdiction and eliminate any need for provincial legislative sanction.

As for the meaning of the peace, order and good government clause in the BNA Act, the decision did not yield the particular benefit sought by federal legal strategists. The legislation was not sustained on broad grounds of inherent national importance or concern. Viscount Haldane was not put away in mothballs. The jurisprudence of Viscount Simon and the *Johannesson* case, which Mr. Macdonald said his government was counting upon, was not accepted by the Court's majority as the key to interpreting peace, order and good government. But the federal government did not come away from the decision empty-handed. To begin with, what I shall call the "Lederman doctrine" on peace, order and good government, adopted by Justice Beetz and supported by a majority of the judges, means that when new matters of legislation are considered distinct and specific enough to justify the residual or "normal" use of the peace, order and good government, they are added to the list of *exclusive* federal powers. The exclusiveness of federal jurisdiction in areas such as aeronautics and radio communications, which are cited as instances of this normal use, was not clear in the past. The Lederman doctrine, while apparently not as favourable to federal power as Viscount Simon's dictum, still is not necessarily unfavourable. While it may have seemed relatively easy to Justice Beetz and his colleagues to apply the criterion of "specificity" retrospectively, I would contend that it is not an easy test to apply prospectively. In the hands of a nationally-minded court it may be surprising what turns out to be specific enough to come under the federal residual power. Besides, it should be noted that considerations of national concern and importance have not been discarded by the Court. Under the Lederman doctrine, national concern is the test for determining whether a new subject with the requisite degree of specificity should be brought under the federal rather than the provincial residual power. Also, as I have tried to explain above, Chief Justice Laskin's opinion, which after all spoke for four of the Court's nine judges, kept Viscount Simon's jurisprudence alive and, in deciding whether the legislation was valid on emergency grounds, made the national dimensions of the economic crisis a prime consideration.

But the Court's handling of the emergency question constitutes a more distinct gain for the federal authorities. The majority's ruling that Parliament does not have to proclaim an emergency or crisis in order to be able to defend legislation successfully in court as emergency legislation increases the maneuverability of federal government leaders. This is especially important with regard to crisis situations related to peacetime economic management when the open admission in Parliament that an emergency or urgent crisis exists might be politically embarrassing to the government. The majority's position means that the federal government does not have to pay the price of that embarrassment in order to secure the emergency argument as the basis for an Act's constitutional validity. To put the matter bluntly, temporary federal legislation may be upheld on emergency grounds if federal lawyers can persuade the Court that there is not enough evidence to conclude that it would have been unreasonable for Parliament to have regarded a matter as an urgent national crisis at the time it passed the legislation. Given the probable deference of most Supreme Court Justices to the judgment of Parliament, this is at least a small gain for federal authority.

It may, however, be a significant loss to those Canadians who care about maintaining parliamentary democracy and constitutionalism. For it must be remembered that all of the judicial decisions upholding federal legislation on emergency grounds (as well as those denying it on these grounds) indicate that "the rule of law as to the distribution of powers" is set aside for the duration of the emergency. One can understand the need for an overriding emergency power to protect the state against threats to its very survival, as well as the reluctance of judges to question a clear determination by Parliament that such an emergency exists. But the constitution as a limit on governmental authority will come to mean very little if it is set aside too easily. At the very least, the better constitutional policy might be to insist, with Justice Beetz, that it should be the responsibility of Parliament rather than the courts to proclaim an emergency.

Finally, what does the *Anti-Inflation* case indicate about the future of judicial review in Canada? First, I think it is likely that the frequency with which constitutional issues are brought before the court will increase rather than decrease. The Supreme Court's almost perfect record in upholding federal laws will not be a serious deterrent to those who wish to challenge federal legislation. For provincial governments, and even more, for private interest groups, constitutional litigation is just one weapon that can be used to fight a larger campaign. Even the Parti Quebecois, for instance, although it has no respect for the Supreme Court as an institution of national government, contemplates constitutional litigation as a tactic in its larger constitutional warfare. If it loses, it can portray the decision as yet further evidence of the hostility of federal institutions to Quebec's interests; if it wins this would vindicate the charge that the federal government is encroaching on areas of provincial jurisdiction. But private individuals and groups may be even likely to provoke constitutional litigation. The rapid growth of the legal profession, more generous rules of standing, the influence of the American example and the new jurisdictional rules under which the Supreme Court's docket is shaped primarily by judicial selection of nationally important cases, all of these factors are likely to generate more privately-initiated constitutional cases. And, as labour's approach to the *Anti-Inflation* case indicates, when these pressure groups litigate constitutional issues they may be inclined to let the constitutional chips fall where they may for the sake of pursuing some short-run advantage on an immediate policy issue.

So the Supreme Court's decision in this case will not deter resort to judicial review in the future. Nor, despite the scant attention given Professor Lipsey's brief, should future litigants in constitutional cases be deterred from supporting their arguments with this kind of social science evidence. None of the judges denied that Professor Lipsey's brief was admissible evidence, and the Chief Justice explicitly acknowledged its relevancy even though he did not find it completely persuasive. Further, where the question of constitutionality turns on the reasonableness of regarding a situation as an urgent national crisis requiring national legislation, what other than empirical arguments can lawyers who wish to challenge the legislation use? I am not suggesting that there will be a sudden revolution in the Supreme Court's style of jurisprudence, but that we will likely see more lawyers using this type of material in future constitutional cases. One leading constitution scholar has suggested that "... the admission of social science briefs in constitutional cases where legislative facts are in issue ... may prove in the long run to be the most influential point of the case."

On a more fundamental plane, the Court's majority in subscribing to Professor Lederman's approach to peace, order and good government, rather than Professor Laskin's (as he once was), have opted to maintain a more traditional style of opinion-writing. The central concern apparent in this style of reasoning is "distilling the essences" of legal categories and characterizing the subject matter of legislation. It is basically the old game of sticking the legislation in the right pigeon-hole. Most of our judges (and probably, still most of our lawyers) find this a more congenial exercise than reasoning about legislative schemes in terms of the necessary requirements of effective national policy-making.

Judicial decisions based on the majority's approach have the *appearance* of being based on narrow, technical, purely legal considerations. But the preference for this style of jurisprudence is based on larger considerations of constitutional policy. Only Justice Beetz gave a clear expression of the underlying policy reason for rejecting the federal government's first submission that the Anti-Inflation Act should be sustained under peace, order and good government as a matter of inherent national importance. "It is not difficult to speculate," he wrote "as to where this line of reasoning would lead: a fundamental feature of the Constitution, its federal nature, the distribution of powers between Parliament and the provincial legislatures, would disappear not gradually but rapidly." So, for policy reasons, a jurisprudential style which would make policy reasons more transparent, is rejected. As a result, Canadians cannot expect judicial reasoning to add very much to the country's stock of constitutional wisdom. The question remains whether this masking of judicial power is in itself a kind of constitutional wisdom.

10.5

DOES FEDERALISM REVIEW MATTER?
Patrick Monahan

... [T]here appear to be a variety of ways in which governments or individuals can avoid or modify the effect of constraints associated with federalism. Federalism is premised on a theory of the exhaustion of powers; if one government is denied jurisdiction over a particular matter, then the other level of government must necessarily possess such jurisdiction. Accordingly, if the Supreme Court finds that legislation enacted by one level of government is *ultra vires* on federalism grounds, there are a variety of regulatory alternatives still available. First, the other level of government may choose to enact the legislation in substantially the same form. Alternatively, the results of the litigation may be reversed by intergovernmental agreement, in which the "winning" level of government delegates to the "loser" part or all of the disputed jurisdiction. Finally, the "losing" level of government may simply reassert regulation over the activity in question through substituting an alternative policy instrument in place of the one struck down by the Court.

This leads to the following fundamental maxim of Canadian federalism: contrary to repeated judicial pronouncements to the contrary, it is *always* possible to do indirectly what you cannot do directly. The only relevant question is whether the costs of indirection are so high that they outweigh the benefits.

Yet this "fundamental maxim" is less of a final conclusion than an invitation to further inquiry. Specifically, having noted the theoretical availability of regulatory substitutes, to what extent do governments actually employ such substitutes in order to avoid the constraining effects of judicial interpretations? The remainder of this chapter is an attempt to offer a general and tentative answer to that important question. I begin by setting out a series of principles which must underpin analysis of this issue. I then apply and test these principles through two case studies of the interaction of government and the judiciary. The focus of these case studies is the series of trade and commerce cases decided by the Supreme Court in the late 1970s and analyzed in Chapter 9. As we observed in Chapter 9, the reasoning in many of these decisions was weak; the Court seemed to have a rather poor understanding of the actual purpose and effect of the legislation being considered. Yet, what we will discover in this chapter is that these decisions appear to have had a very modest impact on the formulation of public policy. Governments have

Politics and the Constitution: The Charter, Federalism and the Supreme Court of Canada (Toronto, ON: Carswell Legal Publications, 1987), from pages 224–240.

been able to overcome the effects of these adverse judicial rulings through intergovernmental agreement or by enacting alternative legislation. Based on the analysis developed in these case studies, I attempt to draw out a series of more general conclusions regarding the instrumental impact of federalism adjudication. ...

2. Federal Product Regulation: The Aftermath of *Dominion Stores* and *Labatt Breweries of Canada Ltd.*

In *R. v. Dominion Stores Ltd. (1980) and Labatt Breweries of Canada Ltd. v. A.-G. Canada (1980)* the Supreme Court had limited federal power to provide for national product standards. In *Dominion Stores*, the Court had ruled that a scheme prescribing grade names and standards associated with those names could not be applied to intraprovincial traders. In *Labatt*, the Court had struck down s. 6 of the Food and Drugs Act, ruling that s. 6 was an impermissible attempt to regulate local trade. Both of these decisions were widely criticized by commentators at the time, who saw the rulings as threatening national product standards and thus as promoting increased consumer ignorance and confusion in the market.

Today, close to a decade after the rulings in these cases, the chaos and confusion which these commentators feared has failed to materialize. This is not to suggest that consumers are now able to obtain accurate and full information on all the products they buy. The point is simply that the feared balkanization of the Canadian market, in which individual provinces would prescribe different standards and specifications for goods sold there, has not developed. There has been little complaint from federal policy-makers about the deterioration of national product standards or calls for urgent legislative or constitutional reform. Neither of the statutes which was the subject of litigation has been amended. In short, the cases appear to have had little or no impact on the manner in which goods are packaged and sold in Canada or on the agenda of public policy-makers. How can we account for the negligible impact of the cases, particularly in light of the predictions of dire consequences which were heard in the months immediately following the release of the decisions?

Consider first the aftermath of the *Dominion Stores* case. The key to understanding the limited impact of this case is the long history of constitutional litigation dealing with the regulation of farm products. Federal-provincial attempts to regulate the marketing of farm products date back to the mid-1930s. The Privy Council had determined that the regulation of intraprovincial trade in natural products was a provincial responsibility, while only Parliament could regulate interprovincial and international trade. The two levels of government had overcome this division of responsibility through interprovincial bargaining and agreement. The relevant standards would be set through federal-provincial agreement; each province would then implement the agreement for products traded locally, while the federal government would enact legislation covering interprovincial and international trade. In this way a common set of product standards would apply across the country, notwithstanding the constitutional division of responsibility.

This system of dovetailing legislation was in place long before the litigation involving *Dominion Stores*. Part II of the Canada Agricultural Products Standards Act established a compulsory scheme of grade names and standards for products moving in interprovincial and export trade. The same set of grade names and standards applied to local traders in Ontario pursuant to the [Ontario]Farm Products Grades and Sales Act. The validity of these provisions was not at issue in the appeal. What was challenged was Part I of the federal legislation, which sought to establish a voluntary system of grade names and standards for products traded locally. It was this voluntary system of grade names which was ruled unconstitutional by the Court.

This legislative background makes it easy to understand why the decision in *Dominion Stores* has had minimal impact on the regulation of natural products. Notwithstanding the Court's ruling, the same set of natural product standards remains validly in force. The only difference is that prosecutions must be brought under Part II of the federal Act or the relevant provincial legislation, depending upon the origin of the product in question. The consequence is that it will be necessary for investigators to obtain information on the origin of the product before laying a charge. But there is no reason in principle why such information could not be obtained.

Perhaps the greatest irony of the case is that there was evidence that the apples which were the subject of the charge in *Dominion Stores* had been traded interprovincially. Thus, although the charge was laid under Part I of the federal Act, the investigators could have proceeded under Part II, which contained compulsory standards for interprovincial traders. Had this latter option been chosen, there would have been no constitutional defence to the charge and the only issue would have been whether the apples complied with the relevant standard. Thus, the constitutional issue was manufactured by a discretionary decision to proceed under Part I of the legislation.

In short, the *Dominion Stores* case was little more than a footnote to the long history of constitutional litigation involving the marketing of farm products. The federal and provincial governments had previously agreed on a package of dovetailing legislation establishing a common set of regulatory standards. The *Dominion Stores* case did not call into question the validity of that federal-provincial arrangement. The only effect of the case was to prevent the federal government from applying a "voluntary" scheme of regulation to products traded locally. Given the continued consensus between federal and provincial governments over the relevant standards to be applied in this area, the impact of the decision has been minimal.

There was no similar set of dovetailing federal-provincial legislation in the *Labatt Breweries* case. Section 6 of the federal Food and Drugs Act purported to set down national standards for all food products, without distinguishing whether they were traded locally or interprovincially. There was no comparable provincial legislation in place. Thus, one might have expected that the Court's ruling that s. 6 was *ultra vires* to have had a fairly significant impact on food products standards. Yet this impact has yet to materialize. In general, food products sold in Canada continue to meet the standards set down in the federal legislation. Federal officials responsible for compliance with the so-called "food recipe" standards report very few violations in the wake of the *Labatt Breweries* case.

What is the explanation for this continued compliance with standards which are apparently unenforceable? An explanation which appears initially plausible is based on the observation that the food industry has an interest in a common set of food standards. A common set of standards enables the industry to signal to consumers the varying nature and quality of products which may otherwise appear indistinguishable. Consider the sale of "ground beef" as an illustration of this signalling function. The quality of ground beef varies according to the fat content of the meat, yet fat content cannot be determined through visual inspection. The solution is to establish different grades of ground beef according to the fat content of the meat (i.e., "lean," "medium" or "regular") and to package and sell the meat accordingly. The industry has a clear interest in establishing such standards since they can then differentiate between and charge appropriate prices for products which appear indistinguishable through visual inspection. Consumers also have an interest in such standards since they obtain accurate information about the quality of the product they are buying and (in the example above) they are given a choice between three grades of ground beef rather than one.

Given the clear consumer and industry interest in establishing labelling standards, one might expect such standards to arise spontaneously in a market. The reason why this does not occur is because of the difficulty in policing compliance with the standards. Once a product standard is established, there is an immediate incentive to attempt to substitute a lower quality product in place of one of higher quality. To return to the ground beef example, once three grades of ground beef have been established, there is an incentive to market "regular" ground beef as either "medium" or "lean" beef and charge a higher price for the product. This incentive to cheat is all the more powerful because consumers are unable to distinguish the quality of the product through visual inspection. The way out of this dilemma is to establish the product standards through legislation. If the product standards are established and enforced by the state, cheaters can be identified and prosecuted. State intervention makes possible the efficiency gains associated with product standards.

This analysis, far from explaining the continued voluntary compliance with the food standards, makes such compliance all the more curious. Given the inability of the federal government to enforce compliance with the standards, why has there not been a dramatic increase in the numbers of sellers seeking to substitute lower quality products in place of higher quality ones?

There are undoubtedly a number of factors which have contributed to the absence of widespread violations of the Act. First, the product standards were already in place and had become widely accepted by the industry as being in its own best interest. Thus, it is hardly surprising that the bulk of the industry would continue to support the product standards even after the result in *Labatt Breweries*. Second, the federal government still possesses considerable authority to enforce the product standards. Since the *Labatt Breweries* litigation, federal officials have sought to enforce the product standards through prosecutions under s. 5 of the Food and Drugs Act, which provides:

> 5. (1) No person shall label, package, treat, process, sell or advertise any food in a manner that is false, misleading or deceptive or is likely to create an erroneous impression regarding its character, value, quantity, composition, merit or safety.

It is arguable that prosecutions under s. 5 are somewhat more difficult than prosecutions under s. 6. Under s. 6, the relevant test was whether an article was "likely to be mistaken" for food for which a standard had been prescribed under the regulations. If it was likely to be mistaken for such food, than it had to comply with the applicable standard. In contrast, s. 5(1) makes it an offence to package food in a manner that is "false, misleading or deceptive or is likely to create an erroneous impression regarding its character." . . . It is arguable that the standard under s. 5 is somewhat higher, since there is an obligation to demonstrate that the labelling of the food is "misleading": it may be, for example, that food has not been labelled in accordance with the regulations, but that it cannot be demonstrated that this improper labelling was "false, misleading or deceptive."

Yet, on further examination, it is apparent that there are also certain broad similarities between the standards established under ss. 5 and 6. Section 6 itself did not directly require compliance with the food standards in the regulations. It was also necessary to demonstrate a "misleading" of the public in order to prosecute under s. 6; the offence in s. 6 was one of packaging, selling or advertising food "in such a manner that it is likely to be mistaken" for food subject to the regulations. Nor was this "misleading" element of the offence a mere *pro forma* requirement. It should be recalled that the trial judge in the *Labatt Breweries* case had found that "the plaintiff's Special Lite beverage ("food") has not been labelled, packaged or advertised in such a manner that it is likely to be mistaken for the beverage "light beer" ("food"). Thus, even though Labatt's Special Lite did not comply with the standard for "light beer," the trial judge was prepared to grant a declaration that there had not been a violation of s. 6 of the Act. In short, while s. 5 of the Act does not permit direct enforcement of the standards in the regulations, neither did s. 6. Instead, both sections depend on some demonstration that there has been a misleading of the public.

This leads to the obvious question: is s. 5 of the Act also vulnerable to a constitutional challenge? While the answer is not altogether free from doubt, it would appear that s. 5 of the Act could be defended as an exercise of Parliament's jurisdiction over "criminal law." The criminal law power has always included the authority to proscribe trade practices contrary to the interest of the community such as misleading, false or deceptive advertising. There is a strong argument to the effect that s. 5 is a valid exercise of that power.

In short, while the federal government can no longer utilize s. 6 in order to enforce the food product standards, it has a relatively close regulatory substitute in s. 5. Moreover, there is an alternative basis for directly and conclusively enforcing the standards set out in the Food and Drugs Act. This alternative is to seek the cooperation of the provinces and to establish a framework similar to that already in place for natural products. Under such a scheme, Parliament could enact food product standards for goods moving in interprovincial and export trade. The provinces would enact parallel standards for goods produced and traded locally. In this way, a common set of food product standards would be binding and enforceable throughout Canada. Federal-provincial negotiations aimed at establishing such a scheme are underway and the federal government expects to introduce legislation setting standards for interprovincial and export trade before the next election.

In summary, neither *Dominion Stores* nor *Labatt Breweries* has had any significant impact on the manner in which goods are marketed or on government policy. The impact of the *Dominion Stores* litigation was minimal due to the existence of dovetailing federal and provincial legislation regulating natural products. As for *Labatt Breweries*, the industry has continued to voluntarily comply with the food recipe standards, notwithstanding the outcome of the litigation. Over the longer term, there are a number of alternative regulatory instruments which can be utilized in order to ensure appropriate compliance with the standards. Neither case seems to have made a great deal of difference for the politics of Canadian federalism.

3. Natural Resource Regulation:
The Aftermath of *CIGOL* and *Central Canada*

In the late 1970s, the Supreme Court appeared to have dealt a body blow to provincial attempts to regulate the natural resource industry. In *CIGOL* (1979), the Court struck down a provincial tax designed to capture the dramatic increase in oil prices resulting from the 1973 Middle East war. In *Central Canada Potash* (1979), the Court ruled invalid a provincial scheme establishing quotas and minimum prices for the production of potash in Saskatchewan. There were howls of protest from the western provinces following these decisions. The provinces complained that fundamental issues of federal-provincial politics were being resolved by an institution "not in the mainstream of the political process." Various premiers claimed that the Supreme Court was "biased" in favour of the federal government and that the method of appointment to the Court had to be changed to allow for provincial participation.

A decade after these controversial decisions, constitutional questions no longer seem to feature in discussions of the energy issue. The public policy agenda has become preoccupied with the global over-supply of oil and the resultant drop in world oil prices. The constraints facing contemporary Canadian governments in the energy field are constraints arising from market forces, rather than from the constitutional jurisprudence of the Supreme Court. Indeed, Quebec, rather than the West, has become the principal advocate of Supreme Court reform. Once again, the obvious question: how did provincial governments, particularly those in the West, manage to overcome the constitutional obstacles which seemed so pressing and problematic less than a decade ago?

Consider first the aftermath and provincial response to the *CIGOL* case. The immediate priority of the province of Saskatchewan was to ensure that it would not have to refund the $500 million collected under the invalid production tax. The government achieved this result by levying an income tax on the oil industry, retroactive to December 31, 1973. This alternative form of tax was constitutionally valid, since income taxes are direct taxes and within the provincial taxing power under s. 92(2) of the BNA Act. The $500 million previously collected by the government under the invalid production tax was to be set off against the liability arising from the income tax. The legislation also imposed limits on the deductability of expenses for the purpose of calculating liability for tax.

This income tax allowed the government to achieve its main goal, which was to ensure that the increase in energy rents resulting from the oil crisis remained in Saskatchewan. But income taxes are more complex and costly to administer than production taxes. In order to levy an income tax there must be a calculation of the "profit" that is subject to tax; a production tax can be levied on the more straightforward basis of the bare number of units produced or sold. Moreover, an income tax presents opportunities and incentive for tax avoidance behaviour by those subject to the tax. Tax avoidance is a marginal consideration in the administration of a production tax. This means that, although the income tax was an adequate regulatory substitute for the production tax struck down in *CIGOL*, it was not a perfect substitute. The income tax was more costly to the government, in terms of the additional resources which had to be committed to enforcement. The income tax also carried with it a social cost — the cost of the resources invested in socially unproductive tax avoidance behaviour by the industry.

Having imposed an income tax as an interim measure, the province continued to press for some form of constitutional amendment to remedy fully its difficulty. Fortuitously for Saskatchewan, by 1981 the federal government badly needed western support for its constitutional reform package. In an attempt to gather support, the federal government agreed to amend s. 92 of the BNA Act, so as to broaden provincial powers over the natural resource sector. The new s. 92(a) of the Act. enacted as part of the constitutional reform package by Westminster in 1982, granted provinces power to make "laws in relation to the raising of money by any mode or system of taxation in respect of . . . non-renewable natural resources. . . ." This amendment eliminated the requirement that a provincial tax be "direct" rather than "indirect."

The constitutional amendment has enabled the province of Saskatchewan to enact the Freehold Oil and Gas Production Tax Act, 1982 as well as the Mineral Taxation Act, 1983. The first Act provides for a production tax on the freehold oil and gas produced in the province; the second Act levies a production tax on the production of specified minerals. In short, the province has now fully regained the constitutional ground it lost in *CIGOL*.

What assessment can be offered of the instrumental impact of the Court's decision? First, it is clear that the decision was not nearly as crippling to provincial regulatory power as had been suggested initially. The province was able to replace immediately the invalid production tax with an income tax, thereby avoiding any significant revenue loss. At the same time, there were nontrivial costs associated with the imposition of an income tax in place of a production tax. In short, while the decision was not the disaster which some had feared, neither was it wholly irrelevant to the formulation of provincial energy policy.

Second, the fact that the result in the case was later reversed by constitutional amendment does not mean that the litigation was thereby rendered meaningless. Because the rule announced by the Court had to some extent limited provincial power, the federal government had been provided with an important constitutional bargaining chip. The federal government was able to play that chip when it was faced with widespread opposition to its constitutional proposals. Had the *CIGOL* litigation been decided the other way, the federal government would have had to have offered some other constitutional concession in order to achieve the same result.

There is a final point that needs to be emphasized, relating to the nature of the federal-provincial bargaining surrounding this issue. The energy issue in the late 1970s and early 1980s was framed and understood in explicitly regional terms, with the resource-rich provinces being pitted against consuming provinces. Federal-provincial bargaining on such a regionally-sensitive issue requires the active involvement of the highest political levels of the respective governments. Further, agreement is impossible without each side being seen to offer significant political concessions to the other. In contrast, the issues arising from the *Dominion Stores* and *Labatt Breweries* litigation have not been perceived as explicitly regional issues. Federal-provincial bargaining on food product standards, for example, is understood as an issue which seems to affect all regions of the country in roughly equal fashion. There are a number of consequences which flow from this difference. First, it is possible to achieve federal-provincial consensus on such "technical" issues without the active involvement of the highest political levels. Second, because the negotiations can be framed in technical rather than political terms, there is no necessity for each side to be seen to be offering "concessions" to the other. These distinctions are important in terms of predicting those cases in which federal-provincial bargaining is likely to be successful; I will return to them in the final section of this chapter.

What of the response to the Supreme Court's decision in the *Central Canada* case? As with *CIGOL*, the ultimate impact on provincial regulatory power was much less severe than had been feared initially. In this case, however, the circumstances which produced this result were largely fortuitous. The provincial regulatory scheme had been enacted in the late 1960s, in response to a serious excess of supply and a drop in the world price of potash. By the time the Supreme Court decision in the case was handed down in 1978, the market for potash had changed. Due in part to the success of the provincial scheme limiting production and fixing prices, the market had stabilized. The industry no longer needed production quotas or price-fixing in order to survive. Thus, the Court's ruling that the provincial scheme was unconstitutional had no appreciable impact on the market or the provincial economy.

Potash producers in Saskatchewan during this period had also been contemplating a constitutional challenge to potash "prorationing fees," levied under the Potash Proration Fees Regulations, 1972. The potash producers had laid the groundwork for this challenge by successfully arguing that a province had to refund money collected under an unconstitutional law. However, in 1979 the producers abandoned their constitutional challenge against the prorationing fees by entering into the Potash Resource Payment Agreement, 1979. Under this agreement, the producers agreed to abandon their constitutional challenges and to render payments to the province in accordance with a fixed schedule. In return, the province agreed not to levy any further proration fees.

It is easy to identify the gains each party obtained from this agreement. The province obtained a guaranteed series of payments from the industry, thus avoiding the uncertainty associated with the pending constitutional challenges. The industry gained the certainty of knowing in advance what rate of tax it would have to pay to the province, avoiding the possibility of sudden, unexpected increases in their tax liability. By entering into this agreement, both parties purchased certainty about the intentions and future behaviour of the other.

In short, by the late 1970s, constitutional constraints had faded in significance in the relationship between the province of Saskatchewan and the potash industry. This situation was in part a product of the market conditions prevailing at the time, which made strict provincial regulation unnecessary. It was also due to the fact that the province and the industry had purchased constitutional peace through the Potash Resource Payment Agreement. The enactment of s. 92(a) of the Constitution Act, 1867 served to confirm provincial power to regulate the potash industry. Section 92(a) grants the province power to enact laws in relation to the management and conservation of non-renewable natural resources. This suggests that, should the market for potash collapse in the future, the province will have ample constitutional authority to restore stability to the market.

4. Conclusion: The Impact of Constitutional Constraint

What general conclusions can be drawn from these case studies of the impact of constitutional adjudication on Canadian government? The first conclusion is obvious: the outcomes of constitutional cases are much less determinative of public policy than is often supposed by lawyers and legal scholars. In each of the cases examined, the constitutional result was initially seen as a significant setback to the losing government. Yet in each instance, the governments concerned have been able to achieve the same regulatory goals through alternative instruments. It must be conceded that in certain instances this conclusion had resulted largely from market forces rather than from the conscious intervention of government. The point remains that there was no instance in which the constitutional rule announced by the Court determined the eventual behaviour of the parties.

This does not mean that constitutional constraints are wholly illusory. As I have emphasized throughout this chapter, often the only means of overcoming a constitutional constraint is through intergovernmental agreement: in such instances, the constitutional decision fixes the initial bargaining position of the parties. In other instances, the alternative regulatory instrument is an imperfect substitute for the device struck down by the Court. The point is simply that constitutional reasons will rarely constitute conclusive reasons against undertaking particular public policies. Federalism does not create regulatory vacuums. There will inevitably be a variety of regulatory instruments or legal arrangements which could be utilized in order to achieve a given policy goal. Constitutional reasons may operate so as to rule out the use of some of those regulatory instruments or legal arrangements. But constitutional constraints will rarely make all of the possible instruments off limits. In this sense, constitutional constraints must be seen in relativistic terms. They operate so as to increase the costs associated with achieving policy goals, forcing government to employ alternative regulatory instruments or else to coordinate efforts with those of other levels of government. Policy-makers are then faced with a choice; either bear the increased costs associated with the alternative instrument or abandon the goal. Constitutional constraints help to shape the legislative demand curve.

10.6

RE CONSTITUTION OF CANADA, 1981:

THE *PATRIATION REFERENCE*
Michael Mandel

This excerpt is reprinted as Reading 2.4.

10.7

KEY TERMS

Concepts

federalism
judicial review
disallowance (s.56)
reservation (s.90)
Peace, Order, and good Government
residual power
emergency doctrine
inherent national importance test
delegation via intergovernmental agreement
regulatory substitute
dovetailing federal-provincial legislation
interpretivist (or textual) approach to constitutional interpretation
noninterpretivist (or "living tree") approach to constitutional interpretation

Institutions, Events, and Documents

Judicial Committee of the Privy Council (1833)
Colonial Laws Validity Act (1865)
Constitution Act, ss. 91 and 92 (1867)
Supreme Court Act (1875)
The Persons Case (1928)
Statute of Westminster (1931)
The Labour Conventions Case (1937)
O'Connor Report (1939)
Amendments to Supreme Court Act (1949)
Anti-Inflation Reference (1976)
R. v. Dominion Stores Ltd. (1980)
Labatt Breweries v. A.-G. Canada (1980)
CIGOL v. Saskatchewan (1977)
Central Canada Potash Co. v. Saskatchewan (1979)

11
Judicial Review and Civil Liberties

The practice of judicial review is unique to liberal democratic nations. The grounding principles of liberal democracy posit that good government is "limited government," and a written constitution enforced by judicial review is a means to that end. While all instances of judicial review are found in liberal democracies, not all liberal democracies use judicial review. Great Britain is certainly a liberal democracy, but it does not have a "written constitution," and consequently English judges do not exercise judicial review. Even some democracies with a written constitution—Belgium, Finland, Luxembourg, Netherlands and Switzerland—deny the power of judicial review to their high courts.[1]

The absence of a written constitution and judicial review does not mean that the government of Great Britain is "unlimited." The doctrine of parliamentary sovereignty notwithstanding, Dicey made it clear that political conventions of self-restraint and fair play, reinforced by public opinion, operate to protect the same fundamental freedoms of the English as judicial review of the U.S. Bill of Rights does for Americans. Dicey clearly preferred the flexibility of an "unwritten constitution" and vesting primary responsibility for the preservation of liberty in an elected, accountable, representative legislature such as Parliament. But he did not rule out the possibility of codifying the fundamental freedoms of the English people. After enumerating the fundamental components of the "rule of law"—"the right to personal freedom; the right to freedom of discussion; the right of public meeting; the use of martial law; the rights and duties of the army; the collection and expenditure of the public revenue; and the responsibility of ministers"—Dicey concluded:

> If at some future day the law of the constitution should be codified, each of the topics I have mentioned would be dealt with by the sections of the code.

In adopting the Charter of Rights and Freedoms in 1982, Canada did what Dicey merely speculated about some 100 years earlier—to entrench

[1] Arend Lijphart, *Democracies: Patterns of Majoritarian and Consensus Government in Twenty-One Countries* (New Haven, CT: Yale University Press, 1984), p. 193.

in a written constitution the rights and freedoms that had previously been preserved through the British-style tradition of an "unwritten constitution." The preamble of the Constitution Act, 1867, declares that Canada shall have "a Constitution similar in Principle to that of the United Kingdom." This declaration meant not just the Westminster system of parliamentary democracy, but also the entire "unwritten constitution" that accompanied it. During its first 93 years Canada indeed had such a constitution, with the one important exception of federalism. In 1960, the Diefenbaker government enacted the Canadian Bill of Rights, thus beginning the transition away from the British approach to the protection of civil liberties toward the American approach. Twenty-two years later, the Trudeau government's enactment of the Charter of Rights completed this transition. Parliamentary supremacy was replaced by constitutional supremacy, enforced by judicial review—or nearly replaced. The last minute compromise leading to the section 33 "legislative override" power preserved a qualified form of parliamentary supremacy.

Civil Liberties and the Courts prior to 1960

From Confederation until 1960, judicial protection of civil liberties was limited to two techniques. The first was the "interpretive avoidance" approach inherited from British judges.[2] When interpreting a statute of Parliament or one of the provinces, the courts always assumed that the legislature intended to respect traditional rights and liberties. If a statute was open to two interpretations, one of which infringed a right or freedom, judges would exercise their discretion to choose the other interpretation. This approach is consistent with parliamentary supremacy, in that the courts do not overrule the legislature by declaring statutes "of no force or effect." "Interpretive avoidance" simply sends a message to parliamentary lawmakers that until they indicate otherwise, by redrafting the statute in more explicit language, the courts will interpret it as indicated. While a determined majority in Parliament could easily override such judicial attempts at protecting civil liberties, in practice this was rare. The *Roncarelli* case (Reading 11.3) and the *Boucher* case (Reading 11.4) are both important examples of the Canadian judiciary's use of the "interpretive avoidance" technique to protect the traditional freedoms of individual Canadians.

The second method of judicial protection of civil liberties prior to 1960 was distinctively Canadian, the use of federalism limitations. Using this "power allocation" method, Canadian appeal court judges ruled intem-

---

[2] The three related approaches of interpretive avoidance, power allocation, and power denial are elaborated by E.E. Dais, "Judicial Supremacy in Canada in Comparative Perspective: A Critical Analysis of *Drybones*" (Paper presented at the Annual Meeting of the Canadian Political Science Association, June 8, 1971).

perate or discriminatory provincial policies *ultra vires* on section 91–92 grounds, when the real issue appeared to be one of civil liberties. For example, in 1938 the Supreme Court struck down the euphemistically titled Accurate News and Information Act, which was an attempt by the Alberta Social Credit government to muzzle newspaper criticism of its economic policies. The Supreme Court ruled that this was legislation in relation to criminal law, and therefore beyond the legislative jurisdiction of any province.[3] Another well-known example of this technique was the 1953 case of *Saumur v. Quebec*.[4] This was one of a series of Jehovah's Witnesses' cases from Quebec, where both provincial and municipal governments were restricting the controversial religious sect. In this instance Quebec City had passed a bylaw prohibiting the distribution of pamphlets in the streets without permission of the Chief of Police. Saumur and many other Jehovah's Witnesses were arrested for violating this bylaw. While normally this type of legislation is clearly within the section 92 powers of the provinces, the punitive intentions behind it were equally clear. In striking down the Quebec bylaw, a number of Supreme Court judges argued that it was legislation in relation to religious freedom, and that this was denied to the provinces either by section 91 (criminal law) or section 93 (denominational rights) of the Constitution Act.

While the "power allocation" approach was successfully used on a variety of occasions to protect civil liberties, there were several drawbacks to this approach. First, whatever powers were denied to provincial governments were logically conceded to the federal government. While this had the disturbing implication that the federal government was free to enact the illiberal policies of the provinces, this never proved to be a practical problem. A more serious objection to this approach was that it forced the judges to use the language of federalism when dealing with the logic of civil liberties. This surreptitious method of reasoning tended to confuse the jurisprudence of both federalism and civil liberties.

There is a third strand of pre-Bill of Rights civil liberties jurisprudence that deserves mention, even though it was never accepted by a Supreme Court majority. Known as the "implied Bill of Rights" approach, it argues that the provisions of the preamble of the Constitution Act—that Canada shall have "a Constitution similar in Principle to that of the United Kingdom"—imported into Canada the traditional rights and freedoms protected by Britain's "unwritten constitution." The previously cited passages from Dicey show the plausibility of this argument. In the *Alberta Press Case*, Justice Duff argued that "the right of public debate" was inherent in a parliamentary system, and that the preamble provided sufficient grounds

---

[3] *Reference re Alberta Statutes*, [1938] S.C.R. 100, more commonly known as the *Alberta Press Case*.

[4] [1953] 2 S.C.R. 299.

to declare the Alberta Press bill inoperative. Similarly in the *Saumur* case Justices Rand, Kellock, and Locke said that the preamble implicitly protected "freedom of religion" from both levels of government. The strength of this approach lies in its correct recognition of the civil liberties dimension of the "unwritten constitution" inherited from Great Britain. But this is also its weakness, since British judges never pretended to have the authority to enforce these freedoms directly against Parliament. It was widely accepted (at least until the Supreme Court of Canada's ruling in the *Patriation Reference*) that constitutional custom and convention could not be judicially recognized or enforced, and the strength of this tradition prevented the "implied Bill of Rights" approach from gaining any general acceptance.

Civil Liberties and the Courts under the 1960 Bill of Rights

In the aftermath of the Second World War, growing awareness of the Stalinist and Nazi atrocities of the preceding decades alarmed Western democracies about the fragile nature of human rights and civil liberties in the mass societies of the twentieth century. This concern was shared by Canadian leaders, who were also troubled by their own harsh treatment of Japanese Canadians during the war years, and the Quebec government's harassment of the Jehovah's Witnesses. After a decade of committee hearings and public discussion, the Diefenbaker government adopted the Canadian Bill of Rights in 1960. (See Appendix 2)

The 1960 Bill of Rights took the form of a statute of Parliament, not an amendment to the Constitution Act. It also applied only to the federal government. The provinces would not consent to additional restrictions on their legislative powers, and Ottawa lacked the authority to impose them unilaterally.

From the start the Bill of Rights was swamped by problems of interpretation. These problems stemmed principally from its legal status as an ordinary statute and the ambiguous wording of its second section. Canadian judges, including those on the Supreme Court, could not agree on what function the Bill of Rights assigned to the courts. Some argued that the Bill of Rights conferred new authority on the courts to declare Parliamentary statutes "of no force or effect," if they conflicted with enumerated rights. According to this interpretation, the Bill of Rights armed the Canadian courts with an American-style "power denial" function. Others thought that the Bill of Rights was essentially a canon of statutory interpretation, a codification of the traditional "interpretive avoidance" method. They pointed to the ambiguous wording of section 2, and the statutory as opposed to constitutional status of the Bill. Implicit in this position was the feeling that if Parliament had intended to terminate or substantially modify the tradition of parliamentary sovereignty in Canada, it would have said so in a much clearer manner.

The Supreme Court's landmark decision in the 1969 *Drybones* case put an end to this particular problem.[5] A majority of the Court took the position that the Bill of Rights did confer authority on the judges to declare offending statutes inoperative. The Court ruled that section 94(b) of the Indian Act denied Drybones his rights to "equality before the law," because it treated him more harshly for public intoxication than other Canadians would have been treated for the same offence, simply because he was an Indian. The *Drybones* decision was hailed as a major development in Canadian constitutional evolution. It seemed to signify an important new restraint on the tradition of parliamentary supremacy and an important new role for the Canadian judiciary in policing Bill of Rights violations.

The high expectations created by *Drybones* were short-lived. Subsequent Supreme Court decisions indicated that the judges were still inclined to defer to Parliament's judgment on substantive issues of criminal procedure. This trend culminated in the Supreme Court's 1974 decision of the *Lavell* and *Bedard* cases.[6] Lavell and Bedard were Indian women who had lost their Indian status pursuant to section 12(1)(b) of the Indian Act. This section provides that Indian women who marry non-Indians lose their status, but no similar disability is imposed on Indian men who marry non-Indians. Lavell and Bedard argued that this violated their right to "equality before the law," since it discriminated against them on the basis of their sex. Based on the *Drybones* precedent, which appeared to prohibit discrimination in the laws based on explicitly prohibited categories such as race and sex, their case seemed very strong. The Supreme Court surprised almost everyone by finding otherwise. A majority of the Court ruled that the right to "equality before the law" meant "equality in the application and administration of the laws." Since there was no question that section 12(1)(b) had been applied to Lavell and Bedard the same as it was applied to all other Indian women, there was no violation of the Bill of Rights. The dissenting justices protested the apparent inconsistency of this interpretation with the *Drybones* precedent, but to no avail.

Civil Liberties and the Courts under the 1982 Charter of Rights

By the late 1970s, Prime Minister Trudeau and his Liberal party were increasingly interested in a constitutionally entrenched bill of rights as a potential "nation-building" device to counter the growing conflict in federal-provincial relations. Trudeau had endorsed the idea of a constitutionally entrenched bill of rights as early as 1967. He argued that a

---

[5] *The Queen v. Drybones*, [1970] S.C.R. 282. Reprinted in the first edition of this book.

[6] *Attorney-General of Canada v. Lavell and Bedard*, [1974] 1 S.C.R. 1349. Reprinted in the first edition of this book.

constitutional bill of rights would enhance national unity by emphasizing what Canadians hold in common—citizenship—now to be defined by a common set of rights against both levels of government.[7] Initially there was no political market for Trudeau's idea. The attachment of Canadian political and legal elites to the tradition of parliamentary supremacy and provincial suspicions of a centralist court were too strong. (Interestingly, Trudeau tried to allay provincial fears by suggesting that Ottawa would be willing to abolish the federal powers of disallowance and reservation in return for provincial support for a bill of rights.) But in the years following the *Lavell and Bedard* (1974) and *Morgentaler* (1975) decisions, feminists and civil libertarian groups became disillusioned with the 1960 Bill of Rights as an effective legal instrument to achieve the kinds of judge-led policy reforms that they observed in the United States and wanted to emulate in Canada. They were attracted to Trudeau's proposals for a new, stronger and broader rights document. Out of these seemingly diverse interests was born the political coalition responsible for the adoption of the Charter of Rights and Freedoms in 1982. (See Appendix 3)

The Charter was a central part of the package of constitutional reforms adopted in 1982, and was the product of an extended process of intergovernmental and interest group politics. The Charter is best understood as a compromise between the advocates and opponents of a greater role for the courts in Canadian politics and policy-making. The Liberal party-feminist-libertarian coalition succeeded in strengthening the role of the courts under the Charter in three specific ways, relative to the 1960 Bill of Rights. First and foremost, the Charter applies to both levels of government, provincial and federal. Second, the Charter is constitutionally entrenched, not just a statute as the Bill of Rights was. Third, the Charter explicitly authorizes the judges to review legislation for violations of enumerated rights (s. 24(1)), and to declare "any law that is inconsistent with the provisions of the Constitution . . . of no force or effect." (s. 52)

The opponents of too great a role for the judges extracted two concessions from the government in return for their support. The first is the "reasonable limitations" clause of section 1, which makes explicit what was already understood to be implicit—that none of the enumerated rights are absolute. The second and more important concession is the section 33 "legislative override," which essentially allows either level of government to "veto" a judicial decision to which they object, if it is based on the fundamental freedoms (s. 2), legal rights (ss. 7-14), or equality rights (s. 15) sections of the Charter. This "legislative review of judicial review," as Russell labels it, is important, because it preserves the principle of parliamentary sovereignty, albeit in a modified form. (See the debate over section 33 in Readings 13.3 and 13.4.)

---

[7] See Pierre Elliot Trudeau, "A Constitutional Declaration of Rights," *Federalism and the French Canadians* (Toronto, ON: MacMillan, 1968), p. 52. Reprinted in the first edition of this book.

The Charter basically amplifies the rights that were already protected by the 1960 Bill of Rights, and the latter mainly codified the rights and freedoms that already existed as common law and as constitutional conventions. What was new about both the Bill of Rights and the Charter was the transfer of the decision-making process from representative legislative assemblies to the courts. As Russell correctly pointed out at the time the Charter was being adopted, "[A] charter of rights guarantees not rights but a particular way of making decisions about rights, in which the judicial branch of government has a much more systematic and authoritative role."[8] The net effect of this evolution, Russell observed, is "its tendency to judicialize politics and to politicize the judiciary." (The latter is discussed in chapter 4.)

Whether the adoption of the Charter to Canada's written constitution would be an evolutionary or revolutionary development depended in the end on the interpretation given it by the Supreme Court. The Court's self-restrained and deferential interpretation of the 1960 Bill of Rights effectively prevented that document from having any significant legal or political impact. Would a similar fate meet the Charter?

A study of the Supreme Court's first one hundred Charter decisions (1982–1989) reveals that the answer to this question is a resounding "no." (See Reading 11.5) In its first one hundred Charter decisions, the Supreme Court upheld the rights-claimant in 35 cases. By contrast, litigants won only five of 34 (15%) Bill of Rights cases in the Supreme Court between 1960 and 1982. Just as the Court's unreceptive attitude toward the 1960 Bill of Rights had the effect of discouraging litigation, the Court's activist jurisprudence under the Charter has stimulated litigation. Since 1987 Charter decisions have accounted for roughly 25 percent of the Court's annual caseload. Another indication of the Court's new activism is the number of statutes that it has declared invalid (in whole or in part): 19 by the end of 1989, compared to just one (in *Drybones*) under the 1960 Bill of Rights.

In trying to assess the impact of the Charter on the political process more generally, Charter litigation can be helpfully divided into two broad categories: attempts to turn cases into causes; and the opposite situation where an interest group attempts to turn its cause into a case. It is the latter that is the truly novel element that the Charter has brought to Canadian politics.

The first category involves mostly criminal cases raising legal rights claims, which account for three-quarters of the Supreme Court's Charter decisions (and a slightly higher percentage of Charter litigation in general). These are typically garden-variety criminal cases that occur spontaneously and whose success depends (at least initially) on the

---

[8] Peter H. Russell, "The Effect of the Charter of Rights on the Policy-Making Role of Canadian Courts," *Canadian Public Administration* 25 (1982), p. 1. Reprinted in the first edition of this book.

ingenuity of the client's lawyer. An entrepreneurial lawyer argues that amongst the otherwise routine facts of a client's case is an important principle of procedural fairness that is protected (or should be protected) by a Charter right. Interest groups are rarely involved at the beginning of these cases, and, with the important exception of the Canadian Civil Liberties Association, are less likely to become involved at appeal stages. These cases are usually not overtly political and would have arisen even in the absence of a charter. The introduction of the Charter just means that they are argued (and sometimes decided) differently.

To say that these cases are not overtly political does not mean that they have not had an important policy impact. To repeat, they constitute three-quarters of all the Supreme Court's Charter decisions. Cumulatively, these decisions have reshaped the Canadian criminal process. Prior to the Charter, comparative studies of the criminal process regarded Canada as placing effective crime control ahead of maximizing "due process" rights of the accused.Since the Charter, the Court's decisions in right to counsel, search and seizure, and exclusion of evidence have moved Canada in the direction of a "due process" model of criminal procedure. Indeed, a recent study found that in four areas—waiver of right to counsel, roadside detention for breathalyzer tests, police lineups and involuntary blood samples—the Canadian Court's decisions favoured the accused more than comparable decisions by the American Supreme Court.[9] However, these decisions (with the exception of *Askov* —see Reading 8.4) have not drawn much attention or political controversy. With the exception of the CCLA, some law professors and the criminal law section of the Canadian Bar Association, the legal rights do not have organized constituencies.

The second group of cases, that is, those involving interest groups trying to turn their cause into a case, is numerically much smaller but politically significant. Some have not arisen spontaneously, but represent a conscious effort of an interest group (LEAF or the NCC) or an individual (Dr. Henry Morgentaler or Joe Borowski) to get a policy issue into the courts for judicial determination. Many would not have occurred at all without the Charter. Most involve Charter rights that do have political constituencies—the section 15 equality-seeking groups such as LEAF; the official minority language groups that litigate under section 23 of the Charter; and aboriginal groups pursuing section 35 claims. Some of these cases are part of systematic litigation strategies pursued by Charter groups. These interest groups may be involved either directly as litigants or indirectly as intervenors or financial sponsors. In many of these cases, the groups/litigants have benefited from the Court's own liberalized rules of standing, mootness and intervenor participation as well as government funding.

---

[9] Robert Harvie and Hamar Foster, "Ties That Bind? The Supreme Court of Canada, American Jurisprudence, and the Revision of Canadian Criminal Law Under the Charter," *Osgoode Hall Law Journal* 28, no. 4 (1990), pp. 729–788.

Collectively, it is this group of cases, with their associated interest group activities, that constitute the "judicialization of politics" predicted by Russell in 1982.

Assessment of the impact of "Charter politics" has been mixed. The Charter appears to have wide support, at least at the symbolic level. An extensive survey of elite opinion conducted in 1987 found strong support for the Charter in every political party and every province of Canada.[10] Mass support for the Charter was indicated by the campaign that defeated the 1987 Meech Lake Accord. Leaders of this campaign successfully rallied opposition to the Accord by alleging that the "distinct society" clause threatened to destroy the Charter in Quebec. Since the failure of the Meech Lake Accord, the Charter's popularity in Quebec has plummeted, at least among political elites, and it has become one of the major obstacles to the preservation of national unity. This is bitter irony, when it is recalled that national unity was advanced as one of the chief justifications for adopting the Charter.

Notwithstanding the "Charter problem" with Quebec, political leaders in English Canada have continued to be very supportive of the Charter, at least until Justice Minister Kim Campbell's public address in May, 1992. (See Reading 11.6) While Campbell's reproaches were mild, it marked the first time that a public figure of national stature—not to mention a Justice Minister—has presented a sustained public critique of the dangers of the Charter politics. When Campbell's remarks are placed in context with her government's cancellation of the Court Challenges Program three months earlier, it suggests that unreflective "Charter worship" may have peaked in English Canada.

While the public, the press and the politicans have been very supportive of the Charter, there has been a vociferous and energetic attack on "Charter Worship" within the academic community. Ironically, most of the criticism has come from the left and the right of the political spectrum. The left-wing critics, drawn mainly from old-school social democrats and Marxists, argue that the "judicialized politics" encouraged by the Charter primarily benefits the middle and upper classes by legitimizing the status quo and sapping energy and resources from a class-based politics whose object is the redistribution of wealth. They also argue that that the liberal, individualistic nature of the Charter threatens the communitarian tradition of Canadian politics and delegitimates state intervention to protect community and promote equality.[11]

---

[10] Paul Sniderman, Joseph F. Fletcher, Peter H. Russell, and Phillip Tetlock, "Political Culture and the Problem of Double Standards: Mass and Elite Attitudes Toward Language Rights in the Canadian Charter of Rights and Freedoms," *Canadian Journal of Political Science* 22, no. 2 (June, 1989), pp. 259–284.

[11] The leading lights of the left school of Charter critics are Michael Mandel, *The Charter of Rights and the Legalization of Politics in Canada* (Toronto, ON: Wall-Thomson, 1989);

Conservative critics argue that the Charter is undermining the practice and the habits of representative democracy, especially government by consensus and coalition-building. They also criticize the Charter movement as promoting a jurocracy that unduly privileges the values of neo-liberal special interests. These critics argue that courts lack both the democratic authority and the institutional capacity to fashion public policies designed to promote "equality of results." The neo-liberal agenda of group equality is seen as fostering an oppressive, expensive and inefficient "rights bureaucracy" that benefits primarily itself.[12]

The common denominator of both left- and right-wing Charter critics is the flight from democratic politics that it encourages. Behind the rhetoric of rights both see a reality of judicial policy-making. Debunking rights rhetoric has become a shared project, and the spoof on the "Charter Worshippers' Society" (Reading 11.7) could have been written by partisans of either camp.

To be sure, the Charter also has its academic defenders. David Beatty has written prolifically and enthusiastically about the Charter, chastising the Supreme Court for being too restrained and deferential in its interpretation of the Charter.[13] Richard Sigurdson has presented a critique of "left-wing and right-wing Charterphobia" and his own defence of the Charter. Sigurdson points to a substantial list of policy changes achieved through Charter litigation: "voting rights for people with disabilities, new rules for people found not guilty by reason of insanity, expansion of the due process rights of alleged perpetators or incarcerated persons, decriminalization of abortion, rollbacks of pay equity caps, rights to UIC benefits for those over 65, limited expansion of benefits to same sex couples, abolition of discriminatory 'spouse in the house rules' for social services." Sigurdson argues, "all of these victories for underprivileged individuals and groups enhance, rather than undermine, the democratic

---

Andrew Petter, "Immaculate Deception: The Charter's Hidden Agenda," *The Advocate* 45 (1987), p. 857; and Allan Hutchinson (with Andrew Petter), "Private Rights, Public Wrongs: The Liberal Lie of the Charter," *University of Toronto Law Journal* 38 (1988), pp. 278–297, and "Rights in Conflict: The Dilemma of Charter Legitimacy," *UBC Law Review* 23 (1989), pp. 531–548.

[12] See Rainer Knopff and F.L. Morton, *Charter Politics* (Toronto, ON: Nelson Canada, 1992). Also Rainer Knopff, *Human Rights and Social Technology: The New War on Discrimination* (Ottawa, ON: Carleton University Press, 1989); and F.L. Morton and Rainer Knopff, "The Supreme Court as the Vanguard of the Intelligentsia: Charter Politics as Post-Materialist Politics," in Janet Ajzenstadt, ed., *Canadian Constitutionalism* (Ottawa, ON: Canadian Study of Parliament Group, forthcoming).

[13] See David Beatty, *Talking Heads and the Supremes: The Canadian Production of Constitutional Review* (Toronto, ON: Carswell, 1990).

character of our society. The fact that they were won in the courts rather than in the legislative arena does not make them less democratic."[14]

As Canada enters its second decade in "Charterland," the debate over the Charter is just beginning to warm up. Canada has lost the instinctive confidence in parliamentary democracy that characterized its political life from Confederation until the 1970s and that contributed to the non-development of the 1960 Bill of Rights. The adoption of the Charter, its activist interpretation by the Supreme Court, and the spirited defence of both—all testify to new support for an increased judicial role in government. There is a perception that constitutional questions are *too important to be left with politicians*. Contrast this new attitude with the opposition to the Supreme Court Act in the 1870s on the grounds that constitutional questions were *too important to be decided by unelected judges*. (See Reading 10.1) This change reflects Canadians' growing disillusion with Parliament and democratic politics.[15] The Charter is clearly here to stay. Further debate will not focus on the existence of the Charter, but on corollary issues such as the appointment of judges, public funding of interest group litigation, the use of the section 33 legislative override, and proper modes of interpretation.

Interpretivism and noninterpretivism—the two competing approaches to constitutional interpretation—have different consequences for judicial oversight of the law-making process.[16] Both recognize that constitutional meaning must be flexible enough to keep up with social change, but they draw opposing conclusions about the permissible scope of judicial updating. The interpretivists stress judicial fidelity to the text and the original understanding of that text as illuminated by the framers' intent. New circumstances may require novel applications of that original meaning, but the new meaning may not contradict or overrule the original meaning. The noninterpretivists do not accept this limitation. They minimize the importance of judicial fidelity to original meaning. For the noninterpretivist, the judge's ultimate responsibility is to keep the constitution in tune with the times, not to keep the times in tune with the constitution. In the law of federalism this approach usually supports judicial deference to legislative decisions, but in Charter cases it is used to encourage the judicial expansion of rights and the corollary overruling of legislative choices.

---

[14] Richard Sigurdson, "Left- and Right-Wing Charterphobia in Canada: A Critique of the Critics" (Paper delivered at the Annual Meeting of the Canadian Political Science Association, University of Prince Edward Island, Charlottetown, PEI, May 31, 1992), p. 23.

[15] This trend is not limited to Canada. See Kenneth M. Holland, *Judicial Activism in Comparative Perspective* (London: Macmillan, 1991), Introduction.

[16] For a fuller discussion, see Rainer Knopff and F.L. Morton, *Charter Politics* (Toronto, ON: Nelson Canada, 1992), pp. 108–110.

11.1

OF THE EXTENT OF THE LEGISLATIVE POWER
John Locke, *The Second Treatise* (1690)

This excerpt is reprinted as Reading 1.2.

11.2

THE RULE OF LAW
A.V. Dicey (1885)

This excerpt is reprinted as Reading 1.4.

11.3

RONCARELLI v. DUPLESSIS
Supreme Court of Canada (1959)

This case is reprinted as Reading 1.1.

11.4

BOUCHER v. THE KING
Supreme Court of Canada (1951)

This case is reprinted as Reading 9.4.

11.5

THE SUPREME COURT'S FIRST ONE HUNDRED CHARTER OF RIGHTS DECISIONS, 1982-1989

F.L. Morton, Peter H. Russell, and Michael J. Withey

Introduction

On April 16, 1982, Canada formally amended its written constitution by adding the Charter of Rights and Freedoms. The Charter explicitly authorized judicial review and the power of all courts to declare offending statutes void. At the time, this constitutional transplant of American-style judicial review into the Canadian hybrid of British-style parliamentary democracy posed important questions of both theoretical and practical interest. Canada had already modified the Westminster model of parliamentary supremacy with an overlay of federalism *cum* judicial review. Within their respective jurisdictions, however, the "exhaustion theory" held that both levels of government were supreme. The Charter appeared to challenge this supremacy, and perhaps the structure of federalism itself. Suffice it to say that in the intervening eight years, the Charter, or more precisely, the Charter through the courts, has had a broad, varied and significant impact on the practice of politics in Canada. In November, 1989, the Supreme Court of Canada handed down its one hundredth Charter of Rights decision. This paper presents a statistical overview of these first 100 Charter cases. It identifies trends with respect both to the Charter's impact on the Court and the impact of the Court's decisions on the Charter.

Statistical analyses of the Supreme Court's Charter decisions can provide an overall picture of the main patterns of a court's work and in this way provide a broader context for interpreting the significance of an individual case or the performance of an individual judge. . . . [B]y identifying patterns not discernible through the study of leading Charter cases, quantitative analysis can generate empirically supported generalizations—that is, new understandings—of how the Charter is affecting the Supreme Court and how the Court is shaping the Charter.

This is not to deny the limitations of quantitative analysis of judicial decision-making. It is not a substitute for jurisprudential analysis. For supreme courts . . . the reasons given to justify a decision are often more

A version of this paper appeared in the *Osgoode Hall Law Journal* 30, no. 1 (1992), pp. 2–52.

important in the long run than a decision's basic outcome or "bottom line."... Statistical analyses treats all cases equally, when in fact they are clearly not all of equal significance. Similarly, statistical classifications of cases in terms of their bottomline outcomes—for example "upholding" or "denying" a Charter claim—do not capture important jurisprudential subtleties....

These limitations qualify but do not negate the value of a statistical approach to the the Supreme Court's first 100 Charter decisions. Statistical studies can make an important contribution to the larger and more complex task of assessing the Supreme Court's Charter jurisprudence. ... We present the following study in the spirit that animated Pritchett's landmark study of the American "Roosevelt Court":

> What is obviously needed is a method in which the analysis is kept from shooting off into the void by being moored to a statistical and factual base, and in which fact-gathering is kept from becoming meaningless by being related to significant analysis.

The Charter's Impact on the Court's Case Load

The Charter has clearly changed the composition of the Supreme Court's case load. Table 1 shows that since the Court's first Charter decision in

Table 1

Charter Decisions by all Supreme Court Decisions, 1981-1989

Year	All SCC Decisions	SCC Charter Decisions	Percent of Total
1981	111	0	0%
1982	117	0	0%
1983	87	0	0%
1984	63	4	6%
1985	83	11	13%
1986	81	11	14%
1987	95	23	24%
1988	104	25	24%
1989	126	29*	23%
	867†	104*	12%

* Only Table 1 uses all Charter decisions through the end of 1989—104 cases. The other tables are based on the first 100 decisions.

† Data provided by Sylvie Roussel, Noel Décary, Aubrey and Associates, *Supreme Court News* (Hull, Quebec).

May, 1984, the volume of Charter cases steadily increased. By 1987 it constituted nearly one quarter of the Court's annual output of decided cases, and has remained at that level since. This means that in a short span of eight years, roughly 25 percent of the Court's time and other resources are now being spent on Charter cases. Significantly, the corresponding percentage for the U.S. Supreme Court is almost identical. During the same time period, the American Court decided 169 Bill of Rights decisions out of a total of 732 written decisions, or 23 percent. This institutional parallel was unthinkable prior to the Charter.

This surge of Charter litigation contrasts sharply with the development of the 1960 Canadian Bill of Rights. From 1960 to 1982, the Supreme Court decided only 34 Bill of Rights cases, an average of slightly over one per year. The high success of Charter claims in the Court's first two years of decision-making, as shown in Table 2, seems to have stimulated use of the Charter. The Supreme Court sent a message to the legal profession and lower court judges that it was prepared to take the constitutionally entrenched rights of the Charter much more seriously than the Bill of Rights. Under the latter, the Supreme Court did not hand down a ruling that supported a rights claim until its 1969 *Drybones* decision, and even this turned out to be the exception not the rule.

The total of 63 cases decided in 1984 represented the Court's lowest annual output since it took over as Canada's highest court in 1949. It was not until 1988 that the Court returned to the 100-plus level which has been its norm since 1949....

The advent of the Charter has not meant an abatement of constitutional cases involving federalism. Indeed, the Supreme Court and lower courts still prefer, where possible, to settle a constitutional case on federalism grounds rather than the Charter. During the period of the Court's first 100 Charter cases, it also decided 31 federalism cases. This means that the Court's constitutional mandate is in this respect actually wider than that of the United States Supreme Court, which has virtually abandoned any active role as an umpire of federalism.

With Charter litigation added to constitutional litigation based on the division of powers, the Supreme Court has become much more concerned with constitutional issues than was the case in the past. It would be a mistake, however, to regard the Canadian Supreme Court, even with its new Charter responsibilities, as simply a "constitutional court." Constitutional cases continue to account for only one-quarter to one-third of the cases it decides. This figure is only slightly lower than the comparable figure for the American Supreme Court for the same time period—44 percent.

On the other hand, the Charter has contributed to the further decline of private law and a corresponding increase in public law cases. As Monahan correctly pointed out, the decline in private law cases decided by the Court dates back to 1974, when appeals as of right in private law cases were abolished. Prior to 1974, private law cases constituted approximately one half of the cases decided by the Supreme Court each year. Since 1974, private law cases have steadily declined to the point where they account for less than a quarter.... To conclude, while the Charter has not made the Supreme Court into an exclusively "constitutional court," it has contributed to the Court's transformation into a decidedly "public law" court.

Outcome of Cases

In the 34 Bill of Rights cases decided by the Supreme Court of Canada between 1960 and 1982, the rights claimant won only five times—a "success rate" of only 15 percent. Table 2 shows how markedly different the Supreme Court has treated rights claims under the Charter. Thirty-five of the first 100 Charter cases were won by the litigant. Once again there is a strong parallel with American experience. During the same time frame, the non-government litigant won 61 of the 169 Bill of Rights decisions handed down by the American Supreme Court, a "success rate" of exactly 36 percent!

During its first two years of Charter decisions (1984 and 1985), the Court awarded victories to a stunning 67 percent (10 of 15) of the Charter claimants who came before it. The success rate of Charter litigants fell off steeply after this initial burst of judicial enthusiasm, averaging 27 percent to 32 percent over the last four years. During these six years, there has been a turnover of six justices, and the Mulroney government has filled all six vacancies. This has tempted some commentators to attribute the sharp drop in Charter success rates to the change in the Court's personnel. David Beatty, for example, has described the six Mulroney appointees as "conservative judges . . . [who] are very deferential to the legislature [and] don't want to hold a law unconstitutional."

Table 2

Outcome of Supreme Court's First 100 Charter Decisions

Year	Charter Claimant Loses	Charter Claimant Wins	Inconclusive	Totals
1984	1	3 (75%)	0	4
1985	3	7 (64%)	1	11
1986	8	3 (27%)	0	11
1987	16	6 (26%)	1	23
1988	17	8 (32%)	0	25
1989 (-Nov.)	16	8 (31%)	2	26
Totals	61	35 (35%)	4	100

This analysis is only superficially persuasive. When the dramatic shift in outcomes first occurred in 1986, there had been only one change in the Court's personnel—LaForest replacing Ritchie. The next Mulroney appointment—L'Heureux-Dubé—had no discernable impact on the Court's Charter work until 1988, the *third* year of lower success rates. Furthermore, the decline in judicial activism after 1985 was common to all the justices, not just the Mulroney appointees. For example, Dickson and Lamer, two of Beatty's "Trudeau liberals," had lower "pro-Charter" records than the Court average in 1989. Finally, when we compare the record of the four Trudeau justices who have left the court since 1988—Estey, Beetz, LeDain and McIntyre—with the four Mulroney replacements—Sopinka, Gonthier, Cory and McLachlin—it is far from evident that the newcomers represent a distinctly more conservative approach to Charter issues. Indeed, McIntyre, a Trudeau appointee, emerged as the Court's most outspoken and consistent proponent of judicial self-restraint. Moreover, McIntyre's Charter performance is perfectly consistent with his voting record in federalism cases, which also discloses a commitment to judicial self-restraint and deference to elected lawmakers. In sum, there is no consistent empirical support for Beatty's thesis that Prime Minister Mulroney has used his appointment power to shape an ideologically "conservative" or self-restrained Supreme Court.

A more probable explanation for the drop in the success rate of Charter claims after 1985 is a philosophical shift among some of the same justices who began the Court's Charter interpretation in 1984. In retrospect, these first two years can be seen as a sort of Charter "honeymoon." Not only were many of these first 15 cases strongly activist, but all save two were unanimous. The written judgments in these decisions manifested a very sanguine—some might say, naively optimistic—view of the Court's new role under the Charter. The Court seemed intent on minimizing any tension between its new mode of American-style judicial activism and its traditional, constitutional functions. The judges seemed to be trying to convince their public—and perhaps themselves—that they were simply carrying out the legal implications of the Charter. The Court wanted to have its cake and eat it too, and, for a brief moment, it did. Like all honeymoons, this one came to an end. As the Court ventured deeper into "Charterland," it was no coincidence that the success rate for Charter cases began to fall precipitously while at the same time the number of dissenting opinions soared. The number of unanimously decided Charter decisions dropped from over 85 percent in 1984–85 to the 60 percent range since then. The falling success rate and growing division on the Court both reflect the same hard reality—the inescapably contentious character of modern judicial review.

The seeds of this change were already present in the Court's 1984 and 1985 Charter decisions. As Monahan observed, these early Charter decisions were characterized by two very different and conflicting tendencies.

On the one hand, the Court repeatedly invoked the rhetoric of judicial activism (especially Lord Sankey's "living tree" metaphor) and repeatedly ruled in favor of Charter litigants. At the same time, the Court drew a sharp distinction between law and politics, characterizing its new role under the Charter as purely legal. Monahan argued that this somewhat schizophrenic behaviour was symptomatic of an underlying "crisis" on the Court over its new role under the Charter and "the relationship between law and politics." Gold has also noted the presence of disagreement in the Court's early Charter decisions, but suggests that it was supressed in order "to establish the legitimacy of judicial review under the Charter." ...

While Monahan's characterization of the problem as a crisis may be overstated, there was clearly a tension between the Court's legalistic pretense and its activist behaviour. In 1986, this tension came to a head for at least some of the justices, who adopted a more cautious or self-restrained approach to their Charter work. This shift was particularly evident in the three cases decided early in 1986 rejecting language rights claims and in the cases rejecting claims of organized labour decided later in 1986 and early 1987.

The growing sense of caution and judicial self-restraint can also be seen in the Court's handling of section 1 "reasonable limitations" claims by the Crown. Section 1 involves what is widely recognized as a highly discretionary "balancing test" between the policy interests of the government and the interest of the litigant in having Charter rights upheld. From 1984 through 1987, the Court rejected all but one of the 11 section 1 defences that were presented by the Crown. By contrast, in 1988 and 1989, it accepted eight of 14. This data simply confirms what was already an open secret: that the Court has become badly divided on how to handle the section 1 issue.

To conclude, the simultaneous drop in the success rate and increase in dissenting opinions after 1985 cannot be explained as an effect of "conservative" Mulroney appointments to the Court. Rather, it represents the working out of the tension between the activist behaviour and legalistic pretense in the Court's earlier decisions. There are real tensions between judicial review of constitutional rights and parliamentary democracy, and it was inevitable that these would surface and produce disagreement among the justices. The same disagreements have fueled constitutional debate in the U.S. for the past 20 years, and the advent of the Charter has brought "an American debate ... to Canada." It has not—at least not yet—brought the corollary American practice of "court packing" into Canadian politics. The most that can be said at this point about the Mulroney Supreme Court appointments is that they have been chosen according to traditional, non-ideological criteria, and they have neither impeded or hastened any prior trends in the Court's approach to Charter interpretation.

Even at the current, lower levels of success, the Charter has served as a catalyst for a new era of judicial activism unparallelled in Canadian history, and on a par with contemporary American practice. ...

A final caveat is in order about the tendency of Beatty and others to use "liberal" and "conservative" as synonyms for "judicial activism" and "judicial self-restraint" when discussing the Charter of Rights. This usage is as misleading as it is common. It reflects a simplistic attitude of, "the more rights, the better," an attitude that fails to grasp either the complexity or ambiguity of "rights." The wrong-headedness of this common practice can be illustrated by comparing judges with legislators. It is simply perverse to describe a politician who supports state intervention to regulate or redistribute private power as a "liberal," and simultaneously to describe a judge who strikes down such laws as a "liberal." Similarly, it is hardly clear why a politician who votes against interventionist, statist projects should be described as a "conservative," while a self-restrained judge who votes to uphold the same laws is described as a "conservative." Judicial activism and judicial self-restraint denote the willingness or reluctance of judges to use the power of judicial review to revise or obstruct the decisions of legislatures and the executive. They may be used with equal facility for either conservative or liberal ends. There is thus nothing to be gained and much to be lost by conflating the two sets of terms. . . .

Treatment of Different Charter Rights

Table 3 shows which Charter rights and freedoms have formed the basis of the Supreme Court's first 100 decisions and how they were decided. The unit of analysis is Charter cases. We have classified each of the 100 cases according to the right or freedom on which the case primarily turned and the outcome in terms of whether the litigant achieved the practical objective of his or her litigation. In civil cases, a "win" denotes the Charter claimant received the remedy requested —the nullification of a statute or regulation, a declaratory judgment, an injuction, and so forth. Likewise in criminal cases, a "win" denotes the Court awarding the Charter litigant/accused the remedy he requested—the exclusion of evidence, the nullification of a statute, a reinstatement of a verdict of "not guilty," an order for a new trial, and so forth. In cases where the Charter claimant receives some but not all of the remedies requested, the result of the case is coded as "inconclusive."

Table 3 clearly shows the extent to which legal rights cases have dominated the Court's Charter agenda—74 of its first 100 decisions. This trend has been evident from early on. Most commentators agree that it favours both the Court and the Charter, as judicial expertise and authority are highest in this area. Also, legal rights cases arise predominantly in the making and enforcement of criminal law—a purely federal jurisdiction— and thus tend not to become embroiled in the politics of federalism or language. This is not to minimize the importance or extent of the changes effected by the Court in this area. As Manfredi has shown, criminal process issues contain important substantive dimensions. The Court has used the Charter to develop a new constitutional code of conduct for Canadian police officers in dealing with suspects and accused persons, and in the process has pushed the Canadian criminal process away from the "crime control" toward the "due process" side of the ledger.

Ironically, while this policy area represents the Court's most extensive *de facto* efforts at law reform, it has thus far escaped public notice. American experience shows that this type of judicial policy-making can become an issue of partisan political conflict. Beginning with Richard Nixon's 1968 presidential campaign, the Republican Party has criticized "liberal" judges for being "soft on criminals" and successfully exploited the "law and order" issue, particulary as it relates to the appointment of federal judges. It will be of both theoretical and practical interest to see if a Canadian political party will try to make a political issue out of the Supreme Court's Charter-inspired reform of the criminal law process.

Table 3

Different Categories of Charter Cases by Result

| | Charter Claimant | | | |
	Wins	Loses	Inconclusive	Totals
Fundamental Freedoms	5	11	0	16
Democratic Rights	0	0	0	0
Mobility Rights	1	2	0	3
Legal Rights*	27	42	5	74
Equality Rights	1	4	0	5
Language and Education Rights**	4	3	0	7
Aboriginal Rights***	0	0	0	0
Totals	38	62	5	105

Note: The following five cases are counted in two categories, thus making the total number of cases 105.

Morgentaler v. the Queen: counted as Legal Rights and Fundamental Freedoms
Black and Co. v. Law Society of Alberta: counted as Fundamental Freedoms and Mobility Rights
Irwin Toy v. A.-G. Quebec: counted as Fundamental Freedom and Legal Rights
Reference re Bill 30 (Ontario): counted as Fundamental Freedom and Equality Right
Borowski v. The Queen: counted as Legal Rights and Equality Rights

* Including s.23(2).
** Includes sections 16-23 of Charter, sections 93 and 133 of BNA Act, s.23 of Manitoba Act and s.16 of Saskatchewan Act.
*** Includes s.25 of Charter and s.35 of Constitution Act, 1982.

Fundamental freedoms are a distant second, accounting for 16 cases. The distinctively Canadian sections of the Charter—mobility rights and language rights—have generated only three and seven cases, respectively. On the other hand, they have been relatively more successful than the other sections. The two unsuccessful mobility rights cases dealt with the extradition of criminals and the rights of non-citizens—issues peripheral to the nation-building objectives of the primary author of section 3, Pierre Trudeau. By contrast, the one successful section 6 case struck down Alberta's restrictions on non-resident lawyers and law firms—precisely the type of interprovincial barrier targeted by Trudeau. Within months of the decision, almost every major law firm in Alberta had announced mergers or associations with large Toronto-based firms.

Nor do the small number of language rights cases accurately reflect their considerable political impact. The Court's 1984 decision in the *Quebec Protestant School Boards* forced the Quebec government to realize that they had lost control of education and culture, and gave them the incentive to enter into new negotiations with Ottawa, negotiations that led eventually to the 1987 Meech Lake Accord. The Supreme Court's 1988 decisions dealing with language rights in Saskatchewan, Alberta and Quebec, and the political responses that they provoked, have in turn contributed heavily to the demise of Meech Lake. In both instances the Supreme Court affirmed the existence of minority language rights, and in both instances the governments affected enacted new legislation that negated the judicial ruling. Critics of Meech Lake seized upon Quebec's use of the section 33 override as an indicator of what to expect under the "distinct society" clause.

Section 15, the multi-pronged equality rights section, did not come into force until 1985. While it has flooded the lower courts with litigation, it has not yet had much of an impact at the Supreme Court level. However, now that the Court has begun in *Andrews* to lay the foundations of equality rights jurisprudence, a larger proportion of cases coming before the Court will likely deal with equality rights.

Nullification of Statutes

Section 32 of the Charter declares that its enumerated prohibitions apply to "all matters within the authority" of Parliament and the legislatures of each of the provinces. Cases such as *Dolphin Delivery* and *Daigle* show that occasionally it is difficult to say where "state action"—and thus the reach of the Charter—ends and "private action" begins. As a basic rule, however, Charter litigation can be directed at three forms of government actions: primary legislation or statutes; secondary legislation or administrative rules and regulations; and the conduct of government officials. Table 4 presents a breakdown of the Court's first 100 Charter decisions according to the "object" of the challenge.

Table 4

Object of Charter Challenge by Result of Case

| | Charter Claimant | | | |
	Wins	Loses	Inconclusive	Total
Statute	18	29	2	49
Conduct	18	32	1	51
Regulation	2	1	0	3
Totals	38	62	3	103*

* total greater than 100 because some Charter cases involve challenges to both statute and conduct, or both statute and regulation, etc.

Executive conduct has been under review in just over 50 percent of the Court's Charter cases. This is significantly lower than the proportion for Charter cases generally. Earlier studies by both Morton and Monahan found that two out of every three Charter cases are challenges to "conduct"—usually the actions of the police in the enforcement of criminal law. The Supreme Court, it would appear, has been more willing to grant leave to appeal when statutes are challenged than when conduct is challenged.

This has implications for the new role of the Court under the Charter. If the Supreme Court followed the trend of the lower courts and heard primarily "conduct cases," it would reduce the potential for direct clashes between the Court and legislatures over the substantive policy choices implicit in most Charter challenges to statutes. It would also weaken the "anti-democratic" critique of judicial review. The Court's decision to hear a roughly equal number of statute and conduct cases has thrust it into a more competitive relationship with Parliament and provincial legislatures, and made the "legitimacy issue" more explicit and thus more difficult to ignore. This may have been a contributing factor to the end of the Court's initial Charter honeymoon described above. The legitimacy issue becomes even sharper when we focus on the judicial nullification of statutes, the subject of Table 5.

Table 5 shows that in the seven years since its adoption, the Supreme Court has used the Charter to strike down a total of 19 statutes, in whole or in part. Remarkably, this figure is almost identical with the number of statutes declared invalid by the U.S. Supreme Court for Bill of Rights violations during the same time period—20.

The 19 Charter nullifications also contrast sharply with the Court's deferential, British-style exercise of judicial review under the 1960 Bill of Rights. Under the latter, the Court struck down only one statute in 22 years—a section of the Indian Act which restricted drinking rights on reserves. The magnitude of this change can be appreciated by comparing this figure to the number of statutes declared *ultra vires* on sections 91–92 federalism grounds during the same time frame, only 10 in 31 cases. The Charter has clearly replaced federalism as the primary basis for the Court's exercise of judicial review.

More provincial legislation (11 statutes) has been declared invalid under the Charter than federal (8 statutes). This is consistent with Morton et al.'s earlier study of all appeal court nullifications under the Charter, which found that the quantitative impact of the Charter on federal and provincial statutes was roughly equal, but that there were some interesting qualitative differences. The invalidated provincial statutes tended to be of a substantive character and more recently enacted. The same trend is present in the federal and provincial statutes declared invalid by the Supreme Court . . .

Seven of the eight nullifications of federal statutes were procedural in character, and half were based on the legal rights provisions of the Charter. By contrast, nine of the 11 nullifications of provincial statutes were substantive in character, and seven of them were based directly or indirectly on French-English minority language and education issues, a perennial source of conflict in Canadian politics.

. . . Five of the eight invalidated federal statutes involved criminal law. Parliament's exclusive power over criminal law makes federal legislation in Canada a prime target for Charter challenges. This contrasts with the United States, where the states have the primary responsibility for making criminal law. As a result, the American Supreme Court's application of the Bill of Rights, via the Fourteenth Amendment, applies primarily to the states. As noted above, most of the federal legislation overturned by the Court on Charter grounds have involved procedural issues and have not involved major policy concerns.

The major exceptions—and they are major—were the *Singh* and *Morgentaler* decisions. The latter is the most famous—or infamous—Charter decision to date. *Morgentaler* overturned the abortion provisions of the Criminal Code and forced the Mulroney government to deal with the

Table 5

Nullification of Federal and Provincial Statutes

Statute	Upheld	Nullified	Total
Federal	16	8	24
Provincial	15	11	26
Totals	31	19	50

politically charged abortion issue. The government struggled for more than two years to frame a new abortion policy. In June, 1990, after several failed attempts, Parliament in a free vote adopted Bill C-43, a compromise measure that left abortion in the Criminal Code but allowed therapeutic abortions when a pregnancy threatened the life or health of the mother. Bill C-43 abolished the old requirement of committee approvals, and left the determination of the threat to health to a woman and her doctor. In this respect, it closley followed Chief Justice Dickson's judgment in the *Morgentaler* decision. . . . [Ed. note: Bill C-43 was defeated by a tie vote in the Senate in February, 1991. The government has made no attempt since then to introduce new abortion legislation.] The legal vacuum created by the government's inaction has led to a variety of different provincial responses to the funding and access issues, and also a series of abortion injunction cases. The most dramatic, *Daigle v. Tremblay*, went all the way to the Supreme Court for an unprecedented emergency hearing during the summer recess of 1989.

The *Singh* decision is less well known but hardly less dramatic in its effects. *Singh* struck down the procedures for hearing applications for refugee status under the Immigration Act and forced the government to provide a mandatory oral hearing for refugee applicants. This decision has had the unintended consequences of creating a backlog of 124,000 refugee claimants; an amnesty for 15,000 claimants already in Canada; $179 million in additional costs; and a new refugee law that some critics say is more unfair than the original one. The new refugee law took effect January 1, 1989. Eighteen months later, the government announced that the "new" Immigration and Refugee Board would quadruple its capacity to keep up with applications. This would allow the Board to hire an additional 280 public servants (to add to the present 496) at an additional cost $20 million. This increase brings the annual budget of the new Board to $80 million.

Only five provinces have lost legislation to Charter challenges: Quebec, British Columbia, Alberta, Saskatchewan and Manitoba. Of the five, Quebec has clearly been most affected. Not only has it had the highest number of nullifications (5), but the statutes affected represented recent policy initiatives that were important to the Quebec government—all but one in the fields of language and education. By contrast, none of the other provincial legislation which has been overturned represented recent policy commitments considered important by the provincial governments. For Quebec, the Court's decisions striking down various sections of Bill 101 have been serious policy setbacks.

In one sense, Quebec presents the clearest example of the counter-majoritarian character of judicial review, where the Court uses the Charter to protect the rights of a local minority against the local majority. From a different perspective, however, the same decisions, particulary in conjunction with the language rights cases from Manitoba and Saskatchewan, show how the Charter, through the Supreme Court, can serve as a vehicle for majoritarian democracy rather than a limitation on it. The American comparison is instructive on this point. In the United States, seven times more state laws (970) have been declared unconstitutional than federal laws (135). In the same time period as our study (1984–1989), 18 state statutes and only two federal statutes were declared invalid for violating the Bill of Rights.

Leading American commentators argue that rather than being a restraint on Congress and the president, the American Supreme Court has more often been "an active participant in the ruling national coalitions that dominate American politics," especially when it comes to curbing state or local policies that are offensive to the ruling national coalition. The Supreme Court's lead in attacking racial segregation in the South is only the most well known example of the use of judicial review to restrain what is perceived as "aberrant" behaviour of regional majorities. The Canadian Supreme Court's activist promotion of national bilingualism at the expense of the preferred unilingual policies of some provincial governments also supports Shapiro's broader comparative thesis that the primary function of judicial review is not legal but political—to "aid the central authorities in breaking into the cake of local custom and bringing [central] government influence down into the villages."

The greater impact of the Charter on provincial law-making also supports earlier predictions about the potential of the Charter to act as a force for policy uniformity throughout Canada. Whether this will serve a "nation-building" function, as its proponents hoped, or be a politically divisive influence, remains to be seen. Judicially mandated policies pleasing to the "central authorities" often do not sit well with local governments. Within Quebec, for example, the Supreme Court's decision in the "French-Only" Public Signs Case triggered a significant increase in support for Bill 101 and restrictions on English-language signs. Support for the separatist Parti Québécois jumped eight percent while support for bilingualism was cut in half. Outside of Quebec, Premier Bourassa's use of the section 33 override to re-instate restrictions on English-language advertising was widely criticized and contributed to the eventual defeat of the Meech Lake Accord. Critics of the Accord effectively argued that the distinct society clause would be used to insulate Quebec's attempts to promote French and suppress English from successful Charter challenges.

The bitter debate over the "distinct society" clause reflects the Charter's disproportionate impact on Quebec. Research conducted in 1987 showed that while the Charter was as popular in Quebec as in the rest of Canada among those who knew about it, considerably fewer people knew about the Charter in Quebec than elsewhere in Canada. The introduction of the Charter without the Quebec government's consent and subsequent developments in judicial and constitutional politics may make the Charter less attractive to Francophone Quebeckers. The Supreme Court's decisions overturning key elements of Quebec's Bill 101 and the hostility directed against Quebec for using the override clause to protect Bill 178 from Charter challenge may contribute to a political environment in which the Charter is increasingly seem by the Quebecois as a constitutional instrument hostile to their primary constitutional concerns.

Judicial Discretion: Reasonable Limitations and the Exclusion of Evidence

Frequently in Charter cases, after the Court has found that a right has been violated, it goes on to a second stage of analysis to consider whether the law abridging the right is a "reasonable limitation" under section 1 or whether, if it is a criminal case, the evidence should be excluded under section 24(2). Both these types of second stage determinations are crucial to the practical outcome of Charter cases. They are also both highly discretionary, and thus reliable indicators of judicial self-restraint or activism. The most significant feature of both tables is the contrast in outcomes between the early years and more recent years, evidence which further supports the thesis that after an initial burst of activism, the Court has moved toward a practice of greater self-restraint.

Section 1 states that the rights and freedoms enumerated in the Charter are "subject to such reasonable limitations prescribed by law as can be demonstrably justified in a free and democratic society." Rather than treat this as a self-evident, declaratory truth (i.e., no right is absolute), the Court has made section 1 an integral step in Charter interpretation. If the Court finds that the statute in question restricts a Charter right, the judges then proceed to determine if this limitation is "reasonable" and "demonstrably justifiable." In its 1986 *Oakes* decision, the Court laid down specific guidelines for applying section 1. The *Oakes* guidelines require that to qualify as a "reasonable limitation," the statute must serve a "pressing and substantial" purpose and that the means used must be proportional to the ends. The *Oakes* guidelines may have structured judicial discretion, but they certainly have not removed it. In practice, *Oakes* amounts to a form of judicial "balancing" of ends and means: do the former justify the latter? Since the practical outcome of a case rides on this section 1 determination, a judge's sensitivity to what Justice LaForest has called "second guessing" legislative choices, is likely to influence how deferential or strict he is in applying the *Oakes* test. How then has the Court exercised its discretion under section 1?

Table 6 shows that from 1984 through 1987, only one of 11 section 1 defences of legislation was accepted by the Court. This is consistent with— indeed it supported—the Court's initial activism. It may also reflect the unpreparedness of government lawyers for section 1 arguments, specifically the use of "extrinsic evidence" (social data) to support the reasonableness of the challenged statute. By contrast, in 1988 and 1989, the Court accepted eight of 14 section 1 defences, more than half. In practical terms, this means that the Charter challenge failed. The Court has also become divided over the treatment of section 1. There have been only four dissents in cases in which section 1 was decisive, and three of these occurred in 1989. Also, the justices differ in the consistency with which they use *Oakes* in responding to section 1 arguments.

[There was] a similar trend for the exclusion of evidence under s.24(2). Section 24(2) represents a significant and potentially controversial innovation in Canadian criminal law. Prior to 1982, Canadian judges accepted Crown evidence even if police obtained it in a manner that violated the rights of the accused. This was consistent with British practice, but diverged significantly from the American practice initiated by the U.S. Supreme Court's 1966 decision *Mapp v. Ohio* to exclude evidence from trial if the police had violated the rights of the accused. In practice, this often meant an acquittal since it was difficult to obtain a conviction without the evidence. After much controversy, the framers of the Charter adopted a compromise wording that would make the exclusion of evidence "conditional" upon the judges' finding that the admission of evidence "would bring the administration of justice into disrepute." Since this determination is far from self-evident, the practical effect of section 24(2) was dependant on how the Supreme Court interpreted it.

From 1984 through 1986, the Court accepted the only two exclusion motions that it heard. Since 1987, it has evenly divided on section 24(2) motions to exclude, rejecting eight and accepting eight. Section 24(2) prompted the first dissent in the Supreme Court's Charter jurisprudence, and has divided the Court in three subsequent cases—more than any other section of the Charter.

The close division in outcomes and the division within the Court on section 1 and section 24(2) arguments reflects the rather discretionary and subjective nature of applying these sections of the Charter. Deciding whether legislation is "reasonable" or whether the admission of unconstitutionally obtained evidence "would bring the administration of justice into disrepute" are not likely to become precise arts. The divisions which

Table 6

The Section 1 Reasonable Limits Defence

	1984	1985	1986	1987	1988	1989	TOTAL
Section 1 defence							
Accepted	0	0	1	0	5	3	9
Rejected	2	4	2	2	4	2	16
Totals	2	4	3	2	9	5	25

have developed within the Court over the Court's proper role under the Charter can be understood as both cause and effect of its changing and divided record on section 1 and section 24(2) issues. . . .

Conclusions

The Charter has ushered in a new era for the Supreme Court of Canada. The year, 1982, marks a turning point for the Court equal in importance to the abolition of appeals to the JCPC in 1949. In only eight years, the Charter has come to constitute roughly one quarter of the Supreme Court's annual work-load. The Court has made a clean break with the British-style judicial self-restraint that characterized its interpretation of the 1960 Canadian Bill of Rights. The Court has upheld Charter claimants in 35 percent of its first 100 decisions, and declared 19 statutes void for Charter infractions. The comparable figures for the Bill of Rights were 15 percent and one statute. In all three of these important respects—composition of docket, success rate and nullification of statutes—there is no longer any appreciable difference between the Supreme Court's Charter work and the American Supreme Court's work under the Bill of Rights.

Like its American counterpart, the Supreme Court now routinely finds itself in the thick of the political process. Seventy-five percent of the Court's Charter work has dealt with legal rights and criminal justice. While most of these decisions have not touched on issues of great public interest, the exceptions are important: abortion and language rights in particular. The impact of the Charter on the provinces has been qualitatively greater than its effect on federal law-making.

Our study confirms a growing dissensus within the Court over Charter interpretation since 1986, and argues that this accounts for the decline of Charter successful Charter challenges after 1985. We document the division on the Court between activists (Wilson and Lamer) and non-activists (McIntyre and L'Heureux-Dubé), and suggest that such division was more or less inevitable, given the inescapably contentious character of modern judicial review. [Ed. note: See Reading 12.3] Comparative data from American experience suggests that such division is to be expected and is even likely to increase.

For the country too, the Charter, which was promoted as an instrument of national unity, is ironically becoming a source of disunity so far as Quebec's relationship to the rest of Canada is concerned. The Supreme Court's application of the Charter, while by no means the sole explanation of this tendency, has been a contributing factor. Among the provinces, Quebec's legislature experienced the most serious reversals in the Supreme Court's first 100 Charter cases. Likewise, the Quebec Court of Appeal has been reversed more often than any other provincial court of appeal. With respect to the Charter, Quebec may already be well on its way to becoming a distinct society.

[Ed. note: The remaining sections of this article are reprinted in Reading 12.3.]

11.6

THE CHARTER AND GOOD GOVERNMENT

A. Kim Campbell,
Minister of Justice and Attorney-General of Canada

The Charter is a very important part of the Canadian legal system and of our system of government generally. In the Charter's early years, the biggest challenge was to ensure that it was given real force, unlike the Canadian bill of rights, and that it was interpreted generously and purposively. The courts have met that challenge and met it well by giving the Charter a large and liberal interpretation. I hope that they will continue to do so.

In the second decade of the Charter, however, there is a second challenge—to ensure that the Charter advances the cause of good government in Canada, and helps to make our uniquely Canadian system of government function well. I would like this afternoon to tell you why I see this as a key challenge and what needs to be done about it. Specifically, I am going to address three themes:

- First, that the Charter has given the courts new and expanded responsibilities.
- Second, that, unless we are careful, Canadians will increasingly look to the courts rather than Parliament to achieve social and political reform and to promote their rights.
- Third, that we must articulate and respect an allocation of responsibility among the courts, Parliament and the executive that reflects our Canadian traditions and circumstances and that assigns to each its proper role in this post-Charter era.

Turning to my first point, by giving Canadians constitutionally-entrenched rights and freedoms, and by making these enforceable by the courts, the Charter has given the courts a much more powerful and visible role in our governmental system. It has also given the courts—which on the constitutional front were previously limited mainly to decisions about the division of powers—a substantive policy role, one which was previously reserved to Parliament. This has led to some tensions and to questions about the proper scope of judicial review in a parliamentary system.

I think we must address these tensions. My concern is that, unless Parliament and the courts understand and respect each other's role, we will evolve towards a system in which courts rather than democratically-

"On the Canadian *Charter of Rights and Freedoms*." Address to the B.C. Civil Liberties Association, May 15, 1992. Reprinted with permission.

elected legislatures are seen as the primary protectors and promoters of our rights and freedoms. In my view, this may be what is happening in the United States. Increasingly, Americans seem to be seeking social and political change through the courts. They may be doing so because they have lost faith in the capacity of the other two branches to achieve the results they desire. Consider, for example, the recent mass demonstrations in front of the United States Supreme Court on the abortion issue. I am concerned that similar developments are taking root here. We appear to have become increasingly rights oriented, increasingly confrontational, and increasingly quick to look to the courts rather than to our elected representatives for social and political reform.

In my view, however, these trends are neither inevitable nor irreversible in Canada. Our adoption of an entrenched Charter of Rights does not mean that Canadians will *necessarily* become more litigious or that courts will *inevitably* replace legislatures as the agents of change. The decision is ours to make. While some hail these developments as proof of an increased sense of "ownership" in the constitution, I think we must be extremely careful not to disregard our constitutional history and attempt to understand our complex political and constitutional framework solely from a post-1982 perspective.

In this regard, I think we must be mindful of one of the most distinctive aspects of Canadian political culture, namely the relationship Canadians have with their government. Unlike their American counterparts, Canadian citizens have not perceived government as being antagonistic to their interests; on the contrary, there is a rich and deeply-imbedded tradition of looking to government to protect a larger societal interest—of relying on government to advance and protect certain basic values. Social and income support programs, equalization payments and regional diversification initiatives are but three of the many examples which could be cited.

I do not think the Charter either represents or requires any radical break from this tradition. Indeed, I think it must be interpreted in light of and consistently with this important element of the Canadian experience. The Charter is much more than a bulwark against the state; it is a statement of the positive relationship between citizens and state. Let's remember that in Canada citizens have invoked state power as much as they have sought to limit it.

Against this background, then, what sort of institutional relationships are appropriate under the Charter? First, I think we must now accept that the Charter has given the courts a policy role, one that goes well beyond the mere adjudication of competing fact situations. Courts are now required to choose from among competing approaches and values. The real question, therefore, is not whether the courts are "making policy," but rather the appropriate limits of the court's policy-making role. In considering the proper limits of the judicial policy function, three main factors must be taken into account:

- First, *the nature of the issues*: Court cases are about the interpretation and application of the law, usually to specific fact situations. They are, in my view, often inappropriate for deciding broad policy issues affecting a large number of people;
- Second, *the nature of the adversarial process itself*. The adversarial process has evolved over the centuries as a formalized process for resolving disputes among parties by ensuring that the facts and the law relevant to the matter at hand are advanced and tested before an impartial arbiter. While this approach has proven its value in resolving differences of fact and in applying the law to those facts, it is not designed to ensure that all of the considerations relevant to value-laden policy decisions are identified. Further, even if all of these considerations are brought out, the adversarial process, with its win/lose result, is not then designed to lead to the finely crafted compromises that are required in our society, and that the parliamentary system is uniquely able to shape.
- Third, *the background of the judges* is important. Judges are invariably eminent members of the bar, highly trained to deal with matters of law. They are, however, usually without training or experience in the broader exercise of policy formulation and may not be in the best position to benefit from those who are.

These considerations should, I think, constrain the policy involvement of courts. This is not to suggest that the courts should refrain from taking policy decisions where they have to, but rather, that they should be very conscious of their role and of the limitations of the legal adjudicative framework within which they work.

If I appear to be placing considerable emphasis on the need for judicial restraint, I am. Bearing in mind the wide-ranging implications of judicial decisions and the fact that those decisions are, to all intents and purposes, the final word as to the meaning of our constitution and the validity of governmental action pursuant to it, I think it important that courts approach their policy role with some degree of circumspection. It is natural for interest groups to demand more, but they are interested in specific results, not the long-term health of the overall system.

At the same time, we must acknowledge that the democratic process is imperfect and at times fails to live up to its responsibilities to the individuals and groups it serves. To my mind, this is the reason why some form of judicial review is necessary. And if this is the *raison d'etre* of judicial review, it equally provides guidance as to the proper limits of the judicial role.

As a general rule, I think judicial intervention will be most appropriate where it serves to strengthen the workings of the democratic process in order to correct failures within that process. Thus, courts can properly intervene where Parliament loses its way, either in disregarding fundamental values enshrined in the Charter or in failing to give sufficient regard to minority interests. Further, where a Charter defect is found, courts can provide guidance to Parliament by setting out the precise nature of the problem, enabling Parliament to reformulate the legislation in a manner consistent with the Charter. In this way, courts can ensure that Parliament carries out its obligations under the Charter without intruding on Parliament's function.

On the other hand, I think it is particularly important that courts show restraint where their decisions will have fiscal implications. It must be open to Parliament to re-assess fiscal priorities where Charter rulings affect the scope of government programs. The more courts become involved in the balancing of competing demands or political interest, the more they risk trenching into the legislative domain.

In this regard, I think there are real dangers to importing into Canada the so-called "doctrine of extension," wherein courts become involved in the implementation of their own decisions. This doctrine is rooted in the American political and judicial context, with its elaborate system of checks and balances. We have a uniquely Canadian Charter and Canadians are entitled to a uniquely Canadian rights jurisprudence. In this context, decisions as to the design of laws, of policies and of programs should, as a general rule, be left to Parliament within the constitutional framework as interpreted by the courts.

Let me give you a few examples of what I have been trying to say. First, let me refer to some instances in which courts may have been somewhat over-zealous and risked encroaching upon parliament's domain. Section 7 guarantees the rights to life, liberty and security of the person, and the right not to be deprived of these except in accordance with principles of fundamental justice. It is clear that the drafters of the Charter intended this section as a guarantee relating to procedural fairness. While the drafters' intent is not determinative, courts have in fact given it little weight. In the *B.C. Motor Vehicle Reference*, the Supreme Court rejected the argument of the Attorney-General of Canada and others that section 7 should be restricted to the examination of the procedural aspects of government action. Instead, the court held that section 7 could also be used to review the substance of legislation. In so doing, the court imported into Canada an American constitutional doctrine known as substantive due process. Not only is this contrary to what Parliament appears to have intended; the substantive use of section 7 is one of the chief bases of policy involvement by the courts and therefore one of the areas in which concern about the legitimacy of judicial review is most prevalent.

Another example I would cite is the series of cases in which the court struck down the constructive murder provisions of the Criminal Code. In these decisions, rather than simply identifying the Charter defects and striking down the provisions, the court effectively held that murder *had* to be defined in a certain way. In my view, the court in so doing, over-stepped the appropriate boundaries of the judicial function. It is for Parliament and Parliament alone to define what murder is. Having found Parliament's definition deficient, the court should simply have struck down the provision and left it to Parliament to try again. The court should set the basic limits, not define the optimum policy result.

Let me now give you an example of what I consider to be a more appropriate model for institutional relationships under the Charter. As most of you will know, the Supreme Court of Canada recently struck down what was commonly referred to as the "rape shield provision," which protected sexual assault complainants from being questioned about their sexual history. You will recall that the court found that Parliament had gone too far in its attempt to protect victims of sexual assault, and had in fact violated the rights of accused to make full answer and defence. Significantly, while the court provided some useful guidance as to what might be an appropriate way of balancing the competing interests, it did *not* attempt to strike this balance itself. It offered a fairly rich set of suggestions, but still left the final determination for Parliament to make, in accordance with its representative function.

In this instance, I believe the various branches of government worked cooperatively, as they were meant to do: the Supreme Court decision affirmed the principles on which Parliament had based its original provisions, but indicated how and why the actual balance struck was deficient. In so doing, it recognized the right and the responsibility of Parliament to go back and examine how best to achieve its objectives in a manner consistent with the Charter. This allowed us to go to the people who were most affected by the legislation and ask them for their opinions. It allowed us to engage in a truly democratic, consultative process whereby the views of many were considered and reflected in a legislative initiative that is consistent with the fundamental principles of the Charter. We have achieved an approach with protection for complainants and victims, while at the same time respecting the right of the accused to a fair trial. Besides illustrating an appropriate role for courts under the Charter, this example highlights the responsibilities of Parliament and the executive under the Charter, and the fundamental role of Parliament in fashioning social compromise and demonstrating leadership.

Parliament has the vital and pre-eminent role in our constitutional system as an arbiter among competing interests in society. Our system of constitutional adjudication must recognize that the difficult political choices and decisions as to how to respond to social needs must remain in the hands of a government responsible through the House of Commons to the people of Canada. We must never lose sight of the central importance of the political process. Nor must we forget that it is legislatures—not courts—which are in the best position to assess competing demands and to conduct the necessary balancing of interests. In this regard, I think we often fail to give sufficient credit to our parliamentary process. It is this process alone which permits consensus decision-making, problem solving and public involvement—reflecting the spirit of practical compromise which is so fundamental to the Canadian way of doing things.

Parliament is, however, more than simply a broker amongst competing interests. It has a positive rule to play as the guardian of the principled commitments of the Canadian community. It also has an enormously important creative role to play in giving material life to the aspirations of the Charter, a role that cannot be fulfilled by the courts. In a very real sense, Parliament and the executive side of government are on the front lines of rights protection in Canada. At the same time, democratic institutions must demonstrate that they deserve the trust, faith and respect of Canadians. Parliament must *act* to promote the larger values and objects of the Charter. Parliamentarians have a vital responsibility to ensure that the laws they pass and other actions they take respect and advance Charter rights and freedoms.

In this regard, I have begun to note a very disquieting trend among legislators to leave difficult decisions to the courts. There is a great temptation to avoid dealing with contentious issues by saying "let's wait until the courts force us to act." This is a defeatist attitude and nothing less than an abdication of Parliament's role as the primary agent of social change in Canada. It ignores the responsibility of legislatures to craft the law—to determine both *what* should be done and *how* it is to be accomplished. We must never forget the profound responsibility of legislators to demonstrate leadership and to make the difficult choices required to govern a nation.

It will be obvious by now that I am trying to make a case for a coherent functional specialization among our governmental institutions in the application of the Charter. But there is one additional element which must not be forgotten, and that is the people whose welfare the Charter was designed to foster and protect. The people of Canada are the real beneficiaries of the Charter, and Canadians are, for good reason, justly proud of it. But the Charter's beneficiaries also have responsibility. Just as courts must be responsible in their disposition of the Charter issues coming before them, so must Canadians be responsible in deciding which issues to put before the courts, for judicial rather than political resolution. I would hope that Canadians will take their decisions carefully, having given due consideration to the effect of a particular course of actions on the welfare of our community and institutions.... If Canadians become too impatient with the workings of our democratic institutions, they will, as I implied earlier, lose their effectiveness.

What conclusions can we draw from what I have been saying? There are several. First, I think we must remain vigilant in ensuring that we do not become overly reliant on the courts to satisfy individual rights. We must not lose our ability to search for consensus and compromise. We must ensure that Canadians do not come to believe that public policy issues can only be resolved by a court decision. In particular, it is our duty to ensure that our political processes remain effective agents of social change, and that Canadians have confidence in the ability of those processes to advance the largest vision of public interest.

Second, we require an appropriate framework of institutional relationships between Parliament, the executive and the courts. This framework should be based on a functional allocation of responsibilities. Each organ of government should encourage and assist the others to fulfil their roles while at the same time respecting the proper limits of its own function.

Third, there is a danger to democratic institutions of over-reliance on courts to effect social change. The long-term effect could be to debilitate the process of problem-solving and policy-making which lies at the heart of democratic governance and upon which its survival depends.

Fourth, we do our courts no favour in asking them to resolve what are essentially political questions. Besides demonstrating a lack of faith in political institutions, judicial involvement in political issues threatens the judiciary's legitimacy. There is a danger that courts will no longer be seen as impartial or neutral arbiters above the fray of political debate; instead they may come to be perceived as active players in the political arena.

Fifth, the approach I am suggesting imposes a heavy responsibility on Parliament, parliamentarians and the executive to ensure that democratic institutions live up to the trust we place in them as protectors and promoters of the rights of Canadians.

Finally, we must define a role for our courts under the Charter which is consistent with our Canadian system of government. Courts are not, and must not become, the exclusive defenders of the values the Charter seeks to protect.

It has been suggested that the Charter of Rights and Freedoms is causing a legal revolution in our country. Reflecting on a decidedly less metaphorical revolution in 18th century France, Edmund Burke made what I consider to be a genuinely profound comment on the relationship between citizens and their laws. He said, if I may paraphrase, *that we should approach the imperfections in our laws as if they were the wounds of a parent.*

Burke's idea resonates with a sense of proprietorship, of membership, of a kind of citizenly solicitude for the laws of the community. I am painfully aware that it may seem arcane and other-worldly to us from the standpoint of a modern cynicism. But Burke was—and still is—I am convinced, absolutely right. The Charter is *one* of the instruments that we have fashioned to help ensure that our governance is more principled and humane. It is part of, an element of, a *system* of government. It cannot replace the other functions with which it must, ultimately, form a working, living, resilient whole.

We cannot simply follow other nations in achieving this integration and balance. We must find our own way, a Canadian way, to provide for a complementary and mutually supportive relationship between our commitment to individual rights and our need for a vital and responsive political culture. This is a tremendous challenge that will require both political leadership and a special kind of understanding and sophistication on the part of Canadian citizens. It forms the great challenge and promise of the next 10 years of the Charter.

11.7

CHARTER WORSHIPPERS' SOCIETY
John Young

> Our Charter, which art in Ottawa,
> hallowed be thy sections.
> Thy judgments come, thy will be done,
> in Halifax, as they are in Whitehorse.
> Give us this day our daily cases,
> and forgive us our lengthy litigations,
> as we forgive those who litigate against us.
> Lead our governments not into the temptation of section 33,
> but deliver us from the evil of true crimes without mens rea.
> For thine is the courtroom,
> the power and the glory,
> forever and ever,
> Ermine.

Note to Members:
The Lord Chief Bishop of Upper Canada will be giving a talk on the doctrine of Charteral Infallibility and the Immaculate Interpretation at noon in the Dickson Room.

For those members who have not completed their penances for imagining Canada without a Charter, a group recitation of the obligatory 20 "Hail Charter, full of Grace" has been organized in the Chapel of Saint Estey of the Assertation, Tuesday at 4:00 p.m.

Be sure to attend this Sunday's service, where I am sure all members will be moved into a state of legal bliss by the worshipful sounds of Bertha Wilson and the Supremes.

*   *   *

Obiter Dicta (Osgoode Hall Law School, January 20, 1992), p. 9. Reprinted with permission.

"The Last Session" (today's Reading)

And when the ministers had gathered the disciples in the Commons, the Prime Minister stood up and taking the Charter in his hand, he opened the book and broke the binding, saying to the lawyers amongst them, "Take, litigate, for this is the body of the law which giveth unto you. Do this in remembrance of me." And taking the ink pot out of the ink well, he said, "Take, writeth out thy bills, for this is the life blood of the profession which shall keepeth our pockets lined." And they were all glad.

Whereupon there was a great pestilence in the land, and the masses didst wailest and criest and there was a great gnashing of teeth. And it did come to pass that the masses sayeth unto the minister, "Minister, minister, we, the disempowered, have not the financial resources to make use of thy wondrous parchment and when we do, more often than not, we get nailed." Whereupon the minister didst sayeth, "O ye of little faith, didst thou thinkest that we shouldst create such a miraculous document if it was not for thine own good? Verily I say unto thee, readest thou the judgments according to Dickson and you shall be glad." And they did, but they weren't.

Here endeth our Reading.

11.8

KEY TERMS

Concepts

constitutional convention
constitutionally entrenched
canon of statutory interpretation
"interpretive avoidance"
"power allocation"
"power denial"
"equality in the application and administration of the laws"
"equal laws"
legislative override clause

Institutions, Events, and Documents

1960 Bill of Rights
Drybones v. the Queen (1969)
A.-G. Canada v. Lavell and Bedard (1974)
Charter of Rights and Freedoms (1982)

12
Judicial Decision-Making

The subject of this chapter is the decision-making processes of appeal courts, and specifically the Supreme Court of Canada. The practicing bar and the general public are interested only in the practical "product" of courts—the final judgment and opinion. However, the character and even the quality of the final product are influenced by the internal procedures of a court—how a court goes about its business. To better understand the judicial process, we must go behind the institutional facade of courts, and examine how appeal court judges actually decide cases and write opinions. (See Readings 12.1 and 12.2)

As we have seen throughout this book, courts, like other institutions, have a particular institutional logic formed by and around their purpose. Their traditional adjudicatory function has moulded the internal decision-making procedures of courts in all common law countries. The notion that the judicial function is "to find the law" led to the practice of *seriatim* opinion-writing, in which each judge gives his or her own "findings" or reasons for judgment. *Seriatim* opinions reflected and reinforced the tradition of judicial independence, which includes the independence of the judges from each other as well as from "outside" influences.

Whatever the merits of *seriatim* opinions in the traditional realm of private law, the practice is open to criticism in the realm of public law, particularly constitutional law, where judicial decisions tend to have a greater impact on public policy. The two principal criticisms of *seriatim* opinions are that they are often confusing and that they erode the authority of the court. The first criticism can be greatly appreciated by any student who has had to wade through the multiple opinions in such Supreme Court decisions as *Saumur* or *Johannesson*, both from the 1950s. In constitutional law cases, it is typical to have a number of public and private policy "actors" looking to the Supreme Court's decisions for guidance as to what is or is not permissible government policy, and what can reasonably be expected in the future. A decision that gives five different reasons for the majority decision is obviously not as helpful as a single "opinion of the court." The multiplicity of opinions also saps the authority of the court. If a final appellate court hands down a single unanimous opinion in a potentially controversial case, it sends a subtle but important message to the "losing" side that continued litigation or resistance to the decision would be futile.[1] Multiple reasons for the same result send a very different message.

Predictably it was the American Supreme Court that first abandoned the practice of *seriatim* opinion-writing. John Marshall, considered the most influential of all American chief justices, persuaded his colleagues that a single "opinion of the court" expressing the majority view would enhance the authority and prestige of the then-fledgling court. Marshall initiated the practice of formal conferences as a means for the judges to share their opinions, to discover common ground as well as differences, and so to facilitate the production of a single "opinion of the court." Until the New Deal court crisis, over 80 percent of the American Court's decisions were unanimous. Since the so-called "constitutional revolution" of 1937, however, concurring and dissenting opinions have steadily multiplied to the point where unanimous decisions account for less than 40 percent of its decisions.

Notwithstanding post-1937 developments, American Supreme Court opinions still tended to be more coherent than the Canadian Supreme Court's continuing practice of *seriatim* opinions, if simply because they were less diverse. This began to change during the 1970s, under the leadership of the late Chief Justice Laskin. Laskin initiated a number of procedural reforms designed to increase the collegiality of the court and reduce the number of separate opinions. Laskin formalized the judges' conferences by scheduling them on a regular basis. He rearranged the Court's schedule so that during their three annual sessions they hear cases for only two out of every three weeks, and no cases are scheduled for Fridays. Last, but in his own opinion not least, he had a private dining room installed, so that the judges could have lunch together and confidentially continue discussing the business before the court that day.

The greater opportunity for informal interaction and discussion among the justices was calculated to enhance the coherence of the Supreme Court's opinion-writing style. While it did not lead to the adoption of a single "opinion of the court" approach, it facilitated a more integrated set of opinions. The justices now know ahead of time one another's positions, and are more inclined to acknowledge points of agreement and disagreement in their respective opinions.

There is some evidence that these reforms have begun to affect the opinion-writing procedures of the Court. Since 1978 there have been six cases where the decision has been delivered simply as an unsigned opinion of "The Court." Prior to this there had only been one such case, the 1969 *Offshore Minerals Reference*. These decisions were unanimous and there

---

[1] The textbook example of this was the U.S. Supreme Court's decision in the 1954 *School Desegregation Case*. Then Chief Justice Warren spent several years "negotiating" with reluctant members of the Court in order to produce a unanimous opinion for a decision that he knew would incite controversy and opposition in the American South.

was no indication of who wrote the opinion. Most of these cases dealt with politically volatile issues—minority language rights in Quebec[2] and Manitoba[3], Quebec's claim to a unilateral veto over constitutional amendments[4] the federal government's claim to unilateral authority to reform the Senate,[5] and Newfoundland's jurisdictional claim to the offshore Hibernia oil fields.[6] The Supreme Court, aware of the political sensitivity of the issues raised in these cases, seems to have adopted a "united front." There has also been several instances of "group authorship" of single majority and dissenting opinions.[7] While unsigned or group-authored opinions remain very much the exception, the Supreme Court has clearly abandoned the classical *seriatim* style of each judge working alone and writing a separate opinion. Justice Wilson's account of the contemporary Supreme Court confirms the attempt to build consensus and the tendency of the judges to concur—perhaps after some bargaining—with the written opinion of another judge. (See Reading 12.1)

An institutional change that may curb the Court's quest for greater collegiality and consensus is the parallel development of the increasing use of "law clerks." A law clerk is typically a recent law school graduate individually selected by a justice to work as a research assistant.Until recently, the use of law clerks was largely an American practice. The Supreme Court of Canada did not hire its first clerk until the late 1960s. By 1978, each justice had one clerk, at which point Chief Justice Laskin hired a second. By 1984, each justice had two clerks, and Chief Justice Dickson then hired an "Adminstrative Director." While modest by American standards—there are now 29 clerks working for the American Court—the trend is clearly in the same direction. The increasing reliance on clerks has tended to bureaucratize the American Court, creating "nine little law firms" inside the court and thus eroding collegiality. (See Reading 12.2) There is no reason not to expect a similar effect from the same trend in Canada.

A related change initiated by Laskin was his preference for the Supreme Court to sit as a full nine judge bench rather than in panels of five. The practice of five judge panels had long been followed, and was defended on the grounds of efficiency. After the Supreme Court assumed final responsibility for overseeing the legal dimensions of Canada's con-

---

[2] *A.-G. Quebec v. Blaikie*, [1979] 2 S. C. R. 1016

[3] *A.-G. Manitoba v. Forest*, [1979] 2 S. C. R. 1032.

[4] [1982] 2 S.C.R. 792.

[5] [1980] 1 S. C. R. 54.

[6] Released March 8, 1984, unreported.

[7] See *Re Exported Natural Gas Tax*, [1982] 1 S.C.R. 1006.

stitutional development in 1949, this practice began to be criticized as introducing a haphazard element into the court's decisions. A case might be decided differently depending on how the five judge panel was selected, a matter totally at the discretion of the Chief Justice. This was considered particularly inappropriate in constitutional cases. Before his appointment as Chief Justice, Laskin had publicly disapproved of the five judge panels for important cases, and he quickly exercised his new administrative prerogative to implement his preferred policy of nine judge panels. The results were significant. In the three terms preceding his appointment nine judge panels heard only 10 percent of the cases argued before the Supreme Court. In the eight years following Laskin's elevation to the chief justiceship the average increased to 36 percent, and since 1976 there have been more nine judge panels than five judge panels.[8] This trend has continued through the 1980s, although seven (not nine) judge panels seem to be the norm.[9] The cumulative effect of this trend has been to increase the authority of the Supreme Court's pronouncements on constitutional issues, and so to make it a more influential participant in the political process.

The description of the American Court's decision-making process (See Reading 12.2) provides a comparative perspective and points to some interesting parallels. Both courts are constrained by the common need to find or build a consensus that can support a majority if not a unanimous judgment. This shared objective induces strategic voting and opinion-writing in both courts. The basic options are the same: join a majority opinion; concur in a majority opinion; or write a dissent. While it is more extensively documented in the American case, it is clear that judges on both courts negotiate with one another, bargaining votes for wording changes, what Justice Wilson describes as "judicial lobbying." Despite the American Court's early leadership in developing the practice of a single "Opinion of the Court," such unanimity is now the exception not the rule. It should be noted that the factors contributing to the decline of consensus on the American Court are increasingly present in the Supreme Court of Canada: control of docket, resulting in more controversial, and thus more divisive, cases being decided; the triumph of the non-interpretivist approach to constitutional interpretation; and the increasing use of law clerks.

A study of the Supreme Court's first 100 Charter of Rights decisions (See Reading 12.3) provides preliminary evidence to support this hypothesis. After an initial "Charter honeymoon," the Supreme Court has become increasingly divided in its Charter decisions. In recent years the Court has

---

[8] S.I. Bushnell, "Leave to Appeal Applications to the Supreme Court of Canada: A Matter of Public Importance," *Supreme Court Law Review* 3 (1982), p. 479.

[9] See Andrew D. Heard, "The Charter in the Supreme Court of Canada: The Importance of Which Judge Hears an Appeal, *Canadian Journal of Political Science* 24, no. 2 (1991), pp.289–307.

achieved unanimity in only 60 percent of its Charter decisions, compared to over 80 percent in its non-Charter decisions. Nor is this disagreement random. Analysis of judicial voting shows that certain judges have been consistently activist in their Charter interpretations while others have repeatedly exercised judicial self-restraint. These findings support the legal realist view that the judge is as important as the (text of the) law in determining the outcome of many cases. This conclusion was echoed by Professor Heard who concluded a similar study: "The unmistakeable conclusion of this study is that the outcome of a Charter claim argued in the Supreme Court of Canada depends to a very large extent upon which judges sit on the panel that hears the appeal."[10]

Another important procedural difference between final appellate courts is the relative importance that they assign to oral and written argument. In Great Britain, written argument is limited to a brief one or two page outline of issues and precedents, while oral argument is unlimited, and typically lasts several days. This practice represents the extension of the adversary process into the appeal courts: counsel for opposing sides do battle before passive and impartial judges. At the other extreme is the American practice of strictly limited oral argument but lengthy and detailed written "briefs." In the U.S. Supreme Court oral argument is restricted to 30 minutes, with a system of flashing lights to warn counsel that time is almost over. Prior to oral argument, however, the American justices receive written briefs of 20 to 100 pages, detailing not just the legal arguments and precedents, but often relevant socio-economic evidence as well. The purpose of oral argument is to allow the judges to questions and to clarify facts and arguments presented in the written briefs. Despite the fact that each lawyer has only 30 minutes, the justices frequently interrupt and ask questions. Unlike the appeals courts in Great Britain, it is the the judges, not the counsel, that control the course of the hearing.

Until recently, Canadian practice fell somewhat between the American and British approaches. Unlike their British counterpart, the Canadian Supreme Court developed the practice of accepting substantial written arguments, known as "factums," prior to oral hearing. Unlike the American Court, however, the Canadian Court historically allowed unlimited oral argument, often running several days. In 1972, Bora Laskin wrote than the written factum was "often subservient" to oral argument. As recently as 1986, the oral argument in the appeal of the Morgentaler abortion case went on for four days.

Perhaps as a result of this experience, the following year the Court decided that unlimited oral argument was a luxury that it could no longer afford. In the years following the adoption of the Charter, the Court fell badly behind in its caseload. The annual number of decisions handed down dropped precipitously and there were delays of 12 months and

---

[10] Ibid., p. 305.

longer between oral argument and delivery of the judgment. In 1987, the Court announced that henceforth oral argument for normal appeals would be limited to two hours, one hour for each side. They also discontinued (except for very rare instances) their traditional practice of a 15-minute oral hearing for parties seeking leave to appeal. Henceforth leave to appeal applications would have to be submitted in writing.

Some members of the Canadian Bar protested that this reform robbed them and their clients of their "day in court." It did, but the protests fell on deaf ears. The Court justified both the elimination of oral hearings for leave applications and the new time limits on oral argument as necessary efficiency measures. It was true that these reforms would save the Court many " judge-hours" that could now be devoted to other tasks. What the Court did not explicitly state was that these other tasks were a consequence of its new and evolving "supervisory" function. The Court was no longer primarily a "court of error," serving as a backup to provincial courts of appeal. Even before the adoption of the 1982 Charter of Rights, the Court had begun to change from an English-style appeals court to a more political role. The reduction of time committed to oral argument was a symptom of this change.

Perhaps no procedural change contributed more to the Supreme Court's new supervisory role than the abolition in 1975 of appeals as of right in civil cases with a value over $10,000. This reform permitted the Supreme Court to control its own docket, to pick and choose which cases raise sufficiently important questions of law or policy to merit the Supreme Court's time and energy. The impact of this change has been dramatic. Between 1970 and 1975, 72 percent of the Supreme Court's docket came from appeals as of right, and only 23 percent by its own decision to grant leave to appeal. This situation was reversed after 1975. Between 1976 and 1980, 75 percent of its cases were chosen by granting leave to appeal, while only 20 percent were heard as a matter of right.[11] This new ratio of appeals by right to appeals by leave remained relatively constant throughout the decade of the 1980s. The contrast between the new and the old Supreme Court was captured by Ian Bushnell's observation that prior to the 1975 reform, "it [was] the litigant who [was] affforded access and he [brought] the legal issue with him," while now "it is the legal problem that determines access, and the litigant is brought along with it."[12] Of course, it is the judges who determine which legal issues are sufficiently important to merit their attention.

An important but not surprising consequence of the Court's control of its docket has been a dramatic increase in the number of constitutional law

---

[11] S.I. Bushnell, "Leave to Appeal Applications to the Supreme Court of Canada: A Matter of Public Importance," *Supreme Court Law Review*, 3 (1982), p. 479.

[12] Ibid., p. 488.

cases it hears annually. Between 1950 and 1975, the Court heard only two to three constitutional cases a year. Beginning in 1975, this number began to increase, reaching an annual rate of 10 or more by 1982. The additional constitutional litigation generated by the Charter of Rights has almost tripled this rate. In November, 1989, the Supreme Court handed down its one hundredth Charter decision. (By April, 1992, this figure was approaching 200.) During this same time, the number of federalism cases has remained substantial: 31 between 1982 and 1989. In sum, approximately 30 percent of the Court's annual docket is now composed of constitutional law.

In 1972, Bora Laskin observed that the "more fixed and formal" internal structure of the American Supreme Court reflected its greater jurisdictional responsibilities. Most of the procedural changes in the Supreme Court of Canada since then—some at Laskin's initiative—may be understood as logical responses to its own growing jurisdictional responsiblities as Canada's final court of appeal. Beginning with the abolition of appeals to the JCPC in 1949, which marked the end of what Laskin sarcastically described as a "captive court", the Supreme Court of Canada has steadily discarded the procedures designed for a middle-tier British appeals court and adapted its procedures to fit its new responsibilities. The adoption of the Charter of Rights in 1982 has further stimulated this institutional "retooling," but the process began long before.

12.1

DECISION-MAKING IN THE SUPREME COURT OF CANADA

Bertha Wilson

This tension [between the judge as an individual member of the Court versus the Court as an institution] is in a rather different category from the others I have mentioned. Some judges think that the best way for an appellate court to operate is for each judge to perform his or her judicial function independently— ideally with each member of the Court writing a separate judgment. Lord Reid was a great advocate of this approach. He believed that the diversity of views expressed, although admittedly making it more difficult to identify the *ratio decidendi* of the case, had the

---

"Decision-making in the Supreme Court," *University of Toronto Law Journal* 36 (1986), from pages 235–238. Reprinted with permission.

advantage of providing greater flexibility in the development of the law. Lower courts could pick and choose from among a variety of different judicial approaches the one that seemed most appropriate to changing social conditions; the others would simply wither away. Indeed, the majority of the Law Lords, when interviewed by Alan Paterson for his book, *The Law Lords*, expressed the view that between the 1940s and the 1970s the Court's attitude to dissenting judgments had changed radically. The pressure to present a united front had gone, and the right and duty of individual expression had become central to Their Lordships' perception of their role. On the other hand, the Judicial Committee of the Privy Council for many years published only one opinion, apparently on the theory that dissenting views would weaken the authority of the tribunal which, notionally at least, was only advising the sovereign on the resolution of the dispute.

Present practice in the Supreme Court of Canada lies somewhere between these two extremes. Different members of the Court hold differing views on the extent to which it is important to develop a consensus on particular legal issues. Is public confidence in the institution enhanced by unanimous judgments? Some think so. Or do strong dissents and separate concurring reasons reflect the potential for growth and change in the system? Is there any merit in 'watering down' a judgment in the interests of unanimity? To what extent should judges try to persuade their colleagues to their point of view? And why do some judges find this process of judicial "lobbying" quite repugnant?

The answers one gives to these questions will depend, I think, on one's concept of what a collegial court is and how it should function. For some reason very little has been said or written on this very fascinating subject. Yet no consideration of the decision-making process of an appellate tribunal is complete without it. If there is, indeed, an obligation on a collegial court to strive for a consensus, or at least to submerge individuality in the interests of fewer sets of reasons, then the dynamics of the Court's process would seem to be extremely important. So let us take a brief look at what happens following the hearing of an appeal.

After argument is concluded the judges retire to a conference room to express their tentative views on the case. It is our practice for each judge to state his or her views in reverse order of seniority, beginning with the most junior judge and concluding with the most senior. The thinking behind this tradition was to avoid the more junior members of the Court simply adopting the views of their elders and betters. I may say that whatever may have been the case in the past, there is very little risk of this happening today; the members of the Court are, as the Chief Justice euphemistically puts it, "fiercely independent." It is interesting to note that the United States Supreme Court does it the other way round, proceeding on the basis of seniority, with the Chief Justice expressing his views first.

The first tentative expression of views at our conference will usually disclose whether there is any prospect of unanimity or whether there is clearly going to be more than one judgment. We decide at this conference who is going to prepare the first draft. This will be a member of the group which appears likely to form the majority. One of that group will normally volunteer or, if there is no volunteer, the Chief Justice will ask one of the group to take it on. The other judges then set aside their record in the case until a draft is circulated. Depending on the complexity of the case and the number of other judgments which a particular judge is working on, it may take several weeks or, regrettably, even months before a judgment is circulated. When this happens the judges on the panel get their papers out again, review their bench notes and any memoranda they may have dictated immediately following the hearing, study the draft, and decide whether or not they are going to be able to concur. They may at this point ask their law clerks to do some additional research.

Sometimes members of the panel will make suggestions for amendment which the author of the draft may accept or reject. Sometimes these suggested amendments are proffered in terms that that judge's concurrence is premised on their adoption. More often than not they are put forward on the basis that the judge views them as an improvement or clarification or as additional support for the result but would be willing to concur in any event. If amendments are made, the draft is recirculated and approval sought for the changes from those proposing to concur. The changes may be dropped at this point or, if not, they may spark concurring reasons.

A member of the Court may find the draft reasons totally unacceptable and will memo his or her colleagues that he or she proposes to dissent. This grinds the process of concurring to a halt since it is viewed as "bad form" to concur with the original reasons until you have seen the dissent. The same process of suggested amendment may take place with respect to the dissenting reasons. Two and maybe three sets of draft reasons are now in circulation. It is agreed at the next court conference that this is an appeal on which judgment should be released soon, on the next judgment day, if possible. The pressure is on. At this point, if not before, the individual judge's approach to decision-making becomes very important. This is particularly so in a court with a very heavy caseload. The ideal would, of course, be if all the judges could spend as much time on the cases assigned to their colleagues as they spend on the ones they are writing themselves. This is simply not possible. As the late Chief Justice Laskin put it: "If the case load is heavy, the tendency will be for judges to concentrate their limited time and their energy on opinions that have been assigned to them; and to show generous institutional faith in opinions in other cases prepared by others." Laskin concluded, therefore, that on a busy court "there is an institutional preference to support a majority result by reasons acceptable to a majority." I have no doubt that this is correct, and it should, of course, be the focal point of our concern about overworked courts. Under the pressure of a heavy caseload, the delicate balance which should exist between judicial independence and collegiality may be displaced and collegiality may give way to expediency. This is an extremely serious matter for an appellate tribunal because the integrity of the process itself is threatened. The only answer is to grant fewer leaves and make sure that the balance between the Court's sitting time and its non-sitting time is appropriate and correct, one that allows adequate time for research and reflection, for conferring with one's colleagues, and for the drafting and redrafting of reasons for judgment.

First drafts have a way of developing a life of their own as they pass through a number of different hands. This is hardly surprising in view of the tensions in the decision-making process which I have been discussing. Nor is it surprising that there are multiple judgments on a court of nine people. Consciously or subconsciously, judges bring their philosophy of judging to bear on their judgments. Yet scant attention has been paid to the presuppositions about the role of the judge on which our different philosophies are based, and to the process by which decisions are reached. I believe this is changing. I think the advent of the Charter is bringing the role of the courts into sharper focus and that one of the benefits may be a more sophisticated appreciation by both lawyers and judges of what we do. Perhaps with that more sophisticated appreciation will go an enhanced sense of responsibility and dedication to our task.

12.2

OPINION-WRITING IN THE U.S. SUPREME COURT
F.L. Morton

Conference: Preliminary Vote and Assignment of Opinions

The Supreme Court hears and decides cases from October through June each year. Normally, all nine judges sit for each case. During the weeks the Court is hearing cases, the judges meet once or twice in private conference to discuss the cases for which they heard oral argument that week. After the discussion, they take a preliminary vote and assign responsibility for writing an opinion. To preserve confidentiality and to maximize candor, the conference takes place behind locked doors, and the proceedings are secret. Only the nine judges are present. For its first 100 years, the conference played an important deliberative role in building consensus

A French version of this paper has been published as "La rédaction des opinions dans la Cour suprême," *Pouvoirs: Révue Française D'Études Constitutionneles et Politiques* 59 (1991), pp. 45–57.

among the judges for a single judgment. In recent decades increasing work-loads and changing norms have undermined the collegial and deliberative character of the conference. Its modern function is to determine if a major-ity of the nine judges support the same result and to assign responsibility for writing an opinion. Consensus, if it is to be found at all, must usually await the negotiation that accompanies the circulation of draft opinions.

Discussion of each case is initiated by the Chief Justice, followed by the eight associate justices in order of seniority. In the contemporary Court, time is a scarce resource, and those judges who choose to discuss a case are expected to limit their remarks to several minutes. Some cases of course receive much more time, others much less. When each judge has had an opportunity to speak, a preliminary vote is taken. Traditionally, the judges voted in reverse order of seniority, so that the most junior judges would not be unduly influenced by the votes of the more experienced judges. In evenly divided cases, this procedure also gave the Chief Justice the strate-gic option of casting a "tie -breaker" vote and thus becoming part of the majority. This custom was gradually discontinued during Earl Warren's tenure as Chief Justice (1953–1969), and today the judges vote in the same order they speak. Judges may still cast their conference vote in a strategic fashion. That is, a judge may vote for a result he does not really favour in order to become a part of the majority and thereby influence the writing of the majority opinion from within. Because the conference vote is tenta-tive, judges are free to change their votes later.

The primary function of the vote is to discover a majority. If the Chief Justice is a member of the majority, he can choose to write the opinion or assign it to another member of the majority. If the Chief Justice is not a member of the majority, then the most senior associate justice from the majority becomes responsible for writing the opinion or assigning it to another member of the majority. Chief Justices often keep the most impor-tant decisions for themselves. For example, Chief Justice Hughes (1930–1941) wrote the majority opinion in the landmark case of *West Coast Hotel v. Parrish* (1937), the decision that brought to an end half a century of "substantive due process" and judicial nullification of state labour regula-tions. Chief Justice Warren wrote the opinion of the Court in the landmark *School Desegregation Case* in 1954. Chief Justice Warren Burger (1969–1986) wrote the opinion of the Court in the 1974 *Watergate Tapes Case*, ordering President Richard Nixon to release the tape-recordings of his telephone conversations. The tape-recordings were so damaging that two weeks after the Court's decision, the President who had appointed Warren Burger as the Chief Justice was forced to resign. While some Chief Justices tend to write more opinions than their colleagues, the difference is small. More importantly, all of the recent chief justices have sought to assign a more or less equal number of opinions to each judge, the annual average being about 14 assigned opinions per judge.

The assignment of opinions is based on a mix of factors. Like conference voting, it has strategic dimensions. The Chief Justice can decrease the probability of a sharply divided court by assigning the opinion to a colleague who is known for moderation and "diplomacy." Such a justice is more likely to write an opinion that accomodates the diversity of opinion and thus unites the court. Specialization can also play a role. Judges with expertise in areas such as criminal law, trusts, administrative law or tax law are more likely to be asked to write opinions in cases dealing with their specialty. Anticipation of public reaction and problems of compliance can also be a factor. One Chief Justice asked a judge from the South to write an opinion that was clearly going to be unpopular in his home region. Similarly, "conservative opinions" have been asigned to "liberal judges" and vice versa. In each case, the Chief hopes that the decision will be made more acceptable to those groups who oppose it by their respect for its author.

Writing and Circulating Drafts: The Search for Consensus

Once as case has been assigned, a judge is responsible for drafting a majority opinion and then circulating it among all the other judges for comment. The initial drafting stage averages about seven weeks, and reveals one of the important institutional changes of the modern Court: the rapid increase in the number and influence of law clerks. While the first clerk was hired in 1882, no judge had more than one clerk until as recently as the 1950s. During the Warren Court era (1953–1969), the average rose to two per judge, and then to three and four per judge during the 1970s. During the 1988–89 term, there were 36 clerks.

While they perform a variety of tasks—screening cases, research, commenting—their most influential role is assisting their respective judges in the drafting of opinions. Even the judges now concede that most first drafts of opinions are done by their clerks. Less clear is the extent to which judges rely on these drafts. This varies with the judge and also with the case. Some judges may only lightly edit a clerk's draft before circulating it among their colleagues. Others may substantially rewrite it. Whatever the case, there is no doubt that cumulatively there has been a very substantial increase in the influence of clerks on the Court's final decisions.

The significance of the growth in the number and influence of clerks is two-fold. Internally, it has contributed to the bureaucratization of the Court, the isolation of the judges from one another, and thus a decline in collegiality. Most commentators now describe the Court as "nine small and independent law firms," each led by a judge, followed by his own pack of clerks, secretaries and messengers. As the caseload increases and judges increasingly rely on their clerks, there is less interaction with one another. Externally, the clerks are a symptom of the increasing political role and influence of the Court. Analysts agree that the rapid post-war growth of the Executive Office and the White House Staff testified to the new power vested in the presidency, although not necessarily the President. In an analogous way, the bureaucratic growth of the "jurocracy" testifies to the growing influence of the Court.

Once a justice is satisfied with his draft opinion, he then circulates it among the other eight judges. Each has the opportunity to comment and recommend changes. This stage of the process is a twentieth-century development, and partially fulfills the role formerly played by judicial conferences—the search for consensus. This stage of the process is characterized by negotiation, compromise and coalition building. A judge may make his support for the opinion conditional upon the author accepting his recommendations for change. To back up his position, a judge may draft and circulate a dissenting or concurring opinion of his own. A threat to dissent or concur is more effective in cases where the Court is closely divided. The author is of course free to accept or reject any and all suggestions. The author must decide whether gaining the support of another judge justifies a change or dilution in reasoning. Unanimity—or at least strong majority support—is much prized, but so is clarity and precision of reasoning. The author must choose. This bargaining process is often lengthy, and it is not unheard of for a judge to circulate as many as 10 revised drafts before gaining the support of his colleagues. While there are many colourful anecdotes of how judges have persuaded colleagues to join an opinion and thereby achieve a single opinion of the Court, the statistical reality is that compromise-based court unity has declined sharply in recent decades.

Options and Strategies in Opinion-writing

Towards the end of the circulation stage, each judge must reach a decision. There are basically three options: to join the majority of his colleagues in the opinion of the Court; to write (or join) a concurring opinion; or to write (or join) a dissenting opinion. By this time, both majority and dissenting (or concurring) opinions have usually been circulated, discussed and revised. When, after consulting his associates, the Chief Justice is satisfied that none of them desires any more time, he orders the case to be listed as one of the decisions to be announced by the Court in the following week.

A unanimous "opinion of the Court" is the preferred mode of decision. It conveys the symbolic values associated with "the rule of law": certainty, stability and impartiality. By speaking with a single voice, the Court also enhances the clarity and authority of its decision. Such clarity and authority are especially prized in decisions that the justices know in advance will be controversial. For example, Chief Justice Earl Warren worked long and hard to achieve unanimous support for the Court's 1954 *School Desegregation Decision*. Knowing that the desegregation order would incite hostility

and resistance in the South, Warren believed that unanimity was imperative to demonstrate the entire Court's commitment to the decision.
Similarly, Chief Justice Burger carried on extensive negotiations with his
eight colleagues to achieve a unanimous decision in the *Watergate Tapes
Case* that led to the resignation of President Nixon.

The political utility of a single opinion has obviously recommended
itself to other constitutional courts. By hiding divisions within a court
from public notice, the use of single, anonymous opinion dissimulates the
political character of judicial decision-making in constitutional courts. The
Conseil Constitutionnel in France, the Supreme Court in Italy, the new
Cour d'arbitrage in Begium, the European Court of Justice, have all adopted
the device of a single, institutional opinion. The German Constitutional
Court began allowing dissents in 1971, but they remain rare. In Canada,
the Supreme Court has used a single (and sometimes anonymous) "Opinion of the Court" in several controversial cases involving federalism and
language issues. Ironically, while the American Supreme Court provided
the original model of the negotiation-based institutional opinion, in recent decades it has found itself increasingly incapable of achieving such
consensus. Precisely because important cases are often the most controversial, unanimity is elusive. Given the increasing tendency toward
concurring and dissenting opinions, the judges are usually happy if they
can just garner solid majority support (e.g., 7–2, 6–3) for the Opinion of the
Court.

A concurring opinion reaches the same result as the majority opinion,
but relies upon different reasoning. When a judge believes that the majority has reached the correct result but for the wrong reason, he can write a
concurring opinion that explains the legal argument he believes supports
the result. While concurring opinions are defended as an aspect of judicial
independence and as a way to illuminate legal issues ignored by the majority, they have the unfortunate consequence of eroding the clarity and
thus the authority of a decision. This is especially true when the number of
judges writing (or joining) plurality opinions prevents the Court from
achieving majority agreement on the legal reasoning to support the result.
In this case, the opinion supported by the most judges (but not a majority)
becomes the "plurality opinion." A plurality opinion explains the outcome of the case at hand, but lacks authority as precedent for future cases.
Needless to say, this complicates the job of lower court judges who look to
the Court for guidance and for public officials who are expected to comply
with the Court's ruling.

A third option is to write (or join) a dissenting opinion. A dissenting
opinion disagrees with both the reasoning and the result of the majority. A
judge uses a dissenting opinon to declare that he would have decided the
case differently and to explain why. Following the common law practice
inherited from Britain, the American Supreme Court has always recognized the right of a judge to write a dissenting opinion as an essential

element of judicial independence; that is, independence from the other judges. However, in its very early years the Court developed an institutional norm strongly favouring a single, institutional opinion of the Court. Dissenting opinions were viewed as a form of "institutional disobedience," and discouraged.

This is not to say that they did not exist, nor to deny that they were influential. Indeed, some of the most famous justices to sit on the Supreme Court are celebrated in part for their influential dissenting opinions. For example, Oliver Wendell Holmes's dissent in the 1905 case of *Lochner v. New York* became the guiding light for the next generation's criticism of the doctrine of "substantive due process" and freedom of contract. In 1937 Holmes's dissenting argument became the majority opinion when the Supreme Court overruled the *Lochner* precedent and renounced further judicial interference with state regulation of labour and industry. Similarly Justice Harlan's dissenting opinion in *Plessy v. Ferguson* (1896)—that "Our Constitution is color-blind and neither knows nor tolerates classes among citizens"—was adopted by the unanimous Court in *Brown v. Board of Education* (1954).

The decision to write a dissenting (or concurring) opinion is not the same as a decision to publish it. The former has long been a regular feature of the circulation stage of the Court's work. Initially it is a posture, a bargaining position, intended to influence other judges to change or at least to accomodate the views of the potential dissenter. The decision to actually publish a dissenting opinion rests on very different calculations. It is unlikely to influence members of the majority opinion, at least in the short term. Indeed, a judge who dissents repeatedly risks alienating other members of the Court, who may come to view a chronic dissenter as an unreliable colleague. This is especially true if the dissenter impugns the intelligence or integrity of the majority opinion. The decision to publish a dissenting opinion usually rests on the hope that it will persuade future judges or future courts to the dissenter's position. The examples of the "great dissenters"—Harlan, Holmes, Brandeis and others—have conferred not only legitimacy but a certain romantic character on dissenting opinions. In this respect, a dissent may be understood as an appeal to future generations.

Historical Trends

The practice of writing a single "Opinion of the Court" originated with the justly celebrated Chief Justice, John Marshall (1803–1836). Until Marshall's appointment, the new Supreme Court operated under the British practice of *seriatim* opinion-writing, according to which each judge normally writes a separate opinion. Marshall was the first to perceive that the Court's prestige and authority would be enhanced if it spoke in a single, unified voice. Over the strong protests of President Thomas Jefferson, a sharp critic of both Marshall and the novel doctrine of judicial review, Marshall persuaded his colleagues to adopt, whenever possible, a single opinion. Under Marshall's leadership, this became the norm for the next 130 years.

Prior to the 1930s, 80 to 85 percent of the Supreme Court's decisions were unanimous. Since then, the rate of unanimity has dropped to 25 to 30 percent. During the last years of the Hughes Court (1937–1940), the Court averaged 179 opinions per year: 144 institutional opinions and 35 separate, concurring and dissenting opinions. Between 1968–1980, the Court issued an average of 331 opinions per year: 138 institutional opinions; 43 separate opinions, 45 concurring opinions and 105 dissenting opinions. Thus after 40 years, there were seven times more separate opinions, four times more dissenting opinions and 10 times more concurring opinions. The severity of the dissensus on the modern Court is also reflected in the rapid increase in plurality opinions, cases in which the Court cannot generate majority-support for an opinion. There were more plurality opinions—116—during the Burger Court years (1969–1986) than during the entire previous history of the Court (61).

There are several causes behind this trend. One cause is institutional. The growing case-load and reliance on clerks has increasingly isolated the judges from one another. This in turn has undermined the the collegial, deliberative character of the Court that in the past supported the norm of suppressing disagreements in order to achieve a unanimous, institutional opinion. A second cause is procedural. Since 1925, the Court has had almost absolute discretion in choosing the cases it hears. Prior to 1925, 80 percent of the Court's docket consisted of cases that it was legally obligated to hear, most of them with little significance beyond the parties to the case. Today this figure is less than five percent. The judges normally exercise their discretion to hear cases that involve legal issues of political importance. Because they are political, these cases are more likely to elicit disagreement and less likely to facilitate compromise.

Least tangible but no less important has been the triumph of the non-interpretivist school of constitutional interpretation, or what Wolfe describes as "modern judicial review"—the transition "from constitutional intepretation to judge-made law." The influence of legal realism has eroded the old model of judicial review as the quest for "the true meaning of the Constitution" and replaced it with judicial adaptation of "constitutional principles" to modern social needs and changing values. While the old model allowed for only one "true meaning," the new model allows for as many meanings as there are judges.

These changes have eroded the old norms that facilitated the production of a single opinion of the Court. The lower dissent rates in the nineteenth century do not reflect greater consensus, but different institutional norms. Nineteenth century judges conceived that their first duty was to produce as near as possible a unanimous opinion of the Court, and were thus more willing to compromise their own views and accomodate those of their associates.

The extensive use of dissenting and concurring opinions is one of the distinctive characteristics of the American Supreme Court. They distinguish the American Court from most comparable constitutional courts in the civil law nations of Europe, where a single institutional opinion is the *de jure* or *de facto* norm. While concurring and dissenting opinions are also found in the courts of other common law nations, the justification is usually judicial independence. By contrast, the use of concurring and dissenting opinions in the American Supreme Court has a distinctively political character. As the statistical trends discussed below reveal, the norms of the modern, post-New Deal Court clearly favour individual opinions over institutional opinions. The freedom and willingness of judges to write concurring and dissenting opinions has political signficance. As O'Brien has observed, "The Court now functions more like a legislative body relying simply on a tally of the votes to decide cases than like a collegial body working toward collective decisions and opinions."

Content: Ratio Decidendi and Obiter Dicta

A final distinctive characteristic of the opinions of the American Supreme Court are their length and content. The average length of opinions has steadily increased from eight pages in the 1930s to seven in 1970 to 11 pages during the 1980s. Since most cases involve several opinions (i.e., the opinion of the Court, perhaps a concuring opinion and a dissent), a single case may easily take 20 or 30 pages in the law reports.

The length of the Court's opinions is readily explained by the long-established practice of not limiting opinions to the facts and *ratio decidendi*—the strict legal ruling—of the case, but to indulge in lengthy flights of *obiter dicta*—statements expressing the judges' opinions about collateral issues—often political—that "flesh out" the narrower legal ruling. Because *obiter dicta* are distinct from the *ratio*, they technically do not constitute binding precedent. However, often it is difficult to determine where the *ratio* ends and the *obiter* begins.

Chief Justice Marshall's lucid and compelling digressions on the nature of federalism and the separation of powers established the practice of allowing the justices considerable latitude in their use of peripheral political or policy analysis in their opinions. The broad scope of the Court's opinions often give them the character of essays or treatises. Compared to the much shorter, formal and sometimes cryptic decisions of the Conseil Constitutionnel, the American court's opinions provide more interesting reading. Indeed, the better opinions constitute a sub-category of American political literature. They are read by university students, discussed in the newspapers, and quoted by politicians. This celebrity is not without its price. The political character of the Court's opinions dissolves the protective veneer of legalism and subjects them to constant scrutiny and frequent criticism. Just as American politicians use public speeches, so the justices can use their written opinions to try to shape public opinion on critical issues of the day. Like their political counterparts, sometimes they succeed and sometimes they fail.

12.3

JUDGING THE JUDGES: CONSENSUS AND DISSENT IN THE SUPREME COURT'S CHARTER DECISIONS

F.L. Morton, Peter H. Russell, and Michael J. Withey

[Ed.note: Preceding sections of this study are reprinted in Reading 11.6.]

Divisions Within the Court

The Supreme Court's initial consensus on the Charter has broken down. Since the opening activist "honeymoon", the Court has become increasingly divided in its approach to the Charter. Table 1 presents the percentage of unanimous Supreme Court Charter decisions in Charter and non-Charter cases. Note first how the former has fallen steadily. Since 1986 there have been dissents in two out of every five Charter decisions. Meanwhile, the percentage of unanimous decisions in non-Charter cases has remained relatively steady in the 80 percent range, which is the same as pre-Charter practice. This means that the growing dissensus on the Court is limited to Charter cases. A 60 percent unanimity rate is still high by American standards. During the same time period as our study, the American Supreme Court was unanimous in only 23.1 percent (39/169) of its Bill of Rights decisions, and 37.7 percent overall (276/732). These figures are consistent with trends over the past four decades. However, prior to the 1930s—that is, before the Bill of Rights became the most active part of the its workload— the American Court also enjoyed unanimity in over 80 percent of its decisions. With the advent of "modern judicial review," its preoccupation with rights and emphasis on judicial discretion, this consensus quickly evaporated. Since these conditions now apply in Canada, the declining consensus on the Canadian Court associated with the advent of the Charter may only be the beginning of a longer trend toward still greater dissensus.

A version of this paper appeared as "The Supreme Court's First One Hundred Charter of Rights Decisions: A Statistical Analysis," *Osgoode Hall Law Journal* 30, no. 1 (1992), pp. 2–52.

Table 1

Unanimity in Charter and Non-Charter Cases

Year	Charter Decisions	Unanimous Judgments	
		Charter	Non-Charter
1984	4	100%	88%
1985	11	82%	83%
1986	11	55%	89%
1987	23	61%	85%
1988	25	64%	85%
1989	26	61%	77%
Totals	100	65%	

"Dissent is usually not a game played in solitude; the great majority of all Supreme Court dissents are concurred in by two, three or four justices." So wrote C. Herman Pritchett about the American Supreme Court. While it is true to a lesser degree of the Canadian Supreme Court, the study of dissenting voting patterns suggests that they are not random but reflect a shared judicial philosphy.

Table 2 presents one way of analyzing the patterns of inter-agreement among the nine justices who participated in a substantial number of the Court's first 100 Charter decisions. The top line records the number of cases in which a justice dissented. The numbers below indicate the number of times the other justices also dissented in the same cases. Solo dissents are shown in brackets. The table is arranged so that each judge is placed closest to those with whom he or she joined in dissent most often and furthest from those with whom they dissented least often. A difficulty in interpreting levels of inter-agreement within the Canadian Supreme Court arises from fact that the full Court rarely participates in decisions. Indeed, nine justices participated in only eight of these first 100 Charter cases. Thus, to some extent, levels of inter-agreement may be affected by the frequency with which justices participate in the same cases. Nonetheless, even with this caveat, a fairly clear pattern emerges from Table 2. There has been a tendency for three justices—Wilson, Lamer and Dickson—to cluster together at one end of the Court, while Justice McIntyre has been relatively isolated at the other end of the Court. McIntyre received some support from L'Heureux-Dubé after she joined the Court in 1987. Note that McIntyre has never been joined in dissent by Wilson, Lamer or Dickson.

Table 2

Pattern of Division: Voting Blocs Inter-agreement in Dissents

1984–1989 Terms	No. of Dissents	Wilson	Lamer	Dickson	Estey	Beetz	LeDain	LaForest	L'Heureux Dubé	McIntyre
		13	9	6	3	3	1	3	3	11
Wilson		(5)								
Lamer		4	(2)							
Dickson		3	3	()						
Estey		1			(1)					
Beetz			1	1		()				
LeDain							()			
LaForest		1	1	1			1	(1)		
L'Heureux-Dubé		1					1		()	
McIntyre		1			1	1	1	1	2	(5)

Ideological Differences Between Justices

While Table 2 indicates how the Court has divided over Charter interpretation, it does not provide any information as to the direction of the division. Tables 3 and 4 leave no doubt about the ideological nature of the cleavage within the Court. Wilson and Lamer are at the more activist end of the court, while McIntyre and L'Heureux-Dubé have been the justices most inclined to favour judicial self-restraint. Table 3 shows the vote orientation of the justices in all of their Charter decisions—unanimous as well as split decisions. Wilson has supported the Charter litigant in over half the cases she has participated in—a startling 53 percent. At the other extreme are L'Heureux-Dubé (15%) and McIntyre (23%), both less than half the rate of Wilson. Lamer, at 47 percent, is closest to Wilson, followed by Estey (47%). The rest of the justices fall into a wide middle ground ranging from 30 percent (LaForest) to 39 percent (Beetz). The Court average is 37 percent.

Table 3

Vote Orientation

| | Votes in support of Individual | | Total no. of Charter Decisions |
	Number	Percent	
Wilson	41	53%	78
Lamer	37	47%	79
Dickson	28	37%	76
Estey	16	47%	34
Beetz	23	39%	59
LeDain	15	36%	42
LaForest	18	28%	65
L'Heureux-Dubé	4	15%	26
McIntyre	17	23%	74
Totals	199	37%	533

Table 4 indicates the same pattern with regard to dissents in split decisions. All of Wilson's and Lamer's dissents have come in decisions in which the Charter claimant has lost, whereas all but one of McIntyre's and L'Heureux-Dubé's dissents have been in cases in which the majority has favoured the Charter claimant.

Table 4

Vote Orientation: Dissents

	Number of Dissents	Outcome of Majority Decision	
		Individual Wins	State Wins
Wilson	13	0	13
Lamer	9	0	9
Dickson	6	1	5
Estey	3	1	2
Beetz	3	1	2
LeDain	1	1	0
LaForest	3	1	2
L'Heureux-Dubé	3	2	1
McIntyre	11	10	1
	52	17	35

It is interesting to observe the position of the then Chief Justice Dickson. Certainly his voting record in Tables 3 and 4 shows that he has leaned towards the more activist end of the Court and has been more inclined than any other justice to join Wilson and Lamer. On the other hand he has not isolated himself at that end of the court and has been able to play the role of an activist-leaning leader on the Court. Evidence for this can be found in the fact that his overall voting record of favouring the Charter claimant in 37 percent of his decisions is almost the same as the overall Court average. Also, he has never dissented by himself.

Table 5 throws further light on the ideological differences within the Court. Table 5 records the tendency of the justices' dissenting and concurring opinions to give a broader or narrower interpretation of the Charter. This table includes concurring opinions, which are often written to mark out a significant departure from the interpretation advanced in the main opinion on either the majority or dissenting side. Hence it is likely to give a fuller picture of the orientation of a justice's Charter jurisprudence. Table 5 shows an even sharper cleavage than the voting tables. Whereas not one of the concurring and dissenting opinions of L'Heureux-Dubé and McIntyre supported a broader interpretation of the Charter section in question, all but three of those in which Wilson, Lamer and Dickson have participated argue for a wider interpretation.

Table 5

**Direction of Charter Interpretation in
Dissenting and Concurring Opinions**

	Broader	Narrower	Same
Wilson	28	2	1
Lamer	11	1	4
Dickson	12	1	3
Estey	2	4	1
Beetz	1	4	5
LeDain	2	4	2
LaForest	5	5	2
L'Heureux-Dubé	0	3	0
McIntyre	0	16	6

The data presented in tables 1 to 5 make it clear that there is growing disagreement on the Supreme Court over how the Charter should be interpreted. The number of unanimous decisions has decreased every year while the number of dissenting opinions has risen steadily. Nor is this division random. The data show a clear pattern of voting blocs. The Court has divided into two wings and a centre. The activist wing is led by Justice Wilson and includes Justice Lamer and usually the Chief Justice. This bloc has provided the most consistent support for Charter litigants, given broader interpretations to Charter rights, and frequently dissented together—usually when the majority votes against the Charter claimant. They are also less likely to accept "section 1 defences" and more likely to exclude evidence under section 24(2).

The other wing exemplifies the philosophy of judicial self-restraint and has been led by Justice McIntyre. While McIntyre lacked reliable allies, he managed to attract all members of the Court to join him in dissent at least once, except for the three members of the activist wing. Since her appointment in 1987, Justice L'Heureux-Dubé has frequently voted with Justice McIntyre. Justice LaForest is an occasional member of this bloc. All of them have been much less likely to support Charter claims, tend to give narrower interpretations of the Charter, are more receptive toward "section 1 defences" and more reluctant to dismiss illegally obtained evidence. The "leader" labels apply to Wilson and McIntyre because they are on the opposite ends of the activist-restraint spectrum in every table but one.

They also "lead" the Court in the number of dissents and the number of solo dissents, yet have never dissented together.

In sum, Wilson and McIntyre have developed very different theories of proper judicial review under the Charter, theories that consistently lead them to very different results. Lamer and Dickson seem to share Wilson's activist perspective, but are less consistent in following it. L'Heureux-Dubé and, to a lesser extent, LaForest, are sympathetic to McIntyre's vision of judicial self-restraint. The other justices have hewn to a more pragmatic, middle ground. These findings support Gold's earlier qualitative studies of the justices' Charter jurisprudence.These differences make it clear that in "border line" cases—and thus far, no cases have involved clear cut violations of well established rights—it is the judge not the Charter that determines the outcome of the case.

This conclusion should come as no surprise to those familiar with the American Supreme Court. Particularly since 1937, it too has fragmented into different voting blocs with even wider discrepancies between the voting records of the judges. On the Burger Court (1968–1986), for example, support for civil liberties claims ranged from a high of 90.6 percent for Justice Douglas to a low of 19.6 percent for Justice Rehnquist.

Canadian and American experiences diverge at this point, however. In the U.S., the perception of federal judges as essentially political actors has given rise to an increasingly partisan competition over judicial appointments. The "Bork Affair" was only the most recent and most visible incident in this struggle. [Ed. note: See Reading 4.6.] Such nakedly partisan attempts to shape the outcome of the Supreme Court's decisions by strategic judicial appointments sits poorly with traditional concepts of judicial independence and impartiality. In practice, however, it is consistent with interest group behaviour in contemporary western democracies. As V.O. Key has written: "Where power rests, there influence will be brought to bear." Courts that act politically will come to be treated politically.

In Canada, however, there has thus far been no evidence that the federal government has let ideological criteria influence its Supreme Court appointments. Nor has there been much popular interest in following the American practice of subjecting the views of Supreme Court justices to public examination before they are appointed. Unlike Americans, it would appear that Canadians prefer to remain in a state of ideological innocence about their judges. This traditional, legalistic view of judges may be the legacy of the dominant English influence in Canadian law prior to 1982. Further evidence of differences within the Court on Charter issues may well transform this condition in the future.

At a minimum, the growing perception of "different judges, different rights" is likely to produce demands that the Supreme Court cease its current practice of sitting in panels of seven or fewer justices—something they did in approximately 75 percent of their first 100 Charter decisions. In these cases, the outcome of a Charter challenge may be largely determined by the selection of justices for the panel that hears the case, rather than the merits of the case. The prospects of a Charter claimant are much better before a five-judge panel which includes Chief Justice Dickson and Justices Lamer and Wilson, rather than one which includes Justices McIntyre, L'Heureux-Dubé and LaForest. Awareness of this fact will generate increasing pressure to organize the Court's work so that all nine justices participate in Charter cases.

12.4

KEY TERMS

Concepts

seriatim opinion writing
"opinion of the court"
majority opinion
dissenting opinion
concurring opinion
plurality decision
judicial collegiality
five and nine judge panels

13

Reconciling Judicial Review and Constitutional Democracy

The readings in this final chapter address some of the fundamental questions about the practice of judicial review. The late Donald Smiley's contribution argues that the real question raised by the constitutional entrenchment of rights is not whether Canadians shall have civil liberties or not, but *who* defines and ranks these liberties. (See Reading 13.1) The principal effect of a document like the Charter is to transfer the primary, although not exclusive, responsibility for such decisions from the legislatures to the courts. Smiley expresses scepticism over the judges' ability to make these kinds of decisions better than Canada's elected legislators. Smiley's argument, written in 1975, accurately reflected the confidence in parliamentary democracy that was widespread in Canada prior to the 1980s. This confidence was shared by legal and judicial elites and accounted in large part for the Supreme Court's extremely cautious and narrow interpretation of the 1960 Bill of Rights.

Smiley's scepticism can be summarized in the following question: What special competences do judges have that elected legislators lack? The late Alexander Bickel, the leading American constitutional scholar of his generation, has answered this question. A justification of judicial review, Bickel argued, must rest on principle, rather than habit and tradition.

> The search must be for a function which might (indeed, must) involve the making of policy, yet which differs from the legislative and executive functions; which is peculiarly suited to the capabilities of the courts; which will not likely be performed elsewhere if the courts do not assume it; which can be so exercised as to be acceptable in a society that generally shares Judge Learned Hand's satisfaction in a "sense of common venture"; which will be effective when needed; and whose discharge by the courts will not lower the quality of the other departments' performance by denuding them of the dignity and burden of their own responsibility.[1]

---

[1] *The Least Dangerous Branch: The Supreme Court at the Bar of Politics* (Indianapolis, IN: Bobbs Merrill, 1962), p. 24.

The potentially unique contribution of judicial review, according to Bickel, is the defence and articulation of a society's fundamental political and ethical principles. In the name of individual liberty, the pursuit of self-interest is given wide range in Western democracies. The executive and legislative branches are purposely made responsive to the resulting clash of interests and groups that is the stuff of democratic politics. Amidst the welter of competing self-interests, the rush and crush of practical affairs, and the ensuing short-term perspective on all matters, it is prudent to have one institution, purposely distanced from the fray, to guard society's fundamental institutions and to protect its organizing ethical principles. Judicial review offers this potential.

The contribution by then Justice Brian Dickson, later the Chief Justice of the Supreme Court of Canada, elaborates one dimension of Bickel's defence of judicial review. (See Reading 13.2) It does not do to say that judicial review is "undemocratic" simply because it sometimes replaces the decisions of a representative assembly with the judgment of nine, non-elected judges. In many instances the principles that the court intervenes to protect—freedom of political speech and press, freedom of association and thought—are indispensable to the very processes that constitute liberal democracy.

Chief Justice Dickson's remarks also reflect the new confidence in courts that supported the Supreme Court's activist and "purposive" jurisprudence in the first decade of the Charter. Unlike the 1960 Bill of Rights, Dickson declared, "there can be no doubt as to the legitimacy of judicial review" under the Charter. While there is no question that the sanguine "Dickson perspective" overwhelmed the sceptical "Smiley perspective" during the 1980s, the debate over the legitimacy of judicial review under the Charter has not disappeared. As Patrick Monahan has pointed out, "The debate is [no longer] over judicial review *per se*, but rather over what type of judicial review can be justified in a democratic polity."[2] As in all practical matters, the legitimacy of the principle does not vouch for the legitimacy of its application.

This new version of the legitimacy debate can arise in the context of a specific Charter decision, such as *Operation Dismantle* (See Justice Wilson's judgment in Reading 7.4, and Monahan's critique); or, more generally, in competing approaches to constitutional interpretation, such as the interpretivism versus non-interpretivism debate. (See Introduction to Chapter 11) It has also arisen in the debate over the section 33 "notwithstanding" (or legislative override) clause of the Charter. John Whyte, former Dean of Law at Queen's University, has forcefully argued for abolishing the legislative override power. (See Reading 13.3) Note that White's argument shares the same optimism about the political capacity of judges that is found in the Dickson reading. In a similar vein, Peter Russell's equally forceful defence of section 33 resonates with the same scepticism of judicial policy-making that

---

2 See Patrick Monahan, *Politics and the Constitution: The Charter, Federalism and the Supreme Court of Canada* (Toronto, ON: Carswell-Methuen, 1987), p. 31.

animated Smiley's earlier critique. The players and the law has changed, but the debate endures.

If, as Whyte (and also former Chief Justice Dickson) alleges, section 33 essentially allows legislatures to violate constitutional rights when they deem it appropriate, it would be hard indeed to justify. If, on the other hand, most Charter litigation is not about the traditional or core meaning of a right, but about its extension to new areas of behaviour, or balancing it against competing and equally important rights, then section 33 appears in a different light. From this perspective, what section 33 allows a government to override is not so much the right itself but the Court's interpretation of that right. Unless one accepts the theory of judicial infallibility, there is nothing intrinsically illegitimate about this. It provides, as Peter Russell has argued elsewhere, a form of legislative review of judicial review.

In fact, section 33 may be properly conceived as only a more formal procedure for giving expression to the ultimate sovereignty of majority public opinion in democratic societies. Contrary to Chief Justice Dickson's (See Reading 13.2), the American Supreme Court has not always had "the final word" in constitutional disputes. The history of the United States is strewn with Supreme Court decisions that have been reversed. This has been accomplished by such various means as constitutional amendment, withdrawal of appellate jurisdiction, statutory reversal (i.e., new legislation), courtpacking and even outright defiance.[3] In this respect, Russell is correct in placing the section 33 override as simply another intermediate step along this continuum. In the final analysis, the debate over section 33 reflects the ambiguous nature of judicial authority. That nature, and the difficult task it imposes on constitutional judges, was captured by Tocqueville's analysis of the American federal courts over one hundred years ago:

> [The power of the courts] is immense, but it is a power springing from opinion. They are all powerful so long as the people consent to obey the law; they can do nothing when they scorn it. Now of all powers, that of opinion is the hardest to use, for it is impossible to say exactly where its limits come. Often it is as dangerous to lag behind as to outstrip it.

> The federal judges therefore must not only be good citizens and men of education and integrity, qualities necessary for all magistrates, but must also be statesmen; they must know how to understand the spirit of the age, to confront those obstacles that can be overcome, and to steer out of the current when the tide threatens to carry them away, and with them the sovereignty of the Union and obedience to its laws.[4]

The written constitution, in the end, is no stronger than the unwritten constitution.

---

[3] Examples of all of these may be found in chapter 6 of Louis Fisher, *Constitutional Dialogues: Interpretation as Political Process* (Princeton, NJ: Princeton University Press, 1988). Indeed, section 33 is functionally almost indistinguishable from the American court-curbing device of Congress withdrawing the Supreme Court's appellate jurisdiction over controversial subjects.

[4] Alexis de Tocqueville, *Democracy in America*, ed. J.P Meyer (Garden City, NY: Anchor, 1969), pp. 150–151.

13.1

COURTS, LEGISLATURES, AND THE PROTECTION OF HUMAN RIGHTS
Donald Smiley

This paper examines in a Canadian context the appropriateness of judicial as against legislative decision in the definition and ranking of human rights. The issue is often put within the framework of proposals for the further entrenchment of human rights in the Canadian constitution. . . . Most provisions related to human rights . . . would necessarily be expressed in general language conferring on the courts of law the responsibility of defining and ranking rights in an ongoing process of judicial review of the constitution. . . .

. . . Most discussions of legislative as against judicial decision with respect to human rights proceed according to conflicting views of what I call democratic fundamentalism.

The first view asserts that, in terms of democratic theory, elected officials have better claims than courts to define and rank human rights as well as to make other important decisions about public policy. Democracy in this view is government in accord with the will of the governed, and the organs of government best able and most likely to act in accord with this will are composed of people who have successfully contested popular elections—and act in anticipation of future elections. I do not find this argument completely convincing. If we look at the operative constitution of any developed political system—the constitution in action as against the constitution of the textbooks of law or civics—we find a complex allocation of discretionary powers. Powers are wielded in various kinds of matters by judges and juries, by political executives and career bureaucrats, by elected legislatures and political parties, by the electorate, by the groups who effect constitutional amendment. And we also find different kinds of procedural rules for reaching various kinds of decisions—unanimous consent in jury verdicts, certain motions in the House of Commons and the most crucial of constitutional amendments, consensual decision-making at federal-provincial conferences and, perhaps, in cabinets, pluralities, bare majorities and extraordinary majorities as so defined, different provisions for quorums, and so on. On this basis, I would see no *a priori* reason stemming from democratic theory which would prevent a democratic community from conferring decisions involving human rights

Courts and Trials: A Multidisciplinary Approach. Edited by M.L. Friedland (Toronto, ON: University of Toronto Press, 1975), from pages 89–101. Reprinted with permission.

on the courts or from enacting provisions respecting such rights other than those which prevail in respect to ordinary lawmaking....

... It seems to me ... that the connection between the preferred procedures for protecting human rights and natural law is historical and psychological rather than logical in the sense that if the imperatives of natural law are binding, surely they bind legislatures as much as courts. Which of the two sets of institutions will better protect such rights is thus a matter of prudential political judgment rather than political philosophy....

... Perhaps some will agree with most of this but still maintain that, on balance, courts will be wiser and more zealous than elected bodies in defining and ranking human rights. In much of the argument for entrenchment there is the underlying premise that the community needs to be saved from the inherently liberal tendencies of public opinion because these create irresistible pressures on elected legislatures. Perhaps. It is my own impression, however, that in Canada the elected political elites are considerably more liberal than are the prevailing sentiments in their respective local, provincial, and national electorates. Again, it is my impression that when we begin to inquire carefully into those institutions of Canadian society under the direct control of the bar and the bench we will find less than a total commitment to humane values. There is a strain of absolutism in recent Canadian proposals for an entrenched Bill of Rights. Prime Minister Trudeau said in 1969, "To enshrine a right in a constitutional charter is to make an important judgment, to give to that right of the individual a higher order of value than the right of government to infringe it." This argument proceeds on the assumption that encroachments on human rights are always unequivocal and disinterested and liberal people will always be able to agree when such encroachments are made. Again, if we take Mr. Trudeau's statement literally, there is the assumption that under all conceivable circumstances entrenched rights are to prevail over other considerations. These absolutist premises are in practice indefensible. In the sphere of human rights there is indeed an economy, and rights have what economists call "opportunity costs," in the sense that to get something of value it is necessary to give up something else of value.

As a non-lawyer, it seems clear to me that if Canadian courts are to assume a more active role in the ranking and defining of human rights there must be profound changes in the Canadian legal culture. Canadian jurists are profoundly in the positivist tradition. But the determination of human rights in particular circumstances is in Peter Russell's terms the "delicate balancing of social priorities." I confess not to know the shape of the new jurisprudence or how judges and legal scholars are going to get us to realize it while maintaining the continuity with past traditions and lines of judicial interpretation that is surely necessary in our kind of polity. I confess also that the break proposed by Atkey and Lyon is too radical for me. But perhaps there should be a warning to enthusiasts for a socially relevant jurisprudence. This approach by its nature downgrades the technical nature of the law, and when members of bar and bench set up shop to articulate the political need and political ideals of the community they enter a world in which others make the same claims. To be blunt: as piety does not make a theologian or pugnacity a military strategist, an increasing social sensitivity among lawyers and judges is no substitute for intellectual discipline in the social sciences and political philosophy.

To return to the main argument of this paper, I quote what I said on a previous occasion:

> Apart from those times where public opinion is inflamed, the democratic legislature is uniquely equipped to make sound judgments about human rights. In my view Parliament has been at or near its best in some of the debates about human rights in the past decade, debates in respect to capital punishment, divorce, abortion, hate literature, official languages. Although the determination of the scope and nature of human rights usually involves some technical considerations, the technical content of reasoned discussion and decision is characteristically not as high as in regard to, say, defence policy or environmental pollution. Thus the major considerations in respect to human rights ordinarily involve the clash of human values, the sense of the community about what is acceptable and the broadest judgments of where society is going. Further, questions involving human rights tend not to be as localized in their incidence as is true of many other public policies and the Member of Parliament may well be more free to act primarily as a member of a deliberative body rather than a voice of particularized constituency interests. Elected politicians working within an environment of public discussion and debate are well equipped to deal wisely with questions of human rights. It is yet to be demonstrated that the Canadian judiciary can do better....

13.2

THE DEMOCRATIC CHARACTER OF THE CHARTER OF RIGHTS

Brian Dickson

It has sometimes been said that the Charter marks an "Americanization" of the Canadian Constitution. It has not always been clear to me whether this is meant as praise, as criticism, or simply as a neutral statement of fact, but however it is intended I think it is only partly true at best....

... The American Constitutional system is sometimes described as one of "judicial supremacy." Whether or not this characterization is strictly

---

From a lecture delivered at the University of Calgary, Faculty of Law, September 13, 1983. Reprinted with permission.

accurate in political science terms, there is no doubt that in a real sense the American judiciary always has the last word. American legislation must conform to the Constitution including the Bill of Rights, and once the Supreme Court has ruled that a given enactment violates the Bill of Rights the legislature's only recourse is to the lengthy and difficult process of constitutional amendment.

The Anglo-Canadian tradition, by contrast, is one of parliamentary sovereignty. A British Parliament is free to pass any legislation it wishes and no court has jurisdiction to invalidate a regularly enacted statute. The only constraints on Parliament in its legislative capacity are political ones. In Canada this concept of parliamentary sovereignty was modified to the extent that the distribution of powers under the British North America Act necessitated giving the courts a mandate to rule on whether a given enactment was within the legislative competence of the enacting parliament. But assuming that the distribution of powers in ss. 91 and 92 of the British North America Act was respected it was generally thought that there was no other limit on parliamentary sovereignty.

It seems clear that the very concept of a bill of rights which would act as a further constraint on Parliament's legislative freedom is in serious conflict with the assumptions of such a theory. The history of the Canadian Bill of Rights perhaps illustrates some of the consequences of this conflict. It is true that in the *Drybones* decision the Supreme Court of Canada held that the Canadian Bill of Rights did provide a mandate to strike down legislation inconsistent with the fundamental freedoms enumerated in the Bill, but that mandate was always controversial. . . . It is sufficient to note that despite the *Drybones* decision the Canadian judiciary proved itself to be very cautious about using the Bill of Rights to override the enactments of democratically-elected legislatures or to expand the ambit of judicial review. . . .

. . . Much of this caution is no doubt to be attributed to the fact that in contrast to the American Bill of Rights, the Canadian Bill was simply an ordinary statute, or at most, in the words of Chief Justice Laskin—a "quasi-constitutional document." The Charter of Rights and Freedoms is, of course, an entrenched constitutional document. Given s. 52, there can be no doubt as to the legitimacy of judicial review. . . .

. . . In the result, while I do not think we have moved to an American model of judicial supremacy, it does seem clear that we have moved somewhat away from pure parliamentary sovereignty. That we have not moved that far away is made clear by s. 33, a provision unique to our constitution which allows for a time-limited legislative override of rights and freedoms guaranteed in sections 2 and 7 through 15 of the Charter. Without in any way denying the provisions of s. 52, s. 33 provides a way for the legislature directly to abrogate constitutionally-entrenched rights. Provided that the proper formalities have been complied with, the only effective constraint on a legislature so-minded to do is a political one, based on its perception

of the electoral consequences of legislating directly in the face of the supreme law of the land. And, of course, the principle of democratic control
has always been the theoretical basis underlying the notion of parliamentary sovereignty.

This does not mean, however, that without s. 33 or insofar as it does not
apply to any parts of the Charter, there is anything necessarily undemocratic about a constitution in which legislative power is constrained by a
judicially-enforced Charter of Rights. In this regard I commend to you a
statement by the Committee on the Constitution of the Canadian Bar Association:

> A democracy is the basis and prerequisite for the operation of the supremacy of Parlia-
> ment. That being so, it would seem justifiable to entrench in a constitution principles
> which are prerequisite to the existence of democracy. Democracy is the periodic determi-
> nation of the common will by the free expression of the genuine and informed will of the
> individual. There must be freedom of thought, conscience and opinion, or there can be no
> expression of the genuine will of the individual. There must be freedom of information,
> assembly and association, or there can be no expression of an informed will of the indi-
> vidual. There must be freedom of speech, or there can be no "expression" of the will of the
> individual at all. There must be universal suffrage and free elections, representation by
> population and required sittings and elections of legislative institutions, or there can be
> no "expression of the common will." The right to privacy is a prerequisite to freedom of
> speech, expression, thought, conscience, opinion, assembly and association. It is incon-
> sistent to guarantee these rights directly when a person's knowledge that his privacy
> may be violated will indirectly inhibit the exercise of the guaranteed rights. All the above
> rights are prerequisites to the proper exercise of democracy, which in turn, is a prerequi-
> site to the proper operation of the principle of the supremacy of parliament. There is,
> therefore, no conflict between the entrenchment of these rights and the principle of the
> supremacy of parliament.

In addition to its commendable eloquence, this statement is noteworthy for its approach to the *Charter* as a purposive document rather
than simply as a text to be analyzed. I think that this is the proper approach to take.

13.3

ON NOT STANDING FOR NOTWITHSTANDING
John D. Whyte

... [W]ith respect to the debate on whether to continue the override clause, the usual starting point has been to advance arguments rooted in Canadian constitutional principle. For instance, a claim made by Professors Peter Russell and Paul Weiler in their opinion piece on the issue is that legislative override is a uniquely Canadian feature of our constitution. What must be being expressed by this observation is that there are other elements of our constitution—other constitutional arrangements that reveal fundamental commitments—that fit well with permitting legislative override of *Charter* protections. Professors Russell and Weiler, in arguing against repeal of the override power, provide a rudimentary explanation of what those commitments are:

> ... nothing in our constitution is so distinctively Canadian as this manner of reconciling the British tradition of responsible democratic government with the American tradition of judicially enforced constitutional rights.

Another version of principled justification of the override clause is to label it as the perfect device for accommodating a regime for vindicating civil rights with the constitutional principle of parliamentary supremacy. Professor Peter Hogg, for example, has explained the clause as "a concession to Canada's long tradition of parliamentary sovereignty."

In my view these attempts to locate a justification for the override procedure in Canadian constitutional theory are wrong for two reasons. First, the principles at work in the design of the Canadian state support not allowing any legislative exemptions from court-enforced rights at least as powerfully as they support including such a power in the constitution. Second, arguments rooted in constitutional principle distract us from enquiry into the actual social goods and bads that are likely to be produced by the practice of exercising the legislative power to override Charter rights. In short, this sort of debate keeps us from choosing a policy that is good because it reflects the actual aspirations of political community.

Looking for the Lesson from Constitutional Theory

The position that is advanced in this paper is that the debate over keeping the override power should be conducted in terms of what will produce the

Alberta Law Review 28, no. 2 (1990), from pages 348–357. Reprinted with permission.

soundest government and fairest society and that we should approach this question by trying to anticipate how effective courts and legislatures actually will be in making various sorts of social and political accommodation. For this reason it is not essential to demonstrate that Canadian constitutional theory requires repeal of an override power for legislatures. What I do want to demonstrate is that the values inherent in our constitutional arrangements do not require (or even tend towards) including in the constitution a trumping authority for legislatures over courts in the complex business of mediating between claims of right and the general social interest.

The basic constitutional principles that I perceive to be at work in the formal structure of the Canadian state are legalism, democracy and federalism. . . .

Legalism

Public authority in Canada derives at least a part of its legitimacy from its legal base. What a government does must accord with what, from a legal perspective, it is entitled to do. This idea that the legitimacy of state power can be measured through legal adjudication is, in our culture, well over half a millennium old. We understand authoritative social relationships to be formed and governed by enforceable promises and the keystone of the system is that enforceability is produced through legal evaluation. In order to produce a system for legal evaluation that has some degree of formality, specialized legal agencies grew up. Furthermore, we attached to those agencies political attributes that were designed to conduce to legal or formal evaluation (as opposed, say, to self-interested evaluation). These attributes were expertise and independence. Of course, we are right to be highly sceptical about the role of expertise and formality when the legal order that requires expertise and formal elaboration is as indeterminate as it is. We are also right to be sceptical about the actual degree of independence from social forces that can be achieved simply through protecting pay and tenure, the devices that are provided by the 1867 Constitution. However, it is not important to this argument that we subscribe to the purity of formalism or complete independence. All that is necessary is to see that they are long-standing constitutional values: it is through the identification of certain ideals and values that we can determine what arguments from principle can be made.

If it is accepted that these values have been recognized in Canadian constitutional ordering then other conclusions might be drawn. The chief one is that our state structure seems to be based on the idea that formal commitments represent binding promises that restrain future power. This idea is perhaps derived from the development of the law of contract. In any event, the commitment to legal enforceability of promises extends to binding governments as well as individuals. Legalism is what makes possible constitutionalism, the process by which political expressions from one age can bind future ages unless equally formal political processes are mustered to remove the constitution constraint. In short, Canadian constitutionalism is not in thrall to the idea that populations are free to determine their own best interests from moment to moment. Judicial control over governmental authority and legislative choices is no alien concept for Canada. We are a nation in which past solemn commitments are allowed to work to the disadvantage of current preferences. For instance, perfectly clear legislative preferences about the administration of laws are frequently frustrated by the prior constitutional commitment to the separation of powers. The separation of powers is seen as a relevant doctrine to the maintenance of a commitment to legalism and the implications of that commitment are tolerated by the people of this democratic state.

My claim is simply this. As a matter of principle we have adopted the notion that there are adjudicable public issues. Furthermore, we have come to terms with these issues being *ultimately* adjudicable—not subject to legislative review and revision. If Canada wants to say about human rights claims that not only are they adjudicable at the first stage of resolution, but they are adjudicable as a matter of ultimate resolution, this would be entirely consistent with our commitment to legalism in public ordering.

However, in the context of the Canadian Charter of Rights and Freedoms, section 33 means, first, that what were once political problems have been transformed into legal problems but, second, that when political interests are sufficiently compelling these issues can revert to being resolved through political choice. This arrangement gives rise to a further principled argument. The idea that some problems may be adjudicated—may be made subject to legal determination—requires there to be substantive constitutional value to be interpreted and applied. It is necessary to the conception of legalism that adjudication of disputes be based on previously expressed normative standards. When there is a sense that there are no constraints, or no interpretative processes (for instance, when there is no textual basis for decision-making), no genuine ajudication is possible. Canada, in enacting the Charter of Rights, accepted that some political problems were capable of adjudication and at the same time, created a normative order (a text, in other words) to ensure that those issues could be resolved through adjudication. The nation expressed its commitment to, first, the rightness of social resolution being produced by the interpretation of rights and, second, the capacity of the terms of the Charter to be interpretable—to be the subject matter of adjudication. This assessment of what was possible and appropriate for adjudication does not fit well with the idea that the ultimate method of resolution of conflicting claims is through a purely political process. In other words, once the advantages of constitutional interpretation were accepted, as a general matter, it is not easy to see why the framers of the 1982 Constitution then saw political judgment to be a preferred form of political accommodation in each and every instance in which political interests wished to suspend the operation of legalism.

Democracy

Judicial enforcement of human rights standards poses a serious challenge to majoritarianism. The advantage of pure majoritarianism is that there is no situation which cannot be responded to and no strategy of social regulation that cannot be tried once a majority of the people wish to act.

The problem with truly entrenched rights is that they undermine the majoritarian principle. Legislative calculations of social need are subject to being substituted by courts which are not representative and are not amenable to majoritarian control. The will of the electors is not sovereign. The question is whether the shift away from majoritarianism through removal of the override power reflects a conception of democracy that is as fundamental as the popular conception of democracy— that state policies ought always to reflect the preferences of a majority of electors.

Democratic theory rests not so much on the mechanisms of expressing political preferences (or who should represent the voters in making political choices) and on who should govern, as it does on deeper conditions such as political participation, equality, autonomy and personal liberty. From the now fully developed constitutional idea that people have the right to participate in public choices it is possible to tease out a series of non-derogable conditions. For example, we know that duly elected and popularly supported governments can, and do, believe that the appropriate conditions for democratic politics include such things as censored political speech, restrictions on political participation, political campaigns that are funded by government, and perhaps most currently, in at least two Canadian jurisdictions, gerrymandering. In considering this list, it is not difficult to see the connection between the use of judicially enforced fundamental rights of speech, equality and due process and the vindication of principles that are designed to protect democratic processes.

Of course it would be wrong to suggest that the whole array of interests identified in the the Charter of Rights are justifiable on the basis that they enhance the democratic process. Some rights (for example, an expanded notion of personal security being protected from substantive injustice under section 7 of the Charter) must be explained by reference to other political commitments. However, the point that needs to be made is that the democratic principle provides a powerful pedigree for judicial control over political choices that erode some fundamental human rights.

Federalism

There are two points to make about Canada's adoption of federalism in organizing state power. The first is that the chief justification for the federal arrangement (and this is particularly true in the Canadian experience) is that it provides protection to minorities from the political choices of national majorities. Federalism is a political arrangement that is designed to blunt the force of majoritarianism because groups within the nation are recognized as having special interests that deserve entrenched protection. It is true that this mode of protection does not entail courts engaging in the same kind of social accommodation as they do under the Charter. Nevertheless, courts do intervene to protect specific constitutionally recognized interests. Federalism is quite simply a substantial check on the exercise of national popular will. As such it is a further instance of seeing our constitutional order as consisting of commitments that have been embraced so that, as we live out our life as a community, certain ideals or images will prevail over power.

The second point is that by looking at the history of court adjudication over federalism we might get a better perspective on the significance of the debate over the override clause. Courts have been involved in disallowing back to work legislation and Sunday closing legislation, in adjudicating refugee claims and rules for qualifying as a profession, and in setting out the modes of proof in criminal liability and the allowable strategies for criminal investigations, each of which produces some disruption of public administration. These outcomes require the abandonment of administrative processes and, sometimes, governmental policies. Indeed, some of these policies have become established within the country as the standard way of accommodating social conflict. Charter decisions that cause an abandonment of established accommodations will produce periods of dislocation and adjustment and could effect long term changes in the distribution of social benefits. However, the capacity of governments to regulate society for the public good has not, yet, been fundamentally hampered by Charter decisions. The major determinants that shape well-being in society are not frequently at stake in Charter decision. For instance, compare the significance of any of the Charter cases alluded to above to the significance of a court decision that prevents a province from controlling trans-boundary environmental damage produced by pollution that is licensed by an adjoining province. Compare any Charter decision with the significance to a province's economic development of deciding that it is unconstitutional to ration production of a resource with a view to sustaining a viable market for the resource. Or compare the impact of any Charter decision with the consequence for a province of limiting its capacity to control the distribution of benefits from its most valuable natural attribute. This is not a country in which governments have never been seriously frustrated in implementing policies that make a difference to the health, wealth and well-being of every person in their jurisdiction. It is not credible to argue that removal of the override clause will produce a shift in the balance of power between political decision-makers and courts that will change the nature of our society. Constitutionalism already exacts a high price on the autonomy of electoral politics. Most Canadians see this as legitimate and fair in order to maintain the integrity of our national commitment to federalism. Undoubtedly the Charter of Rights has produced additional restraints on democratic politics. However, it has not made irrelevant the role of politics in shaping the nature of our society. Our experience under federalism has clearly shown us that politics lives (that political initiatives are vital and that political mobilization makes an important contribution to the well-being of society) even when courts have the authority to protect constitutional values.

As I have stated, it is not my ambition to demonstrate that the override provision cannot coherently be included in our constitutional arrangements. My goal has been simply to show that it doesn't earn its place in the Constitution because of its logical fit with the general constitutional pattern. The most basic features of our constitutional arrangements do not, as it happens, create a logical or principled argument for the legislative override of the Charter of Rights.

Finding a Lesson in Political Practice

. . . The constitutional patterns that we create are, happily, hardly ever pure. There are many visions of a good society and we act wisely when we find ways not to deny the legitimacy and place of perfectly plausible visions. Hence, one of the virtues of the override power is that it has allowed Canada to create a regime for protecting human rights and it has left room for determined legislators to maintain social arrangements that they consider particularly important.

The unfortunate aspect of this benign description of the override clause as a restrained tool, instrument of thoughtful response and balance of constitutional ideologies is its use is simply not likely to be restricted to instances that match this description. The primary reason for wishing to do away with the override clause is that the anxiety that produced the political demand for entrenched rights cannot rationally be calmed in the face of the legislative power granted by section 33. That anxiety is simply this: political authority will, at some point, be exercised oppressively; that is, it will be exercised to impose very serious burdens on groups of people when there is no rational justification for doing so.

Furthermore, the more that we succeed in marginalizing section 33 by pointing to its rare use and speaking of its deployment in extraordinary circumstances only, the more that legislative override will become associated with the intense political moments that produce political oppression.

There are two types of situations in which the Charter of Rights seems a positive constitutional instrument. One is when legislatures neglect to calculate the extraordinary impact of legislative measures on particular individuals. Another is when they know full well the impact on certain people but do not care enough about the problem (or do not have the time or skill to cope with the problem) to tailor the measure to avoid the injury to constitutional rights. Courts applying the terms of the Charter of Rights can give to individuals and groups both a forum to explain the precise nature of the disadvantage, and relief from undue burdens.

The other scenario that impels the entrenchment of rights is one in which fear and distaste by the majority for certain people leads to the oppression of those people. The Canadian historical record reveals a number of instances of political passion directed against conspicuous minorities—Japanese Canadians, Hutterites, Doukhobors, aboriginal peoples, Jehovah's Witnesses, the Acadians, Metis, Roman Catholics, communists and separatists. All of these groups have, at some point, been seen as producing more social disruption and risk than society has been able to bear and all of these groups have been governmentally burdened in order to reduce the fear that has surrounded their presence. In all of these cases the governmental assessment of risk has been facile and overstated. In all of these cases the governmental response has been more than merely disadvantageous to members of these groups. It has been brutal, community crushing, and life destroying. Political passion that is generated by the fear that there are communities whose practices subvert the fabric of our society is powerful and terrifying.

In a recent article, Professor Andrew Petter quotes the famous observation of Judge Learned Hand: "Liberty lies in the hearts of men and women; when it dies there, no constitution, no law, no court can save it; no constitution, no law, no court can even do much to help it." To the extent that this is accepted, the moments of political anger and passion that I fear—the moments of political reaction that we invariably come later to regret—will not be forestalled by the removal of the override powers. There are, however, two ways in which Learned Hand's assessment of the role of the courts in applying constitutionalized human rights is unduly pessimistic.

First, the terms of the Charter of Rights are not totally indeterminate. Judges are not free to reflect the dominant political winds in interpreting rights. The systematic destruction of a group's expression and practices cannot easily be denied as a Charter violation. Judges are, of course, aware of the political passion that is around them, but the values of independence and discipline that we seek to vindicate in appointments do frequently shine through both in this country and in the brave judgments of courts in nations with a longer record of repression than ours. . . .

The second claim to make for the benefit of judicial supervision in moments of oppression is that the calling into play of Charter claims reminds the political community of the costs to fundamental values of political desperation. For the political process, for the people whose rights are being abridged and for the future political environment, the process of identifying carefully and calmly the precise loss of freedoms and rights is a process to be valued above all others in extreme political moments.

It is my view that the Charter, in its normal course, does not substantially rearrange society. In the normal course the Charter's benefits are, in any event, distributed in the same manner as legal services—preponderantly to the wealthy. It seems perverse to advocate the retention of a provision which is most likely to be used to preclude judicial intervention when that process has its strongest moral claim, and when the radically dispossessed will have no route for salvation other than appealing to courts to intervene on behalf of the Charter values of liberty, equality and due process.

13.4

STANDING UP FOR NOTWITHSTANDING
Peter H. Russell

The *Alberta Law Review*'s first annual supplement on constitutional issues included an essay by Professor John Whyte putting the case against the notwithstanding clause in the Canadian Charter of Rights and Freedoms. Whyte's article is the most fully reasoned attack we have had on the Charter's override clause. It is an important contribution to our constitutional debate which certainly deserves a reply from one of those singled out, quite rightly, by Professor Whyte as a defender of the override.

Although I readily confess to being a supporter of the override clause, I am not at all satisfied with Professor Whyte's understanding of the rationale for such a clause. Unfortunately, instead of carefully examining the scholarly writings of those who have defended the override, he cites only a portion of one sentence from an "opinion piece" in the *Toronto Star* by Professor Paul Weiler and myself and a few words from a passage in Professor Hogg's book on the *Constitutional Law of Canada*. The words quoted and the arguments he proceeds to knock down do not come close to providing an acceptable justification of the Charter's notwithstanding clause.

Bad Reasons for the Notwithstanding Clause

The passage quoted from our *Toronto Star* piece draws attention to the distinctively Canadian manner in which the notwithstanding clause balances the British tradition of responsible democratic government with the American tradition of judicially enforced constitutional rights. I would certainly agree with Professor Whyte in dismissing arguments for the override clause that depend primarily on showing that it is distinctively Canadian. I am sure there are plenty of things that are distinctively Canadian that are perfectly dreadful. The point we were making is that the

Alberta Law Review 29, no. 2 (1991), from pp. 293–309. Reprinted with permission.

override gave Canada an opportunity to get the best out of British and American constitutionalism, the two traditions which have profoundly influenced our constitutional development. Professor Whyte, unhappily, may be right, and as English Canada moves ever closer to Charter worship, it may no longer be distinctively Canadian to try to strike a shrewd balance between the wisdom derived from these two parts of our heritage.

It may well be true, as the quotation from Professor Hogg suggests, that political defenders of the override have most often couched their arguments in terms of the need to preserve the principle of parliamentary sovereignty. Again, I am in agreement with Professor Whyte that the case for the override cannot rest on a simple invocation of the principle of parliamentary sovereignty. Even if one were to accept, as this writer does not, a purely Burkean standard for constitutional development and insist that our constitutional future never break from inherited tradition, it simply is not true that the Canadian constitution historically has been based on the principle of parliamentary sovereignty. No Canadian legislature or parliament has ever been sovereign, and I hope none ever shall be. Legislatures in colonial Canada were subject to important imperial controls and since 1867 Canadian legislatures have been subject to judicially enforceable limitations, limitations based on more than preserving the federal division of powers.

Equally unacceptable as a defence of the override is an appeal to simple majoritarianism. The crude utilitarian standard of "the greatest happiness of the greatest number" is an unacceptable ethical foundation for a constitutional democracy. *Liberal* democracy requires much more than giving free play to the preferences of the majority. Professor Whyte delineates a number of the "deeper conditions" of democratic government: "political participation, equality, autonomy and personal liberty." Professor Ronald Dworkin in his contribution to the same issue of the review cogently argues that democratic government should not be founded on a statistical, head-counting, conception of political equality but on a communal understanding in which citizens share equally the responsibilities of determining what is right for their political community.

With all of this I whole-heartedly agree. The override should not be defended on the grounds that appointed judges must never be able to thwart the will of a body elected by the majority. Such an argument would rest on the most simplistic and illiberal conception of democracy, a conception oblivious to the need for checks and balances as a condition of liberty and oblivious to the injustices which a majority may wish to inflict on a minority. Such a simplistic and morally shallow theory of democracy is not held by this defender of the notwithstanding clause, nor, I suspect, by most others who see its merits.

Now, having cleared away the underbrush of unacceptable arguments for the override, I shall attempt to put forward what I regard as the strongest grounds for retaining this provision in the Canadian Charter of

Rights and Freedoms. These are the arguments which Professor Whyte does not address.

The Case for the Override

The major arguments in support of a legislative override turn on considerations about the substantive outcome of decision-making and about the process of decision-making in a liberal democracy. Let me deal first with substantive considerations.

Substantive Considerations

In a nutshell, the argument about the substance of decision-making is as follows. Judges are not infallible. They may make decisions about the limits and nature of rights and freedoms which are extremely questionable. There should be some process, more reasoned than court packing and more accessible than constitutional amendment, through which the justice and wisdom of these decisions can be publicly discussed and possibly rejected. A legislative override clause provides such a process. At the core of this argument is recognition of the kind of questions courts typically deal with in interpreting and applying a constitutional charter of rights. These are questions not about the validity of the core values enshrined in the general language of the Charter—freedom of speech, fundamental justice, equality—but about the proper limits of rights based on these values. It is a truism that no single right should be treated as an absolute. This truism is recognized in section 1 of the Charter which states that all the rights in the Charter are "subject to reasonable limits prescribed by law as can be demonstrably justified in a free and democratic society." It is also recognized in decisions of the Supreme Court of Canada eliminating certain kinds of claims from the definition of the entrenched right or freedom. Thus, it is quite misleading to describe what the courts are doing in deciding Charter cases as "guaranteeing" that citizens enjoy the rights entrenched in the Charter. What judicial review under the Charter guarantees is careful consideration by the judiciary of a citizen's claim that a Charter right or freedom has been unreasonably encroached upon by a law or executive act of government. In dealing with such a claim the court must decide whether it should be upheld or whether it should give way to other important rights or interests with which it conflicts.

Consider the Supreme Court of Canada's decisions on claims based on section 2(b), the freedom of expression section of the Charter. In these cases the Court has determined whether the following were reasonable limits on the constitutional right to freedom of expression:

- a Criminal Code provision requiring that a trial judge, on the request of a complainant in a sexual assault case, ban publication of information identifying the complainant

- an injunction issued by a judge, *ex parte*, prohibiting striking court workers from picketing court houses
- a law prohibiting commercials directed at children under 13
- an order from a labour relations board requiring an employer to write a letter of recommendation about a wrongfully dismissed employee
- a law requiring French-only commercial signs and firm names
- a law prohibiting publication of the details of evidence adduced in matrimonial proceedings.

In the first four of these cases the Supreme Court decided that the limit on free speech was justified and in the latter two that it was not. One does not find in these cases the Court defending citizens against government attacks on what is fundamental to the right of free speech in a democracy, the right to criticize the government and advocate opposition to it. Instead, in each case the Court dealt with an issue at the margin, not at the core, of free speech and whether such a marginal claim should give way to some other value. In effect, in these cases, the Court was making decisions about the policy of free speech—how far this essential democratic right should be extended and under what circumstances and for what purposes it should be subject to restrictions.

In making the case for a legislative override in the Charter, one need not, and indeed should not, argue that the judiciary should play no part in policy decisions such as these. I agree with Professor Whyte that "Canada in enacting the Charter of Rights, accepted that some political problems were capable of adjudication. . . ." But Professor Weiler and I and other defenders of the notwithstanding clause part company with Whyte when he contends that these issues must be "ultimately adjudicable," that once the judiciary has spoken there must be closure on these issues.

Far from it being the case, as Professor Whyte claims, that we Canadians in adopting the Charter committed ourselves to having questions about the limits of rights and freedoms ultimately determined by the courts, our constitution-makers in 1982, through the override clause, provided for a partnership between legislatures and courts. In Professor Weiler's words:

> Under this approach judges will be on the front lines; they will possess both the responsibility and the legal clout necessary to tackle "rights" issues as they regularly arise. At the same time, however, the Charter reserves for the legislature a final say to be used sparingly in the exceptional cases where the judiciary has gone awry.

Under the Charter we can certainly benefit, in ways described by Professor Whyte, by having "rights" issues systematically ventilated in the courts. Most often we will accept the decisions of the courts on these rights issues. But occasionally situations will arise in which the citizenry through a responsible and accountable process conclude that a judicial resolution of a rights issue is seriously flawed and seek to reverse it. These are the situations in which we should enjoy the benefit of the legislative override.

For anyone familiar with the history of judicial review in the United States or in our own country, it is difficult to believe in the infallibility of judges. In American history, the decisions of the Supreme Court in *Lochner* and other early twentieth century decisions denying state legislatures the power to ensure vulnerable workers decent conditions of employment are reminders of the injustice and harm that can flow from judicial decisions interpreting constitutional guarantees. Already under the Charter, several judicial decisions vetoing legislation might be questioned for the harm they inflict on vulnerable groups in Canadian society. One example is the decision of the Ontario Court of Appeal that in certain circumstances it would be an unreasonable limitation on an accused's Charter rights to give effect to the recent amendment of the Criminal Code protecting complainants in sexual assault cases from being forced to give evidence on their prior sexual conduct. [Ed. note: In its 1991 decision in *R. v. Seaboyer and Gayme*, the Supreme Court of Canada reached the same conclusion. In 1992, Minister of Justice Kim Campbell announced amendments to the "rape-shield" law that respond to the *Seaboyer and Gayme* ruling but without using the section 33 override.] Another is the decision of the British Columbia Court of Appeal overturning provincial regulations designed to channel the influx of new doctors to areas of the province where they are most urgently needed, a decision from which the Supreme Court of Canada has denied leave to appeal.

Countries without legislative overrides in their constitutional bills of rights have other means of reversing judicial decisions. In no constitutional democracy is there absolute closure on rights issues once they have been pronounced upon by the judicial branch. The most direct method of reversal is constitutional amendment. But in most constitutional democracies (and most certainly in Canada), amending the constitution is an extraordinarily difficult process which may leave decision-making power in the hands of a small group of people who are indifferent to or beneficiaries of the injustice resulting from a judicial decision. The more usual method of reversing constitutional decisions of the courts, at least in the United States, is to change or threaten to change the composition of the judicial bodies most influential in interpreting the constitution. [Ed. note: see Reading 4.6]

Absent a Canadian-style legislative override, court-packing or court-bashing are the devices to which democratic leaders are most likely to resort when faced with judicial interpretations of the constitution they consider to be seriously unjust and harmful. These devices may yield relatively quick results as was the case with Roosevelt's threat to pack the U.S. Supreme Court, or they may work much more slowly as has been the case with the efforts of Republican Presidents to reverse certain decisions of the Warren Court. In either case court-packing or court-bashing, involving as they do the application of raw majoritarian power to the judicial branch, would seem less appropriate devices than legislative debate and discussion for challenging judicial decisions. The legislative override has the merit, when properly used, of applying reasoned discussion in a publicly accountable forum to the great issues of justice and public well-being at stake.

Now it will be noticed that I have qualified my support of the legislative override by arguing for its superiority "when properly used." By "properly used" I mean when it is invoked only after a reasoned debate in the legislature. This is precisely the point about the override which the Supreme Court of Canada failed to grasp in *Ford* when it upheld Quebec's blanket use of the override. The Court held that in using the override legislatures are not even required to name the rights or freedoms which are to be restricted. By insisting on an entirely formal approach to the override clause, as Professor Lorraine Weinrib has put it,

> The Court thereby defers to a legislative process devoid of its legitimating qualities of reasoned and focussed debate by the people's representatives.

The Supreme Court's approach to the notwithstanding clause, unfortunately and ironically, is a departure from the purposive approach applied to other sections of the Charter. The primary purpose of the override is to provide an opportunity for responsible and accountable public discussion of rights issues, a purpose that may be seriously undermined in legislatures are free to use the override without discussion and deliberation.

At this point it is essential to turn to the second wing of the argument for the Charter, the argument that focuses on the process advantages of the override. It is only when we recognize the contribution an override can make to the quality of democratic government that the inadequacy of the Supreme Court's ruling on section 33 can be fully understood and the merits of the notwithstanding clause fully appreciated.

Process Considerations

A legislative override does not guarantee that we will arrive at the right answers to the questions of political and social justice raised by the Charter. What it can do is to subject these questions to a process of wide public discussion so that the politically active citizenry participate in and share responsibility for the outcome.

The advantage of retaining a role for legislatures in the determination of rights issues is not to ensure that the will of the majority prevails. Even if one accepted a simplistic majority rule conception of democracy (which this writer does not), the decisions of legislatures can rarely be realistically equated with the will of the majority. This is especially true of legislative decisions on the issues of moral conscience and justice raised by questions about the appropriate limits of rights and freedoms. The point of maintaining parliamentary bodies in a democracy is not to ensure that majority preference gets its way on all public issues. Given the wonders of modern electronics, we do not need legislative chambers to register citizens' preferences. No, the fundamental purpose of parliamentary bodies is to facilitate the democratic ideal of government by discussion. A parliament must above all be a "talking place"—that is, after all, the very root meaning of the term. Through media coverage of legislative debates, citizens are engaged in deliberating on public issues. It is through parliamentary institutions that we move closer to experiencing a form of democratic government that is not simply rule of the greater number but that, in the words of Ernest Barker,

> ... elicits and enlists—or at any rate is calculated to elicit and enlist, so far as is humanly possible—the thought, the will, and the general capacity of every member ... a government depending on mutual interchange of ideas, on mutual criticism of the ideas interchanged, and the general capacity of every member.

Much the same democratic ideal is put forward by Professor Dworkin in his recent contribution to this journal. Dworkin rejects what he calls a "statistical democracy" whose institutions are designed simply to ensure that political decisions match the will of the majority. Instead he argues for a "communal democracy" in which

> each citizen insists that his political convictions are in every important sense his business, that it is his independent responsibility to decide what is required of the nation to do well, and whether or how far it has succeeded.

We have much less chance of realizing Barker's or Dworkin's democratic ideal, if, as Professor Whyte insists, we give judges the last word, the ultimate say, on rights issues raised by the Charter. To exclude citizens and their elected legislators from the ultimate determination of these issues is to exclude them from resolving questions of justice which should be at the very heart of political life. As Aristotle taught so long ago,

> It is the peculiarity of man, in comparison with the rest of the animal world, that he alone possesses a perception of good and evil, of the just and the unjust, and of similar qualities: and it is association in a common perception of these things which makes a family and a polis.

Giving judges the last word, the definitive say, on issues of social and political justice is to exclude citizens from participation in the essential activity of a political community.

In making this point I do not mean to denigrate the contribution judicial decisions can make to public discussion and consideration of rights issues. Some Charter critics, in my view, have gone too far in denouncing judicial review under the Charter as excessively elitist and undemocratic. These critics tend to underestimate the extent to which legal aid and the organization of advocacy groups have made litigation much more accessible than in the past as well as the extent to which Charter litigation generates action on law reform issues which are neglected or ignored by legislatures. Also, I would acknowledge that both the presentation of Charter issues before judges and the reasoned decisions of judges on Charter issues can contribute significantly to public understanding of rights issues. But I am not persuaded that these benefits of applying the judicial process to these issues are so great as to justify making adjudication always the ultimate means of resolving rights issues. Court decisions on whether restricting where new doctors supported by public medicare can practice is a justifiable restriction of individual freedom, or on whether a French-only sign law is needed to preserve the predominantly French character of Quebec, may well have contributed to public understanding of these issues. But in a democracy that aspires to government by discussion and full participation of its citizens in questions of social and political justice, court decisions should not close off further debate and decision-making in elected and publicly accountable legislatures.

Legislatures, it is true, may act precipitously and make questionable decisions. On occasion their consideration of rights issues may, to use Professor Whyte's phrase, be unduly influenced by "the dominant political winds." But it is a dreadful distortion to suggest that such impassioned and inconsiderate behaviour is the norm in Canadian legislatures. A reading of legislative debates on justice issues such as capital punishment, criminal procedure, aboriginal rights and language rights does not find legislators simply pandering for popularity. At the same time we should recognize that while judges are free from any pressure to curry favour with the public, they are not altogether free from other institutional biases. The Supreme Court's court opinion in *B.C.G.E.U. v. British Columbia* upholding the power of a judge to restrict the free speech rights of workers does not shine out as a carefully reasoned and balanced consideration of that issue. Professor Dale Gibson's article in the last issue of this journal reveals other instances of judicial bias and self-interest in adjudicating public law issues.

In designing the institutional matrix for making decisions on rights issues it is a mistake to look for an error-proof solution. Both courts and legislatures are capable of being unreasonable and, in their different ways, self-interested. By providing a legislative counter-weight to judicial power the Canadian Charter establishes a prudent system of checks and balances which recognizes the fallibility of both courts and legislatures and gives closure to the decisions of neither. A legislature's decision to use the override, it must be remembered, is not ultimate. It is good for only five years. After five years it can be reviewed but not without re-opening the issue for public debate and discussion.

If we do anything to section 33 of the Charter, we should reform it, not abolish it. There is need to overcome by constitutional amendment that part of the Supreme Court's decision in *Ford* which permits standard-form overrides without any obligation on the legislature to identify the specific legislative provision which in its judgment needs protection or the right or freedom which in its view should not be given priority. Professor Weiler and I have advocated a further amendment which would require that any use of the override be subject to two enactments, one before and one after an election. This would ensure a cooling off period and time for second thoughts. What is even more important, it would also ensure broad citizen involvement, thus contributing to the fundamental process value of the override....

[Ed. note: Russell discusses two test cases: one in which the override was not used but in which he argues that it should have been; the other in which it was used but many people think that it should not have been. The first was the National Citizens' Coalition successful 1984 challenge to the Elections Act, striking down its restrictions on non-party spending during federal elections. The latter was Quebec's use of the override to re-instate its "French-only" public signs law that was struck down by the Supreme Court in its 1989 ruling in *Ford v. A.-G. Quebec*.]

The Perspective of Principle

At the beginning of his article Professor Whyte argues that the future of the override cannot be settled by resort to principle. By this he means that the case for the override cannot be a logical deduction from the "basic constitutional principles" he perceives to be at work in the "formal structure of the Canadian state"—namely, "legalism, democracy and federalism." The elimination of the override, he argues, is at least as consistent with these principles as its retention. Given that the established principles of our constitution cannot settle the issue, the merits of the override should be assessed on a more prudential basis in terms of "the actual social goods and bads" it is likely to produce and "what will produce the soundest government and fairest society."

As I have earlier indicated, I have no difficulty accepting Whyte's suggestion that we not try to judge the override entirely on the basis of our constitutional antecedents. And I agree with him that the override should be judged in terms of what will produce a sound and fair polity for Canadians. But I do take issue with his treatment of what he regards as Canada's basic constitutional principles and their bearing on the override issue.

I have the least quarrel with Whyte's treatment of the federal principle. He is right in viewing federalism as a check on national majoritarianism and pointing out that judicial decisions enforcing the federal division of powers have significantly constrained Canadian legislatures in the past. But he overlooks an important difference between judicial review based on federalism and judicial review based on a bill of rights. Also, he underestimates the impact of the Charter on the workings of Canadian federalism and on the unity of the country.

When courts strike down legislation on federalism grounds, normally this means that one level of government but not the other is precluded from proceeding with a policy. This is a less drastic result than when legislation is struck down on Charter grounds, for then the judicially vetoed policy, absent the override, is placed beyond both levels of government. It is in this sense that removing the override from the Charter would, contrary to Whyte's assertion, entail a greater shift in the balance of power between legislatures and courts than is inherent in the judicial enforcement of federal limits. Secondly, the Charter does have a centralizing effect on Canadian federalism. The article by Morton et al., also in the most recent issue of this journal, tracking the judicial nullification of statutes begins to take the measure of the Supreme Court's capacity under the Charter to impose uniform policies on the provinces. This centralization of policy-making power, from a normative perspective, may at times have clear benefits for Canadian society. At the same time it may reduce the policy pluralism and diversity that many of us value in federalism. Finally, and from the perspective of national unity most seriously, . . . it is most unlikely that we could retain Quebec as a member of the Canadian federation if we were now to insist on removing the override from the Charter. This is not because the majority of Quebeckers are opposed to rights and freedoms but because they want to keep a reasonable measure of control over their cultural security in their own hands.

But Professor Whyte's elucidation of the principle of legalism gives me much more difficulty than his discussion of federalism. For it is here that he seems to slide into the very mode of analysis he has cautioned us to eschew and to argue, in effect, that regardless of "the goods and bads that are likely to be produced" we must be bound by the implications of his principle of legalism.

Whyte's initial formulation of what he calls legalism—namely "the notion that there are adjudicable public issues"—is not problematic. But then he goes on to assert that "we have come to terms with these issues being *ultimately* adjudicable—not subject to legislative review and revision. " Here he seems to be saying that having accepted through adoption of the Charter that a great many public issues which were heretofore dealt with by the "political branches" are now to be subject to adjudication, we are ineluctably committed to giving the judiciary *ultimate* control of these issues. But that surely isn't so. Certainly when the Charter was adopted with an override, we Canadians made no such commitment. The question now before us, using Whyte's own criteria, is whether making Charter issues "ultimately adjudicable" will lead to the soundest and fairest system of government.

For reasons already advanced in this article I believe that in terms of both the substance of rights policy and its process it would not be sound even to try to let all the public issues which may be adjudicated under the Charter be ultimately settled by judges. I say "try" because that is the closest we can come to realizing Whyte's ideal of forever removing issues arising under the Charter from what he calls "a purely political process." The experience of the United States shows what an illusion it is to think that without the possibility of a legislative override, rights issues dealt with by the judiciary are forever withdrawn from the political process. School desegregation was not withdrawn from the American political process after the Supreme Court in *Plessy v. Ferguson* gave its blessing to "separate but equal," any more than Roosevelt's New Deal legislation was removed from the political agenda after being vetoed by the Supreme Court.

But it is difficult to see why even trying to remove rights issues *entirely* from the political process should result in "sounder" or "fairer" laws. Professor Whyte asserts that "the capacity of governments to regulate society for the public good has not, yet, been fundamentally hampered by Charter decisions." Some might consider the damage done in *Wilson* to government's capacity to provide for an equitable distribution of publicly funded medical services, or in *National Citizens Coalition* to government's freedom to follow an election commission's advice on how best to provide fair and effective election laws as already a refutation of Whyte's dictum. But, let us concede that these decisions have not *fundamentally* hampered government from "regulating for the public good." The question remains why is it sound and fair to accept this much judicial damage to effective, socially responsible regulation without the possibility of legislative review and, indeed, risk the possibility that judicial decisions might go further and fundamentally cripple government's effectiveness in providing for the public good? Are the judiciary and the judicial process so inherently superior to the legislature and the processes of ordinary politics that we are justified in running these risks?

Professor Whyte apparently thinks they are. The problem with legislatures, he tells us, is that sometimes they "neglect to calculate the extraordinary impact of legislative measures on particular individuals." Sometimes too, he says, they simply do not care enough about the injury to some persons' right to tailor measures which will minimize the damage. I agree with Whyte that legislatures certainly do these things, and these are precisely the situations in which we may be well served by Charter-based judicial review. But I would submit that judicial review of legislation under the Charter, in turn, has its own limitations and blind spots. Judges often fail to take into account, and indeed sometimes are exposed to the scantiest of submissions on, the relationship of a challenged law to its total social or policy context. In *Wilson*, for example, the British Columbia Court of Appeal, in upholding the "liberty" of new doctors to practice their profession at public expense wherever they wish in the province, did not consider the possible inequity in not extending a similar liberty to other newly graduated professionals in that province or the impact of this decision on the financing of other social programs. Judges considering Charter challenges to legislation and government regulation may, on occasion, minimize the damage which can be inflicted by private centres of social and economic power on the freedom and equality of the most vulnerable groups in a market economy. It is to his credit that Chief Justice Dickson warned against this possibility. But we cannot always count on such enlightened judicial leadership or on its being followed.

The art of living with the Charter and with its override is to get the best out of both the judicial and the legislative process in making decisions on rights issues. However, according to Whyte's principle of legalism, we must now put all our eggs in the judicial basket. A legislative back-up, in his view, is too apt to plunge rights issues back into the grubby, unprincipled, partisan realm of "pure politics." It is here that we encounter what I find most unacceptable in Whyte's argument, his disdain for democratic politics.

In his discussion of the democratic principle Whyte rejects, as I would, a simplistic majoritarian conception of democracy. I agree with him that a liberal democracy requires checks and balances and that judicial review based on a constitutional bill of rights is not inherently undemocratic. Where I differ with him on the democratic principle is on how best to enhance and develop our capacity for democratic citizenship. The attempt to remove rights issues, irretrievably, from the arena of popular politics is to give up on what democratic politics at its best should be—the resolution of questions of political justice through a process of public discussion. As I have written before, it "represents a further flight from politics, a deepening disillusionment with the procedures of representative government and government by discussion as a means of resolving fundamental questions of political justice." For me, the legislative override clause is a way of countering this flight from democratic politics. It is a signal that we Canadians have not yet given up on our capacity for debating and deciding great issues of political justice in a popular political forum.

In the concluding paragraphs of his article Professor Whyte turns to what for many may be the clinching argument against the override—the need for a judicial check against "extreme political reaction." It is in moments of "serious political repression," he contends, that we are most in need of cool judicial guardians to check the passions of democracy. Now, I have no doubt that legislative bodies can act unreasonably and fall under the sway of very repressive forces. In the 1950s we witnessed just that when McCarthyism held sway in the United States. We also witnessed then how ineffective that country's judicial guardians were in checking that repression. But more fundamentally, I would argue that a democracy which puts its faith as much in its politically active citizenry as in its judges to be the guardians of liberty is stronger than one that would endeavour to vest ultimate responsibility for liberty and fundamental rights exclusively in its judiciary.

APPENDIX 1

CONSTITUTION ACT, 1867, ss. 91-92

VI — Distribution of Legislative Powers

Powers of the Parliament

91. It shall be lawful for the Queen, by and with the Advice and Consent of the Senate and House of Commons, to make Laws for the Peace, Order, and good Government of Canada, in relation to all Matters not coming within the Classes of Subjects by this Act assigned exclusively to the Legislatures of the Provinces; and for greater Certainty, but not so as to restrict the Generality of the foregoing Terms of this Section, it is hereby declared that (notwithstanding anything in this Act) the exclusive Legislative Authority of the Parliament of Canada extends to all Matters coming within the Classes of Subjects next hereinafter enumerated; that is to say, —

1. The amendment from time to time of the Constitution of Canada, except as regards matters coming within the classes of subjects by this Act assigned exclusively to the Legislatures of the provinces, or as regards rights or privileges by this or any other Constitutional Act granted or secured to the Legislature or the Government of a province, or to any class of persons with respect to schools or as regards the use of the English or the French language or as regards the requirements that there shall be a session of the Parliament of Canada at least once each year, and that no House of Commons shall continue for more than five years from the day of the return of the Writs for choosing the House: provided, however, that a House of Commons may in time of real or apprehended war, invasion or insurrection be continued by the Parliament of Canada if such continuation is not opposed by the votes of more than one-third of the members of such House.

1A. The Public Debt and Property.
2. The Regulation of Trade and Commerce.
2A. Unemployment insurance.
3. The raising of Money by any Mode or System of Taxation.
4. The borrowing of Money on the Public Credit.
5. Postal Service.
6. The Census and Statistics.
7. Militia, Military and Naval Service, and Defence.
8. The fixing of and providing for the Salaries and Allowances of Civil and other Officers of the Government of Canada.
9. Beacons, Buoys, Lighthouses, and Sable Island.
10. Navigation and Shipping.
11. Quarantine and the Establishment and Maintenance of Marine Hospitals.
12. Sea Coast and Inland Fisheries.
13. Ferries between a Province and any British or Foreign Country or between Two Provinces.
14. Currency and Coinage.

15. Banking, Incorporation of Banks, and the Issue of Paper Money.
16. Savings Banks.
17. Weights and Measures.
18. Bills of Exchange and Promissory Notes.
19. Interest.
20. Legal Tender.
21. Bankruptcy and Insolvency.
22. Patents of Invention and Discovery.
23. Copyrights.
24. Indians, and Lands reserved for the Indians.
25. Naturalization and Aliens.
26. Marriage and Divorce.
27. The Criminal Law, except the Constitution of Courts of Criminal Jurisdiction, but including the Procedure in Criminal Matters.
28. The Establishment, Maintenance, and Management of Penitentiaries.
29. Such Classes of Subjects as are expressly excepted in the Enumeration of the Classes of Subjects by this Act assigned exclusively to the Legislatures of the Provinces.

And any Matter coming within any of the Classes of Subjects enumerated in this Section shall not be deemed to come within the Class of Matters of a local or private Nature comprised in the Enumeration of the Classes of Subjects by this Act assigned exclusively to the Legislatures of the Provinces.

Exclusive Powers of Provincial Legislatures
92. In each Province the Legislature may exclusively make Laws in relation to Matters coming within the Classes of Subject next hereinafter enumerated; that is to say, —

1. The Amendment from Time to Time, notwithstanding anything in this Act, of the Constitution of the Province, except as regards the Office of Lieutenant Governor.
2. Direct Taxation within the Province in order to the raising of a Revenue for Provincial Purposes.
3. The borrowing of Money on the sole Credit of the Province.
4. The Establishment and Tenure of Provincial Offices and the Appointment and Payment of Provincial Officers.
5. The Management and Sale of the Public Lands belonging to the Province and of the Timber and Wood thereon.
6. The Establishment, Maintenance, and Management of Public and Reformatory Prisons in and for the Province.
7. The Establishment, Maintenance, and Management of Hospitals, Asylums, Charities, and Eleemosynary Institutions in and for the Province, other than Marine Hospitals.
8. Municipal Institutions in the Province.
9. Shop, Saloon, Tavern, Auctioneer, and other Licences in order to the raising of a Revenue for Provincial, Local, or Municipal Purposes.
10. Local Works and Undertakings other than such as are of the following Classes:
    (a) Lines of Steam or other Ships, Railways, Canals, Telegraphs, and other Works and Undertakings connecting the Province with any other or others of the Provinces, or extending beyond the Limits of the Province;
    (b) Lines of Steam Ships between the Province and any British or Foreign Country;

(c) Such Works as, although wholly situate within the Province, are before or after their Execution declared by the Parliament of Canada to be for the general Advantage of Canada or for the Advantage of Two or more of the Provinces.

11. The Incorporation of Companies with Provincial Objects.

12. The Solemnization of Marriage in the Province.

13. Property and Civil Rights in the Province.

14. The Administration of Justice in the Province, including the Constitution, Maintenance, and Organization of Provincial Courts, both of Civil and of Criminal Jurisdiction, and including Procedure in Civil Matters in those Courts.

15. The Imposition of Punishment by Fine, Penalty, or Imprisonment for enforcing any Law of the Province made in relation to any Matter coming within any of the Classes of Subjects enumerated in this Section.

16. Generally all Matters of a merely local or private Nature in the Province.

APPENDIX 2

CANADIAN BILL OF RIGHTS, 1960

The Parliament of Canada, affirming that the Canadian Nation is founded upon principles that acknowledge the supremacy of God, the dignity and worth of the human person and the position of the family in a society of free men and free institutions;

Affirming also that men and institutions remain free only when freedom is founded upon respect for moral and spiritual values and the rule of law;

And being desirous of enshrining these principles and the human rights and fundamental freedoms derived from them, in a Bill of Rights which shall reflect the respect of Parliament for its constitutional authority and which shall ensure the protection of these rights and freedoms in Canada;

THEREFORE Her Majesty, by and with the advice and consent of the Senate and House of Commons of Canada, enacts as follows:

PART I

BILL OF RIGHTS

1. It is hereby recognized and declared that in Canada there have existed and shall continue to exist without discrimination by reason of race, national origin, colour, religion or sex, the following human rights and fundamental freedoms, namely,

(a) the right of the individual to life, liberty, security of the person and enjoyment of property, and the right not to be deprived thereof except by due process of law;

(b) the right of the individual to equality before the law and the protection of the law;

(c) freedom of religion;

(d) freedom of speech;

(e) freedom of assembly and association; and

(f) freedom of the press.

2. Every law of Canada shall, unless it is expressly declared by an Act of the Parliament of Canada that it shall operate notwithstanding the Canadian Bill of Rights, be so construed and applied as not to abrogate, abridge or infringe or to authorize the abrogation, abridgment or infringement of any of the rights or freedoms herein recognized and declared, and in particular, no law of Canada shall be construed or applied so as to

(a) authorize or effect the arbitrary detention, imprisonment or exile of any person;

(b) impose or authorize the imposition of cruel and unusual treatment or punishment;

(c) deprive a person who has been arrested or detained

   (i) of the right to be informed promptly of the reason for his arrest or detention,

   (ii) of the right to retain and instruct counsel without delay, or

   (iii) of the remedy by way of *habeas corpus* for the determination of the validity of his detention and for his release if the detention is not lawful;

(d) authorize a court, tribunal, commission, board or other authority to compel a person to give evidence if he is denied counsel, protection against self crimination or other constitutional safeguards;

(e) deprive a person of the right to a fair hearing in accordance with the principles of fundamental justice for the determination of his rights and obligations;

(f) deprive a person charged with a criminal offence of right to be presumed innocent until proved guilty according to law in a fair and public hearing by an independent and impartial tribunal, or of the right to reasonable bail without just cause; or

(g) deprive a person of the right to the assistance of an interpreter in any proceedings in which he is involved or in which he is a party or a witness, before a court, commission, board or other tribunal, if he does not understand or speak the language in which such proceedings are conducted.

3. The Minister of Justice shall, in accordance with such regulations as may be prescribed by the Governor in Council, examine every proposed regulation submitted in draft form to the Clerk of the Privy Council pursuant to the *Regulations Act* and every Bill introduced in or presented to

the House of Commons, in order to ascertain whether any of the provisions thereof are inconsistent with the purposes and provisions of this Part and he shall report any such inconsistency to the House of Commons at the first convenient opportunity.

4. The provisions of this Part shall be known as the *Canadian Bill of Rights*.

PART II

5.(1) Nothing in Part I shall be construed to abrogate or abridge any human right or fundamental freedom not enumerated therein that may have existed in Canada at the commencement of this Act.

(2) The expression "law of Canada" in Part I means an Act of the Parliament of Canada enacted before or after the coming into force of this Act, any order, rule or regulation thereunder, and any law in force in Canada or in any part of Canada at the commencement of this Act that is subject to be repealed, abolished or altered by the Parliament of Canada.

(3) The provisions of Part I shall be construed as extending only to matters coming within the legislative authority of the Parliament of Canada.

6. Section 5 of the *War Measures Act* is repealed and the following substituted therefor:

6.(1) Sections 3, 4, and 5 shall come into force only upon the issue of a proclamation of the Governor in Council declaring that war, invasion or insurrection, real or apprehended, exists.

(2) A proclamation declaring that war, invasion or insurrection, real or apprehended, exists shall be laid before Parliament forthwith after its issue, or, if Parliament is then not sitting, within the first fifteen days next thereafter that Parliament is sitting.

(3) Where a proclamation has been laid before Parliament pursuant to subsection (2), a notice of motion in either House signed by ten members thereof and made in accordance with the rules of that House within ten days of the day the proclamation was laid before Parliament, praying that the proclamation be revoked, shall be debated in that House at the first convenient opportunity within the four sitting days next after the day the motion in that House was made.

(4) If both Houses of Parliament resolve that the proclamation be revoked, it shall cease to have effect, and sections 3, 4 and 5 shall cease to be in force until those sections are again brought into force by a further proclamation but without prejudice to the previous operation of those sections or anything duly done or suffered thereunder or any offence committed or any penalty or forfeiture or punishment incurred.

(5) Any act or thing done or authorized or any order to regulation made under the authority of this Act, shall be deemed not to be an abrogation, abridgement or infringement of any right or freedom recognized by the *Canadian Bill of Rights*.

APPENDIX 3

CANADIAN CHARTER OF
RIGHTS AND FREEDOMS, 1982

Whereas Canada is founded upon principles that recognize the supremacy of God and the rule of law:

Guarantee of Rights and Freedoms
1. *The Canadian Charter of Rights and Freedoms* guarantees the rights and freedoms set out in it subject only to such reasonable limits prescribed by law as can be demonstrably justified in a free and democratic society.

Fundamental Freedoms
2. Everyone has the following fundamental freedoms:
  - (a) freedom of conscience and religion;
  - (b) freedom of thought, belief, opinion and expression, including freedom of the press and other media of communication;
  - (c) freedom of peaceful assembly; and
  - (d) freedom of association.

Democratic Rights
3. Every citizen of Canada has the right to vote in an election of members of the House of Commons or of a legislative assembly and to be qualified for membership therein.

4.(1) No House of Commons and no legislative assembly shall continue for longer than five years from the date fixed for the return of the writs at a general election of its members.
(2) In time of real or apprehended war, invasion or insurrection, a House of Commons may be continued by Parliament and a legislative assembly may be continued by the legislature beyond five years if such continuation is not opposed by the votes of more than one-third of the members of the House of Commons or the legislative assembly, as the case may be.
5. There shall be a sitting of Parliament and of each legislature at least once every twelve months.

Mobility Rights

6.(1) Every citizen of Canada has the right to enter, remain in and leave Canada.

(2) Every citizen of Canada and every person who has the status of a permanent resident of Canada has the right

(a)   to move to and take up residence in any province; and
(b)   to pursue the gaining of a livelihood in any province.

(3) The rights specified in subsection (2) are subject to

(a)   any laws or practices of general application in force in a province other than those that discriminate among persons primarily on the basis of province of present or previous residence; and
(b)   any laws providing for reasonable residency requirements as a qualification for the receipt of publicly provided social services.

(4) Subsections (2) and (3) do not preclude any law, program or activity that has as its object the amelioration in a province of conditions of individuals in that province who are socially or economically disadvantaged if the rate of employment in that province is below the rate of employment in Canada.

Legal Rights

7. Everyone has the right to life, liberty and security of the person and the right not to be deprived thereof except in accordance with the principles of fundamental justice.

8. Everyone has the right to be secure against unreasonable search or seizure.

9. Everyone has the right not to be arbitrarily detained or imprisoned.

10. Everyone has the right on arrest or detention

(a)   to be informed promptly of the reasons therefor;
(b)   to retain and instruct counsel without delay and to be informed of that right; and
(c)   to have the validity of the detention determined by way of *habeas corpus* and to be released if the detention is not lawful.

11. Any person charged with an offence has the right

(a)   to be informed without unreasonable delay of the specific offence;
(b)   to be tried within a reasonable time;
(c)   not to be compelled to be a witness in proceedings against that person in respect of the offence;
(d)   to be presumed innocent until proven guilty according to law in a fair and public hearing by an independent and impartial tribunal;
(e)   not to be denied reasonable bail without just cause;
(f)   except in the case of an offence under military law tried before a military tribunal, to the benefit of trial by jury where the maximum punishment for the offence is imprisonment for five years or a more severe punishment;
(g)   not to be found guilty on account of any act or omission unless, at the time of the act or omission, it constituted an offence under Canadian or international law or was criminal according to the general principles of law recognized by the community of nations;

(h)   if finally acquitted of the offence, not to be tried for it again and, if finally found guilty and punished for the offence, not to be tried or punished for it again; and

(i)   if found guilty of the offence and if the punishment for the offence has been varied between the time of commission and the time of sentencing, to the benefit of the lesser punishment.

12. Everyone has the right not to be subjected to any cruel and unusual treatment or punishment.

13. A witness who testifies in any proceedings has the right not to have any incriminating evidence so given used to incriminate that witness in any other proceedings, except in a prosecution for perjury or for the giving of contradictory evidence.

14. A party or witness in any proceedings who does not understand or speak the language in which the proceedings are conducted or who is deaf has the right to the assistance of an interpreter.

Equality Rights

15.(1) Every individual is equal before and under the law and has the right to the equal protection and equal benefit of the law without discrimination and, in particular, without discrimination based on race, national or ethnic origin, colour, religion, sex, age or mental or physical disability.

(2) Subsection (1) does not preclude any law, program or activity that has as its object the amelioration of conditions of disadvantaged individuals or groups including those that are disadvantaged because of race, national or ethnic origin, colour, religion, sex, age or mental or physical disability.

Official Languages of Canada

16.(1) English and French are the official languages of Canada and have equality of status and equal rights and privileges as to their use in all institutions of the Parliament and government of Canada.

(2) English and French are the official languages of New Brunswick and have equality of status and equal rights and privileges as to their use in all institutions of the legislature and government of New Brunswick.

(3) Nothing in this Charter limits the authority of Parliament or a legislature to advance the equality of status or use of English and French.

17.(1) Everyone has the right to use English or French in any debates and other proceedings of Parliament.

(2) Everyone has the right to use English or French in any debates and other proceedings of the legislature of New Brunswick.

18.(1) The statutes, records and journals of Parliament shall be printed and published in English and French and both language versions are equally authoritative.

(2) The statutes, records and journals of the legislature of New Brunswick shall be printed and published in English and French and both language versions are equally authoritative.

19.(1) Either English or French may be used by any person in, or in any pleading in or process issuing from, any court established by Parliament.

(2) Either English or French may be used by any person in, or in any pleading in or process issuing from, any court of New Brunswick.

20.(1) Any member of the public in Canada has the right to communicate with, and to receive available services from, any head or central office of an institution of the Parliament or government of Canada in English or French, and has the same right with respect to any other office of any such institution where

    (a)   there is a significant demand for communications with and services from that office in such language; or

    (b)   due to the nature of the office, it is reasonable that communications with and services from that office be available in both English and French.

(2) Any member of the public in New Brunswick has the right to communicate with, and to receive available services from, any office of an institution of the legislature or government of New Brunswick in English or French.

21. Nothing in sections 16 to 20 abrogates or derogates from any right, privilege or obligation with respect to the English and French languages, or either of them, that exists or is continued by virtue of any other provision of the Constitution of Canada.

22. Nothing in sections 16 to 20 abrogates or derogates from any legal or customary right or privilege acquired or enjoyed either before or after the coming into force of this Charter with respect to any language that is not English or French.

Minority Language Educational Rights

23.(1) Citizens of Canada

    (a)   whose first language learned and still understood is that of the English or French linguistic minority population of the province in which they reside, or

    (b)   who have received their primary school instruction in Canada in English or French and reside in a province where the language in which they received that instruction is the language of the English or French linguistic minority population of the province, have the right to have their children receive primary and secondary school instruction in that language in that province.

(2) Citizens of Canada of whom any child has received or is receiving primary or secondary school instruction in English or French in Canada, have the right to have all their children receive primary and secondary school instruction in the same language.

(3) The right of citizens of Canada under subsections (1) and (2) to have their children receive primary and secondary school instruction in the language of the English or French linguistic minority population of a province

(a)   applies wherever in the province the number of children of citizens who have
such a right is sufficient to warrant the provision to them out of public funds of
minority language instruction; and

(b)   includes, where the number of those children so warrants, the right to have
them receive that instruction in minority language educational facilities provided out of public funds.

Enforcement

24.(1) Anyone whose rights or freedoms, as guaranteed by this Charter,
have been infringed or denied may apply to a court of competent jurisdiction to obtain such remedy as the court considers appropriate and just in
the circumstances.

(2) Where, in proceedings under subsection (1), a court concludes that
evidence was obtained in a manner that infringed or denied any rights or
freedoms guaranteed by this Charter, the evidence shall be excluded if it is
established that, having regard to all the circumstances, the admission of
it in the proceedings would bring the administration of justice into disrepute.

General

25. The guarantee in this Charter of certain rights and freedoms shall not
be construed so as to abrogate or derogate from any aboriginal, treaty or
other rights or freedoms that pertain to the aboriginal peoples of Canada
including

(a)   any rights or freedoms that have been recognized by the Royal Proclamation of
October 7, 1763; and

(b)   any rights or freedoms that may be acquired by the aboriginal peoples of
Canada by way of land claims settlement.

26. The guarantee in this Charter of certain rights and freedoms shall not
be construed as denying the existence of any other rights or freedoms that
exist in Canada.

27. This Charter shall be interpreted in a manner consistent with the preservation and enhancement of the multicultural heritage of Canadians.

28. Notwithstanding anything in this Charter, the rights and freedoms
referred to in it are guaranteed equally to male and female persons.

29. Nothing in this Charter abrogates or derogates from any rights or
privileges guaranteed by or under the Constitution of Canada in respect
of denominational, separate or dissentient schools.

30. A reference in this Charter to a province or to the legislative assembly
or legislature of a province shall be deemed to include a reference to the
Yukon Territory and the Northwest Territories, or to the appropriate legislative authority thereof, as the case may be.

31. Nothing in this Charter extends the legislative powers of any body or
authority.

Application of Charter
32.(1) This Charter applies
- (a)   to the Parliament and government of Canada in respect of all matters within the authority of Parliament including all matters relating to the Yukon Territory and Northwest Territories; and
- (b)   to the legislature and government of each province in respect of all matters within the authority of the legislature of each province.

(2) Notwithstanding subsection (1), section 15 shall not have effect until three years after this section comes into force.

33.(1) Parliament or the legislature of a province may expressly declare in an Act of Parliament or of the legislature, as the case may be, that the Act or a provision thereof shall operate notwithstanding a provision included in section 2 or sections 7 to 15 of the Charter.

(2) An Act or a provision of an Act in respect of which a declaration made under this section is in effect shall have such operation as it would have but for the provisions of this Charter referred to in the declaration.

(3) A declaration made under subsection (1) shall cease to have effect five years after it comes into force or on such earlier date as may be specified in the declaration.

(4) Parliament or a legislature of a province may re-enact a declaration made under subsection (1).

(5) Subsection (3) applies in respect of a re-enactment made under subsection (4).

Citation
34. This Part may be cited as the *Canadian Charter of Rights and Freedoms.*

Rights of the Aboriginal Peoples of Canada
35. (1) The existing aboriginal and treaty rights of the aboriginal peoples of Canada are hereby recognized and affirmed.

   (2) In this Act, "aboriginal peoples of Canada" includes the Indian, Inuit and Métis peoples of Canada.
. . .

General
52. (1) The Constitution of Canada is the supreme law of Canada, and any law that is inconsistent with the provisions of the Constitution is, to the extent of the inconsistency, of no force or effect.

Index